Introduction to Computers and MS-DOS PCs WITH BASIC

SECOND EDITION

West 2.5 Version

Introduction to Computers Using the IBM® and MS-DOS® PCs

WITH BASIC

STEVEN L. MANDELL ■ SECOND EDITION

West 2.5 Version includes the following software:

WestWord™ 2.5
WestCalc™ 2.5
WestGraph™ 2.5
WestData™ 2.5
WestSoft™ 1.0
Student File Disk

WEST PUBLISHING COMPANY

St. Paul   New York   San Francisco   Los Angeles

Library of Congress Cataloging-in-Publication Data

Mandell, Steven L.
  Introduction to computers using the IBM and MS-DOS PCs with BASIC/West 2.5 software version.

  Includes index.
  1. Computers.   2. Microcomputers   3. BASIC (Computer program language)   4. Computer programs.
  I. Title.
QA76.M274783   1987   004   87-1999
ISBN 0-314-32170-5

IBM® is the registered trademark of International Business Machines Corporation.
MS-DOS® is the registered trademark of Microsoft Corporation.

WestWord™, WestCalc™, WestGraph™, WestData™, and West-Soft™ were developed by Rawhide Software. Copyright © 1987, M & M Productions, Rawhide Software®

Cover Photo: Walter Urei Photography. Photo by Walter Urei.
Composition: Parkwood Composition Service, Inc.
Copy Editor: Joan Compton
Artwork: Carlisle Graphics

Part and Chapter Opening Photos

Part One Courtesy of International Business Machines, Inc., **Chapter 1** Courtesy of Shell Oil Company, **Chapter 2** Photo by Walter Urei, **Chapter 3** Courtesy of Electro Scientific Corporation, **Chapter 4** Courtesy of Hewlett-Packard, **Chapter 5** Courtesy of Blyth Software, **Chapter 6** Courtesy of Apple Computer, Inc., **Chapter 7** Courtesy of U.S. Postal Service, **Part Two** Courtesy of Crown Zellerbach, **Chapter 8** Courtesy of WordPerfect Corporation, **Chapter 9** Courtesy of Compugraphic, **Chapter 10** Courtesy of Hewlett-Packard, **Chapter 11** Courtesy of Texas Instruments, **Chapter 12** Courtesy of Los Alamos National Laboratory, **Chapter 13** Courtesy of Concurrent Computer Corporation, **Chapter 14** Courtesy of Sperry Corporation, **Part Three** Courtesy of Dow Chemical U.S.A., **Section I** Courtesy of Virginia Tech, **Section II** Courtesy of National Computer Camps, **Section III** Courtesy of International Business Machines, Inc., **Section IV** Courtesy of International Business Machines, Inc., **Section V** Courtesy of Honeywell, Inc., **Section VI** Courtesy of Sperry Corporation, **Section VII** Courtesy of New England Digital.

Intext Photo Credits

Fig. 1-1 Courtesy of Chrysler Corporation, **Fig. 1-2a** Courtesy of AT&T Bell Laboratories, **Fig. 1-2b** Courtesy of AT&T Bell Laboratories, **Fig. 1-3** Courtesy of Bethlehem Steel Corporation, **Fig. 1-4** Courtesy of Santa Fe Southern Pacific Corporation, **Fig. 1-5** Photo courtesy of Best Western International, Inc., **Fig. 1-6** Courtesy of Ohio Citizen's Bank, **Fig. 1-7** Courtesy of Brooks Shoe, Inc., **Fig. 1-8** Courtesy of N.Y. Yankees Magazine, **Fig. 1-9** Photograph by John Morgan, **Fig. 1-10** Courtesy of Whirlpool Corporation, **Fig. 1-11** Courtesy of Toshiba's Information Systems Division, Tustin, CA, **Fig. 1-15a** Courtesy of International Business Machines Corporation, **Fig. 1-15b** Courtesy of International Business Machines Corporation, **Fig. 1-16** Crown Copyright, Science Museum, London, **Fig. 1-17a** Courtesy of International Business Machines Corporation, **Fig. 1-17b** Courtesy of International Business Machines Corporation, **Fig. 1-19** Courtesy of Sperry Corporation, **Fig. 1-20** Courtesy of Sperry Corporation, **Fig. 1-21** Courtesy of International Business Machines Corporation, **Fig. 1-22** Photo courtesy of Digital Equipment Corporation, **Fig. 1-23** Courtesy of International Business Machines Corporation, **Fig. 1-24** Courtesy of AT&T Bell Laboratories, **Fig. 2-1** Courtesy of International Business Machines Corporation, **Fig. 2-2** Photo by Walter Urei, **Fig. 2-3** Photo by Walter Urei, **Fig. 2-4** Photo by Walter Urei, **Fig. 2-5** Photo by Walter Urei, **Fig. 2-6** Photo by Walter Urei, **Fig. 2-7** Photo by Walter Urei, **Fig. 2-8** Photo by Walter Urei, **Fig. 2-9** Photo by Walter Urei, **Fig. 2-10** Photo by Walter Urei, **Fig. 2-11** Photo by Walter Urei, **Fig. 2-12** Photo by Walter Urei, **Fig. 3-1** Courtesy of International Business Machines Corporation, **Fig. 3-2** Photo courtesy of Wang Laboratories, Inc., **Fig. 3-3** Courtesy of Honeywell Information Systems, **Fig. 3-4** Courtesy of Cray Research, Inc., **Fig. 3-8** Courtesy of Motorola Inc., **Fig. 3-11** Courtesy of Verbatim Corporation, **Fig. 3-14** Courtesy of Anacomp, Inc., **Fig. 3-15** Photo courtesy of 3M Office Systems Division, **Fig. 3-16** Courtesy of International Business Machines Corporation, **Fig. 3-17** Courtesy of AT&T Bell Laboratories, **Fig. 3-19** Photo courtesy of Wang Laboratories, Inc., **Fig. 3-21a** Courtesy of International Business Machines Corporation, **Fig. 3-21b** Courtesy of Albertson's Inc., **Fig. 3-22** Courtesy of Sperry Corporation, **Fig. 3-23** Photo supplied by New Image Technology, Inc., **Fig. 3-24** Courtesy of AT&T Bell Laboratories, **Fig. 3-25** Courtesy of Texas Instruments, **Fig. 3-27** Courtesy of Dataproducts Corp., **Fig. 3-28** Courtesy of Blyth Software, **Fig. 3-29** Photo courtesy of Hewlett-Packard Company, **Fig. 5-1** Reproduced with permission of AT&T Corporate Archive, **Fig. 5-2** Courtesy of Apple Computer, Inc., **Fig. 5-4** Photo courtesy of Hewlett-Packard Company, **Fig. 5-5** Courtesy of Corona Data Systems, Inc., **Fig. 5-6** The Tower of 1632 from NCR Corp., **Fig. 5-7** Courtesy of Apple Computer, Inc., **Fig. 5-8a** Courtesy of Apple Computer, Inc., **Fig. 5-8b** Courtesy of The Mouse House, Inc., **Fig. 5-8c** Photo courtesy of Hewlett-Packard Company, **Fig. 5-9** Courtesy of Amdek Corporation, **Fig. 5-10** Zenith Data Systems, subsidiary of Zenith Electronics Corp., **Fig. 5-11** Courtesy of Verbatim Corporation, **Fig. 5-12a** Photos courtesy of 3M, **Fig. 5-12b** Photos courtesy of 3M, **Fig. 5-13** Courtesy of Maxtor Corporation, **Fig. 5-14** Courtesy of Interstate Voice Products, **Fig. 5-15a** Photos courtesy of Microsoft Corporation, **Fig. 5-15b** Reprint permission granted by Computer Associates, Micro Products Division, Oct. 1985, **Fig. 5-15c** Courtesy of SAS Institute, Inc., Cary, N.C., **Fig. 5-15d** Smart Software photos

Credits are continued following the index.

CONTENTS-IN-BRIEF

v

CONTENTS

CHAPTER 3

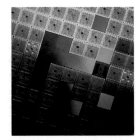

Hardware   **63**

CHAPTER 4

CHAPTER 5

CHAPTER 6

Computers' Impact on Society   **151**

CHAPTER 7

Issues of Concern   187

PART TWO

APPLICATIONS SOFTWARE: USING WESTWORD™ 2.5, WESTCALC™ 2.5, WESTGRAPH™ 2.5, AND WESTDATA™ 2.5   209

CHAPTER 8

Introduction to Word Processing and WestWord™ 2.5   211

CHAPTER 9

Advanced WestWord™ 2.5   **243**

CHAPTER 10

Introduction to Spreadsheets and WestCalc™ 2.5   **277**

CHAPTER 11

Advanced WestCalc™ 2.5   317

CHAPTER 12

Introduction to Graphics and WestGraph™ 2.5   343

CHAPTER 13

Introduction to Data Managers and WestData™ 2.5   **377**

CHAPTER 14

Advanced WestData™ 2.5   **413**

PART THREE   **BASIC SUPPLEMENT**   **B-1**

SECTION I   **Introduction to BASIC**   **B-3**

SECTION II   **Getting Started with BASIC**   **B-19**

SECTION III

Input and Output   B-39

SECTION IV

Control Statements and Subroutines   B-65

SECTION V

Looping   B-91

SECTION VI

Arrays   B-117

SECTION VII

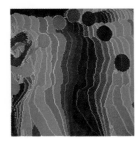

Graphics and Sound   **B-147**

PREFACE

The goal for books in the first edition of this series was to combine computer concepts, application packages and BASIC programming in each textbook. Three versions were offered in the first edition series—one for use with the IBM, Apple and TRS 80 microcomputers. Because of the tremendous proliferation in applications software, and in order to give adoptors a wide range of choices, three second edition texts now focus on the IBM PC and MS-DOS computers, while the fourth text is for use with Apple II computers.

In addition to *Introduction to Computers Using The IBM® and MS-DOS® PCs** with BASIC, Second Edition, West 2.5 Version*, the following texts are available for use with IBM and MS-DOS PCs:

■ Popular Commercial Software Version for WordStar® 2000, WordPerfect®, Lotus® 1-2-3®, and dBase® III (with WestSoft™ 1.0 and Student File Disk)
■ Educate-Ability® 1.1 Version, an integrated software package (with WestSoft™ 1.0 and Student File Disk)

The fourth text in the series is *Introduction to Computers Using the Apple® II with BASIC, Second Edition, West 2.5 Version* (with WestWord™, WestCalc™, WestGraph™, WestData™, WestSoft™ 1.0 and Student File Disk).

Each second edition text retains the strengths of those in the first edition—combining computer concepts with hands-on applications and BASIC programming. The second edition series, however, is improved in structure and substance, thanks to the excellent feedback from instructors who served as reviewers.

New Features

Like books from the first edition, second edition texts are divided into three sections. The first focuses on fundamental computer concepts, the second section

---

*IBM® is the registered trademark of International Business Machines Corporation. MS-DOS® is the registered trademark of Microsoft Corporation.

on applications software, and the final section presents BASIC programming. Although the basic format of the first and second editions is the same, readers familiar with the first edition will notice several changes, including the following for the IBM versions:

■ The chapter on "Getting to Know Your IBM" has been moved from Part Two of the book to Part One. WestSoft™ 1.0, a program containing simulations of a home banking system, personality traits test, ticket office manager, information network, and dental office manager, has been incorporated into the chapter. Moving this chapter to the front of the book enables students to become familiar with the computer right at the start of the course.
■ All the chapters in Part One have been updated and revised to reflect recent changes in technology.
■ Part Two of the book for the West 2.5 Version, the hands-on application software section, focuses on WestWord™, WestCalc™, WestGraph™, and WestData™. One chapter in Part Two is devoted to WestGraph™, while WestWord™, WestCalc™, and WestData™ each have introductory and advanced chapters explaining the software. The 2.5 version of the West software is more sophisticated in design and more professional in appearance than earlier versions.
■ A WestSoft/File disk is included with each book. It contains WestSoft™ 1.0 simulations, and permanent files to be used with problems at the end of each chapter in Part Two. The WestSoft/File disk also contains permanent files to be used with additional problems included in the Instructor's Manual.
■ Part Three, the BASIC section has been rewritten to emphasize structured programming and top-down design.

In the last few years, there has been an explosion in the number of students taking introductory courses on computers. The content of these courses is undergoing constant rethinking and revision. A current trend seems to be to expose students to state-of-the-art professional software. In keeping with this trend, West 2.5 Version software includes many of the features found in popular professional software packages, and this book introduces students to these features in a logical and uncluttered manner. My hope is that students using the text will gain an increased awareness of the usefulness of application packages and acquire the necessary skills to successfully master software packages on their own.

Color coding has been used in the applications software examples and the BASIC programming examples throughout the text to assist the reader. The legend for this coding is shown below:

Light Blue shading	`Computer Output`

Blue	`User Response or Input`

Supplementary Educational Material

A complete instructor's resource package has been designed to reduce administrative efforts. The classroom support for each chapter of the first section includes a detailed Lecture Outline, Answers to Review Questions, and Additional Questions. For the Application Software section, Answers to Exercises in Text and Additional Problems (with answers) are included. The BASIC Programming section includes Answers to Review Questions in Text, Additional Questions, Answers to Debugging Exercises in Text, Answers to Programming Problems in Text and three Additional Programming Exercises per section. All the Answers to Programming Problems in Text are accompanied by flowcharts and actual printouts of the programs. A Test Bank with more than 550 multiple-choice questions is also included in the Instructor's Manual. Answers to questions follow each chapter test. In addition, there are more than fifty Transparency Masters provided in the Instructor's Manual.

WestTutor™ is a computer-assisted instruction package to be used to support the BASIC Programming section. Instructions are provided at the bottom of each screen to direct the student through the tutorial. At the end of a section, checkpoint questions are included to test the student's understanding of the material. The student reads each question and selects an answer. The program indicates whether the correct answer was selected and gives an explanation concerning the correct answer.

Acknowledgments

I was very fortunate to have had several outstanding college educators serve as reviewers for this book. I would like to thank the following people for their invaluable comments:

David Allen
San Antonio College

Clark B. Archer
Winthrop College, South Carolina

Ellis Blanton
University of South Florida

W. Joseph Cochran
University of Southern California

Stanley P. Franklin
Memphis State University

Dwight Graham
Prairie State College, Illinois

Janet Bard Hanson
University of South Florida

Berni Hopper
Clark College, Washington

George Kelley
Erie Community College, City Campus, New York

Beverly Oswalt
University of Central Arkansas

Thomas A. Parkinson
Oakland Community College, Michigan

E. Raydean Richmond
Tarrant County Jr. College, South Campus, Texas

Douglas F. Robertson
University of Minnesota

Lee Tangedahl
University of Montana

Numerous corporations and government agencies supplied the color photographs for this book. Many professionals provided the assistance required for completion of a textbook of this magnitude: Michelle Westlund and Melissa Landon on manuscript development; Sarah Basinger on Part One Computer Literacy; Meredith Flynn, Alan Johnson, and Susan Moran on Part Two Applications Software; Sue Baumann, Irene Bulas, and Sara Fetterman on the BASIC Programming Section; Patricia Busch on the Instructor's Manual; Christine Custer on photographs; Sally Oates, Shannan Benschoter, Linda Cupp, and Kathleen Shields on manuscript preparation; and Robert Slocum on the index.

The design of the book is a tribute to the many talents and great patience of John Orr. One final acknowledgment goes to my publisher and valued friend, Clyde Perlee, Jr. If it were not for his constant encouragement, this project would never have been completed.

Steven L. Mandell

PART ONE

Computer Literacy

CHAPTER 1

Computers
in Our World

Introduction

Figure 1-1
Car With Electronic Map

Forty-five years ago, scientists began to use computers for research, mathematics, and technology. When computers became available commercially, only the largest businesses acquired them, often just for the prestige of owning one. The uses of computers were quite limited in those days. Today, however, it would be hard to name areas in which computers are not being used. Computers have entered almost every aspect of the average American's life.

Think of the many household items that contain some type of computer. Televisions, video recorders, stereos, microwave ovens, and even coffee makers are computer-controlled. Computerized telephones can store and dial up to 100 telephone numbers. Some houses have computers that regulate temperature and energy use. Our cars, too, contain computer devices that govern fuel mixture, control emissions from the car's exhaust system, and tell us to buckle up or take the keys out of the ignition. Some cars even contain electronic maps that help the driver navigate through unfamiliar territory (see Figure 1-1).

More and more American families are buying personal computers for home use. Many people use their personal computers for playing games, but home computer use goes far beyond entertainment. People are realizing the tremendous potential of home computers in gathering information. Using the telephone lines and specially equipped computers, subscribers can call a commercial database such as CompuServe (see Figure 1-2) for information about the stock market, current

Figure 1-2
Commercial Database Menu Screen
With a subscription to a commercial database, personal computer users have the world at their fingertips. These women are checking the week's best-selling fiction books.

Figure 1-3 Computer-Aided Manufacturing
The entire steel-rolling operation of this Bethlehem Steel mill is supervised and monitored from this computerized control center.

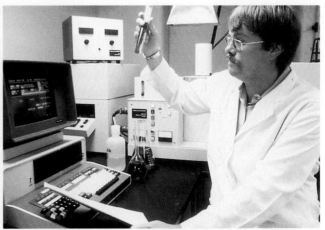

Figure 1-4 Laboratory Testing
A laboratory technician uses computers to aid in research and development.

WORD PROCESSING
The use of computer equipment in preparing text; involves writing, editing, and printing.

COMPUTER
General-purpose electronic machine with applications limited only by the creativity of the humans who use it. Its power is derived from its speed, accuracy and memory.

events, and sports information. In addition, they can do their banking by computer, shop via an electronic catalog, or enroll in accredited college courses through electronic communications systems such as TeleLearning's Electronic University. Other popular home uses include **word processing,** filing, financial planning, and educational games.

In the workplace, computers have made financial analysis, bookkeeping, manufacturing processes, and other functions faster and more efficient. Company executives use personal computers as aids in decision making. Clerks and secretaries use personal computers for preparing documents and keeping records. Manufacturers use computers in designing machines and products, controlling robots, and regulating manufacturing processes (see Figure 1-3).

Scientists build computer models of airplane crashes in order to determine the crash behavior of airplanes. This information helps aircraft designers plan safer seats and windows, and fabrics that decrease fire hazards during a crash. Ecologists use computers for monitoring problems such as acid rain and suggesting solutions for environmental management. Educators use computers in the classroom for performing chemistry experiments that might otherwise be dangerous. Computers are used by medical researchers in testing drugs; by meteorologists for predicting the weather; by musicians for synthesizing and reproducing sounds; by artists for producing graphics; and by students for learning basic skills (see Figure 1-4). Moviegoers may notice an increased sophistication in special effects, thanks to computer scene simulation. Even the farmer of the 1980s benefits from such computer applications as bookkeeping, maintaining animal health and production records, and devising economical feed programs.

This chapter discusses additional examples of computers in our daily lives, and provides introductory material to help you understand the machine we call the **computer.**

Daily Encounters

Businesses, governments, research laboratories, and many other organizations deal with so much information every day that it would be difficult to operate without computers. Most businesses lend themselves to computerization. Historically, the types of jobs most easily computerized have been routine, repetitive jobs. These simple tasks can be performed quickly and accurately by a computer. A good example is the preparation of a company's payroll. The preparer finds each employee's net pay by multiplying the pay rate by the number of hours worked, then subtracting taxes and other deductions. When given accurate data and instructions, the computer can produce paychecks for hundreds of employees quickly and with little error.

Although some organizations use computers only in simplifying their accounting activities, others have benefited from using computers in making decisions. For example, computers can calculate sales forecasts using any number of variables or combinations of variables. A computer can quickly determine how changes in price, inventory level, volumn of advertising, or coupon offers are likely to affect sales.

Some decision-making aspects of a business are not easily computerized. These processes are not routine and are hard to define, so it is difficult to write instructions for the computer. Many businesses are now computerizing risk analysis, one important aspect of business decision making. Risk analysis determines whether a business investment will be profitable. The largest users of computerized risk analysis to date have been oil and utility companies. Utility companies generally use the technique for determining locations for nuclear power stations, and oil companies use it in placing offshore oil-drilling rigs.

Many businesses link their computers by communication lines so that several computers can share data and programs. Connecting computers eliminates the need for duplicating the data stored by each computer. The data is more easily kept up to date, because all changes made to the data on any computer are immediately accessible from the other computers.

Just as computers improve business people's performance, they improve the services offered to consumers. Computers affect the way many businesses, from banks to restaurants to grocery stores, deal with their customers. Airlines, travel agencies, and hotels use extensive networks of computer equipment for scheduling reservations (see Figure 1-5). Some large shopping malls contain computers that act as electronic directories. Through computer use, banks have been able to offer more services to their customers. These services include direct deposit of payments, automatic teller machines, and banking from home (see Figure 1-6).

Manufacturers make extensive use of computers, too. Engineers use computers in drawing plans for products, for machines to build those products, and for machines to build the machines to make the products. During the manufacturing process, computers are used in controlling the operation of machinery. Computers also are helpful in testing prototypes of products. Among the items we use every day that may have been designed by computer are car seats, lenses in sunglasses, sport shoes, and other sports equipment (see Figure 1-7).

The federal government is the largest user of computers in the United States. This fact is not surprising when one considers the many government agencies that

Figure 1-5
A Hotel Reservation Network
Reservation sales agents utilize Best Western International's worldwide computerized network to book room reservations.

Figure 1-6
Automatic Teller Machine
This customer of Ohio Citizen's Bank can use the bank's automatic teller machine at any time of day that is convenient for him.

Figure 1-7
Computer-Aided Design In Sport Shoes A final shoe design is shown on the terminal screen.

collect, process, and store information. Typical examples include the U.S. census taken every ten years; the millions of income tax returns processed every year; the huge databases maintained in the Library of Congress and Federal Bureau of Investigation; and the public assistance and social security systems.

In science and medicine, as in business, computers are used for routine clerical functions. More importantly, computers can make calculations and perform design testing functions in seconds which human beings could not otherwise complete in months. Data analyzed by computers can be collected by satellites for military intelligence and environmental planning; by seismographs for earthquake prediction; by CAT scans for medical diagnosis; and by sensors for determination of toxicity levels.

Educators also are becoming more involved in computer use. A frequently asked question in the past ten years has been: "Will the computer replace the teacher?" The answer, of course, is no. In fact, the opposite is true, because computers can help teachers and students with their work. Computers become private tutors for students who need extra help or additional challenges. Computers are used in helping students learn programming languages such as Pascal or BASIC. Videodisks combined with computers offer a learning aid that includes motion and sound. Using videodisk lessons, students can watch reenactments of the early colonists preparing for the Revolutionary War or the Wright brothers trying out their first airplane. They can interact with lessons on current events and watch news footage from old newscasts.

Computers play important roles in sports, too. In baseball, computers are used to calculate statistics such as batting averages and runs batted in, and to evaluate how pitchers and hitters work together. A computer analyzes the statistics collected during a game so that a manager can predict the most likely moves in a certain situation (see Figure 1-8). For example, a Chicago White Sox coach once determined that a certain left-handed batter for an opposing team almost always got a hit when a left-handed pitcher threw a breaking ball. Bits of information like that can help a team win. In fact, teams are finding computers so successful in analyzing statistics that many maintain secrecy as to how they use the machines.

In professional football, computers are being used in scouting and evaluating other teams and college players. Olympic cyclists wear helmets designed with the aid of computers for efficient aerodynamics. These athletes may also improve their performance after a computer indicates that their pedaling motions are inefficient. Olympic pole vaulters are using the technology to record movements with high-speed video cameras and store the results, in digitized form, in a computer. They can then view their movements on the screen by watching a computerized stick figure (see Figure 1-9).

We have seen how computers can be powerful tools in both large-scale applications and everyday functions of our lives. By knowing how computers work,

Figure 1-8
Collecting Baseball Data
A team manager uses an Apple Computer at the Yankee Stadium to record pitches, hits, and runs of the New York Yankees.

Figure 1-9
Computer Analysis in Pole Vaulting

what they can do, and what their limitations and benefits are, we can use computers to their best advantage.

The Computer's Role In Data Processing

DATA PROCESSING
A set of procedures for collecting, manipulating, and disseminating data to achieve specified objectives.

ELECTRONIC DATA PROCESSING (EDP)
Data processing performed by electronic equipment, such as computers, rather than by manual or mechanical means.

DATA
Facts, the raw material of information.

INFORMATION
Data that has been organized and processed so it is meaningful.

Data processing is nothing new. People have processed data ever since they have had things to count. **Data processing** refers to collecting, manipulating, and distributing data in order to achieve certain goals. Using computers for data processing is called **electronic data processing (EDP),** although EDP usually is known simply as data processing.

The objective of all data processing, whether manual or electronic, is the conversion of data into useful information. The words data and information often are used interchangeably, but in the context of data processing they have different meanings. **Data** refers to raw facts collected from various sources, but not organized or perhaps even defined. Data cannot be used in making meaningful decisions. For example, a bank manager may have little use for a daily list of the amounts of all checks and deposit slips from the branch offices. The manager could, however, use a summary that gives the dollar value and total number of deposits and withdrawals at each branch. Such a summary provides **information,** which is processed data that increases understanding and helps people make intelligent decisions. Information must be accurate, timely, complete, concise, and relevant. It must be delivered to the right person at the right time in the right place. If information fails to meet these requirements, it fails to meet the needs of those who use it and is of little value.

Figure 1-10
Analog Computer

ANALOG COMPUTER
A computer that measures changes in continuous electrical or physical conditions rather than counting data.

DIGITAL COMPUTER
A computer that operates on distinct data by performing arithmetic and logic processes on specific data units.

CHARACTER
A single letter, digit, or special sign (such as $, #, or *).

BIT
Short for *binary digit*, the smallest unit of data which the computer can handle.

HARDWARE
Physical components that make up a computer system.

SOFTWARE
Program or programs used to direct the computer in solving problems and overseeing operations.

PROGRAM
A series of step-by-step instructions which tells the computer exactly what to do.

Analog and Digital Computers

There are two types of computers: analog and digital. **Analog computers** measure changes in continuous physical or electrical states, such as pressure, temperature, voltage, length, number of shaft rotations, or volume (see Figure 1-10). A gasoline pump uses a simple analog device that measures the quantity of gasoline pumped to the nearest tenth of a gallon. More complex analog devices are used in testing and adjusting the performance of electronic equipment.

   Digital computers, by contrast, represent data by discrete ''on'' and ''off'' (conducting/nonconducting or yes/no) states of the computer's electronic circuitry. **Characters** (numbers, letters, and symbols) are stored in binary notation, a code based on the binary number system, which consists of two digits: 1 (on) and 0 (off). Each 1 or 0 is called a **bit,** short for *bi*nary dig*it*, the smallest unit of data a computer can handle. The binary number system is well suited to the on/off states of electric current. A digital computer must convert all data to binary form in order to process it.

   The electronic and electrical parts of a digital computer—that is, the tangible parts of a computer system—are called **hardware.** Examples of hardware are the computer itself, monitors used for viewing data, keyboards, and printers (see Figure 1-11). Hardware is useless without **software,** the instructions or **programs** that direct the equipment in performing various tasks. The hardware and software discussed in this book apply to digital computers.

The Computer Advantage

A computer pulls data from storage, acts on it, and stores it again under the direction of programs that determine the yes/no, conducting/nonconducting, or

Figure 1-11
Computer Hardware

on/off operations of its circuits. It must be given exact, step-by-step instructions for any task it performs. Within the limitations of its circuits, a computer can carry out three basic functions.

1. Arithmetic operations (addition, subtraction, multiplication, and division).
2. Logical comparisons of relationships among values (greater than, less than, or equal to).
3. Storage and retrieval operations.

The manufacturer builds into the computer a basic set of instructions—the **instruction set**—which performs these three tasks. By working with the instruction set, people can direct the computer to perform many tasks. The computer can perform these tasks quickly and reliably and can store vast amounts of data.

INSTRUCTION SET
The fundamental logical and arithmetic procedures that the computer can perform, such as addition and comparison.

Speed Modern computers can perform millions of calculations in one second. Computer speed describes the time required to perform one operation, and is measured in terms of nanoseconds or other small units (see Figure 1-12). A nanosecond is one-billionth of a second. In one nanosecond, electricity can travel 11.8 inches. The smaller the distances in the electronic circuitry of a computer, the shorter the time needed for the computer to perform a task. In the past, the time required for performing one addition ranged from 200 nanoseconds to 4

Figure 1-12
Divisions of a Second

Divisions of a Second		
Unit	Symbol	Fractions of a Second
Millisecond	ms	one-thousandth (1/1,000)
Microsecond	μs	one-millionth (1/1,000,000)
Nanosecond	ns	one-billionth (1/1,000,000,000)
Picosecond	ps	one-trillionth (1/1,000,000,000,000)

microseconds. In the future, it may be 200 to 1,000 times faster. This means that computers can do certain jobs hundreds of thousands of times faster than humans can.

Accuracy   The accuracy of a computer refers to the inherent reliability of its electronic components. The same type of current passed through the same circuits should yield the same results each time. We take advantage of this aspect of circuitry every time we switch on an electric device. When we turn on a light switch, we expect the light to go on, not the radio or a fan. The computer is reliable for the same reason. Its circuitry is reliable. A computer can run for hours, days, and weeks at a time, giving accurate results for millions of activities. Of course, if the data or programs submitted to the computer are faulty, the computer will not produce correct results. The output will be useless and meaningless, illustrating the human error involved. This is called the garbage in–garbage out (GIGO) principle and is fundamental in understanding computer ''mistakes.''

PRIMARY MEMORY
The section of the computer which holds instructions, data, and intermediate and final results during processing.

Storage   Besides being very fast and reliable, computers can store large amounts of data. Some data is held in **primary memory** for use during immediate operations. The amount of data held in primary memory varies among computers. Some small computers hold as few as 16,000 characters, and large computers can

---

Learning Check

1. Many of the jobs that are easily computerized are _____.
   a. decision-making tasks
   b. routine and repetitive
   c. hard to define
   d. used in risk analysis

2. In the context of data processing, what is the difference between data and information?

3. One of the three functions digital computers can perform is _____.
   a. measuring continuous physical and electrical states
   b. manipulating a half bit
   c. providing accurate information
   d. storing and retrieving information

4. When you inquire about machines and programs at a computer store, you might use the terms _____ and _____ respectively.

5. We know that information resulting from EDP is not always accurate. Why, then, is accuracy considered one of the features of using computers?

Answers

1. b 2. The term *data* means raw, unorganized facts. The term *information* means processed data that increases understanding and aids in making decisions. 3. d 4. hardware, software 5. Accuracy refers to the reliability of electrical currents, not to the reliability of human programmers and data entry personnel.

SECONDARY STORAGE
Storage that supplements primary memory and is external to the computer; data is accessed at slower speeds than with primary storage.

hold billions of characters. Data also can be recorded on magnetic disks or tapes; this **secondary storage** makes a computer's "memory" almost limitless. Secondary storage holds data that is not immediately needed by the computer.

Electronic data storage requires considerably less space and less retrieval time than manual methods. Vast quantities of data stored in paper files are extremely bulky and require substantial storage space. Further, the job of manually extracting data from such files becomes more tedious and time consuming as the size of the files increases.

The ability to store, retrieve, and process data, all without human intervention, separates the computer from a simple calculator and accounts for its power and appeal. Whereas humans can perform the same functions as computers, the difference is that the computer can execute millions of instructions reliably in a second and store the results in an almost unlimited memory.

Stages of Data Processing

All data processing follows the same basic data flow: input, processing and output (see Figure 1-13). These stages are described in the following paragraphs.

INPUT
Data submitted to the computer for processing.

Input   **Input** means capturing data and putting it in a form that the computer can understand. Input of data can involve entering new data, changing old data, or deleting data. It involves three steps:

■ **Collecting** raw data and assembling it at one location.
■ **Verifying,** or checking, the accuracy and completeness of data, including both the facts and the programs. This step is very important, since most computer errors result from human error.
■ **Coding** the data into a machine-readable form for processing.

ONLINE
In direct communication with the computer.

OFFLINE
Not in direct communication with the computer.

Data can be entered either online or offline. **Online** entry occurs when the input device used is connected directly to the computer. Some examples are typing on a keyboard, using a scanning device (such as the wand found in a department store or the scanner found in grocery stores), or speaking into a microphone connected to the computer. Some processing and output usually occur during online data entry. **Offline** entry occurs when a device not connected directly to the computer is used for recording data onto tapes, disks, or other storage media. Later, the data is read in batches by another machine directly connected to the computer for processing. Chapter 3 discusses input devices in detail.

PROCESS
To transform data into useful information by classifying, sorting, calculating, summarizing, and/or storing.

CENTRAL PROCESSING UNIT (CPU)
The "brain" of the computer, composed of three sections: arithmetic/logic unit (ALU), control unit, and primary storage unit.

Processing   Once the data has been input, it can be processed. **Processing** occurs in the part of the computer called the **central processing unit (CPU),** which is examined in Chapter 3. The CPU includes the circuitry needed for performing arithmetic and logical operations and holding data in primary memory. Once an instruction or data is stored in primary memory, it stays there until new data or instructions are written over it. The same data can be **accessed** repeatedly during processing, or the same instructions can be used repeatedly while processing many different pieces of data.

ACCESS
To get or retrieve data from a computer system.

Figure 1-13
The Data Flow

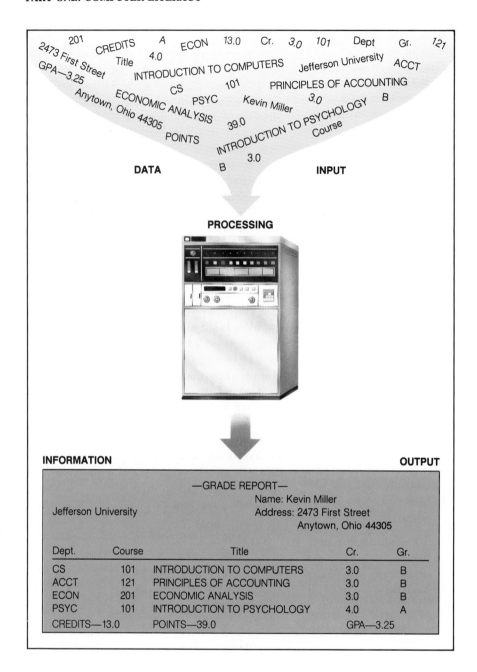

Processing entails several kinds of manipulations (see Figure 1-14):

■ **Classifying,** or categorizing, data according to certain characteristics. For example, sales data can be grouped by salesperson, product, or customer.
■ **Sorting** or arranging the data alphabetically or numerically. An employee file can be sorted by social security number or by last name.
■ **Calculating** results arithmetically or logically, such as computing grade-point averages, bank balances, and payrolls.

**Figure 1-14
Processing Functions**

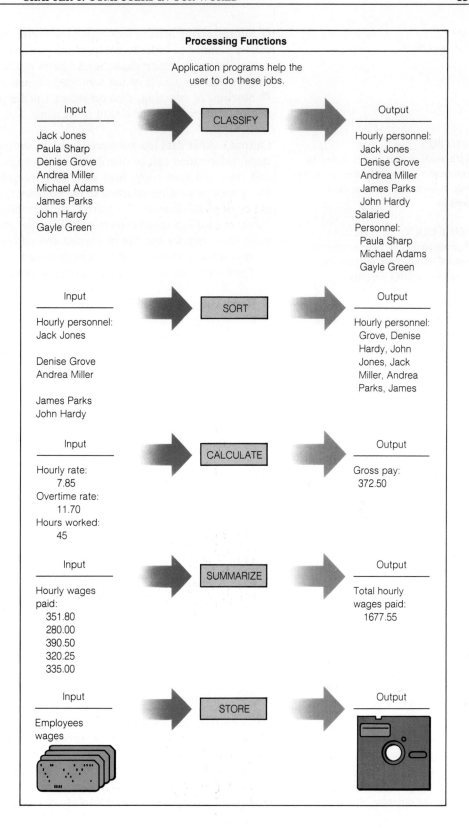

■ **Summarizing** data, or reducing it to concise, usable form. Grade-point averages can be scanned in order to compare the performance of this year's senior class to that of last year's senior class. Sales figures can be summarized in order to compare sales in various outlets of the same department store.

■ **Storing,** or retaining, data on storage media such as magnetic disks, tapes, or microfilm for later retrieval and processing.

OUTPUT
Information that comes from the computer as a result of processing into a form that can be used by people.

SOFT COPY
A temporary, or nonpermanent, record of machine output; for example, a CRT display.

HARD COPY
Output that is printed on some permanent medium, such as paper.

Output   After data has been processed according to some or all of the preceding steps, information can be distributed to the users. There are two types of **output:** soft copy and hard copy. **Soft copy** is information that appears on a television-like screen or monitor attached to the computer. As soon as the monitor is turned off or new information is required, the old information vanishes. **Hard copy** is output printed in a tangible form, such as paper or microfilm. It can be read without using the computer and can be carried around conveniently, written on, or passed to other readers. Printers and plotters produce hard copy, as discussed in Chapter 3.

Three steps are necessary in the output phase of data flow:

■ **Retrieving,** or pulling, data from storage.
■ **Converting,** or translating, data into a form that humans can understand and use (words or pictures displayed on a computer screen or printed on paper).
■ **Communicating,** or providing information to the proper users at the proper time and place, in an intelligible form.

FEEDBACK
A check within a system to see whether predetermined goals are being met.

User requirements for information may change over time. The output is evaluated periodically and the input or processing steps are adjusted in order to ensure that processing results in good information. This procedure is called **feedback.**

Types of Data Processing

BATCH PROCESSING
A method of processing data in which data items are collected and forwarded to the computer in a group.

There are two general types of computer processing. One type is **batch processing,** in which data items are collected over time and processed all at once. In a bank, transactions—deposits, withdrawals, loans, or loan payments—are entered into the computer system as they occur. A summary of the number and dollar amounts of all transactions for one day is processed by batch at night when the bank is closed.

INTERACTIVE PROCESSING
A data processing method by which the user inputs data from the keyboard during processing.

REAL TIME
Descriptive of a system's capability to receive and process data and provide output fast enough to control the outcome of an activity.

Many computer applications, however, require immediate feedback. If the computer is being used for preparing documents or for learning a skill, the user wants to see the results of processing as he or she works. This feedback occurs during **interactive processing.** For example, the user can type a memo, see the words on a screen, and make any necessary corrections. Interactive processing usually occurs online.

Interactive processing often is used for transactions. A person making a plane reservation wants to know immediately what flight is available and at what cost. The computer system also must record the transaction immediately, or a travel agent in another office may sell the same seat to another customer. A bank customer putting money into a savings account wants the amount entered in a passbook now, not tomorrow or next week. Such transactions occur in **real time**—that is, they provide results fast enough to affect the outcome of an activity.

Learning Check

1. Define the term online, with reference to data input, and name its opposite.

2. What input step can help prevent GIGO?

3. Name five kinds of manipulations which can occur during computer processing.

4. Summarizing an entire day's sales at several branch stores often involves batch processing, whereas playing a computer game requires _____ processing.

5. Evaluating data by computer during a rocket launch must occur in _____ time.

Answers

1. *Online* describes data entry via a device directly connected to the computer used to process the data. Its opposite is *offline.* 2. Verification 3. Classifying, sorting, calculating, summarizing, storing 4. Interactive 5. Real

---

Computers Yesterday and Today

By now, we take the computer for granted. We make our plane reservations, use automatic teller machines, and listen to synthesized music, forgetting that true electronic computers are only about 45 years old. The first mechanical calculator was invented just a few hundred years ago.

People have always had ways to figure, sort, compile, store, and classify data. They tied knots in rope to keep track of livestock and carved marks on clay or stone tablets to record transactions. Later, they added and subtracted with an abacus, a device made of beads strung on wires. The abacus, along with hand calculations, was adequate for computation until the early 1600s. Then John Napier designed a portable multiplication tool called Napier's Bones or Rods. The user slid the ivory rods up and down against each other, matching the numbers printed on the rods to figure multiplication and division problems. Napier's idea led to the invention of the slide rule in the mid-1600s.

These tools were useful, but they were anything but automatic. As business became more complex and tax systems expanded, people needed faster, more accurate aids for computation and record-keeping. The idea for the first mechanical calculating machine grew out of the many tedious hours a father and his son spent preparing tax reports. Once this machine was introduced, the way opened for better machines as inventors built upon each succeeding development.

As we trace the history of computers, we see that the concepts of input, processing, and output have not changed. Only the method of entering data, the speed of processing, and the media and display devices for output have advanced.

Early Developments

In the mid-1600s, Blaise Pascal, a mathematician and philosopher, and his father, a tax official, were compiling tax reports for the French government in Paris. As they agonized over the columns of figures, Pascal decided to build a machine that would do the job much faster and more accurately. His machine, the Pascaline, could add and subtract (see Figure 1-15). Much as an odometer keeps track of a car's mileage, the Pascaline functioned by a series of eight rotating gears. Although it had limited uses, it was an improvement over knots, beads, and bones. Yet a market for the Pascaline never grew. Clerks and accountants would not use it. They were afraid it might replace them at their jobs and thought it could be rigged, like a scale or roulette wheel.

About 50 years later, in 1694, the German mathematician Gottfried Wilhelm von Leibniz designed the Stepped Reckoner that could add, subtract, multiply, divide, and figure square roots. Although the machine was not widely used, almost every mechanical calculator during the next 150 years was based on it.

The first signs of automation benefited France's weaving industry when Joseph Marie Jacquard built a loom controlled by **punched cards** (see Figure 1-16). Heavy paper cards linked in a series passed over a set of rods on the loom. The pattern of holes in the cards determined which rods were engaged, thereby adjusting the color and pattern of the product. Prior to Jacquard's invention, a loom operator adjusted the loom settings by hand before each glide of the shuttle, a tedious and time-consuming job.

Jacquard's loom emphasized three concepts important in computer theory. One was that information could be coded on punched cards. A second was that cards could be linked in a series of instructions—essentially a program—thus allowing

PUNCHED CARDS
Heavy paper storage medium in which data is represented by holes punched according to a specific coding scheme.

Figure 1-15
Blaise Pascal and the Pascaline
The Pascaline worked very well for addition, but subtraction was performed by a roundabout adding method.

HIGHLIGHT ▲▲▲▲▲▲▲▲▲▲▲▲▲▲▲▲▲▲▲▲▲

Ada Lovelace

Ada Augusta Byron, Countess of Lovelace, did not lead the kind of life typical of most aristocratic English women during the early 1800s. The daughter of the romantic English poet Lord Byron, Lady Lovelace contributed significantly to modern-day programming concepts.

Lady Lovelace first became involved with the theoretical concepts of computers when she translated a paper on Charles Babbage's analytical engine, a device designed to perform mathematical calculations from coded card instructions. In 1842, at the age of 27, Lady Lovelace began working with Babbage. Several of her ideas were incorporated into the design of the analytical engine.

The most significant of Lady Lovelace's ideas was what is now called the loop. In her studies, Lovelace noticed that the same sequence of instructions often had to be repeated in performing a single calculation. She concluded that only one set of instruction cards was needed if there was a way to loop back to those instructions. A calculation then could be made with only a fraction of the original effort. Lady Lovelace also suggested that Babbage use the binary number system in coding his machine.

Lovelace is now considered to be the first programmer because of her insight into the programming process. In honor of her achievements, a high-level programming language used mostly by the U.S. government was named Ada.

Figure 1-16
The Jacquard Loom
Although other weavers already had designed looms that used punched cards, Jacquard refined the idea and he is credited with the invention.

a machine to do its work without human intervention. A third concept was that such programs could automate jobs.

The first person to use these concepts in a computing machine was Charles Babbage, a professor at Cambridge University in England. As a mathematician, Babbage needed an accurate method for computing and printing tables of the properties of numbers (squares, square roots, logarithms, and so on). Existing tables contained too many mistakes, the results of miscalculations and printing errors. So Babbage designed the Difference Engine, a machine that would compute and print the tables. A model of the machine worked well, but the technology of the day was too primitive for manufacturing metal parts precise enough for a full-sized version.

Later, Babbage envisioned a new machine, the Analytical Engine, for performing any calculation according to instructions coded on cards. The idea for this steam-powered machine was amazingly similar to the design of computers. It had four parts: a "mill" for calculating; a "store" for holding instructions and intermediate and final results; and "operator" or system for carrying out instructions; and a device for "reading" and "writing" data on punched cards. Although Babbage died before he could construct the machine, his son built a working model from Babbage's notes and drawings. Because of the ideas he introduced, Babbage is known as the father of computers.

Punched cards played an important role in the next advance toward automatic machines, a machine used for tabulating census data. Totals from the 1880 census were not completed until 1888; by then the data had little meaning, being so out of date. Therefore, the U.S. Census Bureau asked Dr. Herman Hollerith, a statistician, to develop a faster method of tabulating the data. Hollerith invented a

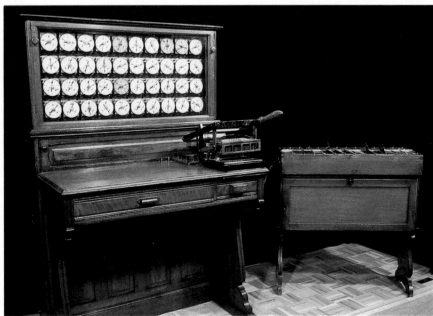

Figure 1-17
Herman Hollerith and the
Tabulating Machine
Once data was punched onto the
cards, a tabulator read the cards as
they passed over tiny brushes. Each
time a brush found a hole, it
completed an electrical circuit and
caused special counting dials to
increment the data. The cards then
were sorted into 24 compartments by
the sorting component of the machine.

Tabulating Machine that read and compiled data from punched cards (see Figure 1-17). These cards were the forerunners of today's standard computer card (see Figure 1-18). Thanks to Hollerith's invention, the time needed to process the 1890 census data was reduced to two and one-half years, despite the fact that the population increased by thirteen million people in the intervening ten years.

Encouraged by his success, Hollerith formed the Tabulating Machine Company in 1896 to supply equipment to census takers in western Europe and Canada. In 1911, Hollerith sold his company, which later combined with twelve others as the Computing-Tabulating-Recording Company (CTR). Thomas J. Watson, Sr., became president of CTR in 1924, and changed the name to International Business Machines Corporation (IBM). The IBM machines made extensive use of punched cards. After Congress set up the Social Security System in 1935, Watson won for IBM the contract to provide machines needed for this massive accounting and payment distribution system. The U.S. Census Bureau also bought IBM equipment.

During the late 1920s and early 1930s, accounting machines evolved which could perform many record-keeping and accounting functions. Although they handled the U.S. business data processing load well into the 1950s, they did little more than manipulate vast quantities of punched cards. These machines were limited in speed, physical size, and versatility.

The first real advance toward modern computing came in 1944, when Howard Aiken's team at Harvard University began designing the Mark I. This machine, the first automatic calculator, used Hollerith's punched card concept and was controlled by instructions coded on punched paper tapes. The U.S. Navy used the Mark I for designing weapons and calculating trajectories until the end of World War II.

Regardless of its role in computer history, the Mark I was outdated before it was finished. Only two years after work on it was begun, John Mauchly and

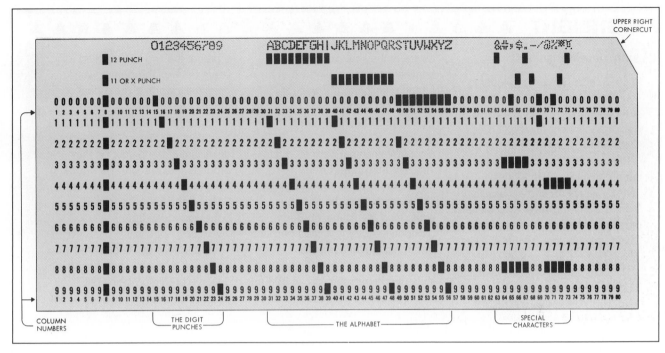

Figure 1-18
A Computer Card

J. Presper Eckert, Jr., introduced the first electronic computer for large-scale, general use at the University of Pennsylvania Moore School of Engineering. This machine was called the ENIAC, short for Electronic Numerical Integrator and Calculator (see Figure 1-19). Although it was invented because of a need for faster ways to calculate artillery trajectories during World War II, ENIAC was finished after the war ended, and was used instead for studying weather, cosmic rays, and

Figure 1-19   The ENIAC
The ENIAC's first job was calculating the feasibility of a proposed design for the hydrogen bomb. The computer also was used for studying weather and cosmic rays.

HIGHLIGHT ▲▲▲▲▲▲▲▲▲▲▲▲▲▲▲▲▲▲▲▲▲▲▲▲▲

John Vincent Atanasoff

In 1973, after 32 years, a federal court declared that the true inventor of the electronic digital computer was John Vincent Atanasoff. Traditionally, John W. Mauchly and J. Presper Eckert, Jr., had received the credit for their work on the ENIAC. Atanasoff and his assistant Clifford Berry, however, completed a prototype of a digital computer seven years before the ENIAC was developed.

The old adage, "Necessity is the mother of invention," held true in Atanasoff's case. He first felt the need for a computing machine while working on his doctorate in math and physics. After Atanasoff completed his degree, he accepted a teaching position at Iowa State University. He became even more

aware of the limitations of conventional calculating when he began monitoring the work of graduate students.

Atanasoff began working on the design of a binary electromechanical device. In late 1939, Atanasoff and Berry completed a prototype computer. Three years later, the two men completed the Atanasoff-Berry Computer (ABC), a limited-purpose electronic digital computer.

At the time, Atanasoff could not interest companies such as IBM and Remington Rand in the computer. Even more disturbing, he failed to obtain patent rights for the invention. This issue came to court as a dispute over patents. Sperry Rand had purchased the rights to Eckert and Mauchly's design and received

a patent the two had applied for years before. The patent was potentially worth a great deal of money in royalties from other companies. Another computer manufacturer, Honeywell, sought dismissal at the patent on the grounds that Mauchly had gone to Iowa to study the ABC before building the ENIAC and had borrowed ideas from Atanasoff's invention.

Regardless of the outcome, Atanasoff, Mauchly, and Eckert all deserve credit for their work. Atanasoff for his initial ideas about using vacuum tubes and binary code and Mauchly and Eckert for having built the first true large-scale general-purpose computer.

---

nuclear energy. It represented the shift from mechanical/electromechanical devices that used wheels, gears, and relays for computing to devices that depended upon electronic parts, such as vacuum tubes and electrical circuitry.

The ENIAC was a huge machine; its 18,000 vacuum tubes took up a space 8 feet high and 80 feet long. It weighed 30 tons and consumed 174,000 watts of power. In 20 seconds, ENIAC performed a mathematical calculation that would have required 40 hours for one person to complete using manual techniques. At the time, the ENIAC seemed so fast that scientists predicted that seven computers like it could handle all the calculations the world would ever need.

STORED-PROGRAM CONCEPT
The idea that program instructions can be stored in primary memory in electronic form so that no human intervention is required during processing.

The ENIAC had one major limitation: Operating instructions had to be fed into it manually by setting switches and connecting wires on control panels called plugboards. This was a tedious, time-consuming, and error-prone task. In the mid-1940s, the mathematician John von Neumann proposed a way to overcome this difficulty. The solution was the **stored-program concept** (discussed further in Chapter 3). Von Neumann believed that both instructions and data could be written in binary notation and stored in the computer's primary memory. This advance decreased the number of manual operations needed in switching programs and other computer operations. Eckert and Mauchly actually conceived the stored-program concept long before von Neumann did, but they did not outline a plan for its use and therefore did not profit from their ideas.

Table 1-1
Summary of Early Calculating
Developments

Person	Motivation	Machine
Pascal	Needed a faster, more accurate way to compute tax reports	Pascaline
von Leibniz	Wanted a faster method for computing	Stepped Reckoner
Jacquard	Thought changing loom settings by hand was tiresome and time-consuming	Loom automated by punched cards
Babbage	Needed accurate mathematics tables	Difference engine, Analytical engine
Hollerith	Worked on a project to finish tabulating the 1890 census faster	Tabulating Machine
Aiken	Helped in designing a machine that aided in calculating artillery trajectories	Mark I
Eckert, Mauchly	Designed a machine meant to be used in calculating artillery trajectories	ENIAC
von Neumann	Recognized the probjem with setting computer instructions by moving switches and wires	EDVAC

Von Neumann's principles spurred the development of the first stored-program computer in the United States, the EDVAC (Electronic Discrete Variable Automatic Computer). This development marked the beginning of the modern computer era and the so-called information society. Subsequent refinements of the stored-program concept have focused on speed, size, and cost. (See Table 1-1 for a summary of early developments.)

Learning Check

1. What was Pascal's contribution to the development of computers?

2. In what three ways was Jacquard's loom important to the development of computers?

3. Who is known as the father of computers?

4. What did the federal government want Herman Hollerith to invent in time for the 1890 census?

5. What need spurred the development of the Mark I and the ENIAC?

6. What was von Neumann's contribution to computer development?

Answers

1. A mechanical calculator, the Pascaline   2. Information could be coded on punched cards, punched cards could be linked to form a "program," and such programs and machines could automate jobs.   3. Charles Babbage   4. A faster method for tabulating census data   5. The need for faster ways to calculate artillery trajectories   6. The stored-program concept

Table 1-2
Hardware Benchmarks
Vacuum tubes gave way to transistors and transistors gave way to chips in the effort to reduce the size of computer components.

Vacuum Tubes	
Mauchly, Eckert, and ENIAC	First electronic digital computer
von Neumann and EDVAC	First stored-program computer
Mauchly, Eckert, and UNIVAC	First general-purpose, large-scale computer used for commercial purposes
Transistors and Magnetic Cores	
Bell Laboratories	Developed first transistor
U.S. Navy and Whirlwind I	First computer used for real-time functions
Integrated Circuits	
Jack S. Kilby	Developed integrated circuit
Robert Noyce	Developed integrated circuit
Ted Hoff and microprocessor	Led to development of microcomputers

The First Generation: 1951–1958

Improvements in computer capabilities are grouped into generations, based upon the electronic technology available at the time. (See Tables 1-2 and 1-3 for reviews of hardware benchmarks and characteristics of the generations.) There is some disagreement among professionals about the exact dates associated with each computer generation. The dates given in this chapter are approximations. The first generation of computers—based upon the designs of the ENIAC and EDVAC—began with the sale of the first commercial electronic computer (see Figure 1-20). This machine, called the UNIVAC I, was developed by Mauchly and Eckert, who had approached Remington Rand for financing. Remington Rand (today Sperry Corporation) bought Mauchly and Eckert's company and entered the computer age with a product that was years ahead of the machines produced by competitors. In 1951, the first UNIVAC I replaced IBM equipment at the U.S. Census Bureau.

Figure 1-20
The UNIVAC I
The most popular business uses for the UNIVAC I were payroll and billing.

Table 1-3
Chracteristics of the Four Generations

Period	Characteristics
First Generation 1951–1958	Vacuum tubes for internal operations. Magnetic drums for primary memory. Limited primary memory. Heat and maintenance problems. Punched cards for input and output. Slow input, processing, and output. Low-level symbolic languages for programming.
Second Generation 1959–1964	Transistors for internal operations. Magnetic cores for primary memory. Increased primary memory capacity. Magnetic tapes and disks for secondary storage. Reductions in size and heat generation. Increase in processing speed and reliability. Increased use of high-level languages.
Third Generation 1965–1970	Integrated circuits on silicon chips for internal operations. Increased primary memory capacity. Common use of minicomputers. Emergence of software industry. Reduction in size and cost. Increase in speed and reliability.
Fourth Generation 1971–Today	Large-scale and very large-scale integration for internal operations. Development of the microprocessor. Introduction of microcomputers and supercomputers. Greater versatility in software. Increase in speed, power, and storage capacity. Parallel processing. Artificial intelligence and expert systems. Robotics.

Another UNIVAC was installed at General Electric's Appliance Park in Louisville, Kentucky. For the first time, business firms saw the potential of computer data processing.

The UNIVAC I and other first-generation computers were huge, costly to buy, expensive to power, and often unreliable. They were slow compared to today's computers, and primary memory was limited. They depended upon the first-generation technology of vacuum tubes for internal operations. The masses of vacuum tubes took up a lot of space and required an air-conditioned environment to dissipate the considerable heat they generated. When a tube burned out, too much time was wasted hunting for it.

Punched cards were used to enter data into the machines. Internal storage consisted of magnetic drums, cylinders coated with magnetizable material. A drum rotated at high speeds, while a device poised just above it either wrote on the drum by magnetizing small spots, or read from it by detecting spots already magnetized. Then the results of processing were punched on blank cards.

Early first-generation computers were given instructions coded in **machine language.** Preparing the program or instructions was extremely tedious, and errors were common. In order to overcome this difficulty, **assembly languages** were developed. Assembly languages consist of mnemonic symbols. For example, ADD

MACHINE LANGUAGE
The only language the computer can execute directly; designates the computer's electrical states as combinations of 0's and 1's.

ASSEMBLY LANGUAGE
Lower-level, symbolic programming language that uses abbreviations rather than groupings of 0's and 1's.

might stand for addition. These symbols were easier for people to use than the strings of 0s and 1s of machine language. Special programs were developed to translate the assembly language into machine language, the only language computers can understand. Commodore Grace Murray Hopper of the U.S. Navy worked with a team that developed the first of these programs.

The public was not yet aware of the amazing computing machines, but this situation changed with the 1952 presidential election. After analyzing only 5 percent of the tallied vote, a UNIVAC I computer predicted that Dwight David Eisenhower would defeat Adlai E. Stevenson. CBS doubted the accuracy of the prediction and did not release the information to the public until the election results were confirmed by actual votes. The electronic prediction became the first in a burgeoning trend that has culminated in today's controversy about predicting election results from East Coast tallies before polls are closed on the West Coast.

Business acceptance of computers grew quickly. In 1953, Remington Rand and IBM led the infant industry, having placed a grand total of nine installations. By the late 1950s, IBM alone had leased 1,000 of its first-generation computers.

The Second Generation: 1959–1964

Four hardware advances in the 1940s and 1950s characterized the second-generation computers: the transistor, magnetic core storage, magnetic tapes, and magnetic disks. Transistors, developed by Bell Laboratories, replaced the vacuum tubes of first-generation machines. A transistor is a small component made of solid material which acts like a vacuum tube in controlling the flow of electric current. Using transistors in computers resulted in smaller, faster, and more reliable machines that used less electricity and generated much less heat than the first-generation computers.

Just as transistors replaced vacuum tubes as primary electronic components, magnetic cores replaced magnetic drums as internal storage units. Magnetic cores consisted of tiny rings of magnetic material strung on fine wires (see Figure 1-21). Each magnetic core was placed at the intersection of a vertical and a horizontal wire. To turn on a core, half the electricity needed was run through each wire. Thus, only at the intersection of specific wires would a core become charged. In this way, groups of cores stored instructions and data.

The development of magnetic cores resulted from the U.S. Navy's need for a more advanced, reliable high-speed flight trainer. Known as Whirlwind I, the Navy project was one of the most innovative and influential projects in the history of the computer. Because of the high speed with which instructions and data could be located and retrieved using magnetic cores (a few millionths of a second), the Whirlwind allowed the real-time processing necessary in flight simulation. The development led to other real-time functions such as air traffic control, factory management, and battle simulations.

MAGNETIC TAPE
A sequential storage medium consisting of a narrow strip of material upon which spots are magnetized to represent data.

MAGNETIC DISK
A direct-access storage medium consisting of a metal or plastic platter upon which data can be stored as magnetized spots.

This new type of internal storage was supplemented by external storage on **magnetic tapes** and **disks.** During World War II, huge, heavy steel tapes were used for sound recording. Plastic magnetic tapes eventually replaced the metal tapes and were used later for recording computer output, recorded as magnetized spots on the tape's surface. Another byproduct of sound recording, the phonograph record, led to the introduction of the magnetic disk, which allows direct access to

Figure 1-21
A Frame of Magnetic Cores
An assembled core unit looked much
like a window screen.

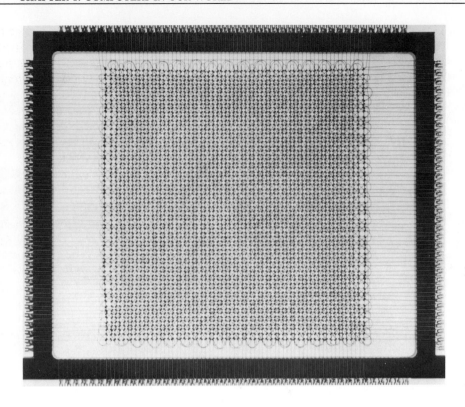

data. Both disks and tapes greatly increased the speed of processing and storage capacities, and eventually replaced punched cards for storage.

During this period, more sophisticated, English-like computer languages such as COBOL and FORTRAN were commonly used.

The Third Generation: 1965–1970

INTEGRATED CIRCUIT
An electronic circuit etched on a small silicon chip less than one-quarter inch square.

SILICON CHIP
Solid-state logic circuitry on a small piece of silicon.

LARGE-SCALE INTEGRATION (LSI)
Method by which circuits containing thousands of electronic components are densely packed on a single chip.

At the same time that transistors were replacing vacuum tubes, Jack S. Kilby of Texas Instruments and Robert Noyce at Fairchild Semiconductor were separately developing the **integrated circuit (IC).** Using their own methods, they discovered that the components of electronic circuits could be placed together—or integrated—onto small chips. Soon, a single **silicon chip** less than one-eighth inch square could hold sixty-four complete circuits. This seems crude to us, since today's chips can contain as many as 500,000 transistors.

The chips marked the third generation of computers, which used less power, cost less, and were smaller and much more reliable than previous machines. Although computers were smaller, their internal memories were larger due to the placement of memory on chips. In early third-generation computers, the density with which components were integrated was known as medium-scale integration (MSI). **Large-scale integration (LSI)** soon followed, which put thousands of components on a silicon chip.

Figure 1-22
A Third-Generation Minicomputer
The development of minicomputers
enabled many small businesses to
acquire computer power, because the
costs were much less than for
mainframes.

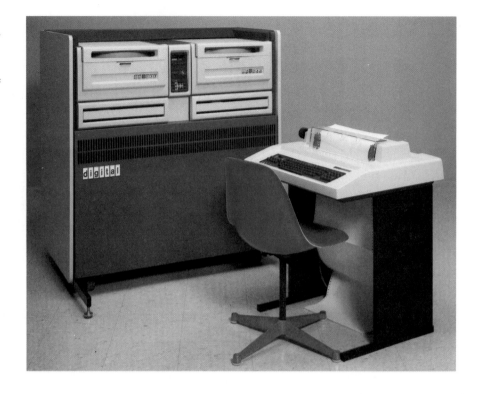

MINICOMPUTER
**A type of computer with the
components of a full-sized system
but with smaller primary memory.**

A major innovation resulted when IBM realized its company was turning out
too many incompatible products. The company responded to the problem by designing the System/360 computers, which offered both scientific and business
applications and introduced the family concept of computers. The first series
consisted of six computers designed to run the same programs and use the same
input, output, and storage equipment. Each computer offered a different memory
capacity. For the first time, a company could buy a computer and feel that its
investment in programs and peripheral equipment would not be wasted when the
time came to move to a machine with a larger memory. Other manufacturers
followed IBM's lead, and before long, over 25,000 similar computer systems were
installed in the United States.

Minicomputers, developed during the second generation, were commonly used
in the 1960s (see Figure 1-22). Although these machines had many of the same
capabilities as large computers, they were much smaller, had less storage space,
and cost less. Use of remote terminals also became common. Remote terminals
are computer terminals located some distance away from a main computer and
linked to it through cables such as telephone lines. Thus it is not necessary to be
in the same room, or even the same building, in order to use the computer.

The software industry also began to emerge in the 1960s. Programs to perform
payroll, billing, and other business tasks became available at fairly low cost. Yet
software rarely was free of "bugs," or errors. The computer industry experienced
growing pains as the software industry lagged behind advances in hardware technology. The rapid advancements in hardware meant that old programs had to be
rewritten to suit the circuitry of the new machines, and programmers skilled enough

Figure 1-23
An IBM Microcomputer

MICROPROCESSOR
A programmable processing unit (placed on a silicon chip) containing arithmetic, logic, and control circuitry.

MICROCOMPUTER
A small, low-priced computer used in homes, schools, and businesses; also called a personal computer.

VERY LARGE-SCALE INTEGRATION (VLSI)
Method by which circuits containing hundreds of thousands of components are packed on a single chip even more densely than with LSI.

SUPERCOMPUTER
Currently the largest, fastest, most expensive type of computer; can perform millions of calculations per second and process enormous amounts of data.

Figure 1-24
A Computer Chip
This 32-bit chip contains almost 150,000 transistors and offers processing power comparable to that of today's minicomputers.

to do this were scarce. Software problems led to computer horror stories, such as a $200,000 water bill or $80,000 worth of duplicate welfare checks.

The Fourth Generation: 1971–Today

Although the dividing lines between the first three generations of computers are clearly marked by major technological advances, historians are not so clear as to when the fourth generation began. They do agree that, in fourth-generation computers, magnetic cores had replaced memory on silicon chips. Even today, however, programmers often refer to main memory as "core."

Engineers continued to cram more circuits onto a single chip in LSI, thus shortening the distance electricity had to travel during data processing. The functions that could be performed with a chip, however, were permanently fixed during the production process. Ted Hoff, an engineer at Intel Corporation, introduced an idea that resulted in a single programmable unit: the **microprocessor** or "computer on a chip." In 1969, working with a team at Intel, Hoff packed the arithmetic and logic circuitry needed for computations onto one microprocessor chip, which could be made to act like any kind of calculator or computer desired. Other functions, such as input, output, and memory, were placed on separate chips. The development of the microprocessor led to a boom in computer manufacturing which gave computing power to homes and schools in the form of **microcomputers** (see Figure 1-23).

As microcomputers became more popular, many companies began producing software that could be run on the smaller machines. Most early programs were games. Later, instructional programs began to appear. One important software development was the first electronic spreadsheet for microcomputers: *VisiCalc,* introduced in 1979. *VisiCalc* vastly increased the possibilities for using microcomputers in the business world. Today, a wide variety of software exists for microcomputer applications in business, school, and personal use.

Currently, **very large-scale integration (VLSI)** has replaced large-scale integration. In VLSI, as many as 500,000 electronic components can be placed on a single silicon chip (see Figure 1-24). This further miniaturization of integrated circuits offers even greater improvements in price, performance, and size of computers. A microprocessor based on VSLI is more powerful than a roomful of 1950s computer circuitry.

Trends in miniaturization led ironically to the development of the largest and most powerful of computers: the **supercomputers.** By reducing the size of circuitry

PARALLEL PROCESSING
A type of processing in which instructions and data are handled simultaneously by two or more processing units.

and changing the design of the chips, companies that manufacture supercomputers were able to create computers powerful enough with memories large enough to perform the complex calculations required in aircraft design, weather forecasting, nuclear research, and energy conservation. Supercomputers process data differently than other computers. Traditional processing occurs serially—that is, all the data is handled bit by bit. Supercomputers, on the other hand, use **parallel processing.** In parallel processing, two or more CPUs or microprocessors work simultaneously on parts of the same problem, so that more than one bit is handled at one time. Computer speed is increased without further miniaturizing the circuits and encountering problems that result when circuits are packed too densely. The technique shows great potential for tackling very large problems with multiple variables. Parallel processing aids further development of speech recognition, interpretation of data from sensing devices, navigation uses, expert systems, artificial intelligence, and new generations of robots. (See Chapters 6 and 7 for more information about robots, expert systems, and artificial intelligence.)

Today's trends in chip design, supercomputers, and computer languages anticipate a fifth generation of computer development. In the effort to increase processing speed and develop ultra-large-scale integration needed in supercomputers, scientists are working on a new generation of chips that can perform more than a million calculations in a single second. Experts predict that, by 1990, a single chip may contain as many as 16 million components. Materials such as gallium arsenide, which achieves speeds five to seven times that of the fastest silicon chips, may be used in developing these new chips.

Some scientists believe that tiny computer circuits can be grown from the proteins and enzymes of living material, such as *E. coli* bacteria. Like other life forms, these "biochips" would require oxygen, and the signals they would send would be similar to those sent and received by our brains. Since biochips would be made from living material, they could repair and reproduce themselves. They would be 10 million times as powerful as today's most advanced computers.

Learning Check

1. What was the distinction given UNIVAC I?

2. What electronic technology characterized each of the four generations of computers?

3. Why was the magnetic core an important development?

4. Name one problem of software during the third generation.

5. What development led to microcomputers?

6. What is the advantage of parallel processing?

Answers

1. It was the first commercial computer. 2. Vacuum tubes, transistors, integrated circuits, and very large-scale integration respectively. 3. It allowed real-time processing. 4. All software had to be rewritten for the new technology. 5. Microprocessors 6. Since it processes more than one bit at a time, it allows faster processing without further miniaturization of circuits.

Biochips might first be used to sense odors that indicate unusual or dangerous conditions. Such chips also could be implanted in a blind person's brain and linked to a visual sensor like a miniature camera, thus enabling the person to see. Some biochips placed in the human bloodstream could monitor and correct chemical imbalances. Although the idea of biochips may seem farfetched at present, scientists continue to experiment.

It is no wonder that writers describe computer chips in terms of angels dancing on the heads of pins and house-by-house maps of the largest cities etched on postage stamps. With the breakneck pace of chip development in the past few years, nothing seems surprising now.

Summary Points

■ Computers are powerful tools in many areas such as business, manufacturing, banking, government, education, and personal use. Most of today's transactions and procedures involve computers.

■ Electronic data processing involves the use of computers in collecting, manipulating, and distributing data to achieve goals.

■ Data refers to unorganized, raw facts. Information is data that has been organized and processed so that it can be used in making intelligent decisions.

■ Analog computers measure changes in continuous physical or electric states, whereas digital computers count data in the form of yes/no, conducting/nonconducting, on/off states of electronic circuitry. The digital computer must convert all data to binary form, which is based on the binary number system of two digits, 0 and 1.

■ The terms *hardware* and *software* describe the physical components of a computer and the instructions or programs respectively.

■ The computer performs three basic functions: arithmetic operations, logic comparisons, and storage and retrieval operations.

■ A computer's internal memory is called primary storage. Media used to hold data outside the computer constitute secondary storage, which makes the computer's memory almost limitless.

■ Converting data into information includes three steps: input, processing, and output.

■ The two types of processing are batch, in which data are collected and forwarded to the computer in groups, and interactive, in which the user communicates with the computer during processing.

■ The first programmable machine was a weaving loom. The same punched-card principle was used later by Hollerith in processing census data.

■ Charles Babbage is called the father of computers because his plans for an analytical engine outlined some ideas important in the design of computers.

■ The Mark I, the first automatic calculator, was the first real advance toward modern computers, although it was out of date by the time it was finished.

■ ENIAC was the first general-purpose electronic computer put to large-scale practical use, but it had no internal memory. A later machine, EDVAC, used internal memory and stored program instructions.

■ First-generation computers used vacuum tubes to control operations. These machines were large and unreliable, and they generated much heat.

■ Second-generation computers used transistors to control operations. Transistors are smaller, more reliable, and faster than vacuum tubes. During this period, computers had magnetic core storage and magnetic tapes and disks for secondary storage.

■ Third-generation computers used integrated circuits to control operations. Integrated circuits are smaller, faster, and more reliable than transistors. Some third-generation computers used large-scale integration (LSI). The third generation also was characterized by the use of minicomputers, remote terminals, and families of computers. The software industry was beginning to emerge.

■ Fourth-generation computers continue to become smaller, faster, and less costly; they are characterized by very large-scale integration (VLSI). The refinement of the microprocessor led to the development of microcomputers.

■ Faster chips and parallel processing will increase the capabilities of computers. Some experts believe that a single chip may contain as many as 16 million components by 1990. Others believe that circuits will be grown into biochips from protein and enzyme material. Parallel processing improves processing speed by allowing one computer to handle more than one bit simultaneously.

Review Questions

1. Name some ways that computers affect you in your job or school today. Relate these examples to applications discussed in the first section of this chapter.

2. Distinguish between data and information in the context of data processing. Give some examples.

3. Define data processing. Why is it often referred to as EDP?

4. Using data that a store might collect when you purchase groceries, describe the five types of manipulations that may occur in the processing stage of EDP.

5. Although computer processing is essentially error-free, mistakes can and do occur. What is meant by the ''garbage in–garbage out'' principle? Name two procedures mentioned in the data flow discussion which could prevent GIGO.

6. Describe two types of storage involved in data processing. Why is the computer's memory almost limitless?

7. From the material in this chapter, name and describe at least two terms that would characterize the computer processing involved in buying tickets to the Olympic Games.

8. Describe how the use of punched cards affected the advance of automation, beginning with the invention of Jacquard.

9. Describe the stored-program concept and explain how it changed computer processing.

10. Based on the material in the text, name at least three factors that usually indicate a new generation of computers.

11. Why has the development of the integrated circuit and large-scale integration made such an impact on the computer industry?

12. How will further development of parallel processing affect use of computers?

CHAPTER 2

Getting to Know Your IBM

Introduction

IBM microcomputers are popular for business applications and for writing and editing. They are powerful enough, yet inexpensive enough, for small businesses to use for financial management, bookkeeping, billing, and professional-looking document preparation. Large businesses also are buying IBM microcomputers for linking to mainframe systems. Workers can use these microcomputers as independent machines for tasks that do not need the power of a mainframe. They can access data from the mainframe system through communication lines. This solution keeps the data in one central location, thus facilitating data integrity by reducing the number of places where the same data must be updated. It also reserves the mainframe for tasks that require its greater capacity.

IBM microcomputers are also popular in schools and homes. A wide variety of software is available for educational, recreational, and home-management purposes.

IBM microcomputers come in several models, including the IBM PC, PC jr. (no longer manufactured), IBM PC/XT, IBM PC/AT, and the IBM PC Convertible. This chapter explains how to begin using the IBM PC and how to care for your computer and disks.

IBM Hardware

DISK DRIVE
The mechanical device used to rotate a disk, floppy disk, or disk pack past a read/write head during data transmission.

MONITOR
A video display device or screen used for showing computer output.

PRINTER
A machine that prints characters or other images on paper.

KILOBYTE (K)
1,024 (2^{10}) storage units, or bytes; often rounded to 1,000.

PRIMARY MEMORY
The section of the computer which holds instructions, data, and intermediate and final results during processing.

In order to run software on an IBM PC, you need three standard pieces of equipment (see Figure 2-1). The main part of an IBM PC is the system unit (see the back of a system unit in Figure 2-2), which holds the computer itself and one or more **disk drives.** A **monitor** and a keyboard also are needed. If you want paper copies of your work, a fourth piece of hardware, the **printer,** will do the job.

The basic IBM PC has 256 **K (kilobytes)** of **primary memory,** but it can be upgraded to 640 k which will allow it to handle almost any type of software. The amount of memory a computer can handle is important because each program requires a specific amount of memory. The software package lists the amount of memory needed, so be sure to check the requirements before buying a program. More memory can be added to an IBM PC by installing additional memory chips or expansion boards containing memory chips (see Figure 2-3). An IBM dealer can give you details about adding memory.

The Monitor

The monitor displays output on a screen that is similar to a television screen. Without it, you could not see what you have typed. IBM PCs usually are equipped with a monochrome monitor or color monitor. A monochrome monitor displays a single color on a black or gray background. Color monitors require a special graphics circuit card that is installed in the computer. Television sets can be used, too, but they display a poorer quality of text than monitors designed for computer use. The type of monitor depends on the purposes for which the computer will be used. (More information about monitors appears in Chapter 5, Microcomputers.)

Figure 2-1
IBM PC Microcomputer

Figure 2-2
Back View of an IBM PC

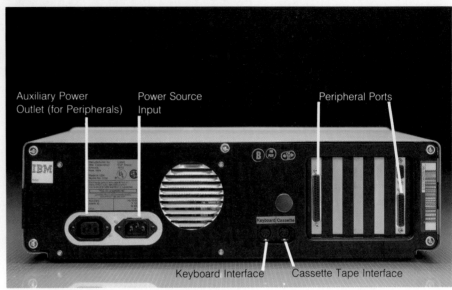

CURSOR
A character (square, vertical bar, or arrow) on a screen which shows where the next typed character will appear; the cursor may flash.

The Cursor   You see your location on the screen by looking for the **cursor.** The cursor for many programs on IBM computers is a tiny horizontal bar (see Figure 2-4). As you type, the cursor moves ahead of each typed character that appears on the screen.

Figure 2-3
A Card of Memory Chips

Figure 2-4
The Cursor

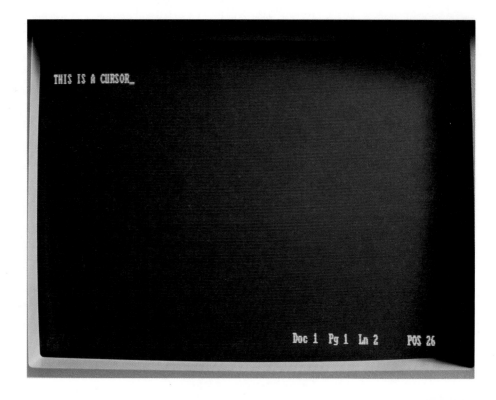

PROMPT
A message or cue that guides the
user during computer processing.

Changing Screen Width When in the DOS mode (DOS is explained later in this chapter), the IBM PC shows 80 columns on the screen. The computer is in DOS mode when you see the A> **prompt.** (Depending on which disk drive you are using, the prompt may be B> or C> instead.) If you are using a color/graphics monitor, you can type the following command to change the screen width from 80 columns to 40 columns:

```
MODE BW40
```

Similarly, you can type the following command to change the screen width from 40 columns to 80 columns:

```
MODE BW80
```

The Keyboard

Before using your IBM computer, you should become familiar with its keyboard. The IBM PC, IBM PC/XT, and older IBM PC/AT keyboards are similar. Each keyboard has the same keys as a regular typewriter (see Figure 2-5). The letter and number keys work the same as a typewriter's keys. Pressing the shift key (marked ⇧) with a letter key produces a capital letter. Pressing the shift key with a number or special character key produces the character shown on the top half of the key. When any key is held down, the character is repeated until the key is

Figure 2-5
The IBM PC Keyboard

released. Because of this feature, be sure that you press keys just long enough for the character to appear on the screen or for the computer to receive the command.

On the left side of the keyboard is a set of ten numbered function keys. The function that each key performs is determined by the software being used. (On the new IBM PC/AT keyboards, these function keys are the top row of keys.)

The keyboard has a numeric keypad on the right side, similar to a calculator's keypad, which also is used for editing purposes. When the Num Lock key in the top row of keys is pressed, the keypad can be to enter numbers 0–9.

Arrow keys for controlling the cursor are located within the numeric keypad. They can be used to move the cursor up, down, to the left, or to the right on the screen. The left arrow key is the same key as the 4, the right arrow key is the same key as the 6, the up arrow key is the same key as the 8, and the down arrow key is the same as the 2. If you make a typing mistake, these keys help you move the cursor to it. Then you can correct the mistake. Mistakes also can be corrected by moving the cursor to the left using the backspace key, which is located in the top row of keys and marked with an arrow pointing left.

The key marked with the ← ↑ symbol, located just to the left of the numeric keypad, is referred to as either the Enter Key or the Return Key. It moves the cursor down to the beginning of the next line. The line of data just typed is entered into the computer's memory.

Other special keys on IBM keyboards are listed in Table 2-1. When two keys are used together, hold down the first one while typing the second. Then release both keys immediately. Do not continue holding them down. The functions of some key combinations vary depending on the software being used. Always read the software documentation to find out the functions of the keys.

FLOPPY DISK
A low-cost, direct-access form of secondary storage made of flexible plastic; also called a flexible disk or diskette.

The Disk Drive

Disk drives can be double-sided or single-sided. A double-sided disk drive can write data to and read data from both sides of a **floppy disk** without the user

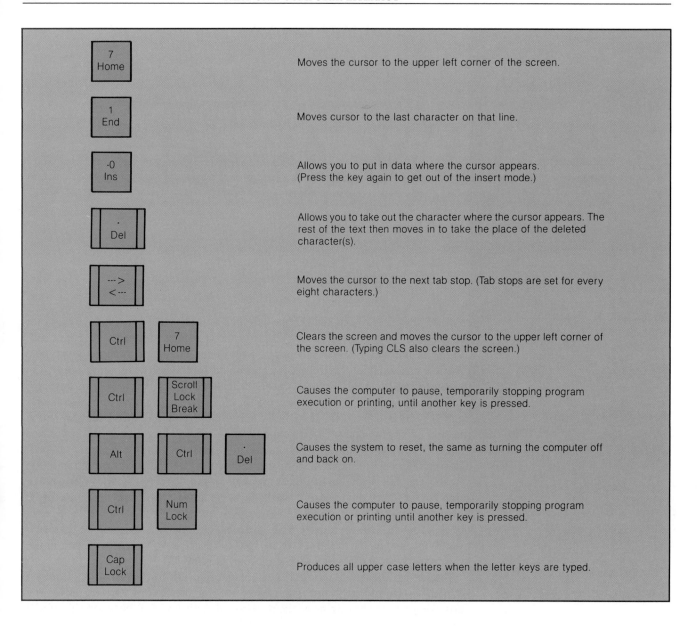

Key	Function
7 Home	Moves the cursor to the upper left corner of the screen.
1 End	Moves cursor to the last character on that line.
-0 Ins	Allows you to put in data where the cursor appears. (Press the key again to get out of the insert mode.)
. Del	Allows you to take out the character where the cursor appears. The rest of the text then moves in to take the place of the deleted character(s).
---> <---	Moves the cursor to the next tab stop. (Tab stops are set for every eight characters.)
Ctrl + 7 Home	Clears the screen and moves the cursor to the upper left corner of the screen. (Typing CLS also clears the screen.)
Ctrl + Scroll Lock Break	Causes the computer to pause, temporarily stopping program execution or printing, until another key is pressed.
Alt + Ctrl + . Del	Causes the system to reset, the same as turning the computer off and back on.
Ctrl + Num Lock	Causes the computer to pause, temporarily stopping program execution or printing until another key is pressed.
Cap Lock	Produces all upper case letters when the letter keys are typed.

Table 2-1
Special Keys and Their Functions

flipping the disk. (See Figure 2-6 for a graphic description of a floppy disk.) A single-sided disk drive can write data to and read data from only one side of the floppy disk at a time. The standard IBM disk drive is a double-sided drive. A diskette drive adapter card must be installed in the system unit for the disk drive to operate. The card can control up to four disk drives.

When two floppy disk drives are used, one drive is called Drive A and the other is called Drive B. Drive A is the drive on the left. A disk should be inserted in Drive A before one is inserted in Drive B. When only one drive is present, it is Drive A.

Figure 2-6
Floppy Disk

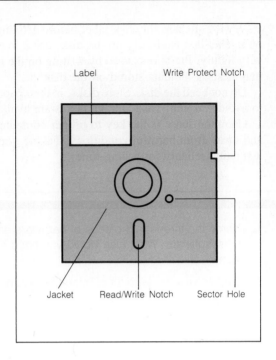

Caring for Your Computer

Taking good care of your IBM computer will help keep it working properly. The computer should be set on a sturdy desk or table. The room should be clean and dry, but not too dry. When the humidity in a room is very low, static electricity may be created, which can destroy the data stored on floppy disks. Extreme heat and cold also may harm the computer. Keep the machine away from direct sunlight. Never set the computer or any hardware on appliances that get hot, such as televisions, and keep hardware away from heating ducts and air conditioners.

Eating and drinking should be avoided near the computer. Crumbs and spilled drinks can make the keyboard keys stick. Dust and dirt from the air can harm the keyboard or cause static. It is a good idea to keep the computer and hardware devices covered with anti-static covers when they are not being used.

When the computer is on, be careful not to move it or jolt it, including the desk or table where it is placed. If the electrical plug is disconnected accidentally, data that has not been recorded on a disk is lost.

Your computer is only as reliable as the data storage medium. Floppy disks always should be handled with care. Never touch the exposed surface of the disk. Hold disks by their labels. Floppy disks can be ruined by extreme temperatures, dust, and eraser crumbs. For example, disks should not be left in a car when it is hot or cold outside. Avoid setting disks near magnets or telephones or on top of computers, disk drives, or television sets. Magnets and electrical devices can destroy data stored on disks.

Always prepare the disk label before affixing it to the disk. If you must write on a label that is already on the disk, use a felt-tip or nylon-tip marker and press very lightly. Pressure caused by writing on the label with a pencil or ballpoint pen may destroy the data stored on the disk.

Do not bend the disk. Store disks, in their paper envelopes, in an upright position to avoid warping. Disk storage boxes are available for this purpose.

Common sense is the key to proper computer care. Keep the equipment clean and away from harmful conditions. Taking good care of the computer will keep it running reliably for a long time.

Learning Check

1. Name the three main pieces of hardware an IBM computer needs to run most software. What else would you need for making paper copies of your work?

2. Explain why the amount of internal memory is an important factor.

3. What key on an IBM keyboard must be pressed to get capital letters? To move the cursor to the next line without typing to the end of the current line?

4. What keys can be used to move the cursor to a mistake for correction? Where are they located?

5. When an IBM computer uses two floppy-disk drives, what names are used to designate them? Into which drive should a disk always be inserted first?

6. Name three things that can harm a computer or its hardware devices.

7. Describe how floppy disks should be handled so that data stored on them remains reliable.

Answers

1. System unit (computer and disk drives), monitor, and keyboard; printer. 2. It determines which software can be used. 3. Shift; Enter. 4. The arrow keys on the numeric keypad, or the backspace key in the top row of keys. 5. Drive A and Drive B; Drive A. 6. Static, heat, spilled food. 7. Hold them by the labels. Never touch the exposed surface of the disk. Use only felt-tip or nylon-tip pens for writing on a label already attached to the disk. Put the disks in their protective paper envelopes and then rest them vertically for storage. Keep them away from extreme heat and cold and magnetic or electrical devices. Keep dust and eraser crumbs away from them.

Getting Started

LOAD
To put a program into a computer's primary memory from a disk or other medium.

Before you can use software with your IBM computer, you need to know how to **load** it. To load a program means to put it into the computer's primary memory. The method used to load software differs from one package to another, so you should read the directions accompanying the software.

Figure 2-7
Removing the Disk from Its
Envelope

OPERATING SYSTEM (OS)
A collection of programs used by
the computer to manage its own
operations.

Many software packages require that some type of operating system software be loaded first. IBM PC DOS 3.10 is one version of the **operating system** that comes with IBM microcomputers. An operating system consists of programs that allow the computer to manage itself. Disk operating system (DOS) is a name given to an operating system that resides on a disk. One of the programs in a DOS, for example, governs the transfer of data to and from disks.

When loading DOS, use Drive A if there are two drives. Hold the disk with your thumb on the label and take it out of its envelope (see Figure 2-7). Gently slide the disk into the slot (see Figure 2-8) on the drive. The oval cutout (read/

Figure 2-8
Inserting the Disk into the Disk
Drive

Figure 2-9
Closing the Disk Drive Door

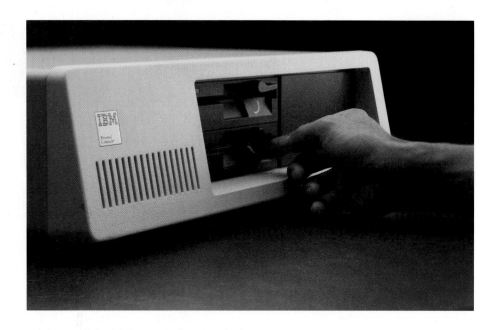

write notch) goes in first. Do not bend or force the disk. When the disk is in all the way, lock the diskette into place by pressing down on the knob to the right of the slot (see Figure 2-9).

Note that IBM also manufactures a diskette drive which has a disk-drive door which you open first and then insert the diskette. Once you insert the diskette, the door must be closed. See Fig. 2-10.

Figure 2-10
Opening the Disk Drive Door

Figure 2-11
Turning on the Power

Now turn on the computer and the monitor. Reach to the right rear side of the computer to find and turn on the power switch (see Figure 2-11).

Switches for most monitors are on the front right-hand side of the monitor. Turn or pull the ON switch of the monitor to the ''on'' position (see Figure 2-12). Then adjust the brightness control knob. Turning the knob to the left usually makes the screen darker. Turning the knob to the right usually brightens the screen.

Figure 2-12
Turning on the Monitor

HIGHLIGHT ▲▲▲▲▲▲▲▲▲▲▲▲▲▲▲▲▲▲▲▲▲▲▲

A Tale of Two Bugs

The story of the first computer bug has become a legend. In the summer of 1945, something went wrong with the Mark II, a large electromechanical machine used by the Department of Defense. Although the machine was not working properly, the operating personnel could find no obvious problems. A continued search revealed a large moth beaten to death by one of the electromechanical relays. The moth was pulled out with tweezers and taped to a log book (now exhibited in the Naval Museum at the Naval Surface Weapons Center, Dahlgren,

Virginia). "From then on," said Rear Admiral Grace Hopper, one of the people working with the machine, "when the officer came in to ask if we were accomplishing anything, we told him we were 'debugging' the computer." So the expressions "bugs in the program" and "debugging the program" became popular in describing programming errors.

Few people realize, however, that the use of the word bug to mean an error is at least 100 years old. Thomas Alva Edison introduced the word in a letter to Theodore Puskas, Edison's representative in France, on November 13, 1878. He wrote:

I have the right principle and am on the right track, but time, hard work, and some good luck are necessary too. It has been just so in all of my inventions. The first step is an intuition, and comes with a burst, then difficulties arise—this thing gives out and then that—"bugs"— as such little faults and difficulties are called—show themselves and months of intense watching, study and labor are requisite before commercial success—or failure—is certainly reached.

So now you have it—A Tale of Two Bugs.

When the computer is turned on, the power indicator on the keyboard and the small light on the front of Drive A both light. The disk drive makes a whirring noise as it reads the disk. After a few seconds, the noise stops and the disk-drive light goes off. *Never remove the disk or press any keys when the disk drive light is on.*

The opening display for your version of IBM PC DOS appears on the screen, as shown in Figure 2-13. First, the computer asks you to input today's date and time. Press the Enter key after you respond to each of these prompts. If you do not want to enter the date and time, press the Enter key twice instead. When the A> prompt appears, you can take out the DOS disk and insert the program disk. At this point, you probably need to type the name of the program in order to access the software. Read the software directions completely and follow them carefully.

Some software disks contain DOS in addition to the program, so it is not necessary to load DOS first. Just insert the disk into Drive A, and then turn on the computer and monitor.

When you are ready to remove a disk from the disk drive, make sure the light on the drive is off and that no noise is coming from the drive. Open the door and gently pull on the disk. Put the disk in its envelope. Turn off the computer and monitor if you are finished using the computer.

Figure 2-13
Opening Display for IBM PC DOS

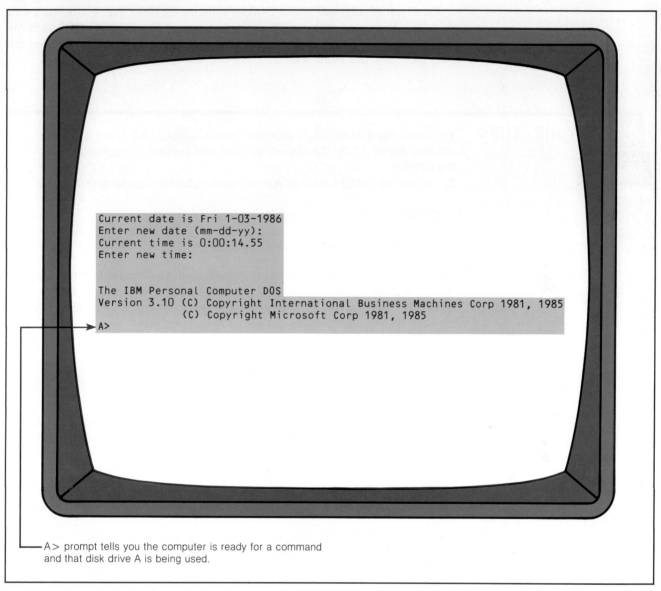

```
Current date is Fri 1-03-1986
Enter new date (mm-dd-yy):
Current time is 0:00:14.55
Enter new time:


The IBM Personal Computer DOS
Version 3.10 (C) Copyright International Business Machines Corp 1981, 1985
              (C) Copyright Microsoft Corp 1981, 1985
A>
```

A> prompt tells you the computer is ready for a command
and that disk drive A is being used.

Initializing a Disk

INITIALIZE (FORMAT)
To prepare a disk so that data and programs can be stored on it.

Before a blank disk can be used for storing data, you must **initialize** or **format** it. Initializing prepares the disk so that data and programs can be stored on it, according to the specifications of the DOS. When a used disk is initialized, everything stored on the disk is erased so that the disk can be used for new data and programs. Never initialize a disk with data stored on it unless you are sure you no longer need the data.

Each type of computer uses a DOS to initialize the disks that will be used with it. A disk initialized with a DOS other than one of the IBM PC DOS versions may not work on an IBM PC. To initialize a disk for an IBM PC, you need the IBM DOS disk that came with the computer and a blank disk.

 YOUR TURN

1. Insert the IBM PC DOS disk into the disk drive. Use Drive A if there are two drives. Close the disk-drive door and turn on the computer and the monitor.

2. When the system prompt A> appears, type the following command:

FORMAT B:/S (for a two-drive system)
or
FORMAT A:/S (for a one-drive system)

Press the Enter key. (The B that you type tells the computer that the blank disk is in Drive B. The A tells the computer that only one drive is being used. The /S, which is optional, copies three operating system files to the disk.

3. The following message appears:

```
Insert new diskette for drive B: (A for one drive)
and strike ENTER when ready
```

Insert the blank diskette in Drive B (or remove the DOS disk and insert the blank disk in Drive A) and close the door. Then press the Enter key. You should see the following message:

```
Formatting . . . Format complete
System transferred
```

along with some information about the byte space available. Remember, never remove a disk while the red light on the drive is still on.

4. The system asks if you need to format another disk. Type a Y if you do, or an N if you are finished.

5. Make a label for the disk. The label should state what the disk will be used for. Remove the disk from the drive, and put the label on the disk.

Initialize a disk using the steps listed above. You will need the IBM PC DOS disk and a blank disk. Be sure to put a label on the disk and put the disk back into its envelope when you are finished. The initialized disk can be used as a backup disk for the programs you will write in Section III of this text.

Disk Operating System Commands

The operating system contains the programs that control the computer (see Chapters 3 and 5). The few operating system instructions held permanently in primary memory do not contain all the programs needed for controlling operations. The remainder of the operating system is stored on a disk, and is loaded into primary memory as described in the last section. Part of this DOS is copied onto a blank disk when the blank disk is initialized using the /S option.

When you type the DOS commands, DOS programs tell the computer what to do. Some of these commands tell the computer to copy the contents of a disk onto another disk, rename a **file,** or erase a file. These commands are explained in Tables 2-2 and 2-3. Table 2-2 lists the steps involved in copying a disk. The DISKCOPY command is useful when you want to create backup disks of the programs you write while working on Section III of this text. The commands in Table 2-3 allow you to work with files stored on the disk.

FILE
A group of related records stored together; a specific unit of data stored on a disk, tape, or other medium.

Table 2-2
Copy a Disk

You should make copies of the disks that hold your files and programs as a precaution in case the originals are damaged or lost. Keep these backup disks in a place where they will not be damaged, and update them each time you update the original files or programs.

Insert the DOS disk into Drive A. Turn on the computer and monitor. Take out the DOS disk and insert the disk to be copied in Drive A and the disk to be copied to in Drive B. Then follow these steps:

1. The command for copying a disk is as follows:

```
DISKCOPY source drive: target drive:
```

You must specify the letter of the source drive (drive containing the disk to be copied) and the letter of the target drive (drive containing the disk to be copied to). For example, to copy the contents of the disk in Drive A onto the disk in Drive B, type the following command and press the Enter key:

```
DISKCOPY A: B:
```

For a system with only one disk drive, specify only one drive as shown. (The program will tell you when to switch disks during the copying process.)

```
DISKCOPY A:
```

2. After copying, the following message appears:

```
COPY ANOTHER (Y/N)?
```

Type Y to continue copying disks on the same drives indicated, or type N if you are finished.

3. When the copying process is completed, use the following command, which checks to see if the disks are identical:

```
DISKCOMP source drive: target drive:
```

To specify drives, follow the same examples that were shown for the DISKCOPY command. The disk in the first drive specified will be compared to the disk in the second drive. Again, for a one-drive system, specify only one drive. (You will have to switch disks again.) If there are any errors, a message indicates the location of the error. Check your user's manual if an error occurs.

Table 2-3
Operating System Commands

The operating system commands appear in uppercase letters in this chart. Do not type the word *filename.ext*; instead, type a name of your own choosing, as shown in the examples. Files sorted using Microsoft IBM DOS are typed with extensions. After the filename, type a period (.) and then an extension such as BAS for programs written in the BASIC programming language, TXT for text files, or DOC for document files. Press the Enter key after typing the complete command. The Enter key signals to the computer that it is time to execute the command.

Command	Example	Job Performed
DIR	DIR	Stands for DIRECTORY; shows the names of all the files stored on the disk.
ERASE *filename.ext* or DEL *filename.ext*	ERASE GRADES. TXT DEL GRADES. TXT	Erases or deletes a program on the disk.
RENAME *drive: old filename.ext new filename.ext*	RENAME A: GRADES.BAS SCORES.BAS	Changes a file's name. The old filename must be typed exactly as in the directory.
COPY *source drive: filename.ext target drive:*	WRONG COMMAND	Makes a copy of one file onto another disk. The file indicated is copied from the source disk to the target disk.

Using WestSoft™ 1.0

SIMULATION
A computer program that imitates a real-life event.

MODEM
A device that modulates and demodulates signals transmitted over communication lines; allows linkage with another computer.

MENU
A list of choices or options shown on the display screen, from which the user selects commands or data for entry into the computer.

The WestSoft software contains simulations of popular computer applications. A computer **simulation** is a program that imitates a real-life event. Thus a simulated program lets the user learn how to do a certain task or how to use a computerized service, such as an information network or home banking service.

The WestSoft programs demonstrate typical steps involved in using a home banking service, taking a personality survey, ordering tickets through a ticket agency, calling an information network, and using an office management system. The home banking system and information network are similar to services offered to people with microcomputers in their homes or offices. Both types of services require that the user have a **modem,** but the WestSoft programs are only simulations, so you do not need a modem.

Four of the programs demonstrate the use of a menu-driven program. That means that you select the next operation from a **menu,** or list of options. In the case of WestSoft, you tell the computer which selection you have chosen by typing the number that appears to the left of the selection. Once you have typed the number, the program automatically goes to that operation. You do not need to press the Enter key after typing menu selections. The same is true for responses to most prompts such as WOULD YOU LIKE INSTRUCTIONS? or ARE YOU SURE? The answer to such prompts is a simple N for no or Y for yes. Other instructions tell you to press the Enter key or Space Bar in order to advance to the next step in a program.

After typing data during a simulation, you must press the Enter key, which tells the computer to process your input. If you make a mistake while typing data, use the backspace key to space back to the error. Make the correction and then finish typing the data.

If you type something that does not follow the rules of the program, you will see a message explaining the mistake. Usually the program does nothing if you type a mistake. If the program does not seem to be doing what you expect, stop and read the directions and then continue. If all else fails, you can restart the WestSoft software, or simply restart the project by pressing the Esc key and returning to the MAIN MENU, where you can select the program again. Pressing the Esc key usually returns the program to the previous menu. This operation and other directions are listed in the help area that appears at the bottom of many screens.

The WestSoft simulations can be used on a IBM PC or compatible with 128K or more of primary memory, using DOS 2.0 or higher.

Loading WestSoft

In order to use the programs, you must first boot the IBM DOS disk unless you are using a self-booting disk. (To create a self-booting disk, you format the disk using the /S option.) Insert the DOS disk into Drive A and turn on the computer and monitor. Press the Enter key in response to the time and date prompts. When the A> prompt appears, remove the DOS disk. Insert the disk labeled *WestSoft* into the disk drive and close the door. Type WESTSOFT after the A> prompt and press the Enter key.

Read the information that appears on the screen, pressing the Space Bar as needed. Soon the WestSoft MAIN MENU appears, as shown in Figure 2-14. (The Information Network and Dental Office programs are on side 2 of the disk. Directions for accessing these two programs appear on the screen when you make your selection from the MAIN MENU on side 1.)

The directions for each WestSoft program assume that you are loading the software for the first time. You may wish to run more than one program during your session at the computer. In that case, when you finish a program, select the EXIT option that appears at the end of that simulation's menu. The software returns to the WestSoft MAIN MENU, so that you can choose another simulation without going through the beginning information again. (The Personality Traits program automatically returns to the MAIN MENU when you are finished with the test.)

When you are ready to exit the WestSoft programs, choose option 6 from the MAIN MENU. Remove the disk from the disk drive, turn off the computer and monitor, and put the disk in its envelope.

WestSoft Home Banking System

The WestSoft Home Banking System simulates a system that enables you to perform some banking tasks using a microcomputer, modem, and telephone lines.

Figure 2-14
WestSoft MAIN MENU

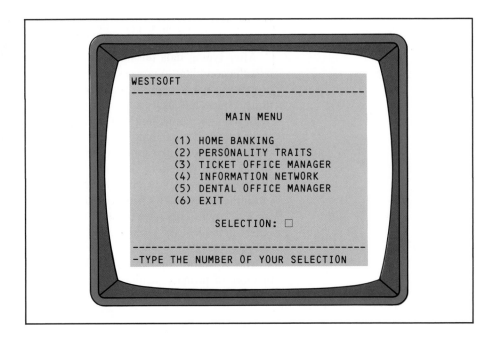

```
WESTSOFT
----------------------------------------

               MAIN MENU

       (1) HOME BANKING
       (2) PERSONALITY TRAITS
       (3) TICKET OFFICE MANAGER
       (4) INFORMATION NETWORK
       (5) DENTAL OFFICE MANAGER
       (6) EXIT

           SELECTION: □

----------------------------------------
-TYPE THE NUMBER OF YOUR SELECTION
```

A home banking system does not allow you to withdraw or deposit money directly, but you can move money from one account to another, check the current balance of your account, and pay your bills. Whereas most home banking systems allow an unlimited number of transactions per month, this demonstration allows eight new transactions before you must restart the program. This means that a total of eight money transfers and bill payments can be done each time the program is used. You can check an account's balance or print account statements as many times as you want.

To experiment with home banking, load the WestSoft program into your computer. Read the beginning screens as they appear. When the WestSoft MAIN MENU appears, type 1 for the home banking simulation. The program asks for a telephone number. The number 352-1616 connects your computer to the bank's computer. Type 352-1616 and press the Enter key.

When the telephone number has been entered correctly, the program asks for your password, which gives you access to your account. Type the password ABC and press the Enter key. If the password is typed correctly, the BANK MENU appears (see Figure 2-15).

The following exercises guide you through some typical home banking transactions.

YOUR TURN   You believe that you have charged too much on your credit card. In order to make sure that the funds in your credit-card account cover the charges, transfer $300 from your savings account to your credit card account.

Figure 2-15
BANK MENU

```
WESTSOFT: HOME BANKING SYSTEM
---------------------------------------------
              BANK MENU

      (1) ACCOUNT STATEMENT
      (2) TRANSFER FUNDS
      (3) ACCOUNT BALANCES
      (4) RATES YOU SHOULD KNOW
      (5) PAY YOUR BILLS
      (6) EXIT PROGRAM

         SELECTION: □
---------------------------------------------
-TYPE THE NUMBER OF YOUR SELECTION.
```

1. Type 2 in order to choose TRANSFER FUNDS from the BANK MENU.
2. The source of the money is the SAVINGS account. Type 2 for SAVINGS.
3. You will put the money in your charge account. Type 3 for CHARGE.
4. The amount you want moved is $300. Type 300, and press the Enter key.
5. A summary of the transaction appears. If it is correct, type Y for yes. The program returns to the BANK MENU. If it is not correct, type N for no and repeat steps 2 through 5. Does the summary tell you the balance in the charge account?

YOUR TURN

You now want to print the charge account statement so that you can refer to it later. Follow these steps for making a paper copy.

1. Make sure that the printer is properly connected to the computer and that there is enough paper. Turn on the printer.
2. Choose ACCOUNT STATEMENT from the BANK MENU by typing 1.
3. You want a statement of the charge account. Type 3 for CHARGE.
4. Type Y when the program asks whether you want to print the statement. If the printer is not properly connected, the program will display an error message.
5. When the printing is finished, what step(s) are needed to return to the WestSoft MAIN MENU?

WestSoft Personality Traits Program*

This project is a simulation of a personality traits test. In this simulation, you use the arrow keys for moving the cursor on the screen.

The test compares the traits you see in yourself with the program's evaluation of your responses to particular situations. In the introductory part of the test, you choose traits that you think describe yourself. Then you answer multiple-choice questions. Finally, during assessment, the test calculates and displays the most significant traits based on your answers to the questions.

Load the WestSoft software into your computer. Read the beginning screens as they are displayed. When the WestSoft MAIN MENU appears, type 2 for the Personality Traits program. The program tells you that the test can be stopped at any time by pressing the Esc key. Now try the following exercises.

YOUR TURN Choose the traits that you believe describe yourself.

1. Type your name. If you make a mistake, use the Backspace key to go back to the error. Then type the data correctly. Press the Enter key to continue.

2. Read the next two screens, which describe the test. Press the Enter key again.

3. A new screen asks you to examine the way you see yourself. In order to mark your responses, you need to move the cursor using the arrow keys. Type X next to each personality trait that you think describes your strongest characteristics. Choose as many traits as you think apply. For example, the cursor first appears in front of the word PATIENT. If patience is one of your more predominant traits, then type the letter X. If not, use the cursor movement commands in order to move to another trait. What key do you press if you want to delete an X?

4. Put the cursor in front of the word PATIENT. What happens if you press a letter other than X?

5. Finish making your selections and press the Enter key.

6. The screen now lists the selections you made. You can edit the list or continue with the test.

YOUR TURN You are now ready for the question/answer part of the test.

1. The screen that you see gives a brief description of this stage. Then press the Enter key to begin this stage of the survey.

---

* *Note:* The material presented in this simulation was not prepared by a psychologist and is not intended to be an accurate assessment of individual personalities. The simulation is structured to acquaint you with the procedures used in many surveys conducted by computer.

2. For each question that appears, choose the answer that most closely describes your actions or feelings by typing the letter that corresponds to your selection. Your response appears on the screen, and the program asks if you are sure. Press Y for yes, or, if you wish to change your response, press N for no and make a new selection. Go on to step 3 before answering all fifteen of the questions.

3. What happens if you press something other than one of the selection letters when the screen displays TYPE SELECTION LETTER.>>?

4. Answer all fifteen questions.

YOUR TURN

1. When you finish the test, a screen appears which reminds you of the upcoming assessments. Press the Enter key to obtain the first page, or screen, of results.

2. This screen displays two columns. The column on the left, labeled TEST SELECTIONS, lists the traits the survey determined to be the most significant in your personality. Your trait selections are listed in the right column. Compare the test results with your perception of yourself. Press the Enter key to continue.

3. The next screen shows four columns. The first column contains a list of the twelve traits evaluated in this survey. The second contains the number of points you acquired for each trait during the test. The third lists the total number of points possible for each trait. The fourth displays your percentage of points out of those possible.

4. Press the Enter key when you are finished reading the results. The next screen displays an option to print the results. Check to see that the printer is properly connected to the computer and that there is enough paper. Turn on the printer and then press Y for a printout. What happens when printing is finished?

WestSoft Ticket-Office Manager

The WestSoft Ticket-Office Manager simulates a type of software used in a ticket office. A ticket-office manager program keeps track of the seats sold, the seats available, and the ticket prices for various events. It also prints the ticket with the event, date, time, seat number, and price of the event. This program does not have all the features available in most real ticket-office software packages, but it will show you how to use a menu, choose ticket options, and print the tickets.

Imagine that you are working at a local ticket office, and customers are inquiring about tickets for several events. Before handling any customer requests, load the WestSoft disk. Read the beginning screens as they are displayed. When the WestSoft MAIN MENU appears, type 3 for the ticket-office manager program. The program then displays the TICKET MENU (see Figure 2-16).

Figure 2-16
TICKET MENU

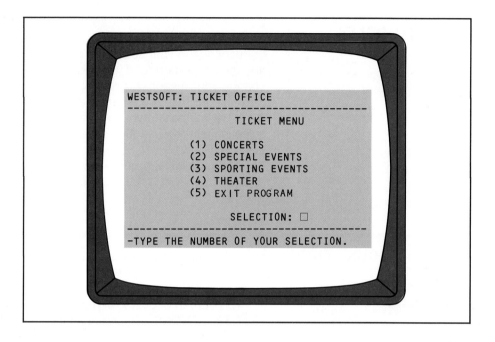

```
WESTSOFT: TICKET OFFICE
----------------------------------------
                TICKET MENU

        (1) CONCERTS
        (2) SPECIAL EVENTS
        (3) SPORTING EVENTS
        (4) THEATER
        (5) EXIT PROGRAM

            SELECTION: □
----------------------------------------
-TYPE THE NUMBER OF YOUR SELECTION.
```

The following exercises guide you through some typical ticket requests.

YOUR TURN

Your first customer would like four tickets to the September 15 matinee showing of *Annie*. Because *Annie* is a play, choose the THEATER option from the TICKET MENU by typing 4. After you have selected the THEATER menu, follow these steps:

1. Choose the option entitled *Annie* from the THEATER MENU by typing 3.
2. The time and date are listed on the screen for five showings of *Annie*. Press M to see more dates. (In this simulation, ten showings are listed for each event.)
3. To select the September 15 matinee showing, you must move the cursor (the highlighted bar) to this date and showing. Use the up arrow key to move the cursor up, and the down arrow key to move the cursor down. Once you have moved the cursor to the September 15 matinee showing, press the Enter key to enter the request.
4. A screen appears with the name of the play, the date, and the time. Now you can enter the section, row, and seat numbers the customer wants. The customer wants section 45, row 26, and seats 12–15. Type the numbers at the appropriate prompts, pressing the Enter key after each.
5. The next screen asks you to enter the number of seats wanted. Type 4 and press the Enter key.

HIGHLIGHT ▲▲▲▲▲▲▲▲▲▲▲▲▲▲▲▲▲▲▲▲▲▲▲

Winning With Antonia Stone

People in prisons, halfway houses, and housing-project community centers are "playing to win" by using microcomputers as learning tools, all because of the efforts of Antonia Stone.

Antonia Stone spent 25 years teaching in public and private schools in New Jersey and New York. As she watched children spend hours playing arcade video games, Stone wondered how she could use computers to motivate culturally disadvantaged students. She believed that computers also would benefit prisoners, who could use their incarceration time for learning useful skills that would give them a better chance in the world upon their release.

As she researched the needs of students and prisoners, she began to develop the concepts behind Playing To Win. Playing To Win is a nonprofit organization dedicated to promoting computer use for the education of minorities, inmates of correctional institutions, juvenile delinquents, and other socially disadvantaged people. Through the organization, Stone helped set up programs at the Fortune Society, a non-residential counseling center in New York City serving ex-offenders and young people in trouble with the law. She also designed programs for the Playing To Win Computer Center in the East Harlem area of New York City, the Massachusetts Department of Corrections, the New

York Public Library's Computer Outreach Project, and the Spofford Juvenile Detention Center in New York City.

Part of Stone's success results from the fact that she hasn't just "dropped" computers into detention centers and prisons. She has studied the situation, set up the proper equipment, trained the teachers and tutors to run the computers and help the students, and changed the programs as needed. By her intense involvement in Playing To Win, she has given many people the core of a new lease on life and a feeling that they can learn skills for a technological age.

---

6. The program tells you to get the printer ready. make sure the printer has enough paper and is connected to the computer. Then turn on the printer. You may press the Esc key at this time to stop the print operation. Otherwise, press the Space Bar to print the tickets.

7. When printing is complete, you are returned to the THEATER MENU. What steps are needed to return to the WestSoft MAIN MENU?

WestSoft Information Network

An information network, or information service, makes a wide variety of information available to microcomputer users. The microcomputer user pays a fee to subscribe to such a system. Subscribers can access world or national news, sports news, weather reports, current facts, and much more. The computer must be connected to a modem so it can get information over telephone lines. (Modems and information services are described in more detail in Chapter 6.) Some of these services, called buyer's services, are electronic mail-order catalogs. Subscribers to these services can order products shown on the screens of their computers.

The WestSoft Information Network is a simulation of a system that contains useful information and shows products available for ordering. Because this is only a simulation, it does not contain nearly as much information as the popular information services.

To see how an information service works, load the WestSoft disk. Read the beginning screens as they are displayed. When the WestSoft MAIN MENU appears, type 4 in order to choose the INFORMATION NETWORK.

The program asks for a telephone number. The number 352-1616 will connect your computer with the information service computer. Type 352-1616 and press the Enter key.

Once you have typed the number correctly, you are asked for your host name, identification number, and password. These codes tell the system, for billing purposes, who is using the service. The codes also ensure that someone else does not access the service through your account, thereby billing the time to you.

When the program asks for your host name (a name supplied by the service), type WIS and press the Enter key. Next, you are asked for your user ID number. Type 7411 and press the Enter key. Finally, you are asked for your password. Type ABC and press the Enter key. When these codes are typed correctly, the NETWORK MENU appears on the screen (see Figure 2-17). You need to go through these same steps every time you want to use the service.

The following exercises give you an idea of how to use an information network and how to make selections from a program that is menu-driven.

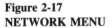

Figure 2-17
NETWORK MENU

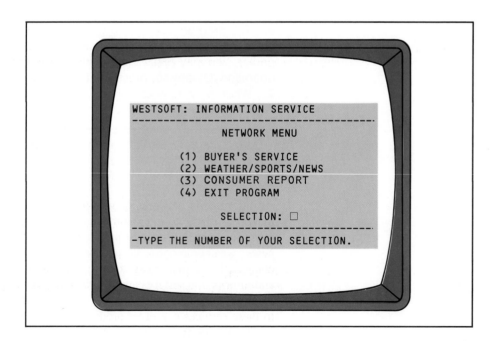

YOUR TURN

You would like to see what products can be ordered through the Buyer's Service this month. To do this, follow these steps:

1. From the NETWORK MENU, type 1 for the Buyer's Service. Read the screen that appears and press the Enter key.
2. The BUYER'S SERVICE MENU appears on the screen. It displays the types of items available. Type the number next to the item in which you are interested.
3. The screen now displays a list of specific brands of the product you choose. The service asks if you want to buy something. If you want to buy, type Y for yes. If not, type N for no. Typing N returns you to the BUYER'S SERVICE MENU.
4. Once you have decided to buy something, type the invoice number and discount price of the item you would like. If you do not make a mistake while typing, you are asked for mailing and billing information (for example, your name and address).
5. Next, the program shows a summary of the order. It asks for information about your method of payment. Respond accordingly. Then you can print a summary of the transaction for your records. Make sure that the printer is connected to the computer and that there is enough paper. Turn on the printer. Type Y to indicate that you want to print the summary, then press the Space Bar to print or the Esc key to stop the PRINT function. When printing is completed, the program returns to the BUYER'S SERVICE MENU.

WestSoft Dental Office Manager

As personal computers have become cheaper and easier to use, many offices that could not afford a larger computer system have computerized their record-keeping systems. Computerization has enabled them to store all the records that formerly occupied an entire filing cabinet on a few disks, and to gain access easily to any of these records. The WestSoft Dental Office Manager uses a dental office as an example, but a similar system could be used in any type of office. This kind of software can be used to maintain records such as client payments and records, personnel files, and accounting files.

Load the WestSoft software into your computer. Read the beginning screens as they are displayed. When the WestSoft MAIN MENU appears, type 5 in order to choose the DENTAL OFFICE MANAGER. The DENTAL MENU appears.

The following exercises demonstrate how to use an office manager program. use today's date when asked to enter the date of a transaction. This version of the dental office manager allows two charges per patient.

YOUR TURN

Chris Allen enters the office to have a tooth filled. The filling costs $40. Enter the charge into his account, using the following steps:

1. Type 1 from the DENTAL MENU to enter a charge into Chris's account.
2. Type the patient's last name and press the Enter key.
3. Type the appropriate data concerning the new charge—the date, type of service, and amount, pressing the Enter key after each entry. *Do not type a dollar sign ($).*
4. The program asks if the information is correct. If the information you typed is correct as displayed, type Y for yes. Otherwise, type N and make the corrections.
5. Return to the DENTAL MENU by pressing the Escape key.

YOUR TURN

Greg Allgair and Jody Katzner both have written to the office requesting copies of their insurance forms. Make the copies using the DISPLAY AN INSURANCE FORM option from the DENTAL MENU.

1. Type 5 from the DENTAL MENU for the insurance form option.
2. Type the last name of the first patient and press the Enter key.
3. When the information appears on the screen, press the F1 function key to print it.
4. When the printer is done, use the left and right arrow keys to move through the list of patients until you find the file for Jody Katzner.
5. When the file appears on the screen, print the form as directed in step 3.
6. Return to the DENTAL MENU.

Summary Points

■ The IBM microcomputers are popular with businesses for performing routine tasks and for linking with larger computers. They are also popular in homes and schools for a variety of educational, recreational, and home-management purposes.
■ The standard parts of an IBM PC microcomputer are the system unit, monitor, and keyboard. The system unit holds the computer itself and the disk drive(s).
■ The number of columns displayed on the color/graphics screen can be changed from 80 to 40 columns and back again while the IBM PC is in the DOS mode by typing the commands MODE BW40 and MODE BW80.
■ The letter and number keys on any IBM computer work the same as a typewriter's keys. Computer-specific keys let you move the cursor (a symbol that

shows your current location on the screen) and perform other functions by entering keystroke commands.

■ In a two-drive IBM PC, the drives are called Drive A and Drive B. A disk should be inserted in Drive A before one is inserted in Drive B. When only one drive is installed, it is Drive A.

■ The best place for a computer is on a sturdy desk or table in a clean, dry room. Keep food, dust, and dirt away from equipment and disks, and avoid creating static electricity around the equipment.

■ Computer equipment should be kept out of direct sunlight, off appliances that get hot, and away from heating ducts and air conditioning units.

■ Floppy disks should be handled with care so they will remain reliable storage devices. Store them vertically in their envelopes, away from heat or cold.

■ Programs are loaded into the computer's memory in several ways. If operating system files are on the disk, you can insert it into the disk drive and turn on the computer. Otherwise, the operating system software must be loaded first.

■ Disks must be initialized (formatted) according to the specifications of the operating system you are using before they can be used to store data.

■ The operating system contains the programs that control the computer. Disk operating system (DOS) programs reside on a disk and are loaded from the disk drive.

■ A program that imitates a real-life event is called a simulation. The purpose of a program simulation is to teach the user how to do a task, or how to use a computerized service such as an information network.

■ Services such as home banking or information networks require modems. A modem is a hardware device that connects one computer to another over telephone lines.

■ A menu is a list of choices or options displayed on the screen. Prompts are messages or cues that guide you as you use the software.

■ Home banking is a service that lets you perform banking tasks using a microcomputer, modem, and telephone lines.

■ Some ticket offices use ticket-office manager software that keeps track of the seats sold, the seats available, and the ticket prices for various events. This software can print tickets with the event, date, time, seat number, and price.

■ An information service or information network makes a wide variety of information available to microcomputer users, such as world or national news, sports news, weather conditions, current facts, and much more.

■ A dental office manager program facilitates the record-keeping, accounting, and billing that occur in a dentist's office. Similar software is used in other offices.

Review Questions

1. What does the symbol K represent?
2. What is the character called which shows your location on the screen?
3. What two things happen when the Return key is pressed?
4. Why would you not continue to hold down the keys that you press to relay a command to the computer, or that you use for typing data?

5. In a two-drive system, how are the drives differentiated and how do you use them?

6. Describe the ideal environment for a microcomputer.

7. Name at least three things to remember in caring for disks.

8. What does the term *load* mean in computer usage?

9. Why is the disk drive light important?

10. What is the purpose of formatting, or initializing, a disk?

11. List the steps involved in formatting a disk.

12. Two features that make programs easier to use are menus and prompts. Describe each, and tell why they make using computers easier.

Review Exercises

1. WestSoft HOME BANKING Exercises

Your telephone bill for April was $112.37. You want to pay the bill from your checking account, but you are not sure there is enough money in the account. Determine the balance of your checking account, transfer more money to the account if necessary, and pay the telephone bill. (The telephone number to call is 352-1616, and the password is ABC.)

a. What steps did you take to check the balance in the checking account?

b. What two steps should you perform to return to the BANK MENU?

c. What did you do to transfer money to your checking account, if you did so?

d. What four steps did you take to pay the telephone bill?

Last month you wrote check #831 to a friend. The check was not cashed, according to last month's bank statement. You want to know whether the check has been cashed since then.

a. What two steps did you take to see the checking-account statement? Was the check cashed?

b. How can you return to the BANK MENU?

c. Transfer $50 from your savings account to your checking account in order to have enough funds to cover expenses you anticipate in the next couple of weeks. List the steps required to perform the task.

2. WestSoft TICKET OFFICE MANAGER Exercises

A customer would like tickets for the October 25 game of the Philadelphia Minutemen hockey team, or the September 16 Detroit Bengals game.

a. What steps would you take to get tickets to the game, once the TICKET MENU is on the screen?

b. Describe what happens when you try to get tickets for the game.

c. What happens when you try to print a ticket for section 45, row 11, and seat 10, for the September 16 Detroit Bengals game?

One customer calls to ask about performances by the Boston Pops.
    a. Who appears with the Boston Pops on September 20?
    b. Who appears with the Boston Pops on September 27?
    c. On what dates and at what times does Thomas Klein appear with the Boston Pops?
    d. What happens when you try to get tickets for the Washington Philharmonic Orchestra?

3.   WestSoft INFORMATION SERVICE Exercises

You are planning a party based on trivia questions, and you need to write questions and answers on cards. Find the answers to these questions, and then write three more questions with their answers based on information provided in this information network. (The telephone number is 352-1616, the host name is WIS, the user ID number is 7411, and the password is ABC.)
    a. Who hold the baseball world-series record for the most home runs? How many home runs did he have?
    b. By what two names was baseball known in the United States before it became baseball?
    c. Which two teams played in the 1934 NFL championship game, and who won?
    d. Which two swimmers tied for the gold medal in the women's 100-meter freestyle at the 1984 Olympics?
    e. According to the surgeon general's report, what are the three long-term health risks of smoking?

4.   WestSoft DENTAL OFFICE MANAGER Exercises

Mark Steiner has mailed a partial payment to the office. The check is for $50. Enter this payment into his account. (This version of the Dental Office Manager allows two payments per patient.) List the steps required to make the payment and return to the DENTAL MENU.

Dave Biesiada drops by the office to tell you that his insurance company will be covering the remainder of his bill. He wants to know how much that is. Write his balance. The money from Dave's insurance company arrives later that day. Enter the new payment and make sure that Dave's new balance is zero.

Tim Newman enters the office for a checkup. The charge is $24, but Tim has only $10.50 in his pocket. He gives you the $10.50 and owes the rest. Enter the new charge and the payment. What is Tim's new balance?

The office manager decides that too many patients have neglected paying their bills. The manager wants to know which patients owe money and how much each owes. List the patients currently in debt and the amount each owes. Begin the search with Christopher Allen's account.

CHAPTER 3

Hardware

Introduction

Computer hardware consists of the physical devices that constitute a computer system. This chapter discusses the classifications of computer systems and the hardware components of a computer system: the central processing unit, the input devices, the output devices, and the storage devices. It also describes the codes in which data are handled during computer operations.

Computer Classifications

Computers are grouped by their amount of memory, capability, price range, and speed of operation. The four major groups of computers are mainframes, mini-computers, microcomputers, and supercomputers.

Defining the point at which one classification ends and the next begins is difficult, because the capabilities of computers in one classification overlap those of computers in the next category. Computers at the low end of the scale have increasingly larger primary memories and can handle an increasing number of **peripheral devices,** such as printers and secondary storage devices.

PERIPHERAL DEVICE
A device that attaches to the central processing unit, such as a secondary storage device, input device, or output device.

Mainframes

During the 1960s, the term mainframe was synonymous with CPU. Today, the word refers simply to a group of computers intermediate in capacity between the minicomputer and the supercomputer.

Mainframes operate at very high speeds and support many input and output devices, which also operate at very high speeds. They can be subdivided into small, medium, and large mainframe systems. Most mainframes are manufactured as "families" of computers. A family consists of several mainframe models that differ in size and power. An organization can purchase or lease a small system and, if processing needs expand, upgrade to a medium or large system, while retaining the existing software and peripheral devices. Purchase prices range from $200,000 to several million dollars for a large mainframe with peripherals. Main-frames are used chiefly by large businesses, hospitals, universities, and banks with large data processing needs (see Figure 3-1).

A mainframe creates a fair amount of heat, so it requires cooling systems. It cannot be plugged into a standard electrical outlet, and therefore it needs special electrical wiring. It may rest on a special platform so that its wires and cables can be housed beneath it. Because a mainframe operates day and night and provides access to a large amount of data, access to it must be controlled for security reasons. These factors add to its cost.

Because of their sophistication and size, mainframe computers require a great deal of support from the vendor, who may invest considerable time and money in helping a customer select and install the system. The vendor spends additional effort training the customer's employees to use the system, servicing and repairing

MAINFRAME
A type of large, full-scale computer capable of supporting many peripheral devices.

Figure 3-1
IBM System/370/158 Mainframe

Figure 3-2
Wang Laboratories' VS85
Minicomputer
A minicomputer system for a small firm may consist of the computer, a visual display terminal, a disk storage unit, and a printer. A large system may consist of hundreds of minicomputers and peripherals tied together by communication channels to meet the needs of a geographically dispersed organization.

the mainframe, and solving any questions and problems. Some major mainframe manufacturers are IBM, Burroughs, Honeywell, NCR, and Sperry.

Minicomputers

Minicomputers were developed in the 1960s to perform specialized tasks. They were smaller, less powerful, and less expensive than the mainframes available at that time, thus offering computer capabilities to organizations that did not need or could not afford mainframe systems. As minicomputers became more sophisticated, their capabilities, memory size, and overall performance overlapped those of mainframes. The more powerful minicomputers are called superminis.

Minicomputers are easier to install and operate than mainframe computers. They take up less floor space than mainframes; they may fit on a desk, or they may be as large as a file cabinet (see Figure 3-2). Minicomputers require few special environmental conditions. They can be plugged into standard electrical outlets and often do not require facilities such as air conditioning or special platforms. Prices for minicomputers range from a few thousand dollars to two or three hundred thousand dollars.

Minicomputers are used in multi-user applications, numerical control of machine tools, industrial automation, and word processing. They are also used in conjunction with communication facilities for sharing data and peripherals or for serving a geographically dispersed organization.

A minicomputer system can easily be enlarged to meet the needs of a growing organization, because it can be implemented in a modular fashion. For example, a hospital might install one minicomputer in its outpatient department for record keeping and another in the pharmacy or laboratory. As additional minicomputers are installed, they can be connected to existing ones to share common data.

In the late 1970s and early 1980s, the minicomputer industry grew at a rate of 35 to 40 percent annually. Today, the market for minicomputers is weakening. The increased capabilities and improved software of **microcomputers** has led to the increased use of microcomputers in traditional minicomputer markets. Many companies now link microcomputers with mainframes or existing minicomputers to hold down equipment investment costs and still meet processing needs. This practice, however, creates new security problems for many corporations, because more people have access to data.

Some major manufacturers of minicomputers include Digital Equipment Corporation (DEC), Hewlett-Packard, Data General, Honeywell, General Automation, Burroughs, Texas Instruments, Wang Laboratories, Prime Computer Inc., and IBM.

Microcomputers

**Figure 3-3
Honeywell PC DP**

When technology advanced to the point at which many circuits could be etched onto a single chip, the microprocessor was developed. A microprocessor is a chip that contains the portions of the CPU that control the computer and perform arithmetic and logic operations. It may also contain some primary storage. The microprocessor became the foundation for the microcomputer, also called the personal computer.

Microcomputers are the most popular type of computer today. They may fit on a desktop or in a briefcase (see Figure 3-3). Some microcomputers designed for home use cost as little as $100, but users can spend many thousands of dollars for state-of-the-art microcomputers and peripherals. Most microcomputers are single-user systems.

One important aspect of microcomputer design involves the development of user-friendly hardware and software, that is, equipment and programs that are easy to use and easy to learn to use. The concern for user friendliness has overflowed into the development of other categories of computers.

Microcomputers are available in computer stores, office supply stores, and department stores. In some cases they are sold in the same way as an appliance, such as a television or video cassette recorder. Packaged software for microcomputers is available, but many users like the challenge of developing their own, and many businesses need custom software.

Chapter 5 provides a detailed discussion of microcomputers.

Supercomputers

Supercomputers are the largest, fastest, most expensive computers currently made (see Figure 3-4). They process data at speeds exceeding 400,000,000 to 600,000,000 operations per second. The Cray-2, for example, operates at speeds of 1.2 billion flops (floating-point operations per second, a measure of optimum computer efficiency). It can perform calculations in one minute which a personal computer could perform in three weeks. By 1992, U.S. supercomputer industries hope to

Figure 3-4
The Cray X-MP Supercomputer

build computers that will reach speeds of 1,000 gigaflops (billions of flops per second).

Research in supercomputer development has become a heated race between the United States and Japan. Whoever develops and commercializes improved supercomputer technology will have the competitive edge in all computer-related industries, an important consideration for both economics and national defense. Some major companies developing supercomputers include Cray Research, Fujitsu, and ETA Systems, Inc.

Only a few supercomputers currently are produced each year, because the manufacturing cost is high and the market is limited. Each machine costs several million dollars to develop and install. In addition, software development for supercomputers is much more complex and expensive, because the design of the machines is so much different from that of less powerful computers. To justify costs this high, an organization must be very large and must need to process millions of instructions very quickly or maintain large databases. Despite these facts, demand for supercomputers is increasing. In 1980, there were only 21 supercomputers in the world. As of 1986, about 150 supercomputers are busy crunching numbers, and the demand for them seems insatiable. Even universities are beginning to install supercomputers for their extensive research projects.

Supercomputers are used to perform lengthy and complex calculations. Scientists use them in weather forecasting, oil exploration, energy conservation, seismology, nuclear reactor safety analysis, and cryptography. In addition, supercomputers are used for simulations in nuclear energy research and for stress tests in automotive and aircraft design.

All categories of computers process data by the same three stages discussed in Chapter 1: input, processing, and output. All computers have a CPU, primary memory, secondary storage devices and media, input devices, and output devices. The following sections discuss these aspects of hardware in general terms.

Learning Check

1. How can mainframe "families" benefit businesses?

2. Why might a business choose a minicomputer rather than a mainframe?

3. What effect have today's microcomputers had on the minicomputer market?

4. Why is supercomputer research of national importance?

Answers

1. Businesses can upgrade easily and still use existing software and peripherals. 2. Mainframes are more expensive and require the added expense of air conditioning, special platforms, and special electrical wiring. Minicomputers can be added in modular form to an organization's existing system. 3. They have weakened the minicomputer market. 4. Whoever leads in supercomputer development will lead in all computer-related industries. In addition, supercomputers are used for research in areas important to national defense.

The Central Processing Unit

CENTRAL PROCESSING UNIT (CPU)
Acts as the "brain" of the computer; composed of three sections—the arithmetic/logic unit (ALU), control unit, and primary memory.

CONTROL UNIT
The section of the CPU which directs the sequence of operations and governs the actions of the various units that make up the computer.

ARITHMETIC/LOGIC UNIT (ALU)
The section of the processor, or CPU, which handles arithmetic computations and logical operations.

A computer stores data temporarily and acts on it. The component that is responsible for this operation is the **central processing unit (CPU).** The CPU is often called the "brain" of the computer. It is a complex collection of electronic circuitry which directs electrical signals to all parts of a computer system. The CPU decides what to do with the instructions that the programmer gives the computer, and ensures that assigned tasks are carried out properly.

The CPU consists of three parts that function together as a unit. These parts are the **control unit,** the **arithmetic/logic unit (ALU),** and primary memory (see Figure 3-5). The CPU is located inside the computer, so primary memory is also called internal storage, primary storage, or main memory. The control unit and the arithmetic/logic unit often are referred to collectively as the processor.

A processor may contain many chips, each with special functions. In a large computer, the processor may be built on several circuit boards in box-like structures or frames, hence the term mainframe. In a microcomputer, the processor is reduced in size to fit onto a single plug-in chip and is referred to as a microprocessor. A microcomputer may contain more than one microprocessor for performing various functions. Whereas primary memory is part of the CPU, typically it is located on separate circuit boards.

Control Unit

The control unit, as the name implies, maintains order and controls the activity that occurs in the CPU. It does not process or store data, but directs the sequence

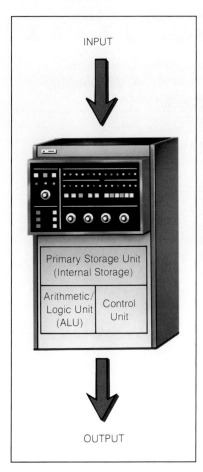

Figure 3-5
Parts of the CPU

of operations. It interprets instructions and produces signals that act as commands for the execution of instructions. The control unit communicates with and directs input equipment and keeps track of the instructions that have been executed. It also sends the results of processing to the designated locations.

Arithmetic/Logic Unit

The ALU manipulates data. It does not store data, but performs arithmetic computations and logical operations. Arithmetic computations performed in the ALU include addition and subtraction, whereas logical operations involve comparisons. The computer makes a comparison and then performs some action based on the result of the comparison. There are six possible results in all: equal to, not equal to, greater than, less than, equal to or greater than, and equal to or less than. For example, a computer might have to deal with the following logic statement: "If the total is not equal to 100, then read more data."

Primary Memory

Memory is a major factor in computer power. The more powerful computers store more data and operate on it in larger amounts. Data in primary memory can be accessed quickly. It is stored as "on" and "off" electrical states. Primary memory is in charge of storing data and programs temporarily in the computer's internal memory. When a program resides in primary memory, it is called a **stored program.** In order for data to be processed, the computer must be able to locate the programs and data in memory. Each piece of data in memory has an address which is a unique, built-in number that identifies its location. The address helps the computer locate the data, just as a post office box number identifies the proper box for depositing letters (see Figure 3-6).

Figure 3-6
Mailbox Representation of Storage
If a programmer specifies that the value in TOTAL TAX is to be subtracted from the value in GROSS PAY, the computer uses its own addressing system to find the proper locations of the data, just as you look under a box number to find the "data" in the post office box that is designated for your mail.

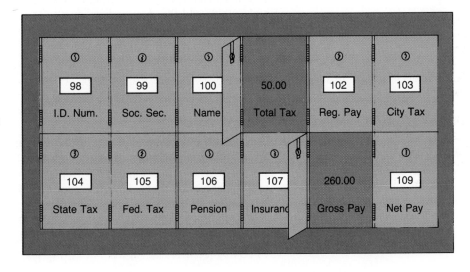

HIGHLIGHT ▲▲▲▲▲▲▲▲▲▲▲▲▲▲▲▲▲▲▲▲▲▲▲▲▲▲

The Connection Machine

It resides inside a 5-foot Lexon plastic cube. It contains 65,536 processors. When the initial kinks are worked out, it will operate at speeds in excess of 1 billion instructions per second—about the power of a Cray X-MP supercomputer. And it costs only one-fourth as much as the Cray X-MP. It is the Connection Machine, brainchild of Daniel Hillis, co-founder of Thinking Machines Corp. of Cambridge, Massachusetts.

This computer not only looks different from most mainframe computers; it *is* different. Packed in a much smaller machine than mainframes and supercomputers, it

is to a conventional mainframe what a supersonic jet is to a bicycle, says Hillis. It scanned three months of Reuters news stories—16,000 articles—in 1/20 of a second. In 3 minutes, it laid out the circuitry for a computer chip containing 4,000 transistors.

The Connection Machine reaches its remarkable speed because of two factors. The first is the thousands of processors that act in parallel, or in concert. Mainframes operate serially (one instruction at a time). The second factor is the manner in which the processors are connected. Each processor is directly or indirectly connected to every other one, in a manner similar to a miniature telephone system.

The links contain 4,096 switching stations and 24,576 trunk lines that can be programmed and reprogrammed without changing the computer's wiring. These connections give the computer its name. Programming such a machine, however, calls for complex instructions that even computer scientists find difficult to write.

Regardless of the difficulties, the Connection Machine offers hope of solving problems in machine vision and artificial intelligence which even today's supercomputers cannot solve. It signals the wave of the future in computer architecture, mimicking the action of the billions of neurons in the human brain.

SOURCE: *Time,* June 9, 1986, p. 64.

STORED PROGRAM
A program held in primary memory in electronic form, which can be executed repeatedly during processing.

Once an instruction or piece of data is stored at a particular location, it stays there until new data or instructions are written over it. The same data can be accessed repeatedly by a single program. In addition, the same instructions can be used repeatedly to process many different pieces of data. Storing programs in this manner—the stored-program concept—enables the computer to call upon the programs instantly and to operate at top speed, with minimal human intervention.

Primary memory holds the program that is being executed, the program's input and output, and the intermediate results of any calculations. When a program is entered into the computer, the control unit sends the program to primary memory. The control unit then retrieves one instruction at a time from the primary memory unit (see Figure 3-7).

Registers

REGISTER
An internal computer component used as a temporary holding area for an instruction or data item during processing.

During data processing, data or instructions may be placed in temporary storage areas known as **registers.** Even though registers are used for holding data, they are not part of primary memory. Registers receive data, hold it, and transfer it very quickly, as directed by the control unit of the CPU. The computer uses registers in all the calculations and manipulations it performs.

Registers perform specific functions and are named according to the functions they perform. An accumulator is a register that accumulates the results of com-

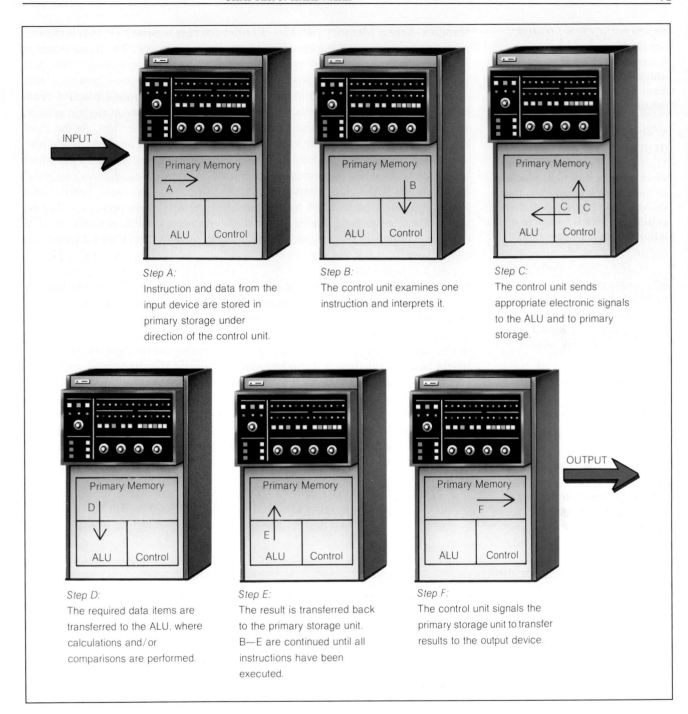

INPUT

Step A:
Instruction and data from the input device are stored in primary storage under direction of the control unit.

Step B:
The control unit examines one instruction and interprets it.

Step C:
The control unit sends appropriate electronic signals to the ALU and to primary storage.

Step D:
The required data items are transferred to the ALU, where calculations and/or comparisons are performed.

Step E:
The result is transferred back to the primary storage unit. B—E are continued until all instructions have been executed.

Step F:
The control unit signals the primary storage unit to transfer results to the output device.

OUTPUT

Figure 3-7
Computer Operations

putations. A storage register holds data being sent to or taken from primary memory. During program execution, each instruction is transferred to an instruction register, where it is decoded by the control unit. The address of a data item called for by an instruction is kept in an address register. General-purpose registers can be used for both arithmetic and addressing functions.

RANDOM-ACCESS MEMORY (RAM)
A form of primary memory in which the contents can be changed many times during processing; volatile or temporary memory.

NONDESTRUCTIVE READ/ DESTRUCTIVE WRITE
The feature of computer memory which permits data to be read and retained in its original state, thus allowing repeated reference during processing. Data is destroyed when it is overwritten by new data.

READ-ONLY MEMORY (ROM)
The part of computer hardware which contains instructions built into the circuitry; it cannot be deleted or altered by stored-program instructions.

PROGRAMMABLE READ-ONLY MEMORY (PROM)
Read-only memory that can be programmed once by the manufacturer or user in order to meet unique requirements.

Random-Access Memory (RAM)   **Random-access memory (RAM)** is the major type of semiconductor memory used in primary memory. The items stored in RAM can be accessed (read) over and over again without destroying them. New instructions or data can be stored (written) over existing ones, however, thus destroying or erasing the old items. This feature is called **nondestructive read/ destructive write.** RAM is volatile, or nonpermanent. It relies on electric current, and if the power fails or is turned off, the contents of RAM are lost. As the name RAM suggests, data and instructions stored in RAM can be accessed randomly.

RAM memory can be added to a computer by installing RAM chips, which usually come mounted on printed circuit boards. In some cases, the user can install the additional RAM chips simply by plugging them into the circuit board. Other RAM chips must be installed by the manufacturer or service personnel. The installation method depends on the design of the machine. Boards, or cards, of RAM chips are commonly used to add memory to microcomputers. (See Chapter 5 for a discussion of the RAM disk.)

Read-Only Memory (ROM)   **Read-Only Memory (ROM)** cannot be changed or deleted by stored-program instructions. ROM instructions are hardwired, or permanently built into circuitry. The only way to change the contents of ROM is to alter the physical construction of the circuits. A microprogram is a sequence of instructions built into read-only memory for carrying out functions that otherwise would be accessed from a secondary storage device. Microprograms usually are supplied by computer manufacturers and cannot be altered by users, but microprogramming allows the basic operations of the computer to be tailored to meet the needs of users. If all instructions that a computer can execute are located in ROM, a complete new set of instructions can be obtained by changing the ROM chip. When selecting a computer, users can get the standard features of the machine plus their choice of the optional features available through microprogramming. Many microcomputers use programs stored in ROM.

A version of ROM that can be programmed before installation to suit the needs of the user is **programmable read-only memory (PROM).** PROM can be pro-

---

Learning Check

1. What do the letters CPU stand for?
2. Which part of the CPU handles mathematical operations?
3. Which part of the CPU interprets instructions and directs the other parts?
4. How is RAM different from ROM?
5. What does the phrase nondestructive read/destructive write mean?

Answers

1. Central processing unit. 2. Arithmetic/logic unit (ALU). 3. Control unit. 4. RAM is volatile; ROM is hard-wired. 5. It means that data can be read repeatedly without destroying or erasing it, but once new data is written over the old data, the old data is destroyed.

Figure 3-8
8-Bit Microprocessor with EPROM

grammed by the manufacturer, or it can be shipped blank for the end user to program. Once programmed, however, its contents are unalterable. PROM gives the end user the advantages of ROM plus the flexibility to meet special needs. PROM technology has one drawback, however: mistakes programmed into the unit cannot be corrected. In order to overcome this drawback, **erasable programmable read-only memory (EPROM)** has been developed. This type of memory unit can be erased, but only by being submitted to a special process, such as being bathed in ultraviolet light (see Figure 3-8).

**ERASABLE PROGRAMMABLE
READ-ONLY MEMORY (EPROM)**
**A form of read-only memory which
can be reprogrammed by a special
process.**

Secondary Storage

Secondary storage, also called auxiliary storage, is storage outside the CPU. It is used for storing large amounts of data at low cost. Access to data in secondary storage can be either direct or sequential, depending on the medium used.

Magnetic tapes provide **sequential-access storage.** This means that the computer must start at the beginning of the tape and read what is stored until it comes to the needed data. In contrast, storage media such as magnetic disks and magnetic drums do not have to be read sequentially; data can be accessed directly. Therefore, these media are called **direct-access storage** media. Direct-access media allow faster retrieval than sequential-access media.

**SEQUENTIAL-ACCESS
STORAGE**
**Secondary storage from which data
items must be read one after
another from the beginning until the
needed data is located.**

**DIRECT-ACCESS STORAGE
(RANDOM-ACCESS STORAGE)**
**Secondary storage from which data
can be located and retrieved
directly, without reading all
preceding data.**

Sequential-Access Media

A **magnetic tape** is a continuous strip of coated plastic tape, wound onto a reel quite similar to that used in reel-to-reel audio recorders. The magnetic tape's plastic base is treated with a magnetizable coating, usually iron oxide. Typically, the tape is one-half inch wide and 400 to 3,200 feet long. Tapes are inexpensive and easy to store. They hold a very large amount of data in a small amount of space, and they can be erased and reused.

MAGNETIC TAPE
**A sequential-access storage medium,
consisting of a narrow strip of
material upon which data can be
recorded as magnetized spots.**

Data is recorded on magnetic tape by magnetizing small spots of the iron oxide coating on the tape. Although these spots can be read by the computer, they are invisible to the human eye. Large volumes of information can be recorded on a single tape. Densities of 1,600 characters per inch are common, and some tapes can hold up to 6,250 characters per inch.

TAPE DRIVE
A device that moves tape past a read/write head.

When a program calls for the information that a tape contains, the tape is mounted onto a **tape drive** (see Figure 3-9). The drive has a **read/write head** that creates or reads the magnetized spots as the tape moves past it (see Figure 3-10). When it is reading, the head detects the magnetized areas and converts them into electrical pulses that are sent to the CPU. When writing, the head magnetizes the appropriate spots on the tape, while erasing any previously stored data.

READ/WRITE HEAD
The electromagnet of a tape drive or disk drive. In reading, it detects magnetized spots; in writing, it magnetizes appropriate areas.

Magnetic tape also is available in cassettes. This form of magnetic tape usually is used with microcomputers for backing up data. Tape cassettes look like those used in audio recording—and some can be used that way—but those made for data storage are made of high-quality, high-density digital recording tape (see Figure 3-11). They are popular with microcomputer users because they can be used with an ordinary cassette player.

Direct-Access Media

MAGNETIC DISK
A direct-access storage medium consisting of a metal platter upon which data can be recorded as magnetized spots.

The **magnetic disk** is a metal platter, usually 14 inches in diameter, coated on both sides with a magnetizable material like iron oxide. Data is stored on the surface of the disk as magnetized spots. In many respects, a magnetic disk resembles a phonograph record, but it has a smooth surface instead of a record's characteristic grooves. A disk drive stores and retrieves data in much the same way as a phonograph. The disk is rotated while a read/write head is positioned above its magnetic surface. Instead of spiraling into the center of the disk like a phonograph needle, however, the read/write head stores and retrieves data in concentric circles called **tracks.** The tracks are concentric, that is, one track never touches another. A typical disk has from 200 to 500 tracks per surface (see Figure 3-12).

TRACK
One of a series of concentric circles on the surface of a magnetic disk.

Figure 3-9
Magnetic Tape Drive
A computer operator mounts tapes on tape drives and pushes the proper button for entry of stored data into the computer.

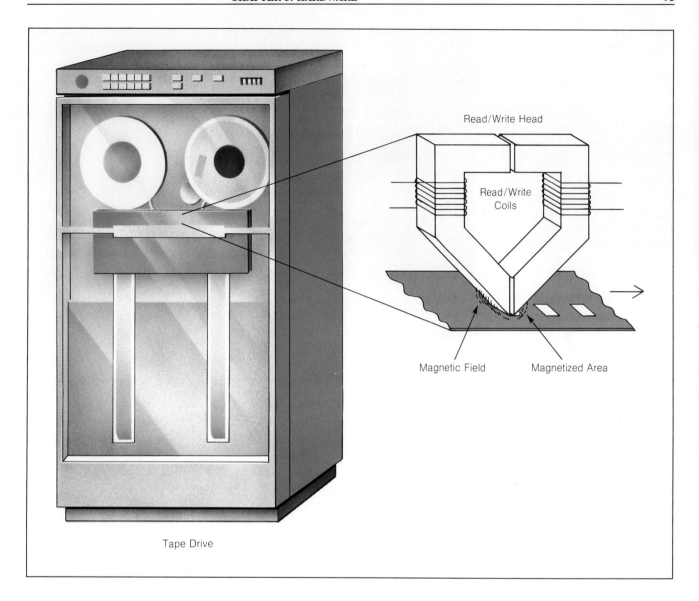

Read/Write Head

Read/Write
Coils

Magnetic Field   Magnetized Area

Tape Drive

Figure 3-10
Read/Write Head
In recording on magnetic media, the
read/write head creates a magnetic
field for either writing or reading data.

The fast access time offered by magnetic-disk storage allows data files to be
changed immediately. In addition, response to inquiries occurs in seconds. Because
disks provide direct access, they are routinely used to store data about which
frequent inquiries are made. Depending upon the type of drive, transfer rates of
up to 850,000 characters per second are possible.

Several disks can be mounted on a center shaft and encased in plastic units.
When assembled in this manner, the unit is called a disk pack. The individual
disks are spaced on the shaft, allowing room for read/write mechanisms to move
between them. The disk pack in Figure 3-13 has eleven disks and provides twenty
usable recording surfaces. The extreme top and bottom surfaces are not used for
storing data because they are likely to become nicked or scratched. A disk pack
may contain five to 100 disks.

Figure 3-11
Cassette Tapes

Figure 3-12
Top View of Disk Surface

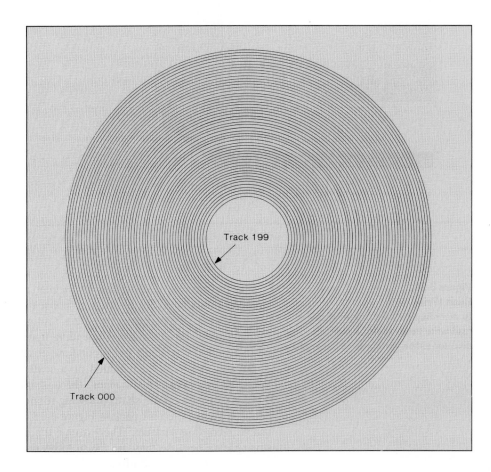

Figure 3-13
Disk Pack Showing Read/Write
Heads on Access Arms

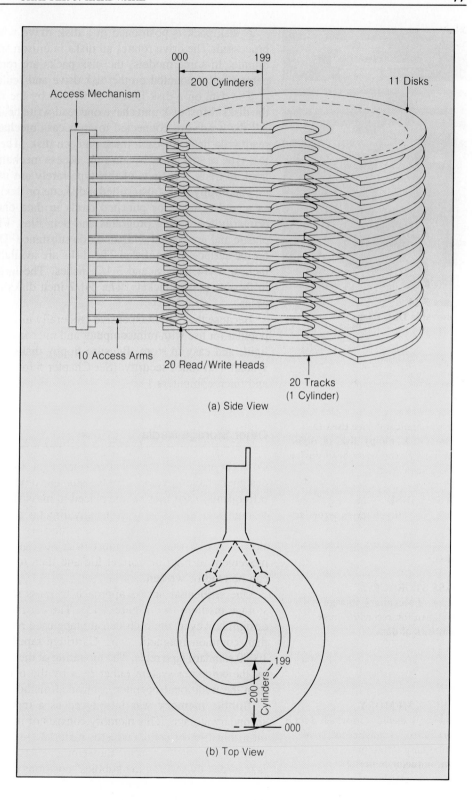

(a) Side View

(b) Top View

Figure 3-14
Removable Disk Packs

DISK DRIVE
The mechanical device used to rotate a disk, floppy disk, or disk pack past a read/write head during data transmission.

FLOPPY DISK
A low-cost, direct-access secondary storage medium made of flexible plastic; also called a flexible disk or diskette.

MASS STORAGE
A type of secondary storage developed for recording huge quantities of data.

BUBBLE MEMORY
A memory medium in which data is represented by magnetized spots resting on a thin film of semiconductor material.

A disk pack is positioned in a **disk drive** when the data on the pack is to be processed. The drive rotates all disks in unison speeds up to 3,600 revolutions per minute. In some models, the disk packs are removable; in others, the disks are permanently mounted on the disk drive and sealed (see Figure 3-14).

The data on a disk is read or written by the read/write heads located between the disks. Most disk units have one read/write head for each disk recording surface. All the heads are connected to an access mechanism. Some disk units have one read/write head for each track on each disk. The access time is much faster with this type of disk unit, because the access mechanism does not need to move from track to track, but units of this type rarely are used because of their high cost.

The **floppy disk** (also called a diskette or flexible disk) was introduced in 1973 as a replacement for punched cards in data entry. Today these disks are used primarily for storing programs and data files. Floppy disks are made of flexible plastic and are coated with an oxide substance. Data is stored as magnetized spots on the surface of the disks. The disks are available in three standard diameters: 8 inches, 5 1/4 inches, and 3 1/2 inches. The larger disks are permanently sealed in flexible plastic jackets. The 3 1/2 inch disks are enclosed in thin, hard plastic cases.

Because they are inexpensive (generally under $2 apiece), floppy disks are very popular for use with minicomputer and microcomputer systems. They are reusable, light, and easy to store. Because floppy disks can be removed, they provide the system with added security. (See Chapter 5 for more information about disk storage and microcomputers.)

Other Storage Media

To meet the need for cheaper storage of very large amounts of data, system designers have developed **mass storage** devices. Large files, backup files, and infrequently used files can be placed in mass storage at a relatively low cost. Mass storage devices allow rapid, usually direct access to data, although the access time is much slower than that of primary memory or magnetic disk. The reason for the slower access time is that most mass storage devices require extensive physical movement to find the correct file and then to mount it mechanically before data can be read or written.

One sequential access approach to mass storage uses a cartridge tape as the storage medium (see Figure 3-15). The cartridges are similar to cassette tapes in design; however, the high-density tape used requires 90 percent less storage space than common magnetic tape. Cartridge tapes can hold the equivalent of up to 1,000 standard tape reels. The mounting of the cartridges is controlled and executed by the computer system rather than by the operator (Figure 3-16), so it is faster than the traditional operator-controlled method.

Bubble memory was introduced as a replacement medium for primary and secondary storage. This memory consists of magnetized spots, or bubbles, resting on a thin film of semiconductor material (see Figure 3-17). The bubbles have a polarity opposite to that of the semiconductor material on which they rest. Data is recorded by shifting the bubbles' positions on the surface of the material. When data is read, the presence of a bubble indicates a 0 bit. The bubbles retain their magnetism indefinitely. Bubble memory can store huge amounts of data. A bubble

Figure 3-15
Cartridge Tapes

memory slightly larger than a quarter can store 20,000 characters of data. Bubble memory is nonvolatile, that is, data is preserved even if the electric power fails.

Many portable computers contain bubble memory. A more common use of bubble memory is for limited storage capabilities in input or output devices. High

Figure 3-16   Mass Storage
A mechanical arm removes a cartridge from its cell when the data stored on it is needed for processing. Because these data cartridges are stored in slots resembling a honeycomb, this type of mass storage sometimes is called honeycomb storage.

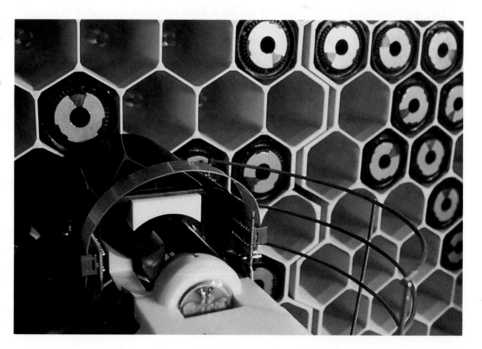

Figure 3-17
Bubble Memory
This bubble memory section is
magnified 1,500 times.

cost and production difficulties have been major factors limiting industry and user acceptance of bubbles.

Laser technology provides an opportunity to store massive quantities of data at greatly reduced costs. A laser storage system can store nearly 128 billion characters of data at about one-tenth the cost of standard magnetic media. In a laser storage system, data is recorded when a laser beam forms patterns on the surface of a polyester sheet coated with a thin rhodium metal layer. To read data from this sheet, the laser reflects light off the surface, reconstructing the data into a digital bit stream. Laser data resists alteration; any attempt to alter it can be detected readily, so it provides a secure storage system. Laser storage does not deteriorate over time and is immune to electromagnetic radiation. Chapters 5 and 6 discuss another development in laser storage technology: the optical disk, or laser disk.

Learning Check

1. Which medium, tapes or disks, allows faster access to data, and why?

2. What is the device that detects and/or puts magnetized spots on tape or disk?

3. Describe a disk pack.

4. What advantages might removable disk packs have over permanent ones?

5. Name three other approaches to secondary storage.

Answers

1. Disks, because they allow direct access to data. Tapes require that data be read from the beginning of the tape, no matter where the needed data is located. **2.** The read/write head. **3.** A disk pack is a series of hard disks mounted on a center shaft. It contains access arms that hold read/write heads in the proper position for each disk side. Usually it is enclosed in a plastic unit. **4.** Removable disk packs allow more data to be accessed by one drive, thereby cutting down on the number of drives needed. The disk packs can be locked away when not in use. **5.** Mass storage; bubble memory; laser storage systems.

Hardware for Input and Output

A computer system includes more than just a central processing unit (CPU). Data must be provided to the computer in a form it can recognize, and output must be translated into a form humans can understand. Input and output are important activities in any computer system, because they are the communication links between people and machines. If the interfaces between people and machines are weak, the overall performance of the computer system suffers.

Input Methods

In order to enter data into the computer—to write instructions, select an operation, ask a question, or update data—you must use an input device. The one with which you are most familiar is the keyboard. The layout of a keyboard is much like that of a typewriter keyboard, except that there are additional keys for specific computer functions. Other data input methods are discussed in the following sections.

Punched Cards Traditionally, data from documents such as time cards, bills, invoices, and checks was transferred onto punched cards and then read into the computer. Today, a few of these documents are still punched cards themselves, because data is keyed directly onto the cards at their source. The most common example is the utility bill. These cards can be read directly into the computer, thus saving time and eliminating errors that can result from retyping the data.

The standard punched card has 80 vertical columns and 12 horizontal rows. Data is recorded as a set of holes punched in a particular column to represent a given character (see Figure 3-18).

Usually, an operator transcribes data from a source document onto cards by pressing keys on a keyboard that resembles an ordinary typewriter. The keypunch machine automatically feeds, positions, and stacks the cards. The data on the cards then is read into the computer by a card reader. Most card readers are photoelectric readers—that is, they detect the positions of the holes in the cards by passing light over them. Even with these automatic functions, keypunching is costly in both time and personnel. For these reasons, punched cards and keypunches are limited in use today.

Figure 3-18   Punched Card

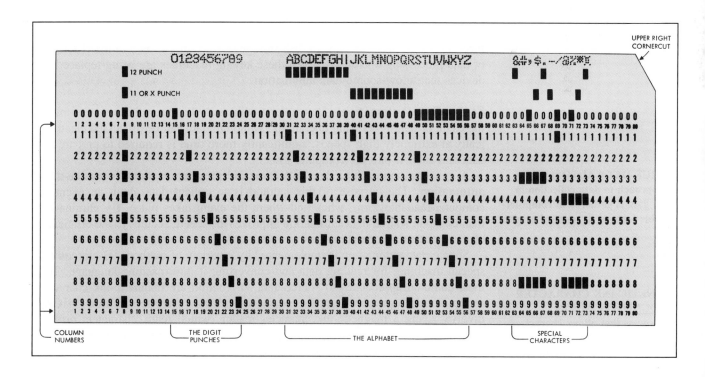

Figure 3-19
Key-to-Disk System

Key-to-Magnetic Media   Key-to-tape and key-to-disk systems were developed for recording data on magnetic media, after it became obvious that magnetic media would soon replace punched cards (see Figure 3-19). With these systems, data is entered from the keyboard and stored as magnetized spots on the surface of a tape of disk. Because the spots retain their magnetism, the data can be stored and used indefinitely. Unlike punched cards, which cannot be repunched, old data on tape and disks can be replaced with new data. Tape and disks also can store much more data than cards, and in a much smaller space. In addition, data stored on tape or disk can be read into the CPU hundreds of times faster than data on cards. Therefore, the use of magnetic tape or disk storage significantly increases the efficiency of data-processing operations. Even these keying machines are being replaced by devices that allow source-data automation.

Source-Data Automation   Data entry traditionally has been the weakest link in the chain of data-processing operations. Although data can be processed electronically at extremely high speeds, significantly more time is required to prepare the data and enter it into the computer system.

A common approach to data collection and preparation today is **source-data automation.** The purpose of this method is to collect data about an event in computer-readable form, when and where the event takes place. By eliminating manual input, source-data automation improves the speed, accuracy, and efficiency of data-processing operations.

Source-data automation is implemented by a variety of methods. Each requires special machines for reading data and converting it into machine language. The most common approaches to source-data automation are magnetic-ink character recognition and optical recognition. **Magnetic-ink character recognition (MICR)** involves using a magnetic-ink character reader, which reads characters printed with ink that contains magnetized particles of iron oxide. Check processing is a major application of MICR. The magnetic-ink characters are printed at the bottom of checks, as shown in Figure 3-20, and can be read by both humans and the

SOURCE-DATA AUTOMATION
An approach to data collection in which data is gathered in computer-readable form at its point of origin.

MAGNETIC-INK CHARACTER RECOGNITION (MICR)
The process that allows characters printed with magnetized ink to be read by a magnetic-ink character reader.

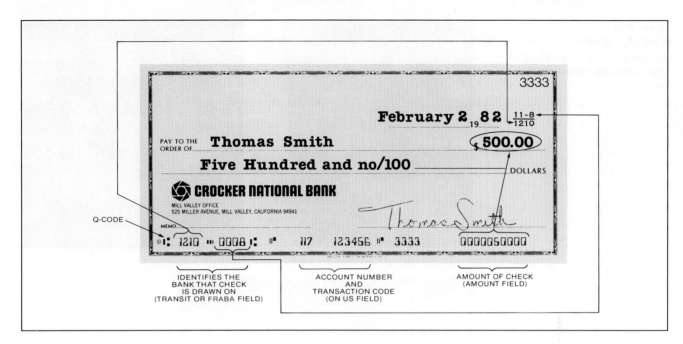

Figure 3-20
Sample Check with Magnetic Ink
Characters

OPTICAL RECOGNITION
A method of electronic scanning
which reads marks, bars, or
characters and converts the optical
images into appropriate electrical
signals.

BAR CODE
A machine-readable code made up
of bars and spaces of varying
widths; often used on packaging of
merchandise and read by optical
scanning devices.

REMOTE TERMINAL
A terminal that is placed at a
location distant from the central
computer.

POINT-OF-SALE (POS)
TERMINAL
A terminal that serves as a cash
register, but also records data for
such tasks as inventory control and
accounting at the location where
goods are sold.

character reader. Between 750 and 1,500 checks per minute can be read and sorted by an MICR device.

Optical recognition uses devices to read marks or symbols coded on paper documents and to convert them into electrical pulses. These pulses then are transmitted directly to the CPU or stored on magnetic tape for input at a later time. Optical character recognition is used extensively in mail sorting, credit card billing, utility billing, and inventory control.

There are several types of optical recognition, but one type we see frequently interprets **bar codes** (see Figure 3-21). A bar code is a pattern of lines which appears on products in grocery and department stores. The code for each product is a unique combination of vertical bars of varying widths and varying spaces between them. The bars represent data such as the product name and manufacturer.

Remote terminals often are used in conjunction with optical recognition. Remote terminals collect data at its source and transmit it to a central computer for processing. Remote terminals that function as cash registers and also capture sales data are called **point-of-sale (POS) terminals.** These terminals have a keyboard for data entry, a panel that displays the price, a cash drawer, and a printer that provides a cash receipt. Some POS terminals have a scanner that reads the bar code stamped on an item. Many supermarkets are equipped with this type of terminal. Other POS terminals are used with wands that read characters from a price tag or other document on clothing and other goods (see Figure 3-22). By using POS terminals and other forms of source-data automation, retailers can update inventory and sales information almost immediately. In many cases, the resulting data source can be read by both humans and machines.

Specialized Input Devices   Traditional input devices, such as those used in source-data automation or with key-to-magnetic media, do not meet the needs of every

Figure 3-21
Bar Code A clerk passes the merchandise over a scanner, which reads a bar code printed on the packages.

Figure 3-22
Optical Recognition with a Wand Scanner Some methods of optical recognition reads specially shaped characters much as the ones shown below.

ABCDEFGHIJKLMN
OPQRSTUVWXYZ,.
$/*-1234567890

Figure 3-23
Spatial Digitizer

SPATIAL DIGITIZER
An input device that can reconstruct a three-dimensional object graphically on a computer's display screen.

TOUCH SCREEN
A computer screen equipped for detecting the point at which it is touched by the user, thus enabling the user to bypass the keyboard.

situation. Special input devices may be required, such as spatial digitizers, touch screens, and voice recognition systems. Other specialized input devices are discussed in conjunction with microcomputers in Chapter 5.

Three-dimensional graphics can be created on a display screen with the use of a **spatial digitizer** (see Figure 3-23). A spatial digitizer allows a user to trace an object with the digitizer's arm or pointer for reproduction on the display screen. The precise measurements are taken electronically, and the object is reconstructed graphically on the screen.

A **touch screen** looks like a normal computer screen, but it can detect a user's touch and can identify the point at which the user actually touches the screen (see Figure 3-24). The touch screen is especially useful when the user has a list of

Figure 3-24
Touch Screen

Figure 3-25
Voice Recognition System

alternatives from which to choose. When the user touches the desired alternative, the computer registers the choice made and continues processing accordingly.

VOICE RECOGNITION SYSTEM
An input system that recognizes certain speech and voice patterns; the user is limited to the patterns that the system is programmed to recognize.

Remote terminals that use audio input, **voice recognition systems,** are suitable for low-volume, highly formal input. Because of the limitations of current technology, voice recognition is best used with short-answer data. The user must speak in short, clearly enunciated words because the computer is programmed to recognize specific voice and speech patterns. In industry, workers can use a voice recognition unit for entering data about inventory or quality control, thus leaving their hands free for sorting products (see Figure 3-25). Research in voice recognition focuses on improving three areas: amount of recognized vocabulary, ability to recognize different voices, and ability to interpret continuous or flowing speech.

Printers

IMPACT PRINTER
A printer that forms characters by physically striking the ribbon, paper, and embossed character together.

NONIMPACT PRINTER
A printer that uses heat, laser, or photographic methods for producing images.

Once data have been fed into the computer by card, tape, disk, or other method, it is processed and output in the way that best suits the user's needs. Output may appear as soft copy on a computer screen, or it may be printed as hard copy, the standard term for permanent printed copy. (Monitors for microcomputers are discussed in Chapter 5.) The type of output device is determined by the needs of the user. In most cases, however, when we refer to output we mean hard copy that has been produced by a printer. There are two general types of printers: **impact printers** and **nonimpact printers.**

Impact Printers   This type of printer uses a striking motion. A hammer mechanism strikes together an inked ribbon, the paper, and the character embossed on a plastic or metal part. Impact printers come in a variety of sizes and shapes.

Figure 3-26
Dot-Matrix Character Set

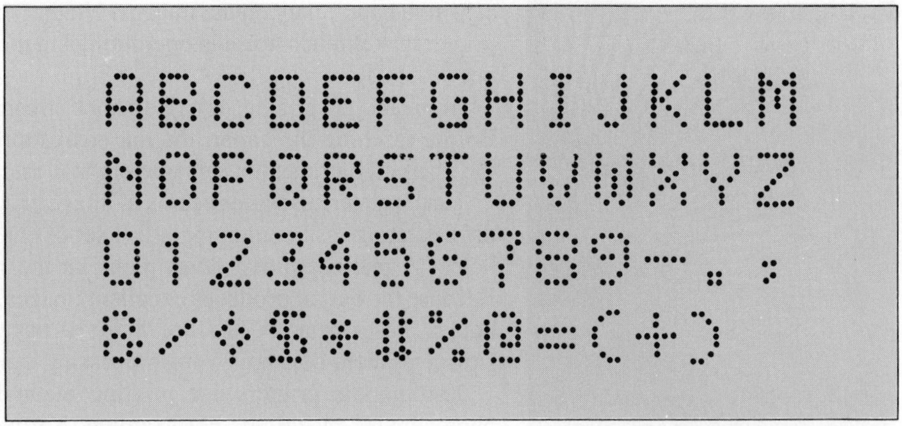

DOT-MATRIX PRINTER
An impact printer that forms characters from a matrix of pins arranged in a rectangular shape. Only the pins necessary for forming a particular character are selected from the matrix.

DAISY-WHEEL PRINTER
An impact printer whose print element is a removable flat wheel of spokes, each with a character embossed at its tip.

Some print one character at a time, whereas others print a line at a time. Printers in the first category include dot-matrix and daisy-wheel printers.

Dot-Matrix (also called wire-matrix) **printers** operate by striking pins in a print element against the ribbon and paper. The pins are arranged in a rectangular matrix, usually seven pins high and five pins wide. Combinations of pins are activated to represent various characters. The dot combinations used to represent numbers, letters, and special characters are shown in Figure 3-26. High-quality, or near–letter-quality, dot matrix images are produced when the matrix contains more pins for the same amount of space or when each character is struck twice. Dot-matrix printers typically can print 100 to 200 characters per second.

Daisy-wheel printers are solid-font printing devices that create a character like a typed character. They use a flat disk or wheel with petal-like projections, each with a single character embossed at the tip (see Figure 3-27). The wheel rotates to bring the desired character into position and is then struck by a hammer mechanism to form an image on paper. Daisy wheels come in several type fonts that can be interchanged quickly. The daisy-wheel printer often is used in word processing systems to give output a typewriter-quality (or ''letter-quality'') appearance. Daisy-wheel printers can print between 15 and 55 characters per second.

Devices that print one line at a time include print-wheel printers, chain printers, drum printers, and band printers. All have multiple sets of characters, so they can print all the characters on a line at once or in very fast succession. These printers are used primarily with mainframes and minicomputers.

Nonimpact Printers   Nonimpact printers do not print characters by means of a mechanical printing element that strikes the paper. Instead, heat, laser, or photographic methods are used in producing the image. Electrostatic, thermal, ink-jet, laser, and xerographic printers are discussed here.

An electrostatic printer forms an image of a character on special paper, using a dot matrix of charged wires or pins. The paper is moved through a solution containing ink particles that have a charge opposite to that of the pattern. The ink particles adhere to each charged pattern on the paper and form visible characters.

Thermal printers generate characters by using heat and heat-sensitive paper. Rods are heated in a matrix. As the ends of the selected rods touch the heat-

Figure 3-27
Daisy Wheel
The daisy wheel produces solid-font characters.

Figure 3-28
Apple Laser Writer
Laser printers are becoming inexpensive enough for small offices and individuals to buy.

sensitive paper, they create images. Neither the electrothermal nor the electrostatic printer makes much noise in operation, and most produce at least 40 to 80 characters per second.

In an ink-jet printer, nozzles shoot streams of charged ink toward the paper. Before reaching the paper, the ink passes through an electrical field that arranges the charged particles into characters at a rate of up to 220 characters per second.

Laser printers use laser beams in image production. The laser beams are reflected off a rotating disk containing a full set of characters or a grid of thousands of tiny holes. A photosensitive drum picks up the images and transfers them to paper. Because the output produces excellent images, the process often is used for printing books. Laser printers produce 8 to 10 pages per minute and are replacing the slower printers of many word processing systems (see Figure 3-28).

Xerographic printers use printing methods like those employed in common photocopying machines. For example, Xerox, the pioneer in this type of printing, has one model that prints on single 8 1/2 × 11-inch sheets of plain paper. Xerographic printers can turn out 4,000 lines per minute.

New printing systems now on the market combine many features of the printing process into one machine, including stacking, routing, hole punching, blanking out of priority information, and perforating. Some printers produce both text and graphic images on plain paper, thus reducing or eliminating the need for preprinted forms.

LaserWriter Plus

Figure 3-29
Flatbed Plotter

Specialized Output Devices

PLOTTER
An output device that typically uses pens to produce hard-copy graphic output, such as drawings, charts, maps, and other images.

Plotters   A **plotter** uses pens to produce hard copies of graphic images, such as bar charts, graphs, organizational charts, engineering drawings, maps, trend lines, supply and demand curves, and other useful graphics.

The two types of plotters are the flatbed plotter and the drum plotter. A flatbed plotter looks like a table with pens mounted on a track (see Figure 3-29). On some plotters, the pens move; on others, the table holding the paper moves. Drum plotters draw on paper that is rolled on a cylinder.

Many plotters operate with a variety of pens—filter-tip, ballpoint, liquid roller, and nylon-tip. For high-quality output, fine drafting pens are used. Output can be produced in four, six, or eight colors. Some plotters can position the pen at as many as 45,000 different points within each square inch of paper.

COMPUTER-OUTPUT
MICROFILM (COM)
A form of computer output in which information from a printer or magnetic tape is placed on microfilm or microfiche.

Computer-Output Microfilm   Sometimes large amounts of information must be printed and stored for future reference. Printing the output on conventional-sized paper would quickly create both a storage and an access problem. A technique that solves this problem is **computer output microfilm (COM).** In this method, photographed images are produced in miniature by the computer. Sometimes the

HIGHLIGHT ▲▲▲▲▲▲▲▲▲▲▲▲▲▲▲▲▲▲▲▲▲▲▲▲▲

Ray Kurzweil and His Amazing Machines

Ray Kurzweil likes to make things. He has made the Kurzweil Reading Machine and the Kurzweil 250, a keyboard that sounds much like a concert grand piano, and he is working on perfecting a voice-activated typewriter. Not the sorts of things most people who like to make things make.

Kurzweil had an early start. When he was 12, he developed a software package that was distributed by IBM. As a high school student he won the prestigious International Science Fair, with a computer program that analyzed musical patterns and used them to generate what he now calls second-rate Mozart. At age 28, he introduced the world's first optical character recognition technology for reading a wide variety of type fonts. The Kurzweil Reading Machine, widely used today in helping visually impaired people read printed matter, uses this technology.

Another popular Kurzweil product is the Kurzweil 250, a digital music synthesizer. The 250 creates a complex model of an acoustic piano sound—rather than an electronic sound—as well as sounds of other musical instruments and human voices. (If you want to know how successful the 250 is, ask Stevie Wonder, whose desire for better acoustic sound imitation in electronic music prompted the development of the machine.)

Kurzweil's current project centers on voice-activated typewriter (VAT) technology. If Kurzweil's VAT machines are successful, people won't have to hunt and peck at the typewriter, and deaf people will be able to use the telephone with complete freedom and flexibility.

output is first recorded on magnetic tape and then transferred to 35-millimeter microfilm rolls or to 4 × 6-inch microfiche cards.

The COM system can store graphics as well as characters, and records at a rate 25 to 50 times that of traditional printing. Another advantage is that it costs relatively little to produce additional microfilm copies.

VOICE RESPONSE UNIT
A device through which the computer "speaks" by arranging half-second records of phonemes, or voice sounds.

VOICE SYNTHESIZER
The output portion of a voice communication system; used to provide verbal output from the computer system to the user.

Voice Output Computer audio output, or **voice response units,** "speak" by arranging half-second records of voice sounds (phonemes) or prerecorded words. This approach is being used in the banking industry for reporting customer account balances, and in supermarkets for informing customers of the amount of each purchase. Audio output is well suited to situations that require short, formal messages.

Some audio systems use **voice synthesizers,** which use a mathematical model of the human voice to create the output. Many people with special needs are using voice synthesizers to improve the quality of their lives. The Kurzweil Reading Machine, designed by Ray Kurzweil to aid the blind, scans a printed page and reads aloud. Other synthesizers are connected to microcomputers and synthesize speech for those who cannot speak.

As of 1986, the quality of speech produced by many voice synthesizers is poor. Continuing research and development efforts will improve both the range of words and quality of speech produced by these devices. Someday, listeners may be unable to tell that audio output and synthesized voices are coming from computers.

Learning Check

1. What approach to data collection involves collecting data at its source at the time an event occurs, in computer-readable form?

2. What is a POS terminal?

3. Why might a touch screen be easy to use?

4. In what three ways must voice recognition be improved?

5. Differentiate between an impact printer and a nonimpact printer.

6. What type of output do plotters primarily produce?

7. Of what advantage is COM?

Answers

1. Source-data automation. 2. Point-of-sale terminal. 3. The user does not have to type or learn special key sequences in order to use the computer. 4. Recognized vocabulary must be expanded, different voices must be able to use the system, and people must be able to talk in continuous speech. 5. An impact printer uses a striking motion in producing an image, whereas a nonimpact printer uses heat, laser, or photographic methods of producing the image. 6. Graphic output. 7. It is cheap and takes up little space.

Data Representation

MACHINE LANGUAGE
The only language the computer can execute directly; a code that designates the computer's electrical states as combinations of 0s and 1s.

When data is entered into a computer through an input device such as a keyboard, it is not in a form that the computer can interpret. Computers cannot understand the complex symbols that humans use. They recognize only a code composed of 0s and 1s, known as **machine language.** Machine language suits the computer because electronic components and storage media represent two states: on/off, conducting/nonconducting, or present/absent. Before the computer can execute the English-like statements of most programming languages, these statements must be translated by special programs into machine language. Machine language uses binary code or one of several other codes based on it.

BINARY NUMBER SYSTEM
The base 2 number system, which uses the digits 0 and 1; convenient for use in computer coding because it corresponds to the two states in machine circuitry.

BINARY REPRESENTATION
Use of a two-state, or binary, system for representing data.

Binary Representation

Because data is represented in the computer by the electrical states of its circuitry, data representation is easily accomplished by using the **binary number system.** In the binary or base 2 number system, there are only two digits: 1 and 0. Using binary numbers to represent data is called **binary representation.**

The binary system is similar to the decimal (base 10) number system that we use every day. Both represent the values of digits as powers of the base, and in both, the digits farther to the left represent larger powers than the digits to the right. For example, the decimal number 3,568 can be analyzed like this:

Figure 3-30
Decimal Place Values

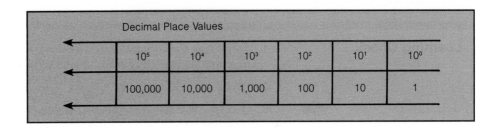

$$8 \times 10^0 = 8 \times 1 \quad \text{or} \quad 8$$
$$6 \times 10^1 = 6 \times 10 \quad \text{or} \quad 60$$
$$5 \times 10^2 = 5 \times 100 \quad \text{or} \quad 500$$
$$3 \times 10^3 = 3 \times 1,000 \text{ or } 3,000$$
$$\overline{3,568}_{\text{base } 10}$$

Each position represents a power of the base 10. The progression of power is from right to left—that is, digits farther to the left in a decimal number represent larger powers of the base 10 (see Figure 3-30).

The same principle holds for binary representation. The difference is that, in binary representation, each position in the number represents a power of 2 (see Figure 3-31). For example, consider the decimal number 11. In binary, the value equivalent to 11 is written as follows:

$$1 \quad 0 \quad 1 \quad 1_{\text{base } 2}$$
$$1 \times 2^0 = 1 \times 1 \text{ or } 1$$
$$1 \times 2^1 = 1 \times 2 \text{ or } 2$$
$$0 \times 2^2 = 1 \times 4 \text{ or } 0$$
$$1 \times 2^3 = 1 \times 8 \text{ or } 8$$
$$\overline{11}_{\text{base } 10}$$

Each digit position in a binary number is called a bit. A 1 in a bit position indicates the presence of a specific power of 2; a 0 indicates the absence of a specific power. As in the decimal number system, the progression of powers is from right to left.

Figure 3-31
Binary Place Values

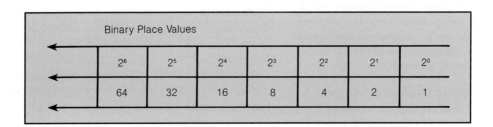

Computer Codes

A single binary digit (0 or 1) cannot represent a number of letter. By using combinations of the two digits, however, computer scientists have developed codes that represent the alphanumeric characters. Many computers use coding schemes that group the bits in order to represent characters.

BYTE
A fixed number of adjacent bits, usually eight, operated as a unit.

A fixed number of adjacent bits operated on as a unit is called a **byte.** Bytes usually are eight bits long. The number of possible combinations of 0s and 1s in eight bits is enough to represent all the characters. For example, one standard coding system codes an upper-case letter B as follows:

$$\text{1 1 0 0 0 0 1 0} = \text{B}$$

bit ↓

byte

Other combinations of 0s and 1s represent the other letters, numbers, and special characters. There are 256 possible bit combinations in an eight-bit code.

EXTENDED BINARY CODED DECIMAL INTERCHANGE CODE (EBCDIC)
An eight-bit code for character representation.

One eight-bit code is known as **Extended Binary Coded Decimal Interchange Code (EBCDIC,** pronounced EP-see-DICK). The 256 (2^8) possible bit combinations in EBCDIC are used to represent uppercase and lowercase letters and additional special characters, such as the cent sign and the quotation mark.

AMERICAN STANDARD CODE FOR INFORMATION INTERCHANGE (ASCII)
A seven-bit standard code used for information interchange among data-processing systems, communications systems, and associated equipment.

The **American Standard Code for Information Interchange (ASCII,** pronounced ASK-ee) is a seven-bit code developed cooperatively by several computer manufacturers in order to establish a standard code for all computers (see Figure 3-33). Because certain machines are designed to accept eight-bit rather than seven-bit code patterns, an eight-bit version of ASCII, called ASCII-8, was also created. ASCII and EBCDIC are similar. The key difference is in the bit patterns used to represent certain characters.

Code Checking

PARITY BIT
A bit added to a byte to detect incorrect transmission of data within a computer system.

Computers do not always function without errors. When errors occur, they must be detected immediately to keep data from being changed. Most computers include an extra bit at each storage location to check for certain kinds of internal errors. This extra bit is called a **parity bit.** Computers can be set to either odd parity or even parity. If a computer is set for odd parity, each character is represented by an odd number of 1 bits. The parity bit is set to 0 if the number of 1 bits in the character is already odd. If the number of 1 bits is even, the parity bit is set to 1, making the total number of 1 bits odd. With even parity, the parity bit is set to either 0 or 1 so that the total number of 1 bits is even.

When the computer checks each character for errors, it checks for the proper number of 1 bits. For example, a computer set for even parity checks for an even number of 1 bits and detects an error in any character that has an odd number of 1 bits.

Figure 3-32
ASCII Code and ASCII Values
The ASCII values in decimal form
often are used in programming. These
are only some of the ASCII
representations, 0–9 and A–Z.

Character	ASCII Code	Decimal Value	Character	ASCII Code	Decimal Value
0	0110000	48	I	1001001	73
1	0110001	49	J	1001010	74
2	0110010	50	K	1001011	75
3	0110011	51	L	1001100	76
4	0110100	52	M	1001101	77
5	0110101	53	N	1001110	78
6	0110110	54	O	1001111	79
7	0110111	55	P	1010000	80
8	0111000	56	Q	1010001	81
9	0111001	57	R	1010010	82
A	1000001	65	S	1010011	83
B	1000010	66	T	1010100	84
C	1000011	67	U	1010101	85
D	1000100	68	V	1010110	86
E	1000101	69	W	1010111	87
F	1000110	70	X	1011000	88
G	1000111	71	Y	1011001	89
H	1001000	72	Z	1011010	90

If an error is detected, the computer may try to repeat the operation in which the error occurred. If the error remains, the computer informs the operator. The computer cannot correct these errors; it can only detect them.

Learning Check

1. What is the number system suited to represent the states of computer circuitry?

2. What does the binary number 11010 stand for in decimal representation?

3. In $1100\underline{0}10_{base\ 2}$, the underlined digit stands for what power of 2? What place is it in?

4. Two binary-based codes used for representing letters, numbers, and special characters are _____ and _____.

5. The extra bit used as a check for some internal errors is called a _____ bit.

Answers

1. Binary number system. 2. 26. 3. 2^3 (2 to the third power); eights. 4. EBCDIC and ASCII. 5. Parity.

Summary Points

■ Computers are categorized by memory capacity, capability, price range, and speed of operation. The four classifications are supercomputer, mainframe, minicomputer, and microcomputer.

■ Advances in technology have blurred the distinctions between these classifications of computers.

■ The component that is responsible for temporarily storing data and acting on it is the central processing unit (CPU). The CPU is made up of the control unit, which maintains order and controls what is happening in the CPU; the arithmetic/logic unit (ALU), which performs arithmetic and logical operations; and primary memory, which holds all data and instructions necessary for processing.

■ Each location in primary memory has a unique address, which allows stored-program instructions and data items to be located by the control unit as it directs processing operations.

■ Random-access memory (RAM) is the major type of primary memory. The nondestructive read/destructive write characteristic of RAM allows a program to be executed as many times as needed, since the program remains intact until another is stored over it.

■ Read-only memory (ROM) is hardwired primary memory. It stores microprograms or other data in a form that cannot be changed. ROM that can be programmed once is called programmable read-only memory (PROM). ROM that can be reprogrammed is called erasable programmable read-only memory (EPROM).

■ Storage located outside the computer is called secondary storage. There are two types of secondary storage: sequential-access and direct-access. Sequential-access storage media must be read from and written to sequentially—that is, from the beginning and in order. Examples are magnetic tapes and tape cassettes. Direct-access storage media allow the user to access data directly at any point. Examples are magnetic disks and floppy disks.

■ Other types of storage include mass storage devices for storing large amounts of data at low cost; nonvolatile bubble memory, in which data are stored as magnetized spots or bubbles on a thin film of semiconductor material; and laser storage, which resists alteration.

■ Traditional input methods include punched cards and key-to-magnetic media systems. These forms of input require an intermediate step, in which data is recorded manually by keypunching or typing from the original source of data.

■ Source-data automation is a technique that allows data to be collected at the source in computer-readable form. Most source-data automation systems use some type of mark or character recognition device, such as the bar code.

■ Remote terminals often are used in conjunction with source-data automation; point-of-sale terminals function as cash registers and capture sales data at the same time.

■ Spatial digitizers, touch screens, and voice recognition systems are 3 devices for specialized input.

■ Traditional output devices produce either hard or soft copy. Hard-copy output is printed on paper, whereas soft-copy output appears on a computer screen.

■ The most common output device is the printer. Printers come in two types:

impact and nonimpact. Impact printers press the print elements against the paper and ribbon. Common impact printers are dot-matrix printers and daisy-wheel printers. Nonimpact printers use a variety of means to create their images, but the print element never touches the paper. Nonimpact printers include electrostatic printers, thermal printers, ink-jet printers, laser printers, and xerographic printers.

■ Other types of output devices include plotters, which produce graphic images with pens; computer output microfilm (COM), in which output is produced on microfilm rather than paper; and voice response units, which "speak" by arranging half-second records of voice sounds (phonemes) or prerecorded words. Some audio systems use voice synthesizers, which use a mathematical model of the human voice to create the output.

■ Data representation in the computer is based on a two-state system or binary number system. This system suits the computer because it matches the on/off, conducting/nonconducting, present/absent states of computer hardware and storage.

■ A bit is one position in a binary number. A byte is a specified number of adjacent bits (usually eight), and a parity bit is used to detect errors in data transmission. Check digits are used to determine the correctness of data entry.

■ Because numeric representation in binary is tedious, coding schemes have been devised which offer shorthand methods of representing binary. Two coding schemes are Extended Binary Coded Decimal Interchange Code (EBCDIC) and American Standard Code for Information Interchange (ASCII).

Review Questions

1. For what purposes might you use a supercomputer? Have you heard of any uses other than the ones mentioned in the text? What are they?

2. What market trend currently is affecting sales of minicomputers?

3. Name the parts of the central processing unit and discuss the functions of each.

4. Relate RAM, the stored-program concept, and nondestructive read/destructive write.

5. Explain the concept of ROM and how it might help prevent unauthorized copying of software.

6. Explain the difference between sequential-access storage and direct-access storage, and give examples of each.

7. What is source-data automation, and how would it benefit a retail store owner? Describe some instances of source-data automation which you have encountered.

8. Differentiate between impact printers and nonimpact printers, and give some examples of each. What factors would you take into consideration when deciding which printer to buy?

9. Describe how computer-output microfilm (COM) might be useful to a large bank.

10. How are characters represented in binary coding methods?

CHAPTER 4

Software Development

Introduction

PROGRAMMING
The process of writing the step-by-step instructions that direct a computer in performing a task.

Computers are capable of performing all kinds of tasks that sometimes seem magical. In order to perform even the simplest task, however, computers need directions from people. **Programming** is the process of giving step-to-step instructions to computers so that the machines will execute the desired tasks.

The earliest computers were programmed by arranging wires and switches within the computer components. Up to 6,000 switches could be set on ENIAC for executing one program. When a new program was to be run, the switches had to be reset. EDSAC, the first stored-program computer, allowed instructions to be entered into primary memory without rewiring or resetting the switches. Instructions were written in codes based on the binary number system. This method of coding was tedious and error-prone. The development of assembly language and high-level, English-like languages has simplified and streamlined the programming process and has increased the variety of problems that can be solved using computers.

This chapter describes the programming process, one part of which is writing the program in a suitable programming language. Also discussed are structured programming techniques, the types of computer programs, and some popular programming languages.

Solving Problems with the Computer

PROGRAMMER
A person who writes the instructions that tell a computer what to do.

Every day you solve problems, many of which have several solutions. Often you solve them without consciously thinking of all the steps involved. For example, traveling from your home to a friend's house involves deciding when to leave and what route to take. When you arrive at your friend's door, any of a number of different decisions could have helped you get there safely.

Computer problem solving is similar. Many solutions exist for a single problem. Some are more efficient than others. In order to develop a good solution to a problem, a **programmer** follows four steps, known as the programming process (see Figure 4-1):

1. Define the problem.
2. Design the solution.
3. Write the program.
4. Compile, debug, and test the program.

Define the Problem

This step is built upon the answers to a number of questions: Who needs information? What kind is needed? What data is needed to yield the information, and where can it be found? Must the data be accumulated in a certain order? In what form should the data be given to the computer, once it has been gathered? In what

Figure 4-1
The Programming Process
Each step of the programming process
must be carefully documented.

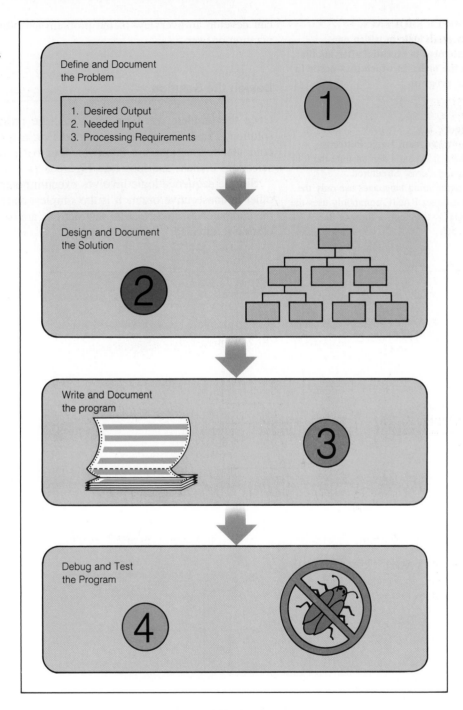

Define and Document
the Problem

1. Desired Output
2. Needed Input
3. Processing Requirements

①

Design and Document
the Solution

②

Write and Document
the program

③

Debug and Test
the Program

④

SYSTEM ANALYST
A person who is the communication
link or interface between users and
technical persons; responsible for
designing software.

form will the information be most useful to the intended users? The answers to
such questions provide the desired output, the needed input, and the processing
requirements for solving the problem.

Not all of these questions can be answered by the programmer. Some guidance
often is needed from management. An information specialist, the **system analyst,**

SIMPLE SEQUENCE
Program logic in which one
statement is executed after another,
in the order in which they occur in
the program.

can develop an overview of the problem and how its solution can help an organization or user.

Design the Solution

Once the problem has been analyzed, the programmer can begin designing a solution. The design requires considerable creativity from the programmer, but all computer instructions are based on four basic logic patterns: simple sequence, selection, branch, and loop (see Figure 4-2).

Simple sequence logic involves executing instructions one statement after another in consecutive order. It is the simplest and most often used pattern. In fact, the computer assumes that all instructions are to be executed in this order unless otherwise directed.

Figure 4-2
Four Program Logic Patterns
These flowcharts demonstrate the four logic patterns. Structured programming languages use only the first three. BASIC commonly uses the GOTO statement, a form of the branch.

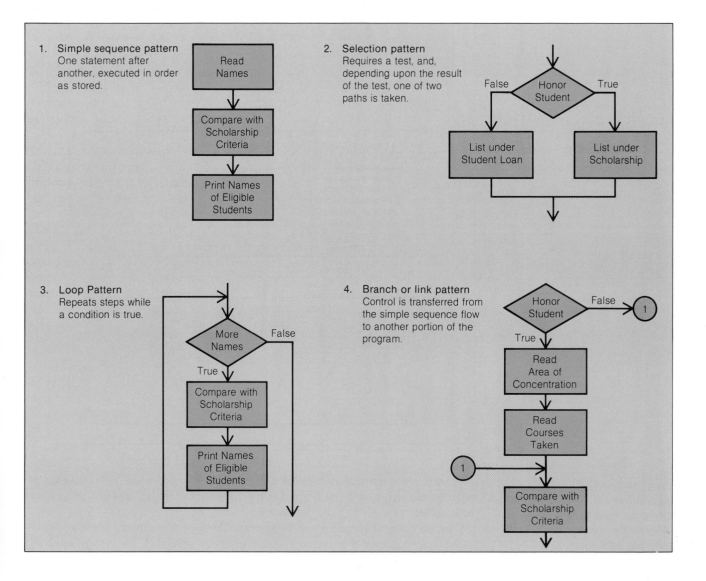

SELECTION
Program logic that requires the computer to make a comparison; the result of the comparison determines which execution path will be taken next.

BRANCH
Program logic used to bypass or alter the normal flow of program execution.

LOOP
Program logic that allows a specified sequence of instructions to be executed repeatedly, as long as stated conditions are met.

ALGORITHM
A set of well-defined instructions that outline the solution of a problem in a finite number of steps.

PSEUDOCODE
An informal, narrative language used for representing the logic of a programming problem solution.

FLOWCHART
A graphic representation in which symbols represent the flow of operations, logic, data, and equipment of a program or system.

The **selection** pattern requires the computer to choose from two or more items. Each choice is based on one of the three comparisons a computer can make: equal to, less than, or greater than. When complex selections must be made, several comparisons can be combined. For example, the computer can select employees who have worked for a company for ten years or longer, or determine whether your checking account is overdrawn.

A variation of selection is the **branch.** The branch pattern allows the computer to skip statements in a program, based on the answer to a question. The branch often is signaled with the command GOTO. Frequent use of branching results in a program that is inefficient and difficult for other programmers to follow. According to many experts, few or no GOTO statements are needed in a well-planned program.

A **loop** pattern directs the computer to loop back through previous instructions in the program. A given set of statements can be performed as many times as needed. By looping, a programmer avoids writing the same set of instructions over and over. For example, a loop might be used in figuring weekly pay for 500 employees or in calculating your telephone bill. Because the loop and selection patterns pass control to another part of a program, statements that signal those patterns are known as control statements or control structures.

In order to avoid writing and using faulty programs, programmers must carefully formulate an outline of the logic used to solve the problem. This outline is called an **algorithm.** An algorithm outlines the desired sequence and details of instructions so they can be checked for errors. Two popular ways of representing algorithms are with pseudocode and flowcharts.

Pseudocode is a brief set of instructions written in prose form in the order that the instructions will appear in the actual program (see Figure 4-3). Pseudocode allows the program planner to focus on the steps required for performing a particular task rather than on the rules of a particular programming language. Pseudocoding is similar to writing an outline or a rough draft for a term paper.

Like pseudocode, the **flowchart** is a skeleton of the program. It is a diagram of the necessary steps, rather than a prose statement. Other names for flowcharts are block diagrams, logic diagrams, and logic charts. Accurate flowcharts, both in their original and updated forms, are good visible records of programs and how they were designed. When drawing flowcharts, programmers should use the stan-

Figure 4-3
Pseudocode for a Payroll Processing Example

```
Begin
Begin loop; perform until no more rec-
ords
        Read employee's name, hours
        worked, and hourly wage
        Calculate gross pay
        Calculate withholdings
        Calculate net pay
        Print check
End loop
Generate summary reports
End
```

CODING
The process of writing a programming problem solution in a programming language.

MACHINE LANGUAGE
A code that the computer can execute directly, and that designates electrical states in the computer as combinations of 0s and 1s.

ASSEMBLY LANGUAGE
A low-level programming language that uses abbreviations called mnemonics, rather than the groupings of 0s and 1s used in machine language.

HIGH-LEVEL LANGUAGE
A language that is oriented more toward the user than the computer system (contrast with low-level language).

LANGUAGE-TRANSLATOR PROGRAM
A system program that translates programming languages other than machine language into machine-executable code.

SOURCE PROGRAM
A program written in a language other than machine language, which must be translated into machine language before execution can occur.

OBJECT PROGRAM
A sequence of machine-executable instructions generated by a language translator program from source program statements.

ASSEMBLER PROGRAM
The translator program for an assembly language program; produces a machine language program that can be executed.

INTERPRETER PROGRAM
A high-level language translator that evaluates and translates a program one statement at a time.

dard flowchart symbols established by the American National Standards Institute (ANSI) and keep the flowcharts complete, up to date, and legible (see Figures 4-4 and 4-5).

Write the Program

Writing the program involves translating the algorithm or flowchart into a programming language. This process is also known as **coding.** The language chosen depends upon what the program is expected to do and what facilities are available to the programmer. A well-written program should be:

■ Easy to read and understand. The program should be written so that another programmer can see quickly what the program does.
■ Reliable. The program should consistently produce the right output.
■ Workable under all conditions. Even when incorrect or inappropriate input data is entered, the program's internal logic should cause it to operate correctly.
■ Easy to modify and update. Programs should be constructed in independent, structured segments, so that a change in one segment does not mandate a change in others. (Structured programming is discussed later in this chapter.)
■ Portable. A program should be usable on other computers with little or no modification.
■ Efficient. Programs should execute as quickly as possible.

Compile, Debug, and Test the Program

After a program has been written, it is submitted to the computer for translation into **machine language. Assembly** and **high-level languages** are used by programmers much more widely than machine language, but these languages cannot be executed directly by computers, so they are converted into machine-executable form by a **language-translator program.** The instructions written by the programmer (the **source program**) are transformed by the language-translator program into machine language (the **object program**).

The translator program for assembly language is an **assembler program,** and a high-level language translator is either an **interpreter program** or a **compiler program.** (Many high-level languages are available in both compiled and interpreted versions.) Translator programs are designed for specific machines and languages. A compiler that translates a program written in FORTRAN into machine language cannot translate COBOL statements, for example.

During the compilation process, the object program is generated and the programmer receives a listing that indicates any errors detected during translation. Compilers translate the source program all at once. Interpreters, on the other hand, translate the source program one instruction at a time. The interpreter reads a program statement by statement—first checking for errors, then translating the statement, and finally executing the statement before proceeding to the next one.

Once the program (or statement, in the case of an interpreted language) has been translated, the programmer must locate and correct any errors before the program will run correctly. This is part of the debugging process. In general,

Figure 4-4
Flowchart Symbols

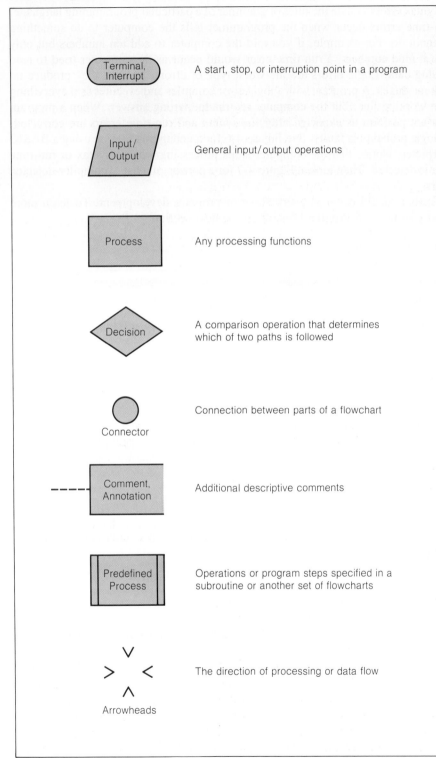

Terminal, Interrupt	A start, stop, or interruption point in a program
Input/Output	General input/output operations
Process	Any processing functions
Decision	A comparison operation that determines which of two paths is followed
Connector	Connection between parts of a flowchart
Comment, Annotation	Additional descriptive comments
Predefined Process	Operations or program steps specified in a subroutine or another set of flowcharts
Arrowheads	The direction of processing or data flow

Figure 4-5
Flowchart
Example

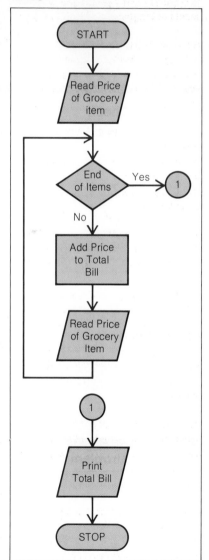

there are three types of computer errors: syntax errors, run-time errors, and logic errors.

Syntax errors violate the rules of grammar of a particular programming language. Run-time errors occur when the programmer tells the computer to do something it cannot do. For example, if you told the computer to add ten numbers but only gave it nine numbers, a run-time error would occur as the computer tried to read missing data. Logic errors are the worst type of errors, because they produce no error messages. A program with a logic error compiles and executes as if everything were working fine, but the computer returns the wrong answer. When a program does not perform as expected after the syntax and run-time errors are corrected, the logic probably is faulty. See Figure 4-6 for a debugging session using a BASIC interpreter. Notice that the computer stops processing when a syntax or run-time error is detected. Then look at Figure 4-7 for a portion of a list of compiler-detected errors.

Testing should occur at every stage of program development. To learn more about testing, read Program Testing in the next section.

Learning Check

1. List the four steps in the programming process.

2. Which logic pattern is illustrated when a professor repeats the same process to calculate a grade for each student in a class?

3. Which logic pattern is illustrated when you decide you have enough money to buy a personal computer?

4. Name two ways in which you can illustrate an algorithm.

5. If you were shopping for a programming language that would translate a program line by line and give you error messages at appropriate spots within the program, what word would you use to describe this language?

Answers

1. Define the problem, design the solution, write the program, and compile, debug, and test the program. 2. The loop. 3. Selection (if MONEY = X, then buy computer). 4. Pseudocode; flowchart. 5. Interpreter.

Structured Problem Solving

In the early days of software development, there were no standards or concrete rules. A programmer's objective was to develop a program that executed properly, without regard for how this was accomplished or who else might read the program. This approach created programs that were unreliable, difficult to follow, and expensive to maintain. Furthermore, without standard design procedures, a pro-

Figure 4-6 A Debugging Session
Using an Interpreter

```
100  REM  *** THIS PROGRAM WILL ADD FIVE GRADES, ***
110  REM  *** CALCULATE THE AVERAGE, AND DETERMINE ***
120  REM  *** A FINAL LETTER GRADE FOR EACH STUDENT ***
130  REM
140  REM  *** PRINT HEADINGS ***
150  PRINT
160  PRNT TAB( 35);"FINAL"
170  PRINT  TAB( 8);"NAME"; TAB( 25);"AVERAGE"; TAB( 35);"GRADE"
180  PRINT
190  FOR J = 1 TO 5
200  REM  *** READ DATA ***
210  READ N,G1,G2,G3,G4,G5
220  REM  *** AVERAGE GRADES ***
230  LET T = G1 + G2 + G3 + G4 + G5
240  LET A = T / 5
250  REM  *** DETERMINE LETTER GRADE ***
260  IF A > = 90 THEN F$ = A
270  IF A > = 80 AND A < 90 THEN F$ = "B"
280  IF A > = 70 AND A < 80 THEN F$ = "C"
290  IF A > = 60 AND A < 70 THEN F$ = "D"
300  IF A < 60F$ = "F"
310  REM  *** PRINT DATA ***
320  PRINT N$; TAB( 27);A; TAB( 37);F$
330  REM
340  REM  *** DATA ***
350  DATA  "FRED J. SMITH",70,65,24,100,98
360  DATA  "JASON JACKSON",97,96,59,78,60
370  DATA  "JOHN S. LAWSON",90,94,88,98,96
380  DATA  "SUSAN EAKINS",83,76,87,89,95
390  DATA  "MARY Q. JOHNSON",66,79,83,75,70
999  END
```

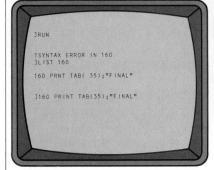

Error 1:
The syntax error is that PRINT is spelled PRNT. When that error is corrected, the program will run until another error is detected.

Error 2:
The computer indicates an error in line 350, but when 350 is listed, we see that it is typed correctly. A review of the program reveals that the error is in line 210, where the variable N should have been typed N$ to show that the variable values are words rather than numbers.

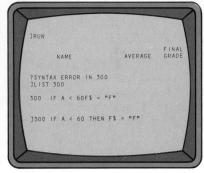

Error 3:
The syntax error in line 300 is the omission of the word THEN.

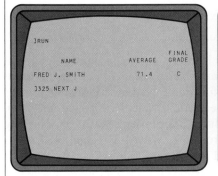

Error 4:
The program runs, but for only one name. Since we know there are five names typed in the DATA list, there must be an error. The NEXT statement has been omitted.

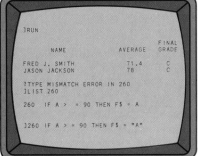

Error 5:
A "TYPE MISMATCH ERROR" is indicated for line 260. Upon examination, we see that the variable name does not match the variable value. Therefore, we change F$ = A to F$ = "A" to show that the variable value is a string.

The program runs correctly

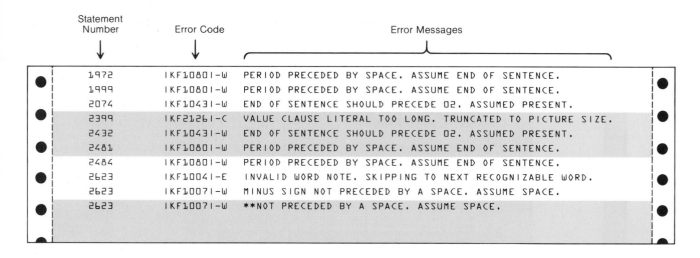

Statement Number	Error Code	Error Messages
1972	IKF1080I-W	PERIOD PRECEDED BY SPACE. ASSUME END OF SENTENCE.
1999	IKF1080I-W	PERIOD PRECEDED BY SPACE. ASSUME END OF SENTENCE.
2074	IKF1043I-W	END OF SENTENCE SHOULD PRECEDE 02. ASSUMED PRESENT.
2399	IKF2126I-C	VALUE CLAUSE LITERAL TOO LONG. TRUNCATED TO PICTURE SIZE.
2432	IKF1043I-W	END OF SENTENCE SHOULD PRECEDE 02. ASSUMED PRESENT.
2481	IKF1080I-W	PERIOD PRECEDED BY SPACE. ASSUME END OF SENTENCE.
2484	IKF1080I-W	PERIOD PRECEDED BY SPACE. ASSUME END OF SENTENCE.
2623	IKF1004I-E	INVALID WORD NOTE. SKIPPING TO NEXT RECOGNIZABLE WORD.
2623	IKF1007I-W	MINUS SIGN NOT PRECEDED BY A SPACE. ASSUME SPACE.
2623	IKF1007I-W	**NOT PRECEDED BY A SPACE. ASSUME SPACE.

Figure 4-7
Compiler-Detected Errors
A programmer receives a list of errors after the entire program has been translated. Once the errors are corrected, the program must be recompiled before it can be executed.

grammer might spend far more time than necessary in determining an appropriate solution and writing the program.

In order to offset these tendencies, programmers defined structured programming techniques in the early 1970s. **Structured programming** encourages programmers to think about the problem first, rather than spending an unreasonable amount of time on debugging later. Structured programming has four goals:

1. Reducing time and costs associated with program development.
2. Increasing programmer productivity.
3. Increasing clarity by reducing complexity.
4. Decreasing time and effort required to maintain a program once it is implemented.

Four methodologies characterize structured programming: top-down design, program documentation, program testing during all states of the problem-solving process, and use of a programming team.

STRUCTURED PROGRAMMING
A collection of techniques that encourage the development of well-designed, less error-prone programs with easy-to-follow logic.

TOP-DOWN DESIGN
A method of defining a solution in terms of major functions to be performed, and breaking down the major functions into subfunctions.

MODULAR APPROACH
A method of simplifying a programming project by breaking it into segments or subunits referred to as modules.

MODULE
A program segment that performs one specified task in a program.

Top-Down Design

The most difficult part of programming is learning how to organize solutions in a clear, concise way. One method of organizing a solution is to define the major steps or functions first and then expand the functions into more detailed steps later. This method, which proceeds from the general to the specific, is called **top-down design.** Top-down design employs the **modular approach,** which means breaking a problem into smaller and smaller subproblems. When the actual program is written, these subproblems can be written as separate **modules,** each of which performs a specific task.

The most general level of organization is the main control module. This overall definition of the solution is critical to the success of the program. Modules at this level contain broad descriptions of the steps in the solution process. These steps are further detailed in several lower-level modules. Depending on the complexity

HIGHLIGHT ▲

Software Prices Dropping?

Back in 1981, Adam Osborne pioneered the concept of inexpensive transportable computers by shipping the first Osborne 1. Now he's at it again. No longer with Osborne Computer Corporation, Adam Osborne is selling inexpensive software primarily through bookstores. His company, Paperback Software International, reflects his philosophy: If people pay a lot of money for

software packages, they don't buy many of them. If the packages are less expensive, they buy a lot more.

Osborne believes the same thing will happen with software as happened with hardware: Inexpensive—and perhaps better—clones of expensive, well-known brands will edge into the market.

Many of the new software packages do not have the perceived value necessary for people to pay hundreds of dollars

per package out of idle curiosity. Customers want to be reassured that software will be useful to them. If a program costs only $50, they may try it without worrying too much about long-term usefulness. When software prices drop, people will realize that low-cost software can be good—and they will buy lots of it. Software essentially will be bought like books, at $25 to $50 per program. So now we will wait and see if Adam Osborne is right.

STRUCTURE CHART
A graphic representation of the results of the top-down design process, displaying the modules and their relationships to one another.

of the problem, several levels of modules may be required, with the lowest-level modules containing the greatest amount of detail. Figure 4-8 shows a diagram of a top-down design for inventory control. The diagram, called a **structure chart,** illustrates the various modules and their relationships to one another. When the program is coded, each box in the structure chart is written as a separate module performing a specific task.

When writing a program in modular form, the programmer uses only three of the four logic patterns: the simple sequence, selection, and loop. The branch pattern (including the GOTO statement) is avoided, thus limiting the amount of jumping around that can occur otherwise. The modules should be small in order to make programming and debugging easier. Each module should have only one entry point and one exit point, so that a programmer can follow the flow of instructions easily. A program whose modules have only one entrance and one exit is called a **proper program.** Programs developed in this manner tend to have fewer errors than unstructured programs, because the logic is readily apparent.

PROPER PROGRAM
A structured program in which each individual segment or module has only one entrance and one exit.

Documentation

DOCUMENTATION
Written material that accompanies a program and includes definitions, explanations, charts, tests, and records of changes to the program.

Documentation is text that explains the program. Sometimes it is listed as a separate programming step, but in fact it should occur during each of the four programming steps. Documentation begins with the initial request for a program and continues throughout the problem-solving process and into program maintenance. It describes what the program should do, what data is needed, how data is identified in the program statements, and how the output is formatted.

In top-down design, documentation describes the modules as well, explaining their individual functions and their relationship to the entire program. Documentation also includes the flowcharts or pseudocode produced during program design, the tests and data used to check the program, and any changes made to the program.

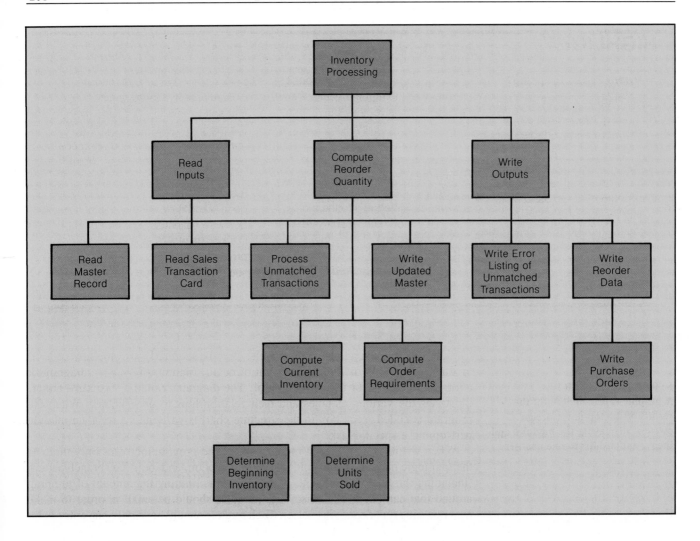

Figure 4-8
Structure Chart for Inventory
Control

Other important documentation provides instructions to program users and lists hardware requirements for running the program. A paper copy of the actual computer program is a part of documentation.

An example of documentation is a user's manual that explains how to use a program or piece of computer hardware. You also use documentation when you follow program instructions that appear on a computer monitor. If you read a copy of the actual computer program, you might also see documentation interspersed throughout.

Program Testing

At each step during the problem-solving process, the program should be tested before going on to the next step. This approach often was ignored during the early years of programming, and testing occurred after an entire program was completed. Corrections were made in a haphazard manner, and major errors often were discovered after the programs were implemented. Software buyers commonly were discouraged by programs that did not work correctly. Today, software developers test their programs more thoroughly, yet errors still occur. Clearly, testing is an important step in developing reliable software.

Testing involves executing the program with input data that is either a representative sample of actual data or a facsimile of it. Even incorrect data can be entered, in order to see how the program reacts. The results should be compared with correct results determined by the programmer. Testing cannot prove that the program will work in all situations, but it decreases the likelihood of problems. Each time a program is modified during testing and debugging, the documentation must be rewritten to reflect the changes.

The Programming Team

CHIEF PROGRAMMER TEAM (CPT)
A method of organization in which a chief programmer supervises the development and testing of software.

A popular method of organizing and managing system projects involves the use of a **chief programmer team (CPT).** The purpose of a CPT is to facilitate the goals of structured programming. Team members review one another's work and the accompanying documentation at each stage of development, making suggestions for changes and improvements. The CPT usually includes a chief programmer (often a system analyst), who is responsible for the overall coordination and development of the project. Depending on the size and complexity of the project, the team may also have a number of regular programmers, each working on a different module, and a librarian who updates the documentation and performs other clerical tasks.

Learning Check

1. The goals of structured programming include reducing the _____ and _____ associated with program development while increasing _____.

2. Top-down design involves breaking a problem into subproblems that can be written as separate _____, each performing a particular task.

3. Name at least one other characteristic of structured programming.

Answers

1. Time; costs; productivity.　2. Modules.　3. Documentation; limited jumping within the program; adequate program testing; the chief programmer team.

Types of Programs

The programming methods we have described are used in generating the two basic types of programs: **system programs,** which coordinate the operation of the computer, and **application programs,** which solve user problems.

HIGHLIGHT ▲▲▲▲▲▲▲▲▲▲▲▲▲▲▲▲▲▲▲▲▲▲▲▲

Programs As Models of the Real World

Computer scientists often try to create programs that resemble or reflect real-life situations. In other words, they attempt to produce programs that correspond closely with the processes they are controlling and which can act, in a sense, as models of the real world.

An article in *Science Digest,* December 1985, reports on the work of Peter Oppenheimer, a research scientist at the New York Institute of Technology Computer Graphics

Laboratory. After studying the crystalline structure of snowflakes, Oppenheimer decided to generate computer images of them. He started with a tiny "seed image." Then he designed a computer algorithm that modified the seed pattern to make a new image, which in turn served as the basis for a new modification. He was able to do this because of a property found in nature, called self-similarity. Self-similarity means that if a small part of an image is magnified, it resembles the geometric structure of the whole.

Using a mathematical definition of self-similarity, computer scientists have been able to construct graphic images that resemble natural phenomena such as Oppenheimer's snowflake images. Oppenheimer says that the logic of the computer scientist reflects the logic of life. In this sense the program is the model, and its output, the images produced, is the test. If the image looks right, then the model must be in some sense a valid image of the real world.

SYSTEM PROGRAM
Instructions written for coordinating the operation of computer circuitry and helping the computer run quickly and efficiently.

APPLICATION PROGRAM
A sequence of instructions written for solving a specific user problem.

System programs directly affect the operation of the computer. They are designed for efficient and fast use of the hardware. System software includes a variety of programs such as operating systems, utility programs, and language translators. A system program may, for example, allocate storage for data being entered into the system. The programs vary from computer to computer and cannot be used without modification on different machines. System programming normally is provided by the computer manufacturer or by a specialized programming firm.

Application programs perform specific data processing or computational tasks for solving an organization's information needs, or help an individual with personal or educational tasks. They can be developed by the user or purchased from software firms. Typical examples of application programs include those used by businesses for inventory control and accounting, and by banks for updates in customer accounts. Application programs also help in preparing documents, drawing graphs, learning new skills, and filing data. Several types of application programs are discussed in Part II of this text.

Operating Systems

OPERATING SYSTEM (OS)
A collection of system programs used by the computer for managing its own operations.

When computer systems were in their infancy, human operators monitored computer operations, decided the order in which the programs would run, and handled input and output devices. Although the processing speeds of CPUs increased, the speed of human operators stayed the same. This situation created time delays and errors. **Operating systems,** developed in the 1960s, eased the problem. An operating system is a collection of programs that the computer uses to manage its own operations at computer speeds. An operating system provides the interface between the user and the applications programs and computer hardware (see Figure 4-9).

Each program in an operating system performs a specific duty. Because all operating system programs work as a "team," idle CPU time is avoided and use of computer facilities is increased. Operating system programs usually are stored on a secondary storage medium (magnetic tape or disk) and are called into primary storage when needed.

Two types of programs make up the operating system: control programs and processing programs. Control programs oversee system operations and perform tasks such as communicating with input/output devices, scheduling tasks, and communicating with the computer operator or programmers. One type of control program, the supervisor program, is the major component of the operating system. It coordinates the activities of all other parts of the operating system. When the computer is first put into use, the supervisor is the first program to be transferred into primary storage from the system residence device. The supervisor schedules input/output operations and allocates channels to various input/output devices. It also sends message to the computer operator, indicating the status of particular jobs, error conditions, and so forth.

Processing programs are executed under the supervision of control programs. Their purpose is to simplify program preparation for the computer system. The principal processing programs are language translators, library programs, and utility programs. The language translator program translates the source programs written by humans into object programs of machine-language instructions. A library program maintains a directory of programs in secondary storage and contains procedures for adding and deleting programs. Utility programs perform specialized functions, such as transferring data from tape to disk, or from tape to printer.

Figure 4-9
Operating System As Interface

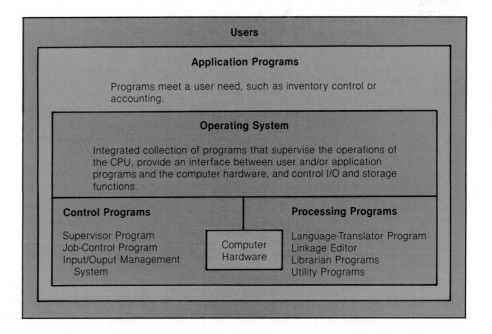

Users

Application Programs

Programs meet a user need, such as inventory control or accounting.

Operating System

Integrated collection of programs that supervise the operations of the CPU, provide an interface between user and/or application programs and the computer hardware, and control I/O and storage functions.

Control Programs

Supervisor Program
Job-Control Program
Input/Ouput Management
  System

Computer
Hardware

Processing Programs

Language-Translator Program
Linkage Editor
Librarian Programs
Utility Programs

Learning Check

1. A program that translates a high-level language into machine language and a program that communicates with a disk drive are examples of _____ programs.

2. Why were operating systems developed?

3. What does the supervisor program do?

4. Besides the type of program mentioned in question 1, what other type of program is there? Give a general or specific example of one.

Answers

1. System. 2. To allow the computer to handle its own operations at its own speed (human operators were too slow). 3. It coordinates the activities of all other parts of the operating system, schedules input/output operations, allocates channels to various hardware devices, and communicates with the computer user. 4. Application program; software used for outlining a paper (for example, *ThinkTank*).

Programming Languages

SYNTAX
The grammatical rules of a language.

Programming languages are used during the coding stage of the programming process. Like the languages we use for everyday speech, programming languages have their own rules. This group of rules governing a language is called **syntax.** A computer program with incorrect syntax cannot run. Some languages are suited for scientific uses, some for business uses, some for artificial intelligence, and so on. Several languages are described in the following paragraphs.

Low-Level Languages

LOW-LEVEL LANGUAGE
A machine-oriented language; machine language and assembly languages are low-level languages.

Low-level languages give the programmer direct control over details of computer hardware. They enable the programmer to specify memory locations, direct input and output operations, and govern the use of registers. Each type of computer has its own low-level languages, which are not transferable to other types of computers. Each instruction in a low-level language must state not only the operation required, but also the storage locations of the data items. For this reason, the programmer must know exactly how the specific computer works.

The lowest-level language is **machine language,** which designates the on/off electrical states of the digital computer. Being so closely linked to computer operations, it is the only language that the computer can execute directly. Programs written in any other language must be translated into machine language before the computer can execute them.

Machine language is the most efficient language in terms of storage area use and execution speed. It allows the programmer to use all of the computer's potential for processing data. Coding a program in machine language, however, is very tedious, time-consuming, and error-prone.

MNEMONICS
**Symbolic names or memory aids;
used in assembly and high-level
programming languages.**

Assembly languages were developed in order to alleviate many of the disadvantages of machine-language programming. When programming in an assembly language, the programmer uses **mnemonics** (symbolic names) to specify machine operations; thus, coding in 0s and 1s is not required. Mnemonics are alphabetic abbreviations for the machine language instructions. For example, STB might stand for *store in register B,* and LDA might stand for *load register A.* Assembly language programs are highly efficient in terms of storage space and processing. Assembly language often is chosen when fast execution is essential, for example, for writing operating systems. In general, one assembly-language instruction is translated into one machine-language instruction. This one-to-one relationship makes it easier—and therefore faster—for the computer to translate the program into machine language than to translate a high-level language into machine language. (See Figure 4-10 for a comparison of machine instructions and assembly instructions.)

High-Level Languages

High-level languages enable the programmer to focus on problem solving rather than on the details of computer operations. They are easier to understand than low-level languages, because they use meaningful words such as READ and PRINT and common mathematical terms and symbols. Although one assembly language statement generally is equivalent to one machine language statement, a single high-level language statement can represent several machine language statements. These features reduce the time needed for writing a program and make programs easier to correct and modify.

During the past 40 years, approximately 400 computer languages have been developed. Many are highly specialized. Their names often are colorful—CLIP,

Figure 4-10
Examples of Assembly Language and Machine Language Codes for Computer Operations

Operation	Typical Assembly Language Codes for Operations	Typical Binary (Machine Language) Codes for Operations
Add memory to register	A	01011010
Add (decimal) memory to register	AP	11111010
Multiply register by memory	M	01011100
Multiply (decimal) register by memory	MP	11111100
Subtract memory from register	S	01011011
Subtract (decimal) memory from register	SP	11111011
Move (numeric) from register to memory	MVN	11010001
Compare memory to register	C	01011001
Compare (decimal) memory to register	CP	11111001
Zero register and add (decimal) memory to register	ZAP	11111000

FLAP, SOAP, SNOBOL, LISP, and TREE, to name a few. Some languages are widely used and have played an important role in the development of the computer industry. Some of the more commonly-used languages are FORTRAN, COBOL, BASIC, Pascal, APL, RPG, C, Ada, Modula-2, FORTH, LISP, and Logo, which are discussed in the following sections.

FORTRAN (FORmula Translator)
The oldest surviving high-level programming language; used primarily for mathematical or scientific operations.

FORTRAN   FORTRAN (FORmula TRANslator) is the oldest surviving commercial high-level programming language. It was introduced in the mid-1950s because programmers needed a language that resembled English.

As the language became accepted, several manufacturers offered variations of FORTRAN which could be used only with their own brands of computers. In response to this problem, ANSI laid the groundwork for a standardized FORTRAN. In 1966, two standard versions of FORTRAN were recognized: ANSI FORTRAN and Basic FORTRAN. A more recent version, FORTRAN 77, enhances the language's usefulness and supports structured programming. In spite of these attempts to standardize FORTRAN, however, most computer manufacturers have continued to offer their own extensions of the language. Therefore, compatibility of FORTRAN programs remains a problem.

In 1957, when the language was first released, computers were used primarily by engineers, scientists, and mathematicians. FORTRAN was designed to meet their needs, and this purpose has remained unchanged. FORTRAN provides extraordinary mathematical capabilities and is executed quickly. FORTRAN is not often used for business purposes, because its capabilities are not well suited to programs involving file maintenance, editing of data, or production of documents. Use of FORTRAN is increasing, however, for business applications that require complex mathematics formulas, such as feasibility studies, forecasting, and production scheduling. FORTRAN does not resemble English as closely as do many high-level languages; therefore, the programs must be well documented so that they are understandable. Figure 4-11 contains a simple FORTRAN program that calculates a payroll.

COBOL (COmmon Business-Oriented Language)
A high-level programming language generally used for business applications.

COBOL   COBOL (COmmon Business-Oriented Language) is the most popular business programming language. Its specifications were established in 1960 by the Conference of Data Systems Languages (CODASYL) Committee, and the first commercial versions of the language were offered that year. One of the objectives of the CODASYL group was to establish a language that could be used on any computer. When several manufacturers began offering their own modifications and extentions of COBOL, the need for standardization became apparent.

In 1968, ANSI established and published guidelines for a standardized version of COBOL that became known as ANSI COBOL. ANSI has revised these standards twice. The 1974 standards are widely accepted, but new ANSI standards for COBOL were published in 1985. These new standards made many changes to the language, including the addition of structured programming facilities. It will be several years before we know how widely accepted and implemented this new COBOL will be.

COBOL is well suited for handling large amounts of data. It is often used in businesses for storing customer or employee information. Since COBOL is standardized, a firm can switch computer systems with little or no rewriting of existing programs.

**Figure 4-11
Payroll Program in FORTRAN**

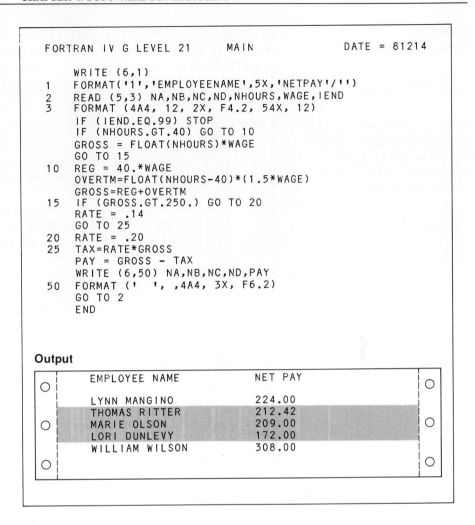

```
FORTRAN IV G LEVEL 21        MAIN              DATE = 81214

        WRITE (6,1)
 1      FORMAT('1','EMPLOYEENAME',5X,'NETPAY'/'')
 2      READ (5,3) NA,NB,NC,ND,NHOURS,WAGE,IEND
 3      FORMAT (4A4, I2, 2X, F4.2, 54X, I2)
        IF (IEND.EQ.99) STOP
        IF (NHOURS.GT.40) GO TO 10
        GROSS = FLOAT(NHOURS)*WAGE
        GO TO 15
 10     REG = 40.*WAGE
        OVERTM=FLOAT(NHOURS-40)*(1.5*WAGE)
        GROSS=REG+OVERTM
 15     IF (GROSS.GT.250.) GO TO 20
        RATE = .14
        GO TO 25
 20     RATE = .20
 25     TAX=RATE*GROSS
        PAY = GROSS - TAX
        WRITE (6,50) NA,NB,NC,ND,PAY
 50     FORMAT (' ', ,4A4, 3X, F6.2)
        GO TO 2
        END
```

Output

```
    EMPLOYEE NAME            NET PAY

    LYNN MANGINO            224.00
    THOMAS RITTER          212.42
    MARIE OLSON            209.00
    LORI DUNLEVY           172.00
    WILLIAM WILSON         308.00
```

Well-written COBOL programs tend to be self-explanatory. This feature makes programs easier to maintain and modify, an important feature because business programs are often expanded and changed. In addition, programmers other than the authors can read COBOL programs, and quickly discern what they do. You can judge the clarity of a COBOL program by looking at the COBOL-coded application in Figure 4-12.

**BASIC (Beginners' All-purpose Symbolic Instruction Code)
A high-level programming language commonly available with interpreter programs; often taught to beginning programmers.**

BASIC   BASIC, an acronym for Beginner's All-purpose Symbolic Instruction Code, was developed in the mid-1960s at Dartmouth College to help students learn how to program. Most computer manufacturers offer BASIC support on their computers, and many companies have adapted BASIC for their data processing needs.

Among BASIC's most attractive features are its simplicity and flexibility. Because BASIC is easy to learn, it can be used by people with little or no programming experience. BASIC can be used for solving a wide variety of problems. A BASIC program is shown in Figure 4-13.

Figure 4-12
Payroll Program in COBOL

```
IDENTIFICATION DIVISION.
PROGRAM-ID. PAYROLL.
INPUT-OUTPUT SECTION.
FILE-CONTROL.
    SELECT CARD-FILE ASIGN TO UR-S-SYSIN.
    SELECT PRINT-FILE ASSIGN TO UR-S-OUTPUT.

DATA DIVISION.
FILE SECTION.
FD  CARD-FILE
    LABEL RECORDS ARE OMITTED
    RECORD CONTAINS 80 CHARACTERS
    DATA RECORD IS PAY-RECORD.
01  PAY-RECORD.
    03  EMPLOYEE-NAME       PIC A(16).
    03  HOURS-WORKED        PIC 99.
    03  WAGE-PER-HOUR       PIC 99V99.
    03  FILLER              PIC X(58).

FD  PRINT-FILE
    LABEL RECORDS ARE OMITTED
    RECORD CONTAINS 132 CHARACTERS
    DATA RECORD IS PRINT-RECORD.
01  PRINT-RECORD            PIC X(132).

WORKING-STORAGE SECTION.
77  GROSS-PAY              PIC 9(3)V99.
77  REGULAR-PAY            PIC 9(3)V99.
77  OVERTIME-PAY           PIC 9(3)V99.
77  NET-PAY                PIC 9(3)V99.
77  TAX                    PIC 9(3)V99.
77  OVERTIME-HOURS         PIC 99.
77  OVERTIME-RATE          PIC 9(3)V999.
77  EOF-FLAG               PIC X(3)      VALUE 'NO'.

01  HEADING-LINE.
    03 FILLER              PIC X         VALUE SPACES.
    03 FILLER              PIC X(21)     VALUE
        'EMPLOYEE NAME'.
    03 FILLER              PIC X(7)      VALUE
        'NET PAY'.

01  OUTPUT-RECORD.
    03 FILLER              PIC X         VALUE SPACES.
    03 NAME                PIC A(16).
    03 FILLER              PIC X(5)      VALUE SPACES.
    03 AMOUNT              PIC $$$$.99.
    03 FILLER              PIC X(103)    VALUE SPACES.

PROCEDURE DIVISION.
MAIN-LOGIC.
    OPEN INPUT CARD-FILE
        OUTPUT PRINT-FILE.
    PERFORM HEADING-ROUTINE.
    READ CARD-FILE AT END MOVE 'YES' TO EOF-FLAG.
    PERFORM WORK-LOOP UNTIL EOF-FLAG = 'YES'.
    CLOSE CARD-FILE
        PRINT-FILE.
    STOP RUN.

HEADING-ROUTINE.
    WRITE PRINT-RECORD FROM HEADING-LINE
        BEFORE ADVANCING 2 LINES.
```

**Figure 4-12
(continued)**

```
WORK-LOOP.
    IF HOURS-WORKED IS GREATER THEN 40
        THEN
            PERFORM OVERTIME-ROUTINE
        ELSE
            MULTIPLY HOURS-WORKED BY WAGE-PER-HOUR
                GIVING GROSS-PAY.
    PERFORM TAX-COMPUTATION.
    PERFORM OUTPUT-ROUTINE.
    READ CARD-FILE AT END MOVE 'YES' TO EOF-FLAG.

OVERTIME-ROUTINE.
    MULTIPLY WAGE-PER-HOUR BY 40 GIVING REGULAR-PAY.
    SUBTRACT 40 FROM HOURS-WORKED GIVING OVERTIME-HOURS.
    MULTIPLY OVERTIME-HOURS BY 1.5 GIVING OVERTIME-RATE.
    MULTIPLY OVERTIME-HOURS BY OVERTIME-RATE
        GIVING OVERTIME-PAY.
    ADD REGULAR-PAY, OVERTIME-PAY GIVING GROSS-PAY.

TAX-COMPUTATION.
    IF GROSS-PAY IS GREATER THEN 250
        THEN
            MULTIPLY GROSS-PAY BY 0.20 GIVING TAX
        ELSE
            MULTIPLY GROSS-PAY BY 0.14 GIVING TAX.
    SUBTRACT TAX FROM GROSS-PAY GIVING NET-PAY.

OUTPUT-ROUTINE.
    MOVE EMPLOYEE-NAME TO NAME.
    MOVE NET-PAY TO AMOUNT.
    WRITE PRINT-RECORD FROM OUTPUT-RECORD
        BEFORE ADVANCING 1 LINES.
```

Output

EMPLOYEE NAME	NET PAY
LYNN MANGINO	224.00
THOMAS RITTER	212.42
MARIE OLSON	209.00
LORI DUNLEVY	172.00
WILLIAM WILSON	308.00

The main criticism of BASIC focuses on the fact that traditionally it has not been a structured programming language. Many popular versions of BASIC do not encourage dividing the program into modules, nor do they contain adequate control statements. Many implementations of BASIC require the use of unconditional branches, commonly signaled by GOTO statements, which can cause program logic to be convoluted and difficult to follow.

Some newer versions of BASIC support the development of structured programs. One of these is True BASIC, which was developed by the original writers of BASIC, John Kemeny and Thomas Kurtz. True BASIC is an economical language that uses English-like commands, yet it provides options that enable programmers to develop properly structured programs. The format of the new BASIC looks

Figure 4-13
Payroll Program in BASIC

```
10 REM THIS PROGRAM CALCULATES A WEEKLY
20 REM PAYROLL FOR FIVE EMPLOYEES
30 PRINT "EMPLOYEE NAME",,"NET PAY"
40 PRINT
50 READ N$,H,W
60 IF N$ = "END OF DATA" THEN 270
70 IF H > 40 THEN 100
80 LET G = H * W
90 GOTO 130
100 LET R = 40 * W
110 LET O = (H - 40) * (1.5 * W)
120 LET G = R + O
130 IF G > 250 THEN 160
140 LET T = .14
150 GOTO 170
160 LET T = .2
170 LET T2 = T * G
180 LET P = G - T2
190 PRINT N$,P
200 GOTO 50
210 DATA "LYNN MANGINO  ",35,8.00
220 DATA "THOMAS RITTER ",48,4.75
230 DATA "MARIE OLSON   ",45,5.50
240 DATA "LORI DUNLEVY  ",40,5.00
250 DATA "WILLIAM WILSON",50,7.00
260 DATA "END OF DATA",0,0
270 END
```

Output

```
RUN
EMPLOYEE NAME              NET PAY

LYNN MANGINO               224.00
THOMAS RITTER              212.42
MARIE OLSON                209.00
LORI DUNLEVY               172.00
WILLIAM WILSON             308.00
```

much like that of Pascal, a language noted for its structure. In addition, ANSI is in the process of adopting new standards for a structured BASIC.

PASCAL
A high-level structured programming language, developed for instructional purposes, but now commonly used in a wide variety of applications.

Pascal Pascal was the first major programming language to implement the ideas and methodology of structured programming. Niklaus Wirth, a Swiss computer scientist, developed Pascal between 1969 and 1970. The first Pascal compiler became available in 1971, and in 1982 ANSI adopted a standard for Pascal. Wirth named the language after the French philosopher and mathematician Blaise Pascal, inventor of the first mechanical adding machine.

Like BASIC, Pascal was developed for teaching programming concepts to students. Often it is the first programming language taught to college-level students; at present, it is the introductory programming course for computer science students at 80 percent of all universities. Pascal is relatively easy to learn, and it is a powerful language capable of performing a wide variety of tasks, including sophisticated mathematical operations. It supports structured programming concepts, such as modular programming and structured methods for controlling loops and selection patterns. These features encourage students to develop good programming habits. Figure 4-14 contains a short program written in Pascal.

Figure 4-14
Payroll Program in Pascal

```
PROGRAM PAYROLL (INPUT,OUTPUT);
VAR HOURS,REGULAR,WAGE,OVERTIME,GROSS,TAX,NETPAY : REAL;
NAME : ARRAY (.1..17.) OF CHAR;
I : INTEGER;
BEGIN
WRITELN('1','EMPLOYEE NAME','                     NET PAY');
WRITELN(' ');
WHILE NOT EOF DO
    BEGIN
    FOR I:=1 TO 17 DO
        READ (NAME(.I.));
        READLN (HOURS,WAGE);
        IF HOURS>40
            THEN BEGIN
                REGULAR:=40*WAGE;
                OVERTIME:=(HOURS-40)*(1.5*WAGE);
                GROSS:=REGULAR + OVERTIME
            END
            ELSE BEGIN
                GROSS:=HOURS*WAGE
            END;
        IF GROSS>250
            THEN BEGIN
                TAX:=0.20*GROSS;
                NETPAY:=GROSS-TAX

            ELSE BEGIN
                TAX:=0.14*GROSS;
                NETPAY:=GROSS-TAX
            END;
    WRITE (' ');
FOR I :=1 TO 17 DO
    WRITE(NAME(.I.);
    WRITELN(NETPAY:12:12);
    END
END.
```

Output

```
      EMPLOYEE NAME              NET PAY

      LYNN MANGINO               224.00
      THOMAS RITTER              212.42
      MARIE OLSON                209.00
      LORI DUNLEVY               172.00
      WILLIAM WILSON             308.00
```

At first Pascal's availability was limited, but more computer manufacturers now are offering Pascal compilers for their machines. Some compilers developed for microcomputers, such as TURBO Pascal, are inexpensive and versatile. Many of these compilers can create intricate, detailed graphics on properly equipped display terminals. This feature is attractive to scientists as well as to business personnel. Many people believe that Pascal has poor input/output capabilities, however, a limitation that makes it less than ideal for applications involving manipulation of large data files.

RPG (Report Program Generator)
A high-level language designed for producing business reports. RPG requires the programmer to record data and operations on specification forms.

RPG RPG (Report Program Generator) was designed in the late 1960s for producing business reports. A programmer using RPG must describe the kind of report desired, but need not specify much of the logic involved. Acting upon this description, a generator program builds a program that produces the report. Instead of coding statements, the programmer completes specification forms, such as those shown in Figure 4-15. The data on these forms is entered into the computer. The RPG generator program then builds an object program that the computer executes.

IBM introduced a new version, RPGII, in the 1970s for use with its IBM System/3 computers. This version has replaced the original RPG. A third version introduced in 1979, RPGIII, provides the capability of processing data stored in a database.

RPG is easy to learn and use. It provides an efficient means for generating reports requiring simple logic and calculations. It is commonly used for processing files for accounts receivable, accounts payable, general ledgers, and inventory. Because RPG requires little main storage space, it is one of the primary languages of microcomputers and minicomputers.

The language has shortcomings, however, among them its limited computational capabilities. Also, RPG is not standardized. RPG programs written for one computer may require significant changes before they can be used on another computer.

C
A high-level structured programming language that includes low-level language instructions; popular because it is portable and is implemented on a wide variety of computer systems.

PORTABLE
Describes a program that can be run on many different computers with minimal changes.

C Developed in 1972, C is rapidly becoming popular for both system and application programming. It has some capabilities similar to those of assembly languages; for example, it can manipulate individual bits and bytes in storage locations. Yet it also offers many high-level language features, such as a wide variety of useful control structures. Therefore, it is sometimes referred to as a middle-level language.

C is popular for several reasons. First, it is independent of machine architecture, so that C programs are **portable.** This means the same program can be run on different computers. Second, C can be implemented on a wide variety of systems, from eight-bit microcomputers to supercomputers such as the Cray-1. Third, it includes many of the structured programming features found in languages like Pascal. Fourth, the compilers are simple and compact. C, however, is a language intended for experienced programmers. Figure 4-16 shows a payroll program written in C.

C was designed by Dennis Ritchie at Bell Laboratories. One of its first uses was in the rewriting of Bell Laboratories' Unix operating system. Unix and its utilities include over 300,000 lines of C source code, a very ambitious programming project. Today, many major microcomputer manufacturers and software developers use C for system programs, utility programs, and graphics applications. C is also useful for text processing and database programs.

Figure 4-15
RPG Program Specification Forms

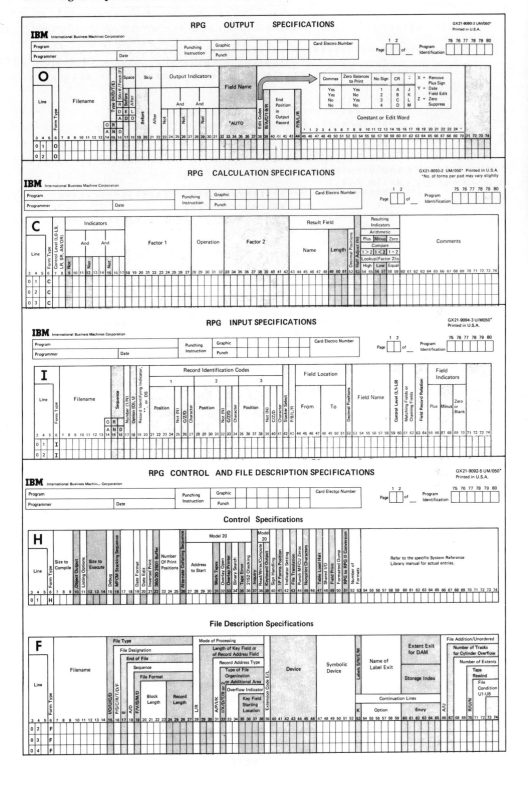

Figure 4-16
Payroll Program in C

```
main()
{
/***************************************************
      This program calculates a weekly payroll.
 ***************************************************/

    double atof();
    float wage, hours, grosspay, tax, netpay;
    char *chwage, *chhours, *name;

    flag = 0;
    printf ("EMPLOYEE NAME              NETPAY \n");
    emplfile = fopen("payroll","r");
    while (1) {
/***************************************************
                procedure read data
 ***************************************************/
        readname(name);
        if (flag)
              break;
        readname(chhours);
        readname(chwage);

/***************************************************
                Calculate gross pay
 ***************************************************/
        wage = atof(chwage);                    /* convert the string */
        hours = atof(chhours);                  /* to a float value   */
        if (hours <= 40)
              grosspay = hours * wage;
        else
              grosspay = hours * wage + (hours - 40.0) * wage * 0.5;

/***************************************************
                Calculate net pay
 ***************************************************/
      if (grosspay > 250)
          tax = 0.2 * grosspay;
      else
          tax = 0.14 * grosspay;
      netpay = grosspay - tax;
```

ADA
A high-level structured programming language developed for use by the U.S. Department of Defense.

Ada Ada is a relatively new programming language developed by the United States Department of Defense (DOD). It is derived from Pascal and is also a structured language. Ada is named in honor of the first programmer, Augusta Ada Byron, Countess of Lovelace and daughter of the poet Lord Byron (see Chapter 1).

The need for a language such as Ada was determined by a DOD study conducted in 1974, which found that in 1973 over $7 billion was spent on software that did not meet the needs of the department. Through further study, the DOD found that no current high-level language met its needs for reliability and portability, and concluded that a new language would have to be developed. In 1980 the DOD approved the initial Ada standard, and in 1983 ANSI approved it.

Ada has the sophistication and reliability (that is, the ability to obtain correct results consistently) that are necessary for programming in critical areas such as defense, weather forecasting, and oil exploration. It is not a beginner's language,

Figure 4-16
(continued)

```
/*****************************************************
                Print the results
*****************************************************/
        printf("%-24s  %7.2f\n",name,netpay);
        }   /* while loop closing bracket */
        fclose(emplfile);
} /* main closing bracket */

/*****************************************************
                Subroutine readname
*****************************************************/
readname(ts)
char *ts;
{
        int cc;
        char *cs;

        cs = ts;
        while ((cc = getc(emplfile)) != EOF)    /*look for EOF */
                {
                if (cc == 13)                    /* return if CR is seen */
                        break;
                if (cc != 10)                    /* do not process LF */
                        *cs++ = cc;              /* build the string */
                }
        if (cc == EOF) flag = 1;                 /* IF EOF we are done */
        *cs = '\0';                              /* make sure we terminate
                                                    a string value */

}
```

Output

```
  EMPLOYEE NAME              NETPAY
  LYNN MANGIN                224.00
  THOMAS RITTER              212.42
  MARIE OLSON                209.00
  LORI SANCHEZ               172.00
  WILLIAM LUOMA              308.00
```

however, and a skilled programmer may take six months to become proficient in the language.

MODULA-2
A high-level structured programming language that is a descendent of Pascal; incorporates low-level language commands.

Modula-2   Modula-2 is a descendant of Pascal. Designed by the creator of Pascal, Niklaus Wirth, Modula-2 contains all aspects of Pascal and is learned easily by Pascal programmers.

As Pascal became widely implemented during the 1970s, it became evident that certain improvements in the language were possible. Wirth proposed the creation of a single, high-level language that also had low-level capabilities for interacting more closely with hardware. In this respect, Modula-2 is similar to C and FORTH.

Modula-2 is a structured language that is easy to modularize and has a wide variety of useful control structures. Because Modula-2 is a new programming language, it remains to be seen how widely implemented it will be.

FORTH

FORTH
A high-level programming language that includes low-level language instructions; used at many astronomical observatories worldwide.

FORTH Working at Kitt Peak National Observatory, Charles Moore developed FORTH in response to a need for an adequate programming language for use in satellite tracking and astronomy. Like C and Modula-2, FORTH often is categorized as a middle-level language. FORTH can be modeled to meet the programmer's particular needs, and it is a very portable language. In FORTH, a programmer can build up a dictionary of programs that can be called up by name for many uses.

FORTH is used at many astronomical observatories around the world. It is also used for guiding automated movie cameras, running portable heart monitors, and simulating radar for the Air Force. In addition, it is being used increasingly for less glamorous tasks such as database management and word processing.

The simplicity of FORTH makes it fast and efficient. Because FORTH systems are interpreted rather than compiled, the programmer can write one word (procedure) at a time and test it thoroughly before writing the next word. FORTH is a strange-looking language, however, and it is hard to read. It also lacks many of the safety features built into other languages, so finding program errors is difficult.

LISP (LISt Processing)

LISP (LISt Processing)
A high-level programming language commonly used in artificial intelligence research and in the processing of lists of elements.

LISP LISP (or LISt Processing) is the language commonly associated with artificial intelligence. Using concepts of lambda calculus (a branch of mathematics) and a new idea in computing called list processing, John McCarthy developed the language in 1960 at the Massachusetts Institute of Technology (MIT). LISP aids in the manipulation of nonnumeric data that change considerably in length and structure during execution of a program. Essentially, LISP performs built-in or user-defined functions on lists.

These lists can contain collections of functions (for example, finding the square or cube of a number), sentences, mathematical formulas, logic theorems, or even complete computer programs. This capability makes LISP a powerful tool in applications such as the generation of mathematical proofs and simulations of human problem-solving techniques. To beginning programmers in LISP, however, the tangle of parentheses used in writing the lists can be confusing.

LOGO

LOGO
An education-oriented programming language designed to allow anyone to begin programming and communicating with computers quickly.

Logo LOGO was designed originally as a teaching tool by Seymour Papert and the MIT Logo group in the late 1960s. Logo's main attraction is that it enables both children and adults to begin programming and communicating with the computer in a short period of time. Logo enables the user to draw images, animate them, and color them using simple instructions. Some instructions involve commanding a triangular object called a turtle, which leaves a graphic trail in its path. The user commands the turtle to draw straight lines, squares, or other objects, which can be combined to form images. Figure 4-17 contains Logo statements that draw a triangular figure inside a square.

The strength of Logo lies in its ability to help the inexperienced user learn logic and programming. Because it is a structured language, it encourages the beginning programmer to develop good programming habits.

Although Logo can help young children learn geometry and programming, it is a powerful language, and learning every aspect of Logo can be difficult. Because Logo is derived from LISP, it handles list processing with ease. Its large memory and file-handling capabilities make it appropriate for advanced applications, such

Figure 4-17
Logo Program for Drawing a
Square with a Triangular Design

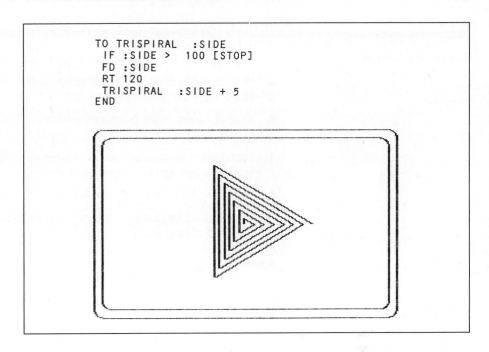

```
TO TRISPIRAL   :SIDE
  IF :SIDE >  100 [STOP]
  FD :SIDE
  RT 120
  TRISPIRAL   :SIDE + 5
END
```

as creating music, performing sophisticated mathematics functions based on trig-onometry and logarithms, and studying physics.

Natural Languages

Computer scientists have long realized that computers cannot achieve their full potential if only a few people know how to use them. Programmers have developed user-friendly software that uses menus and other devices that make computers easier to use. In addition, they are developing ways for people to interact with computers by using natural English, the English used in everyday speech.

Natural languages, or **query languages** as they sometimes are called, are programming languages that enable the user to state queries in English-like sentences. They are used most frequently in conjunction with **databases.** For example, a member of a personnel department might ask, *"How many women hold a position at level 10 or above?"* in order to gain information for reporting purposes. The question then is translated into a form that the computer can use in searching a database for the correct answer. If the natural language processor does not fully understand the inquiry, it may request further information from the user.

Most natural language processors are designed to be used with a vocabulary of words and definitions which allows the processor to translate the English-like sentences into machine-executable form. Currently, natural language sentences are typed at the keyboard; in the future, however, the combination of voice recognition technology and natural languages could result in a very powerful tool for computer users. The ability to interface natural language systems with graphic software also provides a valuable decision making tool for managers. Although limited to mainframe computers in the past, natural language systems are being developed for minicomputer and microcomputer systems.

NATURAL LANGUAGE (QUERY LANGUAGE)
A language designed primarily for novice computer users which allows use of statements very much like everyday speech, usually for the purpose of accessing data in a database.

DATABASE
A collection of data items that are commonly defined and consistently organized to fit the information needs of a wide variety of users in an organization.

Learning Check

1. Explain the advantages of low-level languages.

2. In what circumstance might a programmer choose assembly language rather than a high-level language?

3. In what cases might programs written in FORTRAN be useful to a business organization?

4. Name three languages widely used in teaching beginning programmers, and tell why each is popular for that use.

5. State one major use each for Ada, C, FORTH, and LISP.

6. What type of language is the most English-like? What is the primary use of this type of language?

Answers

1. Low-level languages give the programmer direct control of hardware details. Also they are efficient in terms of memory and execution speed. 2. Assembly language may be chosen when fast execution is essential, but coding directly in machine language is too time-consuming. 3. FORTRAN can be used for business applications that require complex calculations, such as feasibility studies, forecasting, and production scheduling. 4. BASIC is easy to learn, and Pascal and Logo are structured languages that encourage the development of good programming habits. 5. Ada is used in defense-related programming, C is used for writing operating systems, FORTH is used at astronomical observatories, and LISP is used in artificial intelligence studies. 6. Natural or query languages are the most English-like, and they are used in accessing databases.

Summary Points

■ A computer program should be developed using these four steps: define the problem, design the solution, write the program, and compile, debug, and test the program.

■ Defining the problem involves defining the desired output, the needed input, and the processing required for solving the problem.

■ Designing a solution to a problem may require considerable creativity and one or more of four basic logic patterns: simple sequence, selection, loop, or branch.

■ To guard against writing and using faulty programs, programmers use an outline of the program logic called an algorithm. Algorithms can be represented by pseudocode or flowcharts.

■ Writing the program involves coding—writing the algorithm in a programming language. A program should be easy to read, reliable, workable under all conditions, easy to modify and update, portable, and efficient.

■ Compiling, debugging, and testing are the final steps of program development. Compiling means using a special program that translates the program to machine language. Debugging means locating and correcting any errors in the program. Testing means running the program with a wide variety of data in order to see if it performs correctly.

■ Structured programming is characterized by top-down design, good documentation, program testing at all stages of the problem-solving process, and use of a programming team to develop the software.

■ In the top-down approach, a program is broken down into functional modules that follow a hierarchy from general to specific.

■ Program documentation should occur at all programming stages. It facilitates testing and review of programs at the development stages, and simplifies modification and updating of existing programs.

■ Program testing should occur at all programming stages in order to isolate errors early in the process, thereby reducing time and costs.

■ A chief programmer team (CPT) should reduce the time and costs associated with program development, increase programmer productivity, increase program clarity, and decrease time and effort in maintaining a program once it is implemented.

■ The two basic types of programs are system programs, which coordinate the operation of the computer circuitry, and application programs, which solve user problems.

■ An operating system is a collection of programs designed to enable a computer system to manage its own operations. It allocates computer resources among the users, keeps track of the data, and establishes job priorities.

■ Low-level languages, including machine language and assembly language, are machine-oriented and require extensive knowledge of computer circuitry. Machine language is the only language the computer can execute directly. Assembly language uses symbolic names for machine operations, thus making programming less tedious and time-consuming than when machine language is used.

■ High-level languages are user-oriented and allow the programmer to focus on problem solving rather than on details of computer operation. They use meaningful words such as READ and PRINT and common mathematical terms and symbols.

■ Examples of high-level languages are FORTRAN, used for scientific applications; COBOL, the most popular business programming language; RPG, designed for producing business reports; LISP, used in artificial intelligence programming and research; and Ada, a new language developed by the Department of Defense.

■ Languages commonly used in education are BASIC, a language widely implemented on microcomputers, and Pascal and Logo, both structured languages that develop good programming habits.

■ C, Modula-2, and FORTH are high-level languages that contain low-level language capabilities, thereby allowing the programmer to interact closely with the computer's hardware.

■ Natural languages (or query languages) are designed to enable the novice computer user to access the computer's capabilities more easily. English-like sentences are easy to write and understand; they enable the user to access information in a database, for example.

Review Questions

1. List the four steps in the software development process.
2. Discuss some important qualities that make one program better than another.
3. Why should the system analyst consult with the potential program user(s) when developing software?
4. Is is important for a system analyst to have a specific programming language in mind when performing the first two steps of the software development process? Why?
5. What are the four basic logic patterns that the computer is capable of executing? Which of these patterns is avoided in structured programming? Why?
6. What is meant by the term top-down design, and how are structure charts used in this design methodology?
7. At what point in the programming process should documentation be written? What should it include?
8. Contrast the compiler program and the interpreter program.
9. Give several reasons why a programmer might choose a low-level language rather than a high-level language.
10. Name two or three high-level languages that would fulfill the requirements listed in the answer to question 9.
11. Describe some of the key advantages associated with the Pascal language and with the C language.
12. What is the purpose of natural languages? For what type of user are they best suited?

CHAPTER 5

Microcomputers

Introduction

Few technological changes equal the recent impact of microcomputers. In just one decade, microcomputers have evolved from primitive toys for hobbyists to sophisticated machines that far surpass the early mainframe computers in both speed and capabilities. The small machines have become so common that they now appear in every area of our lives, from work to play. This chapter examines the terms and hardware associated with microcomputers and describes some of their unique aspects.

Microcomputers: An Overview

Microcomputers, also called personal computers or home computers, are the smallest computers. They are smaller and less expensive than minicomputers and mainframes. Although they cannot perform as many complex functions as the large computers, their capabilities in terms of speed and memory are rapidly expanding. In fact, a clear distinction no longer exists between the capabilities of some microcomputers and those of the next class of computers, minicomputers. Microcomputers have come a long way since the first commercial microcomputer kit was introduced in 1975.

The New Technology

The invention of the microprocessor ushered in the fourth generation of computers in 1971. The microprocessor is a single chip containing the **instruction set,** that is, the fundamental logic and arithmetic circuitry as well as control capability for memory and input/output access (see Figure 5-1). It controls the arithmetic and logic operations and the sequence in which they are performed. It also controls the storage of data, instructions, and intermediate and final results of processing, much as the CPU of a mainframe computer does. A mainframe's CPU contains a series of integrated circuits, however, and is much more complex than the microprocessor.

The first microprocessor, the Intel 4004, was developed for use in a calculator. It had a very limited instruction set, could not perform many functions, and could handle only four **bits** of data at a time. By 1974, however, microprocessors were faster; they could handle eight bits of data at a time. Early eight-bit chips still in use today are the Zilog Z-80, Intel 8080, MOS 6402, and Motorola 6809. These eight-bit microprocessors were used in the first microcomputers. The number of orders received for the first commercial microcomputer kit, the MITS Altair 8800, indicated that the market for microcomputers was well worth pursuing. Companies such as Apple Computer, Commodore, Atari, and Tandy/Radio Shack began offering preassembled microcomputers for home use.

Microprocessors quickly increased in power while they decreased in size. This combination of power and miniaturization paved the way for microcomputers as

BIT
Acronym for Binary digiT; the smallest unit of data than can be represented in binary notation; a bit can be either a 0 or a 1.

Figure 5-1   Microprocessor
This microprocessor from Bell Labs
has as much processing power as
some minicomputers.

Figure 5-2   Microcomputer
Microcomputers, the least expensive
category of computers, are general-
purpose machines used in homes,
schools, and offices. This Apple IIe is
found frequently in schools.

they exist today. In 1981, IBM introduced the IBM PC with a 16-bit microprocessor. The success of the IBM PC for business uses prompted other microcomputer
manufacturers to develop 16-bit microcomputers. Established manufacturers of
larger computer and communications systems, such as DEC, WANG, Hewlett-
Packard, AT&T, and NCR, entered the microcomputer market. Soon customers
expected even more powerful machines, containing 16-bit microprocessors with
32-bit capabilities (Zilog Z8000, Intel 80286, and Motorola MC68000).

Today, the true 32-bit microprocessor offers faster processing, multi-user capability, minicomputer and mainframe compatibility, and the ability to tackle
enormous tasks such as voice recognition. The Intel 80386 and Motorola MC68020
are examples of these popular chips. Perhaps there will never be a point at which
microcomputers have reached their full potential.

The Machines Themselves

Most microcomputers today are desk-top models (see Figure 5-2). They are small
enough to place entirely on a desk, but too large to carry around easily. A fairly
versatile system includes the computer, a keyboard for input, a disk drive or two
as storage devices, and a monitor and a printer for output. Other **peripheral devices**
can be added to most systems.

Inside the computer is a main system board, often called the motherboard,
which holds the microprocessor, other circuits, and memory chips. The system
board may contain slots for plugging in cards (smaller, add-on circuit boards) that
expand the capabilities of the computer. For example, you can insert cards that
add memory, change the number of characters per line on the monitor, or interface
with printers, modems, voice recognition units, music synthesizers, and bar code

Figure 5-3 Ports
The places where peripheral
equipment can be connected to the
computer are called ports.

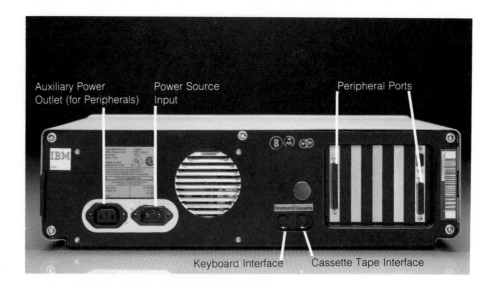

readers. Of course, there is a limit to the number of cards that can be added at once.

Microcomputers also have ports used for plugging in peripherals (see Figure 5-3). A port may be designed for serial communication, in which the bits are transferred one at a time, much as people pass through a turnstile; or for parallel communication, in which the bits are transferred eight at a time, much as cars drive down a multi-lane expressway. Cables for telephone connections and some printers require serial ports, but parallel ports also are used for communicating with printers. "Closed systems"—those that cannot easily be opened for access to the system board—depend almost entirely on ports for expanding the capabilities of the system.

Although most microcomputers are desktop models, there are three other classifications of microcomputers: portables, transportables, and supermicrocomputers.

PORTABLE
A small microcomputer that is light enough to be carried easily and does not need an external source of power.

Portables and Transportables The smallest microcomputers available are **portables.** Portables are light enough to be carried and do not need an external source of power. They are powered by rechargeable or replaceable batteries. Their flat display screens allow them to be slim and therefore easy to carry. Portables usually need some form of direct-access storage medium, such as floppy disks.

Portables can be divided further by size into briefcase and notebook portables. The Hewlett-Packard 110 is a briefcase computer and is noted for being very fast (see Figure 5-4). Radio Shack's TRS-80 Model 100 and Model 200 are even smaller; they are called notebook computers and are used mostly for word processing.

Some portables are capable of performance almost equal to that of small desktop microcomputers as reflected by their prices—from $3000 to $8000. Other portables carry a much lower price tag, between $500 and $2,000.

Each portable has different features, so users must evaluate their particular needs before selecting a portable. Some useful features include built-in **modems** and software for transmitting and receiving data by telephone. Some portables

Figure 5-4
Hewlett-Packard 110 Portable
Computer This computer can fit in
a briefcase, which makes carrying it
on business trips easy.

TRANSPORTABLE
A class of microcomputer smaller
than the desktop models for easier
carrying, but larger than the
portables and therefore bulkier to
carry.

have ports for connecting floppy disk drives, cassette recorders, or bar code readers. Most portables have built-in software such as a word processor, spreadsheet, or database manager (see the section on software later in this chapter). Built-in programming languages such as BASIC may also be included.

Portables are especially useful for reporters, businesspeople, and students. For example, a salesperson might use a portable to compose reports that are sent to the main office via telephone lines. Journalists use portables in similar ways. A reporter can cover an event 2,000 miles from the newspaper's headquarters, write the story using a word processor and a portable computer, and use a modem for sending the article over telephone lines to the editor's desk. Students carry briefcase or notebook computers to classes in order to take decipherable lecture notes and prepare assignments.

Portables should be distinguished from another class of small microcomputers, the **transportables.** Transportables generally are larger than portables but are still small enough to be carried easily. They differ from portables because they require an external power source (see Figure 5-5).

Supermicrocomputers Some microcomputers are so powerful that they can compete with low-end minicomputers These **supermicrocomputers** usually are built around powerful 32-bit microprocessors, and can handle large amounts of data and support more than one user (see Figure 5-6). Because microprocessors are inexpensive compared to the CPUs of minicomputers, supermicrocomputers offer a significant price edge over minicomputers. In fact, the minicomputer market

Figure 5-5
A Transportable Computer

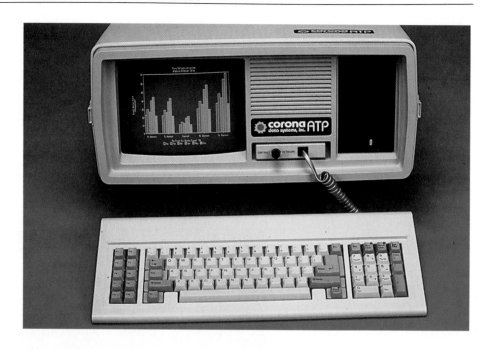

already is weakening as more customers upgrade their systems by linking super-microcomputers to existing minicomputers or mainframes.

Supermicrocomputers must be able to store large amounts of data. Hard disks can store much more data than the floppy disks often used with microcomputers.

Figure 5-6
Supermicrocomputer
The Tower 1632
Supermicrocomputer from NCR

HIGHLIGHT ▲▲▲▲▲▲▲▲▲▲▲▲▲▲▲▲▲▲▲▲▲▲▲▲▲▲

Please! Count Your Eggs Before They Hatch!

An egg counter? You've got to be kidding.

On second thought, when you're faced with counting 700,000 eggs daily, an egg counter would be handy.

Stephen Herbruck of Poultry Management Systems (Saranac, Michigan) developed an egg-counting system about six years ago. The systems use as many as 1,500 photodetectors to record the passage of eggs on conveyors

(deposited there, of course, by obliging hens). The count is transferred to an IBM PC, which records and displays the count. The system saves hiring the one or two persons needed for the full-time job of counting eggs.

This year, Herbruck is testing an extension of his egg counters on his own egg-laying hens (about 1 million of them). The new system is called NOAH (Natural On-Line Animal Housing). NOAH controls all aspects of egg production, including as many as 2,000 devices:

water-flow meters, feed-weighing devices, variable-speed ventilating fan motors, and thermostats. NOAH is outgrowing the IBM PC, so Herbruck probably will switch to the IBM PC/AT. Herbruck can even check the feeding system from a remote NOAH terminal in his home before going to bed.

Now he has to sell the system to other egg production centers—no easy hendeavor.

SOURCE: "Automating America's Heartland," Raeburn, Paul, *High Technology*, December 1985, p. 51.

The prices of hard disk drives have fallen in recent years, making them ideal storage devices for supermicrocomputers.

One problem hindering full-scale implementation of supermicrocomputers is the limited amount of available software. As they gain in popularity, however, there will be more interest in developing software for these machines, just as a great deal of software has been developed for traditional microcomputers.

Learning Check

1. Compare microcomputers with minicomputers and mainframes in terms of size, cost, and capabilities.

2. What event prompted many manufacturers to enter the microcomputer market?

3. What basic equipment makes up a fairly versatile microcomputer system?

4. What features make portable computers useful to salespersons?

5. How are some customers using supermicrocomputers?

Answers

1. They are smaller, less expensive, and have lesser capabilities, although some approach minicomputers in capabilities. **2.** IBM introduced the 16-bit IBM PC. **3.** A computer, key-board, monitor, one or two disk drives, and a printer. **4.** They are lightweight, flat, easy to carry, and do not need an external source of electricity. **5.** They are upgrading their systems by linking microcomputers to existing minicomputers and mainframes.

Understanding the Microchips

In Chapter 1, you learned that a computer's power is derived from its speed and memory and the accuracy of its electronic circuits. This section explains two of those factors—speed and memory—as related to microprocessors. It also discusses the programs that integrate the workings of a microcomputer's circuitry.

The Microprocessor's Speed

The speed with which the microprocessor can execute instructions affects the speed of the microcomputer. Speed depends on several factors, including word size and clock speed.

WORD SIZE
The number of bits than can be manipulated at one time; for instance, an eight-bit microprocessor can manipulate eight bits (one byte) of data at a time.

Word size is the number of bits that can be manipulated at one time. An eight-bit microprocessor, for example, manipulates data in clusters of eight bits (each of which is called a byte). A 16-bit microprocessor can handle 16 bits—two eight-bit bytes of data—at a time. Therefore, a 16-bit microprocessor can manipulate twice as much data as an eight-bit microprocessor in approximately the same amount of time. This does not necessarily mean that there is a direct relationship between word size and speed. A 16-bit microprocessor may not be twice as fast as an eight-bit microprocessor. It may be more than twice as fast in performing some operations, but less than twice as fast in performing others. Generally speaking, however, a 32-bit microprocessor is faster than a 16-bit microprocessor and a 16-bit microprocessor is faster than an eight-bit microprocessor.

The 16- and 32-bit microprocessors are appropriate for business users for two reasons. First, in business, several users often use the same software and data in a system of linked microcomputers. Second, business users often work on several programs at one time and therefore need a large amount of primary memory, which can be handled by the 16- and 32-bit microprocessors. Nonetheless, many eight-bit machines are used. Applications and operating systems (see the section on operating systems) for eight-bit systems are well established, and most users do not require a lot of speed. In addition, eight-bit machines are cheaper.

CLOCK SPEED
The number of electronic pulses a microprocessor can produce each second.

MEGAHERTZ (MHz)
One million times per second; the unit of measurement for clock speed.

The **clock speed** of a microprocessor is the number of electronic pulses the chip can produce each second. Clock speed is built into a microprocessor and is measured in **megahertz (MHz).** (*Mega* means million and *hertz* means times per second, so one megahertz is one million times per second.) The electronic pulses affect the speed with which program instructions are executed, because instructions are executed at predetermined intervals that are timed by these pulses.

As an illustration of this concept, assume that one instruction is executed every 100 pulses. A 4 MHz microprocessor, then can process 40,000 instructions per second (4 million pulses divided by 100 pulses). An 8 MHz microprocessor can process 80,000 instructions, or twice as many as a 4 MHz microprocessor. Thus, the more pulses produced per second, the faster the instructions can be executed. Most microcomputers have clock speeds between 2 MHz and 8 MHz.

Memory

Primary memory is important in microcomputer speed because the more memory directly accessible by the CPU, the faster the machine. In addition, a computer with more memory can use more complex programs. Primary memory consists of thousands of on/off devices, each of which holds one bit. Primary memory consists of RAM and ROM.

RAM   The primary memory that holds the data and programs for immediate processing is a form of semiconductor memory called **random-access memory (RAM).** RAM is the working area of the computer. Because RAM is volatile or nonpermanent, data and programs are erased when the electric power to a computer is turned off or disrupted in some other way. When any changes or results are to be saved, they must be saved on an external form of storage, such as magnetic disks or tapes.

The size of RAM memory is stated in bytes. The most common sizes in microcomputers are 64K (kilobytes), 128K, 256K, 512K and 640K. The sizes are related to the word sizes of microprocessors, in that each microprocessor can access directly only a certain number of bytes of data in primary memory. As the word size increases, so does the amount of RAM that can be handled. Typically, an eight-bit microprocessor can directly access 64K bytes of data and a 16-bit microprocessor can directly access 256K. Many 8- and 16-bit machines are available with more RAM than their microprocessors can directly access. The extra RAM is additional "indexed" memory that can be accessed indirectly at a slightly slower speed than RAM. Just as 16-bit and 32-bit microcomputers are appropriate for business uses, 256K and 512K RAMs are appropriate for holding the increased amount of data and programs that a business user needs to access.

ROM   When functions are built into the hardware of a microcomputer, they are placed in **read-only memory (ROM).** Read-only memory instructions cannot be changed or deleted by other stored-program instructions. Because ROM is permanent, it cannot be occupied by instructions or data read from a disk or tape. ROM and versions—PROM and EPROM—are available for microcomputers. See Chapter 3 for a complete discussion of these chips. ROM programs are also available on cartridges that can be inserted into special slots built into the computer. Programs built into ROM chips or cartridges often are called firmware.

Operating Systems

Without an **operating system,** a computer cannot recognize that a key has been pressed, much less what it means. Several operating systems have been designed for use with microcomputers (see Table 5-1).

Most operating systems are loaded into a computer's RAM from floppy disks, a process called **booting.** The word boot derives from the expression "lift yourself up by your own bootstraps," which essentially is what a computer does. In order to read and write data residing on a disk, the disk operating system must be loaded into memory from the disk where it is kept. The computer has a small program built into ROM which starts the process of reading the operating system code from a disk.

BOOT
To start or restart a computer by reading a small amount of code from a storage device into the computer's memory.

	CP/M	MS DOS	Apple DOS	Unix
Manufacturer	• Digital Research	• Microsoft	• Apple Computer	• Bell Laboratories
Microprocessor	• Intel 8080 • Intel 8085 • Zilog Z-80	• Intel 8088 • Intel 8086 • Intel 8286	• MOS 6502	• Not built around a single family of microprocessors
Features	• First OS for micros • For 8-bit mmicroprocessors • Not easy for beginners to use, but succeeding versions easier • Concurrent DOS new version for 16-bit micro-processors; runs programs written for MS-DOS and 8-bit CP/M	• First licensed for use on the IBM PC • Quickly became most popular for 16-bit machines • Over 100 commputers using it • Not easy for beginners to use	• Designed to be used by nonprofessional computer users • Easy to learn and easy to use • Limited utilities and file usage • Closely tied to Apple's version of BASIC • Apple ProDOS overcomes its problems; ProDOS can be used with hard disks	• First used on minicomputers • Easily adapted for different types of computers • Used on various classifications of computers (micros, minis, mainframes) • Handles multiple usage • Handles several tasks from one terminal • Many utility programs • Not all versions compatible • Few applications for home users

Table 5-1
Operating Systems for Microcomputers

Generally, a person uses the operating system by typing keystroke combinations that direct the computer to copy data, save data, delete data, or get a list of items kept on disks.

Compatibility

The owner of a microcomputer can enhance its capabilities by adding peripheral equipment to the system, such as a disk drive, color monitor, printer, or modem. It is not always necessary to choose peripherals made by the same manufacturer as the microcomputer. Another manufacturer's equipment may have the same or better capabilities at a better price. The peripherals do have to be **compatible,** though. Software also must be compatible. Programs designed for one operating system cannot be used on computers with different operating systems. Compatibility in software includes the ability to read and write data on the same diskette and to use common data files. If one manufacturer's equipment or software can be used with another manufacturer's equipment or software, the two are said to be compatible.

Compatibility can be extended by adding a **coprocessor** to a computer. The coprocessor makes the computer compatible with another operating system. It is a microprocessor that can be plugged into the original computer to replace or work with the original microprocessor. The coprocessor usually comes on a plug-in board or card, along with other chips necessary for it to run. For example, adding a Z-80 board to the main system board makes an Apple IIe compatible with the CP/M operating system. The original microprocessor and the coprocessor share the computer's disk drives, keyboard, and other peripherals.

COMPATIBLE
Descriptive of hardware and/or software that can work together.

COPROCESSOR
A microprocessor that can be plugged into a microprocessor to replace or work with the micrcomputer's original microprocessor.

Learning Check

1. What does it mean to define a microprocessor in terms of the number of bits—eight or 16, for example?

2. How are word size and RAM related?

3. How can a computer be started if the disk operating system is on a disk, but the computer needs it in primary memory in order to read and write data residing on a disk?

4. What characteristic must you look for when buying peripheral equipment or software for use with a certain type of computer?

Answers

1. This refers to the word size—the number of bits which can be handled in one cluster. **2.** As word size increases, so does the amount of RAM that can be handled directly. An eight-bit microprocessor can directly access 64k bytes of data, and a 16-bit microprocessor can directly access 256K. **3.** A small program is built into ROM which starts the process of reading the operating system code from the disk. **4.** Compatibility.

Using Microcomputers

Microcomputers are designed to perform a variety of tasks. The people who buy and use microcomputers are a diverse group—businesspeople, teachers, students, doctors, lawyers, and farmers—and their computing needs are just as diverse. This section describes some of the many equipment and software options available for microcomputers.

Input Devices

The increased use of microcomputers has promoted the popularity of a variety of input and output devices, many of which have become essential for easy use of microcomputers.

The most common input device is indispensable: the keyboard. Most computer keyboards resemble typewriter keyboards in the layout of keys for letters, numbers, and symbols. They also include computer-specific keys, such as control keys, arrow keys, and function keys. Typing combinations of these keys sends commands to the CPU for performing specific tasks, such as moving the **cursor,** printing a document, inserting a sentence, or removing some data. Some keyboards contain a numeric keypad, which enables the user to enter numbers in a manner similar to using an adding machine (see Figure 5-7).

Keyboard entry is too slow or inconvenient for some applications. Devices that allow the user to bypass the keyboard in moving the cursor and in entering data or commands include joysticks, game paddles, mice, graphics tablets, and light pens. See Figure 5-8 for pictures and descriptions of these devices.

Figure 5-7
The Mac⁺ Keyboard

Other input devices formerly used only with minicomputers and mainframes are being adapted for use with microcomputers. These include the voice input devices and scanning equipment discussed in Chapter 3.

Output Devices

The most common output device is the monitor. This device enables users to view information before sending it to the microprocessor for processing, as well as to view information sent from the microprocessor. The information displayed on the monitor can be in either character or graphic form.

A monitor is one of the essential peripherals of a microcomputer system. Monitors generally are divided into three categories: (1) monochrome, (2) composite color, and (3) RGB (red-green-blue).

Monochrome monitors display a single color, such as white, green, or amber, against a dark background. They display text clearly and are inexpensive, ranging from $100 to $300. Most monochrome monitors are composite monitors, so-called for their single video signal.

Composite color monitors display a composite of colors received in a single video signal, and are slightly more expensive than monochrome monitors. They deliver less clarity in displaying text, however, than monochrome monitors. On some, in fact, text is almost unreadable in the 80-column mode. Images on a composite color monitor are less crisp than images on RGB monitors.

RGB monitors receive three separate color signals, one for each of three colors: red, green, and blue (see Figure 5-9). Commonly used for high-quality graphic displays, they display sharper images than the composite color monitors, but they produce fuzzier text than monochrome monitors. They are more expensive than

MONOCHROME MONITOR
A monitor that displays a single color, such as white, green, or amber, against a darker background.

COMPOSITE COLOR MONITOR
A color monitor that displays a composite of colors received in a single video signal.

RGB MONITOR
A monitor that receives three separate color signals, one for each of three colors—red, green, and blue.

(a) Joystick

(b) Mouse

(c) Graphic Tablets

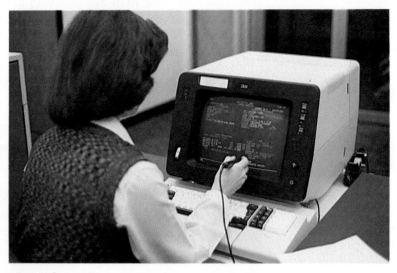

(d) Light Pen

Figure 5-8
Special Input Devices
(a) Joysticks generally are used with game and graphics applications. They allow very fast, multidirectional cursor control. (b) The mouse is a hand-movable input device about the size of a Jell-O box. On the bottom is a small ball like a roller bearing. On top is a pushbutton or two for activating a command. When the mouse is rolled across a flat surface, it sends electronic signals through an input cord to the computer, and the cursor moves accordingly. Using the mouse eliminates a considerable amount of typing. (c) Graphics tablets are flat, boardlike surfaces upon which the user draws, using a pencil-like device. The image is then transmitted to the screen. (d) A light pen is a pen-shaped object with a light-sensitive cell at its end. A person uses the device by touching the light pen to the screen.

Figure 5-9
RGB Monitor

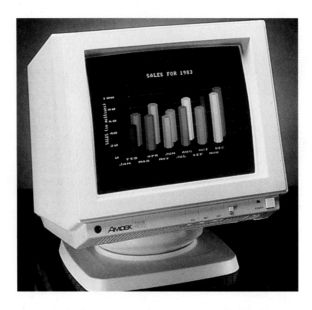

composite color monitors, generally from $500 to $900. An add-on display card is necessary for using RGB monitors with most computers.

Also available are RF modulators, which allow television sets to be used as monitors. Television sets deliver less resolution than any of the other types of monitors discussed here.

Flat panel displays are available for portable computers (see Figure 5-10). They are less bulky and require less power than the cathode ray tubes used in most

Figure 5-10
Flat Panel Display

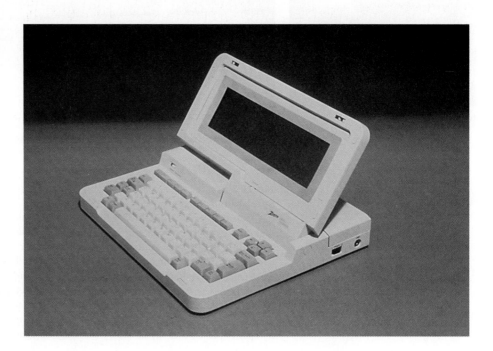

from an angle or in direct lighting makes the image appear faint or even invisible. Two common types of flat panel display technologies are liquid crystal display (LCD) and electroluminescence. LCDs generally show poor contrast and visibility, although new technology is improving them. The electroluminescent panel shows a better display and a wider viewing angle, but also costs more than the LCD. In the future, it is expected that electroluminescent panels will display full color and be readable even in sunlight.

Other common output devices for microcomputers are printers and plotters. The same types of printers and plotters discussed in Chapter 3 are available for use with microcomputers. In fact, the high-quality reproduction, versatile type sizes and styles, and graphics capabilities of laser printers used with microcomputers have fostered a new aspect of computing: desktop publishing (Chapter 6).

Online Storage

The storage media commonly used with microcomputers are cassette tapes and floppy disks. These tapes and disks are inexpensive and small, so they are ideal for microcomputer data storage. They are not suitable for storing large amounts of data, however. Hard disks are more expensive than floppy disks, but they can hold over ten times as much data.

Cassette tapes are popular with microcomputer users because they are inexpensive, easy to store, and in most instances, can be used with a regular cassette player (see Figure 5-11). Data access with cassette tapes is sequential and very slow, so cassettes are used mostly for backing up data held on disks.

Figure 5-11
Cassette Tapes

Figure 5-12
Floppy Disks
Floppy disks are of three sizes:
8-inch, 5 1/4-inch, and 3 1/2-inch.
The 3 1/2-inch disks are enclosed in
hard plastic for protection.

Floppy disks (also called diskettes) offer direct data access, so they are much faster than cassette tapes. These disks come in three sizes and are reusable, lightweight, easy to store, and safe to mail (see Figure 5-12). They are accessed by disk drives, which are either built into the computer or separate units connected to the computer. A 5 1/4-inch floppy disk can hold as much as 1.2 Mb (megabytes) of data. Most microcomputers use 5 1/4-inch or 3 1/2-inch disks. Eight-inch disks also are available.

Hard disks are the most expensive form of storage, but they allow very rapid access to data (see Figure 5-13). They can be shared by more than one microcomputer and offer more flexibility than other media. Hard disks hold more data than cassette tapes or floppy disks. Common capacities range from 5 Mb to 80 Mb, although some very expensive hard disks for special purposes hold over 400 Mb. Data access is faster with hard disks than with floppy disks. Hard disks act more like RAM than secondary storage.

There are two varieties of hard disks: fixed and removable. A fixed disk is a sealed unit that the user cannot open, so it is well protected from dust and other environmental factors. Often the disk drive unit comes installed in the computer. It may contain one or more polished aluminum platters covered with a high-quality magnetic coating. Fixed disks are reliable and hold a large amount of data. A removable disk enables the user to change disks. Each disk is enclosed in a cartridge that is inserted into the hard disk drive. This feature provides security, because the disks can be removed and locked away from the computer. Removable disks are not as popular as fixed disks, however, because most have less capacity than fixed disks.

No matter what type of hard disk is used, a backup system such as floppy disks or tape is necessary. The nature of the copy protection on some software prevents convenient use with hard disks.

The development of optical disks will change the way microcomputers are used in the future. With such tremendous storage capacity (550 Mb on a single 5 1/4-inch disk), they make possible a wide range of training and instructional capabilities

Figure 5-13
Hard Disk Unit

for businesses. Combined with computer data, the video images stored on one optical disk can provide instruction similar to that given in films, yet enable the user to interact through the computer rather than watch passively. The optical disks commercially available today cannot be erased or recorded on, but that situation is expected to change by 1987 or 1988.

Add-Ons

Add-ons are printed circuit boards or expansion boards containing chips that can increase the capabilities of a microcomputer (see Figure 5-14). They are inserted into a slot on the main system board of a microcomputer. Here are some examples

- Changing the number of characters displayed across the width of the screen (usually from 40 characters to 80 characters).
- Adding graphics capabilities to the computer.
- Adding a coprocessor to the computer so that software for a different operating system can be run.
- Adding memory.
- Providing interfaces for input and output devices, such as printers, graphics tablets, joysticks, or mice.
- Acting as a hard disk drive.

Some software and hardware requires the use of one or more add-ons. Some computers are sold with interfaces for RGB monitors and graphics, for example, whereas others need additional boards.

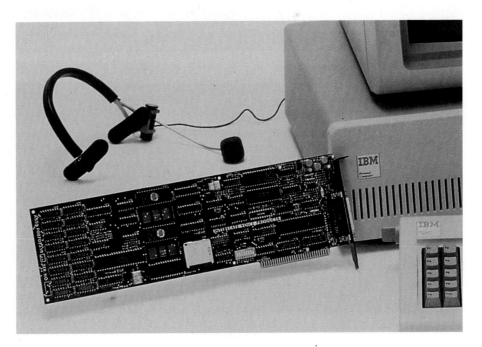

Figure 5-14   Add-ons
A connected speech recognition board.

Software Packages

Figure 5-15
Software Packages
The screens demonstrate the type of display you might see if you were using a similar application. (a) Word Processing (b) Electronic Spreadsheet (c) Business Graphics (d) Data Base

A **software package** is a set of standardized computer programs, procedures, and related documentation necessary for solving problems of a specific application. A wide variety of software is available for managing finances and data, preparing documents, creating art, and learning new skills. Among the popular packages are word processors, data managers, spreadsheets, and business graphics (see Figure 5-15).

Word processing software enables the user to write, edit, format, and print text. Electronic spreadsheets are used for preparing financial data for summaries. Most spreadsheets look like tables, with data and formulas arranged in columns and rows. As the data is changed, the results of the calculations in the formulas change. Data can be filed using data management programs, some of which imitate traditional filing methods: Material is filed by category, and the same data can appear in several files. Other programs provide databases, which allow entry of thousands

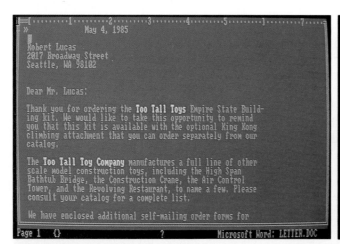

(a) Word processing software

(b) Electronic spreadsheet software

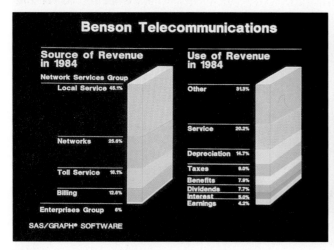

(c) Business graphics software

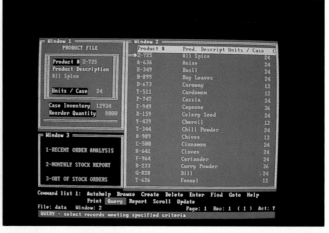

(d) Data base software

of records that can be accessed in many ways. Graphics software packages are designed for displaying data as charts, such as bar charts, line graphs, and pie charts. These four types of software are described in Part II of this text, along with exercises for practicing the skills that these programs require.

INTEGRATED SOFTWARE
Two or more application programs that work together, allowing easy movement of data between the applications.

Integrated Software   Integration suggests the blending of two or more parts into a whole. When the term integration is used in conjunction with software, it means that two or more types of software are blended into one application package. **Integrated software** generally conforms to three standards:

1. The software consists of several programs that would otherwise be separate application packages.
2. The software allows for easy movement of data among the applications.
3. A common group of commands is used for all the applications in the package.

An integrated package may result when several applications are combined into one. For example, a data manager, spreadsheet, and graphics package could be combined to share data and pass data to another application. Integration also can occur when one type of software is enhanced. An example would be the addition of a spelling program, thesaurus, or grammar program to a word processing program.

Utilities and Other Functions   Software can be used for many functions that an office employee or businessperson encounters every day. Some programs provide a calendar for entering appointments and business functions. Others set alarm clocks, dial telephone numbers, or act as calculators and notepads. There are utility programs for programming functions into single keystrokes in order to save time while typing. Such a function may produce a string of characters, such as an often-used sentence or phrase, or a string of commands which performs a task such as backing up or accessing data. Other programs check spelling and grammar and offer alternate word choices.

Utility software may involve a concept called the **RAM disk.** The RAM disk uses a predefined section of computer memory to act as a disk drive. Usually the intent is not to get more storage space, but rather to accelerate access to data. Accessing data on disks is slow compared with accessing data from primary memory. The RAM disk approximates the speed of the microprocessor, therefore increasing the speed of data access.

RAM DISK
A portion of RAM memory that acts temporarily as a disk drive, but approximates the speed of the microprocessor.

The setup process is simple: All that is needed is some spare RAM and RAM disk utility software. Typically a RAM disk uses memory in add-on cards, but it may also allocate part of the original primary memory of a computer. The RAM utility software is available on newer versions of some operating systems (MS DOS 3.0 and Apple ProDOS, for example), but it can be purchased separately instead. The RAM disk is commonly used for holding the utility programs described in the previous paragraph which operate compatibly with word processors or other major application programs. When utility programs are used in this manner, sometimes they are referred to as RAM-resident programs.

Users' Groups

Where can a new microcomputer owner go for help in operating the machine? When a $150 software package will not run, who can identify the problem? Which word-processing package priced under $200 works best on a certain microcomputer?

Questions such as these often baffle the proud new owner of a microcomputer. One answer is a **users' group.** A users' group is a relatively informal group of owners of a particular microcomputer model or software package, who meet or communicate by modem to exchange information about hardware, software, service, and support. Users' groups also may form around applications and related topics, such as real estate, medicine, telecommunications, education, and computer-aided publishing.

USERS' GROUP
An informal group of computer users who meet to exchange information about hardware, software, service, and support.

The value of users' groups comes from the accumulation of knowledge and experience ready to be shared by members. The best evaluation of hardware and software comes from one who has actually purchased and tried it. As software becomes more sophisticated and more hardware becomes available for enhancing microcomputers, users' groups will become even more valuable.

Users' groups also may be beneficial to small companies whose internal computing experience is limited. Top management may join users' groups to learn about new technology and how it can be used in maintaining a competitive position in a particular business field. Individual businesspeople may be interested in improving their individual productivity.

Since users' groups normally do not have telephones or office space, finding a local group is not always easy. Dealers who sell a given microcomputer usually know how to contact users' groups, and groups often post notices and flyers in computer stores. Information on national groups sometimes is included in a microcomputer package when it is sold. Contacting the manufacturer directly also may yield the name of the person to contact about a local group.

Learning Check

1. Describe computer hardware and software that you might use for producing a high-quality bar chart to present a new idea to your boss.

2. Why might flat panel displays be hard to look at for long periods of time?

3. What type of microcomputer storage would you buy to enable two users to access the storage at once.?

4. How are add-ons different from peripherals such as printers, keyboards, and monitors?

5. How does a RAM disk save time?

Answers

1. Computer, RGB monitor, interface for RGB monitor, keyboard, and color plotter (which also might need an interface). 2. Looking at a flat panel display from an angle or in direct lighting makes the image appear faint or even invisible. 3. Hard disk. 4. They are on circuit boards that are inserted into slots inside the computer. The other peripherals are plugged into a port. 5. It allows faster access to data than a disk drive does.

Summary Points

■ Microcomputers are the smallest and least expensive computers. The distinctions between microcomputers and minicomputers are fading as microcomputers become more powerful.

■ The increased power and miniaturization of microprocessors paved the way for the development of microcomputers.

■ The first microprocessors could manipulate four bits of data at a time. Most microprocessors today handle data clusters of eight, 16, or 32 bits.

■ Portable computers can be classified in size as briefcase or notebook. Both types are light enough to be carried and do not need an external power source. Transportables are larger than portables, but still are light enough to be carried. They require an external power source.

■ Supermicrocomputers are less expensive than minicomputers and provide users with high performance at a relatively low cost.

■ The speed of microcomputers depends on word size and clock speed. Word size refers to the number of bits that can be manipulated at one time. Clock speed is the number of electronic pulses the microprocessor can produce each second.

■ Primary memory consists of random-access memory (RAM) and read-only memory (ROM). The amount of RAM is related to the word size of a microprocessor, in that each microprocessor can directly access only a certain amount of data in primary memory.

■ An operating system is a collection of programs used by the computer for managing its own operations. Microcomputers with different operating systems are not compatible.

■ Some popular input and output devices used with microcomputers include joysticks, mice, graphics tablets, light pens, printers, and plotters. Keyboards and monitors are among the essential peripherals for microcomputers.

■ Cassette tapes and floppy disks are the storage media commonly used with microcomputers. Hard magnetic disks are used when large amounts of data must be stored and shared. Optical disks are becoming a popular storage medium for use with microcomputers, although they cannot yet be erased and reused.

■ Add-ons are boards containing chips and printed circuits which are inserted into slots on the main system board for the purpose of adding memory, graphics capabilities, coprocessors, or other capabilities to the computer.

■ Popular software includes programs for word processing, electronic spreadsheets, data management, and graphics. Combinations of programs—such as a data manager, spreadsheet, and graphics package, or a word processor and a spelling program—are called integrated software.

■ Users' groups offer owners advice and information about machines, programs, and topics of special interest such as electronic publishing or telecommunication.

Review Questions

1. What differentiates microcomputers from larger computers?
2. Discuss why a closed system microcomputer might be less flexible than a system that you can open easily. Gain access to a microcomputer at home or at school and tell which type it is.
3. Differentiate between portables, supermicrocomputers, and the desktop models of microcomputers.
4. Explain the role of the microprocessor in the operation of a microcomputer. How is it related to RAM?
5. Explain how word size and clock speed affect the speed of a microcomputer.
6. What is meant by microcomputer compatibility, and how is it determined?
7. Name some input devices that allow you to bypass the keyboard, thus reducing the amount of typing needed.
8. Name three disk concepts or technologies that offer greater capabilities than floppy disks. What is special about each?
9. How can an add-on enhance a microcomputer system?
10. Describe the benefits of joining a users' group.
11. Look through computer magazines and find one specific brand name or picture representing each of the following terms: portable computer, flat panel display, RGB monitor, dot matrix printer, keyboard, graphics tablet, floppy disk, word processor, electronic spreadsheet, database, integrated software, utility program for defining keystrokes, and add-on (for any purpose). To make the project more difficult, find products that are compatible with one another.

CHAPTER 6

Computers' Impact on Society

Introduction

Computers seem to be everywhere, influencing everything we do. Our telephone system is almost completely computerized; we can dial direct to almost any location in the world, and the call is handled by computers. If we need hospitalization or medical tests, we may find ourselves in a room full of computers that monitor our body functions and analyze pictures of our internal organs. To survive at the office, we learn how to use computers for preparing documents, keeping books, and getting information. Whether in art, entertainment, science, medicine, business, government, education, or the home, computers are playing an important and ever-increasing role.

Telecommunications

DATABASE
A collection of data elements that are commonly defined and consistently organized to fit the information needs of a wide variety of users.

People using computers in one location often need to access computers in another location, to obtain or update information or data or to communicate with someone. Salespeople with scanners and POS terminals communicate sales data directly to a centrally located computer as transactions occur. Banks send records of financial transactions from one bank to another and from one computer to another. Officers at local police stations tie in with central **databases** that offer information about known criminals, license plate numbers, or fingerprints. Personal computer owners often communicate with other computer owners electronically rather than by mail or in person. Whatever the purpose, direct communication with a computer reduces delays in the collection and dissemination of data and information.

This section discusses the ways in which computers are linked and some purposes for which people use computer communications.

TELECOMMUNICATIONS
The combined use of communication facilities, such as telephone systems, and data processing equipment.

COMMUNICATION CHANNEL
A pathway along which data is transmitted between sending and receiving devices.

DEMODULATION
The process of retrieving data from a modulated carrier wave.

MODULATION
Technology used in modems to make data processing signals compatible with communication facilities.

Message Transmission

In a data communication system, data is transmitted between microcomputers or computer terminals and a central computer or even between two or more central computers. The use of data processing equipment with communication facilities such as telephone systems is called **telecommunications.** Any such data transmission occurs over **communication channels,** the pathways that carry data from one location to another. Types of communication channels used for data transfer include telegraph lines, telephone lines, microwave links, coaxial cables, communication satellites, and fiber optic cables.

Data is transmitted over communication channels in either analog or digital form. Analog transmission is used on traditional telephone lines: Messages are sent and received over telephone wires in the form of continuous electronic waves that follow the path of the wire. Digital transmission, by contrast, carries data as distinct ''on'' and ''off'' states, just as the computer does.

Analog transmission requires that data be converted from the digital form in which it is stored in the computer to analog form before transmission, in a process

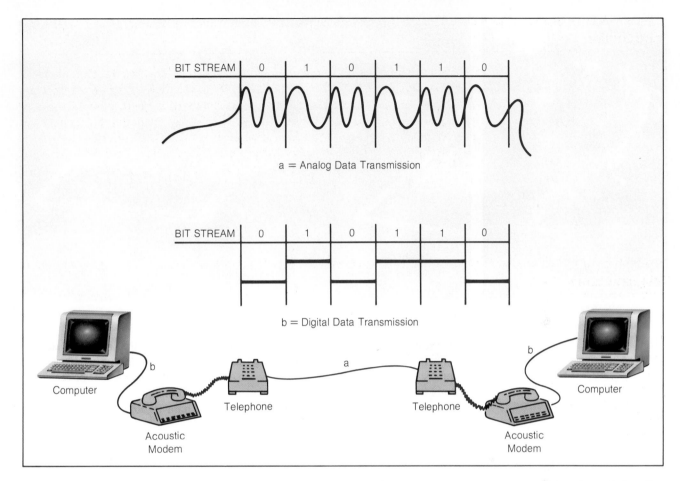

Figure 6-1
Analog and Digital Transmission

MODEM
A device that modulates and demodulates signals transmitted over communication lines; allows linkage with another computer.

called **modulation.** At the receiving end, data must then be **demodulated**—converted from wave form to digital form—before the data is entered into the computer. Both modulation and demodulation are accomplished by devices called **modems,** a term derived from the words modulation and demodulation (see Figure 6-1). Digital transmission requires no data conversion, so it reduces the time required to send messages and creates fewer transmission errors than analog transmission.

Three types of modems are used for preparing data for transmission over telephone lines. A direct-connect modem is attached directly to the computer and to the telephone lines. The user connects with another computer by typing the access numbers on the computer keyboard. An acoustic coupler modem differs from a direct-connect modem in that it must be used with a standard contoured telephone receiver. The receiver of the telephone is placed on two cups built into the modem, thus linking the acoustic coupler with the telephone (see Figure 6-2). An internal modem is built into or plugged directly into the internal circuitry of the computer, and acts similarly to the direct-connect modem.

Message transmission occurs in different modes and at different speeds. A modem must be able to handle the mode and speed of transmission used by the party or service being accessed. These aspects of communication are discussed in the following two sections.

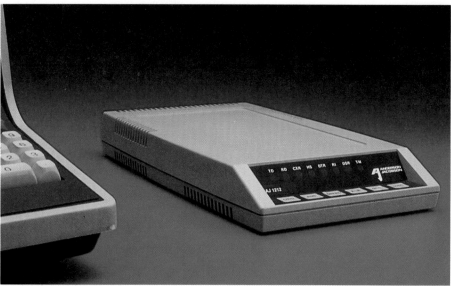

Figure 6-2
Types of Modems

Modes of Transmission   Modems handle the actual transmission of the data in one of three basic modes: simplex, half-duplex, or full-duplex (see Figure 6-3). Simplex transmission is unidirectional, or one-way: Data can be sent or received, but not both. Half-duplex transmission occurs in both directions, but only one way at a time. Full-duplex transmission occurs when data is both sent and received simultaneously.

Speeds of Transmission   The speed at which data is transmitted is referred to as **baud.** Baud is commonly identified as the number of bits per second that can be transmitted over a communication line. Baud rates vary. The most common speeds used with microcomputers are 300 baud and 1,200 baud. A 2,400-baud modem is available for use with microcomputers, but at that speed, poor telephone lines can rob the signal of its strength or introduce noise that distorts the message. Baud rates higher than 2,400 are used only in specialized data transmission.

BAUD
A unit of measurement for transmission speed.

BANDWIDTH
The range of frequencies available for transmission on a given channel; also known as grade.

The grade or **bandwidth** of a channel determines the rate at which the channel can transmit data. A narrow bandwidth channel, such as a telegraph line, transmits data at rates of 45 to 90 baud. Telephone lines have a wider frequency range and fall into the classification of voice-grade channels. They carry data at 300 to 9,600 baud. For high-speed transmission of large volumes of data, broad-band channels transmit data at rates of up to 120,000 baud. Coaxial cables, microwaves, and fiber optic cables (see Figure 6-4) belong in this category.

Software for Transmission

Communication software also is required for data transmission. For example, communication software helps a microcomputer become temporarily a part of the remote computer system with which it is communicating. In effect, the software "tricks" the microcomputer into acting as a part of the remote system. In larger

**Figure 6-3
Transmission Modes**

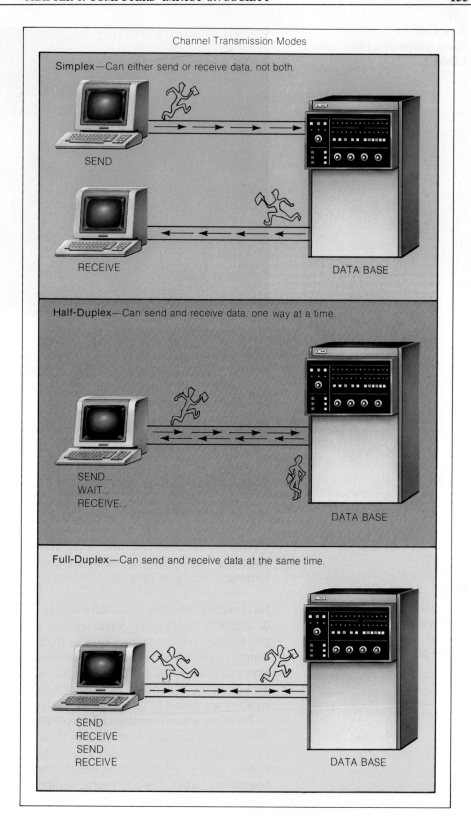

Channel Transmission Modes

Simplex—Can either send or receive data, not both.

SEND

RECEIVE

DATA BASE

Half-Duplex—Can send and receive data, one way at a time.

SEND...
WAIT...
RECEIVE...

DATA BASE

Full-Duplex—Can send and receive data at the same time.

SEND
RECEIVE
SEND
RECEIVE

DATA BASE

Figure 6-4
Cross Section of a Fiber Optic
Cable

systems, communication software manages the communication between the central computer and remote terminals, microcomputers, and other equipment.

Communication software for microcomputers should be able to transmit data in ASCII (American Standard Code for Information Interchange) form. Most information services send their data in ASCII form, and personal computers store their data in this form.

Communication Networks

One of the most popular uses of personal computers is sharing resources and information through the use of commmunication networks. Networks can connect a computer via telephone lines to commercial information services or electronic bulletin boards. They can also link computers within a building or complex, forming a local area network.

INFORMATION SERVICE
A commercial service that offers
information over communication
lines to paying subscribers.

Information Services An **information service** gives the user access to vast databases of information. Some services even enable users to communicate with one another; for example, a user in Rochester, New York, might compete in a computer game against a player in Phoenix, Arizona. Most services require the payment of an initial fee. All services charge an hourly rate, which varies with the time of day and the type of service being used. Passwords and/or identification numbers are issued to subscribers to ensure legitimate access to the service.

There are several commercial network services available to subscribers. Three of the largest are The Source, Dow Jones/Retrieval Service, and CompuServe, Inc. Individuals and businesses subscribe to these and other information services to fill a variety of information needs. They can receive video versions of major newspapers, stock market reports, airline and hotel reservation services, sports news, movie and book reviews, gourmet recipes, foreign language drills, and video catalogs for shopping by computer. Students, researchers, businesses, and private investors all can benefit from using an information service. As the information needs of our society increase, information services will play an important role in fulfilling those needs.

ELECTRONIC BULLETIN BOARD
A smaller, user-run version of the commercial information services, offered at little or no cost to users.

Electronic Bulletin Boards   Computer users also can access **electronic bulletin boards,** which are operated by computer enthusiasts and can be accessed at little or no cost. The thousands of bulletin boards in operation across the United States are used primarily for the exchange of information or programs. People who call a bulletin board may want to try one of the many programs stored on the system. They can also post messages for other users. This option is helpful for finding buyers and sellers for hardware, locating user groups in other communities, and getting evaluations of new software packages.

A bulletin board can be started by practically anyone who has a telephone, a microcomputer, a modem, and communications software. Electronic bulletin boards often are set up for users of a particular computer system, for example, IBM computers. Some bulletin boards are set up for users with special interests rather than for owners of particular computers. For example, there are bulletin boards for writers, lawyers, and pilots. Others have been created to help people research events or to conduct informal polls on political issues.

LOCAL AREA NETWORK
A specialized network of computers and peripherals which operates within a limited geographic area, such as a building or complex of buildings.

Local Area Networks   **Local area networks (LANs)** link computers in the same general area for the purpose of sharing information and hardware (see Figure 6-5). Usually the computers are within 1,000 feet of each other, because they must be connected by a cable hookup, which can be expensive. People at the work stations in a LAN gain more capabilities in word processing, data processing, information retrieval, and communication without duplication of equipment, databases, and activities. LANs are just starting to become popular. Many businesses are installing LANs in order to improve the efficiency of office functions and to facilitate office automation.

Figure 6-5
Local Area Network
Local area networks will continue to gain popularity because of the explosion in microcomputer use in businesses. Portable microcomputers with LAN capability may represent the wave of the future.

Learning Check

1. Name some common communication channels.

2. What function do modems perform, and in what two ways must they conform to the party being accessed?

3. What four items are needed for telecommunications applications?

4. How do information services and bulletin boards differ?

5. What is a LAN, and what purpose does it serve?

Answers

1. Telegraph lines, telephone lines, microwave links, coaxial cables, communication satellites, fiber optic cables. 2. Modems prepare signals for analog transmission. They must be in the same mode and speed as the connecting party. 3. Computer, telephone or telephone lines, communication software. 4. Information services are commercial and charge a fee; they contain large databases. Bulletin boards are usually free and offer specialized information. 5. Local area network; lets users in the same general area share data and hardware.

Automation

Just mentioning the word automation often is enough to start a group of people arguing about the impact of office automation and robotics on jobs. The current availability of robots and electronic office machines makes the argument seem mere rhetoric; automation is here to stay. Automation, with appropriate human intervention, has helped improve operations in offices and manufacturing plants.

The Electronic Office

The office environment is changing rapidly due to developments in communications, information storage and retrieval, and software. Organizations realize that computer technology is efficient, cost effective, and necessary to handle the information revolution. The increasing amount of reporting required by governmental agencies in particular lends itself to computer technology in the office.

Nearly every office function—typing, bookkeeping, billing, filing, and communications—can be done electronically. Among the specific applications are word processing, electronic mail, teleconferencing, telecommuting, and information retrieval. The term applied to the processes that integrate computer and communication technology with traditional office procedures is **office automation** (see Figure 6-6).

OFFICE AUTOMATION
Integration of computer and communication technology with traditional office procedures in order to increase productivity and efficiency in the office.

WORD PROCESSING
The use of computer equipment in preparing text; involves typing, writing, editing, and/or printing.

Word Processing   The most widely adopted office automation technology is **word processing.** An estimated 75 percent of U.S. companies employ some form of word processing, which provides a mechanism for preparing text and bypasses

Figure 6-6
Typical Environment of an
Automated Office

Figure 6-7
Optical Character Recognition Used
for Text Input

OPTICAL CHARACTER
RECOGNITION (OCR)
A method of electronic scanning
which reads numbers, letters, and
other characters and then converts
the optical images into appropriate
electrical signals.

the shortcomings of traditional writing and typing. Like data processing, word processing relieves workers of time-consuming and routine tasks, thereby increasing standards of productivity and quality. It is estimated that, depending on how much typing a secretary does, his or her productivity can be increased by 25 to 200 percent using word processing.

A typical word processing system consists of a computer, keyboard, a visual display device, a storage unit, a printer, and word processing software. A word processing program produces finished copy quickly, in a form that is readable and attractive. The user can edit, rearrange, insert, and delete material electronically until the text is exactly as it should be. Then the text is stored on tape or disk and later printed using a high-quality daisy-wheel printer, laser printer, or draft quality dot-matrix printer. If many form letters must be produced, the secretary has only to type the letter once. When the letter is merged with a file containing names and addresses, an original and personalized letter can be sent to each recipient. Word processing is discussed further in Part II of this text.

The efficiency of a word-processing system can be increased with the addition of an **optical character recognition (OCR)** device (see Figure 6-7). With an OCR scanner, typewritten pages can be read into the computer—a process that saves considerable input time compared to manual retyping. The average operator types text at a rate of 60 words per minute of prepared copy, whereas an OCR can input the same prepared copy at more than 1,000 words per minute. Only the editing needs to be done at the processor's keyboard. OCR scanning relieves a company of some of the expense involved in training operators to use a word processor.

Electronic Mail In large corporations, many messages are exchanged among the members of the organization. Many businesses are using **electronic mail** in order to speed up delivery of the messages and to reduce telephone, paper, and

ELECTRONIC MAIL
Transmission of messages at high speeds over communication channels.

duplicating costs. Electronic mail is the transmission of text at high speeds over telecommunication facilities. It is often used for intercompany communication, and can occur over the company's own communication system or via commercial electronic mail services such as Western Union (EasyLink) and GTE Telenet (Telemail).

The simplest form of computer-based mail system allows one user of the service to send a message to another by placing it in a special storage area in the electronic system. The second user, at his or her own convenience, retrieves the message by printing it on paper or on his or her display screen. The mail can be duplicated, revised, incorporated into other documents, passed along to new recipients, or filed like any other document in the system.

TELECONFERENCE
A meeting that occurs via telephone, electronic, and/or image-producing facilities, thereby eliminating the need for travel.

Teleconferencing   Office communications can be facilitated by another development in electronic technology—**teleconferencing.** Teleconferencing enables people in different geographical locations to participate in a meeting (see Figure 6-8). Satellite technology has enabled corporations with offices in different countries to take advantage of teleconferencing. Businesses can benefit from reduction in travel time and travel costs.

The most basic form of conducting electronic meetings, audio conferencing, consists of a conference call linking three or more people. Ideal for impromptu meetings, audio conferencing requires no major equipment investment, but it is limited to voice communication. Other forms of teleconferencing allow the transmission of graphics onto visual display screens, or one-way and two-way full-motion video involving cameras or picture phones. Teleconferences using video are expensive, and few organizations are willing or able to spend the millions of dollars required to install and upgrade the necessary equipment.

TELECOMMUTE
To work at home and communicate with the office or send data to the office via electronic machines and telecommunications facilities.

Telecommuting   An exciting aspect of the electronic office involves **telecommuting**—commuting to the office by computer rather than in person (see Figure 6-9). Telecommuting offers advantages in cities where office rent is high and mass transit systems or parking facilities are inadequate, and in businesses that do not require frequent face-to-face meetings among office workers. It also has appeal for people with special needs: disabled employees, employees temporarily homebound with injuries or illnesses, parents of young children, pregnant women, retirees who want to remain involved in the work world, and anyone tired of fighting traffic and dressing for success. Many people who telecommute spend one or two days a week at the office to take care of details that require a personal appearance.

Figure 6-8   Videoconference
A videoconference can often save money for corporations that depend on frequent meetings between people at distant branches.

Salespeople and journalists, who are often away from their offices, have already successfully used telecommuting. They type their assignments on portable computers equipped with modems, and then send information over telephone lines to the office. Some companies, such as Blue Cross and Blue Shield of Columbia, South Carolina, have experimented with telecommuting by hiring workers who process claims at home on personal computers. The data then is transmitted to the company's central computers.

Being such a radical departure from past practices, telecommuting is not universally approved. Many employees are not sure they have the discipline to work as well at home as they do in office surroundings. They miss the social interaction of the office and wonder if they will lose out on promotions. Managers fear they

Figure 6-9 Telecommuting
One futurist, Jack M. Nilles, Director of Interdisciplinary Programs at the University of Southern California, estimates that by 1990, 15 to 20 percent of American workers will work from their homes by telecommuting.

will lose control over employees who are out of sight. In addition, labor unions oppose telecommuting; they say telecommuting will trigger an age of electronic sweatshops, with clerical workers receiving piecework wages without any benefits. They also object to "farming out" electronic data entry to workers in countries where labor costs are low, a practice that results in fewer jobs in the United States.

Information Retrieval The final but integral aspect of office automation is information retrieval—getting stored information to users in a form they can understand. In the past, users often had to look through entire reports to locate the information they needed. Now they can use an electronic file management system and avoid this expensive and time-consuming chore. Database management and text management systems allow direct access to company information. The information may be in the form of data, text, images, or voice. The user specifies key words and asks the computer to search for these words in large volumes of text. The computer produces lists telling where the key words appear, and the user assembles the appropriate information in a form he or she can use.

Information retrieval is not limited to sources or files inside a company. Companies also may subscribe to commercial information services, such as CompuServe Inc. or the Dow Jones/Retrieval Service in order to keep up to date on marketing trends, technology, and other important information. Access to commercial services allows workers to obtain information quickly.

Automation in Manufacturing

The computer revolution has done much to increase productivity in industry. Manufacturing, which involves designing and building products, requires extensive planning and scheduling. Computers can help manufacturers handle the routine

HIGHLIGHT ▲▲▲▲▲▲▲▲▲▲▲▲▲▲▲▲▲▲▲▲▲▲▲▲

Desktop Publishing

Is your organization still putting out the same old tired mimeographed in-house newsletter? Well, groan no more. With the use of special software and the new less-expensive laser printers, your organization can produce a snappy, professional-looking newsletter. (That's assuming, of course, that the artist laying out the pages has a good sense of graphic design.)

Arthur Young, one of the "Big Eight" accounting firms, is one company that is taking advantage of desktop publishing. Pamela Davidson, editor of the company's

Micro Newsletter, has spiffed up the publication by using products such as the Macintosh microcomputer, Apple LaserWriter, and Aldus Corporation's PageMaker software. She no longer shells out $79 a page for typesetting and additional charges for pasteup, but instead completes writing and layout in her office. Once the pages are printed on the LaserWriter, they are sent to a commercial printer to be reproduced in quantity.

Although the LaserWriter produces only 300 dots to the inch compared to the 2,000 dots per inch

of professional typesetting equipment, it sure looks a lot better than mimeographed copy. And with the proper software, an editor can design a classy banner for the newsletter, use different fonts and type sizes, right-justify text, lay out multiple columns on one page, and print art on the same page as text. She can even use scanning equipment to digitize photographs for reproduction. Take that, you old mimeographed rag, you!

SOURCE: "New Flash for the Company Newsletter," Michael Antonoff, *Personal Computing,* October, pp. 52–61.

scheduling of inventory, machinery, and labor, and they can automate the assembly line.

MATERIALS REQUIREMENT PLANNING (MRP)
A computerized method of inventory control which involves entering data into a computer and receiving a report based on the data.

Materials Requirement Planning   Inventory control can be handled by a complex system called **materials requirement planning (MRP).** This system consists of programs that enable the manufacturer to enter projected demands and other data into a computer, and to receive reports that list the manufacturing schedule and raw materials needed to make a product that meets those demands. When the blocks of programs are tied together with purchasing and financial applications, such as cost accounting and accounts receivable, they enable a manufacturer to control the entire plant operation.

COMPUTER-INTEGRATED MANUFACTURING (CIM)
An arrangement that links departments within an organization to a central database for greater efficiency in the manufacturing process.

Computer-Integrated Manufacturing   For great savings and efficient operations, manufacturers can tie together design, manufacturing, scheduling, and monitoring functions in a process called **computer-integrated manufacturing (CIM).** CIM is an attempt to connect various departments within a company into a central database. The CIM database can help management run a more coordinated, efficient operation, from raw materials to completed product.

In the United States, no plants currently have a company-wide CIM program. Some operations do employ the CIM concept in certain areas, however. To be successful, CIM requires a long-term commitment from management. Companies experimenting with CIM include Boeing, General Motors, and General Electric. Boeing has saved $2.8 million annually by using CIM to link certain design and manufacturing operations, and GE has found that CIM is most successful when implemented in a step-by-step plan.

ROBOTICS
The science dealing with the construction, capabilities, and applications of robots.

Robotics   A new class of workers is being called upon to perform undesirable work in businesses all over the world. During the 1960s, these workers were assigned simple jobs such as spot welding and spray painting. By the 1980s, their duties were much more complex. They began handling nuclear wastes, moving materials, and mining for coal. These workers are the steel-collar workers, better known as robots.

Robotics is the science that deals with robots, including their construction, capabilities, and applications. Most robots are used for performing tedious, dangerous, or otherwise undesirable work in factories. A typical robot is anchored to a stationary base on the factory floor (see Figure 6-10). It consists of a mobile arm ending in some sort of viselike grip, claw, or other tool that performs the desired task. A second generation of robots possesses tactile sense and crude vision. These robots can "feel" how tightly they are gripping an object and "see" whether there are obstacles in their path. The combination of touch-sensitive grippers and computerized vision has created a robot capable of reaching into a bin of mixed parts, finding a certain object, and picking it up. These actions may sound simple, but they involve a complex series of judgments and movements. Collectively, these robots are called bin-picking robots.

American factories have over 6,000 robots at work; the auto industry is the largest single user of robots in this country. The number of robots in factories is expected to increase rapidly, reaching 150,000 by 1990. General Motors, General Electric, and Westinghouse currently are three leading users of industrial robots. They use steel-collar workers for performing standard jobs such as spot welding and spray painting, as well as more complex jobs such as fitting light bulbs into the dashboards of cars, sorting objects, and assembling electronic parts. Robots also can operate machines, such as stamping mills and electric saws, which otherwise could maim careless workers.

Figure 6-10   Robotics
Robots anchored to the factory floor do routine but often dangerous welding jobs.

Robots operate faster and more efficiently than humans, working around the clock without becoming tired or bored. They do not get hungry or sick or join a union. Robots range in price from $7,500 to $150,000 and have an average lifespan of about eight years. They cost about $5 per hour, whereas human workers might command $20 per hour. Unlike human workers, however, robots lack common sense and may continue making errors that human workers would recognize immediately.

Learning Check

1. What does the term office automation encompass?
2. Name one advantage of word processing.
3. Name two ways of automating communications in an office.
4. What groups of people might need telecommunications?
5. Name two processes that aid in the efficient operation of a manufacturing plant.

Answers

1. It involves using data processing equipment in performing most office functions, including word processing, communications, and information retrieval. 2. It allows a document to be prepared once, personalized for specific circumstances, and printed as an original copy as many times as desired. 3. Electronic mail; teleconferencing. 4. Some examples are disabled employees, parents with small children at home, pregnant women, and retirees who still want some work. 5. Materials requirement planning (MRP); computer-integrated manufacturing (CIM).

Electronic Monitoring

The electronic age has produced many kinds of equipment for use in monitoring chemical and nuclear plants, combustion engine emissions, body functions, air traffic, and many other factors. This section discusses the ways in which computerized monitoring equipment has benefited scientists, physicians, patients, and the general public by maintaining constant vigilance over the changing conditions of our lives.

Monitoring in Science Laboratories

Because of the enormous volumes of data that must be stored and processed for some scientific tasks, scientists use large computers to handle the data and to produce output in a form that is easy to read and interpret. Often these tasks involve monitoring the environment.

Some monitoring requires instantaneous calculations and results. Because the computer can give results in real time—quickly enough to affect the outcome of a situation—computer technology appears in the chemical industry and in nuclear power plants. Immediate awareness of problems in these areas is crucial. For example, a crisis such as the one that occurred at the Three Mile Island nuclear power plant, where the temperature of the nuclear reactor exceeded safe limits and threatened to melt down the core, may be avoided in the future with emergency management systems. The life-endangering gas leak at the Union Carbide plant in Bhopal, India, might have been prevented with computerized warning systems.

An emergency management system developed by Form & Substance, Inc., of Westlake Village, California, was designed for the chemical industry. It contains information such as the properties of the chemicals manufactured at a particular plant site, evaporation rates of the chemicals, the influence of the surrounding land on wind patterns and flow, and backup plans for possible accident situations. The computerized data bank is constantly updated with information supplied by chemical sensors around the plant. These sensors keep track of temperature, toxin levels, and wind velocity and direction (see Figure 6-11). In the event of an emergency, the system supplies instructions and appropriate emergency telephone numbers. Nearby residents are warned automatically through a prerecorded telephone message. While the residents are being warned by the computer, the necessary plant personnel are free to work with civil defense people and to mobilize resources within the plant itself.

Chemical plants are not the only places where emergency management systems are used. The Federal Nuclear Regulatory Commission now requires such systems in nuclear power plants. Although an emergency management system does not guarantee that a crisis can be resolved, it will make emergency evacuation and response much more efficient.

The use of computerized monitoring equipment enables scientists to spend valuable time conducting experiments rather than overseeing the instruments. For

Figure 6-11
Emergency Management System
The SAFER system (left) is an emergency response system that alerts industrial companies to toxic releases that could pose potential harm to the employees and neighboring area. The system displays actions to take in a variety of emergency situations. The display frame (right) illustrates the essential graphic information helpful in an emergency situation.

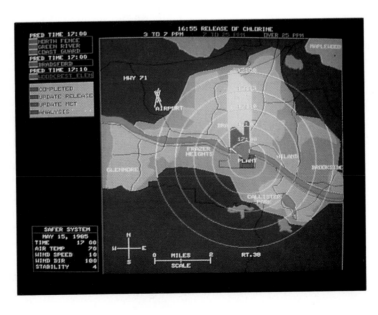

example, computers reduce both the time and cost involved in the study of cells at the California Institute of Technology in Pasadena. Deoxyribonucleic acid (DNA) is a chemical that carries genetic information in human cells. Strands of DNA formerly were synthesized (cloned) by a manual process that took weeks and sometimes months, and cost from $2,000 to $3,000. A computer can perform the same task in less than a day for only $2 to $3! Because the manual procedure involves much repetition, it was easy for technicians to make mistakes. Once the task was turned over to a computer, the mistakes were eliminated and the procedure became more economical.

Another application of scientific instruments involves volcano monitoring. The May 1980 eruption of Mount St. Helens in the state of Washington was predicted by scientists with the help of data analyzed by computers. Devices such as tilt-meters, which show trends in the tilt of the crater floor, and seismometers, which measure harmonic tremors around the volcano, sent data to a laboratory in Vancouver, Washington, every 10 minutes. In the laboratory, computers analyzed the data, thereby helping scientists predict volcanic activity. Because instruments like these are located inside the volcano, volcanic eruptions can be predicted within 30 minutes, so that scientists working near and on the volcano can be evacuated quickly by helicopter. One aspect that cannot yet be predicted, however, is the fury of the eruption and the extent of the mudflow created by the eruption. Mount St. Helens, one of the most extensively monitored volcanos in the world, surprised scientists with the heavy mud flow that followed its eruption.

Monitoring the Human Body

New uses for computers in medicine are emerging daily, while other uses are being improved. Computers have increased the quality of nursing care and the efficiency of monitoring systems. For example, only a few years ago, round-the-clock nursing care was needed for individual critically ill patients. Now computer-controlled machines can monitor life support systems in the intensive care and coronary care units of any hospital. These machines inform doctors and nurses about a patient's vital signs such as heartbeat, blood pressure, respiration, temperature, and pulse. The display for each patient on a monitoring system is shown on a terminal or screen at a nurse's station, so one nurse can oversee many patients rather than just one. When a problem occurs, an alarm is sounded automatically by the computer, and the nurse can initiate appropriate emergency treatment. Besides providing accurate and current information, many of the monitoring systems store data about the patients, which can be retrieved for later study by specialists.

Computer use for intensive care also extends to neonatal units, which specialize in the care of premature and sick newborn babies. In the neonatal unit at New York Hospital, each incubator is equipped with a video screen and keypad. Using the computers, nurses enter and retrieve information needed for treating the infants. Meanwhile, two Hewlett-Packard computers constantly monitor the heartbeat, respiration, and blood pressure of the babies (see Figure 6-12).

Advances in electronic technology have improved implantable monitoring systems for the human body, such as pacemakers. Originally, pacemakers used transistors in controlling the heartbeat. These devices could stimulate the heart only

Figure 6-12
Neonatal Monitoring
Computers are used to monitor infants in neonatal intensive care units.

at fixed pulse rates, even though a healthy heart beats at varying rates. In addition, early pacemakers were heavy, weighing almost 7 ounces. Today's contain microprocessors that enable doctors to enter up to thirty separate functions, such as delay between pulses, pulse width, and energy output per pulse. In this way, a pacemaker can be programmed to deal with a patient's particular heart problems. More sophisticated pacemakers can store heart performance data for retrieval by the physician (see Figure 6-13).

Figure 6-13
Symbios Pacemaker System by Medtronics

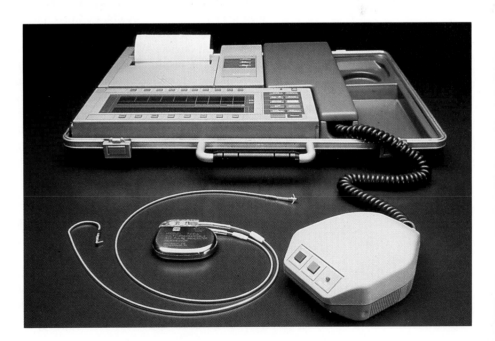

Figure 6-14
The Itrel Spinal Cord Stimulation System This implantable spinal cord stimulator is used for management of chronic, intractable pain. It produces electrical signals that block pain messages traveling to the brain. The stimulator can be programmed at a console or with a hand held programmer.

Another application using microprocessors, still in the experimental stages, involves the controlled release of medication by devices implanted in the body (see Figure 6-14). One device currently undergoing testing is called PIMS (Programmable Implantable Medicine System). PIMS is a 3-inch computer that is programmed to release measured doses of a drug over time. When a drug is taken orally, once or twice a day, it is distributed throughout the whole body; often only a small amount of the drug reaches the correct organ. Also, the amount of the drug present in the bloodstream varies over time as each dose is administered. PIMS and other similar devices are designed to overcome these problems. One experimental device, which is being tested by diabetic patients, dispenses a 40-day supply of insulin from a refillable reservoir using a miniature pump. The reservoir can be refilled with a hypodermic needle. Radiotelemetry and a desktop computer console enable doctors to reprogram the rate at which the pump dispenses medicine. A diabetic's blood sugar level can be monitored closely, and the precise amount of insulin needed can be released into the body. The device has the potential of eliminating some of the life-threatening side effects of diabetes.

The Automated Home

A microcomputer can be dedicated to one particular job, or several microcomputers together can be used for handling many functions in the home. In Arizona, for example, a computer-controlled house has been built as a showcase of home monitoring systems. Called Ahwatukee (a Crow Indian word meaning "house of dreams"), this house is described as the state of the art in technology, ecology, and sociology. Visitors come by the thousands each month to view the house in a half-hour tour.

HIGHLIGHT ▲▲▲▲▲▲▲▲▲▲▲▲▲▲▲▲▲▲▲▲▲▲▲

Nan Davis's New Venture

You may remember reading about Nan Davis and Dr. Jerrold Petrofsky. Nan Davis is the St. Marys, Ohio, woman who in 1982 was the first paraplegic to walk in Petrofsky's laboratory at Wright State University. Her feat was made possible by a walking system that combined computer-controlled electrical stimulation with a lightweight brace and electrically conductive clothing. Since then, the electronic walking system has been improved by the addition of a mechanical backup, a smaller "power pack," and a reduction in the number of individual wires.

By walking, Nan Davis experiences a reduction in the demineralization of bone and an improvement in circulation, both concerns for people confined to wheelchairs. Davis and Petrofsky are involved in an exercise program at Middletown Regional Hospital for people with spinal cord injuries, and Davis is the administrative director of the program.

The program is the first clinical application of therapy that uses a computer for stimulating muscles, thus enabling paraplegics and quadriplegics to exercise their paralyzed limbs. Participants will exercise on a computerized stationary bicycle about 30 minutes per day, three times a week. At the end of their three- to six-week therapy periods, they will purchase the equipment and continue the program at home. In addition to promoting circulation and bone strength, the exercise promotes aerobic conditioning and muscle development. All these benefits serve to help the patients feel healthier, become more independent, and have a better body image.

Five microcomputers are linked to run the five systems in the house. Heating, cooling, and the opening and shutting of doors and windows are the primary functions of the environmental control system. The security system protects against intruders with the use of television cameras, sensors, and a password-controlled front door. The sensors also watch for fire and sound a warning if necessary. An electrical switching system uses sensors to note people moving through the house

Learning Check

1. What is real time, and why is it important to monitoring systems?

2. Name one example of monitoring in science laboratories.

3. Name three uses of monitoring equipment in the medical field.

4. How can monitoring equipment be used in a home?

Answers

1. The term real time describes a situation in which results are received quickly enough to affect the outcome of an event. It is important in monitoring systems because some of these systems are used in situations that could quickly become dangerous to humans and their surroundings. 2. Computer equipment is used for monitoring volcanos. 3. Monitoring life support systems in intensive care units; controlling heart beats; administering correct amounts of medications. 4. To save energy and detect intruders.

and adjusts the lights appropriately. Cost-efficient use of electricity is ensured by the energy management system, and an information storage and retrieval system is provided for personal or home business needs.

Less elaborate systems are available for just about any home user. Among these systems are TomorrowHouse from Compu-Home Systems International in Denver, Colorado; Waldo from Artra Corporation in Arlington, Virginia; and HomeBrain from HyperTeck, Inc., in Whitehouse, New Jersey. Systems such as the ones just named regulate energy consumption, ventilation, and appliance use. Using sensor devices, computers can control the temperatures in all rooms, raise shades, activate switches, and turn on security lights. Some systems are designed to dial the police if a break-in occurs, and turn on a video camera that monitors the area of break-in.

Number Crunching

Computers are very good at number crunching, that is, performing large and complex calculations in a matter of seconds or minutes. Especially in scientific research, weather predictions, and business forecasting, researchers appreciate the number-crunching capabilities of computers. Computers make mathematical calculations and projections in seconds which human beings could not complete unaided in months. Computers gather, compile, and sift statistics to determine similarities and differences that are not apparent to humans. In addition, computers can generate models and make projections without the subjectivity that humans inevitably bring to such tasks. The following sections demonstrate how computers help in making large and complex calculations.

Simulation and Modeling

SIMULATION
Representation of conditions likely to occur in a real-life situation when variables are changed.

MODELING
The process of developing a prototype or mathematical representation of an idea or object in order to design and test it.

EXPERT SYSTEM
Software that uses a base of knowledge in a field of study for decision making and evaluation processes similar to those of human experts in that field.

In science, computers are used for simulating and modeling tasks. The computer is programmed to consider certain facts, which are stored in memory, and then make a decision. The computer makes **simulations** by duplicating the conditions likely to occur when certain variables are changed in a given situation. In the chemistry lab, chemical reactions can be simulated on a computer. One advantage of this type of simulation is that explosive or otherwise dangerous reactions can be discovered without endangering the chemist or destroying the laboratory.

In computer **modeling,** the computer constructs a mathematical model or an image of a prototype of some object on the video screen. Shapes and sizes can be changed easily to alter the model. Computer models are used in many fields, such as astronomy, ecology, engineering, and chemistry. Engineers and designers of airplanes, for example, usually design parts of an aircraft on a computer before building a real model. Many bugs can be worked out on the computer, thus saving considerable time and money.

Some simulations and modeling systems are referred to as **expert systems,** because they plot the best course of action using the same information that experts in a field would use. For example, computer systems programmed to contain the knowledge of geological experts are used to assist oil companies. These systems examine geological data and advise the companies where to drill. Usually, an instrument called a dipmeter is dropped down a hole to measure geological conditions. Human specialists qualified to read the dipmeter are scarce; however, computer expert systems can replace the specialist and dipmeter, and have proven to be almost as successful as the traditional method in determining where to drill for oil.

Weather Predictions

The forecasting of weather is one of the most interesting applications of computers. Several variables, such as air pressure, wind velocity, humidity, and temperature, are fed into huge computers that are programmed to solve complex mathematical equations. These equations describe the interaction of these meteorological variables, thus enabling forecasters to predict the weather and study hurricanes and tornadoes.

The world's weather information is collected by the National Weather Service in Maryland from a variety of locations: hundreds of data-collecting programs (DCPs) placed on buoys, ships, weather balloons, and airplanes; about 70 weather stations; and four satellites (see Figure 6-15). Two of the satellites orbit the earth over the poles to send pictures revealing the movement and shape of clouds. The other two satellites are in stationary orbits above the equator.

The Weather Service's "brain" consists of fourteen computers housed at the meteorological center. These computers receive information from some of the DCPs, whose data is beamed up to the two "stationary" satellites above the equator. The computers also receive information from other DCPs; this information

Figure 6-15
Weather Forecasting
This meteorologist is using Centralized Storm Information System to forecast severe weather across the United States.

travels from ground station to ground station. The fourteen computers use all of this incoming data to construct a mathematical description of the atmosphere. These weather reports—2,000 daily—are sent to local weather offices. Manual processing of this amount of data would take so much time that the results would not be available until the weather conditions had already occurred!

Business Forecasting

Although most business computations can be handled by general accounting software, more complex calculations often are needed in order to help businesses make wise investment decisions. Linear algebra often is used in making business forecasts and preparing schedules for production. A computer aids the businessperson in performing these complex mathematical tasks.

ELECTRONIC SPREADSHEET
An electronic grid, or table, used for storing and manipulating any type of numerical data.

Perhaps the most common use of the computer in financial analysis involves the **electronic spreadsheet.** A spreadsheet is a large grid divided into rows and columns. Spreadsheets are used for designing budgets, recording sales, producing profit-and-loss statements, and performing general accounting and bookkeeping. Although electronic spreadsheets are useful in many areas of business, nowhere are they more helpful than in financial analysis, or forecasting, which determines profit margins, sales, and long-term strategies. The reason for the great impact of the electronic spreadsheet in this area is its ability to answer "What if?" questions quickly and accurately. The spreadsheet does this by recalculating all figures when one or two variables are changed.

For example, if the financial analyst for a jeans manufacturer wants to see how a change in the cost of fabric would affect the financial status of the company, he or she could simply enter the expected costs into the computer. Using an electronic spreadsheet, the computer would quickly recalculate all figures that would be affected by the changed costs, such as the cost to manufacture the jeans and the profit. In very little time, the financial analyst could see how profits would go up or down. Spreadsheets are discussed in detail in Part II of this text.

Graphics

Probably the most familiar use of computer graphics is readily seen on television and motion picture screens. Artists use computers for preparing sports logos, commercials, animated cartoons, and science fiction films. There are many other products of computer graphics, however, including pictures generated from data collected by Landsat satellites; pictures of the insides of our bodies used for medical diagnosis; designs for automobiles and airplane wings; business graphics; and graphics that help analyze dance and exercise motions.

Pictures of Our Earth

Landsat satellites launched by NASA orbit the earth and collect approximately 30,000 overlapping pictures to provide a view of the whole earth. These pictures

Figure 6-16   Landsat
From 570 miles above Tokyo, Japan, this computer-generated Landsat picture defines subtle details in surface geology. Urban areas appear in light blue, Tokyo Bay appears in dark blue, and land under cultivation appears in red.

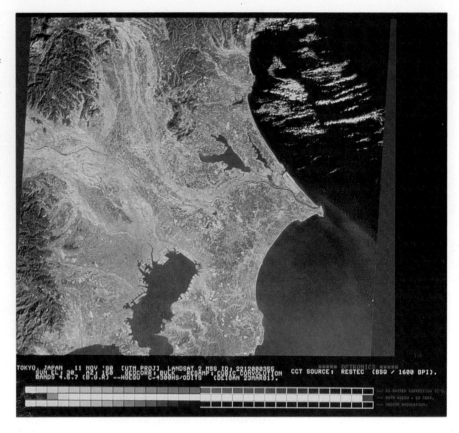

are recorded as digitized electronic pulses, which are broadcast to a ground receiving station. Once received, the data is entered in computer memory and translated into photographs that scientists study (see Figure 6-16). Light patterns and infrared radiation from the sun, which is reflected by the earth, appear on the Landsat pictures and can be detected by the computer. Areas of healthy and sick vegetation can be identified by examining the infrared radiation patterns.

Because the photographs do not show Earth in the same hues that we perceive in our natural environment, they must be enhanced by color. A special color scheme has been adopted: A photograph with red areas indicates healthy vegetation, such as forests and wheat fields, because plants emit high levels of infrared radiation. Areas with a dense human population emit low levels of infrared and are shown as a grayish-blue color. The results of this NASA venture are available to 130 countries. Experts examine the colors and tints to detect mineral deposits, urban areas, and regions of insect infestation or droughts. Landsat photos can even help pick out the best locations for oil drilling.

Graphic Computer-Assisted Diagnosis

Computers often are combined with testing equipment to provide diagnostic tools in hospitals and clinics. Two common diagnostic tools—computerized axial to-

Figure 6-17
CAT Scan Image
A technician studies the image
produced by a CAT scan, which will
help diagnose a medical problem.

**COMPUTERIZED AXIAL
TOMOGRAPHY (CT or CAT)**
**A form of noninvasive physical
testing that combines X-ray
techniques and computers to aid
diagnosis.**

**NUCLEAR MAGNETIC
RESONANCE (NMR) SCANNING**
**A computerized diagnostic tool that
involves sending magnetic pulses
through the body in order to
identify medical problems.**

mography and nuclear magnetic resonance scanning—use graphics in noninvasive (nonsurgical) testing techniques.

Computerized axial tomography (CAP or CT), commonly known as the CAT scan, is a diagnostic aid that joins two tools: X-rays and computerized evaluations of X-ray pictures. A CAT scan can provide clear pictures of cross sections of the body, whereas ordinary X-rays cannot. Using many cross sections together, it is possible for a CAT scan to make a three-dimensional composite of an organ or bone (see Figure 6-17). Computerized axial tomography often is used to assist doctors in reconstructive surgery, because one of the primary concerns in this type of surgery is how the patient will look afterward. Computer-generated pictures can predict the results of reconstructive surgery.

Nuclear magnetic resonance (NMR) scanning may soon replace the CAT scan in hospitals. Unlike X-ray tests or CAT scans, NMR can "see" through thick bones. Moreover, NMR works without radiation. Magnetic pulses sent through the body react differently when they come into contact with different parts of the body. A computer is used to collect the results and to create a detailed picture of the inside of the body. Often NMR scanning is more successful in detecting problems than CAT scanning. Since the procedure does not use radiation, it can be used for testing small children and pregnant women. There are some drawbacks to NMR scanning, however. For example, it does not produce clear images of bones or spot breast cancer.

Both CAT scans and NMR scans enable doctors to conduct tests and make a diagnosis without invading the body through surgery. This approach prevents the patient from having to undergo unnecessary risks associated with surgery, such as infections and fatigue.

CAD/CAM

**COMPUTER-AIDED DESIGN
(CAD)**
The process of designing, drafting,
and analyzing a prospective product
using computer graphics on a video
terminal.

**COMPUTER-AIDED
MANUFACTURING (CAM)**
The use of a computer to simulate
or monitor the steps of a
manufacturing process.

Before a product can be produced, it must be designed. The actual design process can be quite time-consuming and costly. **Computer-aided design (CAD)** enables the engineer to design, draft, and analyze a new product idea using computer graphics on a video terminal (see Figure 6-18).

The designer, working with full-color three-dimensional graphics, can easily make changes so that the product can be tested before the first prototype is ever built. The model can be turned to expose any side or angle, and cross-sectional cuts show interior details on the display screen. The computer model also detects strengths and weaknesses of a product, such as unwanted vibrations on an airplane wing, before the first sample is ever built. A CAD system in the automobile industry can check the designs of automotive parts for poor tolerance between parts and for stress points. This can save a great deal of money by eliminating defective designs before money is spent on building them.

Computer-aided design often is coupled with **computer-aided manufacturing (CAM),** and the combination is known as CAD/CAM. Using CAD/CAM, an engineer can analyze not only the product but also the entire manufacturing process. Problems can be spotted and adjustments made before manufacturing is begun, thus saving the manufacturer large amounts of time and money.

Although CAD and CAM normally are associated with the design of vehicles, these processes also assist in the design and manufacture of artificial joints for humans. These joints are surgically implanted to replace defective joints. A system developed at New York's Hospital for Special Surgery uses a digital computer to read a patient's X-ray in three dimensions. The computer then creates an image on the computer screen of what the implant will look like. The computer includes in the design variables such as the patient's age, ambulatory (walking) condition, allergies, activity level, and other relevant details of the patient's medical history.

Figure 6-18   CAD

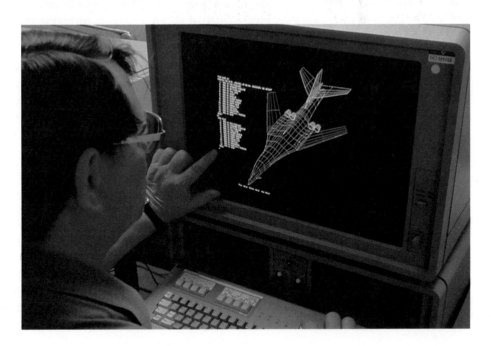

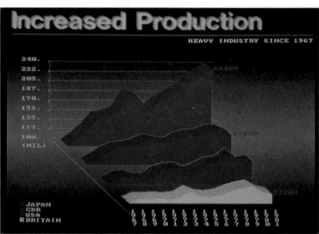

Figure 6-19
Business Graphics
Managers like graphics produced by a computer, such as this pie chart and bar chart, because they summarize information in an easy-to-understand, visual manner.

Business Graphics

Because computers make it so easy to generate and retrieve information, many managers find they suffer from information overload. It is well known in business circles that 80 percent of management decisions are based on 20 percent of the data, but that 20 percent must represent the core data. Finding the right data can be difficult for managers who are flooded with paper. Graphically displayed data helps facilitate decision making. Comparisons, relationships, trends, and essential points can be spotted more easily using graphics.

Business graphics have come a long way from the once-standard black line bar graph. Pie charts, bar graphs, and line and area graphs that are brightly colored and clearly marked can be especially effective in communicating core data (see Figure 6-19). Executives prefer receiving information through graphics because the graphics are attractive and can be understood quickly and easily.

Because these graphs play such a vital role in decision making, many software packages have been developed for use by business managers. The first graphics software package for microcomputers became available in 1979, and the popularity of business graphics software has been growing ever since. Business graphics are discussed in greater detail in Part II of this text.

Graphics for Analyzing Motion

BIOMECHANICS
The application of engineering methodologies to biological systems.

Cameras and computers can be used for analyzing performance in athletics and dance. This process is called **biomechanics.** Sports doctors and biomechanical engineers are creating hardware and software that will help athletes and dancers improve their performance (see Figure 6-20). For example, the Biomechanics and Computer Service Division of the Olympic Training Center, established in 1981, studies sports techniques and bodily stresses during competition. In one procedure, high-speed video cameras record an athlete in competition from two or more angles. The images recorded on video are digitized, and the results are stored in a computer. When these digitized spots are displayed on a computer screen frame by frame,

Figure 6-20   Biomechanics
This equipment in the sports physiology department at the U.S. Olympic Training Center is used to test strength and endurance.

lines connect the dots, creating stick figures that reveal details the human eye cannot see. In gymnastics, for example, the computer reveals exactly how high the athlete leaped, the velocity, and the angle of the arms. Athletes can view the computer screen and see just what they are doing incorrectly. Also, the computer can analyze the data from the digitized images and create graphs showing trends in style. Athletes often find the computer very helpful in improving their performance.

The science of biomechanics also aids dancers, by providing a way of recording dance movements. Traditionally, choreographers have used notation for describing the elaborate dance patterns, but these manual notation methods have not proven adequate and are laborious to perform. A computer graphic system, still in the experimental stage, can record dance by analyzing movements and translating the data into a moving human figure on a computer screen, to be studied and stored for later use. The system allows repetitive steps to be recalled so they do not have to be redrawn each time they are used. Also, the score can be edited instantly.

Education

In the early 1980s, computer experts predicted that there would be millions of microcomputers in schools by the middle of the decade. The experts may have overestimated the numbers somewhat (by the end of 1985 there were about 1,250,000 microcomputers in schools), but there has been steady growth in both the numbers and uses of computers in schools.

Computers also are used for educational purposes outside schools. Businesses and manufacturers are finding that computers help in training their employees, and students can use personal computers for taking college courses at home. In this section, we examine some of the ways computers are helping people to learn new skills and to be successful in school.

Computer Literacy

COMPUTER LITERACY
General knowledge about computers; includes technical knowledge, ability to use computers for problem solving, and awareness of how computers affect society.

The appearance of computers in schools is part of an overall educational plan known as **computer literacy.** Not everyone agrees on a definition of computer literacy, but most say computer literacy includes being able to use computers for solving problems and having a basic understanding of computer terminology and technology. Educators believe that computers will play an important part in our lives in the future. If people know how to use computers, they will be better prepared to cope with the changes that technology brings. Educators, parents, and students have seen the computerization of the workplace and realize that there is no turning back. Some form of computer education is necessary for increased chances of success on the job.

One problem with trying to define computer literacy in terms of specific objectives is that the objectives change constantly as the technology changes. Perhaps this point is best illustrated by reviewing the approach to computer literacy in schools during the past ten years. Early attempts at computer literacy focused on computer history, terminology, and internal operations. Although that information is still recognized as important, the focus has changed from how a computer works to how we can use a computer to help solve problems. In other words, the emphasis has moved from theory to applications. Literacy courses also examine the effect of computers on society, and include discussions on computer manners and ethics, in response to some forms of computer abuse.

Just as students need courses in computer literacy, all teachers need to have some computer training. To meet this need, teachers are attending classes, seminars, and workshops to learn about the new technology. In many classrooms, teachers also are learning from their students, to the surprise and delight of both parties.

Perhaps the hardest fact to accept in the area of computer training is that such education is never complete. The technology has not reached a plateau, and one is not expected soon. Whether the students are children, teachers, or business professionals, the learning process is ongoing. As the technology changes, the definition of computer literacy also changes, and the computer literate individual can never stop learning.

Programming

Computer literacy in some schools focuses on programming. In the past, BASIC has been the primary programming language in schools. Its English-like structure and interactive capabilities make it a good language for beginners. You may recall from Chapter 4, however, that some aspects of BASIC seem to encourage sloppy programming and thinking habits. The recent introduction of the version called

True BASIC offers a more structured style of programming, and one that computer educators find more acceptable for students. The BASIC language does not require the user to be proficient in complex mathematics to be used successfully.

Other popular languages for teaching programming skills are Pascal and Logo. Both emphasize structured programming, and help students develop programming habits encouraged in advanced programming courses in high school and college.

Computer-Assisted Instruction

COMPUTER-ASSISTED INSTRUCTION
The use of a computer to instruct or drill students on an individual or small-group basis.

When computers were first introduced in classrooms in the 1960s, they were used as teaching machines to drill multiplication tables, names of state capitals, and other facts to be memorized. Computers still teach material by repeated question-and-answer presentations of the information, but drills are just one form of **computer-assisted instruction (CAI)** (see Figure 6-21). Included in CAI is a wide selection of software, including the following:

■ Drills for quizzing the student. An example is Math Blaster!, which helps students learn arithmetic facts.
■ Tutorials for introducing students to new material and quizzing them on their understanding of the material. States and Traits, a program that teaches recognition, placement, and geography of the states in the U.S., is an example of a tutorial.
■ Simulations that imitate real-world situations, enabling students to learn through experience and induction without having to take actual risks. An example is Heart Lab, which helps students learn how the heart works.
■ Games for learning new concepts and practicing new skills. An example is Archon, an action-strategy chess program that promotes logical and strategic thinking.
■ Problem-solving software that encourages exploration and application of pre-

Figure 6-21   CAI

vious knowledge. An example is The King's Rule, which encourages the formation and testing of hypotheses, and recognition of patterns and relationships.

Studies have shown CAI to be a powerful learning tool that is particularly effective when used in certain situations. CAI is quite effective when used with either low- or high-achieving students. It is also an effective teaching tool for specific subjects, such as science, math, and foreign languages. CAI works best when used as a supplement to regular classroom instruction, and has been known to have a positive effect on the behavior and attitudes of students. Using computers, students learn at their own rates, receive immediate feedback, and feel comfortable with their impartial "teacher."

Although many good educational programs exist, much of the software advertised for educational use is unimaginative, poor in quality, and even inaccurate. Too often in the past, educators lacked the knowledge necessary to select appropriate software and to develop a comprehensive plan for its use. In addition, the early software was poorly designed because software publishers hurried to be the first to get their products on the markets, and educators had little choice beyond these inadequate packages.

Fortunately, the educational software picture has improved considerably in the last five years, and there are now some excellent packages on the market which are based on sound educational principles. Among these programs are Gertrude's Puzzles and Rocky's Boots, from The Learning Company; The Factory, a simulation program from Sunburst; The Oregon Trail, from the Minnesota Educational Consortium; In Search of the Most Amazing Thing, from Spinnaker Software; and Where in the World is Carmen Sandiego?, from Broderbund Software. Whatever the software chosen, educators need to spend time assessing their goals before selecting and buying a program.

Interactive Video

INTERACTIVE VIDEO
A multimedia learning concept that merges computer text, sound, and graphics by using a videodisk, videodisk player, microcomputer equipment, and software.

The combination of optical disks and computer programming has created a promising tool called **interactive video.** Some educators believe it will replace the computer, the instructional film, and perhaps even textbooks in many fields. Interactive video merges graphics and sound with computer-generated text by linking an optical disk (videodisk), a videodisk player, a microcomputer with a color monitor and disk drive, and computer software. Using this equipment, a person can watch news footage of historical events, learn about the most recent advances in science, and listen to the music of great composers or the speeches of famous people. The interactive process begins when the user responds to computer-generated questions and forms inquiries to input into the system. The videodisk can be accessed at a chosen point, and motion sequences can be shown in slow motion or still frame for observing critical details.

Videodisk technology will change the way we share information. As a student, you may receive a homework package consisting of software on a floppy disk and graphics on a videodisk to play on your equipment at home. As an employee, you could use the same technology for learning how to demonstrate new cars, trade shares on a stock exchange, or maintain and repair large earth-moving equipment. As a hobbyist, you could purchase a videodisk that contains the latest information about your avocation. Interactive video has become so attractive that some people believe the videodisk player will become the most important peripheral device of this decade. The technology will become even more appealing when disks are developed which can be erased and reused.

Networks

Besides using CAI, some schools allow students to access information utilities. Information services such as CompuServe and The Source provide a range of services from electronic mail to online encyclopedias and additional software. Students are able to access sources that are not found in local libraries and find the most current information on a topic. Using information services teaches new computer skills, too—how to gain access to stored data and transfer that data to the user's disks, for example. Once a communication system is set up, schools can link with other schools, thus enabling students to exchange games, newsletters, and student-written programs.

Special networks or services are available for students through ''electronic universities.'' In 1984, for example, the National Education Corporation (NEC) began offering a system called EdNET, which lets personal computer owners study at home. Over forty courses are available to independent-study participants. Students can correspond with instructional specialists as well as take tests via their home computers. Another company, TeleLearning Systems, Inc. of San Francisco, makes over two hundred courses available to home computer users through its Electronic University. Students enrolled in electronic courses must also purchase textbooks and any other required course materials.

Computers on Campus

In a typical dormitory room on a college or university campus, an observer would expect to find an assortment of books, notebooks, pens, pencils, and other traditional aids to learning. But a survey of college campuses and dormitory rooms in this country might also reveal a relatively new learning tool—the microcomputer (see Figure 6-22). Microcomputers are playing an important role in the college experience, as more and more schools are installing microcomputer laboratories and requiring students to purchase these machines.

New students at Dartmouth College are required to buy Apple Macintosh computers to use as freestanding computers and as terminals linked to the **timesharing** system. Drexel University students also must have access to a Macintosh, which means that most must buy the computers either through the university's purchasing plan or by their own means. Stevens Institute of Technology in Hoboken, New Jersey, requires all students to buy a DEC Pro350 computer with dual floppy disk drives and a 10-megabyte Winchester hard disk, with software, for $2100. Students at Dallas Baptist College in Texas carry 3-pound portable computers around campus for word processing, note taking, and computer literacy classes.

Students and professors are finding dozens of uses for these machines. One of the more popular applications for microcomputers is communication. Many schools are investigating the possibility of implementing campuswide networks, and a few already have networks in operation. A campus network offers students and faculty the opportunity to communicate via electronic mail and bulletin boards. Instructors can help students outside class and receive assignments via computer, and students can access online campus library catalogs from their dormitory rooms.

As students become comfortable with computer use in schools and on college

TIMESHARING
An arrangement in which two or more users can access the same central computer resources and receive apparently simultaneous results.

Figure 6-22
Microcomputers on Campus

campuses, computers will become less of a threat and more of a tool, to be used like a telephone, typewriter, or book.

Learning Check

1. Name three applications that take advantage of the number-crunching abilities of computers.

2. How have computer graphics aided in medical diagnosis?

3. How does CAD benefit an industry?

4. How do graphics overcome the problem of information overload for managers of businesses?

5. Name at least five objectives of computer literacy.

Answers

1. Simulations, weather predictions, business forecasting.   2. They allow testing by nonsurgical methods, such as CAT scans and nuclear magnetic resonance scanning.   3. CAD saves time and money involved in building prototypes of products, by allowing an engineer to design and test a product by computer.   4. They present core material in attractive graphs that are easy to read and understand.   5. Using computers for problem solving; learning about the impact of computers on society; discussing manners and ethics involved in computer use; learning computer terminology; learning how a computer works.

Summary Points

■ Data communication is the electronic transmission of data from one location to another, usually over communication channels such as telephone or telegraph lines, coaxial cables, or microwaves. The combined use of data processing equipment and communication facilities, such as telephone systems, is called telecommunications.

■ Telecommunications applications require the use of a computer, telephone or telephone lines, a modem, and communication software.

■ Modems are required for changing digital signals into signals compatible with the communication facilities. The modem must be able to handle the mode and speed of transmission used by the party or service being accessed.

■ Typical telecommunications applications include using information services and accessing electronic bulletin boards.

■ More and more businesses are linking computers and equipment in local area networks, thus enabling the users to share data and hardware.

■ Most office functions—typing, bookkeeping, billing, filing, and communications—can be performed electronically. Some specific computer applications are word processing, electronic mail, teleconferencing, telecommuting, and information retrieval.

■ Manufacturers can automate several aspects of their operations by using materials requirement planning software, the concept of computer-integrated manufacturing, and robotics.

■ Because the computer can provide instantaneous calculations and results, computer technology appears in areas such as the chemical industry, the environment, nuclear power plants, and medical monitoring, alerting people to problems in these areas.

■ Computers are used in intensive care, coronary care, and neonatal units for monitoring life support systems. Patients also benefit from computer monitoring systems if they must use pacemakers or programmable implantable medicine systems (PIMS).

■ Monitoring systems are also available for home use; they help in energy conservation and alert residents to problems such as break-ins.

■ The number-crunching capabilities of computers help scientists and engineers to create prototypes of ideas or objects, and to simulate conditions likely to occur when certain variables are changed in a given situation.

■ By combining data such as air pressure, wind velocity, humidity, and temperature with mathematical models, forecasters can predict the weather. This is accomplished with the help of fourteen computers at the National Weather Service.

■ Businesspeople benefit from the use of computers in figuring the complex and lengthy calculations required for business forecasting, which includes determination of profit margins, sales, and long-term strategies.

■ Landsat satellites launched by NASA orbit the earth and collect pictures to provide a view of the whole earth. Digitized electronic pulses broadcast to a ground receiving station are entered in computer memory and translated into photographs that scientists study.

■ Computerized axial tomography (CAT or CT), commonly known as the CAT scan, and nuclear magnetic resonance (NMR) scanning are diagnostic aids that use computer graphics to help physicians see the insides of our bodies without surgery.

■ Computer-aided design (CAD) is the process of designing, drafting, and analyzing a prospective product using computer graphics on a video terminal. Computer-aided manufacturing (CAM), often teamed with CAD, is the use of a computer to simulate or monitor the steps of a manufacturing process. These processes are used not only in the automotive and aircraft industries, but also in the design and manufacture of artificial joints.

■ Graphics such as bar charts, line graphs, and pie charts can help businesspeople see core material in an attractive form that is easy to read and understand. These graphics can be created quickly and neatly with the assistance of computer software developed especially for that purpose.

■ Graphics also can be used to analyze the motion of dancers and athletes to help improve performance. The term biomechanics describes the combination of computer graphics and biological systems for this type of analysis.

■ The term computer literacy has come to have many definitions, but generally it refers to a basic understanding of computer terminology, how a computer works, and how to use a computer to help solve problems. The objectives of computer literacy change constantly as the technology changes.

■ Computer-assisted instruction (CAI) is the use of a computer to instruct or drill students on an individual or small-group basis. Generally there are five kinds of CAI: drills, tutorials, simulations, games, and problem-solving software.

■ Students also can use computers with information services, electronic universities, and videodisks, to bring the outside world to their homes or schools.

■ Microcomputers are playing an increasingly important role on college campuses. Many colleges and universities are installing microcomputer laboratories and requiring students to purchase microcomputers. Some of their uses include communications, such as accessing library catalogs or exchanging messages and assignments.

Review Questions

1. Explain the role of each of the four elements required for telecommunications applications.

2. How have electronics and computers enhanced communication within a corporation?

3. Define at least four types of computer applications that help manufacturers deal with inventory, design, and manufacture of products.

4. List some applications in which the instantaneous calculations and results possible with computers can help avert a crisis.

5. Discuss some of the ways in which the emergency management system developed by Form & Substance, Inc., can effectively prevent a disaster. What are some possible problems with using emergency management systems?

6. Describe one application of monitoring equipment which frees scientists from routine tasks and enables them to spend valuable time conducting other experiments.

7. Name and explain five ways computers are being used in the diagnosis and treatment of patients.

8. Discuss how the National Weather Service uses computers to forecast the weather.

9. How are managers victimized by information overload, and how can they deal with this problem?

10. Define the term computer literacy. Why is it so hard to define? What is CAI? List and explain the five types of CAI discussed in this chapter.

11. Discuss some ways in which people can use computers for education in settings other than public schools.

CHAPTER 7

Issues of Concern

Introduction

The impact computers have on our lives goes beyond automated banking, required computer literacy courses, and television commercials. Society itself is rapidly changing as computers become commonplace. Many issues have arisen which are both personal and controversial. No clear-cut answers have been found to questions concerning privacy, computer ethics, and computer crime, for example, but the next few years should bring about more discussion and legislative action on such issues.

Privacy

PRIVACY
The right of an individual to be left alone; as related to data processing, the right of an individual to control various aspects of personal data.

Computers are the main means by which businesses and governments collect and store personal information on credit, employment, taxes, and other aspects of people's lives, and many people have access to this information. Thus, the issue of **privacy** is an important concern. Since the early 1970s in particular, people have worried about the amount of information being gathered about them. As a result, some laws and regulations have been enacted regarding privacy and the use of information about individuals.

Databases

Data regarding the average American appears in thirty-nine federal, state, and local government databases and in forty private-sector files (see Figure 7-1). Computers have made data collection and storage easier; they have also made the exchange of data quick, easy, and inexpensive.

The federal government is the largest collector of such data. Anyone who has served in the armed forces, had a physical or mental disability, committed a crime, received government aid, owned a boat, traveled to foreign countries, or completed an income tax return is listed in the government's databases (see Figure 7-2). The fact that most of these records are accessible by social security number makes it easy for the federal government to sweep the files for matches that indicate a violation of federal regulations. The Internal Revenue Service, for example, is bound by law to share its information with thirty-eight different offices in the government. Social Security and IRS files are scanned for names and addresses of people who have defaulted on student loans or avoided court-ordered child support payments. Other government cross-checks reveal government employees who claim welfare, or match welfare recipients with their bank accounts.

Schools, banks, credit agencies, hospitals, insurance groups, and private businesses also are finding it easier to use computers for storing records. These records probably contain the most comprehensive data maintained about individuals. Information entered into these records may include test scores, periodic performance evaluations, results of physical and psychological examinations, stays in hospitals

Figure 7-1 Databases
Source of data: "How Your Privacy Is
Being Stripped Away" *U.S. News
and World Report,* April 30, 1984

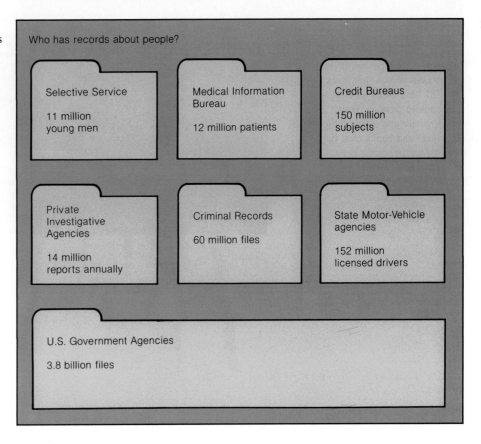

or clinics, transfers and promotions, personal references, salaries, prompt-
ness in paying bills, and disciplinary actions.

Release of such information may be embarrassing and may even cause economic
or psychological harm to an individual. Yet unauthorized people often see the
data, and organizations use the data for unauthorized purposes. The amount of
data and the easy access to that data have led to several major concerns about
privacy:

■ Too much information about individuals is being collected and stored, and some
of it is irrelevant to an organization's goals.

■ Data often is not accurate, complete, or current. Errors are hard to trace, and
can be even harder to correct.

■ Organizations make decisions only on the contents of computerized records.

■ Security of the stored data can be a problem.

Despite the problems involved in data collection, organizations need certain
data. Businesses need to know a potential employee's background in order to
choose the best person for a job. Banks need to know a customer's financial
background before granting a loan. Hospitals need data that ensure the proper
treatment of patients. Corporations need to know consumer's buying habits in

Figure 7-2
Tapes at the FBI's National Crime Information Center
Some critics worry that the name of an innocent person may work its way into FBI files. Such an error could cause untold damage, both economically and psychologically, if employers and banks used that knowledge against the person.

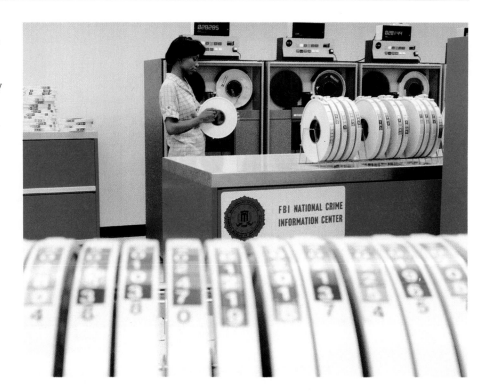

order to make decisions regarding new products and effective advertising. The government—as seen by the list matching practices—uses data to locate abusers of government services, thus benefiting taxpayers. Using computers in data collection can save time, reduce costs, increase efficiency, alert organizations to risks, and help in decision making by providing the most current information. Therefore, the right balance must be found between an organization's need for information and an individual's right to privacy.

Privacy Legislation

Since the early 1970s, several laws have been enacted which protect privacy by controlling the collection, dissemination, and transmission of personal data. Most of these laws have been passed by the federal government, in order to protect against abuse by the government's own record-keeping agencies (see Figure 7-3). The most sweeping federal legislation is the Privacy Act of 1974, which protects the privacy of individuals about whom the federal government maintains data. Although this act was a step in the right direction, it was criticized for its failure to reach beyond the federal government to abuses by state and private institutions. The act contains the following provisions:

■ Individuals must be able to determine what information about them is being recorded and how it will be used.
■ Individuals must be able to correct wrong information.

Figure 7-3
Privacy Legislation

Legislation	Provisions
Freedom of Information Act of 1970	Gives individuals access to data about themselves in files collected by federal agencies.
Fair Credit Reporting Act of 1970	Gives individuals the right to access data about themselves.
	Gives individuals the right to challenge and correct erroneous data.
Privacy Act of 1974	Provides individuals with the right to determine what data is recorded by a government agency and how it will be used.
	States that individuals must be provided with a method of correcting or amending incorrect data.
	Requires organizations to ensure the reliability of collected data and take precautions to prevent misuse.
	States that data collected for one purpose may not be used for another without the consent of the individual involved.
Family Education Rights and Privacy Act of 1974	Regulates access to computer-stored records of grades and behavior evaluations in public and private schools.
Right to Financial Privacy Act of 1978	Limits government access to customer records of financial institutions.
	Protects to some degree the confidentiality of personal financial data.
Comprehensive Crime Control Act of 1984	Prohibits individuals from knowingly accessing a computer without authorization to obtain information protected by the Right to Financial Privacy Act of 1978 or information contained in the file of a consumer reporting agency.
	Prohibits individuals from knowingly accessing a government computer and using, modifying, destroying, or disclosing information stored in the computer or preventing the use of the computer.

■ Information collected for one purpose cannot be used for another purpose without the consent of the individual involved.

■ Organizations that create, manipulate, use, or divulge personal information must ensure its reliability and take precautions against its misuse.

Most states also have adopted laws addressing the privacy issue. Unfortunately, relatively few information privacy violation cases have been litigated either on the state or federal level. Because one problem of privacy violation is that information is transferred and disclosed without the knowledge or consent of the subjects, people are not likely to know how their personal records are being used and may not realize they have a claim to take to court. Furthermore, privacy litigation is something of a contradiction in terms: By taking claims to court, litigants may expose private aspects of their lives to a far greater extent than the initial intrusion did.

Learning Check

1. To what aspects of personal data does privacy refer?

2. Name at least ten situations in which data would be collected about a person.

3. Why has the Privacy Act of 1974 been criticized?

4. What is one difficulty of challenging a privacy violation?

Answers

1. The amount collected, the accuracy, the use, and the security of the data. 2. Serving in the armed forces; having a physical or mental disability; committing a crime; traveling under a passport; receiving government aid; filing an income tax return; attending school; being employed; being in the hospital; borrowing money. 3. It fails to extend to abuse of data by state and local agencies. 4. Taking a privacy violation to court may expose private aspects of a person's life to a far greater extent than the initial intrusion did.

Crime and Security

Computers play a role in activities on both sides of the law. They can help in preventing and solving crimes, thus working toward the good of society. Just as easily, they can be used for illegal purposes. Some persons who commit crimes with the aid of computers are computer hobbyists armed only with a home computer, modem, and telephone. Others are programmers who insert hidden instructions into programs, or seemingly respectable employees ranging from data entry clerks to top executives who stumble on a method of increasing their bank accounts by manipulating computerized company data.

Computer crimes are difficult to detect, and the laws protecting victims are few. For this reason, organizations and individuals should investigate methods of securing their hardware, software, and data. Failure to do so can lead to loss or alteration of data, loss of money, and even the ruin of the system.

Computer Crime

Computer-related crime is more of a problem than most people realize. Americans are losing billions of dollars every year to high-technology thieves whose activities go undetected and unpunished. Estimates of losses range from at least $2 billion to more than $40 billion each year. No one really knows how much is being stolen, but the total appears to be increasing rapidly.

What is meant by the term computer crime? Although there is no consensus, a broad but practical view defines computer crime as a criminal act that poses a greater threat to a computer owner than it would to a nonowner or a crime that is accomplished by using a computer. The perpetrator may manipulate input to the computer, change computer programs, or steal data, computer time, and software.

HIGHLIGHT ▲▲▲▲▲▲▲▲▲▲▲▲▲▲▲▲▲▲▲▲▲▲▲

Monitoring in the Workplace

If you have ever had a heart attack, you're probably thankful that a computer was monitoring your body functions while you were in the hospital. But how would you like to have your work monitored by a computer while you're on the job? Naturally, many employers are enthusiastic about the idea. Knowing that someone is watching you all the time can be unsettling, but computer monitoring is fast becoming an industry standard.

The monitoring system connects workstations to computers to keep tabs on a worker's production. Many employers are using the technique to speed up the work pace and to determine pay raises and promotions. Postal workers are monitored as they key in zip code numbers from each piece of mail. The person who oversees the work watches on a computer monitor that indicates immediately when a zip code is keyed incorrectly. Optical scanners at checkout counters in

the Maryland-based Giant Food store chain eliminate pricing guesses by employees and improve inventory control; they also track the workers' speed. In long-haul trucking, on-board computers can track a driver's average speed and number of stops for a freight line employer.

Critics of the monitoring systems maintain that keeping such a close watch over an employee's work habits leads to increased stress, fatigue, and high employee turnover. They also say that the system can easily be abused, citing the case of an 18-year veteran telephone operator who was fired because a computer detected she was taking more than the average 30 seconds per caller. Although she was reinstated the next day due to a top-level protest by the Communication Workers of America, the experience made a deep impression. "To make me responsible for the amount of time customers take is unfair," she said. "What am I supposed to do

. . . I can't just cut them off."

Some workers appreciate the discipline imposed by monitoring, however, and mention that computer monitoring is less obtrusive than the constant presence of a supervisor. The tighter control resulted in more accurate data and more prompt completion of work.

Many employers say that computer monitoring is not an issue because they have other ways of measuring output. Traditional monitoring measures the quality of the final product, however, whereas computers monitor measurable work as it is being performed. Experts say that arguments over computer monitoring have just begun. As Michael Smith, professor of industrial engineering at the University of Wisconsin, says: "Nothing frightens people more than if they know that someone is going to be watching them all the time."

SOURCE: "Is Your Friendly Computer Rating You on the Job?" *U.S. News and World Report,* February 18, 1985, p. 66

Sometimes the actual hardware or software is damaged. Because computer crimes often are committed by professional people or office employees—people who have easy access to computer systems and data—they are called white-collar crimes. The four categories of computer crimes are sabotage, theft of services, property crimes, and financial crimes. See Figure 7-4 for definitions and examples of these crimes.

A growing concern is that computer systems will become the targets of terrorists, because of the crucial roles that computers fill in the conducting of a nation's business and military affairs. The awareness that a criminal in one country could tap into computers in another country, in order to switch goods or funds to a third country, is raising questions of law as well as security. In fact, the ease with which computers can transfer data across national borders is creating a security dilemma with a dimension all its own.

Figure 7-4
Computer Crimes

Crime	Definition	Examples
Sabotage	Crime directed against hardware or software; physically damages the equipment; requires no special expertise on the part of the criminal.	Flooding the computer room; smashing equipment; damaging stored data or electronic equipment magnetically; planting self-destroying instructions in the software.
Theft of services	Crime that consists of using company computer time, services, or equipment for personal uses.	Acquiring mailing lists or customer lists from a company's computer to use for resale or competitive ventures; using company equipment for freelance work after working hours; using timesharing systems by unauthorized access.
Property crimes	Crime in which computer equipment, software, or company merchandise is stolen.	Stealing computer hardware or making copies of company software for resale or personal use; stealing merchandise by creating dummy accounts to which merchandise is sent, causing checks to be paid out for the receipt of nonexistent merchandise.
Financial crimes	Crime in which computers and software are used to manipulate financial data in the company to the benefit of the perpetrator.	Manipulating the writing of checks, so that multiple checks are sent to the same person or legitimate checks are rerouted to a false address; inserting software instructions that siphon off small amounts from accounts and place them in the perpetrator's account; creating favorable credit ratings for clients.

The unique threat of computer crime is that criminals often use computers to conceal not only their own identities but also the existence of the crimes. Law officers are concerned about the fact that solving computer crimes seems to depend on luck. Many computer crimes are never discovered because company executives do not know enough about computers to detect them. Other crimes are concealed in order to avoid scaring customers and stockholders. It is difficult for a company to admit that its computer systems are not crime-proof.

Perhaps 15 percent of computer thefts are reported to police. Many of these reports do not result in convictions and jail terms, however, because the complexities of data processing mystify most police officials, prosecutors, judges, and jurors. To make matters worse, courts often are lenient in sentencing computer criminals.

The federal government has been slow to pass legislation that deals with computer crime because of disagreements about what computer crime is, how often it occurs, and what to do about it. In 1984, President Ronald Reagan signed into law the Comprehensive Crime Control Act of 1984. This act prohibits individuals from knowingly accessing a computer without authorization in order to obtain information protected by the Right to Financial Privacy Act of 1978 or information contained in the file of a consumer reporting agency. It also prohibits individuals from knowingly accessing a government computer and either using, modifying, destroying, or disclosing information stored in the computer or preventing the use of the computer.

The Comprehensive Crime Control Act follows legislation that many states have enacted regarding a definition of computer crime and penalties for abusing computer use. For example, the Massachusetts state government has passed legislation imposing punishments of up to five years in prison and $20,000 in fines for anyone convicted of damaging computers or software, keeping or destroying software without authorization, entering a computer system with the intent to defraud, or manipulating data to get money, property, or services.

Regardless of the existing laws, it remains largely up to the organization to provide security for its systems and to deal with dishonest or unethical behavior.

Security

Most security problems are caused unintentionally by omission, errors, and accidental destruction. In addition, computer systems, along with data in storage, are vulnerable to hazards such as fire, natural disasters, and environmental problems. Many of these problems would occur less frequently if the proper controls existed. Some problems can be avoided entirely by careful planning, sufficient personnel training, and a well-run computer installation. Other problems, such as computer crime, can be difficult to control completely. Some common security measures are described in the following paragraphs.

■ Organizations should define standards for computer use, with penalties that discourage unethical behavior. Any dishonest or unethical behavior should be dealt with immediately.
■ In order to gain access to company data, authorized users should use special passwords that change periodically.
■ Employees should discontinue careless practices. For example, passwords should not be taped to desks or drawers. Printouts disclosing sensitive financial data or program segments should not be discarded in wastebaskets.
■ Employee responsibilities should be separated. For example, the person who writes orders should not also be the person who authorizes payments.
■ Standards should be established for hiring and training personnel. Persons hired for sensitive computer work should be fully investigated.
■ Data can be translated into a scrambled code, a process called **encryption.** Data transmitted to or from remote terminals is encrypted (scrambled) at one end and decrypted (unscrambled) at the other. Only authorized users can get the data in its unscrambled form.
■ Telephone access to data can be restricted by using a dial-back security measure. Dial-back requires the user to telephone the computer, give a password, and then hang up. If the user and password check out, the computer calls the user back and

ENCRYPTION
The process of encoding data or programs to disguise them from unauthorized personnel.

allows access. This measure ensures that the user is calling from an approved location and that the password corresponds to that location.

■ Backup copies of data should be stored outside the organization's location. Recovery procedures should be established.

In order to deter crime, some organizations have combined several security measures. Access to a computer is granted only after the user passes four tests, which ask for the following:

1. Something the user knows, such as a password.
2. Something the user alone can supply, such as a fingerprint.
3. Something the user alone can do, such as write a signature.
4. Something the user has, such as a magnetic card or electronic key.

Computer security cannot be ignored at home, either. Home computers often contain confidential information that must be protected, such as financial, medical, and insurance information about family members. Also, more business materials will be kept on home computers as more workers participate in telecommuting. Home users also need to employ simple measures that guard against theft and damage to hardware or software.

Just how much security a computer system should have depends on four factors:

■ The value of the hardware.
■ The value of the software and data.
■ The cost of replacing the hardware, software, or data.
■ The cost of the security controls.

Although security precautions reduce the risk of destruction, damage, or theft of computer hardware or software, their cost should be kept within the range that the organization is able and willing to pay.

Computer Mistakes: Who Is Responsible?

We have all heard the story about the man who was declared dead because of a computer error. Social security payments stopped, pension benefits ceased, and the infamous cycle of red tape set in. "So sorry, but if the computer claims you are deceased, you *are* deceased. Computers do not make mistakes . . ."

Of course, computer errors do happen. Some can be humorous, but others are downright annoying. If we have an unhappy experience, we want to know who actually made the mistake and who is responsible for it.

There are several common ways of generating a computer error. By far the most common is using incorrect data. If the data going into the program is wrong, the information coming out will be just as wrong. Incorrect input can come from two sources: (1) the typist mistypes the data, or (2) the person who gathers the data does not check its accuracy. An order from Army officials near Colorado

Learning Check

1. How might a computer crime be committed?

2. What features are included in the Comprehensive Crime Control Act of 1984?

3. Name two inexpensive security measures that could prevent unauthorized persons from obtaining sensitive data.

4. What factors should be considered in deciding just how much security is enough?

Answers

1. By manipulating input to the computer; by changing computer programs; by stealing data, computer time; or by physically damaging the hardware or software. 2. The act prohibits individuals from knowingly accessing a computer without authorization in order to obtain information protected by the Right to Financial Privacy Act of 1978, or information contained in the file of a consumer reporting agency. It also prohibits individuals from knowingly accessing a government computer and using, modifying, destroying, or disclosing information stored in the computer or preventing the use of the computer. 3. Changing passwords often and not taping them to desk drawers or other easily accessible places; being careful about what is discarded in wastebaskets. 4. The factors focus on costs: the value of the hardware; the value of the software and data; the cost of replacing the hardware, software, or data; and the cost of the security controls.

Springs, Colorado, for example, once resulted in the delivery of a ship's anchor to a land-locked U.S. Army base:

The anchor's journey began in early March 1985, when a $6.04 incandescent lamp was requisitioned by computer. Instead of typing the correct order number, 2040-00-368-4972, a clerk at the maintenance unit typed 2040-00-368-4772, the order number for "anchor, marine fluke." Because the order number did correspond to an available item, the computer validated the order. It was shipped from Sharpe Army Depot in Lathrop, California, and arrived at Fort Carson, Colorado, on March 25. Someone astutely observed that it was not a lamp. It was a $28,560 anchor, probably built for use on a destroyer or light cruiser.

Another common cause of computer errors is that the program does not anticipate every possibility. For example, if a program does not take into account the possibility that the current year may be a leap year, a bank's customers could lose one day's interest.

Sometimes this type of error can occur on the system level. That is, rather than an individual program neglecting a possibility, a system might leave out an entire program. A few years ago, the courts faced such a situation:

A North American Van Lines driver drove for over 70 hours in an eight-day period, in violation of an Interstate Commerce Commission rule. The fatigued driver was involved in an accident in which a motorist was killed. The motorist's widow sued North American for negligence, because the company's computer system did not include a program to detect violations of the 70-hour rule. The justices agreed with the motorist's widow, and she was awarded $10 million.

The third type of error occurs when the input is right and the program logic is right—but the answer is wrong. These errors can result if the programmer does not consider the limitations of real and integer arithmetic. Similar errors also can be generated by a power surge. Theoretically, even cosmic rays could interfere with computer operations, but that possibility is very slight.

The fourth type of computer error results from a program designed in such a way that it does not give the same response that a human being would give in the same situation. A prime example involved a stop payment order on a check. A corporate customer of a large bank ordered a stop payment on check number 896, dated February 27, for $1,844.48. The actual amount of the check, however, was $1,844.98. When the computer processed the check, it noted this $.50 difference and did not stop payment. This error resulted in a lawsuit in which the judge ruled that, because a human operator would not have issued payment on the check, the bank was liable for the amount.

A fifth kind of error involves ''hackers'' who enter a system and change data. Errors can range from altered dosages of drugs or radiation treatments for hospital patients to a few cents siphoned from bank accounts.

Problems and errors also can occur when a new computer system is installed. Consider the case of the Internal Revenue Service and the 1984 income tax returns. The new computer system was scheduled to arrive in the summer of 1984. The IRS twice changed the specifications on the original order, however, requiring more sophisticated equipment each time. As a result, the computers were not ready until November 1984, only a few weeks before the first returns began to arrive. IRS employees scrambled to implement the new system. Equipment malfunctioned, and at the last minute IRS programmers still were rewriting the new software so that it would process data more quickly. As a result, errors occurred, refund checks were late, and many people had to refile their income tax returns. In this situation, the IRS committed a basic mistake of the computer age: It failed to provide sufficient backup during conversion to a new system. The IRS did not have the money or programmers to process tax returns on its old machines in case of emergency.

There is little legal guidance in dealing with computer mistakes. Because the use of computers is relatively new, many states have few, if any, laws pertaining to such errors. Court decisions often are based on Uniform Commercial Code regulations that have to be newly applied—and the rulings are by no means consistent.

As a result, legal responsibility for computer errors may be difficult to determine. Is the programmer personally responsible for errors that are written into the program? Or does the company using the program assume responsibility when it purchases the program? Should the typist be held personally responsible for input errors? Or is it management's responsibility to check the information once it is processed? Can an organization be ruled not responsible for a problem that occurs because a hacker enters its computer system and changes or erases data? Or is it the organization's responsibility to keep backup data and check validity often? And how often is *often?* Can we really expect computers to act as human beings would?

Responsibility is an important issue, because computer errors can be far more serious than most people think. Businesses declare bankruptcy because of computer errors. An insurance company survey showed that 90 percent of all businesses that depend on computers, and that experience a major loss of service due to a computer error, go out of business after that loss.

Computer errors have done more than ruin businesses. Computer errors have endangered people's health, and they have ruined reputations through faulty credit checks. If people, computer systems, and programs are imperfect on a small scale, imagine what could happen when computers have control over much larger aspects of our lives. Imagine what might happen if a computer-controlled space defense shield (Star Wars) system were implemented. Imagine what could happen in a nuclear energy plant run by computers. Under such circumstances, it would be crucial for people to discover errors before the computer does and to determine who is responsible for checking for errors.

Computer Ethics

The issue of computer ethics has become increasingly important as more and more Americans gain access to computers. Any computer user might engage in unethical practices, both at work and at home. For this reason, some code of ethics for computer use is essential.

Violations of ethical behavior range from a minor infringement to the commission of a major crime. As examples, think about the following questions and the ethical issues they involve:

■ Should an employee use the company computer for personal use?
■ Should an employee look at the records of other employees out of mere curiosity?
■ Should a company be allowed to add personal information not related to work performance to an employee's computer records?
■ How rigid should a company's policy be regarding monitoring employees by computer, such as keeping track of a typist's speed and mistakes, the number of times people leave their workstations, or the amount of time used in each telephone call at a reservations desk?
■ Is is merely unethical to tap online information networks without paying the fees, or is it also a crime?
■ What are the legitimate uses (if any) of programs that break copy-protection codes on software?
■ If a copy of a program appears on an electronic bulletin board, is it acceptable to download it if the user suspects it is copyrighted software?

These questions and many related ones concern employees, employers, teachers, students, and parents. The answers constitute the standard of moral conduct use, or the degree to which people adhere to computer ethics.

SOFTWARE PIRACY
The unauthorized copying of a copyrighted computer program.

One particular problem in ethics involves **software piracy.** A recent survey by Future Computing Inc. of Dallas revealed that piracy cost vendors $1.3 billion in lost revenues between 1981 and 1984. The firm also predicted lost revenues of $800 million for 1985, and estimated that for every authorized copy of business software for personal computers there is one pirated copy in use. Some experts believe these estimates are conservative.

Most current legal cases regarding copyrights involve illegal bulletin board uses, corporate misuses of software, and pirates who copy popular programs for resale. These cases are heavily prosecuted. In most cases, however, individuals who copy other hobbyists' software for personal use are not taken to court. Their behavior is more a matter of personal ethics, like driving 60 miles per hour when the national speed limit is 55. These people are unlikely to be caught, but they have knowingly violated a law.

Copying software that has been copyrighted is illegal. Software is protected by the U.S. Copyright Act of 1978. Although the creator of an original work is considered to possess the copyright from the moment the work is fixed in some concrete form, he or she gains additional protection by registering the work with the Copyright Office. Registration ensures for the copyright owner the right to bring suit against copyright violators. The creator registers a program by completing Copyright Office registration form TX, paying a ten-dollar fee, and submitting a copy or identifying portion of the program to the Copyright Office.

A copyright notice protects the owner's copyright. In the notice, the symbol ©, the word *Copyright,* or the abbreviation *Copr.* should appear with the name of the copyright owner and the year of the work's first publication. The law makes it illegal to copy a licensed software program except for archival use, which means that one backup copy may be made (see Figure 7-5).

Software vendors have protected their products in other ways besides copyright registration. Many vendors have designed protection codes to make copying disks more difficult. The problem with protecting a disk is that it prevents consumers from making a backup copy, which is legal. It also prevents use of the software with hard disk drives. One trade group is suggesting a hardware device that would be attached to a personal computer. A hard-to-duplicate key purchased with legitimate software would be inserted into the device before the software could be used.

Figure 7-5
Piracy in Other Situations

Object code	Copyright protects the object code, that is, the instructions that actually run the computer. These instructions reside in the operating system, application program, or ROM (read-only memory). A court precedent set in the case of *Apple Computer, Inc. v. Franklin Computer Corporation* extended the copyright protection to the object code. Apple charged Franklin with copyright violations for duplicating the operating system programs contained in the Apple II. Apple was granted an injunction to prevent Franklin from selling the Ace 100, the computer that contained the duplicated operating system.
Databases	With over 2,000 commercial and government databases available for online searching, billions of dollars worth of data now are accessible with a microcomputer and modem. The easy access to the databases and the difficulty in detecting downloading activities makes copyright infringements easy. Whereas downloading data for temporary use or with a downloading license agreement is legitimate, downloading for commercial use or resale is illegal. Copyright infringement cases of databases to date have involved the reproduction of 80 to 100 percent of a program.

Despite these attempts to discourage software piracy, experts believe the battle will never be won. That prediction probably extends to other matters of ethical behavior, such as unauthorized use of databases and unethical computer-related behavior on the job. For these reasons, computer users need to devise a code of ethics governing their own behavior. Such a code of ethics measures behavior against conscience. After all, the best protection against computer hardware and software abuse is a high standard of personal behavior.

Learning Check

1. What is the most common type of computer error?

2. Name two other ways in which computer errors can occur.

3. How does copyright registration protect the owner of a copyright?

4. What is the meaning of the phrase *computer ethics*?

Answers

1. Using incorrect data.   2. The program may not anticipate every possibility; a program may not give the same response as a human being in the same situation.   3. It gives the owner the right to bring suit against copyright violators.   4. It refers to an individual's standard of behavior regarding computer use.

Identification of Computer and Security Needs

SYSTEM ANALYST
The person who is responsible for the analysis, design, and implementation of computer-based information systems.

Compared to the problematic issues of privacy, computer crime, and errors, concerns about meeting an organization's computing needs seem tame. Yet making the correct decisions regarding computer needs can help an organization overcome difficulties related to these other issues.

In order to identify computer and security needs, a business may employ the services of a **system analyst.** The system analyst deals with the materials, procedures, machines, and people that produce information the corporation needs for making decisions about its business.

To design a system properly, the analyst uses an organized approach called the system approach, which involves five steps: analysis, design, programming, implementation, and audit and review (see Figure 7-6). The analyst performs a detailed investigation of a system which uncovers the objectives of the organization and the best ways for accomplishing these objectives. Some of the factors a system analyst might consider are what types of hardware is needed, whether to develop software in-house or purchase it, and what specific personnel may be needed. The system analyst also guides the organization's decisions about security, procedures for computer use, and policies for access to company data. Once these recommendations are made, the system is designed, the software is prepared, and the system is implemented.

Figure 7-6
The System Approach

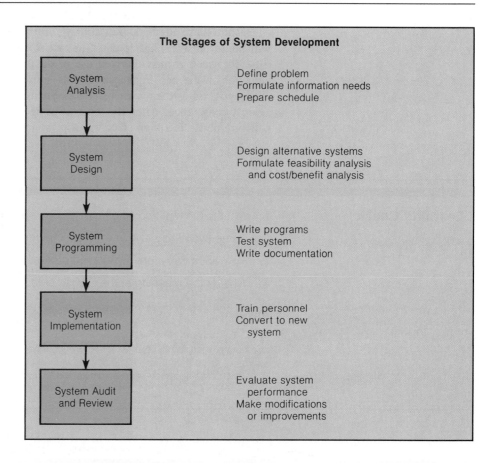

The Stages of System Development

System Analysis
- Define problem
- Formulate information needs
- Prepare schedule

System Design
- Design alternative systems
- Formulate feasibility analysis and cost/benefit analysis

System Programming
- Write programs
- Test system
- Write documentation

System Implementation
- Train personnel
- Convert to new system

System Audit and Review
- Evaluate system performance
- Make modifications or improvements

During the entire process, and after the system is implemented, feedback—audit and review—occurs. The purpose of feedback is to determine whether certain standards have been met within the system. If not, the inputs or processes in the system may need to be changed.

The system analyst may also evaluate a firm's goals, priorities, and general requirements and make suggestions about the kinds of information that could be helpful to its managers. This process is part of establishing a **management information system (MIS),** which uses computers to help managers make better decisions. An MIS differs from a simple data processing system. Simple data processing is used primarily for collecting and manipulating data and producing reports, whereas the purpose of an MIS is to provide managers with useful information that specifically supports their decision-making tasks. To be useful, the MIS must provide relevant information to the appropriate manager at the right time.

Planning a system for an organization is not an easy task, because many factors must be considered. What are the goals of an organization? What are its information needs? Which level of management needs what information? How often are certain types of reports needed? How will the system be implemented so that conversion occurs in a friendly, nonthreatening manner? Will the system require monitoring of employees' work? How will the system meet workers' needs for self-worth,

MANAGEMENT INFORMATION SYSTEM (MIS)
A formal network that uses computers to provide information to support structured managerial decision making.

comfort at workstations, and manageable stress levels? Will suggestions from employees at all levels be considered and implemented? Will the benefits of a new system outweigh the costs?

Artificial Intelligence and Automation

Costs and benefits are primary concerns of managers who are considering implementing devices to improve automation at their companies. The costs and benefits that a manager evaluates, however, may be quite the opposite of the goals of employees. As the technology of automatic devices advances, the rift between management and employees, and between professionals and clients, may widen.

Artificial Intelligence Applied

The term *number crunching* was born in the vacuum tube era of computing, when mathematicians, scientists, and engineers used computers to manipulate huge amounts of numerical data. Even today, number crunching is what most computers do best. As programmers and developers of computer languages become more proficient at designing sophisticated software, however, number crunching will give way to more conceptual applications. Scientists will need faster computers with new designs in order to use the new software ideas. Many people call this new level of computer power the fifth generation.

New computers and languages will only begin to imitate human intelligence at higher levels of abstraction. This type of intelligence exhibited by machines is called **artificial intelligence (AI).** Because human intelligence itself is not clearly understood, current AI programs incorporate just a few aspects of it. The most common AI applications are **expert systems.** These systems are specific to a particular field, and make evaluations, draw conclusions, and recommend action based on a huge database of information in that field (see Figure 7-7).

An example is Dr. Lawrence Weed's medical diagnosis program, called the *Problem-Knowledge Coupler (PKC)*. The patient and doctor enter history, symptoms, and test results on the computer. By making cross-references, the computer responds with a list of diseases the patient might have, thus helping the doctor decide on a diagnosis and treatment. Other expert systems include CADUCEUS II, an internal-medicine diagnostic program; ONCOCIN, which advises physicians on the best combination of therapies for cancer patients; PROSPECTOR, an electronic geologist; and a program currently being developed called TRADER'S ASSISTANT, which will help brokers assess the stock market. Many experts in AI contend, however, that expert systems do not qualify as true AI. Intelligence involves coping with change and incorporating new information to improve performance, and expert systems do neither.

Advances in AI will lead to further automation in the workplace. Intelligent computers could be used to read books, newspapers, journals, and magazines and to prepare summaries of the material. They could scan mail and sort all letters but those with the most illegible addresses. Principles of AI also are used in improving **voice recognition** systems so that they can accept larger vocabularies, different

ARTIFICIAL INTELLIGENCE (AI)
Intelligence exhibited by a machine or software; a field of research aimed at developing techniques whereby computers can be used for solving problems.

EXPERT SYSTEM
Software that uses a base of knowledge in a field of study for decision-making and evaluation processes similar to those of human experts in that field.

VOICE RECOGNITION
The ability of electronic equipment to recognize speech and voice patterns.

Figure 7-7
MENTOR
The MENTOR system uses artificial intelligence to diagnose maintenance procedures in large central air-conditioning units.

voices, and continuous or flowing speech. Robotics will benefit from AI programming in the areas of robot vision, touch, and mobility. Additional skills will enable robots to take over even more jobs normally performed by human workers.

Questions and (No) Answers

Are people ready for the marvelous machines that AI makes possible? How will people react to expert systems that seem to do jobs better than the experts do? Let's look at medical expert systems as an example.

No human being can be expected to remember every minor symptom of every known disease or ailment, but a computer program can do so easily. It can signal drug incompatibilities and patient allergies, and it can react quickly to changes in a patient's condition. It can help a physician keep up to date on treatments, drugs, and diseases. There may also be negative effects of using expert systems. Some experts fear that medical systems will dehumanize medical practice or become crutches for incompetent physicians. Others ask if the role of physicians will decrease as expert systems are more commonly used. Still others wonder how the use of robots in surgery will affect jobs in medicine.

Manufacturing jobs have been lost due to improved robotics and scanning and voice recognition devices. In 1984 and 1985, two million manufacturing jobs were affected by the use of robots, optical scanners, microchips, and other electronic devices. Of those devices, 17,000 were robots. With unemployment in the United States continuing throughout the 1980s, loss of jobs due to robots remains a problem for workers and management alike.

Can all displaced workers be retrained and relocated? What kinds of jobs will they hold? Most of the new jobs by 1995 will be in retailing and service industries.

HIGHLIGHT ▲▲▲▲▲▲▲▲▲▲▲▲▲▲▲▲▲▲▲▲

Seymour Cray

Tremendous number crunching capabilities are required for processing scientific data and conducting research in artificial intelligence. It was Seymour Cray's ambition to build a super-fast, super-powerful computer that would meet these needs.

As a young engineer, Cray worked for Engineering Research Associates and then for Remington Rand when it purchased ERA. Later, he was employed by the Univac Division of Sperry Rand Corporation. When William Norris founded Control Data Corporation (CDC) in 1957, Cray left Sperry to become a director at CDC.

Cray's first project at CDC was the 1604 computer. It was so successful in the scientific community that CDC built a private research laboratory for Cray in his hometown of Chippewa Falls, Wisconsin. There Cray continued his work and in 1963 introduced the powerful 6600, a machine that was adopted immediately by the U.S. Weather Bureau and the Atomic Energy Commission.

Cray became well known as a leading designer of large-scale computers. In 1972 he resigned from CDC and founded Cray Research, Inc., to design, develop, manufacture, and market large-capacity, high-speed computers. Cray Research introduced the Cray-1 in 1976. Next came the Cray X-MP. By 1985, over 100 Cray supercomputers were in use around the world, accounting for nearly 70 percent of the supercomputer market.

Seymour Cray was determined to build a supercomputer even faster and more powerful than the Cray-1 or Cray X-MP. He succeeded: In 1985, the Cray-2 was introduced. It is six to twelve times faster than the Cray-1 and has an internal memory of two billion bytes. Currently, Cray is devoting his time to the development of the Cray-3, which will have an eight-billion-byte memory. It is scheduled to be finished in 1988.

Only 11 percent of the 16 million new jobs will be in high technology, and only 6 percent of the 123 million people now currently employed in the U.S. are working in high-technology fields.

Some experts believe, however, that further loss of jobs will be due to attrition rather than layoffs. They argue that even if 2 million jobs are displaced, that accounts for only 2 percent of total employment. They also say that, in some instances, technology has made it possible to keep jobs in the U.S. For example, automating a plant has made it possible to produce a product here for less than it would cost to send the work to Asian countries.

Regardless of which experts we believe, the use of robots, scanning machines, and other devices improved by AI create very real concerns. Just how many jobs can be performed well by machines and software? Will implementation of AI principles in robots, automation, and expert systems eliminate certain skilled occupations? Is the use of automated equipment likely to affect a worker's sense of worth and purpose (see Figure 7-8)? How will automation affect the social aspect of transactions at banks and other institutions? Once such technology is implemented, is it likely to be disbanded in order to restore employment to displaced workers? Could the goals of sophisticated AI software and devices ever conflict with the goals of humans?

AI technology and the changes it creates could eventually improve the quality of life, but not until certain conflicts have been resolved.

Figure 7-8
Automation

Learning Check

1. What jobs does a system analyst do?

2. How does an MIS differ from a simple data processing system?

3. How are the principles of artificial intelligence used in automation?

4. What problems does automation present?

Answers

1. Analyzes an organization for data processing needs; suggests a design of equipment, material, people, and procedures for implementing a system. 2. A data processing system is used primarily for collecting and manipulating data and producing reports. An MIS provides managers with useful information that specifically supports their decision-making tasks. 3. They are used in developing expert systems; improving voice recognition systems to include larger vocabularies, a variety of voices, and the use of continuous speech; and improving vision, touch, and mobility of robots. 4. Problems related to automation concern workers being displaced by automation, and uncertainty about changes in the jobs available for humans in the future.

Summary Points

■ Some major concerns about privacy involve the amount of information collected and stored, the accuracy and recency of the information, the security of the stored information, and the uses to which it is put.

■ The Privacy Act of 1974 is the major piece of federal legislation passed to protect the privacy of the individual. It addresses these four major concerns on the federal level.

■ Computer crime is a growing concern because it is difficult to detect and because it results in loss of money and information. Tighter computer security measures are needed.

■ Both computer crime and privacy have been addressed by the Comprehensive Crime Control Act of 1984. This act deals with unauthorized access to computers for illegitimate purposes.

■ It is hard to determine who is responsible for computer mistakes. This issue is particularly important in systems that govern sensitive aspects of our lives, such as monitoring nuclear plants.

■ Computer ethics refers to an individual's standards of behavior when using computers. It includes such practices as accessing restricted data, copying copyrighted software, using company computers for personal reasons, and downloading data from commercial databases.

■ The system analyst can help a company identify security needs and suggest procedures to discourage unethical use of a company's computers. He or she may also recommend equipment, people, materials, and procedures needed to improve the collection, storage, and dissemination of information in the company.

■ A management information system (MIS) can help managers make better decisions by providing useful information from the company's databases.

■ Artificial intelligence is intelligence exhibited by a machine. It is used in preparing expert systems, improved voice recognition systems, and improved robot vision, mobility, and touch. These uses can affect the quality and number of jobs, because they enable businesses to automate certain functions.

Review Questions

1. Why has the issue of privacy become so important, and how can the problems associated with the storage and use of personal data be resolved?

2. List the organizations, companies, institutions, and government agencies that you think have computer records about you. Does the number make you uncomfortable? Why?

3. What is computer crime? Discuss some ways that computers are related to the perpetration of crimes.

4. What is meant by the phrase computer ethics? Describe some situations in which individuals apply their personal codes of ethics to computer use.

5. Describe some measures that your company or school could impose which would decrease software piracy, computer crime, and unauthorized access to data.

6. Discuss ethical and unethical uses of programs that unlock copy protection codes on licensed software.

7. Discuss some approaches that software developers could use to discourage piracy, other than copy protection programmed onto the disk itself.

8. Name the five major types of computer errors, and give examples that you may have experienced or read about.

9. Data about us is held in many databases, kept by government agencies, schools, employers, and credit bureaus. Sometimes data is traded among these organizations. Discuss the possible implications if one bit of incorrect data enters the trading system.

10. Describe how the protection of software copyright should be extended to other areas of computer use.

11. Explain the types of decisions which a system analyst might help a company make.

12. Describe some applications of artificial intelligence and expert systems, and tell how they might lead to a decrease in jobs.

13. Discuss how much of an obligation management and factory owners have toward workers who have been displaced by robots or other automation.

14. Computer-assisted diagnosis might increase speed and accuracy of medical diagnoses, especially in an emergency situation. It also might pose great threats to the patient's privacy, and might decrease the physician's familiarity with and recall of diagnostic information. All of these factors must be considered before a hospital implements computer-assisted diagnosis. In your opinion, are the advantages or the disadvantages greater? On what information do you base your answer?

PART TWO
Applications Software: Introduction to WestWord™, WestCalc™, WestGraph™, and WestData™

CHAPTER 8

Introduction to Word Processing and WestWord™ 2.5

Outline

Introduction

It is human nature to look for easier ways to get things done. Writing instruments, for example, have evolved from rocks and twigs to what many people thought to be the ultimate writing machine—the typewriter. But the evolution has not stopped; the computer revolution has brought with it the word processor.

To gain a little perspective, think of the difference between writing with a pen and pad and writing with a typewriter. This comparison approximates the difference between using a typewriter and using a word processor. In terms of speed, power, and capabilities, the word processor is to the pen and pad what the Ferrari is to the Model T.

One of the major advantages of word processing is that the words typed are not committed to paper immediately. First they are displayed on a video screen, where they can be manipulated easily by electronic means. Word processors have made it simple to insert or delete text and to move text from one place to another without having to retype or spend hours cutting and pasting. Gone are the days of overflowing wastepaper baskets and irritating correction paper or fluid. A word processor enables the writer to be completely satisfied with what has been written before one word is printed on paper.

This chapter will introduce you to word processing. It will also instruct you on how to get started using WestWord 2.5, a word processor developed by Rawhide Software Inc.

Definitions

WORD PROCESSOR
A program or set of programs designed to enable the user to enter, manipulate, format, print, store, and retrieve text.

WORD PROCESSING
The act of composing and manipulating text electronically.

WORD PROCESSING SYSTEM
The hardware and software used for word processing.

DEDICATED SYSTEM
A computer equipped to handle only one function, such as word processing.

A word processor is a program (software) or set of programs that enables you to write, edit, format, and print text. As you type on a keyboard, the words appear on the screen for you to see. Mistakes can be corrected easily because the text has not yet been put on paper. Words, sentences, and even entire paragraphs can be moved by special commands. Nothing is printed until you are satisfied with the results.

Word processing refers to the actual act of composing and editing text. The words are composed and rearranged in your mind; the word processor and the hardware simply provide a convenient way to display, store, edit, and recall the work you have done. Word processing has two primary functions: text editing (entering and manipulating text) and print formatting (telling the printer how to format the printed copy).

A **word processing system** comprises both the hardware and software used for word processing. There are two general types of word processing systems: **dedicated systems,** which are microcomputers equipped to handle only word processing; and multipurpose microcomputers, which are equipped to handle a wide variety of processing tasks including word processing. In the early days of word processing, the serious user's only choice was a dedicated system. With the development of faster and more sophisticated microcomputers, however, came the development of microcomputer-compatible word processors such as West-

Word 2.5. Today most, if not all, microcomputers on the market have a word processor available for them.

Although a word processor is actually a program or programs, many people refer to the combination of both software and hardware as a word processor. Table 8-1 provides a quick reference to other terms that you may encounter when reading about word processors.

Uses of Word Processors

Word processors are used in homes, businesses, schools, and many other places. At home, they can be used to write school reports, letters, or the minutes from a meeting. Most word processors for home use are simpler and have fewer features than those designed for business use.

Word processors can take over much of the paperwork involved in running a business. They produce reports, letters, brochures, legal papers, and other important documents. A word processor can print a form letter thousands of times, with a different name and address inserted in each copy to make each letter more personal.

Word processors have revolutionized the publishing industry. Books, newspapers, and magazines can be produced faster and with fewer mistakes. Sometimes these documents are not printed on paper until they are ready to be distributed. Writers enter text at computer terminals, and editors review the work at their terminals. Then designers lay out the pages electronically, choosing the type style,

---

Learning Check

1. A _____ is a program (software) or set of programs designed to enable a user to enter, manipulate, format, print, store, and retrieve text.
   - *a.* word processor
   - *b.* word processing
   - *c.* word-processing system
   - *d.* dedicated system

2. The two general types of word processing systems are _____ and _____.

3. A _____ includes both the hardware and software that enable a user to write, edit, format, and print text using a computer.
   - *a.* word processor
   - *b.* word processing
   - *c.* word processing system
   - *d.* dedicated system

4. Word processing is the act of _____ and _____ text on a computer.

5. A dedicated system handles a wide range of processing tasks, including word processing. (True or False?)

Answers

1. a 2. dedicated systems; multipurpose microcomputers 3. c 4. composing; editing 5. False

Table 8-1
Frequently Encountered Word
Processing Terms

Term	Definition
Automatic pagination	A feature that enables a word processor to number the pages of the printed copy automatically.
Block	A group of characters, such as a sentence or paragraph.
Block movement	A feature that allows the user to define a block of text and then perform a specific operation on the entire block. Common block operations include block move, block copy, block save, and block delete.
Boldface	Heavy type, for example, **this is boldface.**
Character	A letter, number, or symbol.
Character enhancement	Underlining, boldfacing, subscripting, and superscripting.
Control character	A coded character that does not print but is part of the command sequence in a word processor.
Cursor	The marker on the display screen indicating where the next character can be displayed.
Default setting	A value used by the word processor when it is not instructed to use any other.
Deletion	A feature by which a character, word, sentence, or larger block of text can be removed from the existing text.
Document-oriented word processor	A word processor that operates on a text file as one long document.
Editing	The act of changing or amending text.
Format	The layout of a page; for example, the number of lines, margin settings, and so on.
Global	An instruction that will be carried out throughout an entire document, for example, global search and replace.
Header	A piece of text that is stored separately from the text and printed at the top of each page.
Incremental spacing	A method by which the printer inserts spaces between words and letters to produce justified margins; also called *microspacing*.
Insertion	A feature in which a character, word, sentence, or larger block of text is added to the existing text.
Justification	A feature for making lines of text even at the margins.
Line editor	The type of editor that allows the user to edit only one line at a time.
Memory-only word processor	A word processor that cannot exchange text between internal memory and disk during the editing process.
Menu	A list of commands or prompts on the display screen.

Table continued on next page

Table 8-1
Continued

Term	Definition
Page-oriented word processor	A word processor that operates on a text file as a series of pages.
Print formatting	The function of a word processor which communicates with the printer to tell it how to print the text on paper.
Print preview	A feature that enables the user to view a general representation on the screen of how the document will look when printed.
Screen editor	The type of editor that enables the user to edit an entire screen at a time.
Screen formatting	A function of a word processor which controls how the text will appear on the screen.
Scrolling	Moving a line of text onto or off the screen.
Search and find	A routine that searches for, and places the cursor at, a specified string of characters.
Search and replace	A routine that searches for a specified character string and replaces it with the specified replacement string.
Status line	A message line above or below the text area on a display screen which gives format and system information.
Subscript	A character that prints below the usual text baseline.
Superscript	A character that prints above the usual text baseline.
Text buffer	An area set aside in memory to hold text temporarily.
Text editing	The function of a word processor that enables the user to enter and edit text.
Text file	A file that contains text, as opposed to a program.
Virtual representation	An approach to screen formatting which enables the user to see on the screen exactly how the printed output will look.
Word wrap	The feature in which a word is moved automatically to the beginning of the next line if it goes past the right margin.

size, and column width. Finally, the document is printed for the first and only time.

Schools are increasing their use of word processors. Students can write essays or reports on the computers in their classrooms. Teachers can format tests and worksheets on a computer much faster than on a typewriter. School secretaries also can use word processors to prepare school reports and letters.

No matter how word processors are used, they enable the writer to think more about organizing ideas than about the mechanics of writing. A word processor makes it much easier for a person to revise a document before it is printed.

Guide to WestWord™ 2.5

The remainder of this chapter demonstrates the use of WestWord 2.5, a word processing program that is powerful yet easy to use. With WestWord 2.5, you can create memos, letters, reports, and term papers.

The directions in this chapter are written for computers with two floppy disk drives. Each of the following sections introduces a different feature of West-Word 2.5. At the end of each section there is a hands-on activity marked **YOUR TURN**. Be sure to read the section carefully *before* trying the hands-on activity. Do not try out the program functions as you read through the explanatory sections. Wait for the **YOUR TURN** at the end of each section.

On the IBM PC, the key marked ←⏎ is referred to as the <Return> key. Throughout this chapter, when you are instructed to press the <Return> key, press the key marked ←⏎. WestWord 2.5 also uses the ten function keys on the left side of the keyboard to activate most of its functions. Each function key may activate more than one function. Four separate function menus appear beneath the work screen, and the function keys activate the functions listed in the menu that is currently on the screen. Also, the <Ctrl> key is pressed with some of the function keys to activate additional functions.

A few other keys are important in using WestWord 2.5. The <Num Lock> key is used to control the ten-key number pad on the right side of the keyboard. If the <Num Lock> key is pressed once, the pad is used for writing numbers to the screen. If it is not pressed, or if it is pressed twice, it allows the keypad to be used for cursor control. The <←> key, which will be called the <Backspace> key, erases mistakes by backspacing the cursor over them. (The <Backspace> key must not be confused with the left arrow cursor control key.) The <Esc> key enables you to exit most program functions after they have been activated. The <Ctrl> and <Alt> keys on the left side of the keyboard are used in combination with other keys to activate functions. That is, you press the <Ctrl> or <Alt> key and hold it down while pressing the key that accompanies it to activate the function.

The following symbols and typefaces appear throughout the chapter:

Type **b**	**Boldface** is used to designate characters or text that you should type to the screen usually in response to a prompt.
Press the <F10> key	The angle brackets (< >) are used to signify a specific key on the keyboard. Press the key whose name is enclosed by the angle brackets.
ENTER FILENAME	All capital letters indicate text that is displayed on the computer screen. They also indicate WestWord commands.
Type `Job Opening`	Typewriter font indicates input that is to be entered into a document.

Getting Started with WestWord 2.5

BOOT
To load an operating system into a computer's main memory.

To **boot** the computer and start WestWord 2.5, you need an IBM DOS diskette (version 2.0 or higher), a West Instructional Software diskette, and a data diskette—a formatted blank disk where you will store the documents you create. The following steps explain how to start WestWord 2.5 on your computer.

1.   Insert the DOS diskette in drive A (usually the left or top drive). Insert your data diskette in drive B (usually the right or bottom drive). Turn on the monitor and computer and press the <Return> key in response to the time and date prompts (to bypass them). When the A> prompt appears, take the DOS diskette out of drive A and insert the West Instructional Software diskette into drive A. Type **WEST** after the A> and press the <Return> key.

2.   Read the information that appears on the screen. Press the <Return> key when you have read the information, and then read the next screen that appears. At the bottom of the screen are the words *Author's name* and a highlighted box. Type **MANDELL** and press the <Return> key.

3.   The Opening Menu appears. Using the up < ↑ > or down < ↓ > arrow keys, move the highlighting to WESTWORD. Press the <Return> key. The West-Word 2.5 Main Menu appears (see Figure 8-1).

Figure 8-1
WestWord 2.5 Main Menu

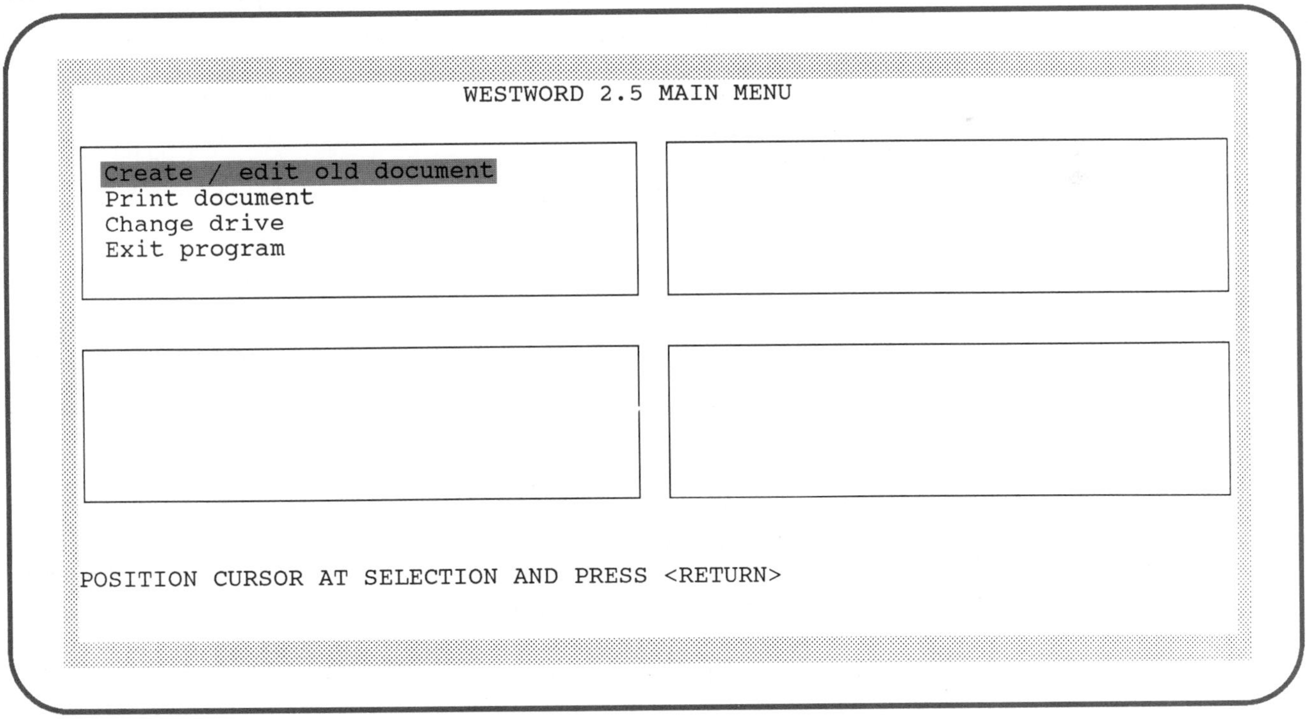

```
                    WESTWORD 2.5 MAIN MENU


    ┌─────────────────────────────┐   ┌─────────────────────────────┐
    │ Create / edit old document  │   │                             │
    │ Print document              │   │                             │
    │ Change drive                │   │                             │
    │ Exit program                │   │                             │
    └─────────────────────────────┘   └─────────────────────────────┘

    ┌─────────────────────────────┐   ┌─────────────────────────────┐
    │                             │   │                             │
    │                             │   │                             │
    │                             │   │                             │
    │                             │   │                             │
    └─────────────────────────────┘   └─────────────────────────────┘

 POSITION CURSOR AT SELECTION AND PRESS <RETURN>
```

YOUR TURN

In the following exercise, you are going to start up WestWord 2.5 on the computer, access the WestWord Main Menu, and then exit the program.
Follow the directions given previously for starting up WestWord on your computer. WestWord's Main Menu appears on the screen. Read the menu.

Use the up < ↑ > or down < ↓ > arrow keys to highlight EXIT PROGRAM
Press <Return>

The Opening Menu appears.

Use the up < ↑ > or down < ↓ > arrow keys to highlight EXIT TO DOS
Press <Return>

When the red lights on the disk drives are off, it is safe to remove the disks from the drives. Never remove a disk from a drive when the red light is on. You might damage the disk, or worse, the computer.
When you have removed the disks from the drives, shut off the computer.

Learning Check

1. WestWord 2.5 uses _____ to activate most of its functions.
   a. letter keys   c. function keys
   b. menus   d. the ten-key number pad

2. Most function keys have _____ function(s).

3. What key controls the ten-key number pad on the right side of the keyboard?

4. What is displayed below a blank work screen in WestWord 2.5?

5. What key can be used to erase mistakes?

Answers

1. c 2. more than one 3. The <Num Lock> key 4. A function menu 5. The <Back-space> key

Creating A New Document

WestWord 2.5 files can store memos, letters, term papers, or virtually anything that can be stored in traditional files kept in filing cabinets. Documents written or edited on the monitor screen are saved on a disk. Once saved, the document can be reentered for further writing or editing.

The Main Menu includes four options: CREATE/EDIT OLD DOCUMENT, PRINT DOCUMENT, CHANGE DRIVE, and EXIT PROGRAM (refer to Figure 8-1). All the files created with WestWord 2.5 must be saved on your data disk in drive B, because there is not enough space on the West Instructional Software disk in drive A to save documents. To change to drive B, use the up $<\uparrow>$ or down $<\downarrow>$ arrow keys to highlight the CHANGE DRIVE option on the Main Menu. Press <Return>. The following prompt appears:

WHAT IS THE DIRECTORY FOR YOUR USER FILES?

Type **b** for drive B. The Main Menu returns to the screen. Once this procedure has been completed, when a file is saved, it is stored on the data disk in drive B.

To begin using WestWord 2.5, you must either create a new document or edit an existing one. The exercises in this section go step by step through the processes of creating and editing documents.

Naming a Document

The first step in creating a new file is to select the CREATE/EDIT OLD DOC-UMENT option from the Main Menu and press <Return>. The Document Operations Menu appears on the screen (see Figure 8-2). Above the menu is a directory

Figure 8-2
Document Operations Menu

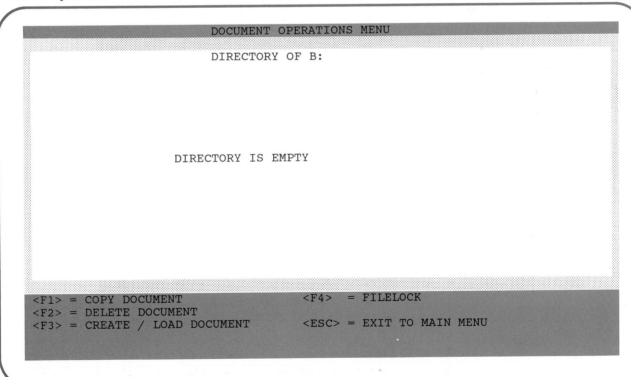

```
                    DOCUMENT OPERATIONS MENU

                        DIRECTORY OF B:




            DIRECTORY IS EMPTY








 <F1> = COPY DOCUMENT               <F4>  = FILELOCK
 <F2> = DELETE DOCUMENT
 <F3> = CREATE / LOAD DOCUMENT      <ESC> = EXIT TO MAIN MENU
```

that lists the names of the files stored on the data disk in drive B. Because you have just started using a new data disk, the directory currently is empty.

Press <F3> to create a new document. When the prompt ENTER FILENAME appears at the bottom of the screen, type a name for the file. Try to name the file something that will remind you of its contents. There is an eight-character limit on filenames. A filename can include all the letters of the alphabet, the numbers 1 through 9, and any of the special characters on the keyboard except for the period. Correct errors in the filename by using the <Backspace> key. Press <Return> once the name has been entered. A blank work screen with a blinking cursor in the upper left-hand corner appears above an editing menu.

YOUR TURN

In this exercise, you are going to start WestWord 2.5, change the disk drive to B, and name a document. Use the explanations in the previous section to complete the following steps:

Boot the computer and start WestWord 2.5.

The Main Menu appears.

Select the CHANGE DRIVE option
Type **b**

The Main Menu returns to the screen.

Select the CREATE/EDIT OLD DOCUMENT
Press <Return>

The Document Operations Menu appears.

Press <F3> for CREATE/LOAD DOCUMENT

The ENTER FILENAME prompt appears.

Type **jobmem**
Press <Return>

Although filenames always appear on the screen in capital letters, you can enter them in either upper- or lower-case letters.
The editing window appears on the screen (see Figure 8-3).

Entering Text

Before entering text into a document, you should become familiar with what appears on the computer screen. WestWord 2.5 divides the computer screen into

STATUS LINE
A message line above or below the text area on a display screen which gives format and system information.

EDITING WINDOW
The area on a computer screen that contains the typed words in a document; also, the area in which changes can be made in a document.

MENU
A display of available choices or selections to help guide the user through the process of using a software package.

CURSOR
The marker on the display screen indicating where the next character can be displayed.

SCROLLING
Moving a line or lines of text onto or off the screen.

Figure 8-3
The WestWord 2.5 Editing Window and Editing Menu

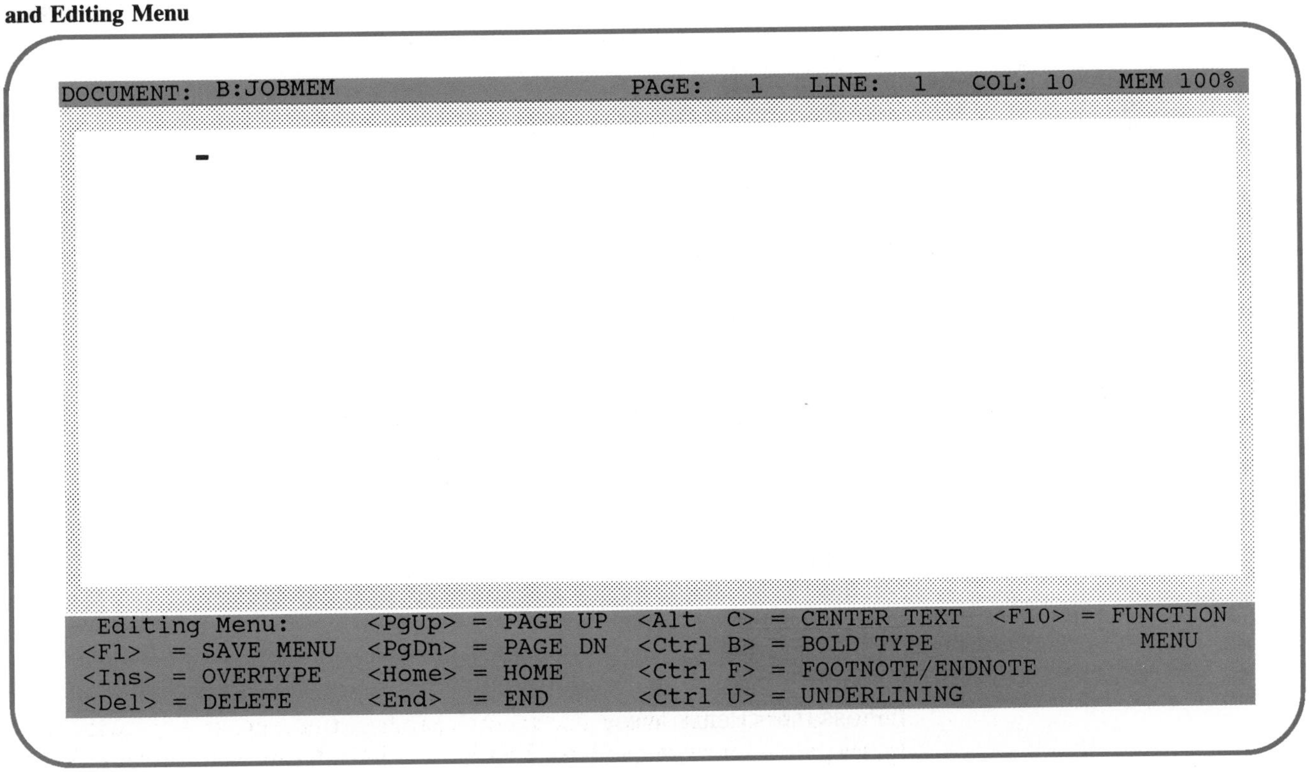

three areas: the **status line**, the **editing window**, and the Editing **Menu** (refer to Figure 8-3).

The status line is at the top of the screen. At the left of the status line is the letter of the drive, followed by the name of the document currently being created or edited. On the right side of the status line is format information about the document: the page number of the text on the screen, and the line and column number where the **cursor** currently is located.

In the right corner of the status line is the word MEM with a number that represents the percentage of remaining memory in the current file. When a file is first started, this percentage is 100, because none of the memory has been used. As data is entered, this percentage decreases. When the memory for a particular file is close to being full, a message appears on the screen giving you a warning to that effect. The maximum size of the files created with WestWord 2.5 depends on the memory capacity of the computer being used (see Table 8-2). If the computer has 128K of memory, approximately three pages of data can be stored before the memory runs out. If the machine has more than 128K, more data (up to 30 pages) can be stored. Longer documents can be accommodated by linking several shorter files together for printing. In order to save some space for additions that may be made while editing, it is a good idea to use only about 80 percent of the available space in a file.

The editing window takes up the major portion of the screen. The editing window displays the words as they are typed. All editing of a document takes place in the editing window, which can contain eighteen lines of text. When you type a document that is longer than eighteen lines, the lines at the beginning of the document **scroll** off the top of the screen to make room for any additional lines.

```
DOCUMENT:  B:JOBMEM                        PAGE:   1   LINE:   1   COL: 10    MEM 100%
 ___




 Editing Menu:        <PgUp> = PAGE UP   <Alt  C> = CENTER TEXT    <F10> = FUNCTION
 <F1>  = SAVE MENU    <PgDn> = PAGE DN   <Ctrl B> = BOLD TYPE              MENU
 <Ins> = OVERTYPE     <Home> = HOME      <Ctrl F> = FOOTNOTE/ENDNOTE
 <Del> = DELETE       <End>  = END       <Ctrl U> = UNDERLINING
```

Table 8-2
WestWord 2.5 File Limit

Amount of Memory Available	Per Document	Maximum Size of Four Files Chained Together
128K*	3 pages and 4 lines	12 pages and 16 lines
256K*	60 pages and 25 lines	241 pages and 46 lines
Over 256K	69 pages and 15 lines	268 pages and 6 lines
Number of footnotes	25	100

*Based on: 54 lines per page double spaced

WORD WRAP
The feature by which a word is moved automatically to the beginning of the next line if it goes past the right margin.

DEFAULT SETTINGS
Programmed parameters that a software package uses when no other parameter has been specified (for example, margin settings for printing).

At the bottom of the screen is the Editing Menu, which lists all the commands that can be used for editing the document on the screen.

When entering text, you need to use both upper- and lower-case letters. If the letters are all capitals when you begin typing, press the <Caps Lock> key. Letters should appear in both upper- and lower-case. Pressing the <Caps Lock> key again produces all capital letters.

The <Return> key does not need to be pressed when the end of a line is reached. WestWord 2.5 has a feature called **word wrap**, which automatically moves a word to the beginning of the next line if it crosses the right margin. The <Return> key is used to begin new paragraphs and to add blank lines to the text.

Features such as margins, tabs, and spacing are set automatically according to **default settings**. These settings can be changed easily, but for now you should just use the default settings.

YOUR TURN

You are going to enter a memo. Type the following memo exactly as it appears here. The errors are intentional, and you will correct them in a later exercise. Make sure to type the errors exactly as you see them. Do not worry about any errors you might make as you type, because these also can be corrected later.

Type TO:
Press the <Tab> key twice
Type Ms. Kim Landon
Press <Return>
Type FROM:
Press the <Tab> key once
Type Dr. Nancy Dillon
Press the <Return> key
Type DATE:
Press the <Tab> key once
Type December 12, 1987
Press the <Return> key

Type SUBJECT:
Press the <Tab> key once
Type Job Opening
Press the <Return> key three times

Notice that each time <Return> is pressed, characters that look like arrowheads appear on the screen. These are <Return> markers to indicate where in the document the <Return> key was pressed. They do not show up on printed documents. Now type the body of the memo as follows. (Remember—do not press <Return> at the end of every line. Word wrap will take care of that automatically.)

As your advisor, I want to help you in any way possible with your job hunt. Since graduation is only six short months away, I'm sure finding a job is a top priority for you right now. I just received some information from the placement service office that I would like to pass along to you. I think this information will help you in your job-search efforts.
Press <Return> twice to begin a new paragraph

Notice as you type the next paragraph that the first lines of the memo scroll off the top of the screen.

The placement service is sponsoring a cerees of semenars designed to help upcoming graduates locate potential employers, write cover letters and resumes, and improve interviewing skills. There is no cost for attending this semenar, but if you plan to attend, you must register with the placement office no later than Monday, February 17. These semenars will be divided up according to majors. The semenar for Accounting majors is scheduled for Saturday, February 21.

Press <Return> twice to begin a new paragraph

I hope you plan to attend this semenar. I think it will be well worth your time.

When finished, your screen should look like Figure 8-4. Leave the memo on the screen. In the next exercise, you will save this memo.

Saving a Document

To save a WestWord 2.5 document, press the <F10> key for FUNCTION MENU from the Editing Menu. Next, press <F1> for SAVE MENU from the Function

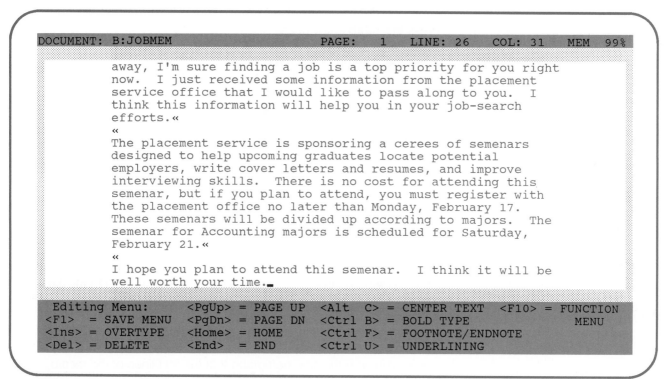

```
DOCUMENT: B:JOBMEM                    PAGE:   1   LINE: 26   COL: 31   MEM  99%

        away, I'm sure finding a job is a top priority for you right
        now.  I just received some information from the placement
        service office that I would like to pass along to you.  I
        think this information will help you in your job-search
        efforts.«
        «
        The placement service is sponsoring a cerees of semenars
        designed to help upcoming graduates locate potential
        employers, write cover letters and resumes, and improve
        interviewing skills.  There is no cost for attending this
        semenar, but if you plan to attend, you must register with
        the placement office no later than Monday, February 17.
        These semenars will be divided up according to majors.  The
        semenar for Accounting majors is scheduled for Saturday,
        February 21.«
        «
        I hope you plan to attend this semenar.  I think it will be
        well worth your time._

  Editing Menu:       <PgUp> = PAGE UP   <Alt  C> = CENTER TEXT   <F10> = FUNCTION
  <F1>  = SAVE MENU   <PgDn> = PAGE DN   <Ctrl B> = BOLD TYPE               MENU
  <Ins> = OVERTYPE    <Home> = HOME      <Ctrl F> = FOOTNOTE/ENDNOTE
  <Del> = DELETE      <End>  = END       <Ctrl U> = UNDERLINING
```

Figure 8-4
Entering Text in the JOBMEM
Document

Menu. The Save Menu with five save options appears at the bottom of the screen (see Figure 8-5). While this submenu is on the screen, no editing can be performed on the document.

Pressing <F2> saves the document and exits to the Document Operations Menu. Pressing <Esc> activates WestWord's Main Menu.

Pressing <F3> abandons a document without saving it. After you press <F3>, the prompt ARE YOU SURE? (Y/N) appears. To exit to the Document Operations Menu without saving the document, type **Y** and press <Return>. An abandoned document cannot be retrieved, so be absolutely certain you do not want to save the document before typing **Y** and pressing <Return>.

To save the document without exiting, press <F4>. The document is saved on the data disk, but also remains on the screen so that you can continue to work on it. Pressing <Esc> from the Save Submenu also allows you to continue working on the document, but without saving it.

YOUR TURN   You are going to save the memo you created in the last exercise. The JOBMEM file should be on your screen. The Editing Menu should be at the bottom of the screen.

Press <F10> for FUNCTION MENU
Press <F1> for SAVE MENU

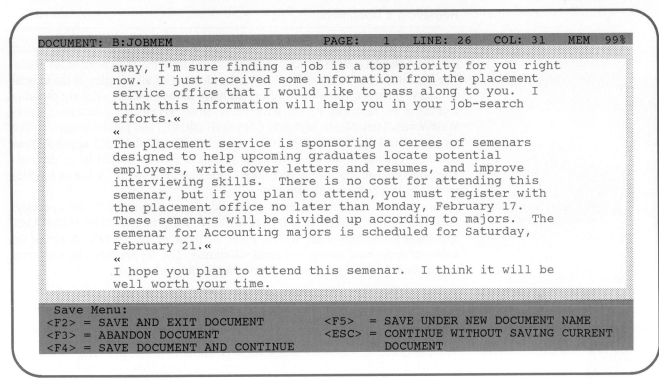

```
DOCUMENT: B:JOBMEM                     PAGE:    1   LINE: 26   COL: 31   MEM   99%

         away, I'm sure finding a job is a top priority for you right
         now.  I just received some information from the placement
         service office that I would like to pass along to you.  I
         think this information will help you in your job-search
         efforts.«
         «
         The placement service is sponsoring a cerees of semenars
         designed to help upcoming graduates locate potential
         employers, write cover letters and resumes, and improve
         interviewing skills.  There is no cost for attending this
         semenar, but if you plan to attend, you must register with
         the placement office no later than Monday, February 17.
         These semenars will be divided up according to majors.  The
         semenar for Accounting majors is scheduled for Saturday,
         February 21.«
         «
         I hope you plan to attend this semenar.  I think it will be
         well worth your time.

  Save Menu:
  <F2> = SAVE AND EXIT DOCUMENT          <F5>  = SAVE UNDER NEW DOCUMENT NAME
  <F3> = ABANDON DOCUMENT                <ESC> = CONTINUE WITHOUT SAVING CURRENT
  <F4> = SAVE DOCUMENT AND CONTINUE              DOCUMENT
```

Figure 8-5   The Save Submenu

The Save Menu appears.

 Press <F2> for SAVE AND EXIT DOCUMENT

The Document Operations Menu returns to the screen. In the editing window under the words DIRECTORY OF B is listed JOBMEM. The file JOBMEM has been saved on your work disk in drive B.

 Press <Esc> to access the Main Menu
 Select EXIT PROGRAM
 Press <Return>

The Opening Menu appears on the screen.

 Select EXIT TO DOS
 Press <Return>

When the red light on the disk drive goes off, it is safe to remove your data disk and the West Instructional Software disk. After removing the disks, turn off the computer and monitor.

Retrieving a Document

To edit a document that already exists, start up WestWord on the computer. Select the CREATE/EDIT OLD DOCUMENT command from the WestWord Main Menu. The Document Operations Menu appears with a list of all the files in the current directory. If the file you want to edit is not listed in the directory, you are probably looking at the directory for the wrong disk drive. To change directories, access WestWord's Main Menu, highlight CHANGE DRIVE, and press <Return>. The prompt WHAT IS THE DIRECTORY FOR YOUR USER FILES appears. Your data disk containing all the documents you have created should be in drive B. Type **b** to change the current directory to the disk in drive B. A list of the files on that disk appears in the directory.

To retrieve a file, find the name of the file you wish to access in the directory. Press <F3> for CREATE/LOAD DOCUMENT. The prompt ENTER FILENAME appears at the bottom of the screen. Enter the name of the file to be retrieved (in lower- or upper-case letters) and press <Return>. The file appears with the cursor in the home position (at the very beginning of the document).

YOUR TURN

You are going to retrieve the JOBMEM document. Insert the West Instructional Software disk in drive A and your data disk in drive B. Start WestWord 2.5 on the computer. The WestWord Main Menu should be on your screen.

Select CHANGE DRIVE
Press <Return>

The following prompt appears: WHAT IS THE DIRECTORY FOR YOUR USER FILES?

Type **b**

The Main Menu appears.

Select CREATE/EDIT OLD DOCUMENT
Press <Return>

The Document Operations Menu appears with the directory of drive B. The JOBMEM file should be listed in the directory.

Press <F3> for CREATE/LOAD DOCUMENT

The prompt ENTER FILENAME appears.

Type **jobmem**
Press <Return>

The first eighteen lines of the memo and the Editing Menu appear on the screen. You are now going to exit from this file.

Press <Esc>

The Save Submenu appears.

Press <F2> for SAVE AND EXIT DOCUMENT

The Document Operations Menu appears.

Press <Esc> for EXIT TO MAIN MENU

The WestWord 2.5 Main Menu appears.

Select EXIT PROGRAM
Press <Return>

The Opening Menu appears.

Select EXIT TO DOS
Press <Return>

When the system prompt appears and the red lights on the disk drives are off, remove the disks and turn off the computer and monitor.

Learning Check

1. Why is it important to remember to choose the CHANGE DRIVE selection from WestWord's Main Menu before beginning work on a document?

2. What keys do you push to save and exit a document?

3. How long can a filename be in WestWord 2.5?

4. What is the feature called which automatically moves words to the next line if they run over the right margin?

5. When is it safe to remove disks from the disk drives on your computer?

Answers

1. There is not enough space on the program disk to store any additional files. **2.** Press <Esc> and then <F2> when the Save Submenu appears. **3.** Eight characters. **4.** Word wrap. **5.** When the A> or B> prompt appears on the screen and the red light is off.

Preparing to Edit a Document

TEXT EDITING
The function of a word processor which enables the user to enter and edit text.

A document that has been saved on disk can be edited using the **text-editing** function of a word processor. This is the function that probably comes to most people's minds first when thinking about word processing. The most fundamental aspect of this function is the word processor's ability to accept and store internally the text that is typed in at the keyboard. Without this ability, all the other functions and procedures would be useless.

The following section describes the procedures necessary to prepare for editing a document.

Copying a Document

Before editing a document, it is a good idea to make a copy of the file and to make changes to the copy rather than the original. That way, if all or part of the document is accidentally deleted, or if anything else happens to damage the document, the original file still exists. Another copy of the original file can then be made, and the editing procedure can be started over again.

To copy a document that already exists, access the directory for drive B. The name of the file to be copied should appear in the directory. If it does not, make sure the West Instructional Software disk is in drive A and your data disk is in drive B. Return to the Main Menu and select drive B by using the CHANGE DRIVE command.

When the Document Operations Menu appears, Press <F1> for COPY DOCUMENT. The message FILE TO COPY FROM appears at the bottom of the screen over the prompt ENTER FILENAME. Type the name of the file to be copied and press <Return>. Next, the message FILE TO COPY TO appears over the prompt ENTER FILENAME. Enter a new name for the copy and press <Return>. The new file is added to the directory.

The name given to the copy has to be different from the name of the original file. If the same name is entered at both the FILE TO COPY FROM and FILE TO COPY TO prompts, the following message appears: FILE ALREADY EXISTS DO YOU WISH TO OVERWRITE IT? (Y/N). Entering **Y**, for yes, and pressing <Return> simply copies the original to itself. Typing **N**, for No, and pressing <Return> at the prompt returns the Document Operations Menu to the screen. At this point, the copy procedure can be started over again. The new filename entered for the copy must be different from the filename of the original.

 YOUR TURN

You are going to make a copy of the file JOBMEM. Take the steps necessary to start WestWord 2.5 on the computer. Make sure that your data disk is in drive B and that the drive currently being accessed is drive B. Start with the Document Operations Menu on your screen. The file JOBMEM should be listed in the directory.

Press <F1> for COPY DOCUMENT

The prompt FILE TO COPY FROM and ENTER FILENAME appear on the screen.

Type **jobmem**
Press <Return>

Next the prompts FILE TO COPY TO and ENTER FILENAME appear on the screen.

Type **newjob**
Press <Return>

Both the JOBMEM and NEWJOB files are listed in the directory. Now you are ready to load the document.

Press <F3> for CREATE/LOAD DOCUMENT

The prompt ENTER FILENAME appears.

Type **newjob**
Press <Return>

The memo you keyed in appears in the editing window (see Figure 8-6).

Figure 8-6
Copying the JOBMEM Document

```
DOCUMENT:  B:NEWJOB                          PAGE:    1    LINE:    1    COL: 10    MEM   99%

           TO:        Ms. Kim Landon«
           FROM:      Dr. Nancy Dillon«
           DATE:      December 12, 1987«
           SUBJECT:   Job Opening«
           «
           «
           As your advisor, I want to help you in any way possible with
           your job hunt.  Since graduation is only six short months
           away, I'm sure finding a job is a top priority for you right
           now.  I just received some information from the placement
           service office that I would like to pass along to you.  I
           think this information will help you in your job-search
           efforts.«
           «
           The placement service is sponsoring a cerees of semenars
           designed to help upcoming graduates locate potential
           employers, write cover letters and resumes, and improve
           interviewing skills.  There is no cost for attending this

    Editing Menu:      <PgUp> = PAGE UP   <Alt  C> = CENTER TEXT   <F10> = FUNCTION
  <F1>  = SAVE MENU    <PgDn> = PAGE DN   <Ctrl B> = BOLD TYPE                MENU
  <Ins> = OVERTYPE     <Home> = HOME      <Ctrl F> = FOOTNOTE/ENDNOTE
  <Del> = DELETE       <End>  = END       <Ctrl U> = UNDERLINING
```

Cursor Movement

Before starting to work on a file, you need to be able to control the cursor position. There are several ways to control the position of the cursor. One way is to use the arrow keys in the numeric keypad on the right side of the keyboard. The down arrow $<\downarrow>$ key moves the cursor one line down. The up arrow $<\uparrow>$ key moves the cursor one line up. The left arrow $<\leftarrow>$ key moves the cursor one position to the left, and the right arrow $<\rightarrow>$ key moves the cursor one position to the right. (Do not confuse the left arrow key with the <Backspace> key.)

The arrow keys are useful for moving the cursor short distances. If the cursor needs to be moved a long distance, however, using the arrow keys may be inefficient. Other keys located in the numeric keypad can move the cursor quickly from one part of the document to another. The following table lists these keys and describes their functions. Some of these keys also are defined in the Editing Menu.

Key	Cursor position
<Home>	Pressing <Home> moves the cursor to the beginning of the first line on the screen.
<Ctrl> <Home>	<Ctrl> and <Home> pressed together take the cursor to the very beginning of the document.
<End>	Pressing <End> moves the cursor to the first position in the bottom line of the screen.
<Ctrl> <End>	<Ctrl> and <End> pressed together take the cursor to the very end of the document.
<PgUp>	Pressing <PgUp> moves the cursor one screen back toward the beginning of the document.
<PgDn>	Pressing <PgDn> moves the cursor one screen forward toward the end of the document.
<Crtl> <PgUp>	<Ctrl> and <PgUp> pressed together move the cursor one page back toward the beginning of the document.
<Ctrl> <PgDn>	<Ctrl> and <PgDn> pressed together move the cursor one page forward toward the end of the document.

Remember, the keypad can be used to move the cursor only when the <Num Lock> key is off. If the numbers 2, 4, 6, or 8 appear on the screen when you are trying to move the cursor, then the <Num Lock> key is on. Press it once and use the <Backspace> key to delete the numbers.

YOUR TURN

You are going to use the cursor movement keys to move the cursor around the document NEWJOB. The NEWJOB file should be on the screen, and the cursor should be located on page 1, line 1, column 10.

Press the down arrow $<\downarrow>$ key three times

The cursor should be under the *S* in *Subject*. Look at the status line at the very top of the screen. The cursor should be on page 1, line 4, column 10.

Press <Home>

The cursor moves back to page 1, line 1, column 10.

Press <PgDn>

The first 18 lines of the letter scroll off the top of the screen. The cursor is now in page 1 on line 19, column 10.

Press the right arrow <→> key 22 times

The cursor is now under the *a* in *plan*. The status line should read line 19, column 32.

Press <PgUp>

The cursor returns to the beginning of the document.

Press <Ctrl> and hold it down while pressing <End>

The cursor moves to the last line of the document.

Press <Ctrl> and hold it down while pressing <Home>

The cursor is back to the beginning of the document. Continue practicing moving the cursor, using all of the cursor movement keys. In particular, you should practice using the commands that require the <Ctrl> key to be held down while pressing <End>, <Home>, <PgUP>, and <PgDn>.
When you are done, save and exit NEWJOB.

Editing a Document

INSERTION
A word processing feature in which a character, word, sentence, or larger block of text is added to the existing text.

DELETION
A word processing feature in which a character, word, sentence, or larger block of text may be removed from the existing text.

Text editing functions include the ability of the word processor to **insert** and **delete** characters, words, lines, paragraphs, and larger blocks of text. The insert and delete modes are probably two of the most commonly used text-editing features of any word processor. Most word processors, including WestWord 2.5, also allow blocks of text to be moved and copied. These features make it easier to rearrange and retype documents.

Removing Text

Text from a WestWord document can be removed in a number of ways. The <Backspace> key, the <Del> key, the <Ins> key, and the MARK TEXT and

Learning Check

1. The most fundamental aspect of the text-editing function of a word processor is _____.

2. Why is it a good idea to make a copy of a file before you begin editing it?

3. What indicates where you are working in a document?

4. Where are the cursor-control keys located?

5. After you have entered the last word of a document, what key combination moves the cursor back to the beginning of the document?

Answers

1. Its ability to accept and store internally the text that is typed in at the keyboard 2. If the file is accidentally damaged in some way, the original still exists so that additional copies can be made and edited. 3. The cursor. 4. On the numeric keypad on the right side of the keyboard. 5. <Ctrl> and <Home> together.

DELETE commands all can be used to remove text. The best method to use depends on the particular text to be removed, its location, and its length. It also depends on your individual typing style. All these methods are explained in this section.

Pressing the <Backspace> key moves the cursor one space to the left, removing characters from each position that it passes. If the <Backspace> key is held down, it continues to remove characters until released. The <Del> key removes the character immediately above the cursor.

The <Ins> key can be used for removing and replacing text at the same time. If the <Ins> key is pressed once, OVT (Overtype) appears in the lower right corner of the screen. If WestWord is in the Overtype mode, text can be changed by typing over the characters above the cursor. For example, if the cursor were under the *d* in the sentence "The dog ran up the street" and OVT were on the screen, typing **cat** would produce the sentence "The cat ran up the street." If you typed *elephant*, however, the new sentence would read "The elephantup the street." For one word to replace another using Overtype mode, the two words must have the same number of letters. Usually you should not work in Overtype mode, because important information could easily be written over. Pressing the <Ins> key again returns WestWord to Insert mode. In this mode, characters that are added appear to the left of the cursor. Existing text moves to the right to make room for the characters being entered, so no characters are deleted or replaced.

To remove larger blocks of text, use the MARK TEXT and DELETE commands from the Function Menu. Position the cursor under the first letter of the text to be deleted. Press <F10> to access the Functions Menu (see Figure 8-7). Press <F5> to begin marking the text. The word MARK appears in the lower right corner of the screen, to remind you that the MARK TEXT command currently is activated. Use the cursor control keys (right, left, or down arrow) to highlight text. When

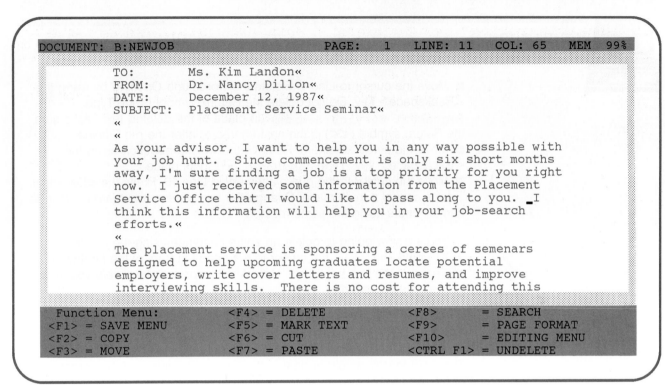

Figure 8-7
The Functions Submenu

the text to be deleted is highlighted, press <F5> again to end the text marking. To delete the highlighted text, press <F4>.

Once the MARK TEXT command is started by pressing the <F5> key once, no other procedure can be performed until <F5> is pressed again to complete the MARK TEXT command. If you press <F5> once and then try to enter text, nothing happens. If you press <F5> once and highlight some text, and then try to delete it by pressing <F4> without first pressing <F5> again, a warning appears at the bottom of the screen, reminding you to finish the procedure. If this happens, press the space bar to return to the document and complete the MARK TEXT command by pressing <F5> a second time. The word MARK at the bottom of the screen should disappear, indicating that the MARK TEXT procedure has ended. Press <F4> to delete the text.

If text that you do not want deleted is accidentally marked, press <Esc> to cancel the procedure. The Functions Menu remains on the screen, and the MARK TEXT command can be started all over again.

If text is accidentally deleted using the DELETE function, you can undelete up to twenty lines using the UNDELETE function. This function is activated by pressing <Ctrl> and <F1>. If more than twenty lines are deleted, only the first twenty lines are recalled. The UNDELETE function can recall only the most recently deleted text.

When the Functions Menu is no longer needed for making changes to the document, pressing <F10> returns the Editing Menu to the screen.

YOUR TURN

You are going to practice editing a document. Start with the NEWJOB file on the screen.

■ Move the cursor to Line 4. Delete the words *Job Opening* by using the <Backspace> key. Do not delete the Return symbol (<<). Type `Placement Service Seminar` in place of the deleted text. Make sure the Return symbol (<<) is the next character after the *r* in *Seminar*.
■ Move the cursor to Line 8. Remove the word *graduation* using the <Backspace> key. Type `commencement` in its place.
■ Move the cursor to the *p* in *placement* in Line 10. Press the <Del> key. Type a capital P in its place. Change the *s* in *service* and the *o* in *office* to capital letters using the same method.

You are now going to delete an entire sentence using the MARK TEXT command. Move the cursor to the space in front of the *I* in the last sentence of the first paragraph (*I think this information will help you in your job-search efforts.*)

Press <F10> for FUNCTION MENU
Press <F5> for MARK TEXT

The word MARK should appear in the lower right corner of the screen. Using the arrow keys, move the cursor to the period at the end of the sentence. The entire sentence, including the period, should be highlighted. The Return symbol that follows the period should not be highlighted.

Press <F5> to end the MARK TEXT command
Press <F4> for DELETE

Move the cursor to Line 13. You are going to make several corrections in this line using the Overtype mode. Move the cursor to the *p* in *placement*.

Press <Ins> to turn the Overtype mode on

The word OVT should appear in the lower right corner of the screen. Type a capital `P`. Move the cursor to the *s* in *service*. Type a capital `S`. Move the cursor to the *c* in *cerees*. Type `seri`. The word should now be *series*. Move the cursor to under the second *e* in *semenars*. Type `i`.

Press <Ins> to turn the Overtype mode off

Move the cursor to Line 17. Change *semenar* to *seminar*. In Line 18, capitalize the *p* in *placement* and the *o* in *office*.
Move the cursor to the *T* in *These* in Line 19. You are going to delete the entire sentence (*These semenars will be divided up according to majors.*) using the MARK TEXT command.

Press <F10> for FUNCTION MENU
Press <F5> for MARK TEXT

Press the right arrow key until the entire sentence, including the period, is highlighted
Press <F5> to end the MARK TEXT command
Press <F4> for DELETE

Type this sentence to take the place of the sentence you just deleted: Each seminar will focus on a different major. In Line 19 change *semenar* to *seminar*.

Move the cursor to Line 23. Change *semenar* to *seminar*. Using the <Backspace> key, delete the words *I think* in the last sentence of the memo. Change the lower-case *i* in *it* to a capital I. The last sentence should now read, *It will be well worth your time*.

Activate the Save Menu by pressing <F1> and save the revised NEWJOB file.

Moving Blocks of Text

In addition to deleting words or lines, the MARK TEXT function can be used to move words, sentences, paragraphs, or any designated block of text around on the page quite easily. This function simplifies making major revisions to any document.

To move a block of text, position the cursor under the first letter of the text to be moved. Activate the Functions Menu, if necessary, by pressing <F10>. Press <F5> for MARK TEXT. Use the right arrow <→> and down arrow <↓> keys to highlight the text. When all of the text that you want to be moved is highlighted, complete the MARK TEXT function by pressing <F5> again. Move the cursor to the position in the document where the text is to be moved, and activate the MOVE function by pressing <F3>. The text is deleted from its current position and reappears beginning at the position of the cursor.

If you want to copy the same block of text somewhere else in a document, highlight the text to be reproduced using the MARK TEXT function. Place the cursor at the position in the document where the text is to appear again, and press <F2> to activate the COPY function. The text is copied beginning at the cursor's position. The COPY Function can only be used once on a marked block of text. To copy the block of text again, remark it using the MARK TEXT function.

YOUR TURN

In this exercise, you are going to practice moving text using the MARK TEXT function. If necessary, start WestWord and load the NEWJOB file.

Using the MARK TEXT command, mark the following sentence as a block of text: "As your advisor, I want to help you in any way possible with your job hunt." Be sure the two spaces following the period at the end of the marked sentence are also highlighted.

Move the cursor to the word *I* in the sentence that begins, "I just received some information . . ."

Press <F3> for MOVE

Now you are going to copy a block of text to a new location. Select the entire first paragraph as a block of text. Include both Return symbols at the end of the paragraph in the highlighted area (see Figure 8-8). Move the cursor to the end of the last sentence in the memo.

Press <Return> twice
Press <F2> for COPY

You decide you do not like this paragraph in its new location. Use the MARK TEXT command to block the last paragraph in the memo. Include the two Return symbols that appear at the end of the paragraph in the highlighting.

Press <F4> for DELETE

The paragraph should remain as the opening paragraph to the memo.

Mark the sentence in the second paragraph that begins, "There is no cost for attending this seminar . . ." as a block of text. The highlighting should start with the *T* in *There* and it should include two spaces following the period at the end of the sentence.

Move the cursor to the Return symbol that follows the period at the end of the last sentence in the second paragraph (see Figure 8-9).

Press the <Space Bar> twice
Press <F3> for MOVE

Save the revised NEWJOB document.

Printing a Document

Before printing a document, make sure the paper is lined-up correctly in the printer. If the paper is not properly aligned before the printer is turned on, the margins will not be correct in the printed document. Once the paper is set correctly, turn the printer on. Make sure the printer is online. After the printer has been turned on, do not adjust the paper.

Access the Main Menu of WestWord 2.5 and use the cursor keys to highlight PRINT DOCUMENT. Press <Return>. The Printer Selection Menu appears. Enter the number that corresponds to your printer and press <Return>. If your printer is not listed, enter **13** for OTHERS.

Next, the prompt NUMBER OF FILES TO BE PRINTED (1 – 4) appears. Type the number of files that you wish to print and press <Return>. Two or more files can be chained together and printed as one document. When the prompt ENTER FILENAME appears, enter the name of the file (or files) to be printed and press <Return>.

The prompt PRINT THE FIRST PAGE MARKER (Y/N) appears. If you want the first page numbered, type **Y** and press <Return>. If not, type **N** and press <Return>. The process for creating footnotes and endnotes is covered in the next

Figure 8-8 Copying a Block of Text

```
DOCUMENT: B:NEWJOB                    PAGE:   1   LINE: 13   COL: 10   MEM  99%

          TO:        Ms. Kim Landon«
          FROM:      Dr. Nancy Dillon«
          DATE:      December 12, 1987«
          SUBJECT:   Placement Service Seminar«
          «
          «
          Since commencement is only six short months away, I'm sure
          finding a job is a top priority for you right now.   As your
          advisor, I want to help you in any way possible with your job
          hunt.  I just received some information from the Placement
          Service Office that I would like to pass along to you.  «
          «
          The Placement Service is sponsoring a series of seminars
          designed to help upcoming graduates locate potential
          employers, write cover letters and resumes, and improve
          interviewing skills.  There is no cost for attending this
          seminar, but if you plan to attend, you must register with
          the Placement Office no later than Monday, February 17.

 Function Menu:          <F4> = DELETE          <F8>      = SEARCH
 <F1> = SAVE MENU        <F5> = MARK TEXT       <F9>      = PAGE FORMAT
 <F2> = COPY             <F6> = CUT             <F10>     = EDITING MENU
 <F3> = MOVE             <F7> = PASTE           <CTRL F1> = UNDELETE
```

Figure 8-9 Moving a Block of Text

```
DOCUMENT: B:NEWJOB                    PAGE:   1   LINE: 20   COL: 67   MEM  99%

          SUBJECT:   Placement Service Seminar«
          «
          «
          Since commencement is only six short months away, I'm sure
          finding a job is a top priority for you right now.   As your
          advisor, I want to help you in any way possible with your job
          hunt.  I just received some information from the Placement
          Service Office that I would like to pass along to you.  «
          «
          The Placement Service is sponsoring a series of seminars
          designed to help upcoming graduates locate potential
          employers, write cover letters and resumes, and improve
          interviewing skills.  There is no cost for attending this
          seminar, but if you plan to attend, you must register with
          the Placement Office no later than Monday, February 17.   Each
          seminar will focus on a different major.  The seminar for
          Accounting majors is scheduled for Saturday, February 21.«
          «

 Function Menu:          <F4> = DELETE          <F8>      = SEARCH
 <F1> = SAVE MENU        <F5> = MARK TEXT       <F9>      = PAGE FORMAT
 <F2> = COPY             <F6> = CUT             <F10>     = EDITING MENU
 <F3> = MOVE             <F7> = PASTE           <CTRL F1> = UNDELETE
```

chapter. If the document does contain footnotes or endnotes, the next prompt is: DO YOU WISH NOTES TO BE <F>OOTNOTES or <E>NDNOTES? (F/E). Type in **F** or **E**, and press <Return>. The document is then printed.

YOUR TURN

You are going to print the NEWJOB file. Take the necessary steps to activate the WestWord 2.5 Main Menu.

Use the < ↓ > key to highlight PRINT FILE
Press <Return>

The prompt NUMBER OF FILES TO BE PRINTED (1 – 4) appears.

Type **1**
Press <Return>

The prompt ENTER FILENAME appears.

Type **newjob**
Press <Return>

The prompt PRINT THE FIRST PAGE MARKER (Y/N) appears.

Type **N**
Press <Return>

After the file is printed, the Main Menu appears on the screen. Your printed document should look like Figure 8-10.

Learning Check

1. The ___ function of a word processor allows the user to enter and edit text.
2. What functions need to be activated to move blocks of text in a document?
3. If the <Ins> key is pressed once, _____ appears in the lower right corner of the screen.
4. If text is deleted by accident, the _____ function allows the first twenty lines of text to be recovered.
5. Text that is highlighted by accident with the MARK TEXT function can be unhighlighted using _____.

Answers

1. text-editing 2. MARK TEXT (<F5>) and MOVE (<F3>) 3. OVT 4. UNDELETE (<Ctrl> and <F1> together) 5. <Esc>

```
TO:       Ms. Kim Landon
FROM:     Dr. Nancy Dillon
DATE:     December 12, 1987
SUBJECT:  Placement Service Seminar


Since commencement is only six short months away, I'm sure
finding a job is a top priority for you right now.   As your
advisor, I want to help you in any way possible with your job
hunt.   I just received some information from the Placement
Service Office that I would like to pass along to you.

The Placement Service is sponsoring a series of seminars
designed to help upcoming graduates locate potential
employers, write cover letters and resumes, and improve
interviewing skills.   Each seminar will focus on a different
major.   The seminar for Accounting majors is scheduled for
Saturday, February 21.   There is no cost for attending this
seminar, but if you plan to attend, you must register with
the Placement Office no later than Monday, February 17.

I hope you plan to attend this seminar.   It will be well
worth your time.
```

Figure 8-10
The NEWJOB Document

Select EXIT PROGRAM
Press <Return>

The Opening Menu appears.

Select EXIT TO DOS

The system prompt A> appears. When the red lights have gone off on the disk drives, remove your disks from the computer and turn the computer off.

Summary Points

■ Word processing is the act of composing and manipulating text with the aid of a computer.

■ A word processor is a program (software) or set of programs which enables users to write, edit, format, and print data.

■ A word processing system includes both the hardware and software needed to operate a word processor. There are two general types of word processing systems: (1) dedicated systems, which can handle only word processing, and (2) multipurpose systems, which are equipped to handle various processing tasks including word processing.

■ Word processors can be used in many different environments, such as businesses, schools, and homes. Uses for word processors include writing business letters, school reports, and letters.

■ The two primary functions of a word processor are text editing (entering and manipulating text) and print formatting (telling the printer how to format the printed copy).

■ Common writing and editing features of a word processor include cursor positioning, word wrap, scrolling, insertion, replacement, deletion, block movements, undo, and save.

WestWord 2.5 Exercises

1. Starting up WestWord 2.5
    a. Assuming your computer is shut off, describe all the necessary steps to start WestWord 2.5. Start WestWord on your computer. How are most of its functions activated?
    b. When is it safe to remove the disks from the disk drives on your computer?

2. Creating a New Document
    a. What actions do you have to take to begin working on a new document in WestWord 2.5? Do what is necessary to begin entering text into a document.
    b. How do you tell where you are in a document? Locate the status line on your screen.

3. Entering a Document
    a. Create a new document and name it SOAP.
    b. Type the following paragraph as shown. The errors in it are intentional and will be corrected later in this exercise, so make sure that you type the errors.

```
    A soap opera deal with the plights and problems
brought about in the lives of its permanent
principal characters by the advent and interference
of one group of individuals after another. Thus, a
soap opera ia an endlesss sequence of narratives
whose only cohesive element is the eternal presence
of bedeviled and beleagured principal characters. A
narative, or story sequence, may run from eight
weeks to several months. The ending of one plot is
always hooked up with the beginning of the next,
but the connection is unimportant and soon
forgotten. Almost all the villains in the small
town daytime serials are emigres from the old
cities--gangsters, white-collar criminals,
```

```
designing women, unnatural mothers, cold wives, and
selfish, ruthless, and just plain cursed rich men.
They always come up against a shrewdness that
outwits them or destroys them, or a kindness that
wins them over to the god way of life.
```

E.B. White, ''Soapland''

4. Using the Editing Commands
   a. Correct the following typing mistakes in the file created in Exercise 3:
   ■ Add an *s* to *deal* in the first sentence.
   ■ In the second sentence, change *ia* to *is* and remove the extra *s* from *endless*.
   ■ In the third sentence, correct the misspelled word *narative*.
   ■ Use the down arrow $<\downarrow>$ key to move to the end of the text. Change *god* to *good* in the last sentence.
   b. Delete the following sentence, using the MARK TEXT function and the DELETE function: ''A narrative, or story sequence, may run from eight weeks to several months.'' (*Note:* Make sure you delete the two spaces following this text.)
   c. Move the cursor to the beginning of the paragraph. Mark the first sentence and place it at the end of the text, using the MOVE function.

5. Saving and Retrieving a Document
   a. You want to save the work you have completed and quit WestWord. What steps do you take to do this? Save the document and quit WestWord.
   b. You decide to restore the sentence that you previously removed, so you need to reboot WestWord to retrieve the file containing the document. Describe the steps required to do this. Retype the sentence at the appropriate place and save your document again.

6. Review

Name all of the WestWord 2.5 functions that you have used in this chapter.

WestWord 2.5 Problems

1. To complete the following problem, you need to use the ORDER file included on your student learning file disk, the DOS disk, and the program disk. Start WestWord. Insert the learning disk with the ORDER file on it in drive B.

2. Take the steps necessary to activate WestWord's Main Menu. Change the disk drive to drive B so that you will be able to access the ORDER file, and so that your work will be saved to the learning disk rather than the program disk.

3. Make a copy of the ORDER file and name it ESSAI. Describe the steps you follow to copy the file.

4.   Retrieve the ESSAI file and use it to answer the remaining questions.

5.   The document is an order to a publishing firm. Assume that you are Helen Turoff, the documentalist. You want to use the same format in the ORDER file to order another magazine. Because you made a copy of the ORDER file, you can make changes to it and still have the original format saved. Change the date of the order to the current date.

6.   Using the MARK TEXT and DELETE functions, delete the supplier address and replace it with the following new address:

```
Midwest Publishing
112 Lassalle Street
Chicago, IL 60610
```

7.   Change the word *monthly* to *weekly*.

8.   Add the following to the beginning of the first sentence: `Starting next month,`. Change the *P* in *Please* from upper- to lower-case.

9.   Add the following name to the list of persons receiving the subscription:

```
Mark Steiner
M.I.S. Department
```

10.   Using the MARK TEXT and DELETE functions, delete the following sentence: "I am accepting your special offer—$15 for the first subscription, $8 for each additional copy."

11.   Save and print your work.

CHAPTER 9

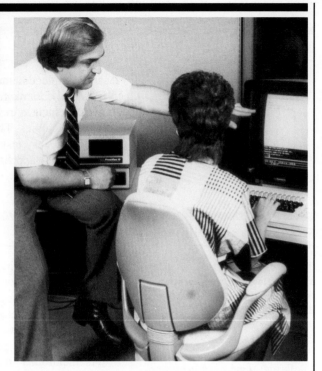

Advanced
WestWord™ 2.5

Introduction

Many simple documents, such as memos and letters can be created with the WestWord commands learned in the previous chapter. Other types of documents, however, such as resumes or term papers, require the use of WestWord's more advanced features. These features can make the creation of a complicated document a relatively easy task. This chapter explains how to use print formatting features to enhance the appearance of a document, and how to add footnotes to a document.

Formatting a Document

PRINT FORMATTING
The function of a word processor which tells the printer how to print the text on paper.

PRINT ENHANCEMENTS
Variations such as underlining and boldfacing; some word processors also include superscripting and subscripting as print enhancements.

The **print formatting** function of a word processor involves a variety of features that communicate with the printer to tell it how to print the text on paper. Some of the more common print formatting features include the ability to set margins and tab stops; to select single- or double-spaced text; to mark page breaks; and to perform **print enhancements** such as underlining and boldfacing. Figure 9-1 illustrates a typical page format.

As mentioned in the previous chapter, WestWord has default settings that automatically format a document. Sometimes, however, it is necessary to create a format with different margins, tab settings, and line spacing. The exercises in this chapter guide you through the process of formatting a document.

Setting Tabs, Margins, and Line Spacing

WestWord's Page Format Menu (see Figure 9-2) enables the user to adjust the line spacing, margins, and tab settings of a document. This menu also includes a quotation function that enables the user to add single-spaced, indented block quotations to a document without changing the existing page formats.

To access the Print Formatting Menu from the Editing Menu, press <F10> for FUNCTION MENU. The Function Menu appears on the screen. Press <F9> for PAGE FORMAT and the Page Format Menu appears on the screen. Table 9-1 lists the options included in the Page Format Menu, along with the function each option performs.

While the Page Format Menu appears on the screen, no work can be performed in the text editing window. For example, if you try to enter text into a document while the Page Format Menu is on the screen, nothing happens. You can work on the document only if the Function Menu or the Editing Menu is on the screen.

The format for a document must be planned before the document is entered into WestWord. The settings for left and right margins cannot be changed after a document is entered. If you attempt to change the margin settings after the document has been entered, you may lose the format established for the entire document. The first step you should take after entering the filename of a new document is to set the left and right margins, if they are to be set somewhere other than the default settings.

Line spacing, top and bottom margins, and tab settings can be adjusted after a document has been entered.

Figure 9-1
A Typical Page Format

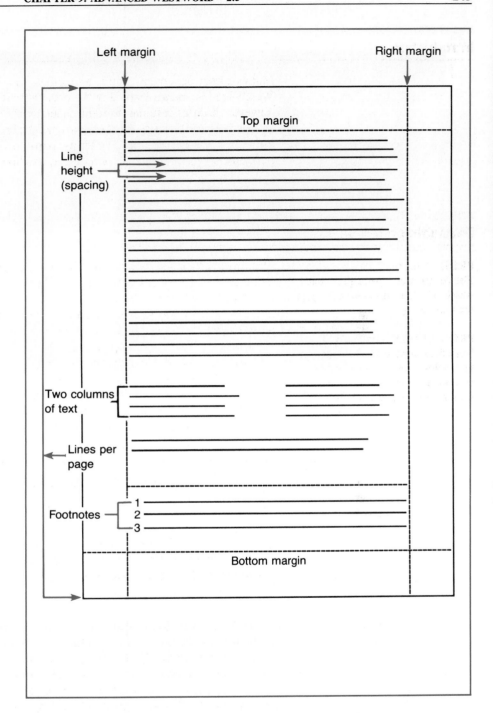

WestWord's default setting for line spacing is single spacing. To change the line spacing of a document, first access the Page Format Menu. Once the Page Format Menu is on the screen, press <F2>. The prompt ENTER LINE SPACING (1–5) appears at the bottom of the screen. A document can have up to five spaces between lines. Type the desired number of spaces (from 1 to 5) and press <Return>. The Page Format Menu returns to the screen, and the line spacing is changed

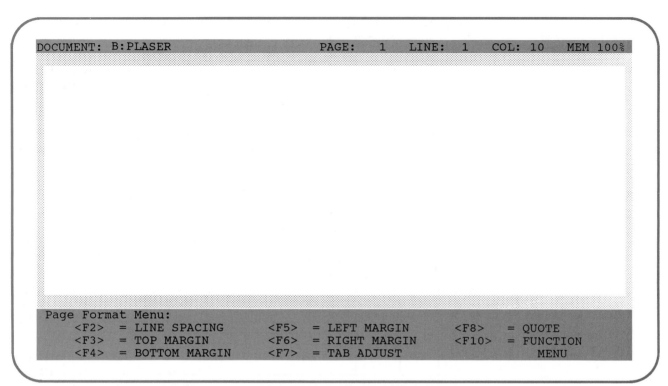

```
DOCUMENT: B:PLASER                    PAGE:   1    LINE:   1    COL: 10    MEM 100%
```

```
Page Format Menu:
    <F2>  =  LINE SPACING        <F5>  =  LEFT MARGIN        <F8>   =  QUOTE
    <F3>  =  TOP MARGIN          <F6>  =  RIGHT MARGIN        <F10>  =  FUNCTION
    <F4>  =  BOTTOM MARGIN       <F7>  =  TAB ADJUST                    MENU
```

Figure 9-2
The Page Format Menu

throughout the entire document. Note that the line spacing on the screen remains single. When the document is printed, however, it is printed double-spaced if the line spacing is set at 2, triple-spaced if the line spacing is set at 3, and so on.

WestWord's default setting for a top margin is 4. This setting provides a top margin of 1-1/4 inches. To change this setting, access the Page Format Menu and press <F3> for TOP MARGIN. The prompt ENTER TOP MARGIN (0–20) appears.

A top margin setting of 0 provides a 1/2-inch top margin, the smallest top margin a document can have. There are six lines of type to an inch, so if the top margin is to be 1-1/2 inches, enter **6** at the ENTER TOP MARGIN prompt. The

Table 9-1 Options from the Page Format Menu

Command	Description
<F2> for LINE SPACING	Sets the spacing between lines. Can be set for a spacing of 1 to 5 lines.
<F3> for TOP MARGIN	Sets the top margin. Can be set so that there are up to 20 lines in the top margin.
<F4> for BOTTOM MARGIN	Sets the bottom margin. Can be set so that there are up to 20 lines in the bottom margin.
<F5> for LEFT MARGIN	Sets the left margin. Can be set so that there are up to 20 spaces in the left margin.
<F6> for RIGHT MARGIN	Sets the right margin. Can be set so that there are up to 20 spaces in the right margin.
<F7> for TAB ADJUST	Sets the tab spacing. Can be set so that there are up to 30 spaces between tabs.
<F8> for QUOTE	Sets a single-spaced block quotation, with both sides indented.
<F10> for FUNCTION MENU	Accesses the Function Menu.

top margin is already 1/2 inch; entering 6 at the prompt provides another inch. For a total top margin of 2 inches, enter **9** at the prompt.

In order to ensure that the document is printed with the correct top margin on each page, you must line up the paper with the printer head before turning the printer on. Once the printer is turned on, do not make any adjustments. If adjustments have to be made, turn the printer off, make the adjustments, and turn the printer back on.

The bottom margin is set the same way as the top margin. First, access the Page Format Menu. Then press <F4> for BOTTOM MARGIN. The prompt ENTER BOTTOM MARGIN (0–20) appears. The default setting for the bottom margin is 4, which provides a bottom margin of 1-1/4 inches.

A bottom margin setting of 0 provides a 1/2 inch bottom margin. Therefore, the method used to compute the number to enter at the ENTER BOTTOM MARGIN prompt is the same as the one used to compute the top margin. Subtract 1/2 inch from the desired bottom margin and, assuming there are six lines to an inch, compute how many lines are needed to make up the remainder. This is the number to be entered at the prompt.

It is important to remember that the left and right margins must be set before the document is entered. The command to set the left margin is <F5> on the Print Format Menu. The prompt ENTER LEFT MARGIN (1–21) appears. The number entered at the prompt depends on whether the printer types 10, 12, or 17 characters per inch. For example, if the printer types 10 characters per inch, entering 10 at the prompt produces a 1-inch left margin. If the printer prints 12 characters per inch, entering 18 produces a left margin of 1-1/2 inches.

The right margin is set in a manner similar to the left margin. The Page Format Menu must first be accessed. Press <F6> for RIGHT MARGIN. The prompt ENTER RIGHT MARGIN (58–78) appears. The width of a standard piece of paper is 8-1/2 inches, so if the printer types 10 characters per inch, 85 characters fit across the width of the page ($10 \times 8.5 = 85$). The numbers next to the ENTER RIGHT MARGIN prompt represent the minimum and maximum column numbers that can be used for the right margin. If 85 characters fit across the width of the paper, column 85 is at the right edge of the paper. WestWord automatically inserts a right margin of 7 characters; therefore, the last column where the right margin can be set is 78. Table 9-2 lists entries for the left and right margin prompts that will set the margins at 1, 1-1/2, and 2 inches. Printers that produce 10, 12, and 17 characters per inch are included in the table.

Remember, in order for the printed document to match the page format you establish, the paper in the printer has to be properly aligned. If the paper is not properly aligned, the margins on the printed document may not be correct.

Table 9-2
Entries for the Left and Right Margin Prompts

Margin Width	Left Margin Entry			Right Margin Entry		
1 inch	10	12	17	75	73	68
1-1/2 inches	15	18	25	70	67	60
2 inches	20	24	34	65	61	
Printer Characters Per Inch	10 CPI	12 CPI	17 CPI	10 CPI	12 CPI	17 CPI

To set the tab spacing, access the Page Format Menu and press <F7> for TAB ADJUST. The prompt ENTER TAB SPACING (2–30) appears. The default setting for tabs is 5 spaces. That is, a tab stop is set automatically at column 5, 10, 15, 20, and so on. To change the default setting for tab stops, enter the number of spaces that should appear between tab stops (from 2 to 30) and press <Return>.

The final command on the Page Format Menu, QUOTE, will be covered later in this chapter. Pressing <F10> for FUNCTION MENU returns the Function Menu to the screen. Remember, no work can be done on the document while the Page Format Menu is on the screen. Every time a formatting change is completed, you should return the Function Menu or the Editing Menu to the screen.

YOUR TURN

For this hands-on exercise you are going to create a new document. Figure 9-3 depicts the final document.

Start up WestWord on the computer
Select CHANGE DRIVE from WestWord's Main Menu
Type **B**
Select CREATE/EDIT OLD DOCUMENT from WestWord's Main Menu
Press <F3> for CREATE/LOAD DOCUMENT

The prompt ENTER FILENAME appears on the screen.

Type **PLASER** (for Placement Service)
Press <Return>

A blank text editing window appears. You are now ready to begin formatting the document. You are going to change the left and right margins. Assuming that your printer types 10 characters per inch, you will specify a 1-1/2-inch left margin and a 1-inch right margin.

Press <F10> for FUNCTION MENU
Press <F9> for PAGE FORMAT
Press <F5> for LEFT MARGIN

The prompt ENTER LEFT MARGIN appears. If the printer types 10 characters per inch, then 15 equals 1-1/2 inches. WestWord automatically inserts one space, however, so the number to be inserted is 14 ($15 - 1 = 14$).

Type **14**
Press <Return>
Press <F6> for RIGHT MARGIN

The prompt ENTER RIGHT MARGIN appears. The right margin is to be 1 inch, which is equal to 10 characters, so the number to be entered is 75 ($85 - 10 = 75$).

Type **75**
Press <Return>

The Placement Service Office is pleased you are attending one
of our job placement seminars. This is the third year we have
sponsored these seminars and they have proven to be quite
successful.

The seminar for Accounting majors is Saturday, February 22
from 8:00 a.m. to 5:00 p.m. The following introduces you to
the people leading the seminar and outlines the day's
schedule.

Seminar Staff:

Dr. Kate Clifford, Head of Placement Service. Dr Clifford has
been the head of the Placement Service Office at Ohio State
for over fifteen years. Before coming to Ohio State, she
worked for the executive recruiting firm, Cyphers and Porter,
Inc.

Mr. Keith Goldman, Audit Manager, Thales Electronic, Inc.
As Audit Manager, Mr. Goldman is responsible for hiring close
to twenty auditors a year. Mr. Goldman's published articles
include, "Marketing Your Accounting Degree," and "The Hiring
Trend in Accounting."

Schedule:

I.   8:00-8:30 Registration

II.   8:30-10:00 Locating Employers

        A.   What are the Job Opportunities
        B.   Informational Interviews
        C.   Talking to Everybody Can Get You a Job

III.   10:00-12:00 Cover Letters and Resumes

        A.   The Content of a Resume
        B.   The Form of a Resume
        C.   How to Write a Cover Letter

IV.   Break for Lunch

V.   1:00-2:00 Interviewing Skills

        A.   How to Make a Positive First Impression
        B.   Being Prepared for Any Interview Question
        C.   Knowing What Questions You Should Ask

VI.   2:00-5:00 Utilizing Placement Service

        A.   Using the Career Library
        B.   Interviews Through the Placement Office

Figure 9-3
Letter from the Placement Service
Office Using Various Formatting
Commands

The left and right margins are now set. Next, you are going to change the
tab spacing. The tabs for this document need to be set every 8 spaces. The
Page Format Menu should still be on the screen.

Press <F7> for TAB ADJUST

The prompt ENTER TAB SPACING appears.

Type **8**
Press <Return>

You are now ready to begin typing the document. Enter the text exactly as it appears here. Press <F10> to activate the Function Menu so that you can begin entering text. Type the following:

```
The Placement Service Office is pleased you are
attending one of our job placement seminars. This is
the third year we have sponsored these seminars and
they have proven to be quite successful.

The seminar for Accounting majors is Saturday,
February 22 from 8:00 a.m. to 5:00 p.m. The
following introduces you to the people leading the
seminar and outlines the day's schedule.
```

Press <Return> twice to create space and then type:

```
Seminar Staff:
```

Press <Return> twice to create space and then type:

```
Dr. Kate Clifford, Head of Placement Service. Dr.
Clifford has been the head of the Placement Service
Office at Ohio State for over fifteen years. Before
coming to Ohio State, she worked for the executive
recruiting firm, Cyphers and Porter, Inc.

Mr. Keith Goldman, Audit Manager, Thales Electronic,
Inc. As Audit Manager, Mr. Goldman is responsible
for hiring close to twenty auditors a year. Mr.
Goldman's published articles include, ''Marketing
Your Accounting Degree,'' and ''The Hiring Trend in
Accounting.''
```

Press <Return> twice to create space and then type:

```
Schedule:
```

Press <Return> twice to create space. The following schedule is in outline form. After typing each Roman Numeral and the following period, press the <Tab> key before typing the text on that line. Double-space after each line by pressing <Return> twice. Type:

```
I.    8:00-8:30 Registration

II.   8:30-10:00 Locating Employers
```

251

You are now going to add second level headings to the outline. Before typing the "A," "B," and "C," press the <Tab> key once to indent all the second level headings. Type the following:

```
A.  What are the Job Opportunities
B.  Informational Interviews
C.  Talking to Everybody Can Get You a Job
```

Press <Return> twice to create space. Type the rest of the outline as it appears below. Remember, for the first level headings, press the <Tab> key after typing each Roman Numeral and the following period. For second level headings, press the <Tab> key before typing the line.

```
III.  10:00-12:00  Cover Letters and Resumes

      A.  The Content of a Resume
      B.  The Form of a Resume
      C.  How to Write a Cover Letter

IV.   Break for Lunch

V.    1:00-2:00  Interviewing Skills

      A.  How to Make a Positive First Impression
      B.  Being Prepared for Any Interview Question
      C.  Knowing What Questions You Should Ask

VI.   2:00-5:00  Utilizing Placement Service

      A.  Using the Career Library
      B.  Interviews Through the Placement Office
```

Look over the document carefully. The format should match Figure 9-3. If it does not match, make the necessary corrections. Save the document and print it.

Print Enhancements

A print enhancement is any special printing effect. Print enhancements such as underlining or boldfacing can improve the appearance of a document. As explained in the previous chapter, whether or not you can use the WestWord print enhancements depends on the type of printer you are using.

WestWord enables the user to bold or underline sections of text that are being entered for the first time or that have already been entered. The UNDERLINE and BOLD functions are found on the Editing Menu. To underline text that is being entered for the first time, press <Ctrl> and U together before typing the word or phrase. A special character (§) appears on the screen. This character indicates that whatever follows it is going to be underlined when printed; the actual underline does not appear on the screen. Type the word or phrase to be underlined. At the end of the word or phrase, press <Ctrl> U again. Another § symbol appears, indicating that the UNDERLINE command is no longer active. Whatever text is included between those two symbols will be underlined when the document is printed.

The BOLD command works the same way as the UNDERLINE command. When the word or phrase to be bolded is reached, press <Ctrl> B for BOLD TYPE. A special character that looks something like a laughing face (☺) appears on the screen. Type the word or phrase to be bolded. When the end of the word or phrase is reached, press <Ctrl> B again. Another laughing face symbol appears, and the BOLD function is turned off. Whatever is included between the two symbols is bolded when the document is printed.

As mentioned in the previous chapter, whether or not you can use the WestWord print enhancements depends on the type of printer you are using. When printing a document, the Printer Selection Menu appears after selecting PRINT DOCU-MENT from the WestWord Main Menu. If the printer you are using is listed in the Printer Selection Menu, enter the number that corresponds with your printer and press <Return>. The printers that are listed will print underlines, boldface, and superscripts. If your printer is not listed, experiment with selecting the printers that are listed. Your printer might be compatible with one of them. If it is, it will print the print enhancements when the printer with which it is compatible is selected. If you try selecting each of the printers listed and your printer still does not print the print enhancements, then select OTHERS. If OTHERS is selected, then underlining and boldfacing will not print. Superscripts will print, but they will appear on the line of text rather than raised slightly above it.

WestWord also has a centering function that allows text to be centered on the line. The CENTER function is also found in the Editing Menu. To use the centering function, first type the text to be centered. With the cursor at the end of the text, press <Alt> C at the same time. The text immediately moves to the center of the line.

YOUR TURN

For this exercise, a resume is created utilizing many of the print enhancements. Figure 9-4 depicts the completed resume. Create a new document and name it KIMRES (for Kim's resume).

Press <Ctrl> B for BOLD TYPE
Type KIM LANDON
Press <Ctrl> B to turn off the BOLD function
Press <Return>

The address needs to be on the right side of the resume. Use the tab key to move the cursor over to position 45.

Type 322 Spring Road
Press <Return> and then tab to position 45

Figure 9-4 Resume Using Several Print Enhancements

```
KIM LANDON
                                    322 Spring Road
                                    Columbus, Ohio  44322
                                    (614) 555-1214

                       Objective

To develop skills in managerial accounting with a major
corporation and to become a controller.

                       Education

B.S. Accounting, Ohio State University, 1985
Minor:  Economics with emphasis in corporate finance
Significant courses include:

     Accounting                 Business
Financial Accounting       Topics in Corporate Management
Cost Accounting            Industrial Economics
Advanced Accounting        Management Information Systems
Advanced Federal Tax Law   Business Communications

                      Experience

Summers
Intern, Price Waterhouse, Columbus, Ohio, 1986
Worked on various audit assignments, including stock
inventory at Mills International.

Intern, Johnson & Johnson, Cincinnati, 1985
Worked in the budget department on data collecting for the
preparation of the next-fiscal-year budget.

College
Assistant, University Financial Aid Office, 1986
Reviewed applications for financial aid; verified their
conformity with tax returns and other supportive documents.

Orientation Leader, University Admissions Office, 1985
Met with prospective students and their parents; conducted
tours of campus; wrote reports for each orientation meeting.

                  Computer Experience

Proficient in running Lotus 1-2-3 and WordStar on an IBM PC.

                      Activities

Alpha Beta Psi
Student Senator, Served on budget committee, 1985-1986

                      References

Credentials and references available upon request.
```

Type `Columbus, Ohio 44322`
Press <Return> and then tab to position 45
Type `(614) 555-1214`
Press <Return> twice
Type `Objective`
Press <Alt> **C** for CENTER TEXT
Press <Return> twice
Type `To develop skills in managerial accounting with a major corporation and to become a controller.`
Press <Return> twice
Type `Education`
Press <Alt> **C** for CENTER TEXT
Press <Return> twice
Type `B.S. Accounting, Ohio State University, 1985` (press <Return>)
Type `Minor: Economics with emphasis in corporate finance`
Type `Significant courses include:` (press <Return> twice)
Press the <Tab> key once
Press <Ctrl> **U** for UNDERLINING
Type `Accounting`
Move the cursor to column 45
Type `Business`
Press <Ctrl> **U** to turn off the UNDERLINING function
Press <Return>

Enter the following by typing the Accounting class on the left first, then tabbing over to column 40 to type the Business class on the same line. Press <Return> after typing each Business class.

`Financial Accounting`	`Topics in Corporate Management`
`Cost Accounting`	`Industrial Economics`
`Advanced Accounting`	`Management Information Systems`
`Advanced Federal Tax Law`	`Business Communications`

Press <Return> twice
Type `Experience`
Press <Alt> **C** for CENTER TEXT
Press <Return> twice
Press <Ctrl> **U** for UNDERLINING
Type `Summers`
Press <Ctrl> **U** to turn off the UNDERLINING function
Press <Return>
Type `Intern, Price Waterhouse, Columbus, Ohio, 1986` (press <Return>)
Type `Worked on various audit assignments, including stock inventory at Mills International.` (press <Return> twice)

Type Intern, Johnson & Johnson, Cincinnati, 1985
  (press <Return>)
Type Worked in the budget department on data
  collecting for the preparation of the next-fiscal-
  year budget. (press <Return> twice)
Press <Ctrl> **U** for UNDERLINING
Type College
Press <Ctrl> **U** to turn off the UNDERLINING function
Press <Return>

Type the following:

Assistant, University Financial Aid Office, 1986
  (press <Return>)
Reviewed applications for financial aid; verified
  their conformity with tax returns and other
  supportive documents. (press <Return> twice)
Orientation Leader, University Admissions Office,
  1985 (press <Return>)
Met with prospective students and their parents;
  conducted tours of campus; wrote reports for each
  orientation meeting. (press <Return> twice)

Type Computer Experience
Press <Alt> **C** for CENTER TEXT
Press <Return> twice
Type Proficient in running Lotus 1-2-3 and WordStar
  on an IBM PC.
Press <Return> twice
Type Activities
Press <Alt> **C** for CENTER TEXT
Press <Return> twice
Type Alpha Beta Psi (press <Return>)
Type Student Senator, Served on budget committee,
  1985-1986 (press <Return> twice)
Type References
Press <Alt> **C** for CENTER TEXT
Press <Return> twice
Type Credentials and references available upon
  request.

Look the format over carefully. The format should match Figure 9-4. If it
does not match, make the necessary corrections. When you are satisafied
that the document matches Figure 9-4, save and print the KIMRES
document.

Learning Check

1. The Page Format Menu is accessed by pressing _____.

2. The first step in changing any of the margins is to activate the _____ function.

3. The UNDERLINE function is activated by _____.

4. Text can be centered by _____.

5. The BOLD TYPE function is activated by _____.

Answers

1. <F9> from the Function Menu 2. PAGE FORMAT (<F9>) 3. pressing <Ctrl> and U together. 4. activating the CENTER TEXT function (pressing <Alt> and C together) 5. pressing <Ctrl> and B together

Cut and Paste

As explained in the previous chapter, WestWord's MOVE and COPY functions allow text to be moved around within a document, thus making it much easier to edit a document. Another WestWord feature that simplifies editing is the CUT/PASTE function. CUT and PASTE are two separate functions but they are used together to perform a single CUT/PASTE operation. They enable the user to move text from one document into another document easily. This feature allows separate documents to be combined.

Before you can use CUT and PASTE, the document that contains the block of text must be on the screen. Position the cursor under the first letter of that text, and press <F6> from the Function Menu to activate the CUT function. Use the arrow keys to highlight the text. Then press <F6> again to deactivate the CUT function. The highlighted text is written to memory, and the highlighting disappears.

The text is now ready to be moved into another document. Save and exit the file that text has been cut from, and open the file containing the document where the text is to be inserted. The margins of this file have to be as wide as the margins of the text about to be inserted. If they are not, a warning message appears. Place the cursor where the text is to be reproduced in the new document. Press <F7> to activate the PASTE function. The text is written into the document.

CUT and PASTE also can be used within a document, but the MOVE and COPY functions are much more efficient for this purpose. CUT and PASTE was designed to facilitate the moving of large blocks of text from document to document.

 YOUR TURN

In this exercise you are going to use WestWord's CUT and PASTE functions to move information from one file to another. You want to create a file of educational material about Kim Landon for later use, possibly in a data base. Create a new file and name it EDATA.

You are going to add an introduction to the material to be pasted in from the KIMRES document to the EDATA document. Type the following:

```
The material stored herein is designed to help
authorized individuals gather information about
prospective employees' educational backgrounds.
```

Press <Return> twice
Press <Ctrl> **U** for UNDERLINING
Type Landon, Kim
Press <Ctrl> **U** to turn off the UNDERLINING function
Save and exit the EDATA document

You now need information from KIMRES in EDATA. Rather than retyping the information, you can use the CUT and PASTE functions to move the information. Before you can do that, however, you need to make a copy of the KIMRES file.

Press <F1> for COPY document
Type **kimres**
Press <Return>
Type **kimres2**
Press <Return>
Load the KIMRES2 document

Position the cursor in column 10 of line 11. The word "Education" is centered on this line.

Press <F10> for the FUNCTION MENU
Press <F6> for CUT

Using the down arrow key < ↓ >, highlight through line 21. All the courses listed under "Significant courses include" should be highlighted.

Press <F6> to end the CUT command

The highlighting disappears from the screen.

Save and exit the KIMRES2 document
Load the EDATA document

Position the cursor two lines under "Landon, Kim." This should be line 7.

Press <F10> for the FUNCTION MENU
Press <F7> for PASTE

All the text just highlighted appears in the EDATA document.

Save and exit the EDATA document.

More Advanced Features

WestWord includes sophisticated features that are not mandatory for all documents. If mastered, however, they can be convenient time-savers. These features, which are covered in the remainder of this chapter, can help you create professional-looking documents with little effort.

Footnotes and Endnotes

The FOOTNOTE/ENDNOTE function is found in the Editing Menu. To create a footnote or an endnote, press <Ctrl> and **F** together when the end of the paragraph or quotation has been reached. The Footnote/Endnote Menu appears at the bottom of the screen (see Figure 9-5). To create either a footnote or an endnote, press <F3> for CREATE FOOTNOTE/ENDNOTE. The prompt AUTHOR'S NAME appears. Type the author's name and press <Return>. The prompts TITLE, LOCATION OF PUBLICATION, PUBLISHER, DATE OF PUBLICATION, and PAGE NUMBER(S) follow. Enter the appropriate information after each prompt and press <Return>. The Footnote/Endnote Menu returns, and a reference number appears at the end of the paragraph or quotation.

The Footnote/Endnote Menu can be activated from either the Function Menu or the Editing Menu, even though <Ctrl F> is not listed as an option in the Function Menu. To exit from the Footnote/Endnote Menu, press <F10>. The

Figure 9-5
The Footnote/Endnote Menu

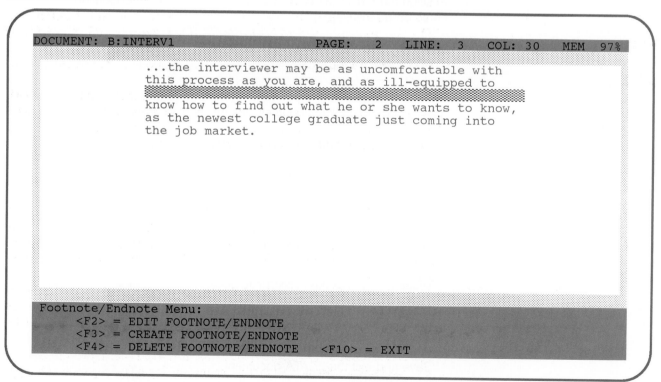

DOCUMENT: B:INTERV1   PAGE: 2 LINE: 3 COL: 30 MEM 97%

   ...the interviewer may be as uncomfortable with
this process as you are, and as ill-equipped to
know how to find out what he or she wants to know,
as the newest college graduate just coming into
the job market.

Footnote/Endnote Menu:
  <F2> = EDIT FOOTNOTE/ENDNOTE
  <F3> = CREATE FOOTNOTE/ENDNOTE
  <F4> = DELETE FOOTNOTE/ENDNOTE <F10> = EXIT

Editing Menu returns to the screen if the Footnote/Endnote Menu was activated from the Editing Menu. The Function Menu returns to the screen if the Footnote/Endnote Menu was activated from the Function Menu.

If a reference is being repeated and you wish to use the abbreviation Ibid. rather than retyping the entire note, simply type **Ibid.** after the first prompt, AUTHOR'S NAME, and press <Return> after the following prompts without entering anything. Be sure to capitalize the *I*, or a string of commas will appear for the following fields, rather than just the period that needs to follow the abbreviation. If the footnote or endnote does not require a page number, press <Return> after the PAGE NUMBER(S) prompt. Otherwise, enter the appropriate page number(s) at the prompt.

Footnotes or endnotes are placed automatically at the bottom of the page or at the end of the document, respectively, according to the guidelines in *The Chicago Manual of Style*. The notes are numbered automatically as well. When the finished document is printed, a prompt appears asking whether the notes are to be footnotes or endnotes.

If you need to edit a footnote or endnote that has already been created, press <F2> for EDIT FOOTNOTE/ENDNOTE from the Footnote/Endnote Menu. The prompt ENTER NUMBER OF NOTE appears. Enter the number of the note and press <Return>. Each footnote/endnote prompt appears with the text that was entered next to it. Even though only one correction may need to be made, all of the entries up to the one being edited have to be entered again. Once the correction has been made, pressing <Esc> returns the Footnote/Endnote Menu to the screen; the remaining note entries do not have to be reentered. If the EDIT FOOTNOTE/ENDNOTE function is activated by accident, press <Esc> to get out of the command and preserve the note as it is.

A footnote can be deleted by pressing <F4> for DELETE FOOTNOTE/ENDNOTE from the Footnote/Endnote Menu. The prompt ENTER NUMBER OF NOTE appears. Enter the number of the note and press <Return>. The footnote is deleted, and the other footnotes and their referents are renumbered automatically to reflect the change.

If a footnote is deleted accidentally, using the <Backspace> key, the MARK TEXT and DELETE functions, or any way other than through the Footnote/Endnote Menu, the automatic renumbering does not work. If that happens, all of the notes following the change have to be renumbered manually.

Automatic Quotation Indentation

In a research paper, long quotations typically are single-spaced and indented five spaces from the right and left margins. WestWord's QUOTE function automatically changes the page formatting to reset the margins and the line spacing for the quotation.

To use the QUOTE function, position the cursor at what will be the beginning of the first line in the quotation. That is, make sure to press <Return> so that there is a space between the quotation and the text that precedes it. Press <F9> from the Function Menu to activate the Page Format Menu. Press <F8> to activate the QUOTE function. The letters QUOT appear in the lower-right corner of the screen, the Function Menu returns, and the text editing window goes blank. Type the quotation in the text editing window. When the quotation is entered, press <F9> to activate the Page Format Menu again. Then press <F8> again and the quotation is inserted into the document. The cursor is positioned at the end of the quotation. You can create the footnote or endnote for the quotation either when you enter the quotation or right after returning to the document. Once the document has returned to the screen, press <Return> to create space between the quotation and the text that will follow it.

If a quotation that has already been entered needs to be edited, place the cursor under the first letter in the first word of the quotation. Activate the MARK TEXT command by pressing <F5> from the Function Menu. Use the arrow keys to highlight the entire quotation, and then press <F5> again to end the MARK TEXT command. Press <F9> to activate the Page Format Menu. Press <F8> for QUOTE. The quotation just highlighted appears in the text editing window, and any necessary changes can now be made. This is the only way you can edit a quotation that has been entered into a document using the QUOTE command. If you try to edit the quotation in normal text entry mode, the spacing in the quotation is changed. Some keys and functions are disabled, however, while the quotation appears by itself in the text editing window. The Overtype mode (<Ins> key), for instance, does not work. The MOVE, CUT, and PASTE functions should not be used either, because they may cause spacing problems within the quotation and the document. The arrow keys, the <Backspace> key, and the <Del> key are the principal editing tools in this mode. Once the quotation has been edited, press <F8> again to return to the main document.

To delete a quote, you must first delete its corresponding footnote as explained in the previous section. After the footnote has been deleted, place the cursor under the first letter in the first word of the quotation. Activate the MARK TEXT command by pressing <F5> from the Function Menu, highlight the entire quotation using the arrow keys, and press <F5> again to end the MARK TEXT command. Once the entire quotation is highlighted press <F4> for DELETE.

Search

SEARCH AND FIND
A routine that locates a specific string of characters and places the cursor at that string.

SEARCH AND REPLACE
A routine that searches for a given character string and replaces it with a specified replacement string.

GLOBAL SEARCH AND REPLACE
A search and replace operation that is carried out throughout the entire document, without user intervention.

If you have ever written a long document and discovered that a key term has been misspelled throughout, you know how difficult and time-consuming it can be to correct the mistake. Most word processors, like WestWord, have alleviated this problem by incorporating various types of search routines. The most basic is the **search and find** routine. The user enters the specific character string to search for, and the program positions the cursor at the first occurrence of that string. Most programs also provide the option of continuing the search to find each successive occurrence of the specified string.

Another type of search routine is the **search and replace** routine, in which the word processor searches for each occurrence of a specified string and replaces it with a specified replacement string. Usually there are two options for this search routine. In the first option, the cursor moves to the first occurrence of the string to be replaced, and the program asks the user if that particular occurrence of the string should be replaced. The user responds accordingly at each successive occurrence of the string. The second option is called **global search and replace**. The word processor finds each occurrence of a specified string and replaces it with the replacement string, without user intervention.

WestWord incorporates all three of these search routines. To use the SEARCH feature, place the cursor at the beginning of the document. Activate the Function Menu and press <F8> for SEARCH. The Search Menu appears at the bottom of the screen (see Figure 9-6). First, the prompt GLOBAL SEARCH: (Y/N) must be answered. If you want the program to find every occurrence of a word, type **Y** and press <Return>. If only the first instance of the word is to be found, type **N** and press <Return>. After the next prompt, SEARCH FOR, enter the character string that is to be searched for and press <Return>. WestWord can search for a string that is up to 40 characters long. After the prompt REPLACE WITH, enter whatever string is to replace the existing string.

If a global search is being performed, when the first instance of the string is located, the program highlights it. The prompt REPLACE THIS TEXT? (Y/N) appears at the bottom of the screen. Type **y** and press <Return> to make the correction. If that particular occurrence of the string is not to be replaced, type **n** and press <Return>. Repeat this procedure until NO MORE SEARCH VALUES FOUND {END OF DOCUMENT} appears at the bottom of the screen.

If you do not want the string to be replaced automatically by a string that you define in advance, type **n** at the GLOBAL SEARCH prompt. Enter the word you wish to change after the SEARCH FOR prompt. At the REPLACE WITH prompt, press <Return> without entering anything. The program locates the first instance of the character string and highlights it. Then the program asks: CONTINUE WITH SEARCH? (Y/N). Type either **Y** or **N**. In either case, the Function Menu returns to the screen and the cursor is positioned under the first character of the highlighted word. At this point, you can delete the character string and enter a replacement string if desired. To find the next instance of the character string,

Figure 9-6
The Search Menu

```
DOCUMENT: B:INTERV1              PAGE:   1   LINE:   1   COL: 10   MEM  98%

                 §Interviews:   Wretched or Rewarding?§«
      «
          For many people, interviews have a peculiar Dr. Jekyll
      and Mr. Hyde quality to them.  While these people are job
      hunting, they anxiously await the phone call or letter
      issuing the coveted invitation for an interview.  After all
      their hard work of scouting out the job market, finding
      openings in their field, writing resumes and cover letters,
      an interview seems like a well-deserved reward.  But, once
      attained, the golden interview turns into a nerve-shattering
      monster.  Sleepless nights are spent worrying over such
      questions as, what will I wear, what will I say, what if
      they ask a question I can't answer?  All of a sudden, the job
      hunter feels like the hunted as visions of the mighty
      interviewer, whose sole purpose is to expose all the
      interviewee's inadequacies, become inescapable.«
          Interviews do not have to turn into such horrible
      monsters.  Exposing some of the myths about interviews helps

SEARCH FUNCTION:      FOR NO REPLACEMENT PRESS <RETURN> AT (Replace with:)
      Global Search:   (Y/N)
      Search for:
      Replace with:
```

press <F8> to activate the SEARCH function again. Each time you reactivate the SEARCH function, you must enter a character string at the SEARCH FOR prompt.

The WestWord SEARCH function locates only the exact uppercase or lowercase match. For example, if *She* is the character string, WestWord does not find the string *she*. When searching for a string that is capitalized occasionally in a document, you need to perform two searches in order to find all occurrences of the string: one search for the string with all lowercase letters, and a second search for the string with the first letter capitalized.

YOUR TURN

In this hands-on exercise, you are going to create the first two pages of a paper that includes footnotes. If necessary start up WestWord on the computer. The Document Operations Menu should be on the screen. Create a new document. Name it **INTERV1**. A blank text editing window should be on the screen. First, change the page format from single to double spacing.

Press <F10> for FUNCTION MENU
Press <F9> for PAGE FORMAT
Press <F2> for LINE SPACING
Type **2** at the ENTER LINE SPACING prompt
Press <Return>
Press <F10> to return to the Function Menu
Press <F10> again to return to the Editing Menu

Now you are going to enter the title of the paper.

Press <Ctrl> **U** for UNDERLINING
Type Interviews: Wretched or Rewarding?
Press <Ctrl> **U** again to turn the UNDERLINING function off
Press <Alt> **C** for CENTER TEXT
Press <Return> twice

Type the following:

    For many people, interviews have a peculiar Dr.
Jekyll and Mr. Hyde quality to them. While these
people are job hunting, they anxiously await the
phone call or letter issuing the coveted invitation
for an interview. After all their hard work of
scouting out the job market, finding openings in
their field, writing resumes and cover letters, an
interview seems like a well-deserved reward. But,
once attained, the golden interview turns into a
nerve-shattering monster. Sleepless nights are
spent worrying over such questions as, what will I
wear, what will I say, what if they ask a question I

```
can't answer?  All of a sudden, the job hunter feels
like the hunted as visions of the mighty
interviewer, whose sole purpose is to expose all the
interviewee's inadequacies, become inescapable.
     Interviews do not have to turn into such horrible
monsters.  Exposing some of the myths about
interviews helps to alleviate the fear we all attach
to the interviewing process.
     Often, the interviewee has a totally inaccurate
image of the interviewer.  Many prospective
employees assume the interviewer is highly skilled
in conducting interviews.  This is not necessarily
the case as Richard Boles points out in the
following quotation:
```

Now you are ready to type the first quotation. The cursor should still be in the space following the colon after the word *quotation*.

> Press <Return>
> Press <F10> to activate the Function Menu
> Press <F9> to activate the Page Format Menu
> Press <F8> for QUOTE

The text editing window is blank except for a shaded area and the blinking cursor. The Function Menu now appears at the bottom of the screen. The shaded area is the page break symbol. Type:

```
...the interviewer may be as uncomfortable with this
process as you are, and as ill-equipped to know how
to find out what he or she wants to know, as the
newest college graduate just coming into the job
market.
```

You now need to insert the first footnote.

> Press <F10> to activate the Editing Menu
> Press <Ctrl> **F** for FOOTNOTE/ENDNOTE

The Footnote/Endnote Menu appears at the bottom of the screen.

> Press <F3> for CREATE FOOTNOTE/ENDNOTE

The prompt AUTHOR'S NAME appears at the bottom of the screen.

> Type **Boles, Richard**
> Press <Return>

The prompt TITLE appears.

Press <Ctrl> **U** to activate the UNDERLINE command
Type **What Color Is Your Parachute**
Press <Ctrl> **U** again to end the UNDERLINE command
Press <Return>

The prompt LOCATION OF PUBLICATION appears.

Type **Berkeley**
Press <Return>

The prompt PUBLISHER appears.

Type **10 Speed Press**
Press <Return>

The prompt DATE OF PUBLICATION appears.

Type **1983**
Press <Return>

The prompt PAGE NUMBER(S) appears.

Type **181**
Press <Return>

The Footnote/Endnote Menu reappears on the screen. The number 1 automatically appears at the end of the quotation.

Press <F10> for EXIT

The Editing Menu appears. Both the quotation and the note that identifies that quotation are now entered. You need to end the QUOTE function. The letters QUOT still appear in the lower-right corner of the screen.

Press <F10> to activate the Function Menu
Press <F9> to activate the Page Format Menu
Press <F8> to end the QUOTE function

The cursor is in the space following the quote in the document (see Figure 9-7).

Press <Return>

Type:

```
This is not the impression most people looking for
jobs have of those who have the power to hire or not
hire them.
   Boles explains why interviewers may be so
uncomfortable with the process:
```

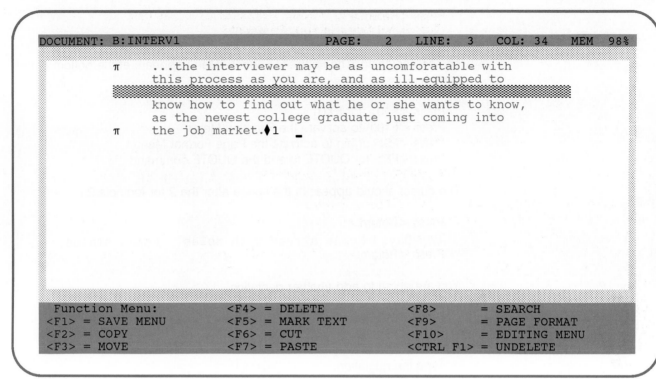

DOCUMENT: B:INTERV1   PAGE: 2   LINE: 3   COL: 34   MEM   98%

π   ...the interviewer may be as uncomforatable with
        this process as you are, and as ill-equipped to

        know how to find out what he or she wants to know,
        as the newest college graduate just coming into
π   the job market.♦1   _

Function Menu: <F4> = DELETE   <F8>   = SEARCH
<F1> = SAVE MENU   <F5> = MARK TEXT   <F9>   = PAGE FORMAT
<F2> = COPY   <F6> = CUT   <F10>   = EDITING MENU
<F3> = MOVE   <F7> = PASTE   <CTRL F1>   = UNDELETE

Figure 9-7
Entering Footnotes and Endnotes

You are now going to enter another quote.

> Press <Return>
> Press <F9> to activate the Page Format Menu
> Press <F8> for QUOTE

> Type the following quote:

> The odds are very great that the executive who does
> the interviewing was hired because of what they
> could contribute to the company, and not because
> they were such a great interviewer. In fact, their
> gifts in this arena may be rather miserable.

You are now going to enter the note for this quote.

> Press <F10> to activate the Editing Menu
> Press <Ctrl> **F** for FOOTNOTE/ENDNOTE
> Press <F3> for CREATE FOOTNOTE/ENDNOTE

The prompt AUTHOR'S NAME appears.

> Type **Ibid.**

Make sure to spell *Ibid* correctly, including the uppercase *I*.

Press <Return>

When the remaining footnote prompts, appear press <Return> without entering anything. The Footnote/Endnote Menu appears at the bottom of the screen.

Press <F10> for EXIT
Press <F10> to activate the Function Menu
Press <F9> again to activate the Page Format Menu
Press <F8> for QUOTE to end the QUOTE command

The cursor should appear in the space after the *2* for footnote 2.

Press <Return>
Type David Roman agrees with Boles. Roman states:
Press <Return>

You are going to add another quotation.

Press <F9> to activate the Page Format Menu
Press <F8> for QUOTE

Type the quotation:

As interviewers, ... managers ... may be out of
their element. They're in the business of running a
... department, not of interviewing job applicants.

Now you are going to enter the footnote.

Press <F10> to activate the Editing Menu
Press <Ctrl> **F** for FOOTNOTING
Press <F3> for CREATE FOOTNOTE/ENDNOTE
Type **Roman, David** at the AUTHOR'S NAME prompt
Press <Return>
Type **"Why MIS/DP Job Interviews Go Wrong"** at the TITLE prompt
Press <Return>

At the next prompt, LOCATION OF PUBLICATION, press <Return> without entering anything, because this is a magazine article rather than a book. The PUBLISHER prompt appears. The name of the magazine is going to be entered at this prompt, and it must be underlined.

Press <Ctrl> **U** to activate the UNDERLINE command
Type **Computer Decisions**
Press <Ctrl> **U** again to end the UNDERLINE command
Press <Return>
Type **November 19, 1985** at the DATE OF PUBLICATION prompt
Press <Return>

Type **66** at the PAGE NUMBER(S) prompt
Press <Return>

The Footnote/Endnote Menu returns to the screen.

Press <F10> for EXIT
Press <F10> to activate the Function Menu
Press <F9> to activate the Page Format Menu
Press <F8> for QUOTE to end the QUOTE command

The cursor should be in the space after the *3* for the third quotation.

Press <Return>

Type:

```
Since the person running the interview is probably
just as uncomfortable as you are, there are several
things you as an interviewee can do to take
advantage of the situation and turn the interview
into a pleasant and rewarding experience.
```

You have finished typing the document, but you now discover that you have misspelled a name throughout the text. The spelling of the author's name is *Bolles*, not *Boles*. Press <Ctrl> <Home> to move the cursor to the very beginning of the document (page 1, line 1, column 10). The Function Menu should be on the screen.

Press <F8> for SEARCH
Type **Y** at the GLOBAL SEARCH prompt
Press <Return>
Type **Boles** at the SEARCH FOR prompt
Press <Return>
Type **Bolles** at the REPLACE WITH prompt
Press <Return>

The program finds the first occurrence of the name Boles and highlights it. The prompt REPLACE THIS TEXT appears.

Type **Y**
Press <Return>

The program finds the second occurrence of Boles and highlights it. The prompt REPLACE THIS TEXT appears.

Type **Y**
Press <Return>

The program finds the third occurrence of Boles and highlights it. The prompt REPLACE THIS TEXT appears.

Type **Y**
Press <Return>

The next prompt reads: NO MORE SEARCH VALUES FOUND, PRESS <SPACE BAR> to CONTINUE.

Press the space bar

The Function Menu returns to the screen. You now need to use the EDIT FOOTNOTE/ENDNOTE function to change the misspelled name Boles in the footnote.

Press <F10> to activate the Editing Menu
Press <Ctrl> **F** for FOOTNOTING
Press <F2> for EDIT FOOTNOTE/ENDNOTE

The prompt ENTER NUMBER OF NOTE appears. The misspelled name is in note 1.

Type **1**
Press <Return>

The AUTHOR'S NAME prompt appears with the name Boles, Richard beside it.

Type **Bolles, Richard**
Press <Esc> to avoid having to retype the rest of the footnote

The Note Menu appears on the screen.

Press <F10> for EXIT

Now you decide the word *interviewee* is too informal for this paper. The cursor should be at the very beginning of the document (page 1, line 1, column 10). The Function Menu needs to be on the screen.

Press <F8> for SEARCH

Since there is no one word that will take the place of interviewee, do *not* do a global search. You are going to enter each correction individually.

Type **N** at the GLOBAL SEARCH prompt
Press <Return>
Type **interviewee** at the SEARCH FOR prompt
Press <Return>
Press <Return> again at the REPLACE WITH prompt without typing anything

The program finds the first occurrence of the word *interviewee*. The prompt

CONTINUE WITH SEARCH appears. You have to make a correction, so you are not going to continue.

Type **N**
Press <Return>

The cursor is under the *i* in the word *interviewee's*. Use the right arrow key to move the cursor so that it is under the apostrophe. Next, use the <Backspace> key to delete the word *interviewee*. You do not have to delete the apostrophe or the *s*.

Type `applicant`

The word *applicant's* appears in place of the word *interviewee's*. Now resume your search.

Press <F8> for SEARCH
Type **N** at the GLOBAL SEARCH prompt
Press <Return>
Type **interviewee** at the SEARCH FOR prompt
Press <Return>
Press <Return> again at the REPLACE WITH prompt

The second occurrence of interviewee is found. The CONTINUE WITH SEARCH prompt is on the screen.

Type **N**
Press <Return>

Using the right arrow key, move the cursor to the space after the last *e* in *interviewee*. Using the <Backspace> key, delete the word *interviewee*.

Type `person being interviewed`
Press <F8> for SEARCH
Type **N** at the GLOBAL SEARCH prompt
Press <Return>
Type **interviewee** at the SEARCH FOR prompt
Press <Return>
Press <Return> again at the REPLACE WITH prompt
Type **N** at the CONTINUE WITH SEARCH prompt
Press <Return>

Using the right arrow key, move the cursor to the space after the second *e* in *interviewee*. Using the <Backspace> key, delete the word *interviewee*.

Type `prospective employee`

You also need to change the word *an* to *a*. Move the cursor so that it is under the *n* in *an*.

Press <Del>

Save and exit INTERV1.

Press <Esc> for EXIT TO MAIN MENU

Select PRINT DOCUMENT from the WestWord Main Menu

The Printer Selection Menu appears. Enter the number that corresponds to the printer you are using and press <Return>.

Type **1** at the NUMBER OF FILES TO BE PRINTED prompt
Press <Return>
Type **INTERV1** at the ENTER FILENAME prompt
Type **Y** at the PRINT THE FIRST PAGE MARKER prompt
Press <Return>

The prompt DO YOU WISH NOTES TO BE <F>OOTNOTES or <E>NDNOTES appears.

Type **F** for footnotes
Press <Return>

When you have finished printing the paper, exit WestWord and then exit to DOS. Remove your disks and turn off your computer.

File Locking

WestWord's file locking feature enables the user to protect existing documents. When a file is locked, no permanent changes can be made to it. A locked file can be viewed and printed, and changes can be made on the screen, but those changes *cannot* be saved. This feature can be useful if other people might use your work disk, because it prevents accidental changes to documents. There is also a special password lock that your instructor can use to lock practice documents. These files cannot be unlocked unless the correct password is entered.

To lock an existing file, activate the Document Operations Menu. Press <F4> for FILELOCK. The prompt ENTER FILENAME appears on the screen. Enter the name of the file that is to be locked and press <Return>. The Document Operations Menu remains on the screen.

A locked file can be a nuisance if data in the file needs to be changed. With WestWord, however, the file can be unlocked as easily as it can be locked. To unlock a file, simply repeat the same procedure used to lock it. The FILELOCK function works like an on/off switch. Pressing <F4> and entering the filename once locks the file. Pressing <F4> and entering the filename a second time unlocks the file. Once a file has been unlocked, changes can be made and saved.

If you have made extensive changes to a locked file without realizing that the file is locked, there is a special function that allows the modified file to be saved under a different name. Press <F1> to access the Save Menu. Press <F2> for

SAVE AND EXIT. A message appears, stating that the file is locked and cannot be saved unless it is saved under a new name. Press <F5> for SAVE UNDER NEW DOCUMENT NAME. The prompt ENTER FILENAME appears. Enter the new name under which the modified document is to be saved, and press <Return>. The new name appears over the modified document in the status line. You can now save and exit the document, as well as make additional changes. Both the locked document and the new document are listed in the directory.

YOUR TURN

In this hands-on exercise, you are going to lock the INTERV1 file. Select CREATE/EDIT OLD DOCUMENT from the WestWord Main Menu. When the Document Operations Menu appears, select <F4> for FILE LOCK. When the prompt ENTER FILENAME appears, type **INTERV1** and press <Return>. The file is now locked and protected against accidental changes. You can tell it is locked because an asterisk appears next to the file name INTERV1 in the directory.

Learning Check

1. What function do you activate to create a footnote?

2. How do you number footnotes in WestWord?

3. What function do you activate to create an endnote?

4. How do you change the page formatting in a research paper to accommodate a long quotation?

5. How do you lock a file?

Answers

1. FOOTNOTE (<Ctrl> and F together). 2. They are numbered automatically. 3. FOOTNOTE (<Ctrl> and F together). 4. QUOTE (<F8> from the Page Format Menu). 5. Activate the LOCK FILE function (<F5>) from the Document Operations Menu).

Summary of Frequently Used WestWord 2.5 Menus

1. WestWord 2.5 Main Menu

```
                    WESTWORD 2.5 MAIN MENU

  ┌─────────────────────────────┐   ┌─────────────────────────────┐
  │ Create / edit old document  │   │                             │
  │ Print document              │   │                             │
  │ Change drive                │   │                             │
  │ Exit program                │   │                             │
  └─────────────────────────────┘   └─────────────────────────────┘

  ┌─────────────────────────────┐   ┌─────────────────────────────┐
  │                             │   │                             │
  │                             │   │                             │
  │                             │   │                             │
  └─────────────────────────────┘   └─────────────────────────────┘

  POSITION CURSOR AT SELECTION AND PRESS <RETURN>
```

2. Document Operations Menu

```
  <F1> = COPY DOCUMENT              <F4>  = FILELOCK
  <F2> = DELETE DOCUMENT
  <F3> = CREATE / LOAD DOCUMENT     <ESC> = EXIT TO MAIN MENU
```

3. Editing Menu

```
   Editing Menu:      <PgUp> = PAGE UP   <Alt  C> = CENTER TEXT   <F10> = FUNCTION
  <F1>  = SAVE MENU   <PgDn> = PAGE DN   <Ctrl B> = BOLD TYPE             MENU
  <Ins> = OVERTYPE    <Home> = HOME      <Ctrl F> = FOOTNOTE/ENDNOTE
  <Del> = DELETE      <End>  = END       <Ctrl U> = UNDERLINING
```

4. Function Menu

```
 Function Menu:           <F4> = DELETE          <F8>      = SEARCH
<F1> = SAVE MENU          <F5> = MARK TEXT       <F9>      = PAGE FORMAT
<F2> = COPY               <F6> = CUT             <F10>     = EDITING MENU
<F3> = MOVE               <F7> = PASTE           <CTRL F1> = UNDELETE
```

5. Page Format Menu

```
Page Format Menu:
     <F2>  = LINE SPACING      <F5>  = LEFT MARGIN      <F8>  = QUOTE
     <F3>  = TOP MARGIN        <F6>  = RIGHT MARGIN     <F10> = FUNCTION
     <F4>  = BOTTOM MARGIN     <F7>  = TAB ADJUST               MENU
```

6. Note Menu

```
Footnote/Endnote Menu:
     <F2> = EDIT FOOTNOTE/ENDNOTE
     <F3> = CREATE FOOTNOTE/ENDNOTE
     <F4> = DELETE FOOTNOTE/ENDNOTE    <F10> = EXIT
```

7. Save Menu

```
 Save Menu:
<F2> = SAVE AND EXIT DOCUMENT       <F5>  = SAVE UNDER NEW DOCUMENT NAME
<F3> = ABANDON DOCUMENT             <ESC> = CONTINUE WITHOUT SAVING CURRENT
<F4> = SAVE DOCUMENT AND CONTINUE           DOCUMENT
```

Summary Points

■ Common print formatting features of word processors include automatic page numbering, creation of footnotes, tab and margin settings, line spacing, and print enhancements.

■ Search functions facilitate the correction of errors that are repeated throughout a document.

■ Locking files can protect documents against accidental changes.

WestWord 2.5 Exercises

1. Changing a Document's Formatting

a. What are the steps required to change the formatting for a WestWord document? Start up WestWord on your computer to begin a new document. Open a new file and call it CHEMTEST.
b. Describe the process for setting margins. Set the left and right margins for your document at 15 and 65 respectively.
c. How do you change the line spacing in a document? Change to double spacing for this exercise.
d. Center and underline the title of your document: Monitoring Chemical Spills
e. Type the following as you see it, two spaces below the title. Type the errors just as you see them. They will be corrected later in the exercise.

Since a recent chemical spill at the Union Carbide plant in Bhopal, India resulted in the deaths of more than 2,000 people, cemical companies have become much more interested in computerized tracking and warning systems designed to protect communities around their plants. The old method for predicting the path and level of toxicity of a cemical cloud (still in use at most cemical plants) involves the use of lengthy charts and tables and relies on human calculations.

Safer Emergency Systems, Inc., has designed computerized emergency systems for 25 cemical plants. The system combines a computer, a 19-inch color graphics screen, and a printer with sensors placed at key locations in the plant to detect leaks early and sound alarms in the central computer. A tower placed on a rooftop or in a nearby open field has sensors that help plot the temperature and direction of a cemical cloud.

2. Cutting and Pasting

a. How do you move blocks of text from one file to another? Move the second paragraph of CHEMTEST into a new file. Name the new file CHEM2.
b. Go back to CHEMTEST and copy the second paragraph at the end of the document. The last two paragraphs of the document are now identical.

3. Search

a. What is the SEARCH function used for? How do you activate it? Use the

SEARCH function to correct the misspelling *cemical* throughout CHEMTEST (the correct spelling is *chemical*).

b. What do you have to do differently in using the SEARCH function if you want to type the correction to each error located rather than having the computer make the replacement automatically?

4. Quotation and Footnotes

a. What is the procedure for inserting block quotations in a WestWord document? After the first paragraph of CHEMTEST, add the words According to Dale Johnson: and insert the following quotation:

        ...the old methods of detecting chemical clouds
        are woefully inadequate. It's like we are in the
        21st century with the chemicals we are using, yet
        still in medieval times with our safety precau-
        tions.

b. What is the procedure for inserting footnotes in a WestWord document? Insert the following footnote after the preceding quotation:

        Johnson, Dale. Safety with the Computer, Bowling
        Green: No Socks Press, 1985, p. 74.

c. Return to the document. Now use the FOOTNOTING function again to edit the footnote. Change *1985* to *1986*.

5. Review all of the functions you have used in this chapter.

WestWord 2.5 Problems

1. To complete the following problem, you need to use the JOB file included on your student file disk, the DOS disk, and the program disk. Start WestWord. Insert the student file disk with the JOB file on it in drive B.

2. Change to drive B using the CHANGE DRIVE command in the Main Menu.

3. Highlight the CREATE/EDIT OLD DOCUMENT selection in the Main Menu and press <Return> to access the Document Operations Menu and the directory.

4. Make a copy of the JOB file and name the copy REQUEST. Describe the steps taken to copy the file. Use the REQUEST file to answer the remaining questions. Retrieve the REQUEST FILE.

5. Read the REQUEST file. REQUEST is a solicited application letter used to

answer an advertisement for an accounting job. Assume that you have just graduated from your college with a major in marketing rather than accounting. You are looking for a job in the marketing field. Delete the sender address using the MARK TEXT and DELETE functions. Replace it with your own address.

6. Change the date to the current date.

7. Delete the company address and replace it with the address of a company that you know.

8. Delete the phrase "Daily Mirror on April 9" from the first sentence of the letter. Insert the following to take its place: in the Tribune No. 350. (Make sure that the word Tribune is underlined.)

9. Using the SEARCH function, replace all occurrences of the word "accounting" with the word "marketing."

10. In the second paragraph, delete "Ohio State University" and type the name of your college.

11. Delete the following sentence:

As an intern at Price Waterhouse, I worked on the audit of Mills International.

12. Insert the following in place of the sentence just deleted:

As a project assignment, I conducted a market survey on fast food business in Northwest Ohio. This survey was used for the implementation of a new fast food chain in the area.

13. Move the cursor to the name of the applicant. Replace the name Kim Landon with your own name.

14. Print the letter.

15. Now that you have seen a hard copy of the letter, you would like to make some changes to the format design. Make the following changes:
  a. Change the top margin from 1 inch to 1-1/2 inches.
  b. Set the left margin so that it is 1-1/2 inches wide (15).

16. Print the letter again.

CHAPTER 10

Introduction to Spreadsheets and WestCalc™ 2.5

Introduction

SPREADSHEET
A ledger or table used in a business environment for financial calculations and for the recording of transactions.

SPREADSHEET PROGRAM
A set of computer instructions which generates and operates an electronic spreadsheet.

A manual **spreadsheet** is used to record business transactions and to perform calculations. A **spreadsheet program** uses a computer's memory capability to solve mathematically oriented problems. With a spreadsheet program, columns of numbers can be set up to keep track of money or objects.

Without a computer and spreadsheet program, you would use a pencil, a piece of paper and perhaps a calculator to solve mathematical problems. Computers can calculate at the speed of electricity, which is a useful capability with more complicated formulas. Suppose that, after finishing your tax returns, you realize you did not include income you received from a temporary job. Every calculation following that part of the form is incorrect. With a spreadsheet program, you can simply insert the forgotten number and have the program recalculate all the totals. With the ability to calculate, store, print, merge, and sort numeric information, a spreadsheet is an extremely useful tool.

This chapter looks at some of the features that make spreadsheet programs so popular. It also provides instructions on how to get started using WestCalc 2.5, a spreadsheet program developed by Rawhide Software Inc.

Definitions

ELECTRONIC SPREADSHEET
A large computerized grid divided into rows and columns; uses computer storage and computational capabilities for financial analysis.

Ledger sheets are used primarily by accountants and business managers for financial calculations and the recording of transactions. A spreadsheet is actually a ledger sheet like the one shown in Figure 10-1. Ledger sheets have columns in which the numbers are written to keep them in line.

An **electronic spreadsheet** is a grid of columns and rows used to store and manipulate numeric information by means of a computer. The grid appears on the

Figure 10-1
Ledger Sheet

		HOME BUDGET				
		Expenses:				
		Rent		235 00		
		Food		100 00		
		Gas		97 00		
		Electric		75 00		
		Phone		25 00		
		Car		100 00		
		TOTAL EXPENSES		632 00		

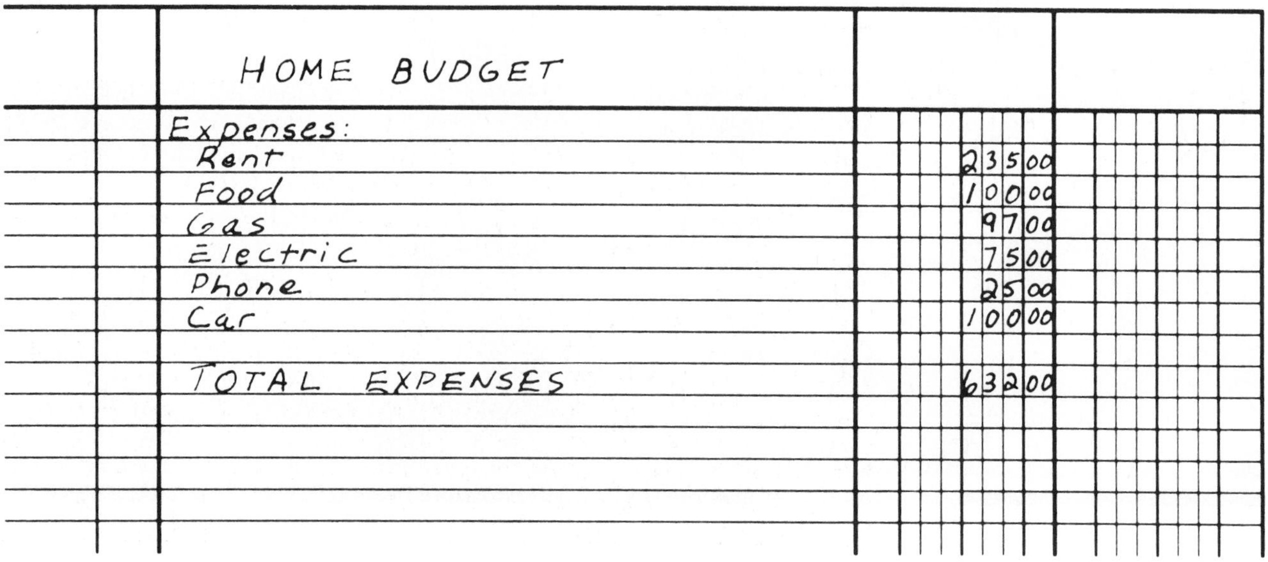

display screen, and data is stored in the computer's memory. Probably the most significant advantage of an electronic spreadsheet over the traditional spreadsheet is the ability to store not only numbers, but also formulas for calculating numbers. One number in a formula can be changed easily without reentering the entire formula.

WORKSHEET
The grid of rows and columns created using a spreadsheet software package. The worksheet falls within the row and column borders.

Some software packages, like WestCalc, refer to an electronic spreadsheet as a **worksheet**. For the remainder of this chapter, the word worksheet refers to the grid of rows and columns used by WestCalc to store and manipulate numeric data. Table 10-1 provides a quick reference to other terms used in connection with electronic spreadsheets.

VALUE
A single piece of information used in the calculations of a spreadsheet.

A spreadsheet program is a set of computer instructions which generates and operates an electronic spreadsheet. With a spreadsheet program, the computer can solve complex mathematical calculations. Numbers, or **values**, are entered into **cells** formed by the columns and rows. Each cell relates to a certain storage location in the computer's memory. **Labels** also can be entered to tell the user what the numbers mean (see Figure 10-2).

CELL
A storage location within a spreadsheet.

Formulas, as well as values, can be entered into cells. A formula is a mathematical expression that can contain numbers from other cells as well as constant numbers. If one number in a cell is changed, the program automatically recalculates any formula that uses that number.

LABEL
Information used for describing some aspect of a spreadsheet.

Because electronic spreadsheets instantaneously recalculate formulas, they can be used to ask "what if" questions, such as the following:

FORMULA
A mathematical expression used in a spreadsheet.

■ How will my budget be affected if I spend $50 more at the grocery store each month?
■ How will my bank balance be affected if the interest earned by my savings account goes up 1/2 percent?
■ How will my income change if I take a job working on commission rather than salary?

With a spreadsheet program, the computer instantly adjusts the values affected by the changed number. If you used a manual spreadsheet instead, you would have to recopy all the numbers by hand. A spreadsheet program calculates and displays in seconds what it would take a person several hours to do.

Table 10-1
Terms Associated with Electronic Spreadsheets

Term	Definition
Cell	A storage location within a spreadsheet used to store a single piece of information relevant to the spreadsheet.
Coordinates	The location of a cell within a spreadsheet; a combination of the column letter and row number.
Formula	A mathematical expression used in a spreadsheet.
Label	Information used for describing some aspect of a spreadsheet. A label can be made up of alphabetic or numeric information, but no arithmetic can be performed on a label.
Value	A single piece of numeric information used in the calculations of a spreadsheet.
Window	The portion of a worksheet which can be seen on the computer display screen.

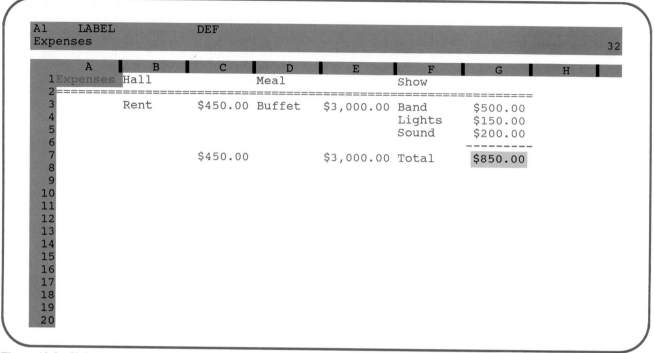

Figure 10-2   Values and Labels. Columns A, B, D, and F contain labels. Columns C, E, and G contain values.

Uses of Spreadsheets

People in decision-making positions frequently use spreadsheets. Managers are responsible for making sure their companies run smoothly, and spreadsheets help them to manage money, goods, and employees.

The spreadsheet stores business data, such as sales figures, expenses, payroll amounts, and prices. A manager can enter formulas to calculate profits and losses, for example, or to compute the percentage of profits paid in taxes. Any calculation that a manager normally would figure by hand can be included in the spreadsheet.

A number in a spreadsheet can be changed to show how that change affects the other numbers. For example, an increase in the cost of a material used in manufacturing can be entered into a spreadsheet to show how that increase affects profits. The spreadsheet program saves time by automatically recalculating formulas when the numbers in cells change.

By using a spreadsheet, instead of a calculator, pencil, and paper, a manager can spend more time thinking about how to run the business. The answers to "what if" questions are quickly calculated. This ability has made electronic spreadsheets popular in business.

Home computer owners also can benefit from using spreadsheets, which simplify any task that requires calculating numbers. One common use of a spreadsheet program is to keep track of household expenses. The program can figure the percentage of each paycheck that goes to rent, electricity, and food. You can see which expenses increase and decrease each month, for example, or how much should be saved each month for a family vacation or a new appliance.

A spreadsheet program can keep track of a team's weekly bowling scores. It can record and tally donations to an organization. It can keep track of your grades at school and determine the marks you need to get the final grades you want.

Complex spreadsheets are used in science and engineering to cut down on the trial and error involved in research. Scientists use the spreadsheet programs to calculate the outcomes of their experiments under various conditions.

Learning Check

1. An electronic spreadsheet is made up of _____ and _____ used to store and manipulate numeric information.

2. _____ are numbers used in the calculations of a spreadsheet.

3. _____ are mathematical expressions that can contain numbers from other cells and constant numbers.

4. One reason why spreadsheets are so popular in business is that they can quickly calculate answers to "_____" questions.

5. A(n) _____ is the location of a cell within a spreadsheet.

Answers

1. columns; rows   2. Values   3. Formulas   4. what if   5. coordinate

---

Guide to WestCalc™ 2.5

COORDINATE
The location of a cell within a spreadsheet.

CELL POINTER
The highlight that indicates the active cell in a spreadsheet.

ACTIVE CELL
The cell on a spreadsheet which is currently available for use; the active cell is indicated by the cell pointer.

CONTROL PANEL
The portion of the spreadsheet which provides status and help information. The control panel is composed of a status line, an entry line, and a prompt line.

The remainder of this chapter introduces WestCalc 2.5, an instructional spreadsheet program that includes many functions to help users enter, move, label, display, and calculate numbers. The hands-on exercises in the chapter provide step-by-step instructions on how to build a worksheet.

Identifying Parts of the Worksheet

When a new WestCalc worksheet is loaded into the computer, a screen like the one shown in Figure 10-3 appears. The numbers listed down the left side of the grid represent rows, and the letters listed across the top of the grid represent the columns.

Each cell in the spreadsheet has a cell address or **coordinate**. The coordinate of a cell consists of a letter for its column and a number for its row. For example, the coordinate or cell address C4 is the cell where column C and row 4 intersect. The **cell pointer** is a highlighted bar that indicates which cell or cells are active or can accept information. The cell indicated by the cell pointer is called the **active cell**. In Figure 10-3, the cell pointer is in cell A1; therefore, A1 is the active cell.

The top three lines of the screen are the **control panel**. The first two lines of the control panel constitute the status area. The first line in the status area provides

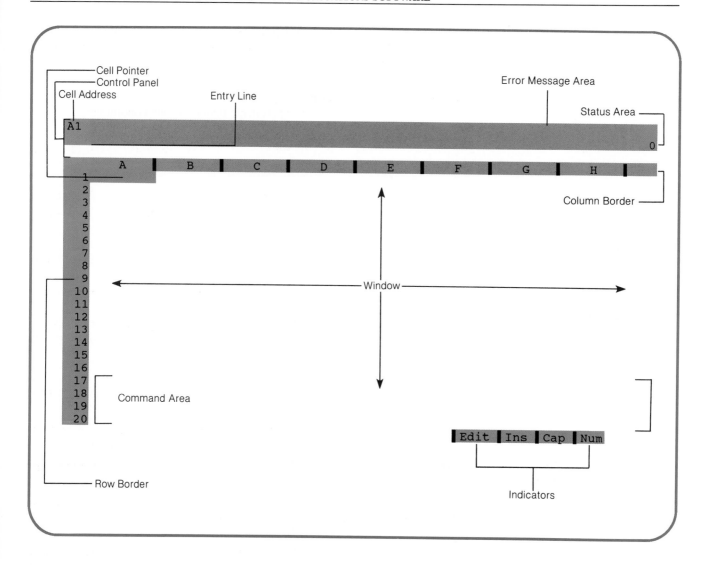

Figure 10-3
A Blank WestCalc Worksheet

information such as the cell address, whether the cell contains a label, value, or formula, and how the cell is formatted. The second line displays the cell contents.

The third line of the control panel, the entry line, displays data as it is typed in at the keyboard. The entry line is called a work line, because the data appearing there can be edited and changed before the <Return> key is pressed. Once the <Return> key is pressed, however, the data moves from the entry line to the second line of the control panel and enters the worksheet.

The error message area is in the upper right corner of the status area. If a mistake is made, an error message provides a brief description of what has gone wrong. The command area is at the bottom of the screen. This is where WestCalc's various menus are displayed.

At the bottom right corner of the screen are the indicators. Any of the five indicators may be displayed: EDIT, INS, CAPS, NUM, or SCRLL. If the <Num Lock> key is on, NUM is displayed; if the <Caps Lock> key is on, CAPS is displayed; if the <Scroll Lock> key is on, SCRLL is displayed. If the <Ins>

key has been pressed, INS is displayed and insertions can be made to the contents of the active cell. If the <F2> key has been pressed, EDIT is displayed and the contents of the active cell can be edited.

Getting Started With WestCalc 2.5

Some of the procedures for using WestCalc 2.5 depend on whether you are using a system with two floppy disk drives or one with a hard disk drive. The directions in this chapter are for a system with two floppy disk drives. Differences for systems with a hard disk drive are written in difference boxes.

Each of the following sections introduces one or more features of WestCalc. At the end of each section, there is a hands-on activity marked **YOUR TURN.** Be sure to read each section carefully before trying the hands-on activity.

The key on the IBM PC keyboard marked ↵ is the <Return> key, sometimes called the <Enter> key. Whenever you are instructed to press the <Return> key, press the key marked ↵ .

Throughout this chapter, the following symbols and typefaces appear:

Type **C12** — **Boldface** is used to designate characters or text that you should type to the screen usually in response to a prompt.

Press the <Return> key — The angle brackets (<>) are used to signify a specific key on the keyboard. Press the key whose name is enclosed by the angle brackets.

WestCalc Tip: — This phrase introduces important information needed to run WestCalc successfully.

Type MONTHLY BUDGET — Typewriter font indicates input that is to be entered into the worksheet.

CELL(S) — All capital letters indicate text that is displayed on the computer screen.

To start WestCalc, you need a DOS disk, a West Instructional Software disk, and a formatted disk to use as a data disk. Follow these steps whenever you need to start WestCalc:

1. Insert the DOS diskette in drive A (usually the left or top drive). Insert your data diskette in drive B (usually the right or bottom drive). Turn on the monitor and computer and press the <Return> key in response to the time and date prompts (to bypass them). When the A> prompt appears, take the DOS diskette out of drive A and insert the West Instructional Software diskette into drive A. Type **WEST** after the A> and press the <Return> key.

2. Read the information that appears on the screen. Press the <Return> key when you have read the information, and then read the next screen that appears. At the bottom of the screen are the words Author's name and a highlighted box. Type **MANDELL** and press the <Return> key.

3. The Opening Menu appears. Using the <↑> or <↓> keys if necessary, move the highlighting to WESTCALC. Press the <Return> key. The West-Calc 2.5 Main Menu appears (see Figure 10-4).

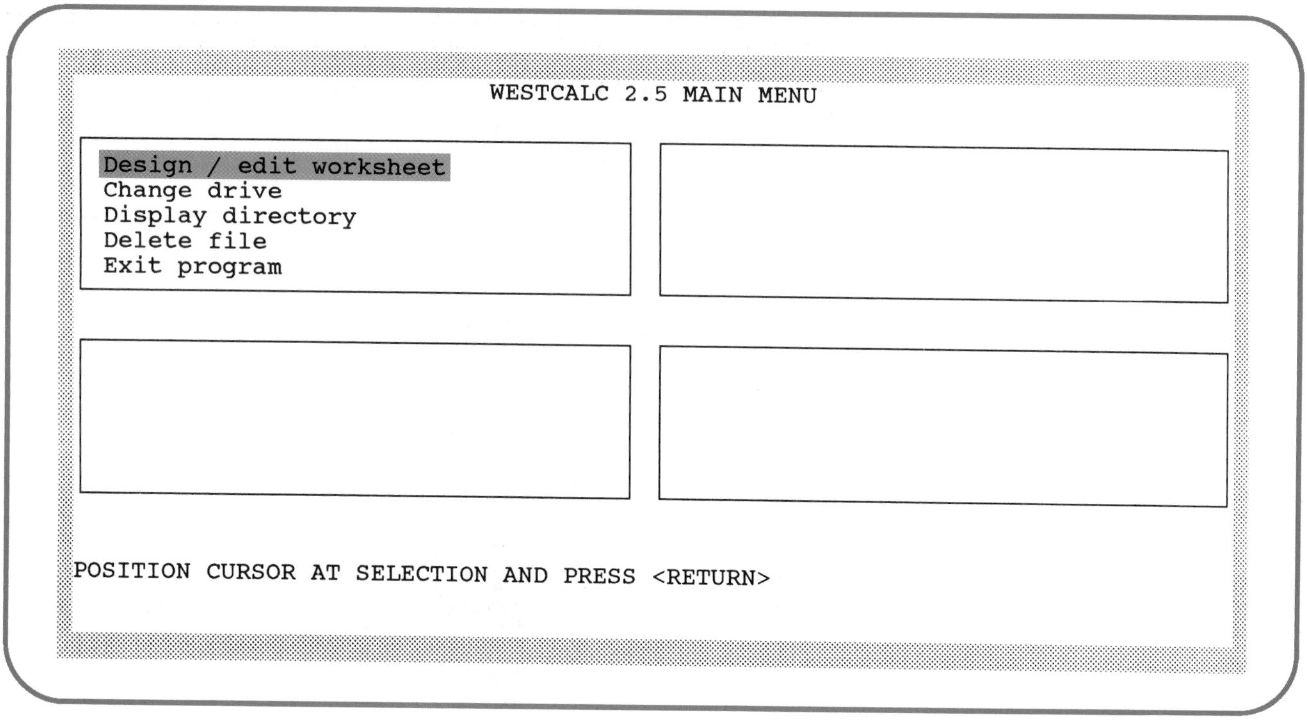

```
                    WESTCALC 2.5 MAIN MENU

 ┌──────────────────────────────┐   ┌──────────────────────────────┐
 │ Design / edit worksheet      │   │                              │
 │ Change drive                 │   │                              │
 │ Display directory            │   │                              │
 │ Delete file                  │   │                              │
 │ Exit program                 │   │                              │
 └──────────────────────────────┘   └──────────────────────────────┘

 ┌──────────────────────────────┐   ┌──────────────────────────────┐
 │                              │   │                              │
 │                              │   │                              │
 │                              │   │                              │
 └──────────────────────────────┘   └──────────────────────────────┘

 POSITION CURSOR AT SELECTION AND PRESS <RETURN>
```

Figure 10-4
The WestCalc 2.5 Main Menu

Hard Disk Differences: To start WestCalc directly from the hard disk, save the West Instructional Software disk to a directory in drive C. Then follow these steps to start WestCalc:

1. At the system prompt (C>) type **CD\ (name of directory where WestCalc is located)**. Press <Return>.
2. Type **West** and press <Return>. The menu comes up.

The Main Menu includes five options: DESIGN/EDIT WORKSHEET, CHANGE DRIVE, DISPLAY DIRECTORY, DELETE FILE, EXIT PROGRAM. All the files created with WestCalc 2.5 must be saved on your data disk in drive B because there is not enough space on the West Instructional Software disk in drive A to save files. To change to drive B, use the up < ↑ > or down < ↓ > arrow keys to highlight the CHANGE DRIVE option on the Main Menu. Press <Return>. The prompt DIRECTORY NAME appears at the bottom of the screen.

Type **B**
Press <Return>

The Main Menu returns to the screen. Once this procedure has been completed, when a file is saved, it is stored on the data disk in drive B. This procedure only has to be done once at the beginning of every work session.

To begin using WestCalc, move the highlighting to DESIGN/EDIT WORK-SHEET and press <Return>. A blank worksheet appears with the Commands

Menu at the bottom. After looking at the Commands Menu, press <Esc> for ABORT. The Commands Menu disappears. Nothing can be entered or edited on the worksheet while the Commands Menu is on the screen.

YOUR TURN

Start WestCalc. The WestCalc 2.5 Main Menu should appear on the screen.

Use the < ↑ > or < ↓ > key to highlight CHANGE DRIVE
Press <Return>

The prompt DIRECTORY NAME appears.

Type **B**
Press <Return>

The WestCalc 2.5 Main Menu returns to the screen. Move the highlighting to DESIGN/EDIT WORKSHEET and press <Return>. A blank worksheet with the Commands Menu at the bottom appears. Read the Commands Menu.

Press <Esc> for ABORT

The Commands Menu disappears from the screen.

Moving Around the Worksheet

WINDOW
The portion of an electronic spreadsheet which can be seen on the computer display screen.

The WestCalc worksheet contains 256 columns, which are labeled A through IV, and 256 rows, which are numbered 1 through 256. The part of the worksheet that appears on the screen at one time is the **window**. For example, in Figure 10-3, cells A1 through H20 appear in the window.

There are several ways to move around the WestCalc worksheet and to see parts of the worksheet outside the window. The first is by using the pointer-movements keys located on the numeric keypad at the right side of the keyboard. Table 10-2 lists the pointer-movement keys and describes their functions.

> *WestCalc Tip:* Since the WestCalc worksheet is so large, you might become "lost" on it. If this ever happens, simply press <Home> to reorient yourself on the worksheet.

The other way to move the cell pointer around the worksheet is by using the GoTo command, which is one of the commands in the Commands Menu. By

Table 10-2
Pointer-Movement Keys

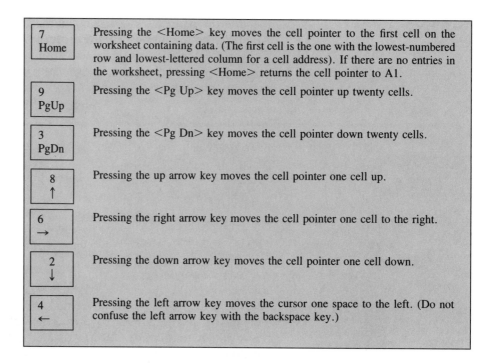

7 Home	Pressing the <Home> key moves the cell pointer to the first cell on the worksheet containing data. (The first cell is the one with the lowest-numbered row and lowest-lettered column for a cell address). If there are no entries in the worksheet, pressing <Home> returns the cell pointer to A1.
9 PgUp	Pressing the <Pg Up> key moves the cell pointer up twenty cells.
3 PgDn	Pressing the <Pg Dn> key moves the cell pointer down twenty cells.
8 ↑	Pressing the up arrow key moves the cell pointer one cell up.
6 →	Pressing the right arrow key moves the cell pointer one cell to the right.
2 ↓	Pressing the down arrow key moves the cell pointer one cell down.
4 ←	Pressing the left arrow key moves the cursor one space to the left. (Do not confuse the left arrow key with the backspace key.)

typing a slash (/) to activate the Commands Menu and then pressing <F3> for the GoTo command, you can move the cell pointer to any cell on the worksheet. For example, if the cell pointer is in cell A1 and you want to go to cell R30, simply type / and press <F3>, type **R30**, and press <Return>. The cell pointer immediately moves to cell R30. The GoTo command quickly moves the cell pointer long distances in the spreadsheet.

YOUR TURN   Start with a blank WestCalc worksheet on the screen. If necessary, press <Esc> to remove the Commands Menu from the screen. Practice moving the cell pointer by doing the following:

■ Press the down arrow key three times. The cell address should be A4.
■ Press the right arrow key ten times. The cell address should be K4.
■ Press <Pg Dn>. Watch the row border. The cell pointer remains in the same column while the row numbers change. The new cell address should be K24.
■ Press <Ctrl> <→>. The cell address should be Q24.
■ Press <Home>. The cell pointer should return to A1.
■ Press <F3>, the GoTo key. (If you need to refresh your memory, type a slash (/) first to display the Commands Menu.) Type **L24** and press <Return>. The cell pointer immediately moves to cell L24. Check the cell address to make sure that is the location of the cell pointer.
■ Press <Pg Up>. The cell address should be L4.

■ Press <Home>. The pointer returns to A1.

■ Press <F3>. Type **Z199** and press <Return>.

■ Press <Home>.

■ Continue practicing moving the cell pointer with the pointer movement keys and with <F3>. When you have finished practicing, press <Home> to return to A1.

Menus and Menu Options

Typing the slash key (/) activates WestCalc's Commands Menu, which appears at the bottom of the computer screen (see Figure 10-5). The Commands Menu has nine options. Each option corresponds to one of the function keys on the left side of the keyboard. Table 10-3 lists the Commands Menu options.

In addition to the Commands Menu, WestCalc has several submenus as noted in Table 10-3. That is, when you select any of options <F4> through <F8> from the Commands Menu, a submenu with additional options appears at the bottom of the screen. For example, if the Format option <F6> is selected from the Commands Menu, a submenu with seven additional options appears at the bottom of the screen in the command area. The same function keys <F1> through <F9> are used to execute commands from the submenu, but they execute different commands.

If a menu is activated by mistake, or if you begin to use an option and decide you do not want that option, you can press the <Esc> key to back out of any

Figure 10-5
The WestCalc Commands Menu

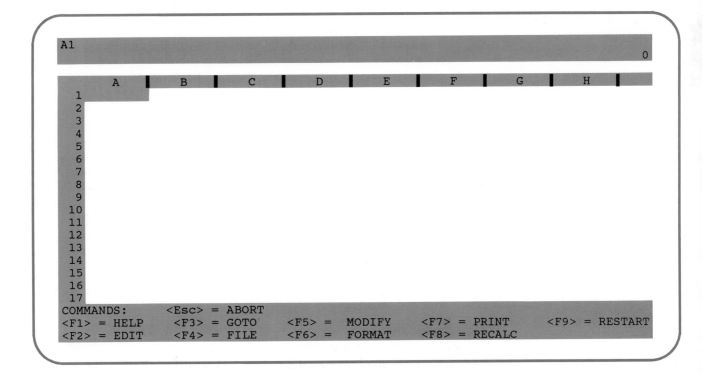

Table 10-3
WestCalc Main Menu Options

Key	Command	Description
F1	Help	Activates a help screen with information relevant to the operation currently being executed on the worksheet.
F2	Edit	Enables the user to edit the contents of a cell.
F3	GoTo	Enables the user to move the cell pointer to a specified cell address.
F4	File	Provides several options relating to a file. (A submenu is displayed.)
F5	Modify	Provides several options for modifying a worksheet. (A submenu is displayed.)
F6	Format	Provides several format options for displaying the contents of a cell. (A submenu is displayed.)
F7	Print	Enables the user to print a hard copy of a worksheet. (A submenu is displayed.)
F8	Recalc	Enables the user to recalculate all the cells in a worksheet containing formulas. (A submenu is displayed.)
F9	Restart	Erases the current worksheet and displays a blank worksheet.
Esc	Escape	Cancels the last command entered. Also used to exit the worksheet and return to the WestCalc Main Menu.

selection one menu at a time. Each time <Esc> is pressed, the current menu or submenu is replaced with the one previous to it.

YOUR TURN

Start with a blank WestCalc worksheet on the screen.

■ Type a slash (/). The WestCalc Commands Menu appears. Press <F5>, the Modify command. The Modify Menu appears in the command area. Notice that the function keys <F2> through <F8> now activate commands different from those they activated in the Main Menu. For example, <F5> now activates the Insert command.
■ Press <F5> again. The Insert Menu appears in the command area.
■ Press the <Esc> key to move WestCalc back one command level. The Modify Menu is now in the command area.
■ Press the <Esc> key again. The Commands Menu is back in the command area. Press <Esc> one more time. The Commands Menu disappears from the command area.
■ Continue to practice moving through the Commands Menu and the submenus by pressing the function keys and the <Esc> key.
■ When you have finished practicing, return a blank worksheet to the screen by using the <Esc> key.

Saving and Retrieving Files

Worksheets are saved permanently in files on your data disk. Once saved, a file can be retrieved at any time to be used and changed as necessary. To save a worksheet in a file, call up the Commands Menu and press <F4> for the File command. Press <F4> again for the Save command.

The prompt ENTER FILENAME appears in the command area. A filename can be up to sixteen characters long, and it can be a combination of letters and numbers. Try to give the file a name that indicates the information contained in that worksheet. Type the name of the file and press <Return>.

To retrieve an existing file, call up the Commands Menu. Press <F4> for File and <F3> for Load. The prompt ENTER FILENAME appears in the command area. Type the name of the file to be retrieved and press <Return>.

If you want to see a list of all the files that have been saved, press <F4> for File from the Commands Menu. Then press <F2> for Directory. A box appears on the screen which lists all the files that have been saved on that data disk. Once you have finished looking at the filenames, press the <Esc> key.

YOUR TURN

Start with a blank WestCalc worksheet on the screen. Make sure the cell pointer is in cell A1.

Type `WestCalc`
Press <Return>

The name WestCalc has been entered into the worksheet. To save this worksheet, do the following:

Type /
Press <F4>
Press <F4> again
Type **Practice**
Press <Return>

Now you are going to exit from the worksheet.

Press <Esc>

The prompt ARE YOU SURE YOU WANT TO QUIT NOW? appears.

Type **Y**
Press <Return>

The WestCalc Main Menu appears. Highlight DESIGN/EDIT WORKSHEET and press <Return>. Now you are going to retrieve the file you just saved.

Press <F4>
Press <F3>
Type **Practice**
Press <Return>

The worksheet with the name WestCalc in cell A1 should appear on the screen.

Saving An Amended File

Once a worksheet has been created, it can be retrieved and changes can be made to it. Data can be added or deleted, values and labels can be changed, and so on. Once a previously saved file has been retrieved and amended, there are two methods by which to save it.

The first method is to save the amended file as a new file. In this case, the original file remains saved on the data disk and can be retrieved again if necessary. The second method is to replace the original file with the amended file, so that only the amended file is saved. The original file is erased from memory.

To save an amended file, first select the File command from the Commands Menu. Next, select the Save command. The prompt ENTER FILENAME appears. To save the amended file as a new file, type a different filename and press <Return>. The amended file is saved under the new filename, and the original file also remains on the disk.

To replace the original file, type the same filename and press <Return>. The message FILE ALREADY EXISTS appears, along with the prompt OVERWRITE IT? (Y/N). You can cancel the Save command, thus keeping the original file intact, by typing **N** for no. Typing **Y**, for yes, erases the original file and replaces it with the amended file.

YOUR TURN Start with the PRACTICE worksheet on the screen. The name WestCalc is in A1.

> Go to A2
> Type `Practice File`
> Press <Return>

The PRACTICE file has now been amended, because new data has been entered into A2. To save the amended file, do the following:

> Type /
> Press <F4>
> Press <F4> again

The prompt ENTER FILENAME appears. If you wanted to save the amended file as a separate file from the original PRACTICE file, you would type in a new filename. In this exercise, however, you will replace the original PRACTICE file with the amended PRACTICE file.

> Type **Practice**
> Press <Return>

The prompt OVERWRITE IT? (Y/N) appears. Type **Y** for yes. The command area disappears, and the new PRACTICE worksheet remains on the screen.

Deleting a File

The command to delete a file is found on the WestCalc Main Menu. Highlight DELETE FILE from the Main Menu and press <Return>. The prompt FILE NAME appears on the bottom of the screen. Enter the name of the file and press <Return>. The Main Menu stays on the screen.

To check to make sure that the file was deleted, highlight DISPLAY DIREC-TORY and press <Return>. A list of all the files saved on the disk appears in a window. The name of the deleted file should no longer appear in the directory.

YOUR TURN

You are going to delete the PRACTICE file. The PRACTICE worksheet should still be on the screen.

Type /
Press <Esc> for ABORT
Press <Esc> again
Type **Y**
Press <Return>

The WestCalc Main Menu appears. Highlight DELETE FILE and press <Return>. The prompt FILE NAME appears.

Type **Practice**
Press <Return>

Now highlight DISPLAY DIRECTORY and press <Return>. The filename PRACTICE should not appear in the Data File Listing. Press the <Space Bar> to remove the directory window from the screen.

Getting Help With WestCalc 2.5

WestCalc includes Help windows that provide information about how to use the program. To call up a Help window, press <F1> from the Main Menu. <F1> is the Help key; it always activates a Help window. As soon as <F1> is pressed, an explanation of the current activity appears on the screen. After reading the information provided by the Help window, press <Esc>.

WestCalc also provides help with error messages that appear on the screen. Error messages are brief descriptions of whatever mistake has been made.

YOUR TURN

The WestCalc Main Menu should be on the screen. Highlight DESIGN/EDIT WORKSHEET and press <Return>.

   Press <F3>

WestCalc prompts you to enter the address.

   Type **G350**
   Press <Return>

The error message INVALID CELL COORDINATE appears at the bottom of the screen. You tried to enter 350 as a row number, but the worksheet only goes up to row 256. Press <Esc>.

   Press <F3>
   Press <F1>

A Help window explaining the GoTo command appears. Read it and then press <Esc> twice.

   Press <F6>
   Press <F1>

A Help window explaining the Format command appears. Read it and then press <Esc> twice.
   Select other Help windows and read them. When you are familiar with the Help command, press <Esc> to return to the worksheet. Leave a blank worksheet on the screen.

WestCalc Tip: When using WestCalc you are bound to make a mistake at some point. When you make a mistake, don't panic. First try pressing <F1>. The Help window provides useful information on whatever function or command is being performed when the <F1> key is pressed. If you still don't know what to do, press the <Esc> key to terminate your last command. Repeatedly pressing the <Esc> key eventually terminates all the commands. Once the command area disappears, you can start all over.

Quitting a File and Quitting the Access System

When you no longer want to work on a particular worksheet, you need to leave WestCalc. Be sure to save the file before leaving WestCalc. Once the file is saved, press <Esc> to leave the Commands Menu, if necessary. Press <Esc> again. The prompt ARE YOU SURE YOU WANT TO QUIT NOW? (Y/N) appears in the command area. Pressing the <Return> key or typing **N** at this point cancels the Quit command and returns you to the worksheet.

Typing **Y** and pressing <Return> at this point takes you to the WestCalc Main Menu. Highlight EXIT PROGRAM and the Opening Menu appears on the screen.

If you want to stop working on the current worksheet but you do not want to leave the WestCalc program, press <F9> from the Commands Menu for the Restart command. Again, make sure the current file has been saved before pressing <F9>. The prompt ARE YOU SURE? (Y/N) appears in the command area. Pressing <Return> or typing **N** cancels the Restart command. Typing **Y** puts a new, blank worksheet on the screen.

YOUR TURN

A blank worksheet should be on the screen. If necessary, press <Esc> to remove the Comands Menu from the screen.

> Press <Esc>

The prompt ARE YOU SURE YOU WANT TO QUIT NOW? appears.

> Type **Y**
> Press <Return>

The WestCalc Main Mehu appears. Move the highlighting to EXIT PROGRAM and press <Return>. The Opening Menu appears.

Learning Check

1. The _____ is the part of the worksheet that appears on the screen at one time.

2. The GoTo key is _____.
   a F1   c. F5
   b. F3   d. F7

3. The Help key is _____.
   a. F1   c. F5
   b. F3   d. F7

4. Typing the slash (/) key calls up the _____.

5. The top three lines of the WestCalc worksheet are called the _____.

Answers

1. window 2. b. 3. a. 4. Commands Menu 5. control panel

Creating a Worksheet

You have already learned how to move around the WestCalc worksheet and how to use menus and submenus. You have used several commands, and you have entered data into the worksheet. This section introduces more commands and basic worksheet operations by having you create a monthly budget.

Entering Labels

As explained at the beginning of the chapter, any one of three categories of data can be entered in a cell: a label, a value, or a formula. Labels are most commonly letters or words. They are used as titles or captions to help identify the items in a column or row.

Data can be entered only when the worksheet is in the Ready mode—that is, when the command area is off the screen. If the command area is on the screen, WestCalc is waiting for a command to be entered and therefore is not in the Ready mode. If you try to enter a label or other data while the command area is on the screen, WestCalc beeps and nothing is entered. Before entering data, check to make sure the worksheet is in the Ready mode.

Entering a label in a cell involves three steps. First, the cell pointer has to be moved to the cell where the label is to be entered. The GoTo command or the pointer-movement keys can be used to move the cell pointer. Next, the label is typed. As soon as you start typing a label, the word LABEL appears in the status area, and the label itself appears in the entry line.

The final step is to store the label in the cell by pressing the <Return> key or one of the pointer-movement keys. The label moves from the entry line to the status area, and it appears in the appropriate cell on the worksheet.

Using the pointer-movement keys to store a label can save time, because these keys perform two functions. If <Return> is pressed, the label is stored, but the cell-pointer remains in the same cell. In order to make the next entry, you need to move the cell-pointer to a new cell. If the appropriate pointer-movement key is used to store a label, however, the label is stored and the cell-pointer also moves one cell in the direction the arrow is pointing. For example, if labels are going to be entered in cells A1, A2, A3, and A4, you can save keystrokes by pressing the down arrow key after each label is typed. The cell-pointer immediately moves to the cell where the next label is to be entered.

A typing error can be corrected before the <Return> key or one of the cell-pointer keys is pressed by using the <Backspace> key, which is located to the left of the <Num Lock> key. The <Backspace> key has a left arrow on it, but you should not confuse it with the left pointer-movement key, because <Backspace> is outside the numeric keypad and does not have a number on it. Each time <Backspace> is pressed, one character is erased. After erasing the mistake, retype and store the label.

There are two ways to edit data already stored in a cell. One way is to go to the cell where the label is located, retype the entire label, and store it. The new label replaces the old one. Once a label has been replaced, it is erased from memory and cannot be retrieved. The second way is to use the Edit command.

To use the Edit command, go to the cell to be edited, type /, and then press <F2>. The Edit indicator appears in the bottom right corner of the screen, and the entry is copied to the entry line. Corrections can now be made on the entry line using the <Backspace> key. The <Return> key must be used to enter the corrected data into the cell.

DEFAULT SETTING
The setting that a software package automatically uses when no other setting is designated by the user.

The **default setting** for the width of a cell in WestCalc is nine characters. That is, unless otherwise specified, a cell can hold only nine characters. For labels, however, WestCalc uses an automatic spill-over feature: If a label longer than nine characters is entered, it automatically spills over into the next cell.

YOUR TURN

Start with a blank WestCalc worksheet on the screen. Make sure the worksheet is in the Ready mode and the current cell address is A1.

Type MONTHLY BUDGET
Press <Return>

The title MONTHLY BUDGET spills over into cell B1 because it is longer than nine characters. The cell pointer remains in cell A1.

Go to cell A3. Use either the GoTo command (<F3>) or the down arrow pointer-movement key. When you are instructed to go to a specific cell, always check the cell address to make sure the cell pointer is in the correct cell.

In cell A3 type Income
Press <↓>

Notice that the cell pointer automatically moves one cell down, to cell A4.

Press the space bar twice and type Take-Home Pay.
Press <↓> three times. The cell address should read A7.
Type Expenses
Press <Return>

By now you should be familiar with the three steps involved in entering a label: going to a specific cell location, typing the label, and pressing either the <Return> key or one of the pointer-movement keys. For the remainder of the chapter, whenever you are instructed to "Enter A Label in A1", this means: go to cell A1, type A Label, and press either <Return>, <↓>, <↑>, <←>, or <→> as appropriate.

Enter Rent in A9.
Enter Phone in A10.
Enter Food in A11.
Enter Personal in A12.
Enter Clothing in A13.

Enter `Transportation` in A14.
Enter `Student Loan` in A15.
Enter `Car Loan` in A16.
Enter `Insurance` in A17.
Enter `Savings` in A18.
Enter `TOTAL` in A20.
Enter `Budgeted` in C7.
Enter `Actual` in D7.
Enter `Difference` in E7.
Enter `Per of Income` in G7.

Now practice using <F2>, the Edit command.

Type **/**
Press <F3> for GoTo
Type **G7**
Press <Return>
Press <F2>

Notice columns A, B, and C scrolled off the screen. The Edit indicator appears, and the label moves into the entry line.

Press <←> 10 times, or until the cursor is one space to the right of the *r* in *Per*.
Press the <Backspace> key 3 times to erase *Per*.
Type **%**

Press the <Ins> key so you can insert a space. The Ins indicator appears. Press the space bar once. Press the <Ins> key again to turn off the Ins indicator. Press <Return>.
   Go to A1 to view the entire worksheet. It should look like Figure 10-6. Save the worksheet under the filename BUDGET1.

Entering Values

Like all spreadsheet programs, WestCalc processes labels and values differently. A value, unlike a label, can be used in an arithmetic calculation. A label can spill over into several cells, but a value must be confined to one cell. Because WestCalc distinguishes labels from values, care must be taken in making entries.
   The first character of an entry identifies it as either a label or a value. Because most labels are words, WestCalc assumes that, if the first character of an entry is a letter, the entry is a label. If the first character is a number, WestCalc assumes the entry is a value. For the most part, the following rules apply:

■ If the first character is one of the following, the entry is interpreted as a value: 0 1 2 3 4 5 6 7 8 9 + − (.
■ If the first character is any character other than those listed above, the entry is interpreted as a label.

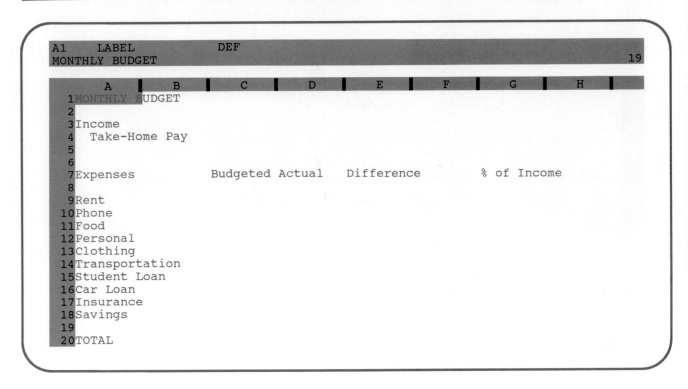

```
A1      LABEL           DEF
MONTHLY BUDGET                                                                    19

          A       B       C       D       E       F       G       H
   1MONTHLY BUDGET
   2
   3Income
   4  Take-Home Pay
   5
   6
   7Expenses          Budgeted Actual    Difference       % of Income
   8
   9Rent
  10Phone
  11Food
  12Personal
  13Clothing
  14Transportation
  15Student Loan
  16Car Loan
  17Insurance
  18Savings
  19
  20TOTAL
```

Figure 10-6
Entering Labels in the BUDGET1 Worksheet

Values are entered into a cell in the same manner described for labels. The worksheet must be in the Ready mode. The cell-pointer is moved to the appropriate cell, the number is typed into the cell, and the number is stored in the cell by pressing <Return> or one of the pointer-control keys.

Values also are edited the same way as labels. A value can be edited with the <Backspace> key before it has been stored in the cell. After a value has been stored, it can be changed either by typing a new entry or by using the <F2> command.

YOUR TURN Start with the BUDGET1 file on your screen. For this hands-on exercise, you are going to enter numbers into cells on the worksheet.

Enter 1100 in C4

Notice that the word VALUE appears in the status area as soon as a number is typed.

Enter 240 in C9.
Enter 20 in C10.
Enter 200 in C11.
Enter 100 in C12.
Enter 70 in C13.
Enter 120 in C14.
Enter 40 in C15.

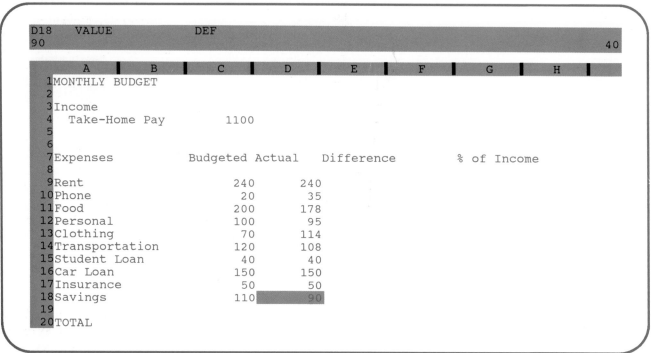

Figure 10-7
Entering Values in the BUDGET1
Worksheet

Enter 150 in C16.
Enter 50 in C17.
Enter 110 in C18.
Enter 240 in D9.
Enter 35 in D10.
Enter 178 in D11.
Enter 95 in D12.
Enter 114 in D13.
Enter 108 in D14.
Enter 40 in D15.
Enter 150 in D16.
Enter 50 in D17.
Enter 90 in D18.

When all the values have been entered, your worksheet should look like
Figure 10-7.

Ranges

RANGE
A rectangular block of one or more cells in the worksheet which is treated as one unit.

A **range** is a rectangular block of one or more cells in the worksheet which WestCalc treats as one unit. A range can be composed of a single cell, one row, one column, or a block of rows and columns that form a rectangle (see Figure 10-8). Ranges are one of the valuable assets of electronic spreadsheets. Instead

Figure 10-8
Ranges

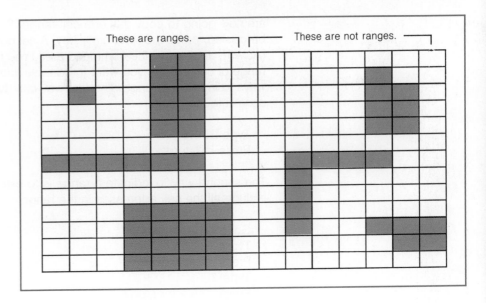

of performing a particular function on one cell at a time, the user can define a range of cells and a function can be performed on the entire range. For example, ranges can be used to copy, move, or erase entire sections of a worksheet.

YOUR TURN   Start with the BUDGET1 worksheet on the screen.

    Go to cell A5
    Type **' =**

Look at the control panel. The single quotation mark does not appear in the entry line; just the equal sign appears. The words LABEL REPEATING DEF are in the Control Panel.

    Press <Return>

Notice that, even though the equal sign (=) was typed only once, the double lines fill the entire cell. That is because the single quotation mark key was pressed first. In WestCalc, the single quotation mark functions as a repeating label prefix. Whatever is typed after the single quotation mark repeats itself until it fills the entire cell.

    Type **/**
    Press <F5> for Modify
    Press <F3> for Copy

The message FROM CELL(S) [A5:A5] appears in the command area. A5 is the current location of the cell-pointer. It is also a one-cell range. You are now going to copy this one-cell range. Since A5 is the only cell to be copied, press the <Return> key. A second prompt line, TO CELL(S) [A5:A5], appears in the command area. You now need to indicate the range of cells where you want the double lines copied to. There are two ways to indicate a range. The first way is to type the cell addresses that constitute the range.

Type **B5:H5**
Press <Return>

The second way to indicate a range is to extend the highlighting to include all the cell addresses in the range.

Go to A8
Type **'-**
Press <Return>
Type **/**
Press <F5> for Modify
Press <F3> for Copy

The prompt FROM CELL(S) [A8:A8] appears in the command area. Again, this one-cell range is what you want to copy, so press <Return>. TO CELL(S) [A8:A8] now appears in the command area. This time you are going to indicate the range by expanding the highlighting. Notice the command <F3> for Mark/Range in the top line of the command area. Press <F3>. The command area disappears and the word MARK appears in the lower-right corner of the screen. Move the cell pointer to B8.

The range must first be anchored before the highlighting can be expanded. Typing a period (.) after the cell address where the highlighting is to begin anchors the highlighting. That is, it indicates the address of the first cell in the range.

Type a period (**.**) to anchor the first cell of the range in cell B8

Notice that the word SET now appears in the lower-right corner of the screen. You can tell that a range is anchored if the word SET appears. The period itself does not appear on the screen.

Press <→> six times

Notice that the highlighting now extends through the range of cells A8–H8.

Press <Return>

Pressing <Return> confirms the range indicated by the highlighting. The single line is copied into that range of cells.

> *WestCalc Tip:* If the range is anchored in the wrong cell, press <Esc> to release the range. The command area reappears. Press <F3> again to mark the correct range.

Entering Formulas

Formulas are mathematical expressions. When writing formulas with WestCalc, you can use addition, subtraction, multiplication, division, and exponentiation, as well as advanced financial and statistical analysis. Formulas can contain references to particular cells (using their cell addresses) and can indicate mathematical operations to be performed on the values within those cells.

Formulas are entered on a worksheet—by typing them into cells. A formula typically is created by entering either a value or a cell address, then a mathematical operator, then another value or cell address, and so on. The mathematical operators most frequently used in formulas are:

    +   add
    −   subtract
    *   multiply
    /   divide

Once a formula has been entered into the cell, press <Return>. The <Return> key has to be pressed. If you press an arrow key rather than the <Return> key, the formula is not entered into the cell. If this happens, move back to the cell where the formula is to be entered. Press <Esc> and then press <Return>.

Formulas often contain cell addresses. For example, a formula might be A5 + A6 + A7. Because formulas are values, and WestCalc assumes an entry beginning with a letter is a label, formulas starting with a cell address must begin with a plus sign (+) to indicate that what follows is a formula, not a label. The previous example would be entered into a worksheet as + A5 + A6 + A7. The first plus sign does not appear on the entry line. Instead, the words VALUE FORMULA DEF appear in the control panel as soon as the first plus sign is entered.

YOUR TURN

Start with the BUDGET1 worksheet on your screen. For this hands-on exercise, you are going to enter formulas into cells on the worksheet. First, you are going to enter formulas by typing the numbers.

    Go to C20
    Type **240 + 20 + 200 + 100 + 70 + 120 + 40 + 150 + 50 + 110**

Notice that the words VALUE FORMULA appear in the status area.

    Press <Return>

The formula moves from the entry line into the status area, and the sum (1100) appears in cell C20. The next formula is entered using cell addresses rather than numbers.

Go to D20
Type **+D9+D10+D11+D12+D13+D14+D15+D16+D17+D18**

Remember, the plus sign (+) has to be the first character typed to indicate to WestCalc that this is a value, not a label. The first plus sign should not appear as part of the formula in the status area.

Press <Return>

Again, the sum appears in the cell where the formula was entered, even though you used cell addresses rather than numbers in the formula.

The column titled Difference shows the difference between what was budgeted for the month and what was actually spent. Enter formulas in cells E9 through E18 to show this difference.

Go to E9
Type **+C9−D9**
Press <Return>

The formula appears in the status area, and the difference appears in cell E9.

Go to E10
Type **+C10−D10**
Press <Return>

Because $15.00 more was actually spent than was budgeted, the number appears as a negative.

Go to E11
Type **+C11−D11**
Press <Return>

Continue to enter formulas into cells E12 through E18 to calculate the difference between what was budgeted and what was actually spent.
Save the amended worksheet.

Formatting Cells

Values in a WestCalc worksheet can be formatted. That is, they can be made to appear with dollar signs, with commas, or rounded off to a certain number of decimal places. Either one cell or a range of cells can be formatted.

Table 10-4
Format Codes for Displaying Values

Code	Description
A	A is WestCalc's default for the value display.
G	G stands for general. The general format specifies whether or not the value appears with an embedded comma, how many decimal places are displayed (0 to 7), and whether or not there is a floating decimal point.
I	I stands for integer. The integer format specifies that the numeric data does not contain decimal points. The option of displaying embedded commas is available.
D	D stands for dollar. The value is displayed as currency.
U	U stands for user-defined. The user selects one of nine options.

To format a cell, first press <F6> for the Format command from the Commands Menu. Then press <F7> for Value Display. The prompt VALUE DISPLAY FORMAT CODE (A/G/I/D/U) appears in the command area. Table 10-4 lists these format codes and the functions they perform.

YOUR TURN

Start with the BUDGET1 worksheet on the screen.

Go to C9
Type **/**
Press <F6> for Format
Press <F7> for Value Display

The VALUE DISPLAY FORMAT CODE prompt appears in the command area. Type **D** for Dollar. Next the prompt BLANK WHEN ZERO appears. Type **N**. The prompt DECIMAL PLACES appears. The default setting is 2. Press <Return> to accept the default setting. The prompt FLOATING-POINT appears. Press <Return> to accept the default setting, which is N (no).

The prompt CELL(S) [C9:C9] appears. You are now going to format a range of cells. Press <F3> for MARK RANGE, and type a period (.) to anchor the range. The word SET appears in the right corner of the screen.

Press the < ↓ > key nine times or until the range reaches C18
Press <→> twice

The range from C9 to E18 is now selected, as indicated in the entry line.

Press <Return>

All the values in cells C9 through E18 now appear in the currency format. Notice that the negative numbers now appear within parentheses, rather than having a negative sign in front of them.

The column titled % of Income is used for figuring out what percentage of the monthly take-home pay was actually spent on each of the budgeted expenses. The formula used to figure this percentage is the actual amount spent divided by the monthly take-home pay. For example, the formula to be entered into G9 is 240/1100 or D9/C4. Enter the appropriate formulas into cells G9 through G18. Remember, if you use cell addresses in your formulas, you must use the + prefix. The + prefix will not appear in the status area.

If you forget to enter the + prefix and WestCalc identifies the formula as a label, you will have to erase the cell contents. To erase the contents of a cell, make sure the cell pointer is on the cell to be erased. If necessary, type / for the Commands Menu. Press <F5> for MODIFY and <F8> for BLANK. The address of the cell whose contents are to be erased should appear next to the CELL(S) prompt. Press <Return>. Start over entering the formula remembering to use the + prefix.

Next, format cells G9 through G18 using the Percent format option.

Type /
Press <F6> for Format
Press <F7> for Value Display
Type **U** for User Defined

A window with the Value Display Options appears.

Type **3** to select the percent sign option
Type **Y** for the percent sign to be displayed
Type **8** to select the decimal places option
Type **0** for no decimal places
Press <Return>

There now should be a Y beside option 3, Percent sign, and a zero beside option 8, Decimal places. Type **0** (zero) to exit the Value Display Options window.

Press <F3> to mark the range to be formatted
Move the cell pointer to G9
Type **.** to anchor the range
Move the cell pointer to G18 so that the range G9 through G18 is selected
Press <Return>

The percentages appear in column G. Save the amended BUDGET1 worksheet.

Erasing a Cell

Erasing a cell or a range of cells on a WestCalc worksheet is easy. First, select <F5> (the Modify command) from the Commands Menu. Then select <F8> for

Blank. The prompt CELL(S) appears. The Mark/Range command <F3> can then be used to select the range to be erased.

If a value that has been used in a formula is erased, the formula using that value automatically recalculates without the value.

YOUR TURN   Start with the BUDGET1 worksheet on your screen.

Go to A12
Type **/**
Press <F5> for Modify
Press <F8> for Blank

The prompt CELL(S) [A12:A12] appears in the command area. Only one cell, A12, is to be erased, so press <Return>.

Enter Spending $ in A12

Save the amended worksheet BUDGET1.

Learning Check

1. To activate the Edit command from the Commands Menu, press ____.
   a. F1   c. F5
   b. F2   d. F10

2. If the first character of an entry is a number, WestCalc assumes the entry is a ____.

3. A ____ is a rectangular block of cells in a worksheet which WestCalc treats as one unit.

4. If the entry in a formula is a cell address, the formula must be preceded with a ____.

5. The ____ key functions as a repeating label prefix; whatever is typed after it repeats itself until it fills the cell.

Answers

1. b. 2. value 3. range 4. plus sign (+) 5. single quotation mark

---

Changing the Appearance of a Worksheet

It is important to have a worksheet that is easy to read. WestCalc options such as being able to align labels, adjust column widths, and insert and delete rows and

Table 10-5
Justify Options

Option	Purpose
D	D stands for Default. Selecting D accepts the default setting for the cell(s) in the specified range.
L	L stands for Left. Labels are aligned on the left side of the cell.
R	R stands for Right. Labels are aligned on the right side of the cell.
C	C stands for Center. Labels are centered within the cell.

columns help to create a neat and easily understandable worksheet. These options are discussed in the following sections.

Aligning Labels

The alignment of a label—whether it aligns on the left side of the cell, is centered within the cell, or is aligned on the right side of the cell—can be set by using the Format command from the Commands Menu. After pressing <F6> for Format, press <F2> for Justify. Table 10-5 lists the Justify options and explains their functions.

Numbers can also be used as labels, but either a space or a double quotation mark (″) must precede the first number. For example, if you wanted to use 1986, 1987, and 1988 as labels, WestCalc will read them as values, not labels, unless a space or double quotation mark is the first character typed when the label is entered into the cell. You can type the following into the cells: ″1986, ″1987, ″1988. (The double-quotation sign does not appear in the status area. It does not appear in the cell as part of the label either.)

YOUR TURN   Start with the BUDGET1 worksheet on your screen.

Go to A7
Type **/**
Press <F6> for Format
Press <F2> for Justify
Type **R** for Right
Press <F3> to mark the range of cells
Type **.** to anchor the range at A7
Press <→> seven times, or until the range of cells from A7 through H7 is selected

Press <Return>

Move the cell pointer through row 7. Notice that the letter R now appears in the status area.

Go to A7
Type **/**
Press <F6> for Format
Press <F2> for Justify
Type **C** for Center
Press <F3> to mark the range of cells
Type **.** to anchor the range at A7
Enter the range of labels A7 through H7
Press <Return>

Notice that the letter C now appears in the status area.

Save the amended worksheet BUDGET1.

Adjusting Column Widths

The default column width in WestCalc is nine characters. The column width can be adjusted, however, from 1 to 72 characters. The width of individual columns can be set, or the width of all the columns in the worksheet can be set.

YOUR TURN   Start with the BUDGET1 worksheet on your screen.

Go to C4

In the previous hands-on exercise when cells were changed to the dollar format, cells C4, C20 and D20 were not formatted. You are now going to format these cells. Do not worry about the message that will appear in the cell. Just continue with the exercise.

Type **/**
Press <F6> for Format
Press <F7> for Value Display
Type **D** for Dollar
Press <Return> to accept the default answer, **N**, to the prompt BLANK WHEN ZERO
Press <Return> to accept the default setting at two decimal places
Press <Return> to accept the default answer (no) to the FLOATING-POINT prompt
Press <Return> again to accept a range of one cell, C4.

Notice that the message TOO BIG now appears in C4. Changing the format to Dollar added characters to 1100, and it is not too long to fit in the column at its present width. Look at the control panel. Notice that, even though TOO BIG appears on the worksheet, WestCalc still has the value 1100 stored in cell C4.

Keep the cell pointer at C4. You are going to change the width of the column so that the actual value, rather than TOO BIG, appears on the worksheet in cell C4.

Type /
Press <F5> for Modify
Press <F7> for Width

The prompt ENTER DESIRED COLUMN WIDTH (1-72) [9] now appears in the command area. The current width of the column is 9. Type **10** and press <Return>.

The prompt COLUMNS [C:C] now appears in the command area. You need to change the width of both columns C and D.

Press <F3> to mark the range
Type . to anchor the range at column C
Press <→> once to move the range to column D
Press <Return>

The current column width for columns C and D is now 10. The value $1,100.00 now appears on the worksheet in C4. A column width of 10 is enough space for this value.

Go to C20
Format C20 and D20 as Dollar, carried out to two decimal places

Because the column-width is now 10, the values rather than the words TOO BIG immediately appear in C20 and D20.

Column F is too wide. Move the cell pointer to column F. The cell pointer can be on any cell in the column, because the width of the entire column is going to change. Change the width to 3. When the prompt ENTER DESIRED COLUMN WIDTH (1-72) appears, type **3** and press <Return>. You only want to change the width of column F, so press <Return> when the COLUMNS [F:F] prompt appears. Column A scrolls off the screen. Press <Home> to view the whole worksheet.

Save the amended worksheet BUDGET1.

Inserting and Deleting Rows and Columns

Sometimes the appearance of a worksheet can be enhanced by adding a row or column. Perhaps a row or column has to be added to accommodate additional data, or data that is no longer relevant has to be deleted from a worksheet. The process of adding or deleting rows and columns on a WestCalc worksheet is a simple task that involves pointing to the location where the row or column is to be added or deleted.

To add a row or column, first position the cell pointer to the right of where a column is to appear or under where a row is to appear. Select <F5> for Modify from the Commands Menu. Press <F5> again for Insert. The option of selecting row or column insertion appears next. After you select R or C, mark the range of rows or columns to be inserted, using the <F3> Mark/Range command. If only one row or column is to be inserted, simply press <Return>. After the <Return> key is pressed, the program adds the row or column.

Deleting a row or column is similar to adding a row or column. Press <F5> for Modify from the Commands Menu. Next press <F6> for Delete. Then you choose to delete either rows or columns, and you indicate the range of rows or columns to be deleted. Pressing the <Return> key deletes the range.

Be very careful when deleting rows and columns. Once a row or column is deleted, it is erased from memory and cannot be retrieved. Accidentally deleting a row when you intended to delete a column could be disastrous.

YOUR TURN

Start with the BUDGET1 worksheet on the screen. You are going to delete row 6 from the worksheet.

> Go to A6
> Type **/**
> Press <F5> for Modify
> Press <F6> for Delete
> Type **R** for Row
> Press <Return> because you want to delete row 6 only.

Now, you are going to add a row between the label Take-Home Pay and the double lines.

> Go to A5
> Type **/**
> Press <F5> for Modify
> Press <F5> for Insert
> Type **R** for Row
> Press <Return> since you want to add one row only.

Your worksheet should look like Figure 10-9 when completed.

> Save the amended BUDGET1 file.

Printing a Worksheet

There are times when it is useful to have a hard copy of a worksheet. Printing a WestCalc worksheet is described in this section.

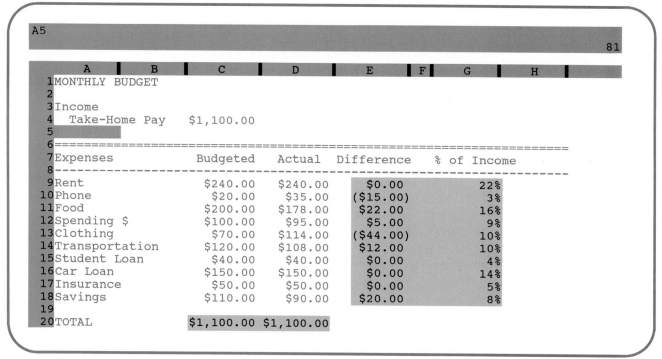

```
A5
                                                                          81

         A     B        C        D        E     F   G        H
 1MONTHLY  BUDGET
 2
 3Income
 4  Take-Home Pay     $1,100.00
 5
 6==========================================================================
 7Expenses          Budgeted   Actual   Difference   % of Income
 8--------------------------------------------------------------------------
 9Rent               $240.00   $240.00     $0.00         22%
10Phone               $20.00    $35.00   ($15.00)         3%
11Food               $200.00   $178.00    $22.00         16%
12Spending $         $100.00    $95.00     $5.00          9%
13Clothing            $70.00   $114.00   ($44.00)        10%
14Transportation     $120.00   $108.00    $12.00         10%
15Student Loan        $40.00    $40.00     $0.00          4%
16Car Loan           $150.00   $150.00     $0.00         14%
17Insurance           $50.00    $50.00     $0.00          5%
18Savings            $110.00    $90.00    $20.00          8%
19
20TOTAL            $1,100.00 $1,100.00
```

Figure 10-9
Changing the Appearance of the
BUDGET1 Worksheet

Before printing a worksheet, save the file so that the hard copy will include the latest changes or additions. Check to see if the printer is connected to the computer, is online, and has plenty of paper. Press <F7>, the Print command, from the Commands Menu. The Print Menu appears next. Press <F3> to print all or part of the worksheet as it appears on the screen. The prompt CELL(S) [A1:A1] appears in the command area. Press <F3> to mark the range of cells to be printed, and press <Return>. WestCalc begins printing the worksheet.

YOUR TURN   You are going to print the entire BUDGET1 worksheet.

Type /
Press <F7> for Print
Press <F3> to print the worksheet as it is displayed
Press <F3> again to mark the range of cells to be printed

Move the cell pointer to A1.

Type . (period) to anchor the range
Press <→> 7 times to select columns A through H
Press < ↓ > 19 times to select rows 1 through 20

The entire worksheet should now be highlighted.

```
MONTHLY BUDGET

Income
   Take-Home Pay    $1,100.00

=================================================================
Expenses            Budgeted   Actual   Difference   % of Income
-----------------------------------------------------------------
Rent                $240.00   $240.00     $0.00         22%
Phone                $20.00    $35.00   ($15.00)         3%
Food                $200.00   $178.00    $22.00         16%
Spending $          $100.00    $95.00     $5.00          9%
Clothing             $70.00   $114.00   ($44.00)        10%
Transportation      $120.00   $108.00    $12.00         10%
Student Loan         $40.00    $40.00     $0.00          4%
Car Loan            $150.00   $150.00     $0.00         14%
Insurance            $50.00    $50.00     $0.00          5%
Savings             $110.00    $90.00    $20.00          8%

TOTAL             $1,100.00 $1,100.00
```

Figure 10-10
The BUDGET1 Worksheet

Press <Return>

The BUDGET1 worksheet is printed. It should look like Figure 10-10.

Learning Check

1. When you are adding a row or a column to a WestCalc worksheet, the cursor must be positioned to the right of where a column is to appear and under where a row is to appear. (True or False?)

2. To change the alignment of a label in a cell, use the _____ command from the Commands Menu.

3. If a heading beginning with a number is to be used as a label, the label prefix _____ must precede it.

4. The default column width in WestCalc is _____ characters.
   a. 6   c. 8
   b. 9   d. 10

5. When a row has been deleted accidentally from a WestCalc worksheet, it can be retrieved. (True or False?)

Answers

1. True 2. <F6> Format 3. " (double quotation mark) 4. b. 5. False

Summary Points

■ A spreadsheet program simulates the operations of a calculator and stores the results in the computer's memory.

■ An electronic spreadsheet is displayed as a table of columns and rows.

■ The three items that can be entered into an electronic spreadsheet are labels, values, and formulas.

■ A formula is a mathematical expression that is assigned to a cell in the spreadsheet.

■ The two major areas of a worksheet are the control panel and the window. The control panel displays important information about the worksheet. The window is the currently displayed portion of the worksheet.

WestCalc 2.5 Exercises

To complete the following exercises you need a DOS disk, a West Instructional Software disk, and a formatted disk that will be your data disk.

1. Starting WestCalc
   a. Assuming your computer is shut off, describe all the necessary steps to start WestCalc. Go ahead and start WestCalc on your computer.
   b. Put your data disk in drive B. Change drives to disk drive B.
   c. Load a blank worksheet.

2. Moving through the worksheet and entering data

Now that a worksheet is displayed, you are going to practice moving through the worksheet.

   a. The cell pointer is positioned on cell A1. Enter the words `last name` into that cell. Describe the steps you use to do this. Which key do you press to go to B1?
   b. In B1, type `first name` and press $<\downarrow>$. Where is the cell pointer positioned after this action? Which key do you press to go to A2?
   c. Use the GoTo command to go to cell L130. Enter the number `145.6`.
   d. Use the <Home> key to return to cell A1.

3. Building a new worksheet

Now you are going to enter a new worksheet. First, type / to activate the Commands Menu. Then press <F9> for Restart and type **Y** to clear the screen and start a new worksheet. This command deletes the information you previously entered. Assume that you want to prepare the following report on the total quantity of items ordered by customers during the past week. In the report, X stands for a figure to be computed.

Summary of Products Ordered During Week 30

PRODUCT NAME	CODE	MON	TUE	WED	THR	FRI	TOT
Skirts	1	80	90	50	70	110	X
Shorts	2	120	130	110	140	150	X
Blouses	3	30	30	20	60	70	X
Shirts	4	180	170	150	180	180	X
Socks	5	110	105	120	140	150	X
Jeans	6	165	170	140	150	170	X
Total		X	X	X	X	X	X

a. Make sure the cell pointer is positioned at cell A1, and start typing the title of the report: Summary of Products Ordered During Week 30. In which cell(s) is the text displayed? What is it called when a label takes up more than one cell?

b. Start typing the labels. Move the cell pointer to cell A3. Type PRODUCT NAME and press <→>. Where is the cell pointer positioned now? Type the next label, CODE, and press <→> again. Continue typing all the labels in row 3.

c. Move the cell pointer back to cell A3. What happens to the cell entry? Type /, <F5>, and <F7> to set the width of column A to 15 characters. Describe all the steps taken to change the column width.

d. Move the cell pointer to cell A5. You are now ready to enter the data for each line.

    1. Type the first product name and press <→> to move the pointer to the right.

    2. Type the code and press <→> again to move the cell pointer to the right.

    3. Type the quantities ordered during the week for product 1 in the appropriate cells.

    4. Repeat steps 1 through 3 for each of the remaining products.

e. You are now ready to compute the totals and complete the report.

    1. Start with the totals per day. For this purpose, move the cell pointer to cell C12. Total orders for the first day are equal to the formula +C5+C6+C7+C8+C9+C10. Enter this formula.

    2. Enter the appropriate formulas in cells D12, E12, F12, and G12.

    3. Move the cell pointer to H5. This cell should contain the total for skirts ordered during week 30, that is, the sum of cells B5 through G5. Enter the appropriate formula in cell H5.

    4. Enter the appropriate formulas in cells H6, H7, H8, H9, H10, and H12. What is the grand total of products ordered during the week?

f. To improve the appearance of the report, you want to draw a horizontal line between the last line of data and the totals. Move the cell pointer to cell C11. Type '-. What appears in the cell? Copy this cell entry to the remaining cells through H11.

4. The report is now ready. Save the worksheet under the name SALES30.

5. Print the report.

6. When you have finished, return to DOS.

WestCalc 2.5 Problems

You are an administrative assistant in the sales department. The manager asks you to prepare a variance report in order to analyze each division's activity and the performance of the sales force during the past year. This variance report will compare how the actual sales varied from the projected sales. To complete the problem, you need to use the WestCalc system disk and the SALES file included on your Student File Disk.

> **Hard Disk Differences:** To be able to access the SALES File, you should copy the Student File diskette onto the hard disk.

1. Using the appropriate steps, start WestCalc and insert the Student File Disk with the permanent files into drive B.

2. Retrieve the file SALES and save a copy of it under the name NEW. From now on, use the file NEW. The original data will always be in the file SALES if you need to start over or if you want to work through the questions again.

3. Retrieve the file NEW. You now have access to the data provided to you by the manager. Move the cell pointer through the worksheet to familiarize yourself with the information. Notice that this worksheet contains the amount of forecasted and realized sales for the previous calendar year.

4. You want to compute all the totals per division and per quarter, and the grand total for the year. First, compute the annual forecasted sales for each division.
a. Go to cell F7. Enter the formula that finds the total of the Northwest division's yearly forecasted sales.
b. Enter the formulas in cells F8, F9, and F10 that find the total yearly forecasted sales for the East Coast, Midwest, and Central division, respectively.

Next, compute the total forecasted sales per quarter and the total for the year.

c. Go to B12. Enter the formula that finds the total of all the divisions' forecasted sales in the first quarter.
d. Enter the formulas in cells C12, D12, and E12 which find the totals for all the divisions' forecasted sales in the second, third, and fourth quarter respectively.

e. Go to F12. Compute the total forecasted sales for all the divisions for the entire year.

Repeat steps a through e for realized sales, starting at cell F15.

5.   Now you want to compute the variances per quarter and per division. Variances are deviations of the actual results from what was expected. For one quarter, the variance is equal to realized sales minus forecasted sales. For example, the formula to compute the variance for the Northwest division in the first quarter is B15–B7.

a. Go to B23. Enter the formula that computes the variance for the Northwest division in the first quarter.

b. In cells C23, D23, and E23, enter the formulas that compute the variances for the Northwest division in the second, third, and fourth quarter respectively.

c. Follow the same procedure to find the variances for the East Coast, Midwest, and Central divisions.

d. In cells B28, C28, D28, and E28, compute the total variance per quarter.

e. In cells F23, F24, F25, and F26, compute the total variance per division.

f. In cell F28, compute the total variance for the entire company for the entire year.

6.   Now that you have finished building the worksheet, you would like to improve its appearance.

a. Insert a row below the subtitles (Forecasted sales, Realized sales, and Variance report).

b. Insert a column before the Total Y1 column.

c. Increase the first column width to 15, in order to be able to read the words *East Coast* completely.

d. Type `Thousands $` under the main title.

e. Above each total line, draw a horizontal line, using the repeating label prefix (`'-`). Start at column B.

f. Below each total line, draw a double line, using the repeating label prefix (`'=`).

7.   Save and print the report.

8.   Look over the report. What are your first conclusions concerning the activity of the firm? Which division has performed best? Do you think that there is a problem with the company's forecasts?

CHAPTER 11

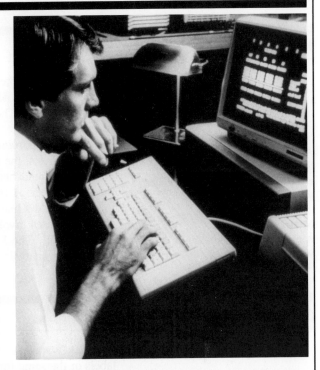

Advanced
WestCalc™2.5

Introduction

SPREADSHEET ANALYSIS
A mental process of evaluating information contained in an electronic spreadsheet; also called what-if analysis.

MODEL
A numeric representation of a real-world situation.

The previous chapter covered the fundamentals for creating a basic worksheet. WestCalc also has advanced features that simplify the task of creating more complex worksheets. These features, such as copy and move functions, are covered in this chapter.

Another important concept covered in this chapter is **spreadsheet analysis** or what-if analysis: the mental process of evaluating information contained within an electronic spreadsheet. It often involves comparing various results generated by the spreadsheet. A **model**, in terms of a spreadsheet, is a numeric representation of a real-world situation. For example, a home budget is a numeric representation of the expenses involved in maintaining a household and therefore can be considered a model. The hands-on exercises in this chapter provide an introduction to spreadsheet analysis.

Copy and Move

Complex worksheets often contain some repetitive data. For example, the same labels or the same formulas may be repeated. Instead of requiring the user to type the same data two or three times, WestCalc has a copy feature that enables the user to copy any cell or cells in the worksheet and move them to any other part of the worksheet.

To use the Copy command, press <F5> from the Commands Menu. Then press <F3>. The prompt FROM CELL(S) appears in the command area. Using the <F3> command, mark the range of cells to be copied. Next, the prompt TO CELL(S) appears in the command area. Type the cell address of the first cell in the range where the data is to be copied, and press <Return>. All the data moves automatically to the new range, which need not be equal in size to the range that was copied.

 YOUR TURN

Because you are now familiar with WestCalc commands, the hands-on exercises in this chapter use an abbreviated method to indicate what comands are to be selected. For example, the instructions

/ <F5> <F3>

indicate you should type a slash (/) and then press <F5> and <F3>. Once you are familiar with the commands in the Commands Menu, you do not have to type a slash before using these commands. For example, if you press <F5> without first typing a slash, you activate the Modify submenu.

In this exercise you will be using dates as labels. Remember, WestCalc will read the dates as numbers rather than labels unless the double quotation mark label prefix is the first character entered. The quotation mark will not appear in the entry line, but as soon as you press the key the word LABEL will appear, indicating the entry is a label, not a number. The double quotation mark will not appear in the cell.

Start with a blank worksheet on the screen. Enter the following labels in the cells indicated:

Cell	Label
A1	INCOME
A3	Rent
A5	Apt. #1
A6	Apt. #2
A7	Apt. #3
A9	Total
A11	EXPENSES
A13	Repairs
B3	''1983
C3	''1984
D3	''1985
E3	''1986
F3	''1987
G3	''1988

You are now going to copy cells B3 through G3 and move them to B13 through G13. You will also copy cells A5 through A9 and move them to A15 through A19.

Go to B3
/ <F5> <F3>

When the FROM CELL(S) prompt appears, press <F3> **.** (type a period). Move the cell pointer to G3. Press <Return>. When the prompt TO CELL(S) appears, type **B13.** Press <Return>. The labels are copied automatically to cells B13 through G13.

Go to A5
/ <F5> <F3>
Using the <F3> command, select the range A5 through A9
Press <Return>
Type **A15**
Press <Return>

The labels are copied to cells A15 through A19.

Save this worksheet as EXAMPLE on your data disk.

> ***WestCalc Tip:*** Before copying a range, make sure there is no data in the range where the data will be copied to. If there is data in that range, the Copy command writes over it and the original data is irretrievably lost.

Formatting an Entire Worksheet

In some cases, the format for an entire worksheet may be the same. For example, every value in a particular worksheet may be currency. Instead of changing individual cells to the dollar format, you can format the entire worksheet once. All the values in that worksheet will appear as currency.

The Worksheet must be formatted before any values are entered into it. The user-defined, value display option enables the user to format the entire worksheet. To format the entire worksheet, access the Value Display submenu by pressing <F6> for Format and <F7> for Value Display.

When the Value Display submenu appears, the prompt VALUE DISPLAY FORMAT CODE (A/G/I/D/U) [A] is in the command area (see Figure 11-1). Type **U** for user-defined. The Value Display Options Window appears (see Figure 11-2).

Select the options you would like displayed for all the values in the worksheet. For example, if all the values are to appear as currency, you would enter three options: **2** for Dollar sign and press **Y** for yes; **8** for decimal places and **2** for two

Figure 11-1
Formatting an Entire Worksheet

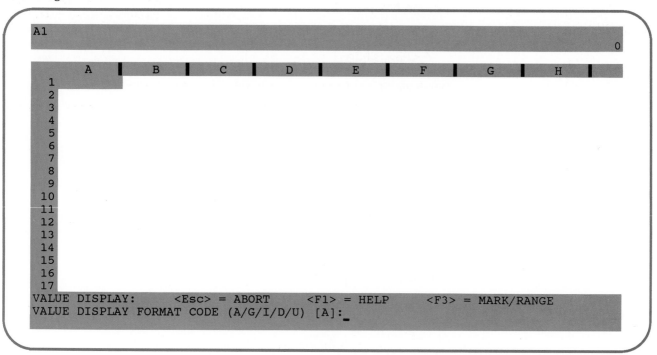

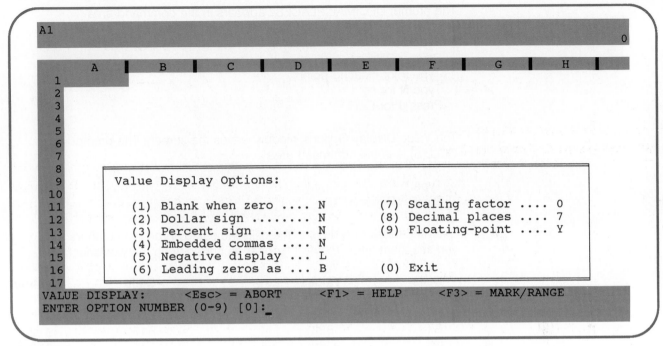

Figure 11-2
The Value Display Options Window

decimal places; and **9** for Floating point and **N** for no. Once all the options have been selected, type **0** to exit from the Value Display Options Window.

The final step in formatting an entire worksheet is to indicate the range for the display just selected. The prompt CELL(S) appears at the bottom of the command area. Since the entire worksheet is to be formatted, type *****. The asterisk is a global symbol that indicates the entire worksheet is to be formatted. Press <Return>. Any values entered into the worksheet will be displayed according to the options selected from the Value Display Options window.

YOUR TURN   Start with the EXAMPLE file on the screen. You are going to format the entire worksheet so that all the values entered will appear as currency.

    / <F6> <F7> <U>

The Value Display Options window appears. Since all the values are to be currency, the options you are going to select are Dollar sign, Decimal places, and Floating point. The ENTER OPTION NUMBER prompt is in the command area.

    Type **2** for Dollar sign

The prompt DOLLAR SIGN? appears in the command area.

    Type **Y** for yes
    Type **8** for Decimal places

The prompt DECIMAL PLACES? appears in the command area.

> Type **2**
> Press <Return>
> Type **9** for Floating point
> Type **N** for no
> Press **0** for Exit

The Value Display Options window leaves the screen. The prompt CELL(S) is in the command area.

> Type *****
> Press <Return>

Enter the following values in the cells indicated. Type the numbers as you see them here. They will appear as currency on the worksheet.

Cells	Values	Cells	Values
B5	2280	B15	250
B6	4080	B16	190
B7	3880	B17	312
C5	2460	C15	235
C6	4260	C16	285
C7	4060	C17	345
D5	2700	D15	310
D6	4500	D16	308
D7	4300	D17	296
E5	3000	E15	433
E6	4800	E16	507
E7	4600	E17	472

When completed, your worksheet should look like Figure 11-3.

> Save the amended EXAMPLE file.

Functions

FUNCTION
A built-in formula or process included in a spreadsheet program. When a function is used in a formula, a calculation is automatically performed. For example, a sum function automatically adds a range of numbers.

In the previous chapter, you learned how to enter formulas by typing them. Using WestCalc's function commands is a quicker and more accurate way to enter certain formulas. **Functions** are built-in formulas that perform specialized calculations. They reduce the number of keystrokes needed to enter a formula and thus reduce the likelihood of error.

A WestCalc function has two parts. The first part is the name of the function, the second part is an argument enclosed by parentheses. The argument indicates what data the function uses. This argument could be a specific number or numbers, a formula, or a range of cells, depending on the function. Table 11-1 lists some of the more commonly used functions.

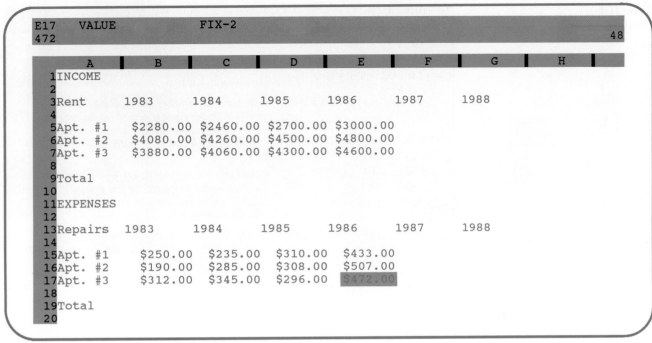

	A	B	C	D	E	F	G	H
E17	VALUE		FIX-2					
472								48

1 INCOME
2
3 Rent   1983   1984   1985   1986   1987   1988
4
5 Apt. #1 $2280.00 $2460.00 $2700.00 $3000.00
6 Apt. #2 $4080.00 $4260.00 $4500.00 $4800.00
7 Apt. #3 $3880.00 $4060.00 $4300.00 $4600.00
8
9 Total
10
11 EXPENSES
12
13 Repairs 1983   1984   1985   1986   1987   1988
14
15 Apt. #1 $250.00 $235.00 $310.00 $433.00
16 Apt. #2 $190.00 $285.00 $308.00 $507.00
17 Apt. #3 $312.00 $345.00 $296.00 $472.00
18
19 Total
20

Figure 11-3 The EXAMPLE File

YOUR TURN

Start with the EXAMPLE file on the screen. You are going to use the SUM function to find the total income from rent in 1983 and the total expenses spent on repairs in 1983.

> Go to B9
> Enter **+SUM(B5:B7)**
> Press <Return>

The total of cells B5, B6, and B7 immediately appears in cell B9.

> Go to B19
> Enter **+SUM(B15:B17)**
> Press <Return>

Your worksheet should look like Figure 11-4. Notice that the formula using the SUM function is in the status area.

> Save the amended EXAMPLE file.

Copying Formulas

Previously you used the Copy command to copy and move labels in the EXAMPLE file. The Copy command also can be used to copy formulas, as explained in this section.

Table 11-1
Functions

Function	Example	Description
AVG	+AVG(B5:B10)	Calculates the average of the numbers in the range specified by the argument. In this example, the function would find the average of the numbers in cells B5 through B10.
COUNT	+COUNT(B5:B10)	Determines the number of non-blank cells contained in the range specified by the argument. In this example, the function would find the number of non-blank cells in the range B5 through B10.
SUM	+SUM(B5:B10)	Determines the sum of the numbers in the range specified by the argument. In this example, the function would find the sum of the numbers in cells B5 through B10.
ROUND	+ROUND(B5,2)	Rounds the value specified in the first part of the argument to the number of decimal places specified in the second part of the argument. In this example, the value in B5 is rounded to two decimal places.

When a cell containing a formula is copied, WestCalc does not copy the value displayed in the cell on the worksheet. Rather, WestCalc copies the formula displayed in the status line and automatically inserts the appropriate argument or

Figure 11-4
Using Functions

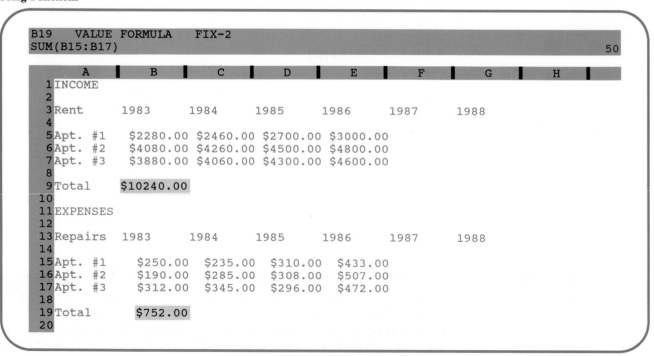

arguments. For example, suppose that a worksheet contains a list of values in columns B, C, and D, and a sum for each column needs to be calculated. First, the SUM function is used to calculate the total for column B. Then the formula is copied into columns C and D to calculate the totals for those columns. When the formula is copied, WestCalc automatically inserts the appropriate range of cells for each total.

YOUR TURN

Start with the EXAMPLE file on the screen. You are going to copy the formula in B9 into C9, D9, and E9. You also will copy the formula in B19 into C19, D19, and E19.

Go to B9
/ <F5> <F3>

When the prompt FROM CELL(S) appears, press <Return> to copy just the formula in B9. When the prompt TO CELL(S) appears, press <F3>. Move the cell pointer to C9. Type a period (.) to anchor the range, and move the cell pointer to E9. Press <Return>.
    The totals for columns C, D, and E immediately appear. Go to C9 and look at the formula in the status area. It should say SUM(C5:C7). WestCalc automatically changed the argument from (B5:B7) to (C5:C7) when the formula was copied into cell C9.

Go to B19
/ <F5> <F3>
Press <Return>
Press <F3>
Move the cell pointer to C19
Type .
Move the cell pointer to E19
Press <Return>

The totals immediately appear in cells C19, D19, and E19. Your worksheet should look like Figure 11-5.

Save the amended EXAMPLE file.

Freezing Titles

To this point, all the worksheets with which you have worked fit within the window. Larger and more complex worksheets may not fit within the window. As a user moves around a large worksheet, columns and rows of information scroll off the computer screen. This is generally not a problem, unless titles identifying the

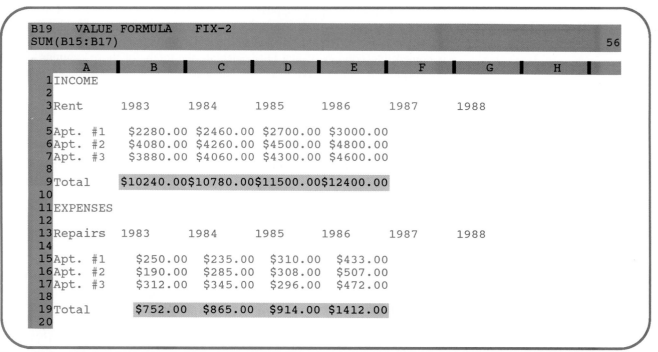

B19   VALUE FORMULA   FIX-2
SUM(B15:B17)   56

	A	B	C	D	E	F	G	H
1	INCOME							
2								
3	Rent	1983	1984	1985	1986	1987	1988	
4								
5	Apt. #1	$2280.00	$2460.00	$2700.00	$3000.00			
6	Apt. #2	$4080.00	$4260.00	$4500.00	$4800.00			
7	Apt. #3	$3880.00	$4060.00	$4300.00	$4600.00			
8								
9	Total	$10240.00	$10780.00	$11500.00	$12400.00			
10								
11	EXPENSES							
12								
13	Repairs	1983	1984	1985	1986	1987	1988	
14								
15	Apt. #1	$250.00	$235.00	$310.00	$433.00			
16	Apt. #2	$190.00	$285.00	$308.00	$507.00			
17	Apt. #3	$312.00	$345.00	$296.00	$472.00			
18								
19	Total	$752.00	$865.00	$914.00	$1412.00			
20								

Figure 11-5
Copying Functions

information contained in the rows and columns also scroll off the screen. A screen full of numbers with no identifying labels would be terribly confusing. With WestCalc, the <Scroll Lock> key can be used to freeze titles. If a row or column of titles is frozen, those titles do not scroll off the computer screen.

The cell pointer must first be positioned in the row or column to be frozen. After positioning the cell pointer, press the <Scroll Lock> key located in the upper right corner of the keyboard. The SCRLL indicator appears in the lower right corner of the screen. Pressing the right arrow key <→> keeps the column where the cell pointer is located frozen. Pressing the down arrow < ↓ > key keeps the row where the cell pointer is located frozen. The only keys that are operative when the SCRLL indicator is on the screen are the right arrow and down arrow keys. To unfreeze the titles, press the <Scroll Lock> key again.

YOUR TURN   Start with the EXAMPLE file on your screen. You are going to freeze column A.

Go to A1
Press <Scroll Lock>

Column A is now frozen and will not scroll off the screen. Suppose you want to start projecting some costs for 1988. To do that, you need to move to column G.

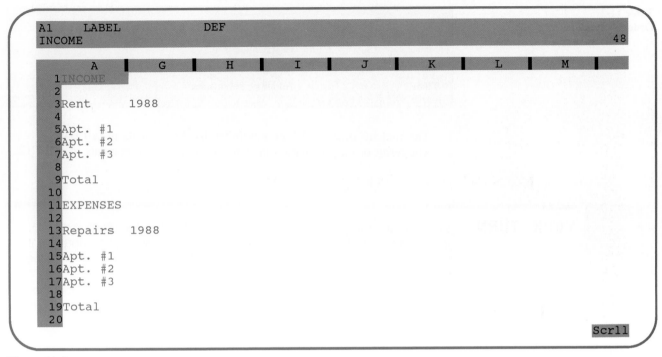

```
A1      LABEL              DEF
INCOME                                                                    48

             A        G         H         I         J         K         L         M
 1INCOME
 2
 3Rent         1988
 4
 5Apt. #1
 6Apt. #2
 7Apt. #3
 8
 9Total
10
11EXPENSES
12
13Repairs    1988
14
15Apt. #1
16Apt. #2
17Apt. #3
18
19Total
20                                                                       Scrll
```

Figure 11-6
Freezing Titles

Using the right arrow key, scroll across the screen until 1988 is the only year that appears on the worksheet.

Your screen should look like Figure 11-6. Notice that column A remains on the screen. Without those titles, the worksheet would not make much sense. Press <Scroll Lock> again to unfreeze the titles.

Order of Precedence

PRECEDENCE
In a spreadsheet program, the order in which calculations are executed in a formula containing several operators.

For more complex formulas, WestCalc performs calculations in a specific order of **precedence**. The order of precedence, or order of operations, is the order in which calculations are performed in a formula that contains several arithmetic operators. Table 11-2 shows operators that can be used in WestCalc formulas, together with the order in which those operations are performed. If a formula contains two or more operations that have the same precedence, they are performed sequentially from left to right.

There is a way to override the order of precedence listed in Table 11-2: Operations contained within parentheses are calculated before operations outside the parentheses. The operations within the parentheses are performed according to the order of precedence. For example, the formula (C12*B12) + C12 is calculated in the following order:

Table 11-2
Order of Precedence

Order	Operator	Operation
First	^	Exponentiation
Second	* /	Multiplication, Division
Third	+ −	Addition, Subtraction

1. The contents of cell C12 are multiplied by the contents in cell B12.
2. The result of the calculation in step 1 is added to the contents of cell C12.

YOUR TURN

Start with an empty worksheet on the screen. For this hands-on exercise, you are going to design a model that will help the owner of an apartment building project the income that each unit in the building will generate per month.

First, you are going to change the column width of the entire worksheet and enter all the labels. When completed, the range of the whole worksheet will be A1 through F17.

/ <F5> <F7>

When you are prompted to ENTER DESIRED COLUMN WIDTH, type **10** and press <Return>. When the columns prompt appears, type **A:F** and press <Return>. Now enter the following labels in the cells indicated:

Cells	Label
A1	''803 NORTH WOOSTER, BOWLING GREEN, OHIO
	(Remember, any number used as a label must be preceded by the '' symbol)
B3	Yearly
D3	Projected
E3	Projected
F3	Projected
B4	Increase
D4	Income
E4	Income
F4	Income
A5	Unit
B5	Rate
C5	''1987
D5	''1988
E5	''1989
F5	''1990
A7	Apt #1
A8	Apt #2
A9	Apt #3
A10	Apt #4
A11	Apt #5

A12   Apt #6
A13   Apt #7
A15   Average
A17   Total

Next, change cells B7 through B13 to Percent format, carried out one decimal place.

Go to B7
/ <F6> <F7> **U**

The Value Display Options window appears. Type **3** and **Y** for the percent option. Type **8** and **1** and press <Return>, for one decimal place. Type **0** (zero) to exit from the options window. The CELL(S) prompt appears. Press <F3> and type a period (**.**). Move the cell pointer down to B13. Press <Return>.

The rest of the worksheet should be formatted as currency, carried out to 0 decimal places.

Go to C7
/ <F6> <F7> **D N**

When the prompt DECIMAL PLACES? appears, type **0** (zero) and press <Return>. When the CELL(S) prompt appears, press <F3> and type a period (**.**). Move the cell pointer to F17. Press <Return>.
Enter the following values in the appropriate cells.

Cells	Values
B7	.065
B8	.08
B9	.065
B10	.05
B11	.08
B12	.05
B13	.10
C7	250
C8	530
C9	275
C10	350
C11	540
C12	325
C13	750

To find the average rent for the apartments in this building, use the AVG function.

Go to C15
Enter **+AVG(C7:C13)**
Press <Return>

Copy this formula into cells D15 through F15.

> Go to C15
> / <F5> <F3>
> When the prompt FROM CELL(S) appears, press <Return> to copy cell C15.
> When the prompt TO CELL(S) appears, type **D15:F15**. Press <Return>.

Notice that $0.00 appears in cells D15, E15, and F15. This is because the formulas entered into those cells include the contents of cells that are currently empty.

To find the total rent per month for each year, use the SUM function.

> Go to C17
> Enter **+SUM(C7:C13)**
> Press <Return>

Copy this formula into cells D17 through F17.

> Go to C17
> / <F5> <F3>
> Press <Return> to copy cell C17
> Type **D17:F17**
> Press <Return>

Because the cells in columns D, E, and F are currently empty, $0.00 appears in cells D17 through F17.

You now need to enter a formula that finds the new monthly rent given the yearly increase percentage rate for each apartment.

> Go to D7
> Enter **(C7*B7)+C7**
> Press <Return>

Because of the order of precedence, the operation within the parentheses is performed first. This operation (C7*B7) finds the amount the rent increases each month, given the yearly increase rate. That amount is then added to the current rent, which is the value in C7. The result is the rental cost for the apartment in 1988. This formula can now be copied into cells D8 through D13.

> Go to D7
> / <F5> <F3>
> Press <Return> to copy from D7
> Type **D7:D13**
> Press <Return>

Notice that after formulas were entered into column D, $0.00 in cell D15 was replaced by a value. Now formulas need to be entered into cells E7 and F7.

```
F7      VALUE FORMULA    FIX-0 C
(E7*B7)+E7                                                           79
```

	A	B	C	D	E	F	G
1	803 NORTH WOOSTER, BOWLING GREEN, OHIO						
2							
3		Yearly		Projected	Projected	Projected	
4		Increase		Income	Income	Income	
5	Unit	Rate	1987	1988	1989	1990	
6							
7	Apt #1	6.5%	$250	$266	$284	$302	
8	Apt #2	8.0%	$530	$572	$618	$668	
9	Apt #3	6.5%	$275	$293	$312	$332	
10	Apt #4	5.0%	$350	$367	$386	$405	
11	Apt #5	8.0%	$540	$583	$630	$680	
12	Apt #6	5.0%	$325	$341	$358	$376	
13	Apt #7	10.0%	$750	$825	$907	$998	
14							
15	Average		$431	$464	$499	$537	
16							
17	Total		$3,020	$3,248	$3,495	$3,762	
18							
19							
20							

Figure 11-7
The RENT Worksheet

Go to E7
Enter **(D7*B7)+D7**
Press <Return>
Go to F7
Enter **(E7*B7)+E7**
Press <Return>
Copy the formula in cell E7 into cells E8 through E13
Copy the formula in cell F7 into cells F8 through F13

To make the worksheet easier to read, you will center the values in cells B7 through F17 under the column headings.

/ <F6> <F2> **C**
When the prompt CELL(S) appears, type **B7:F17**
Press <Return>

When completed, your worksheet should look like Figure 11-7. Save this worksheet under the filename RENT.

Spreadsheet Analysis

Once a worksheet has been created, it is easy to experiment with various options. After changes are made, WestCalc automatically recalculates the worksheet to reflect those changes. Numerous alternatives to a single plan can be projected and evaluated, a feature that makes the spreadsheet an invaluable tool in decision-making.

YOUR TURN

Start with the RENT file on the screen. You are going to experiment with what-if analysis by making changes to the Yearly Increase Percentage Rate and to the rent for each unit.

The owner of this apartment building is thinking of hiring a building manager in 1988, but she cannot afford to pay a building manager's salary unless the total income per month from the apartments is $3,800. The owner wants to know if raising the Yearly Increase Rate for each unit by 1 percent would generate enough income to hire a building manager in 1988. Change the values in cells B7 through B13 to reflect a 1 percent increase in the Yearly Increase Rate. Could the owner afford to hire a building manager in 1988? If not, what year could the owner afford to hire a building manager?

The other option for increasing income is to raise the rent. Increase each apartment's rent in column C by $30.00 per month. Now what year can the owner afford to hire a building manager?

Continue to experiment with what-if analysis. When you have finished, do not save the amended file. Instead, save the file in its original form, as it was before you began experimenting with what-if analysis. Pressing <Esc> and typing **Y** without saving the amended worksheet saves the RENT worksheet as it was originally entered.

Retrieve the original RENT file and print it. It should look like Figure 11-8.

File Locking

WestCalc's file locking feature allows the user to protect existing documents. When a file is locked, no permanent changes can be made to it. A locked file can be viewed and printed and changes can be made on the screen, but those changes cannot be saved. This feature can be useful in instances when other people might be using your data disk. They cannot accidentally change your document, and, neither can you.

There is also a special password lock that your instructor can use to lock practice documents. These files cannot be unlocked unless the correct password is entered. This feature protects practice documents so that they do not have to be rewritten if you accidentally activate the DELETE FILE function or another function that might cause permanent damage to the file.

To lock an existing file, activate the Commands Menu. Press <F4> for FILE and <F7> for LOCK. The prompt ENTER FILENAME appears. Enter the name of the file to be locked and press <Return>. The File submenu returns to the

```
803 NORTH WOOSTER, BOWLING GREEN, OHIO
```

Unit	Yearly Increase Rate	1987	Projected Income 1988	Projected Income 1989	Projected Income 1990
Apt #1	6.5%	$250	$266	$284	$302
Apt #2	8.0%	$530	$572	$618	$668
Apt #3	6.5%	$275	$293	$312	$332
Apt #4	5.0%	$350	$367	$386	$405
Apt #5	8.0%	$540	$583	$630	$680
Apt #6	5.0%	$325	$341	$358	$376
Apt #7	10.0%	$750	$825	$907	$998
Average		$431	$464	$499	$537
Total		$3,020	$3,248	$3,495	$3,762

Figure 11-8
The Rent File

screen. To unlock a locked file, activate the Commands Menu. Press <F4> for FILE and <F8> for UNLOCK. The prompt ENTER FILENAME appears. Enter the name of the file to be unlocked and press <Return>.

If you have made extensive changes to a locked file without realizing that the file is locked, the locked file can be saved under a different name. The command to save a file is <F4> for FILE and <F4> for SAVE. The prompt ENTER FILENAME then appears. If the name of a locked file is entered, the error message FILE IS LOCKED appears, but the ENTER FILENAME prompt remains on the screen. To save the file, enter a different filename and press <Return>. Both the locked document and the new document—which has a different filename from the locked document—will be saved on the data disk.

YOUR TURN

In this exercise you are going to lock the RENT file. Retrieve the RENT file if it is not on your screen. If necessary, activate the Commands Menu.

> Press <F4> for FILE
> Press <F7> for LOCK

The prompt ENTER FILENAME appears.

> Type **RENT**
> Press <Return>

The File Submenu returns to the screen. The RENT file is now locked.

Learning Check

1. In _____, various results generated by the spreadsheet are often compared.

2. A(n) _____ is a numeric representation of a real-world situation.

3. The _____ value display option enables the user to format an entire worksheet.

4. A built-in formula already stored in a spreadsheet program is called a(n) _____.

5. The order in which calculations are performed in a formula with several operators is called the _____.

Answers

1. spreadsheet analysis 2. model 3. user-defined 4. function 5. order of precedence

Summary of Frequently Used WestCalc 2.5 Menus and Submenus

Main Command Menu	Submenus
<F1> Help	
<F2> Edit	
<F3> Goto	
<F4> File →	<F1> Help <F2> Dir <F3> Load <F4> Save <F5> Load Partial <F6> Change Directory
<F5> Modify →	<F1> Help <F2> Find <F3> Copy <F4> Move <F5> Insert <F6> Delete <F7> Width <F8> Blank
<F6> Format →	<F1> Help <F2> Justify <F3> Protect <F4> Unprotect <F5> Visible <F6> Invisible <F7> Value Display
<F7> Print →	<F1> Help <F2> Options <F3> Print Display <F4> Print Cell Contents
<F8> Recalc →	<F1> Help <F2> Turn Auto-Recalc Off <F3> Manual-Recalc
<F9> Restart	

Summary of WestCalc 2.5 Commands

A. Main Menu Commands		
Command	*Key*	*Description*
EDIT	\<F2\>	Modifies the contents of a cell without requiring the user to retype the entire entry.
GOTO	\<F3\>	Moves the cell pointer to a specified cell.
FILE	\<F4\>	Retrieves and saves files. Lists all currently saved files. Sets the current directory drive.
MODIFY	\<F5\>	Finds, moves, and copies data. Inserts and deletes rows and columns. Changes column widths. Erases a cell or a range of cells.
FORMAT	\<F6\>	Aligns data within the cells. Protects cells against being deleted, adjusted, or shifted. Sets cells so their contents are not visible on the screen. Formats the way the contents of a cell is displayed on the screen.
PRINT	\<F7\>	Prints all or part of a worksheet on paper.
RECALC	\<F8\>	Turns off the Auto-Recalc feature, which automatically recalculates all of the cells that contain formulas every time a numeric entry is read into the worksheet.
RESTART	\<F9\>	Erases the worksheet currently in the WestCalc spreadsheet program and replaces it with a blank worksheet.

B. File Menu Commands		
Command	*Key*	*Description*
DIRECTORY	\<F4\> \<F2\>	Provides a list of all the WestCalc files saved on the disk.
LOAD	\<F4\> \<F3\>	Loads a worksheet that was previously saved into the WestCalc spreadsheet program.
SAVE	\<F4\> \<F4\>	Saves on disk the worksheet currently in the WestCalc spreadsheet program.
LOAD PARTIAL	\<F4\> \<F5\>	Loads into the WestCalc spreadsheet program a specified range of cells from a worksheet previously saved.
CHANGE DIRECTORY	\<F4\> \<F6\>	Changes the directory (disk drive) to be used for data files.

Summary of WestCalc Commands Continued

C. Modify Menu Commands

Command	Key	Description
FIND	\<F5> \<F2>	Searches for a specified string of characters.
COPY	\<F5> \<F3>	Copies a specified range of cells.
MOVE	\<F5> \<F4>	Moves a specified range of cells from one part of the worksheet to another part of the worksheet.
INSERT	\<F5> \<F5>	Inserts a row(s) or column(s) in the worksheet.
DELETE	\<F5> \<F6>	Deletes a row(s) or column(s) from the worksheet.
WIDTH	\<F5> \<F7>	Changes the width of one or more columns.
BLANK	\<F5> \<F8>	Erases the contents of a cell or range of cells.

D. Format Menu Commands

Command	Key	Description
JUSTIFY	\<F6> \<F2>	Aligns the contents of a cell(s) within the cell. The contents can be centered or lined up at the right or left side of the cell.
PROTECT	\<F6> \<F3>	Sets a cell(s) so that it cannot be deleted, adjusted, or shifted.
UNPROTECT	\<F6> \<F4>	Clears a cell(s) so that it is no longer protected.
VISIBLE	\<F6> \<F5>	Clears a cell(s) so that it is no longer invisible.
INVISIBLE	\<F6> \<F6>	Sets a cell(s) so that its contents are not displayed on the screen.
VALUE DISPLAY	\<F6> \<F7>	Sets the format in which values are displayed on the screen (dollar, percent, integer, number of decimal places, etc.).

E. Print Menu Commands

Command	Key	Description
OPTIONS	\<F7> \<F2>	Sets printer options.
PRINT DISPLAY	\<F7> \<F3>	Prints the worksheet as it is displayed on the screen.
PRINT CELL CONTENTS	\<F7> \<F4>	Prints cell formats and definitions.

**Summary of
WestCalc Commands
Continued**

F. Recalc Menu Commands		
Command	*Key*	*Description*
AUTO-RECALC	\<F8\> \<F2\>	Sets the Auto-Recalc feature to off or on.
MANUAL-RECALC	\<F8\> \<F3\>	Forces a manual recalculation.

Summary Points

■ Spreadsheet analysis, which often involves comparing various results generated by a spreadsheet, is the mental process of evaluating information contained within a spreadsheet.

■ A model is a numeric representation of a real-world situation.

■ Functions, built-in formulas included in a spreadsheet program, save time by reducing the number of keystrokes needed to enter a formula and also reduce the likelihood of error.

■ Formulas involving several operators are calculated according to the order of precedence. Parentheses are used to override the order of precedence.

WestCalc 2.5 Exercises

In this exercise, you are going to design a model to help you keep track of your performance and determine your final grade in the courses you are taking. Assume that you are a Business major taking the following courses during the Fall semester:

Course	Credit Hours
ACCT 221	3
MIS 200	3
POLS 360	3
ECON 310	3
STATS 210	3

1. At the DOS A\> prompt, insert the West Instructional Software disk in drive A and your data disk in drive B. Start WestCalc and load a new worksheet.

2. Move the cell pointer to cell A1 and enter `Fall Semester`. Move the cell pointer to cell A3 and enter `Course`. In the next cell to the right, enter `Cr. Hrs.`. Then move the cell pointer to cell D3 and enter `Assignments`.

3. Starting at cell C5, and leaving a blank column between assignment numbers, enter your assignment list in row 5 as follows:

```
1  2  3  4  5  TOT.  TOT.POS.  PERC.
```

What is the cell address of TOT.POS?

4. Enter your course list and the credit hours allocated to each course. Start entering the information for the first course, ACCT 221, in cells A7 and B7. Repeat this procedure for the other courses, but make sure you leave a blank row between courses.

5. Now assume that your grades for the semester are as follows:

COURSE	1	2	3	4	5	TOT.	TOT.POS.
ACCT 221	180	80	95	178			600
MIS 200	180	190	170	190	188		1000
POLS 360	45	47	80				200
ECON 310	75	180	140	184			650
STATS 210	150	180	170				600

Enter the data in the appropriate cells.

6. Compute your total for each course in column M, using the SUM function. Then move to the PERC. column and compute your percentage for each course, which is equal to +TOT./TOT.POS. Format cells Q7 through Q15 to percent, with two decimal places.

7. What is your standing in Accounting 221? In Economics 310?

8. In order to improve the appearance of the spreadsheet, you would like to change your column widths.
   a. Reduce the size of columns C, E, G, I, and K to 4 characters.
   b. Reduce the blank columns (between the columns with data) to 2 characters.

9. You realize that in MIS 200, your professor gave a last assignment that does not show in your records. The assignment was worth 50 points and you received a grade of 47. Insert a column before the Total column to include this new assignment. Type the assignment number (6) and your grade in the appropriate cells. Change the total possible points for the course, and correct the formula in order to include this new grade in your total. What is your standing in MIS now?

10. Save your work using the File Save command. Name your file GRADE.

11. Print your work using the Print command.

WestCalc 2.5 Problems

To complete the following problems, use the INCOME file included on the Student File disk. Start WestCalc if necessary, and insert the Student File disk in drive B.

> *Hard Disk Differences:* To be able to access the INCOME file, you should copy the Student File diskette onto the hard disk.

1. Select the File Load command. When asked the name of the file to load, type INCOME. You should see the worksheet with the title INCOME STATEMENT on the screen. Select the File Save command. When asked the name of the file to save, type INCOME1. When you do this, the file INCOME is copied to INCOME1. From now on, you are going to use the file INCOME1 and keep the file INCOME intact in case you want to start over again or you make a mistake. Use the File Load command again to retrieve the file INCOME1.

2. The file INCOME1 contains the summary of income statements for L & T CO. for the past seven years. You will have to update it and make a comparative analysis of the data.

    a. Use the arrow keys to move around the worksheet and discover the structure of the model. Look closely at column D. This column contains simple entries in cells D6, D7, D10, D13, and D16, and formulas for totals and subtotals in cells D9, D12, D15, and D18. This structure is the same for all years.

    b. Go to cell D3 and enter the following: `(Thousand dollars)`

    c. Now assume that you have just received the following data for 1986:

NET SALES	1 650.41
COST OF GOODS SOLD	1 251.30
GENERAL EXPENSES	214.68
INTEREST EXPENSE	15.65
STATE TAXES	73.26
COMMON SHARES	27 500
DIVIDENDS PAID	29 900

You are going to update the worksheet in column B.

- Go to cell B4 and type the label `1986`. Center the label.
- Enter the numbers in the appropriate columns.
- Then copy the formulas from cells D9, D12, D15, and D18 to the equivalent cells in column B. As you can see, the totals are updated as you enter the formulas.

3. Now you would like to compute the differences between years for the following items: NET SALES, COST OF GOODS SOLD, GROSS PROFIT, GEN. ADM.EXPENSES, and NET INCOME

a. Start with the differences between 1986 and 1985.
- Move the cell pointer to cell E4 and type the label D86/85.
- Move the cell pointer to cell E6 to calculate the first difference in NET SALES. The formula should be: **(B6 − D6)/D6**. Type the formula into that cell.
- Copy this formula to the cells corresponding to the other items for which a difference is requested (E7, E9, E10, E12, E13, E15, E16, E18).

b. Change the format of the cells in that range to the percent format.
- Move the cursor to cell E6.
- Select the Format Value Display command. Percent is a user-defined format.
- Set the decimal places to 2. Set the format so the percent sign is displayed.
- When asked for the range of cells, type **E6:E18**. You should see all the differences displayed on the worksheet in the PERCENT format.

c. Now compute the differences for the remaining years.
- Enter the column titles as follows:

Cell	Title
G4	D85/84
I4	D84/83
K4	D83/82
M4	D82/81
O4	D81/80
Q4	D80/79

- The formulas have already been computed once, so use the Copy command to copy them to the appropriate cells for the remaining columns.
- Change the format of the cells to Percent, as in step 3b, to display the differences using the Percent format.
- Move the cell pointer to cell A20. Enter **' =** (using the repeating label prefix). Copy this cell entry to the range B20–R20 to draw a horizontal line.

4. Compute the income per share and the dividends per share for each year. Start with 1986.

INCOME PER SHARE = NET INCOME/COMMON SHARES
DIVIDEND PER SHARE = DIVIDENDS PAID/COMMON SHARES

a. Define the formulas with their cell addresses and enter them in the appropriate cells. For the year 1986, the formula +B18/B21 would go in cell B23 and the formula +B25/B21 would go in cell B27.

b. Copy the formulas to the remaining columns.

c. You would like to show a $ sign before INCOME/SHARE, DIVIDENDS PAID, and DIVIDEND/SHARE. Format the range of cells B23 through P27 to the dollar format with two decimal places.

5. Use the File Save command to save the changes you have made to this file. When asked if you want to overwrite it, type **Y**.

CHAPTER 12

Introduction to Graphics and WestGraph™ 2.5

Introduction

We live in a society where information is a fundamental resource. Businesses today depend on information about inventory, sales, market potential, customer credit, and other subjects. Schools and other institutions have to keep track of a growing amount of information concerning people involved in their organization and operations. Individuals need to manage bank accounts, bills, and tax information and to communicate this information to others. In order for the information to be valuable, it must be clear, concise, and easy to understand. One of the clearest ways to communicate numerical data is through the use of graphs and charts.

A graphics package is a computer program that enables the user to display data in picture form. With bar graphs, line graphs, and pie charts, the relationships among groups of numbers can be seen at a glance. For example, the athletic director of a high school might want to analyze football game attendance over a season to determine which opponents drew the biggest crowds. A business graphics package can display that information in picture form, as a bar or line graph or a pie chart. Each game's attendance is represented in the picture as a bar, line, or pie-chart slice. The games with the biggest attendance are obvious at a glance, because the segments representing them are longer or larger than those for games of smaller attendance. There is no need to read and compare a long list of numbers; the picture says it all, very quickly. This chapter introduces you to the use of graphics packages. In addition, it instructs you on how to get started using WestGraph 2.5, a graphics package developed by Rawhide Software Inc.

Definitions

Graphics software packages are designed to enable the user to display images on a computer monitor and to print the images with a printer. A variety of images can be produced, ranging from simple bar graphs to complicated designs in a wide selection of colors.

PIXELS
Individual dots on the display screen which can be turned on or off.

RESOLUTION
The number of pixels on a display screen. The greater the number of pixels, the higher the resolution.

SIMULATION
The process of creating a model of an object on the display screen, thus making it easy to change the design without building an actual model.

Using a graphics package can be as simple as selecting shapes from a menu of options, or as complex as controlling the individual dots (**pixels**) on the display screen. Turning the pixels on and off forms the images on the screen. Some display screens contain as few as 1,920 pixels, whereas others have 128,000 or more. By controlling which pixels are on and off, the user can create images as detailed as the computer allows. The greater the number of pixels in the screen, the higher the quality, or **resolution,** of the image. The higher the resolution, the clearer or sharper the images will be when displayed.

There are three basic types of graphics packages: design graphics packages, creative drawing and painting packages, and analytical business graphics packages.

Design graphics packages are used by architects, engineers, and other design professionals for drawing plans. These design aids are much faster than conventional drafting tools, such as T squares and french curves. Some packages include a **simulation** feature, which allows models of objects and their uses to be created on a display screen. An original design created and saved on a disk can be modified easily and saved under a new name.

Creative drawing and painting packages enable artists to produce pictures quickly, without many of the problems associated with traditional painting and drawing techniques. Paint never drips or runs, and colors never fade. New programs include ''air brushing'' and tone blending features, which make it even harder to distinguish computer art from more traditional renderings.

Business graphics packages help the user develop charts and **analytical graphics** for financial analysis. These programs transform numeric data into charts and graphs. Market analysis, sales forecasts, and comparisons of stock trends, as well as business and home financial planning all can be aided through the use of a business graphics package. Most packages enable the user to create bar and line graphs and pie charts to summarize financial information.

ANALYTICAL GRAPHICS
Charts and graphics used for financial analysis and other types of numerical comparison.

Learning Check

1. What is a graphics software package?
2. Graphs and charts provide an effective means of communicating _____.
3. What are the three major types of graphics packages?
4. The _____ feature of a design graphics package allows models of objects and their uses to be created on a display screen.
5. In a business graphics package, how is numeric data summarized?

Answers

1. A computer program that displays data in picture form. 2. numeric data 3. Design graphics packages, creative drawing and painting packages, and business graphics packages. 4. simulation 5. Through the use of line and bar graphs and pie charts.

Guide to Using WestGraph™ 2.5

The remainder of this chapter demonstrates the use of WestGraph 2.5, which is simple to use and also versatile. It is a business graphics package designed to demonstrate the use of business graphics to students. Line and bar graphs and pie charts can be created to communicate financial information effectively.

The directions in this chapter are written for computers with two floppy disk drives and a graphics monitor. The computer must also be equipped with either an IBM Enhanced Graphics Adapter card or a Hercules graphics card. If your computer is configured differently, ask your teacher for help in translating these directions.

Each of the following sections introduces a different feature of WestGraph. At the end of each section there is a hands-on activity marked **YOUR TURN**. Be sure to read the section carefully before trying the hands-on activity. Do not try to perform the functions on the computer as you go through the instructional sections. Wait for the **YOUR TURN** sections.

The key marked ←⌐ is referred to as the <Return> key. WestGraph also uses the arrow keys, which are located in the numeric keypad on the right side of the keyboard. If numbers appear on the screen when you press the arrow keys, press the <Num Lock> key once. When entering numbers into WestGraph, use the numbers along the top of the keyboard and not the keypad numbers. Some of the function keys from the left side of the keyboard also are used in WestGraph. In most cases, the <Esc> key cancels a function.

The following symbols and typefaces appear throughout this chapter:

Type **b**	The information in boldface should be typed to the screen, usually in response to a prompt.
Press the <Backspace> key	The angle brackets <> are used to signify a specific key on the keyboard. Press the key whose name is enclosed by the angle brackets.
HOW MANY DATASETS	All capital letters indicate phrases that are displayed on the computer screen. They also indicate WestGraph commands.
Sales Comparisons	Typewriter font indicates input to be entered into a WestGraph file.

Getting Started With WestGraph 2.5

In order to use WestGraph 2.5, you need an IBM DOS diskette (version 2.0 or higher) and a West Instructional Software diskette. The following steps explain how to start WestGraph.

1. Insert the DOS diskette in drive A. Insert the data disk—a formatted disk that will store the documents you create—in drive B. Turn on the monitor and computer and press the <Return> key in response to the time and date prompts. When the A> prompt appears, take the DOS diskette out of drive A and insert the diskette labeled West Instructional Software into drive A. Type **West** after the A> and press the <Return> key.

2. Read the information that appears on the screen. Press the <Return> key when you have read the screen. Read the next screen that appears. At the bottom of the screen, AUTHOR'S NAME appears with a highlighted box next to it. Type **Mandell** and press the <Return> key.

3. The West Instructional Software Opening Menu appears (see Figure 12-1). Using the up or down arrow keys, move the highlighting to WESTGRAPH. Press the <Return> key. The WestGraph Main Menu appears.

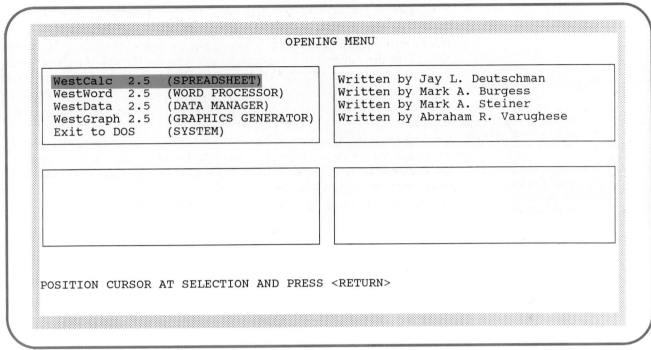

```
                              OPENING MENU

   WestCalc  2.5  (SPREADSHEET)        Written by Jay L. Deutschman
   WestWord  2.5  (WORD PROCESSOR)     Written by Mark A. Burgess
   WestData  2.5  (DATA MANAGER)       Written by Mark A. Steiner
   WestGraph 2.5  (GRAPHICS GENERATOR) Written by Abraham R. Varughese
   Exit to DOS    (SYSTEM)




  POSITION CURSOR AT SELECTION AND PRESS <RETURN>
```

Figure 12-1 West Instructional Software Opening Menu

YOUR TURN

In this exercise you are going to practice starting WestGraph on the computer and exiting from the program.

■ Insert the DOS diskette in drive A. Insert your data diskette in drive B. Turn on the monitor and computer. Press the <Return> key in response to the time and date prompts. When the A> prompt appears, take the DOS diskette out of drive A and insert the diskette labeled West Instructional Software into drive A. Type **West** after the A> prompt. Press <Return>.

■ Read the information on the screen and press the <Return> key. Read the information on the next screen. Type **Mandell** at the AUTHOR'S NAME prompt. Press <Return>.

■ The West Instructional Software Opening Menu appears. Use the down arrow key to select WESTGRAPH. Press <Return>. The WestGraph 2.5 Main Menu appears on the screen (see Figure 12-2).

■ Look over the Main Menu. When you have finished, use the down arrow key to select EXIT PROGRAM. Press <Return>.

■ The Opening Menu appears. Select EXIT TO DOS and press <Return>.

■ When the red lights on the disk drives are off, it is safe to remove the disks from the drives. Never remove a disk from a drive when the red light is on. You could damage the disk, or worse, the computer.

■ When you have removed the disks from the drives, shut off your computer.

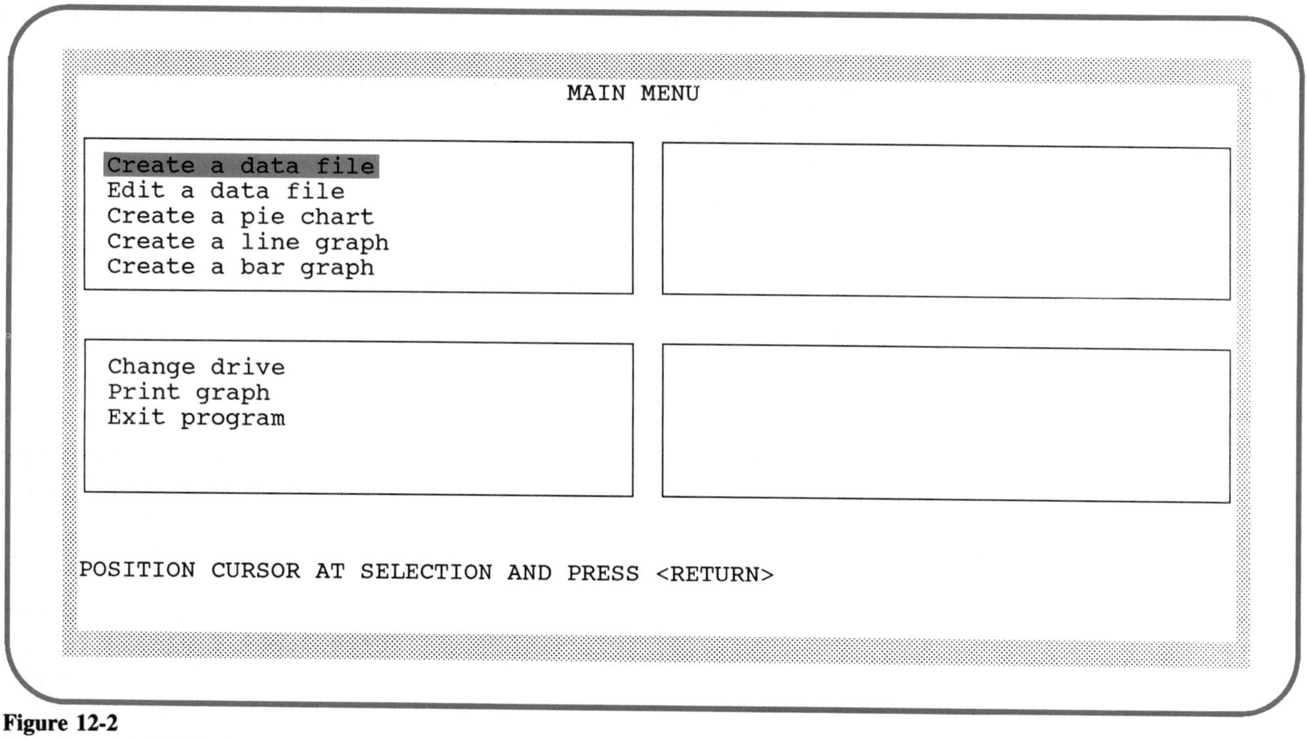

```
                          MAIN MENU

   ┌─────────────────────────┐   ┌─────────────────────────┐
   │ Create a data file      │   │                         │
   │ Edit a data file        │   │                         │
   │ Create a pie chart      │   │                         │
   │ Create a line graph     │   │                         │
   │ Create a bar graph      │   │                         │
   └─────────────────────────┘   └─────────────────────────┘

   ┌─────────────────────────┐   ┌─────────────────────────┐
   │ Change drive            │   │                         │
   │ Print graph             │   │                         │
   │ Exit program            │   │                         │
   │                         │   │                         │
   └─────────────────────────┘   └─────────────────────────┘


   POSITION CURSOR AT SELECTION AND PRESS <RETURN>
```

Figure 12-2
WestGraph 2.5 Main Menu

Learning Check

1. What must be done before you start up WestGraph on your computer?
2. Which disk drive should contain the WestGraph program disk?
3. What do you have to type to access the West Instructional Software Opening Menu?
4. How do you select choices from the Opening and Main menus?
5. When the West Instructional Software disk is in drive A, what should be in drive B?

Answers

1. You must boot up DOS. 2. Drive A (usually the left or top one). 3. Mandell. 4. By first highlighting them, using the up and down arrow keys, and then pressing <Return>. 5. A formatted disk to store files.

Data Files

WestGraph can create line and bar graphs and pie charts that quickly and accurately illustrate the relationships among numbers. Before graphs can be created, however, numbers and explanations of what those numbers mean must be entered into a data file.

The first step in creating a data file is to access WestGraph's Main Menu. There are eight choices on the menu:

CREATE A DATA FILE
EDIT A DATA FILE
CREATE A PIE CHART
CREATE A LINE GRAPH
CREATE A BAR GRAPH
CHANGE DRIVE
PRINT GRAPH
EXIT PROGRAM

Before working with WestGraph, you should always change directories. When WestGraph is first started, the **default** drive is drive A. The West Instructional Software diskette is in drive A. There is not enough room on this diskette to save the files you are going to create, so you must change the default drive to drive B, where your data disk is located.

To change the default drive to drive B, highlight CHANGE DRIVE in WestGraph's Main Menu using the up or down arrow keys and press <Return>. The prompt WHAT IS THE DRIVE FOR YOUR USER FILES appears. Type **b** (for drive B). Press the space bar. WestGraph's Main Menu returns to the screen. Your files will now be saved to your data disk in the B drive.

YOUR TURN

In this exercise, you are going to change the default drive to drive B. Start WestGraph on the computer. The West Instructional Software Diskette should be in drive A and your data disk should be in drive B.

When the WestGraph 2.5 Main Menu appears, select CHANGE DRIVE and press <Return>. The prompt WHAT IS THE DRIVE FOR YOUR USER FILES appears.

Type **b**
Press the Space Bar

The WestGraph 2.5 Main Menu returns to the screen.

Entering Data

Before you can create a graph or a chart, you must first enter a data file of numerical information upon which to base the graph or chart. To enter this numerical information, select CREATE A DATA FILE from the WestGraph 2.5 Main Menu and press <Return>. The directory for your data disk in drive B appears on the screen. (If you have not yet created any files, the screen will say DIRECTORY IS EMPTY.) The prompt ENTER FILENAME appears at the bottom of the screen.

Enter a name that reminds you of the file's contents. The name can be up to eight characters long. It can contain any of the letters and numbers on the keyboard, and any of the special characters (such as *,#,$,%,&) except for the period. Correct any errors in the filename by using the <Backspace> key. Press <Return> after the name has been entered correctly.

A series of screens follows. The prompt on the next screen is HOW MANY DATASETS (1,2,3, or 4). Datasets are divisions within a file for storing numerical information upon which to build separate graphs. Information can be stored to create up to four separate graphs in one file. For instance, if you wanted to graph the monthly sales of four companies for comparison on a bar or line graph, you would need four datasets. Enter the number of datasets needed for the file being created and press <Return>.

The prompt TITLE appears on the next screen. The title of a graph can be up to 30 characters long. This title appears over the graph or chart when it is generated on the screen or printed on paper. The title should describe the graph. For example, a graph comparing the sales of four companies in 1985 might be called SALES COMPARISONS, 1985. Press <Return> after entering the title.

The data entry screen appears next (see Figure 12-3). DESCRIPTION appears over a box containing the number 1 and the blinking cursor. The description is a label that identifies each bar in a bar graph, each point on a line graph, or each slice in a pie chart. Often the description refers to the period covered by the graph. For example, in the SALES COMPARISONS, 1985 graph, the descriptions would be the months of the year. Up to 12 descriptions can be entered. Usually descriptions have to be abbreviated, because they are limited to five characters each.

Figure 12-3
Data Entry Screen

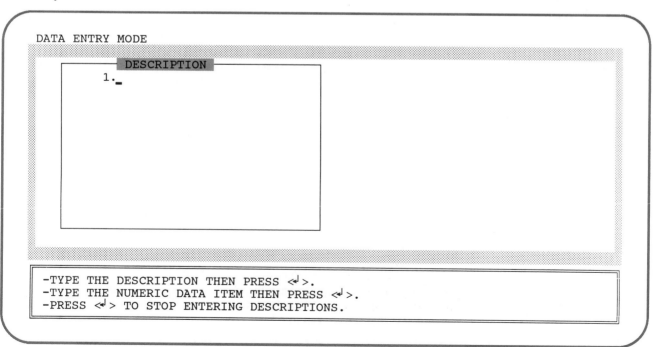

Enter the description and use the <Backspace> key to correct any errors. Press <Return> when the description has been entered correctly. The cursor moves to the next description number. Enter the second description and press <Return>. If fewer than 12 descriptions are to be entered, press <Return> twice after the last description is entered. If you do not notice an error in a description until after the <Return> key is pressed, you must wait and use the edit mode to correct it.

The next screen is the graph definition screen (see Figure 12-4). The purpose of the graph definition screen is to enter numerical data corresponding to each description just entered in the data entry screen. All entries on the graph definition screen must be numeric. In the SALES COMPARISONS, 1985 graph example, the descriptions are the months of the year from January through December. That is, when the data entry screen appeared, Jan was entered after the number 1, Feb was entered after the number 2, and so on. The sales figures corresponding to January, February, March, and so on are entered in the graph definition screen. For example, the sales figures for January are entered next to the 1 on the graph definition screen.

A graph definition screen must be entered for the number of data sets established at the HOW MANY DATASETS (1, 2, 3, or 4) prompt. Be careful to remember what each dataset represents. In the SALES COMPARISONS, 1985 graph example, each dataset represents one company. The user needs to know which dataset represents which company, because the datasets are not named until the graph is created.

After entering the last numeric definition of the last dataset, press <Return>. WestGraph's Main Menu returns to the screen, and the data file is complete. Graphs and/or charts can be created using the information in the data file.

Figure 12-4
Graph Definition Screen

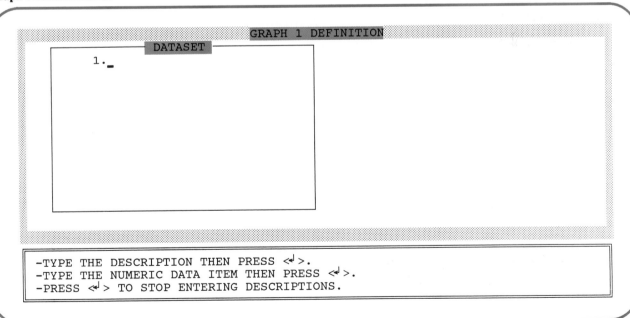

YOUR TURN

You are writing a report on the academic achievements of graduates who attended college on athletic scholarships. Alan, Len, Gail, and Alicia are four students who did attend college on athletic scholarships. You want to compare their semester grade-point averages to see if any patterns exist for the semesters when these students were participating in their sports. In the report, you want to use a line graph that compares their semester grades. In order to create this graph, you need to know the grade-point average for each student for each semester:

	S1	S2	S3	S4	S5	S6	S7	S8
Alan	3.0	3.0	3.0	3.5	3.0	3.25	3.5	4.0
Len	2.5	2.75	2.0	2.5	1.75	2.75	2.5	3.25
Gail	2.0	3.75	2.5	3.75	2.0	3.0	2.5	3.5
Alicia	3.5	3.75	4.0	3.0	3.25	3.5	3.75	4.0

With this information you are ready to create a data file. The WestGraph 2.5 Main Menu should be on your screen.

Select CREATE A DATA FILE from the Main Menu.

The directory of drive B appears on the screen, along with the prompt ENTER FILENAME.

Type **grades**
Press <Return>

The prompt HOW MANY DATASETS (1, 2, 3 or 4) appears. You will have four datasets—one for each student.

Type **4**
Press <Return>

The prompt TITLE appears (see Figure 12-5).

Type ATHLETIC SCHOLARSHIPS
Press <Return>

The graph definition screen appears. In this case, the descriptions are the eight semesters that the four were in college. The eight semesters are going to be grouped by years: first semester freshman year, second semester freshman year, first semester sophomore year, second semester sophomore year, and so on through the second semester of the senior year. There is a five-character limit on the descriptions, so they need to be abbreviated. FR1 represents first semester freshman year, FR2 second semester freshman year, and so on. The blinking cursor should be next to the 1 in the description box.

Figure 12-5
Entering the Title of a Graph

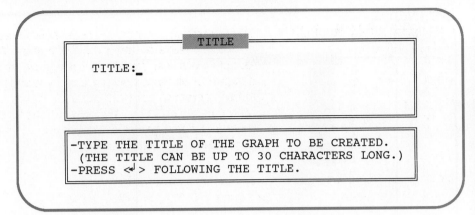

Type FR1
Press <Return>
Type FR2
Press <Return>
Type S01
Press <Return>
Type S02
Press <Return>
Type JR1
Press <Return>
Type JR2
Press <Return>
Type SR1
Press <Return>
Type SR2
Press <Return>

Your screen should now look like Figure 12-6.

Press <Return> again

The graph 1 definition screen appears. This screen is used for entering the data set for graph 1, which is going to be the graph for Alan's grade point averages. The cursor is blinking beside 1. Enter the first semester, freshman year GPA for Alan, because on the data entry screen 1 corresponds to FR1.

Type 3.0
Press <Return>

The cursor moves to 2, which is used for entering the second semester, freshman year GPA. That figure for Alan is 3.0.

Type 3.0
Press <Return>
Type 3.0

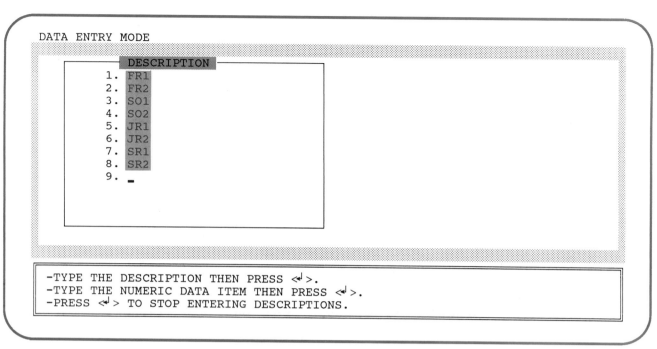

```
DATA ENTRY MODE

              ┌─DESCRIPTION─┐
         1.  FR1
         2.  FR2
         3.  SO1
         4.  SO2
         5.  JR1
         6.  JR2
         7.  SR1
         8.  SR2
         9.  _




-TYPE THE DESCRIPTION THEN PRESS <↵>.
-TYPE THE NUMERIC DATA ITEM THEN PRESS <↵>.
-PRESS <↵> TO STOP ENTERING DESCRIPTIONS.
```

Figure 12-6
Entering Data into the Graph
Definition Screen

Press <Return>
Type 3.5
Press <Return>
Type 3.0
Press <Return>
Type 3.25
Press <Return>
Type 3.5
Press <Return>
Type 4.0

A GPA for each of the eight semesters has now been entered for Alan. Your screen should look like Figure 12-7. Press <Return>. The graph definition screen for graph 2 appears. Repeat the procedure used to enter Alan's GPAs, using the GPAs for Len. When the graph definition screen for graph 3 appears, enter Gail's GPAs. When the graph definition screen for graph 4 appears, enter Alicia's GPAs. When you press <Return> after entering Alicia's GPA for semester 8, the graph definitions are complete. The Main Menu appears on the screen, and the entire data file GRADES is now complete.

Editing a Data File

To edit an existing data file, select EDIT A DATA FILE from the Main Menu and press <Return>. The directory for files on the disk appears on the screen,

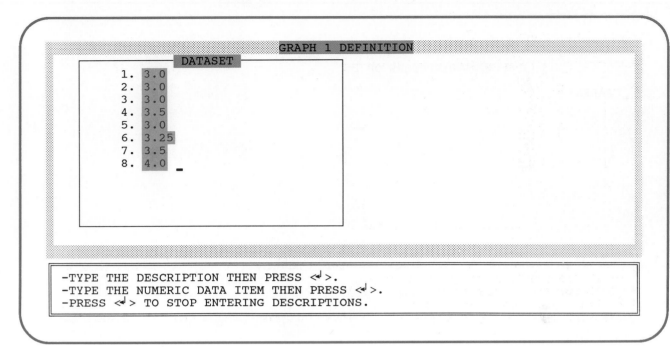

```
                    GRAPH 1 DEFINITION
          ┌ DATASET ─────────────────────┐
          │  1.  3.0                      │
          │  2.  3.0                      │
          │  3.  3.0                      │
          │  4.  3.5                      │
          │  5.  3.0                      │
          │  6.  3.25                     │
          │  7.  3.5                      │
          │  8.  4.0  _                   │
          │                               │
          │                               │
          │                               │
          └───────────────────────────────┘

  ┌─────────────────────────────────────────────┐
  │ -TYPE THE DESCRIPTION THEN PRESS <↵>.         │
  │ -TYPE THE NUMERIC DATA ITEM THEN PRESS <↵>.   │
  │ -PRESS <↵> TO STOP ENTERING DESCRIPTIONS.     │
  └─────────────────────────────────────────────┘
```

Figure 12-7
Entering Data Into the GRADES File

along with the Editing Menu, which contains four choices: <F1> for EDIT FILE, <F2> for DELETE FILE, <F3> for LOCK/UNLOCK FILE, and <Esc> for EXIT TO MAIN MENU (see Figure 12-8). To edit a data file, press <F1>. The prompt ENTER FILENAME appears. Enter the name of the file to be edited and press <Return>. The file must exist in the directory, or the error message FILENAME DOES NOT EXIST appears.

If the file exists, the TITLE screen appears with the title of the graph. The blinking cursor is under the first letter of the first word of the title. If an error exists in the title, retype the title and press <Return> to continue through the editing procedure. If the title does not need to be edited, use the appropriate arrow key to move the cursor all the way through the title. When the cursor is on the right side of the title, press <Return> to leave the title as it is and move on. If <Return> is pressed before the cursor is moved to the end of the title, the title is deleted. If this happens, the editing procedure has to be started over again so that the title can be retyped.

The edit data screen appears next (see Figure 12-9). A box labeled DESCRIPTION and a box labeled DATASET appear beside the prompt EDIT DESCRIPTION (Y/N). If any of the descriptions needs to be edited, type **Y**. The individual descriptions appear in the description box beside the prompt ARE THE ENTRIES OK (Y/N). Type **N** to move the cursor underneath the first description. Use the <Tab> key to move down the list of descriptions to the one that needs editing. When the cursor is in the line of the description that needs editing, type the correct description and press <Return>. The prompt ARE THE ENTRIES OK (Y/N) appears again. If the entries are now correct, type **Y** and press <Return>. If not, type **N** and repeat the procedure.

Once the descriptions have been edited to satisfaction and **Y** has been entered at the ARE ENTRIES OK (Y/N) prompt, the prompt EDIT DATASETS (Y/N)

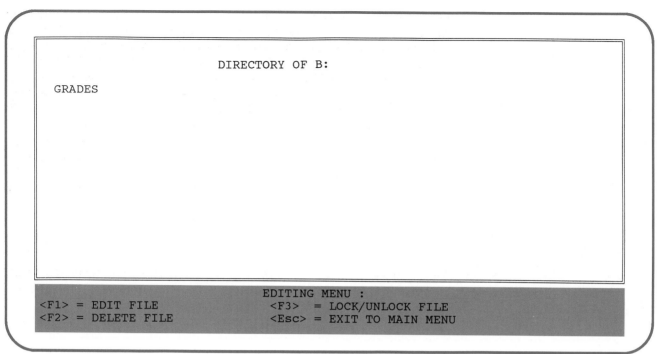

Figure 12-8
The WestGraph Editing Menu

appears. If **Y** is entered here, the following prompt appears: GRAPH 1, 2, 3, or 4? FILE HAS × GRAPHS. (The × here will be replaced on the screen by the number of datasets in the file being edited.) Enter the number of the graph to be

Figure 12-9
The Edit Data Screen

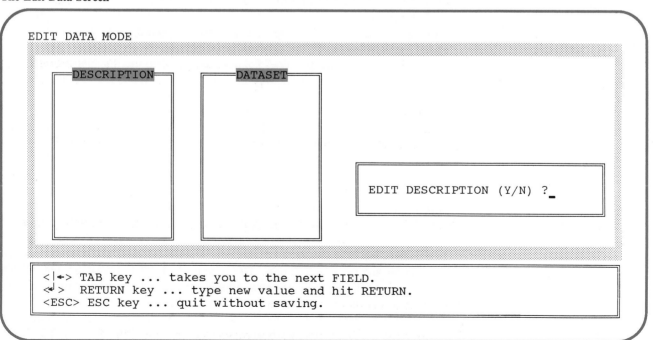

edited and press <Return>. If there is only one graph in the file and a number greater than 1 is entered, for example, an error message indicates an invalid request.

Datasets are edited the same way as descriptions. After you have entered a response to the GRAPH 1, 2, 3, or 4 prompt, the ARE THE ENTRIES OK (Y/N) prompt appears. Type **N** to move the cursor to the first entry in the dataset box. Use the <Tab> key to move down the list to the entry that needs editing. Type the correct entry and press <Return>. The prompt ARE THE ENTRIES OK (Y/N) appears again. If the entries are now correct, type **Y** and press <Return>. If not, type **N** and repeat the procedure. When a **Y** is entered in response to this prompt, the prompt EDIT MORE GRAPHS (Y/N) appears. Entering **Y** starts the editing procedure over again at the EDIT DESCRIPTION prompt. Entering **N** ends the editing procedure. The directory for the files on your work disk appears on the screen.

YOUR TURN

After you have finished working on the GRADES file, you discover you made an error when entering two of the GPAs. The sophomore year GPAs for Len were actually 1.0 for the first semester and 1.5 for the second. You are going to edit the GRADES file to reflect this change. The WestGraph Main Menu should be on your screen.

Select EDIT A DATA FILE
Press <Return>
Press <F1> for EDIT FILE
Type **grades** at the ENTER FILENAME prompt
Press <Return>

The title of the graph appears. The title does not need to be edited.

Press <Tab>

The edit data screen appears. The blinking cursor is next to the prompt EDIT DESCRIPTION (Y/N). The descriptions do not need to be edited.

Press **N**

The EDIT DATASETS (Y/N) prompt appears. The datasets need to be edited.

Press **Y**

The GRAPH 1,2,3, or 4 prompt appears. Dataset 2 contains Len's grades.

Type **2**
Press <Return>

The data entries for graph 2 appear in the dataset box.

Press the <Tab> key twice to move the cursor to entry 3.

You are now ready to enter the correction.

Type 1.0
Press <Return>

The cursor automatically moves to number 4.

Type 1.5
Press <Return>

All the corrections have been made. Use the <Tab> key to move through the remaining numbers. The prompt ARE THE ENTRIES OK (Y/N) appears.

Press **Y**

The prompt EDIT MORE GRAPHS (Y/N) appears. If there are typing errors that you want to correct, press **Y**. If all the entries for the file are correct, press **N**. The directory for the files on your work disk appears.

Press <Esc>

The WestGraph Main Menu returns to the screen.

Deleting a Data File

If a data file will no longer be used for creating graphs or charts, deleting that file is a simple process. First, select EDIT A DATA FILE from the WestGraph Main Menu. When the Editing Menu appears, press <F2> for DELETE FILE. The prompt FILE TO DELETE: ENTER FILENAME appears. Enter the name of the file to be deleted and press <Return>.

The prompt ARE YOU SURE? (Y/N) appears next. This prompt appears as a precaution because once the file has been deleted it cannot be restored. If the file is to be deleted, type **Y** for yes and press <Return>. The file is then deleted and its name is removed from the directory.

Locking a Data File

WestGraph has a feature that allows an existing file to be locked in order to protect it from accidental changes. When a locked file is accessed, it appears on the screen just as an unlocked file appears. Changes and adjustments can be made to the file, but those changes are only on the screen and not on the disk. If you try to save the changes, a prompt appears, indicating that the file is locked and cannot be changed.

There are two ways to make changes to a locked file. The first way is to unlock the file before it is accessed. The second way is to access the locked file, make the necessary changes, and then save the file under a different name.

To lock a file, choose EDIT A DATA FILE from the Main Menu. The directory for the disk appears, along with the Editing Menu. One option in the Editing Menu is <F3> for LOCK/UNLOCK FILE. Press <F3>. The prompt FILE TO LOCK/ UNLOCK : ENTER FILENAME appears. Enter the name of the file to be locked and press <Return>. The Editing Menu returns to the screen. Files that are locked appear in the Directory with an asterisk next to their name. To unlock a file, simply press <F3> for LOCK/UNLOCK FILE again, and enter the name of the file to be unlocked.

To save changes to a locked file in a file with a new name, edit the locked file. When the editing procedure is completed, the following message appears:

THIS DATA FILE IS LOCKED. IN ORDER TO UPDATE IT YOU MUST FIRST UNLOCK IT. WHEN YOU PRESS THE SPACE BAR, THE PROGRAM WILL ASK YOU TO TYPE IN A NEW FILE NAME TO SAVE CHANGES.

Press the space bar, enter a new name for the file, and press <Return>. The new file is saved, and its name appears in the directory.

YOUR TURN

Because you do not intend to modify the information in the GRADES file, you want to lock the file to protect the information from accidental change. The WestGraph Main Menu should be on your screen.

Select EDIT A DATA FILE
Press <Return>

The Editing Menu appears on the screen.

Press <F3> for LOCK/UNLOCK FILE
Type **grades** at the ENTER FILENAME prompt
Press <Return>

The Editing Menu returns to the screen. The GRADES file is now locked.

Press <Esc>

The WestGraph Main Menu appears on the screen.

Select EXIT PROGRAM from the Main Menu
Press <Return>

The Opening Menu appears on the screen.

Select EXIT TO DOS (SYSTEM)
Press <Return>

The system prompt appears. When the red lights are off on the disk drives, remove the disks from your computer and turn it off.

Learning Check

1. What are data sets?

2. Descriptions generally refer to _____.

3. What kind of data is entered into a dataset?

4. How do you delete a data file?

5. How do you lock and unlock a file?

Answers

1. Divisions within a file for storing numerical information to build separated graphs. **2.** The period covered by the graph. **3.** Numerical data only. **4.** Access the directory for your work disk, and press <F2> from the Editing Menu to activate the DELETE FILE function. **5.** Access the directory for your work disk, and press <F3> to activate the FILE LOCK function. You unlock a file by repeating the lock procedure.

Graphs

Once all the information needed to create a graph has been entered into a data file, displaying the graph using WestGraph is a very simple operation. Line and bar graphs are suitable for comparing numerical data, such as the GPAs in the previous section. The descriptions entered in the data entry screen run horizontally along the bottom of the graph. The numbers entered in the graph definition screen are plotted on the graph over their respective descriptions. When the graph is drawn, the relationship between the numbers is easy to see. The graphs can be produced with or without a grid of horizontal lines drawn at intervals across the screen or page.

Line and bar graphs also include a vertical line along the left side of the graph which sometimes has a label at the top of it. This line contains reference numbers. Suppose, for example, that the reference numbers on the side of a graph are 1 through 10, with 1 at the bottom of the line and 10 at the top. The label at the top of the line is THOUSANDS. In this case, the reference numbers 1 through 10 actually stand for the numbers 1,000 through 10,000. MILLIONS, 1/THOU-SANDS, and 1/MILLIONS are other labels that can be used. If no label appears above the line, the numbers on the vertical line may be assumed to represent the actual values.

Creating Line and Bar Graphs

To create a line or bar graph, select CREATE A LINE GRAPH or CREATE A BAR GRAPH from the Main Menu. The directory appears, along with the prompt ENTER FILENAME. Enter the name of the file to be used for creating the graph and press <Return>.

If a line graph is being created, the line definition screen appears; if a bar graph is being created, the bar definition screen appears (see Figure 12-10). There are three boxes within these definition screens. The first is the box labeled GRAPH. The words GRAPH 1, GRAPH 2, GRAPH 3, and GRAPH 4 appear in the graph box, if four datasets were defined in the file being used, with the letter N next to them. If only one dataset was defined, GRAPH 1 appears in the graph box.

All the datasets in the file can be graphed for comparison, or the datasets can be graphed one at a time and then the separate graphs can be compared. The Ns in the graph box stand for no, which tells WestGraph not to create that particular graph. Entering Y to replace the N indicates to WestGraph that the graph is to be created. For example, suppose there are four graphs and you want to display all of them on one screen. When the definition box first appears, the blinking cursor is in the graph box next to the words GRAPH 1. Type **Y**. The cursor automatically moves down to the next GRAPH. Enter **Y** next to GRAPH 2, GRAPH 3, and GRAPH 4. If you do not want a certain dataset graphed, type **N**.

The cursor then moves down to the LEGEND box. A name must be provided for each of the datasets being graphed. The purpose of the LEGEND box is to provide each dataset with its own unique symbol in a line graph, or its own unique shading pattern in a bar graph. These devices clearly distinguish the datasets from one another when they are graphed. Enter a name and press <Return> for each dataset.

After each dataset has been given a name, the cursor moves to the third box, which is the TYPE box. The TYPE box includes two options, STACKED and GRID. The stacked feature can be used only with bar graphs. In a stacked graph, all datasets are graphed in one column, one on top of the other. Each dataset is distinguished in the column by its shading pattern or, on a color monitor, by its color. A legend at the bottom of the graph identifies each shading pattern. The length for each section of the column corresponds to the numeric value of the

Figure 12-10
The Definition Screen for Creating a Bar Graph

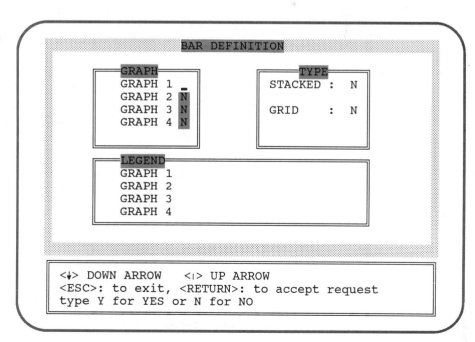

dataset being graphed. Stacked graphs generally are not as clear or easy to understand as graphs with separate columns. If you want the graph to be stacked, type **Y** when the cursor appears next to the word STACKED. If the graph is not to be stacked, type **N**. The cursor then moves to the word GRID. If you want the graph to be placed on a grid, type **Y**. If not, type **N**.

The screen then goes blank except for a message that states: REMEMBER TO PRESS THE SPACE BAR ONCE THE GRAPH HAS BEEN DISPLAYED IN ORDER TO RETURN TO THE MAIN MENU. The graph is then plotted on the screen. At the bottom of the screen is a legend. On a line graph, this legend identifies the special symbol used to identify each dataset. The data points are plotted above the corresponding descriptions (such as JAN, FEB, FR1, or FR2), using the appropriate symbols. In a bar graph, the legend identifies the shading pattern used to represent each dataset. Each of the datasets graphed is plotted using its individual shading scheme to fill in the bar. The height of the bar above each description is determined by the numeric data entered for that description.

In both line graphs and bar graphs, the title of the graph is displayed at the top of the screen. To leave the graph and return to the Main Menu, press the space bar.

YOUR TURN

In this exercise, you are going to create both a line graph and a bar graph using the GRADES file.

Insert the DOS disk in drive A
Insert your data disk in drive B
Turn on the computer and monitor
Press the <Return> key in response to the date and time prompts

The A> prompt appears.

Remove the DOS disk from drive A
Insert the West Instructional Software disk in drive A
Type **West**
Press <Return>
Type **Mandell**
Press <Return>
Select WESTGRAPH from the Opening Menu
Press <Return>
Select CHANGE DRIVE from the WestGraph Main Menu
Press <Return>
Type **b** at the WHAT IS THE DRIVE FOR YOUR USER FILES prompt
Press the space bar

The WestGraph Main Menu should be on the screen.

Select CREATE A LINE GRAPH
Press <Return>
Type **grades** at the ENTER FILENAME prompt

The Line Definition screen appears. The blinking cursor is next to GRAPH 1 in the GRAPH box. All four datasets (Alan, Len, Gail, and Alicia) are going to be graphed.

Type **Y** next to GRAPH 1
Type **Y** next to GRAPH 2
Type **Y** next to GRAPH 3
Type **Y** next to GRAPH 4

The cursor moves next to GRAPH 1 in the LEGEND box. If you recall in the GRADES file, dataset 1 corresponds to Alan's GPAs, dataset 2 corresponds to Len's GPAs, dataset 3 corresponds to Gail's GPAs, and dataset 4 corresponds to Alicia's GPAs. These are the names you will type into the legend box.

Type `Alan`
Press <Return>
Type `Len`
Press <Return>
Type `Gail`
Press <Return>
Type `Alicia`
Press <Return>

The cursor moves to STACKED in the TYPE box. This is a line graph, so it cannot be stacked.

Type **N**

The cursor moves to GRID. You want to see this graph displayed on a grid.

Type **Y**

The message REMEMBER TO PRESS THE SPACE BAR ONCE THE GRAPH HAS BEEN DISPLAYED IN ORDER TO RETURN TO THE MAIN MENU is briefly displayed. Then the Class of '84 Scholarship line graph is displayed.

Notice that the title of the graph is at the top of the screen. At the bottom of the screen is the legend that identifies the symbols being used for Alan, Len, Gail, and Alicia respectively. The numbers running vertically along the left side of the screen represent the grade-point averages. The descriptions FR1, FR2, SO1, SO2, and so on run horizontally along the bottom of the graph.

Find FR1 on the graph, and look above it to compare the GPAs of the four students for the first semester of their freshman year. By using the reference numbers at the left, together with the legend at the bottom of the screen, you can see that Gail had a 2.0 GPA, which was the lowest of all four students. Len had a 2.5 GPA and Alan had a 3.0 GPA. Finally, Alicia had a GPA of 3.5, the highest of the four students.

Spend some time looking over the graph. Once you think you are familiar

with the line graph, press the space bar. The WestGraph Main Menu returns
to the screen. Now you are going to create a bar graph.

  Select CREATE A BAR GRAPH
  Press <Return>
  Type **grades** at the ENTER FILENAME prompt

The BAR DEFINITION screen appears.

  Type **Y** next to GRAPH 1
  Type **Y** next to GRAPH 2
  Type **Y** next to GRAPH 3
  Type **Y** next to GRAPH 4

The cursor moves into the LEGEND box.

  Type Alan
  Press <Return>
  Type Len
  Press <Return>
  Type Gail
  Press <Return>
  Type Alicia
  Press <Return>

The cursor moves into the TYPE box.

  Type **N** next to STACKED
  Type **N** next to GRID

The message reminding you to press the space bar when you have finished
viewing the graph appears for a brief time. Then the bar graph appears.
Notice that the legend at the bottom of the screen provides the shading
pattern for each bar. Four bars, one for each student, are grouped above
each description (FR1, FR2, SO1, SO2, and so on). When you have finished
looking at the graph, press the space bar. The WestGraph Main Menu
returns to the screen.

Printing Line and Bar Graphs

The command to print a graph is found on the WestGraph Main Menu. Before
beginning the procedure to print a graph, make sure the computer you are using
is connected to a dot matrix printer and the printer has paper and is online.

   After you select PRINT GRAPH and press <Return>, the directory for your
data disk appears on the screen with the prompt ENTER FILENAME. Enter the
name of the file being used to create the graph and press <Return>. The prompt
PIE, LINE, OR BAR GRAPH? (P/L/B) appears. Type **L** to print a line graph or

B to print a bar graph. If the computer is not connected to a printer, the message **PRINTER NOT READY** appears. If this message appears, check to make sure the printer is turned on and online. After checking the printer, press the space bar to retry the operation. Press <Esc> to stop the operation and the WestGraph Main Menu returns to the screen.

If the computer is connected to a printer and online, the Bar Definition screen appears if **B** was entered at the PIE, LINE, OR BAR GRAPH prompt. The Line Definition screen appears if **L** was entered at the prompt. A graph has to be defined every time it is viewed or printed. To print a graph, respond to the definition screens exactly as you did to display the graph. After you type **Y** or **N** beside the word GRID in the TYPE box, the graph is displayed on the screen and printed. After the graph is printed, the WestGraph Main Menu appears on the screen.

YOUR TURN

In this exercise, you are going to print a line graph from the GRADES file. The WestGraph Main Menu should be on the screen.

> Select PRINT GRAPH
> Press <Return>
> Type **grades** at the ENTER FILENAME prompt
> Press <Return>

The prompt PIE, LINE, OR BAR GRAPH? (P/L/B) appears.

> Type **L**

The Line Definition screen appears. The blinking cursor is next to GRAPH 1 in the GRAPH box. All four datasets (Alan, Len, Gail, and Alicia) are going to be graphed.

> Type **Y** next to GRAPH 1
> Type **Y** next to GRAPH 2
> Type **Y** next to GRAPH 3
> Type **Y** next to GRAPH 4

The cursor moves next to GRAPH 1 in the LEGEND box. Dataset 1 will correspond to Alan's GPAs, dataset 2 to Len's GPAs, dataset 3 to Gail's GPAs, and dataset 4 to Alicia's GPAs. Type these names into the legend box.

> Type `Alan`
> Press <Return>
> Type `Len`
> Press <Return>
> Type `Gail`
> Press <Return>
> Type `Alicia`
> Press <Return>

The cursor moves to STACKED in the TYPE box. This is a line graph, so it cannot be stacked.

> Type **N**

The cursor moves to GRID.

> Type **N**

The graph is plotted on the screen and printed. Your printed graph should look like Figure 12-11. After the graph is printed, the WestGraph Main Menu returns to the screen.
Now you are going to print the bar graph.

> Select PRINT GRAPH from the WestGraph Main Menu.
> Press <Return>
> Type **grades** at the ENTER FILENAME prompt
> Press <Return>
> Type **b** at the PIE, LINE, OR BAR GRAPH prompt

The BAR DEFINITION screen appears.

> Type **Y** next to GRAPH 1
> Type **Y** next to GRAPH 2
> Type **Y** next to GRAPH 3
> Type **Y** next to GRAPH 4

The cursor moves into the LEGEND box.

> Type Alan
> Press <Return>
> Type Len

Figure 12-11
The Class of '84 Scholarship Line Graph

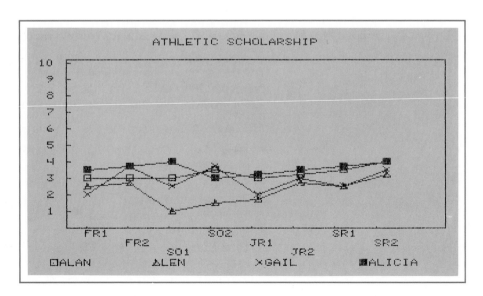

**Figure 12-12
The Class of '84 Scholarship Bar
Graph**

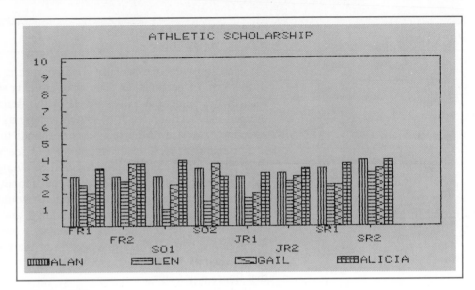

Press <Return>
Type Gail
Press <Return>
Type Alicia
Press <Return>

The cursor moves into the TYPE box.

Type **N** next to STACKED
Type **N** next to GRID

The bar graph is displayed on the screen, and it is also printed. Your printed bar graph should look like Figure 12-12. After the graph is printed, the WestGraph Main Menu appears.

Learning Check

1. What is established in the line or bar definition screen?

2. Stacking usually is reserved for what kind of graph?

3. Where do you find the command to print a graph?

4. How do you return to the Main Menu from the graph on the screen?

5. How are datasets distinguished from one another in graphs?

Answers

1. How many datasets are to be graphed; what the legends for each of those datasets is to be; whether you wish the graphs to be stacked; and whether or not you want the graphs to be placed on a grid. 2. Bar graphs. 3. On the WestGraph Main Menu. 4. By pressing the space bar. 5. By their shading or pattern color.

Pie Charts

Pie charts provide an especially effective means of communicating numerical data in the form of percentages. The chart itself is simply a circle that represents the total of the numerical values of all of the descriptions combined. The circle is divided into sections, each of which represents the percentage value of one description. The size of the section corresponds to the percentage.

For example, a company might want to see which month of the year was the most profitable. The descriptions would be the months of the year, and the dataset value for each description would be that month's profit. When the pie chart for this company was generated, the sections would vary in direct proportion to the profits. If December's profit was $50,000 and June's profit was $25,000, the section of the pie representing December would be twice as big as the section representing June. Beside each section of the pie would be the numerical dataset value (such as 50,000 or 25,000), along with the percentage of the total amount that figure represents.

With WestGraph, up to three of the sections of a pie chart can be "exploded," or separated from the rest of the chart. This feature enables the user to set off the most important facts in a chart, making them more obvious and the graph easier to understand.

A pie chart, unlike a line graph or bar graph, can represent only one dataset. The data files used to create pie charts can have up to four datasets, but only one dataset at a time can be used to create a pie chart. You can use the same data file to create line graphs, bar graphs, and pie charts, but the material used to create line and bar graphs is not always appropriate for creating pie charts. For example, the purpose of the GRADES file used earlier was to compare the grades of four students. Unlike a line graph or bar graph, the pie chart could accommodate only one student at a time. The entire pie would represent the sum of all the GPAs for one student. Each slice of the pie would compare the GPA for one semester to the sum of all the GPAs. The pie chart would not provide any useful information in this situation.

Creating Pie Charts

To create a pie chart, you must first create a data file of information. The procedure is the same as described earlier. First, select CREATE A DATA FILE from the WestGraph Main Menu and press <Return>. The prompt HOW MANY DATASETS (1, 2, 3 or 4) appears on the screen. Enter the number of datasets to be created and press <Return>. Next, the TITLE screen appears. Type a title for the graph and press <Return>.

The data entry screen appears next, with the cursor next to the 1 in the DESCRIPTION box. The descriptions will identify each slice in the pie chart when it is created. Remember that descriptions are limited to five characters each. If fewer than 12 descriptions are to be entered, press <Return> twice after the last description is entered.

The graph definition screen appears next. The numerical data that corresponds to each description needs to be entered. You need to repeat this procedure for the number of datasets established at the HOW MANY DATASETS prompt. After entering the last numeric definition of the last dataset, press <Return>. West-Graph's Main Menu returns to the screen. The data file is complete, and a pie chart can be created from the information in the file.

Select CREATE A PIE CHART from the WestGraph Main Menu. The directory for your data disk appears on the screen, along with the prompt ENTER FILE-NAME. Enter the name of the file being used to create the pie chart and press <Return>. The PIE DEFINITION screen appears (see Figure 12-13). Inside the large box labeled PIE DEFINITION there are two smaller boxes. The first is the GRAPH box. Type a **Y** beside the GRAPH representing the dataset to be graphed. If there is only one dataset, just the words GRAPH 1 appear in the GRAPH box.

The next box is the TYPE box. The words EXPLODE and REGULAR appear in this box. After **Y** is entered beside one of the options in the GRAPH box, the word EXPLODE in the TYPE box is highlighted. Up to three sections of the pie chart can be separated from the graph for purposes of emphasis. To select the sections to be exploded, press <Return> while EXPLODE is highlighted. If you do not want any sections to be exploded, then use the down arrow key to move the highlighting down to REGULAR and press <Return>. If REGULAR is se-lected, the pie chart is plotted as soon as <Return> is pressed.

If EXPLODE is selected, a box appears on the screen with a prompt that says WEDGES TO EXPLODE (MAX. IS 3). Type the number of wedges to be exploded (1, 2, or 3) and press <Return>. The first description and value in the chart are then highlighted. If this wedge is to explode, then press <Return> while it is highlighted. If not, use the arrow keys to move up and down the list to select the exploding wedges. The highlighting can be moved only with the up and down arrow keys. It does not move automatically after <Return> is pressed.

Once a description and value have been selected, an asterisk appears to the left of the description. When you press <Return> after selecting the last wedge, the

Figure 12-13
The Definition Screen for Creating a Pie Chart

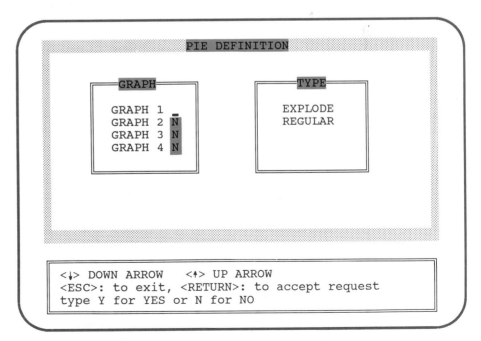

chart is plotted on the screen with the indicated sections exploded from the rest of the circle. Press the space bar to return to the Main Menu.

YOUR TURN

You have been asked to create a pie chart comparing the fund-raising efforts of a number of extracurricular groups at Carter High School. The first step is to establish a data file containing the numerical information necessary to build the chart. The information needed is the amount of money raised by each student organization. Following is a list of the groups that participated in the fund raising and how much each group raised:

Athletic Booster Club	$17,000
Annual Staff	$11,000
Drama Society	$ 3,000
Agricultural Society	$ 2,500
Honor Society	$ 800
Science Club	$ 1,200
Home Economics Society	$ 1,700
TOTAL	$37,200

With this information, you are ready to build the data file. The WestGraph Main Menu should be on your screen.

Select CREATE A DATA FILE
Press <Return>
Type **funds** at the ENTER FILENAME prompt
Press <Return>

The prompt HOW MANY DATASETS (1, 2, 3, or 4) appears. You need only one dataset to create this chart. Remember, you can use only one dataset for each pie chart.

Type **1**
Press <Return>

The TITLE screen appears.

Type CARTER HIGH FUND YEAR
Press <Return>

The description screen appears. The descriptions for this pie chart are going to be the abbreviated names of the extracurricular groups. The limit for descriptions is five characters, so the following abbreviations will be used:

BOOST for the athletic booster club
ANNUA for the annual staff

DRAMA for the drama society
AGRIC for the agricultural society
HONOR for the honor society
SCIEN for the science club
HOMEC for the home economics society

You are ready to enter these descriptions in the description box. The cursor should be next to the number 1.

Type BOOST
Press <Return>
Type ANNUA
Press <Return>
Type DRAMA
Press <Return>
Type AGRIC
Press <Return>
Type HONOR
Press <Return>
Type SCIEN
Press <Return>
Type HOMEC
Press <Return>
Press <Return> again

The dataset box appears on the screen. You are going to enter the amount raised by each organization beside the corresponding number in the dataset box. Dollar signs and commas are not entered into the dataset box. Remember, if you notice a mistake after having pressed the <Return> key, finish entering the remaining figures. When the data file creation procedure is finished, use the EDIT A DATA FILE command from the Main Menu and correct the error. The cursor should be next to 1 in the dataset box.

Type 17000
Press <Return>
Type 11000
Press <Return>
Type 3000
Press <Return>
Type 2500
Press <Return>
Type 800
Press <Return>
Type 1200
Press <Return>
Type 1700
Press <Return>

The WestGraph Main Menu returns to the screen. The data file is complete, and you are ready to create the pie chart.

Select CREATE A PIE CHART
Press <Return>
Type **funds** at the ENTER FILENAME prompt
Press <Return>

The pie definition screen appears. EXPLODE is highlighted immediately in the TYPE box. You want the wedges for the two groups who raised the most money to be set apart from the rest of the pie chart, so you are going to select the EXPLODE option.

Press <Return>

The prompt WEDGES TO EXPLODE (MAX. IS 3) appears.

Type **2**
Press <Return>

You want to highlight the first two descriptions, because these are the groups who raised the most money. The highlighting is on the first group.

Press <Return>
Press the down arrow key to move the highlighting to the second group
Press <Return>

The graph is plotted on the screen.

Printing Pie Charts

Printing a pie chart is very similar to printing a line or a bar graph. Before beginning the procedure, make sure that the computer you are using is connected to a printer, and that the printer has paper and is online. Select PRINT GRAPH from the WestGraph Main Menu and press <Return>.

The directory for your data disk appears on the screen with the prompt ENTER FILENAME. Enter the name of the file being used to create the graph and press <Return>. The prompt PIE, LINE, OR BAR GRAPH? (P/L/B) appears. Type **P** to print a pie chart. If the computer is not connected to a printer, the message PRINTER NOT READY appears. If this message appears, check to make sure the printer is turned on and online. After checking the printer, press the space bar to retry the operation. Press <Esc> to stop the operation and return the WestGraph Main Menu to the screen.

If the computer is connected to a printer and online, the pie definition screen appears. A graph has to be defined every time it is to be viewed or printed. To print a graph, respond to the definition screens exactly as you did to display the graph. When the pie definition screen appears, type **Y** next to the graph to be printed. Select the type of pie chart, either EXPLODE or REGULAR. If EXPLODE is selected, you must select the wedges that are to be separated from the rest of the pie chart. The graph is then displayed on the screen and printed. After the graph is printed, the WestGraph Main Menu appears on the screen.

YOUR TURN

You are going to print the pie chart for the FUNDS file. The WestGraph Main Menu should be on your screen.

> Select PRINT GRAPH
> Press <Return>
> Type **FUNDS** at the ENTER FILENAME prompt
> Type **P** at the PIE, LINE, OR BAR GRAPH prompt

The pie definition screen appears. EXPLODE is highlighted immediately in the TYPE box. You want the two groups who raised the most money to be set apart from the rest of the chart when the chart is printed.

> Press <Return>

The prompt WEDGES TO EXPLODE (MAX. IS 3) appears.

> Type **2**
> Press <Return>

You want to highlight the first two descriptions, because these are the groups who raised the most money. The highlighting is on the first group.

> Press <Return>
> Press the down arrow key to move the highlighting to the second group
> Press <Return>

The pie chart is plotted on the screen and it is printed. Your pie chart should look like Figure 12-14 when it is printed. The WestGraph Main Menu returns to the screen. Exit WestGraph and turn off the computer and monitor.

Learning Check

1. Pie charts are especially effective in communicating what kind of data?
2. How many sections of a pie chart will WestGraph allow you to explode?
3. What is a major difference between pie charts and line and bar graphs?
4. Why would you want to explode sections of a pie chart?
5. How do you move up and down the list of descriptions and values when selecting those you wish to explode in a pie chart?

Answers

1. Numerical data in the form of percentages. 2. Up to three. 3. A pie chart can display only one dataset at a time, whereas with line and bar graphs you can graph up to four at a time. 4. To set them off from the other sections for emphasis. 5. Use the up and down cursor keys.

Figure 12-14
The Carter High Fund Year Pie
Chart

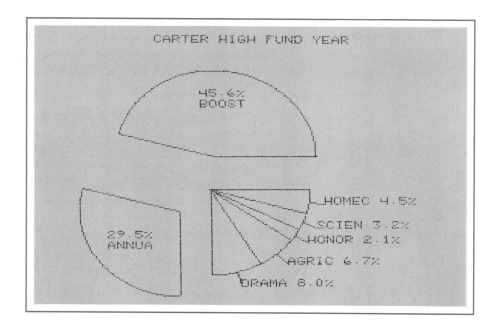

Summary Points

■ Graphics software packages enable the user to display images on a computer monitor and to print these images on paper.

■ There are three basic types of graphics packages: design graphics, creative drawing and painting graphics, and analytical business graphics.

■ One of the clearest ways to communicate numeric data is through the use of charts and graphs.

■ Business graphics packages can be used for a wide range of applications—from creating financial summaries for businesses to planning personal finances.

WestGraph 2.5 Exercises

To complete the following exercises, you will need a DOS disk, the West Instructional Software diskette, the WestSoft/File disk, and your data disk.

1. Assuming that your computer is shut off, describe all the steps necessary to start WestGraph. Go ahead and start WestGraph on your computer, and place your file disk in drive B. What steps are necessary to access WestGraph's Main Menu? Access WestGraph's Main Menu on your computer.

2. What actions do you have to take to begin creating a new data file in WestGraph? Take the necessary steps to begin creating a new data file. Name the data file TEST1. Describe in the proper order the purpose of each screen following the

Main Menu as you create a data file. Place one dataset in TEST1. Title the graph **TEST GRAPH**. Use the months of the year as descriptions, and type the numbers 10 through 120 by tens in ascending order beside each of the dataset numbers. For example, type **10** beside 1, **20** beside 2, and so on. The entry at 12 should be **120**.

3. What steps are necessary to edit a data file? Do what is necessary to change the title of the graph to **TESTGRAPH**. How do you create a line or a bar graph from a data file? Create a bar graph of the TEST1 file. Label the legend SALES. How do the steps required to create a pie chart differ from those required to create a bar or line graph? Create a pie chart using the TEST1 file.

4. What do you do to print a hard copy of a bar graph? Print a bar graph created from the TEST1 file. What do you have to do to print a pie chart? Print a pie chart created from the TEST1 file.

5. You have been asked to create a graph summarizing the monthly sales of a department store. The name of the store is A Mart. The figures for the year are as follows:

January = $84,000　　July = $81,000
February = $75,000　　August = $91,000
March = $69,000　　September = $93,000
April = $78,000　　October = $97,000
May = $82,000　　November = $104,000
June = $88,000　　December = $114,000

Create and print the graph or chart that will best illustrate which months are the best sales months for A Mart.

WestGraph 2.5 Problems

The file called SPRBREAK contains data about the locations and costs of hotels. The following data is stored in the SPRBREAK file:

	Description	Numeric Data
BW-FL	(Best Western-Fort Lauderdale)	667.5
BP-FL	(Beach Plaza-Fort Lauderdale)	797.5
PL-FL	(Park Lane-Fort Lauderdale)	582.5
FL-FL	(Fort Lauderdale-Fort Lauderdale)	707.5
HI-FL	(Holiday Inn-Fort Lauderdale)	857.5
BWC-R	(Best Western Continental-Reno)	557.5
HID-R	(Holiday Inn Downtown-Reno)	627.5
HIL-R	(Hilton-Reno)	627.5
MGM-R	(MGM Grand-Reno)	682.5
SAV-R	(Sands Hotel-Reno)	782.5

1. You are going to make a copy of the SPRBREAK file. Insert the WestSoft/ File disk into drive B. Select the EDIT A DATA FILE option from the Main Menu. Press the <F1> key (edit file) and enter the filename SPRBREAK in response to the prompt. Press <Return>. When the title of the graph appears, press the <Tab> key. Type **N** in response to the next three prompts. When the prompt appears telling you the file is locked, press the <Space Bar> and type NEWBREAK in response to the ENTER FILENAME prompt. Press <Return> and <Esc> to return to the Main Menu.

2. Select the CREATE A PIE CHART option from the Graphics Menu, and create a pie chart using the NEWBREAK data file. Which hotel has the largest slice of the pie? Which has the smallest? What percentage of the total do the Fort Lauderdale hotels have? Which two Fort Lauderdale hotels account for 18 percent of the pie?

3. Select the CREATE A LINE GRAPH OPTION from the Graphics Menu, and create a line graph using the NEWBREAK data file. Which hotel costs the most? Which costs the least? Which of the Fort Lauderdale hotels costs over $750? Which of the Fort Lauderdale hotels costs under $750?

4. Select the CREATE A BAR GRAPH option from the Graphics Menu, and create a bar graph using the NEWBREAK file. Which hotel costs the most? Which costs the least? Which of the Reno hotels costs the most? Which of the Reno hotels costs over $650? Which of the Reno hotels costs under $650?

CHAPTER 13

Introduction to Data Managers and WestData™ 2.5

Introduction

DATA MANAGER
A data management software package that consolidates data files into an integrated whole, allowing access to more than one data file at a time.

Schools, hospitals, restaurants, and all types of businesses store data. The ability to sort, retrieve, and analyze data quickly and efficiently can easily make the difference between a company's success and failure. In the past, the most common way to organize data was to store the records in folders in file cabinets. Today, however, computers provide other options. Computers make it possible to store vast amounts of data and to access it in seconds. They have streamlined the record-keeping process, thus reducing the amount of wasted time, effort, and space.

Data managers are software packages that computerize record-keeping tasks. In this chapter, data managers and their operations are explained. This chapter also introduces WestData 2.5, a data management tool developed by Rawhide Software, Inc.

Definitions

FIELD
A subdivision of a record that holds a meaningful item of data, such as an employee number.

RECORD
A collection of related data fields that constitutes a single unit, such as an employee record.

FILE
A group of related data records, such as employee records.

A data management software package is used to organize files. Data managers use secondary storage devices, such as floppy disks, to store the type of data that is kept in folders and envelopes in a manual filing system.

It is easy to understand how data is stored in a filing cabinet. Folders with related data are kept in the drawers of the cabinet. Each folder has a label that identifies its contents. The contents of each drawer may be related to a certain topic. To find one data item, you need to select the appropriate drawer and then find the specific folder containing the needed information.

A data manager records data electronically on floppy disks or magnetic tapes. Instead of people looking through drawers and folders for a certain item, the computer searches the disk or tape for it.

Each data item, such as a student name, an insurance policy number, or the amount of a bill, is called a **field.** A group of related fields forms a **record.** Your school, for example, may keep a record about each student. A student record might contain fields, such as the student's name, home address, parents' names, class standing, courses taken, and grade-point average.

A **file** is a group of related records. For example, all the student records in a school make up one file. The school may have other files, for teacher records, financial records, school-board members, and other types of data.

Data managers are useful because they perform many tasks faster and more easily than manual filing systems. Most data managers can perform the following functions:

- Add or delete data within a file
- Search a file for specific data
- Update or change data in a file
- Sort data into a specified order
- Print all or part of the data in a file

DATA REDUNDANCY
Repetition of the same data in several different files.

DATABASE
A grouping of independent files into one integrated whole that can be accessed through one central point. A database is designed to meet the information needs of a wide variety of users within an organization.

Because different files may contain the same information, data redundancy can occur and cause problems for a business. **Data redundancy** is the duplication of data in different files. Because of the duplication of data and the difficulty of keeping one piece of information—such as an employee address—current in several files, large companies began to develop database packages. A **database** consolidates various independent files into one integrated unit, while allowing users access to the information they need. Each data item is stored once, so it is easy to maintain. Users can search for, update, add, or delete data on all the records at one time.

Database packages store data that can be accessed in many ways. A university database might be accessed by personnel in the admissions, registrar's, financial aid, and deans' offices. A college dean might request the names of students who will graduate with academic honors, whereas the financial aid director might need a listing of all students participating in a work-study program.

Since microprocessors were introduced, data managers have become popular with businesses as well as with home users. The following section discusses various uses of data managers.

Uses of Data Managers

In homes, data managers can be used to create and organize a computerized address book, holiday card list, or recipe file. A data manager can be used for just about any type of record-keeping. Collectors of coins, stamps, baseball cards, or any other items can maintain up-to-date files of their collections.

Data managers keep home records in a compact form. Instead of having numerous notebooks and folders that must be maintained manually, the user can enter new data into the computer. Files can be stored on floppy disks or on cassette tapes.

Besides storing files in a compact form, data managers can find and retrieve data much faster than people can retrieve data manually. Data managers can be used to prepare reports for filing taxes. For example, a field labeled TAX DEDUCTIBLE in a data record can indicate whether a transaction is tax-related. At tax time, the data manager can pick out the tax-related transactions and print a report listing only those transactions. Some other home uses of data managers include keeping personal records, creating mailing lists, keeping appointment calendars, and indexing books in a personal library.

In business, data managers are replacing the traditional manual filing systems. A data manager can maintain employee records, control inventory, and print reports listing suppliers and customers. A small sporting goods retail store, for example, can computerize its inventory to improve sales through more efficient and timely record-keeping. By recording daily sales in a database, a manager can determine when stock levels are low and reorder items before inventory shortages occur. Thus, the store can maintain an ample supply of items at all times and can avoid losing sales due to inventory shortages.

Some data managers perform mathematical tasks. They can total the values of the same field in each record, find averages, or identify records with the lowest or highest value in a field. A data manager with mathematical capabilities can determine dollar sales of an item for a certain period. The mathematical features of a data manager also can be used for inventory control, by calculating and displaying inventory subtotals and totals for tax reporting at the end of the year.

A major benefit of computerized record-keeping is the time saved both in updating records and in searching for information. Data managers free employees to concentrate on tasks that can be done only by humans, such as talking to customers or planning new displays.

Some data managers are designed for use in special situations, for example, in creating mailing lists. A data manager with this capability might store data, such as people's names, addresses, interests, hobbies, and purchases. (People's interests and hobbies can be determined by studying the products they order or the magazines they receive.) Next, the data manager might sort and print a list of people who order a sewing or craft item or who receive craft catalogs. The data manager would print mailing labels for all names on the list. More sophisticated data managers can be used with word processors to produce personalized form letters for individuals or organizations found on the mailing lists. The data manager supplies the names and addresses that are inserted in the letter.

Learning Check

1. A _____ is a meaningful item of data, such as an employee address.
    a. database   *c.* field
    b. record   *d.* file

2. A _____ is a collection of related data fields that constitutes a single unit, such as all the relevant data about one employee.
    a. database   *c.* field
    b. record   *d.* file

3. A grouping of independent data files into an integrated whole is a _____.
    a. database   *c.* field
    b. record   *d.* file

4. A _____ is a group of related data records.
    a. database   *c.* field
    b. record   *d.* file

5. By storing each data item only once, thus eliminating the need to store the same information in many different files, a database reduces problems caused by _____.

Answers

1. c 2. b 3. a 4. d 5. data redundancy

Guide to WestData 2.5

The remainder of this chapter focuses on how to use WestData. WestData is a data management program with which you can easily perform many functions of database management.

Some of the WestData procedures depend on whether you are using a system with two floppy disk drives or one hard disk drive. The directions in this chapter are for a system with two floppy disk drives.

Each of the following sections introduces one or more features of WestData. At the end of each section, there is a hands-on activity, marked with the symbol **YOUR TURN**. Be sure to read the section carefully *before* trying the hands-on activity.

The key on the IBM PC keyboard marked ↵ is the <Return> key, sometimes called the <Enter> key. Throughout this chapter, when you are instructed to press the <Return> key, press the key marked ↵.

The following symbols and typefaces appear throughout this section:

Type **b**	**Boldface** is used to designate characters or text that you should type to the screen, usually in response to a prompt.
Press the <F10> key	The angle brackets (< >) are used to signify a specific key on the keyboard. Press the key whose name is enclosed by the angle brackets.
ENTER FILENAME	All capital letters indicate text that is displayed on the computer screen. They also indicate WestWord commands.
Type `Job Opening`	Typewriter font indicates input that is to be entered into a file.

Getting Started with WestData 2.5

BOOT
To load an operating system into a computer's main memory.

To **boot** the computer and start WestData, you need a DOS disk (version 2.0 or higher), the West Instructional Software diskette, and a formatted data disk for storing data.

1. Insert the DOS disk into drive A. Close the disk drive door. Turn on the monitor and computer.

2. When asked to type the date and time, press the <Return> key to bypass the prompt.

3. When the system prompt (A>) appears on the screen, remove the DOS disk from drive A. Insert the West Instructional Software diskette into drive A and close the disk drive door.

4. Insert your data disk into drive B. Close the disk drive door.

5. Type **West** and press the <Return> key.

6. Read the opening screen. Press the <Return> key when you have finished reading it. Read the next screen. Type **Mandell** and press the <Return> key. The Opening Menu appears on the screen.

7. Using the < ↓ > key, move the highlighting on the screen to WestData. Press the <Return> key. The WestData 2.5 Main Menu appears on the screen.

 YOUR TURN

Turn on and boot your computer. Start WestData. The WestData 2.5 Main Menu should be on your screen.

Designing a Database File

WestData's Main Menu has 17 command options (see Figure 13-1). To select an option, move the highlighting to the desired command using the < ↑ >, < ↓ >, <→>, or <←> keys; then press <Return>.

Figure 13-1
The WestData 2.5 Main Menu

```
                    WESTDATA 2.5 MAIN MENU
         (DATA FILES)                        (REPORT FILES)

  ┌──────────────────────────────┐  ┌──────────────────────────────┐
  │ Design a data file           │  │ Design a report file         │
  │ Edit a data file definition  │  │ Display a report file        │
  │ Delete a data file           │  │ Delete a report file         │
  │ Copy a data file             │  │ Copy a report file           │
  │                              │  │ Print a report file          │
  └──────────────────────────────┘  └──────────────────────────────┘

         (DATA RECORDS)                        (UTILITIES)

  ┌──────────────────────────────┐  ┌──────────────────────────────┐
  │ Input data to a record       │  │ Lock / Unlock files          │
  │ Edit data in a record        │  │ Mailing labels               │
  │ Display a record             │  │ Change drive                 │
  │ Delete a record              │  │ Exit program                 │
  │                              │  │                              │
  └──────────────────────────────┘  └──────────────────────────────┘


  POSITION CURSOR AT SELECTION AND PRESS <RETURN>
```

DEFAULT SETTING
A setting that a software package automatically uses when the user does not designate another setting.

WestData automatically **defaults** to, or accesses, drive A when first started. The data disk onto which you save all the files you create is in drive B, so the default drive has to be changed. The CHANGE DRIVE command tells WestData to access another drive when reading from or writing to disk files. The default drive needs to be set to B only once during a work session.

To change the default drive, move the highlighting to CHANGE DRIVE and press the <Return> key. The prompt WHAT IS THE DIRECTORY FOR YOUR USER FILES appears at the bottom of the screen (see Figure 13-2). Type **B** and press the <Return> key to continue.

 YOUR TURN

The WestData 2.5 Main Menu should be on your screen. Move the highlighting to CHANGE DRIVE. Press the <Return> key.

When the prompt WHAT IS THE DIRECTORY FOR YOUR USER FILES appears, type **B** and press the <Return> key. The WestData 2.5 Main Menu returns to the screen.

Once the default drive has been changed to B, you can create a data file. Move the highlighting to the option DESIGN A DATA FILE and press <Return>. The directory for drive B then appears on the screen. This directory is divided into

Figure 13-2
Changing Drives

```
                    WESTDATA 2.5 MAIN MENU
        (DATA FILES)                        (REPORT FILES)

  Design a data file                  Design a report file
  Edit a data file definition         Display a report file
  Delete a data file                  Delete a report file
  Copy a data file                    Copy a report file
                                      Print a report file

        (DATA RECORDS)                        (UTILITIES)

  Input data to a record              Lock / Unlock files
  Edit data in a record               Mailing labels
  Display a record                    Change drive
  Delete a record                     Exit program


 POSITION CURSOR AT SELECTION AND PRESS <RETURN>
         WHAT IS THE DIRECTORY FOR YOUR USER FILES?:_
```

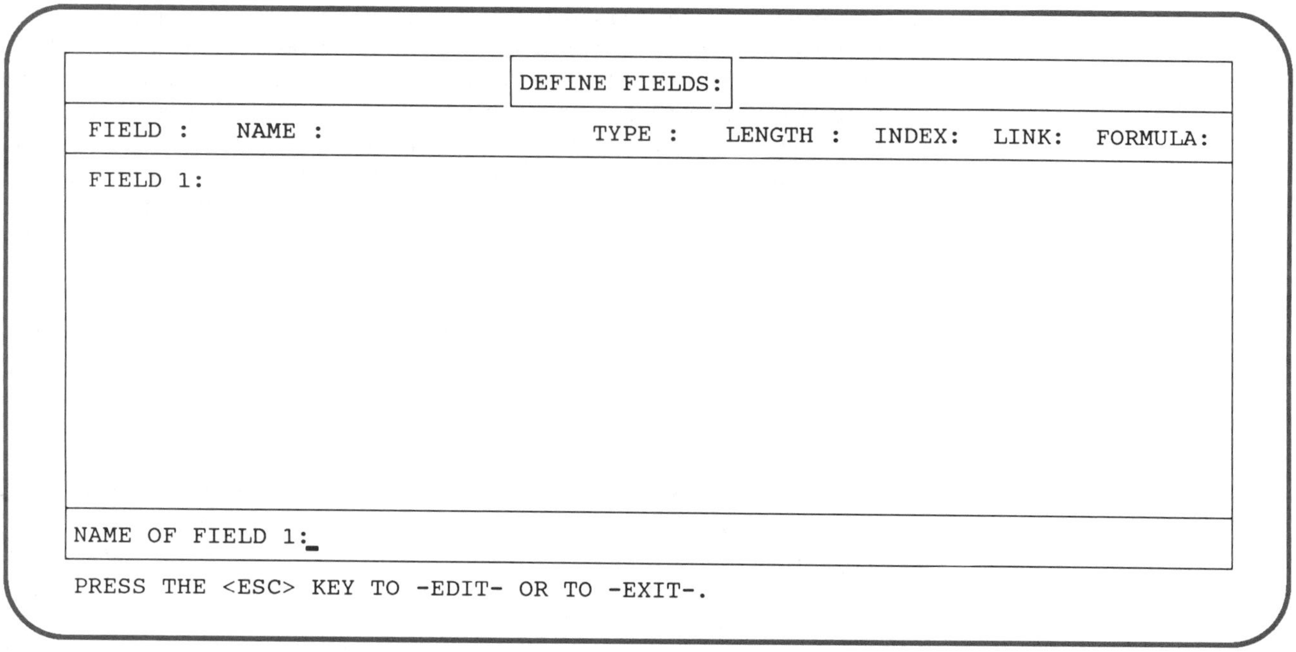

```
                         ┌─────────────────┐
                         │ DEFINE FIELDS:   │
    ┌────────────────────┴─────────────────┴──────────────────────────────┐
    FIELD :    NAME :                TYPE :   LENGTH :  INDEX:  LINK:  FORMULA:
    ├──────────────────────────────────────────────────────────────────────┤
    │ FIELD 1:                                                               │
    │                                                                        │
    │                                                                        │
    │                                                                        │
    │                                                                        │
    │                                                                        │
    │                                                                        │
    │                                                                        │
    ├──────────────────────────────────────────────────────────────────────┤
    │ NAME OF FIELD 1:_                                                      │
    └──────────────────────────────────────────────────────────────────────┘
      PRESS THE <ESC> KEY TO -EDIT- OR TO -EXIT-.
```

Figure 13-3
Field Definition Form

two boxes: the box on the left is the directory of data files, and the box on the right is the directory of report files. The prompt ENTER FILENAME appears at the bottom of the screen. Enter a name for a data file and press <Return>. The field definition form then appears on the screen (see Figure 13-3).

A field is a particular item or type of data which is stored in a file. The purpose of a field definition is to specify all the fields needed for the file being created. Typical fields are such things as first name, last name, street address, phone number, and order number, but almost any useful category or classification can be a field.

WestData asks for six categories of information on each field. The first category is the field NAME. The name of a data field can be up to 25 characters long. Characters include letters, numbers, and symbols.

The second category is the field TYPE. Four types of data fields can be defined, depending upon the kind of information being stored in the field:

A for Alphanumeric
N for Numeric
D for Date
M for Money

The third category is the field LENGTH. The length of the data field is the maximum number of characters allowed in that field. The maximum length of an alphanumeric or numeric field is 60 characters. If a field has been designated as a date field, WestData automatically enters its length as 8. If a field is designated as a money field, WestData automatically enters its length as 10.

The fourth category of information is the field INDEX. Indexed fields are used as cross references for other files; therefore, if a field is going to be used as a cross reference, it must be indexed. Indexed fields also are used to identify and retrieve specific records for displaying, editing, and inputting. Therefore, only fields that are unique identifiers, such as social security numbers, should be indexed. Each file should have at least one indexed field. To index a field, press **Y** (for yes) and the <Return> key after the INDEX FIELD? (Y/N) prompt appears. Responding with a **Y** to the first INDEX FIELD prompt causes the number "1" to appear on the screen in the INDEX column. The next **Y** response causes a "2" to appear, and so forth. Responding with an **N** to the prompt causes a zero to appear in the INDEX column. A field that is indexed takes up more space in the computer's memory than a field that is not indexed, so you should answer **Y** to the INDEX FIELD prompt only if the value stored in the field will be needed as a cross reference or as a means of record retrieval.

The next field category is LINK. A link is a pointer that directs the program to search for a value in another file. You can press either **Y** or **N** when the LINK FIELD? (Y/N) prompt appears. Linking a field determines whether the program should look in another file for a particular data item, so you should answer **Y** to the LINK FIELD prompt only if data is needed from another file. Linking of files is explained in more detail in Chapter 14.

The sixth and final category is the FORMULA for the field. In some cases, it is useful to combine numbers in different fields. A formula enables the user to define the ways in which numbers in fields should be combined. When the prompt FORMULA FOR FIELD appears, enter either **Y** or **N**. The formula, $1+2+4*5$, for example, means "add field 1 + field 2 + field 4 and multiply the result by field 5." The formula feature works only with integer numbers. Decimal numbers entered into a formula are truncated. This feature is discussed in more detail later in the chapter.

Once all the fields for the record have been defined, press <Esc>. A prompt appears in a box at the bottom of the screen, offering the user one of three options: editing the fields, saving the file, or returning to the Main Menu without saving the file. The prompt says: PRESS <E> AND <RETURN> TO EDIT FIELDS, <S> AND <RETURN> TO SAVE FILE, OR PRESS <ESC> TO RETURN TO THE MAIN MENU.

The edit option provides the opportunity to correct any mistakes made while entering data in the fields. To use the edit option, press <E> and <Return>. The field definition screen reappears. The prompt NAME OF FIELD 1 reappears at the bottom of the screen, followed by the name entered in the first field. To correct any mistakes, use the <→> key to scroll through the file until the mistake appears after the prompt at the bottom of the screen. Then type in the correction. When all corrections have been made, press <Esc> and the prompt PRESS <E> AND <RETURN> TO EDIT FIELDS, <S> AND <RETURN> TO SAVE FILE, OR PRESS <ESC> TO RETURN TO THE MAIN MENU appears again.

Pressing <S> and <Return> saves the edited file. A screen appears, listing all the fields in the file. Each field is followed by brackets with periods between the brackets. Each period represents one character or space in the field. After a few seconds, the WestData 2.5 Main Menu reappears on the screen.

Pressing <Esc> after the prompt appears returns the program to the Main Menu without saving the file.

YOUR TURN

You are about to create a file to keep track of books in a personal library. For each book, keep the following information:

Number	Allocated sequentially to each new book
Title	Title of the book
Last Name	Author's last name
First Name	Author's first name
Purchase Month	Month when the book was purchased
Purchase Year	Year when book was purchased
Cost	Amount paid for the book
In/Out	Keeps track of whether the book is in your library or is loaned out to a friend

The WestData 2.5 Main Menu should be on the screen. The DESIGN A DATA FILE command should be highlighted.

Press <Return>

The directory for drive B appears on the screen. The prompt ENTER FILENAME appears at the bottom of the screen.

Type **LIBRARY**
Press <Return>

The field definition form appears on the screen. The prompt NAME OF FIELD 1 should be at the bottom of the screen with the blinking cursor next to it. You are going to start defining eight fields in the field definition form.

Type Number
Press <Return>

The prompt TYPE OF FIELD 1 appears at the bottom of the screen with the blinking cursor next to it.

Type **N** for numeric
Press <Return>

The prompt LENGTH OF FIELD 1 appears at the bottom of the screen with a blinking cursor next to it. The field length for the Number field is 3, because it is doubtful that you will own more than 999 books.

Type **3**
Press <Return>

The prompt INDEX FIELD? appears next.

>Type **Y**
>Press <Return>

The prompt LINK FIELD? appears.

>Type **N**
>Press <Return>

The prompt FORMULA FOR FIELD 1? appears.

>Type **N**
>Press <Return>

All the categories for field 1 have been entered, so the prompt NAME OF FIELD 2 appears next at the bottom of the screen. All the information you entered regarding field 1 now appears at the top of the screen. Enter the information on the remaining fields as follows. If you notice a typing mistake before you have pressed <Return>, use the <Backspace> key to delete the necessary characters. Retype the entry. If you notice an error after pressing <Return>, use the edit function to correct the error when you are defining the fields. Notice that no length is listed for Field 7. That is because field 7 is designated as type M, for Money. As soon as you enter M at the TYPE prompt and press <Return>, WestData automatically provides the field with a length of 10 and immediately moves to the INDEX FIELD prompt.

Field #	Name	Type	Length	Index	Link	Formula
2	Title	A	25	Y	N	N
3	Last Name	A	15	N	N	N
4	First Name	A	15	N	N	N
5	Purchase Month	N	2	N	N	N
6	Purchase Year	N	2	N	N	N
7	Cost	M		N	N	N
8	In/Out	A	1	N	N	N

After you have entered the data on field 8, the prompt NAME OF FIELD 9 appears. There is no field 9, so press <Esc>. The prompt PRESS <E> AND <RETURN> TO EDIT FIELDS, <S> AND <RETURN> TO SAVE FILE, OR PRESS <ESC> TO RETURN TO THE MAIN MENU appears at the bottom of the screen.

>Type **S**
>Press <Return>

A screen listing all the fields for the LIBRARY file appears next. The periods between the brackets indicate the length of each field. After a few seconds, the WestData 2.5 Main Menu appears on the screen.

Manipulating Records

Inputting Data to Records

Once all the fields in a file have been defined and edited, data can be entered into records. Start with WestData's Main Menu on the screen. Move the highlighting to INPUT DATA TO A RECORD and press <Return>. A list of all the data and report files in the directory appears on the screen, along with the prompt ENTER FILENAME. Type the name of the file into which the records are to be entered and press <Return>.

The data entry form appears on the screen (see Figure 13-4). The name of the file appears at the top of the screen. A list of all the fields defined in the field definition form appears below the filename. Notice the periods between the brackets next to each field name, except for the first field, where the cursor is blinking. These periods represent the length of each field. For example, if a field has a length of 10, 10 periods appear between the brackets that follow the field name.

The cursor is between the brackets next to the first field name. Type the data that goes into the first field of the first record and press <Return>. The cursor jumps to the next field. Continue entering data into the fields. Use the <Backspace> key to correct any typing mistakes before pressing <Return>.

After the last field has information entered into it and the <Return> key is pressed, the prompt ARE ALL DATA FIELDS CORRECT? (Y/N) appears at the bottom of the screen. If any errors were made, enter **N**. The cursor returns to the

Figure 13-4
Inputting Data to RECORDS File

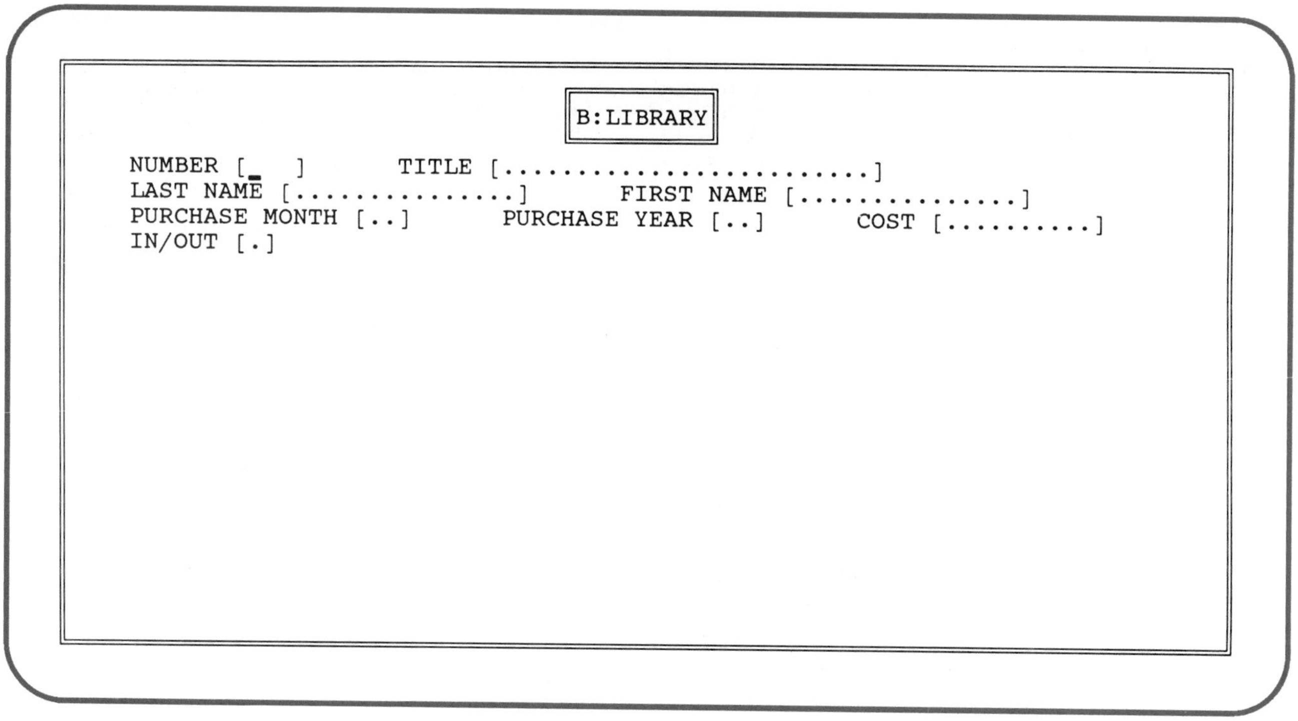

```
                          ┌─────────┐
                          │B:LIBRARY│
                          └─────────┘
NUMBER [_  ]      TITLE [........................]
LAST NAME [..............]      FIRST NAME [...............]
PURCHASE MONTH [..]    PURCHASE YEAR [..]    COST [..........]
IN/OUT [.]
```

first field. If the entry in the first field is correct, press the <→> key to move the cursor from field to field through the record.

Do not press the <Return> key to move through the record. If the <Return> key is pressed instead of the <→> key, the entry for that field is deleted. If that happens, move through the rest of the record using the <→> key. When the prompt ARE ALL DATA FIELDS CORRECT appears, type **N**. Then use the <→> key to move to the field that was erased and enter the data for that field again. Continue using the <→> key to move from field to field in the record.

Once all the fields are correct, enter **Y** when the prompt ARE ALL DATA FIELDS CORRECT appears. A new prompt, DO YOU WISH TO ADD MORE RECORDS, follows at the bottom of the screen. If you enter **Y**, a new data entry form appears. Enter the information for the next record. When all the records are complete, enter **Y** at the ARE ALL DATA FIELDS CORRECT prompt. The WestData 2.5 Main Menu returns to the screen.

YOUR TURN

You are going to enter records into the LIBRARY file. The WestData 2.5 Main Menu should be on your screen.

Use the arrow keys to move the highlighting to the option INPUT DATA TO A RECORD. Press <Return>. The current directory appears on the screen. The prompt ENTER FILENAME appears at the bottom of the screen.

    Type **LIBRARY**
    Press <Return>

The data entry form for the LIBRARY file appears on the screen, and the blinking cursor is next to the NUMBER field. You are now ready to create records for the LIBRARY file by entering data into all of the fields. If you notice a typing error before you press the <Return> key, use the <Backspace> key to correct the error. If you notice an error after pressing the <Return> key, make a note of it. You will have an opportunity to edit each record as it is created.

    Type 1
    Press <Return>

The blinking cursor moves next to the TITLE field.

    Type A Short Course in PL/C
    Press <Return>
    Type Clark
    Press <Return>
    Type Ann
    Press <Return>
    Type 07
    Press <Return>

Type 86
Press <Return>
Type 25.00
Press <Return>
Type 0
Press <Return>

The prompt ARE ALL DATA FIELDS CORRECT? (Y/N) appears at the bottom of the screen. Examine all the entries you made. If you find any errors, type **N**. The blinking cursor moves to the first field, NUMBER. If the error is not in the NUMBER field, move the cursor to the next field by pressing the <→> key. If you press the <Return> key instead of the <→> key, your entry is deleted. If that happens, continue moving through the record, pressing the <→> key and correcting any errors you find. When you get to the end of the record and the prompt ARE ALL DATA FIELDS CORRECT? (Y/N) appears, type **N** and return to the field that was deleted, using the <→> key. Enter the data into the field again and continue pressing the <→> key until you reach the end of the record. Once all the fields are entered correctly, type **Y** at the prompt ARE ALL DATA FIELDS CORRECT? (Y/N).

After you type **Y**, WestData saves the record just entered. The prompt DO YOU WISH TO ADD MORE RECORDS? (Y/N) appears at the bottom of the screen. Type **Y**. Another data entry form appears on the screen. You are now going to add 13 more records to the LIBRARY file. At the end of each record, look it over carefully and correct any errors you find before pressing **Y** in response to the ARE ALL DATA FIELDS CORRECT? (Y/N) prompt. Enter the following information:

No.	Title	Last Name	First Name	PMo	PYr	Cost	In/Out
2	Accounting Today	Asman	Mark	01	87	50.50	O
3	Advanced Structured COBOL	Welburn	Tyler	10	85	35.00	I
4	Business Policies	Christensen	Roland	01	84	45.00	O
5	COBOL for the 80s	Spence	John	11	85	28.00	I
6	Computers Are Fun	Rice	Jean	02	83	34.00	I
7	Consumer Behavior	Williams	Terrel	01	84	40.00	I
8	Economics	McConnel	Campbell	12	83	65.00	I
9	International Marketing	Kramer	Roland	09	84	52.00	O
10	Introduction to BASIC	Mandell	Steven	01	83	54.00	I
11	Using 1-2-3	Leblond	Geoffrey	04	86	21.50	I
12	Discovering PC DOS	Worcester	Clark	07	86	18.50	I
13	Harbrace College Handbook	Hodges	John	10	84	16.75	O
14	Facts from Figures	Moroney	M	11	85	16.00	I

Once all the records have been entered, type **N** at the prompt DO YOU WISH TO ADD MORE RECORDS? (Y/N). The WestData 2.5 Main Menu returns to the screen.

Displaying Records

Once records have been added to a data file, WestData can display them one at a time so that the contents of each record can be checked. To display records, use the arrow keys to highlight the DISPLAY A RECORD option from the WestData 2.5 Main Menu and press <Return>.

A directory for the current disk drive appears, along with the prompt ENTER FILENAME. Type the name of the file containing the records to be displayed and press <Return>. The file structure for that file appears at the top of the screen. The prompt INDEX FIELD NAME appears at the bottom of the screen. The field that is entered must be an indexed field; otherwise, the message INVALID INDEX, PRESS ANY KEY AND TRY AGAIN appears at the bottom of the screen. Enter the name of an indexed field and press <Return>. The cursor moves to the index field in the file structure at the top of the screen. Enter the contents of that field for the first record to be displayed. Press <Return>. Be sure to enter the contents of the field exactly as it was entered in the record, including capitalization and spacing; otherwise, the record you wish to view may not appear. The entire record appears at the top of the screen (see Figure 13-5).

Once a record is on the screen, you can scroll through the entire file. Pressing the <→> key moves the following record onto the screen. The <←> key moves the preceding record onto the screen. Any corrections that need to be made to the file should be noted while you are scrolling through the screen. You can make corrections by returning to the Main Menu and selecting the EDIT DATA IN A RECORD option.

Figure 13-5
Displaying a Record for the LIBRARY File

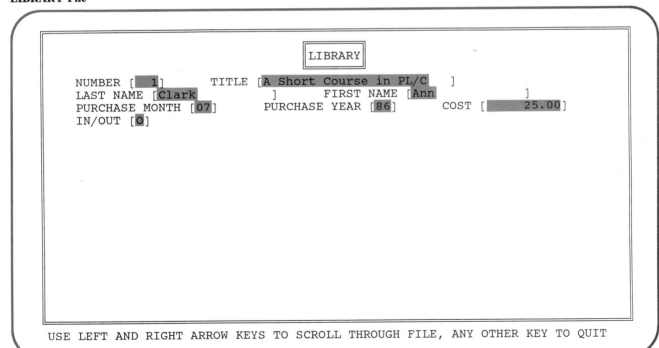

```
                              ┌─────────┐
                              │ LIBRARY │
                              └─────────┘
   NUMBER  [    1]      TITLE [A Short Course in PL/C    ]
   LAST NAME [Clark         ]       FIRST NAME [Ann          ]
   PURCHASE MONTH [07]   PURCHASE YEAR [86]     COST [      25.00]
   IN/OUT [O]




   USE LEFT AND RIGHT ARROW KEYS TO SCROLL THROUGH FILE, ANY OTHER KEY TO QUIT
```

To exit from the display record mode, press <Esc>. The WestData 2.5 Main Menu returns to the screen.

YOUR TURN

You are going to scroll through the LIBRARY file to see if you made any typing errors. The WestData 2.5 Main Menu should be on your screen.

Select DISPLAY A RECORD
Press <Return>
Type **LIBRARY** at the ENTER FILENAME prompt
Press <Return>

The structure for the LIBRARY file appears at the top of the screen. The prompt INDEX FIELD NAME appears at the bottom of the screen. The field that you enter must be an indexed field.

Type **TITLE**
Press <Return>

The cursor appears next to TITLE at the top of the screen. The book *A Short Course in PL/C* is the first book in the record.

Type A Short Course in PL/C
Press <Return>

The entire record for this book appears on the screen. Read through the record to make sure all the entries are correct. If there are errors, make a note of them. They will be corrected in a later exercise.

Press the <→> key

The next record in the file, record 2 for the book *Accounting Today*, appears on the screen. Read through this record, noting any errors. Continue scrolling through the file using the <→> key. If you want to go back to look at a record, use the <←> key.

Note: Because the field TITLE is alphanumeric, the records scroll in alphabetical order. If the field entered is numeric, the records scroll in numeric sequence.

When you reach the end of the file, the message NO ENTRIES FOUND PRESS <SPACEBAR> TO CONTINUE appears. Press the spacebar and the prompt USE LEFT AND RIGHT ARROW KEYS TO SCROLL THROUGH FILE, ANY OTHER KEY TO QUIT appears on the screen. Press any key and the WestData 2.5 Main Menu reappears.

Editing Records

Once data records have been added to a file, the records can be modified or edited using the EDIT DATA IN A RECORD command from the WestData 2.5 Main Menu. Move the highlighting to the EDIT DATA IN A RECORD command and press the <Return> key.

A list of all the files in the directory appears on the screen, along with the ENTER FILENAME prompt. Type the name of the file to be edited and press <Return>. The structure of the record appears at the top of the screen. The prompt INDEX FIELD NAME is at the bottom of the screen. Enter the name of the indexed field in the active file and press <Return>. Be sure to enter only the name of an indexed field. If you enter the name of a nonindexed field, a message saying INVALID INDEX, PRESS ANY KEY AND TRY AGAIN appears at the bottom of the screen. After an indexed field is entered and <Return> is pressed, the cursor moves to the indexed field.

The next entry determines which record will be recalled for editing. To recall a particular record for editing, type the information stored in the indexed field of the record and press <Return>. Once again, the information has to be entered exactly as it was entered in the record, including capitalization and spacing. If the information entered matches an existing record, all the entries for that record appear at the top of the screen. If the information entered does not match an existing record, the program searches through the records and finds the next value in ascending order (numeric or alphabetic). All the entries in that record then appear on the screen. If there are no more records, the message NO ENTRIES FOUND PRESS <SPACEBAR> TO CONTINUE appears at the bottom of the screen.

When the entries for a record appear at the top of the screen, the blinking cursor appears under the first space or character in the first field. Use the <→> key to move to the field to be edited and type the new entry. Once the entry has been made, use the <→> key to move to the end of the record. Do not use the <Return> key to move the cursor to the end of the record. Pressing <Return> deletes the data stored in the field.

The prompt ARE ALL DATA FIELDS CORRECT appears. If they are correct, type **Y**. The WestData 2.5 Main Menu returns to the screen. If they are not correct, type **N**. The cursor returns to the first field and the editing process can be started again.

YOUR TURN

Two of your friends have returned books they borrowed from you, and another friend has borrowed three books. The books *Business Policies* and *Harbrace College Handbook* were returned to you. *Computers are Fun*, *Economics*, and *Using 1-2-3* were borrowed. In this exercise you are going to edit the LIBRARY file to reflect these changes. The WestData 2.5 Main Menu should be on your screen.

    Select EDIT DATA IN A RECORD
    Press <Return>

The directory of your data disk appears on the screen, along with the prompt ENTER FILENAME.

>   Type **LIBRARY**
>   Press <Return>

The structure for the LIBRARY file appears on the screen. At the bottom of the screen is the prompt INDEX FIELD NAME. You have the titles of all the books that were either returned or borrowed, so you are going to enter the TITLE field.

>   Type **TITLE**
>   Press <Return>

The cursor moves to the top of the screen to the TITLE field.

>   Type Business Policies
>   Press <Return>

All the entries for the record containing *Business Policies* in the Title field appear on the screen. Press the <→> key seven times to move the cursor to the IN/OUT field. Currently there is an O for Out in this field. You are now going to change it to an I, because that book has been returned. The cursor should be under the O.

>   Type I
>   Press <Return>

The prompt ARE ALL DATA FIELDS CORRECT appears at the bottom of the screen. Look over the record to make sure all the entries are correct.

>   Type **Y**

The WestData 2.5 Main Menu returns to the screen. You are now going to edit the remaining four files.

>   Select EDIT DATA IN A RECORD
>   Press <Return>
>   Type **LIBRARY** at the ENTER FILENAME prompt
>   Press <Return>
>   Type **TITLE** at the INDEX FIELD NAME prompt
>   Press <Return>
>   Type Harbrace College Handbook
>   Press <Return>
>   Use the <→> key to move the cursor to the IN/OUT field
>   Type I
>   Press <Return>

The prompt ARE ALL DATA FIELDS CORRECT appears.

Type **Y**

You have now recorded the two books that were returned. Next, you need to record the three books that were borrowed.

Select EDIT DATA IN A RECORD
Press <Return>

Type **LIBRARY** at the ENTER FILENAME prompt
Press <Return>
Type **TITLE** at the INDEX FIELD NAME prompt
Press <Return>
Type `Computers are Fun`
Press <Return>
Use the <→> key to move to the IN/OUT field
Type `0`
Press <Return>
Type **Y** at the ARE ALL DATA FIELDS CORRECT prompt

The WestData 2.5 Main Menu returns to the screen.

Select EDIT DATA IN A RECORD
Press <Return>
Type **LIBRARY** at the ENTER FILENAME prompt
Press <Return>
Type **TITLE** at the INDEX FIELD NAME prompt
Press <Return>
Type `Economics`
Press <Return>
Use the <→> key to move to the IN/OUT field
Type `0`
Press <Return>
Type **Y** at the ARE ALL DATA FIELDS CORRECT prompt

The WestData 2.5 Main Menu returns to the screen.

Select EDIT DATA IN A RECORD
Press <Return>
Type **LIBRARY** at the ENTER FILENAME prompt
Press <Return>
Type **TITLE** at the INDEX FIELD NAME prompt
Press <Return>
Type `Using 1-2-3`
Press <Return>
Use the <→> key to move to the IN/OUT field
Type `0`
Press <Return>
Type **Y** at the ARE ALL DATA FIELDS CORRECT prompt

The WestData 2.5 Main Menu returns to the screen. Your records are now updated. Use the EDIT A DATA FILE command to correct any errors you found while doing the exercise.

Adding Records

Once a data file has been created, adding new records to it is a simple process. Select INPUT DATA TO A RECORD from the Main Menu and press <Return>. The directory of the current disk drive appears, along with the prompt ENTER FILENAME. Type the name of the file to which the records are going to be added. Press <Return>. The record structure appears, with the cursor next to the first field name. Type the entries for the new record, pressing <Return> after an entry is made for each field.

After you have made an entry for the last field and pressed the <Return> key, the prompt ARE ALL DATA FIELDS CORRECT appears. Look over the data fields carefully. If a mistake was made, enter **N**. The cursor moves back to the first field. Use the <→> key to move the cursor to the field containing the error, and enter the information again. Use the <→> key to move to the end of the record. When the prompt ARE ALL DATA FIELDS CORRECT? appears again, enter **Y**. The prompt DO YOU WISH TO ADD MORE RECORDS? appears (see Figure 13-6). If there are more records to add, enter **Y**. Otherwise, enter **N** and the WestData 2.5 Main Menu returns to the screen.

Figure 13-6
Adding Records to the LIBRARY File

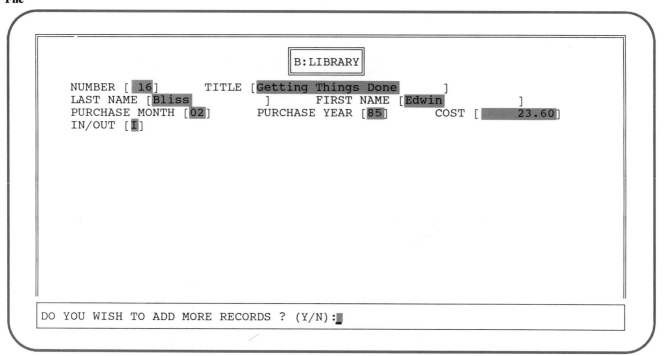

YOUR TURN

You discovered six books that should be added to your LIBRARY file. In this exercise, you are going to add six new records to the LIBRARY file. The WestData 2.5 Main Menu should be on your screen.

Select INPUT DATA TO A RECORD
Press <Return>
Type **LIBRARY** at the ENTER FILENAME prompt
Press <Return>

The record structure for the LIBRARY file appears. The following information needs to be added to the file:

No.	Title	Last Name	First Name	PMo	PYr	Cost	In/Out
15	Financial Accounting	Eskew	Robert	09	86	38.80	I
16	Getting Things Done	Bliss	Edwin	02	85	23.60	I
17	Intermediate Algebra	Mangan	Frances	09	84	22.30	I
18	Management	Glueck	William	07	86	28.45	I
19	Learning to Program in C	Plum	Thomas	07	86	48.90	I
20	Information Systems	Burch	John	01	86	52.60	I

The cursor should be next to the NUMBER field.

Type 15
Press <Return>

The cursor moves to the next field, which is the TITLE field.

Type Financial Accounting
Press <Return>
Type Eskew
Press <Return>
Type Robert
Press <Return>
Type 09
Press <Return>
Type 86
Press <Return>
Type 38.80
Press <Return>
Type I
Press <Return>

The prompt ARE ALL DATA FIELDS CORRECT? appears. Look over all the data fields. If they are not correct, type **N** and make the necessary changes.

If they are correct, type **Y**. The prompt DO YOU WISH TO ADD MORE RECORDS? appears. Type **Y** and enter records 16, 17, 18, 19, and 20, using the information on the books provided above. After the last record is added, type **N** when the prompt DO YOU WISH TO ADD MORE RECORDS? appears. The WestData 2.5 Main Menu returns to the screen.

Deleting Records

Deleting a record from a WestData file is a simple procedure. Select DELETE A RECORD from the WestData 2.5 Main Menu and press <Return>. A directory of the current disk drive appears, along with the prompt ENTER FILENAME. Type the name of the file from which the record is to be deleted and press <Return>. The record structure for the file appears on the screen, along with the prompt INDEX FIELD NAME.

Any field that was entered as an indexed field when the file was first created can be used to access the record that is to be deleted. Enter the name of an existing indexed field and press <Return>. Make sure that the field name entered matches the original field name exactly. The cursor moves to the designated field. Enter the contents of the field which identifies the record to be deleted, and press <Return>. The record containing that field appears at the top of the screen. The prompt DO YOU WISH TO DELETE THIS RECORD appears at the bottom of the screen. To delete the record, type **Y**.

If the record is not the one to be deleted, type **N**. The prompt USE LEFT AND RIGHT ARROW KEYS TO SCROLL THROUGH FILE, ANY OTHER KEY TO QUIT appears at the bottom of the screen. Pressing the <←> key activates the previous record, and the <→> key activates the following record. These two arrow keys can be used to move through the entire file until the record to be deleted is found. As each new record appears on the screen, the prompt DO YOU WISH TO DELETE THIS RECORD appears at the bottom of the screen. If you do not wish to delete a particular record, type **N** and scroll to the next record. Once the record to be deleted is reached, type **Y**.

The prompt USE LEFT AND RIGHT ARROW KEYS TO SCROLL THROUGH FILE, ANY OTHER KEY TO QUIT returns to the screen. If there is another record to be deleted, scroll through the file to find it. Otherwise, press any other key and the WestData 2.5 Main menu returns to the screen.

YOUR TURN   You have decided to sell one of your books, and you want to delete the record from the LIBRARY file. The book you have decided to sell is *Intermediate Algebra*. You think this book is record 15. The WestData 2.5 Main Menu should be on your screen.

Select DELETE A RECORD
Press <Return>
Type **LIBRARY** at the ENTER FILENAME prompt
Press <Return>

The record structure appears at the top of the screen and the INDEX FIELD NAME prompt is at the bottom of the screen. You think the book you want to sell is record number 15, so you are going to use the NUMBER field to recall the record.

Type **NUMBER**
Press <Return>

The cursor moves to the NUMBER field at the top of the screen.

Type 15
Press <Return>

Record 15 appears at the top of the screen. The prompt DO YOU WISH TO DELETE THIS RECORD appears at the bottom of the screen. Record 15 is not the record for *Intermediate Algebra*, so you do not want to delete this record.

Type **N**

The prompt USE LEFT AND RIGHT ARROW KEYS TO SCROLL THROUGH FILE, ANY OTHER KEY TO QUIT appears on the screen.

Press <→>

Record 16 appears on the screen, with the prompt DO YOU WISH TO DELETE THIS RECORD? Record 16 is not the record for *Intermediate Algebra* either.

Type **N**
Press <→>

Record 17 appears on the screen, with the prompt DO YOU WISH TO DELETE THIS RECORD? Record 17 is the record for *Intermediate Algebra*.

Type **Y**

The prompt USE LEFT AND RIGHT ARROW KEYS TO SCROLL THROUGH FILE, ANY OTHER KEY TO QUIT appears on the screen. There are no other records you want to delete, so press any other key. The WestData 2.5 Main Menu returns to the screen.

Formulas

In some cases, it is useful to manipulate numeric data stored in fields in a record. For example, an employer might want to compute the gross pay due each employee. WestData makes it possible to manipulate numeric data with the formula option.

The formula category is the last one in the field definition form. There are two possible ways to enter formulas into a data file: while the file is being designed, or while it is being edited. To enter a formula, respond with a **Y** to the FORMULA FOR FIELD prompt in the field definition form. Next, press <Return> and the prompt ENTER FORMULA appears. Enter a formula using the following symbols to represent mathematical operations:

+   add
−   subtract
*   multiply
/   divide

After entering a formula, press <Return> and save the file design or continue with the field definitions.

YOUR TURN

You are going to create two files, COMPANY and WAGES. You will use the formula function in the WAGES file in this exercise. Both files will be needed for the printing exercise in the section titled **Displaying and Printing Reports**.

Highlight the DESIGN A DATA FILE option in the WestData 2.5 Main Menu.

Press <Return>

The ENTER FILENAME prompt appears on the screen.

Type **COMPANY**
Press <Return>

Use the following information for the COMPANY file design. Save the file design and return to the Main Menu.

COMPANY file design

Field #	Name	Type	Length	Index	Link	Formula
1	Company Name	**A**	**25**	**Y**	**N**	**N**
2	Phone #	**N**	**8**	**N**	**N**	**N**

Highlight the INPUT DATA TO A RECORD option on the Main Menu, and input the following records in the COMPANY file.

Records for COMPANY FILE

Company Name	Phone #
CONSOLIDATED PRODUCTS	555-1497
ACME PLUMBING	555-4190
HARRIS INSURANCE	555-8233
ENERGY SAVERS INC.	555-6352

Enter the following information about the first six fields in the WAGES file design. When you have completed the file design, save the design and return to the Main Menu.

WAGES file design

Field #	Name	Type	Length	Index	Link	Formula
1	Employee Name	A	25	Y	N	N
2	Pay Rate	N	2	N	N	N
3	Hrs Mon	N	2	N	N	N
4	Hrs Tues	N	2	N	N	N
5	Hrs Wed	N	2	N	N	N
6	Hrs Thurs	N	2	N	N	N
7	Hrs Fri	N	2	N	N	N

Highlight EDIT A DATA FILE DEFINITION on the Main Menu.

Press <Return>

The directory for drive B appears on the screen. The prompt ENTER FILENAME appears at the bottom of the screen.

Type **WAGES**
Press <Return>

The field definition form appears on the screen, and the blinking cursor appears after the NAME OF FIELD 1 prompt under the first letter of EMPLOYEE. Use the <→> key to scroll through the file until the NAME OF FIELD 8 prompt appears.

Type Total Hrs
Press <Return>
Type **N**
Press <Return>
Type **3**
Press <Return>
Type **N**
Press <Return>
Type **N**
Press <Return>
Type **Y**

A prompt ENTER FORMULA FOR 8 appears.

> Type **3+4+5+6+7**
> Press <Return>
> Type Gross Pay
> Press <Return>
> Type **N**
> Press <Return>
> Type **4**
> Press <Return>
> Type **N**
> Press <Return>
> Type **N**
> Press <Return>
> Type **Y**

A prompt ENTER FORMULA FOR 9 appears.

> Type **2*8**
> Press <Return>

Save the changes to the file design and return to the Main Menu.

Highlight the INPUT DATA TO A RECORD option on the Main Menu, a'
input the following records in the COMPANY file.

Records for WAGES file

Employee Name	Pay Rate	Hrs Mon	Hrs Tues	Hrs Wed	Hrs Thurs	Hrs Fr
STEVENS, MICHAEL	12	8	9	8	10	8
WOLFORD, SCOTT	9	8	8	8	0	8
RAMIRIZ, CARLOS	12	8	9	9	10	8
LANKY, ANGELA	11	8	8	8	10	8
GAUTIER, JENIFER	9	8	8	10	8	8
LABINO, TONY	9	8	8	8	8	8
CHIN, WAN	10	9	10	10	8	8
BENINGTON, ERIC	8	8	8	8	8	8
OATES, SALLY	12	8	8	9	8	8
HADDAD, ALICE	8	8	8	8	8	8

Notice that the Total Hrs and Gross Pay fields are automatically filled in as
you enter each record because of the formulas you entered earlier.

Reports

Designing Reports

A WestData record can contain a lot of information; one record can hold up to 25 data fields. The data in a file has to be managed in a way that is efficient for the user. Sorting through 25 fields of information for every record is not very efficient. WestData has a report function that enables a user to group the data contained in a file in a manner that is most efficient for the user's purposes.

To design a report, select the DESIGN A REPORT FILE option from the WestData 2.5 Main Menu and press <Return>. The directory appears on the screen, listing existing data and report files. The prompt ENTER A FILENAME BY WHICH TO CALL THIS REPORT: ENTER FILENAME is at the bottom of the screen. Enter a name for the report and press <Return>.

The prompt DO YOU WANT HEADING INFORMATION? (Y/N) appears. If heading information is required for the report, press **Y** and <Return>. Press **N** if heading information is not required. The prompt following a **Y** response is ENTER FILENAME FOR HEADING INFORMATION: ENTER FILENAME. This prompt is requesting a filename from which to select data that will appear in the report heading. Enter a filename and press <Return>.

The prompt ENTER FIELD NAME OR FIELD NUMBER PRECEDED BY # SIGN OR PRESS <S> TO SAVE REPORT DESIGN (EXAMPLE-ADDRESS OR #1) is requesting the user to enter either the name of the field to appear in the report heading, or the number of the field preceded by a number sign (for example, #3).

After entering the field name or number, press <Return>. The name of the first field to appear in the report heading appears at the top of the screen. The next prompt appears: NEXT FIELD UNDER OR BESIDE THE LAST FIELD? (U/B) PRESS <S> AND RETURN TO SAVE REPORT DESIGN, OR PRESS <ESC> TO RETURN TO THE MAIN MENU. The purpose of this prompt is to determine how the heading information for the report will look on the screen, or how it will look on paper when it is printed. The fields can be arranged either horizontally or vertically. Type **U** for a vertical arrangement or **B** for a horizontal arrangement, and press <Return>. Each field entered for the report heading appears at the top of the screen after it is entered. Up to six fields can appear in any report heading. After the last heading field has been entered, type **S** and press <Return> to save the report design.

A prompt then appears: ENTER FILENAME FOR BODY INFORMATION: ENTER FILENAME. This prompt is requesting a filename from which to select data that will appear in the report body. Enter a filename and press <Return>. The prompt ENTER FIELD NAME OR FIELD NUMBER PRECEDED BY # SIGN OR PRESS <S> TO SAVE REPORT DESIGN (EXAMPLE-ADDRESS OR #1) appears next. After entering the field name or number, press <Return>. The name of the first field to appear in the report body appears at the top of the screen.

The next prompt appears: PRESS <C> AND RETURN TO CONTINUE, PRESS <S> AND RETURN TO SAVE REPORT DESIGN, OR PRESS <ESC>

TO RETURN TO THE MAIN MENU. To continue entering body information, type **C** and press <Return>. WestData accepts up to four fields of information in a report body. At least one of the fields entered *must* be an indexed field. When the report design is complete, type **S** and press <Return> to save the report design. The program returns to the Main Menu.

YOUR TURN

You want to create a report that keeps track of the employees' pay rate, total hours worked, and gross pay. The WestData 2.5 Main Menu should be on your screen.

> Select DESIGN A REPORT FILE
> Press <Return>

The directory for drive B appears on the screen, and the prompt ENTER A FILENAME BY WHICH TO CALL THIS REPORT: ENTER FILENAME appears at the bottom of the screen.

> Type **REPORT1**
> Press <Return>

A prompt appears at the bottom of the screen: DO YOU WANT HEADING INFORMATION? (Y/N)

> Type **Y**
> Press <Return>

The prompt ENTER FILENAME FOR HEADING INFORMATION: ENTER FILENAME appears at the bottom of the screen.

> Type **Company**
> Press <Return>

The prompt ENTER FIELD NAME OR FIELD NUMBER PRECEDED BY # SIGN OR PRESS <S> TO SAVE REPORT DESIGN (EXAMPLE-ADDRESS OR #1) appears at the bottom of the screen.

> Type **#1**
> Press <Return>

The prompt NEXT FIELD UNDER OR BESIDE LAST FIELD? (U/B) PRESS <S> AND RETURN TO SAVE REPORT DESIGN, OR PRESS <ESC> TO RETURN TO THE MAIN MENU appears at the bottom of the screen.

> Type **B**
> Press <Return>
> Type **#2**
> Press <Return>
> Type **S**

Press <Return>

The prompt ENTER FILENAME FOR BODY INFORMATION: ENTER FILENAME appears at the bottom of the screen.

> Type **WAGES**
> Press <Return>

The prompt ENTER FIELD NAME OR FIELD NUMBER PRECEDED BY # SIGN OR PRESS <S> TO SAVE REPORT DESIGN (EXAMPLE-ADDRESS OR #1) appears. The four fields to be included in this report are Employee Name, Pay Rate, Total Hours, and Gross Pay.

> Type **#1**
> Press <Return>

The prompt PRESS <C> AND RETURN TO CONTINUE, PRESS <S> AND RETURN TO SAVE REPORT DESIGN, OR PRESS <ESC> TO RETURN TO THE MAIN MENU appears.

> Type **C**
> Press <Return>
> Type **#2**
> Press <Return>
> Type **C**
> Press <Return>
> Type **#8**
> Press <Return>
> Type **C**
> Press <Return>
> Type **#9**
> Press <Return>

The report design just created appears at the top of the screen.

> Type **S**
> Press <Return>

The WestData 2.5 Main Menu returns to the screen.

Displaying and Printing Reports

Once a report design has been created, it can be used to manipulate the information in the file and to display it in a number of useful ways. To display a report, select DISPLAY A REPORT FILE from the WestData 2.5 Main Menu. The directory for drive B appears on the screen, along with the ENTER FILENAME prompt at the bottom of the screen. Select the report file to be displayed from the DIREC-TORY OF REPORT FILES and type the name at the ENTER FILENAME prompt.

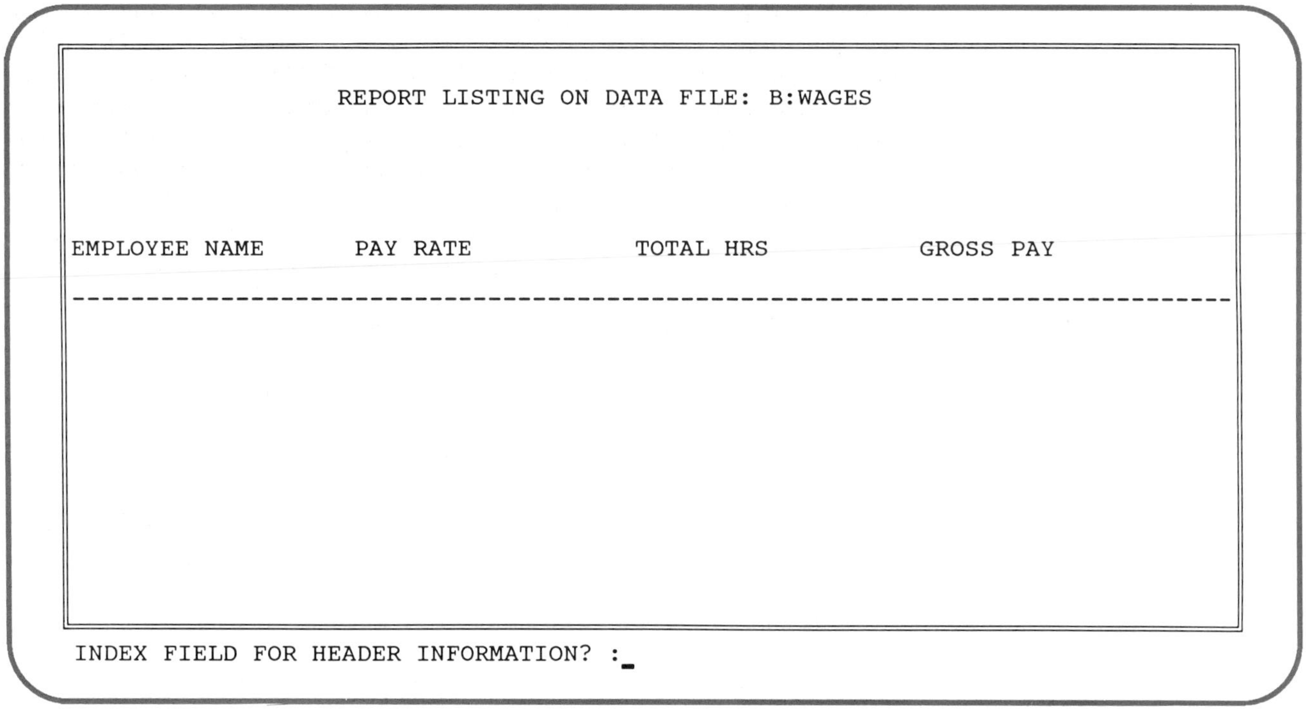

```
┌─────────────────────────────────────────────────────────────────┐
│                                                                   │
│              REPORT LISTING ON DATA FILE: B:WAGES                 │
│                                                                   │
│                                                                   │
│                                                                   │
│ EMPLOYEE NAME      PAY RATE         TOTAL HRS        GROSS PAY     │
│ ----------------------------------------------------------------- │
│                                                                   │
│                                                                   │
│                                                                   │
│                                                                   │
│                                                                   │
│                                                                   │
│                                                                   │
│                                                                   │
│                                                                   │
│                                                                   │
 INDEX FIELD FOR HEADER INFORMATION? :_
```

Figure 13-7
Displaying a Report

The report design appears at the top of the screen, and the prompt INDEX FIELD FOR HEADER INFORMATION is at the bottom (see Figure 13-7). The prompt is asking for an index field to be used as a means of organizing data. The purpose of displaying a report is to extract, from all the data in a file, only the information the user wants to see at one time. One of the fields in the report design has to be selected as the index field for organizing the report headers. Enter the name of the index field and press <Return>.

Next the prompt ENTER THE SEARCH VALUE appears. The search value is a value stored in the indexed field. When performing a numeric search, enter the beginning search value and press <Return>. When performing an alphabetic search, type an indexed name exactly as it was entered in the record and then press <Return>. The report header information appears on the screen.

Next, the prompt INDEX FIELD FOR BODY INFORMATION appears. This prompt is asking for the name of the indexed field that is used to organize the data in the body of the report. Enter a name and press <Return>. When performing a numeric search, enter the number for the beginning search value and press <Return>. When performing an alphabetic search, hold down the <Shift> key and type **A**. Then press <Return>.

The prompt ENTER THE ENDING SEARCH VALUE appears. The ending search value is the last value stored in the indexed field that the user wants to find. For a numeric search, enter the number ending the search and press <Return>. For an alphabetic search, hold down the **Z** key until the cursor moves off the screen. Then press <Return>.

If no values between the beginning and ending search values exist in the index field, the message NO ENTRIES FOUND PRESS <SPACEBAR> TO CONTINUE appears. Press the space bar and the WestData 2.5 Main Menu returns to the screen. If there are values in the index field between the beginning and ending search values, the contents of the fields in the report design appear on the screen.

To print a hard copy of a report, your computer must be connected to a printer. Highlight PRINT A REPORT FILE on the WestData 2.5 Main Menu and press <Return>. A directory for the active drive appears on the screen, with the prompt ENTER FILENAME at the bottom of the screen. Enter the name of a report file listed on the DIRECTORY OF REPORT FILES. Press <Return>. Next, repeat the same steps you used when displaying a report.

YOUR TURN

You are going to print a copy of the REPORT1 file. Begin with the WestData 2.5 Main Menu on the screen. Highlight PRINT A REPORT FILE.

Press <Return>

A directory for drive B appears on the screen, with the prompt ENTER FILENAME at the bottom of the screen.

Type **Report1**
Press <Return>

The report design for the body of the report appears on the screen, along with the prompt INDEX FIELD FOR HEADER INFORMATION.

Type **COMPANY NAME**
Press <Return>

The prompt ENTER THE SEARCH VALUE appears.

Type CONSOLIDATED PRODUCTS
Press <Return>

The printer prints the heading information for the report. A prompt INDEX FIELD FOR BODY INFORMATION appears.

Type **EMPLOYEE NAME**
Press <Return>

The prompt ENTER BEGINNING SEARCH VALUE appears.

Type **A**
Press <Return>

The prompt ENTER THE ENDING SEARCH VALUE appears.

Hold down the <Shift> key.
Press **Z** until the cursor moves off the screen.
Press <Return>

The body of the report is printed.

Summary Points

■ A data manager (data management software package) can be used for the same purposes as a manual filing system: to record and file information.
■ Data managers can be used in the home for such tasks as creating a computerized holiday card list or recipe index file, helping balance a checkbook, or keeping a personal appointment calendar.
■ Computerized home records can be kept in a compact form. Also, data managers can find the data much faster than people can.
■ In many businesses, data managers have replaced traditional filing systems consisting of papers, folders, and filing cabinets. Data managers have many uses, such as keeping employee and inventory control records and lists of customers and suppliers. Data managers enable businesses to update and maintain records quickly and efficiently.
■ Some data managers perform mathematical tasks. They can total the values of the same field in each record, find the average of the values in the same field, or find records with the lowest or highest value in the field.
■ A major benefit of computerized record-keeping is that time is saved, both in updating data and in searching for information. Data managers free employees to concentrate on tasks that can be done only by humans.
■ Some specialized uses of data managers include preparing mass mailings and creating form letters in conjunction with word processors.

WestData 2.5 Exercises

To complete the following exercises, you will need a DOS disk, the West Instructional Software diskette, and your data disk.

1. Start WestData. Describe the steps required. At the WestData 2.5 Main Menu, use the command to set the default directory to drive B.

2. Assume you have been hired by Kenneth Fretwell, D.D.S., to establish a database management system for his office using WestData. You will create a file called PATIENTS. Using the DESIGN A DATA FILE option, name the file and define the following seven fields:

Field	Field Name	Type	Length	Index	Link	Formula
1	Name	A	20	Y	N	N
2	Address	A	15	Y	N	N
3	City	A	10	N	N	N
4	St	A	2	N	N	N
5	Zip	N	5	N	N	N
6	Age	N	2	Y	N	N
7	Balance	M		Y	N	N

3. After you have defined the fields, use the edit function to check for typing errors. Next, save the file and return to the Main Menu.

4. Input the following data in the PATIENTS file.

Name	Address	City	St	Zip	Age	Balance
Busch, David	552 Wallace	Columbus	OH	78654	27	58.60
Busch, Patricia	552 Wallace	Columbus	OH	78654	28	0
Allen, Tom	67 Curtis	Columbus	OH	78653	78	8.90
Spires, Eileen	890 Pine	Columbus	OH	78651	56	120.00
Jenkins, Dave	10 W. Wooster	Columbus	OH	78123	13	93.50
Weaver, Pamela	16 Clough	Columbus	OH	78654	10	0
Busch, Bradley	552 Wallace	Columbus	OH	78654	7	25.00
Bentley, William	77 Palmer	Dayton	OH	89213	45	0

5. Using the DISPLAY A RECORD option, scroll through all the records to check for mistakes. If you find any incorrect entries, make a note of them and use the EDIT DATA IN A RECORD command to correct them.

6. Add the following records to the PATIENTS file:

Name	Address	City	St	Zip	Age	Balance
Lukes, Wilma	909 Clough	Columbus	OH	78653	89	280.00
Swartz, Douglas	9 Main	Dayton	OH	89213	32	46.90
Plazer, Linda	12 Vine	Columbus	OH	78651	25	176.00
Bressler, Ann	25 Baldwin	Columbus	OH	78653	25	0

7. Tom Allen and William Bentley changed dentists. Delete their records from the file.

8. The Busch family (David, Patricia, and Bradley) moved. Their new address is 41 Normandie in Columbus. Update their records, assuming their zip code will be the same.

9. Dr. Fretwell is going to start a No Cavities Club for children under the age of 16. Create a report design that displays the Name and Age fields. Name the report file AGE. Use the AGE report file to display all the patients under the age of 16. Who are the eligible patients?

10.   Dr. Fretwell needs a report that lists the balance owed by the patients. Create another report design that displays the Name and Balance fields. Name the report file BALANCE. Use the BALANCE report file to display the patients who owe over $100. Who are they? Who are the patients with a zero balance?

11.   Print a hard copy of the BALANCE report.

WestData 2.5 Problems

To complete the following problems, you will need a DOS disk, the West Instructional Software diskette, and the WestSoft/File disk. Boot up the computer, load the West Instructional Software diskette, and insert the WestSoft/File disk into drive B.

One of the WestData files on the WestSoft/File disk is called PAYROLL. There are a total of fifteen records in the PAYROLL file. Listed below are the contents of those fifteen records.

Records in PAYROLL file

Record #	Social Security Number	Last Name	First Name
1	999-90-5055	ARNOUX	ANN
2	999-99-7885	SHROEDER	COLLEEN
3	555-50-7098	KOST	MICHAEL
4	555-57-8432	GRANDEL	PASCAL
5	555-55-3089	CLAY	CHRISTOPHE
6	555-50-6924	KODES	ISABELLE
7	555-55-5430	VARTEL	SUZY
8	555-55-2908	MAY	WENDY
9	555-55-4567	MAZUR	MARY ANN
10	555-86-5631	URBA	JOHN
11	999-99-3254	TABLER	LORI
12	999-55-8731	WEBER	DENINE
13	999-55-5529	WATTS	PHILIP
14	999-99-8416	O'BRIEN	KELLY
15	999-99-9991	WICKS	ALAN

Record #	Address	City	State	Zip
1	SECOND STREET	BOWLING GREEN	OH	43402
2	122 SPRING STREET	TOLEDO	OH	43602
3	20200 PORTAGE ROAD	BOWLING GREEN	OH	43402
4	10200 SUGAR RIDGE	TOLEDO	OH	43607
5	2000 HILL AVENUE	TOLEDO	OH	43607
6	318 MAIN STREET	FREMONT	OH	43500
7	1830 REYNOLDS ROAD	TOLEDO	OH	43605

Record #	Address	City	State	Zip
8	115 E COURT STREET	BOWLING GREEN	OH	43402
9	320 E SANDUSKY	FINDLAY	OH	43102
10	12 MAIN STREET	HURON	OH	44839
11	135 HIGH STREET	TOLEDO	OH	43615
12	12 POWELL STREET	CLYDE	OH	43410
13	230 N MAIN STREET	WOODVILLE	OH	43469
14	21 WOOD ROAD	NORTH BALTIMORE	OH	43302
15	500 MERRY AVENUE	TOLEDO	OH	43609

Record #	Birthdate	Status	Job Title
1	01/26/57	F	PROGRAMMER
2	02/10/54	F	SYSTEM ANALYST
3	08/06/52	F	SECRETARY
4	10/15/56	P	WRITER
5	11/12/54	P	WRITER
6	09/01/51	F	WRITER
7	08/22/55	F	PROGRAMMER
8	12/25/54	F	PROGRAMMER
9	07/15/57	F	SECRETARY
10	12/15/52	F	ARTIST
11	01/26/56	P	REVIEWER
12	03/02/54	P	PROGRAMMER
13	02/26/45	F	DIRECTOR
14	02/12/52	F	PHOTOGRAPHER
15	12/01/52	P	WRITER

1. Assume you are working in the payroll department of your company. The company uses a file called PAYROLL to store information such as name, address, job title, and hourly wages. The fields Social Security Number and Last Number are indexed in the PAYROLL file. If the PAYROLL file were not locked, what are two ways you could display the file's structure? Select the DISPLAY A RECORD option for the PAYROLL file. How many fields are there in the file?

Look at the above records for the PAYROLL file. How many alphanumeric fields are there in the file? How many numeric fields? How long is the Job Title field?

2. Next, you are going to examine the records of the employees. Display the first five records. What steps must you take to display the first five records? What is the name and job title of the employee that corresponds to record 5? What is the name of the last employee in the file?

3. Using the PAYROLL file, design, display, and print a report listing the following information: Social Security Number, Birthdate, Job Title, and Status.

CHAPTER 14

Advanced WestData™ 2.5

Introduction

In the previous chapter, the fundamentals of data management were discussed along with some basic functions of WestData 2.5, such as creating data files, inputting data into records, and printing reports. WestData 2.5 also has several advanced features that enable users to manipulate data in other ways. This chapter includes a discussion of features such as editing data files, copying and deleting data files, locking files, and printing mailing labels.

Link
A pointer that directs the program to search for a value in another file.

The **LINK** function, briefly introduced in Chapter 13, is explained more fully in this chapter. The LINK function enables users to take data from two or more existing files and create an entirely new data file. Because data often is stored in many different files, the LINK function is particularly useful in creating files for specialized purposes from data stored in existing files.

Exercises following each feature provide an opportunity to practice using the advanced WestData features.

Editing Data Files

After a data file has been created, sometimes it is necessary to make changes to the basic design of the file. A new data field may be needed in a file, or certain fields may become obsolete. With WestData, it is possible to change a basic file design. Fields can be added or deleted and field definitions can be changed.

To make changes to an existing data file design, highlight the EDIT A DATA FILE DEFINITION option from the WestData 2.5 Main Menu and press <Return> (see Figure 14-1). A screen appears with a directory listing data files on the left and report files on the right. The prompt ENTER FILENAME appears at the bottom of the screen. Type in the name of the data file to be edited and press <Return>. The field definition form appears next, along with the prompt NAME OF FIELD 1. The name entered in field 1 appears after the prompt, with the blinking cursor located under the first letter of the name. To edit the file, use the <→> key to scroll through the field characteristics. Retype any incorrect entries when the entry is highlighted.

To add a field, use the <→> key to scroll through the file until you reach the field number in the file where you want to add a new field. When the NAME OF FIELD prompt appears, press the <F1> key (located in the upper-left corner of the keyboard) and the name that appears after the prompt disappears. (The name is not being deleted; it is stored in memory while a new field is being added.) Enter a new field name and press <Return>. Continue entering data about the new field after each subsequent prompt appears, and press <Return> after each entry. After the last prompt for the new field is answered and <Return> is pressed, the next field (the one that disappeared when you pressed <F1>) reappears. Field numbers for the remaining fields in the file are adjusted automatically to reflect the addition of the new field.

```
                        WESTDATA 2.5 MAIN MENU
            (DATA FILES)                            (REPORT FILES)
   ┌─────────────────────────────┐      ┌─────────────────────────────┐
   │ Design a data file          │      │ Design a report file        │
   │ Edit a data file definition │      │ Display a report file       │
   │ Delete a data file          │      │ Delete a report file        │
   │ Copy a data file            │      │ Copy a report file          │
   │                             │      │ Print a report file         │
   └─────────────────────────────┘      └─────────────────────────────┘

            (DATA RECORDS)                           (UTILITIES)
   ┌─────────────────────────────┐      ┌─────────────────────────────┐
   │ Input data to a record      │      │ Lock / Unlock files         │
   │ Edit data in a record       │      │ Mailing labels              │
   │ Display a record            │      │ Change drive                │
   │ Delete a record             │      │ Exit program                │
   │                             │      │                             │
   └─────────────────────────────┘      └─────────────────────────────┘


 POSITION CURSOR AT SELECTION AND PRESS <RETURN>
```

Figure 14-1
Selecting EDIT A DATA FILE
DEFINITION

To delete a field, use the <—→> key to scroll through the file until the field number appears with the name of the field that you want to delete. Press the <F2> key (located in the upper-left corner of the keyboard) and the field is deleted from the file. Field numbers for the remaining fields in the file are adjusted automatically to reflect the change to the file. After editing the fields in the file, press <Esc>. Then type **S** and press <Return> to save the changes to the file and return to the Main Menu.

 YOUR TURN

You are going to edit the field definitions in the LIBRARY FILE created during an exercise in Chapter 13. Begin with the WestData 2.5 Main Menu on the screen. Access drive B. Highlight EDIT A DATA FILE DEFINITION.

Press <Return>

The directory for drive B appears on the screen. The prompt ENTER FILENAME appears at the bottom of the screen.

Type **LIBRARY**
Press <Return>

The field definition form appears on the screen. At the bottom of the screen, the blinking cursor appears after the NAME OF FIELD 1 prompt under the first letter of NUMBER.

> Press the <F2> key

The field name disappears from the screen and the next field appears and becomes field 1. Now you are going to re-enter the information about the NUMBER field.

> Press the <F1> key
> Type Number
> Press <Return>

The prompt TYPE OF FIELD 1 appears at the bottom of the screen with the blinking cursor next to it.

> Type **N** for numeric
> Press <Return>

The prompt LENGTH OF FIELD 1 appears at the bottom of the screen with a blinking cursor next to it.

> Type **3**
> Press <Return>

The prompt INDEX FIELD? appears next.

> Type **Y**
> Press <Return>

The prompt LINK FIELD? appears.

> Type **N**
> Press <Return>

The prompt FORMULA FOR FIELD 1? appears.

> Type **N**
> Press <Return>

Because all the categories for field 1 have been entered, the prompt NAME OF FIELD 2 appears with a field name following the prompt.
 Use the <→> key to scroll through the field definitions until the NAME OF FIELD 3 prompt appears.

> Press <→> twice

The LENGTH OF FIELD 3 prompt appears.

> Type **25**
> Press <→>

The number 25 replaces 15 in the length column for field 3. Use the <→> key to scroll through the file to field 4 and change the length of field 4 to 25.

Save the edited file and return to the Main Menu.

> Press <Esc>
> Type **S** and press <Return>

Copying Data Files

Occasionally, it is useful to copy a data file. For example, a user may want to experiment with editing a file design while retaining the original file design. The COPY A DATA FILE option enables the user to duplicate a data file under another name.

To activate this function, highlight the COPY A DATA FILE option on the Main Menu and press <Return>. The directory of data and report files appears on the screen. The prompt ENTER THE NAME OF THE FILE YOU WISH TO COPY FROM: ENTER FILENAME is located at the bottom of the screen (see Figure 14-2). The prompt is requesting the name of the file that will be copied. Type the name of the file to copy and press <Return>. Another prompt appears at the bottom of the screen: ENTER THE NAME OF THE FILE YOU WISH TO COPY TO: ENTER FILENAME. This prompt is requesting the user to assign a name to the copied file. Enter a new name for the copied file and press <Return>. The file is then copied and the program returns to the Main Menu.

 YOUR TURN

You are going to make a copy of the LIBRARY file. Begin with the WestData 2.5 Main Menu on the screen.

Use the arrow keys to highlight the COPY A DATA FILE option. Press <Return>. The current directory appears on the screen. The prompt ENTER THE NAME OF THE FILE YOU WISH TO COPY FROM: ENTER FILENAME appears at the bottom of the screen.

> Type **LIBRARY**
> Press <Return>

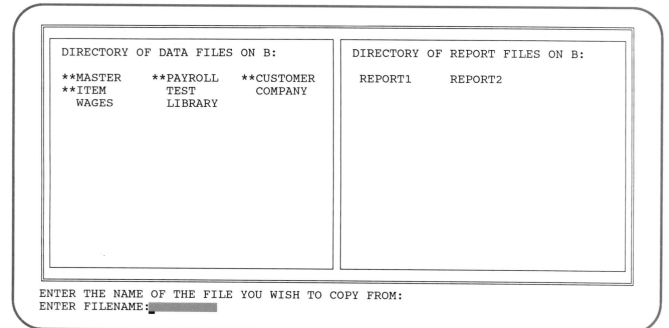

Figure 14-2
Copying a Data File

A new prompt, ENTER THE NAME OF THE FILE YOU WISH TO COPY TO: ENTER FILENAME, appears at the bottom of the screen.

Type **LIBRARY1**
Press <Return>

The program copies the LIBRARY file as LIBRARY1 and returns to the Main Menu.

Deleting Data Files

In the process of learning how to use a data manager, students often create many practice files to test special program features. Disks can quickly become filled with these practice files. WestData enables the user to delete a file that is no longer needed.

To delete a file, select the DELETE A DATA FILE option from the Main Menu and press <Return>. The directory for the active drive appears on the screen with a listing of data and report files. The prompt FILE TO DELETE: ENTER FILENAME is at the bottom of the screen. Enter the name of a file that appears on the directory of data files list and press <Return>. Another prompt, ARE YOU SURE? (Y/N)

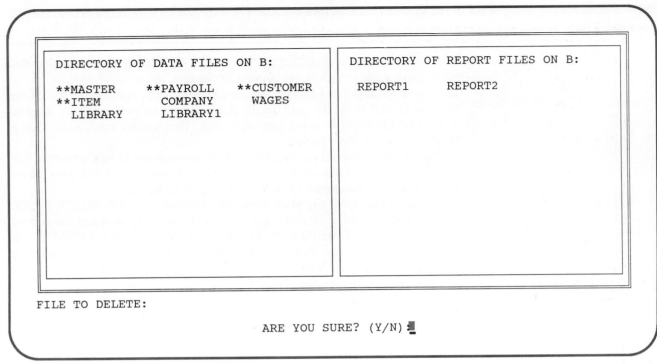

```
DIRECTORY OF DATA FILES ON B:        DIRECTORY OF REPORT FILES ON B:

**MASTER    **PAYROLL    **CUSTOMER      REPORT1      REPORT2
**ITEM        COMPANY      WAGES
  LIBRARY     LIBRARY1
```

```
FILE TO DELETE:

                          ARE YOU SURE? (Y/N)
```

Figure 14-3
Deleting a Data File

appears (see Figure 14-3). Type **Y** or **N** and press <Return> again. A **Y** response to the prompt causes the program to delete the file from the directory, whereas an **N** response returns the program to the Main Menu and leaves the file intact.

YOUR TURN

You are going to delete the LIBRARY file from the disk. Use the arrow keys to highlight the DELETE A DATA FILE option on the Main Menu and press <Return>. The current directory appears on the screen once again. The prompt FILE TO DELETE: ENTER FILENAME appears at the bottom of the screen.

Type **LIBRARY1**
Press <Return>

The prompt ARE YOU SURE? (Y/N) appears at the center of the bottom of the screen.

Type **Y**
Press <Return>

The program returns to the Main Menu and the LIBRARY1 file is deleted.

Locking Files

WestData has a file-locking feature that enables the user to protect existing data files. When a file is locked, no permanent changes can be made to it. A locked file can be displayed and printed, but no changes can be made to the file design or to the records in the file until the file is unlocked. The locking feature is useful if other people might be using your work disk. They cannot accidentally change your files, and neither can you.

There is also a special password that instructors can use to lock a practice file. These files cannot be unlocked unless the correct password is entered. This feature protects practice documents from being damaged accidentally.

To lock a file, go to the Main Menu and highlight LOCK/UNLOCK FILES. Press <Return> and a directory appears, listing the data and report files on the active drive. The prompt FILE TO LOCK/UNLOCK: ENTER FILENAME is at the bottom of the screen. Enter the name of the file that is to be locked and press <Return>. The Main Menu reappears on the screen, and the file selected at the ENTER FILENAME prompt is now locked.

A locked file can be unlocked as easily as it can be locked. Simply repeat the same procedure used to lock it. The LOCK/UNLOCK procedure works like an on/off switch. Once a file is locked, an asterisk appears in front of the filename in the directory to indicate that it is locked. Two asterisks appear in front of files that instructors have locked using special passwords (see Figure 14-4).

Figure 14-4
Directory with Instructor-Locked
Files

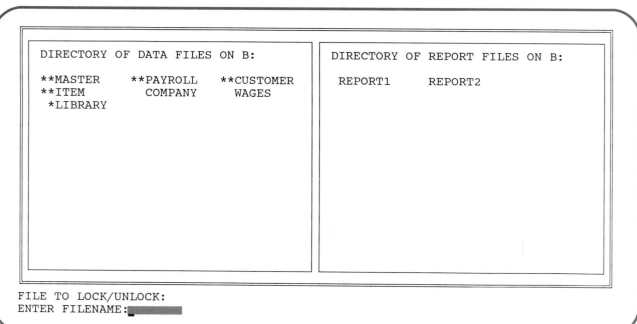

YOUR TURN

You are going to practice locking and unlocking a file. Begin with the WestData 2.5 Main Menu on the screen. Use the arrow key to highlight the LOCK/UNLOCK FILES option.

Press <Return>

The directory for drive B appears on the screen. The prompt FILE TO LOCK/ UNLOCK: ENTER FILENAME is at the bottom of the screen.

Type **LIBRARY**
Press <Return>

The Main Menu reappears on the screen. Use the arrow keys to highlight INPUT DATA TO A RECORD.

Press <Return>

The directory for drive B appears on the screen, and there is an asterisk in front of the LIBRARY file. The prompt ENTER FILENAME appears at the bottom of the screen.

Type **LIBRARY**
Press <Return>

A message appears at the bottom of the screen, stating: THIS DATA FILE IS <LOCKED>. IN ORDER TO UPDATE IT YOU MUST FIRST UNLOCK IT.

Press <Esc>

The program returns to the Main Menu. Use the arrow keys to highlight the LOCK/UNLOCK FILES option.

Press <Return>

The directory for drive B appears on the screen, with the FILE TO LOCK/ UNLOCK: ENTER FILENAME prompt at the bottom of the screen.

Type **LIBRARY**
Press <Return>

The program returns to the Main Menu and the LIBRARY file is unlocked.

Linking Files

Data managers store data in many different files. Sometimes it is necessary to create a new file using data stored in existing files. WestData makes it possible to do this with the LINK function. In Chapter 13, a link was described as a pointer that directs the program to search for a value in another file. To understand the linking of files, consider the following example.

Suppose the registrar at a university has a file called STUDENT which stores, among other things, the name, address, phone number, social security number, and GPA for each student. Also suppose that the university library has a file called BOOKS which lists the names of students who have books overdue at the library. Data stored about each student in the BOOKS file includes student name, book title, due date, and amount of fine.

Now suppose the head librarian at the university wants to send overdue notices to all students who have overdue books. It is possible for the librarian to create a third file using data stored in fields in each of the existing files, STUDENT and BOOKS. The third file, called OVERDUE, can be created using the LINK function. The OVERDUE file will contain student names, addresses, Social Security numbers, book titles, due dates, and amounts of fines.

To create the OVERDUE file, the librarian must designate which fields will receive data from another file. This procedure must take place during the file design process. Fields that receive data from other files are called linked fields. For example, by knowing a student's name, the librarian can find out the student's address and social security number if address and social security number are designated as linked fields in the OVERDUE file. The following exercise sets up files to use the link function.

YOUR TURN

Begin with the WestData 2.5 Main Menu on the screen. You are going to use the link function by creating three files: STUDENT, BOOKS, and OVERDUE. Using the arrow keys, highlight the DESIGN A DATA FILE option and press <Return>. Design a file called STUDENT using the following information.

STUDENT File Design

Field #	Field Name	Type	Length	Index	Link	Formula
1	Student Name	A	30	Y	N	N
2	Address 1	A	25	N	N	N
3	Address 2	A	25	N	N	N
4	SS #	N	11	N	N	N
5	Year	N	1	N	N	N
6	GPA	N	4	N	N	N

Save the file design and return to the Main Menu. Using the arrow keys, highlight the INPUT DATA TO RECORD option and press <Return>. Type the following records into the STUDENT file.

Records for STUDENT File

Student Name	Address 1	Address 2	SS #	Year	GPA
Faulks, Tim	78 Main St.	Miami, FL	343-61-1101	4	3.20
Bulas, Irene	908 W. Summit	Cygnet, OH	289-89-4672	3	3.00
Klein, Tom	12 Young St.	Hampton, NC	278-45-7891	4	2.55
Wilcox, Bill	6 Williams Rd.	Fremont, TX	524-68-4099	1	2.00
Ornelas, Tina	123 First St.	Canton, OH	468-71-9002	2	3.12
Lord, Pamela	98 Pike St.	Oregon, OH	208-46-4096	4	3.78
Busch, Brad	32 Bradner	Columbus, OH	782-28-1598	3	3.70
Weaver, Chris	909 Clough	Portage, OH	411-69-4774	2	2.15
Bressler, Ann	45 S. Like St.	Palma, PA	789-22-6615	1	2.08
DeSalvo, Liz	9 W. Second St.	Hamler, ME	879-43-6291	4	2.22

After all the records are entered, type **N** in response to the prompt DO YOU WISH TO ADD MORE RECORDS? The WestData 2.5 Main Menu returns to the screen.

Next, you are going to design a file called BOOKS with the following information. Using the arrow keys, highlight the DESIGN A DATA FILE option and press <Return>. Begin designing the BOOKS file.

BOOKS File Design

Field #	Field Name	Type	Length	Index	Link	Formula
1	Student Name	A	30	Y	N	N
2	Book Title	A	30	N	N	N
3	Due Date	N	8	N	N	N
4	Fine	M		N	N	N

Save the file design and return to the Main Menu. Use the arrow keys to highlight the INPUT DATA TO A RECORD option and press <Return>. Type the following records into the BOOKS file.

Records for BOOKS file

Student Name	Book Title	Due Date	Fine
Faulks, Tim	Computer Games	10/20/87	.75
Bulas, Irene	Learning dBase III	10/02/87	.50
Klein, Tom	Science Fiction	10/12/87	1.00
Wilcox, Bill	Apple II	10/12/87	.25
Ornelas, Tina	Modern Science	10/12/87	2.50
Lord, Pamela	Calculus	10/20/87	.50
Busch, Brad	Trigonometry	10/02/87	.25
Weaver, Chris	Design and Analysis	10/11/87	.75
Bressler, Ann	Geometry Made Easy	10/12/87	1.25
DeSalvo, Liz	Home Computers	10/20/87	1.25

After all the records are entered, press **N** in response to the prompt DO YOU WISH TO ADD MORE RECORDS? The WestData 2.5 Main Menu returns to the screen.

Next, you are going to design an OVERDUE file that will contain data stored in both the STUDENT and BOOKS files. Using the arrow keys, highlight the DESIGN A DATA FILE option and press <Return>.

Type **OVERDUE**
Press <Return>
Type Student Name
Press <Return>
Type **A**
Press <Return>
Type **30**
Press <Return>
Type **Y**
Press <Return>
Type **N**
Press <Return>
Type **N**
Press <Return>

The prompt NAME OF FIELD 2 appears next. Enter the following information about field 2.

Type Address 1
Press <Return>
Type **A**
Press <Return>
Type **25**
Press <Return>
Type **N**
Press <Return>
Type **Y**
Press <Return>

The prompt NAME OF LINK FIELD IN ACTIVE FILE appears at the bottom of the screen (see Figure 14-5). The active file is the file currently on the screen (OVERDUE). You are going to enter the name of an existing field in that file.

Type Student Name
Press <Return>

The prompt NAME OF REFERENCE FILE appears at the bottom of the screen. The reference file is an existing file from which the Address 1 information will come.

```
┌─────────────────────────────┬─────────────────┬──────────────────────────┐
│                             │ DEFINE FIELDS:  │                          │
├─────────────────────────────┴─────────────────┴──────────────────────────┤
│ FIELD :    NAME :                    TYPE :   LENGTH :   INDEX:  LINK:  FORMULA: │
├───────────────────────────────────────────────────────────────────────────┤
│ FIELD 1:   STUDENT NAME                A         30          1       N       N  │
│ FIELD 2:   ADDRESS 1                   A         25          0       Y          │
│                                                                           │
│                                                                           │
│                                                                           │
│                                                                           │
│                                                                           │
│                                                                           │
├───────────────────────────────────────────────────────────────────────────┤
│ NAME OF LINK FIELD IN ACTIVE FILE:_                                        │
├───────────────────────────────────────────────────────────────────────────┤
│ PRESS THE <ESC> KEY TO -EDIT- OR TO -EXIT-.                               │
└───────────────────────────────────────────────────────────────────────────┘
```

Figure 14-5
The LINK FIELD Prompt

Type **STUDENT**
Press <Return>

The prompt NAME OF INDEX FIELD IN REFERENCE FILE appears at the bottom of the screen. The index field in the reference file is Student Name. Student Name will direct the program to search for the data Address 1 in the STUDENT file.

Type Student Name
Press <Return>

The prompt NAME OF DATA FIELD IN REFERENCE FILE appears at the bottom of the screen. You must enter the name of the data field that you want retrieved from the STUDENT file and placed in the OVERDUE file.

Type Address 1
Press <Return>

The prompt FORMULA FOR FIELD 2 appears at the bottom of the screen.

Type **N**
Press <Return>

The prompt NAME OF FIELD 3 appears next. Enter the following information about field 3.

Type `Address 2`
Press <Return>
Type **A**
Press <Return>
Type **25**
Press <Return>
Type **N**
Press <Return>
Type **Y**
Press <Return>

The prompt NAME OF LINK FIELD IN ACTIVE FILE appears at the bottom of the screen. The active file is the file currently on the screen (OVERDUE).

Type `Student Name`
Press <Return>

The prompt NAME OF REFERENCE FILE appears at the bottom of the screen. The reference file is the file from which the Address 2 information will come.

Type **STUDENT**
Press <Return>

The prompt NAME OF INDEX FIELD IN REFERENCE FILE appears at the bottom of the screen. The index field in the reference file is Student Name which, once again, directs the program to search for data.

Type `Student Name`
Press <Return>

The prompt NAME OF DATA FIELD IN REFERENCE FILE appears at the bottom of the screen. You must enter the name of the data field that you want retrieved from the STUDENT file and placed in the OVERDUE file.

Type `Address 2`
Press <Return>

The prompt FORMULA FOR FIELD 3 appears at the bottom of the screen.

Type **N**
Press <Return>

The prompt NAME OF FIELD 4 appears next. Enter the following information about field 4.

Type `SS #`
Press <Return>
Type **N**
Press <Return>

Type **11**
Press <Return>
Type **Y**
Press <Return>
Type **Y**
Press <Return>

The prompt NAME OF LINK FIELD IN ACTIVE FILE appears at the bottom of the screen. The active file is the file currently on the screen (OVERDUE).

Type `Student Name`
Press <Return>

The prompt NAME OF REFERENCE FILE appears at the bottom of the screen. The reference file is the file from which the student name information will come.

Type **STUDENT**
Press <Return>

The prompt NAME OF INDEX FIELD IN REFERENCE FILE appears at the bottom of the screen. The index field in the reference file is Student Name.

Type `Student Name`
Press <Return>

The prompt NAME OF DATA FIELD IN REFERENCE FILE appears at the bottom of the screen. You must enter the name of the data field that you want retrieved from the STUDENT file and placed in the OVERDUE file.

Type `SS #`
Press <Return>

The prompt FORMULA FOR FIELD 4 appears at the bottom of the screen.

Type **N**
Press <Return>

The prompt NAME OF FIELD 5 appears next. Enter the following information about field 5.

Type `Book Title`
Press <Return>
Type **A**
Press <Return>
Type **30**
Press <Return>
Type **N**
Press <Return>

Type **Y**
Press <Return>

The prompt NAME OF LINK FIELD IN ACTIVE FILE appears at the bottom of the screen. The active file is the file currently on the screen (OVERDUE).

Type Student Name
Press <Return>

The prompt NAME OF REFERENCE FILE appears at the bottom of the screen. The reference file is the file from which the title information will come.

Type **BOOKS**
Press <Return>

The prompt NAME OF INDEX FIELD IN REFERENCE FILE appears at the bottom of the screen. The index field in the reference file is Student Name.

Type Student Name
Press <Return>

The prompt NAME OF DATA FIELD IN REFERENCE FILE appears at the bottom of the screen. You must enter the name of the data field that you want retrieved from the BOOKS file and placed in the OVERDUE file.

Type Book Title
Press <Return>

The prompt FORMULA FOR FIELD 5 appears at the bottom of the screen.

Type **N**
Press <Return>

The prompt NAME OF FIELD 6 appears next. Enter the following information about field 6.

Type Fine
Press <Return>
Type **M**
Press <Return>
Type **N**
Press <Return>
Type **Y**
Press <Return>

The prompt NAME OF LINK FIELD IN ACTIVE FILE appears at the bottom of the screen. The active file is the file currently on the screen (OVERDUE).

Type Student Name
Press <Return>

The prompt NAME OF REFERENCE FILE appears at the bottom of the screen. The reference file is the file from which the title information will come.

Type **BOOKS**
Press <Return>

The prompt NAME OF INDEX FIELD IN REFERENCE FILE appears at the bottom of the screen. The index field in the reference file is Student Name.

Type Student Name
Press <Return>

The prompt NAME OF DATA FIELD IN REFERENCE FILE appears at the bottom of the screen. You must enter the name of the data field that you want retrieved from the BOOKS file and placed in the OVERDUE file.

Type Fine
Press <Return>

The prompt FORMULA FOR FIELD 6 appears at the bottom of the screen.

Type **N**
Press <Return>

Save the file design and return to the Main Menu.
You have created a new file, OVERDUE. To input records to the OVERDUE file, use the arrow keys to highlight the INPUT DATA TO A RECORD option on the Main Menu.

Press <Return>
Type **OVERDUE**
Press <Return>

The cursor appears in the first field, Student Name.

Type Bulas, Irene
Press <Return>

Data immediately appears in the remaining fields. The data for the remaining fields came from the STUDENT and BOOKS files. Input the following data to records in the OVERDUE file:

```
Faulks, Tim      Klein, Tom       Wilcox, Bill
Ornelas, Tina    Lord, Pamela     Busch, Brad
Weaver, Chris    Bressler, Ann    DeSalvo, Liz
```

When you have finished inputting records to the OVERDUE file, save the file and return to the Main Menu.

Mailing Labels

One of WestData's useful features includes the ability to make customized mailing labels. This feature is extremely useful for mass mailings, but customized labels also can be used for other applications, such as labeling bottles, cans, or packages.

To activate the mailing labels feature, highlight MAILING LABELS on the WestData 2.5 Main Menu and press <Return>. The directory for the active drive appears, and the prompt ENTER A DATA FILENAME: ENTER FILENAME appears at the bottom of the screen. Enter the name of a data file that appears in the directory and press <Return>. The following prompt appears on the screen: ENTER THE FIELD NUMBERS TO PRINT ON THE LABEL (TERMINATE LIST WITH 0): LABEL LINE #1 (see Figure 14-6).

The blinking cursor appears after the prompt. Enter the field number of the information that is to appear on the first line of the label and press <Return>. The LABEL LINE # prompt changes from 1 to 2. Enter the field number of the information that is to appear on the second line of the label. Press <Return> again. WestData allows up to six fields of information to appear on each label, so continue entering up to six fields. If fewer than six fields are entered, type 0 (zero) in response to the LABEL LINE # PROMPT after the last field number is

Figure 14-6
Creating a Mailing Label

```
 ┌──────────────────────────────────────────────────────────────────────────┐
 │ ┌────────────────────────────────────┬─────────────────────────────────┐  │
 │ │ DIRECTORY OF DATA FILES ON B:       │ DIRECTORY OF REPORT FILES ON B: │  │
 │ │                                     │                                 │  │
 │ │ **MASTER    **PAYROLL    **CUSTOMER │    REPORT1     REPORT2          │  │
 │ │ **ITEM        COMPANY      WAGES    │                                 │  │
 │ │   LIBRARY     STUDENT      BOOKS    │                                 │  │
 │ │   OVERDUE                           │                                 │  │
 │ │                                     │                                 │  │
 │ │                                     │                                 │  │
 │ │                                     │                                 │  │
 │ │                                     │                                 │  │
 │ │                                     │                                 │  │
 │ │                                     │                                 │  │
 │ │                                     │                                 │  │
 │ └────────────────────────────────────┴─────────────────────────────────┘  │
 │ ENTER THE FIELD NUMBERS TO PRINT ON THE LABEL (Terminate list with 0):     │
 │ Label line #1:█                                                            │
 └──────────────────────────────────────────────────────────────────────────┘
```

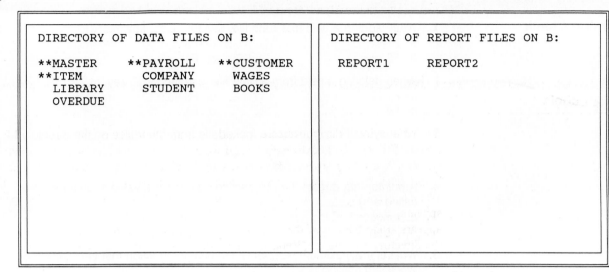

```
DIRECTORY OF DATA FILES ON B:          DIRECTORY OF REPORT FILES ON B:

**MASTER     **PAYROLL   **CUSTOMER      REPORT1      REPORT2
**ITEM         COMPANY     WAGES
  LIBRARY      STUDENT     BOOKS
  OVERDUE
```

```
ENTER THE FIELD NUMBERS TO PRINT ON THE LABEL (Terminate list with 0):


ENTER THE BEGINNING SEARCH VALUE:_
```

Figure 14-7
Printing a Mailing Label

entered and press <Return>. When designing a label remember this rule—at least one of the fields entered *must* be an indexed field.

The next prompt, ENTER THE NUMBER OF SPACES BETWEEN LABELS, appears at the bottom of the screen. Enter the number of blank spaces that will separate each label and press <Return>. A prompt asks DO YOU WISH TO HAVE A TEST RUN? TYPE **N** in response to this prompt and press <Return>, unless the computer you are using is connected to a printer. If your computer is connected to a printer, a **Y** response enables you to print one label to check and see if all the information is correct.

If you have entered **N** in response to the test prompt, another prompt, INDEX FIELD NAME, appears. Enter an indexed field name from the selected file and press <Return>. The prompt ENTER THE BEGINNING SEARCH VALUE appears at the bottom of the screen (see Figure 14-7). If the indexed field is alphanumeric, enter a letter (use upper or lower case to match the indexed field entry) and press <Return>. If the indexed field is numeric, enter a number and press <Return>. The prompt ENTER THE ENDING SEARCH VALUE appears next. Enter either a letter or a number and press <Return>. The printer begins printing the labels.

YOUR TURN   You are going to print mailing labels using the STUDENT file. Highlight MAILING LABELS on the WestData 2.5 Main Menu and press <Return>. The directory for the active drive appears, and the prompt ENTER A DATA FILENAME: ENTER FILENAME appears at the bottom of the screen.

Learning Check

1. When adding a field to a data file, use the _____ key.
   a. F1   *c.* F3
   b. F2   *d.* F4

2. When deleting a field from a data file, use the _____ key.
   a. F1   *c.* F3
   b. F2   *d.* F4

3. What symbol distinguishes a locked file from other files on the directory?
   a. #   *c.* •
   b. ^   *d.* *

4. A pointer that directs the program to search for a value in another file is called a(n) _____.
   a. function   *c.* link
   b. index   *d.* connector

5. What is the maximum number of fields of information that can appear on a WestData mailing label?
   a. two   *c.* six
   b. four   *d.* eight

Answers

1. a 2. b 3. d 4. c 5. c

Type **STUDENT**
Press <Return>

The prompt ENTER THE FIELD NUMBERS TO PRINT ON THE LABEL (TERMINATE LIST WITH 0): LABEL LINE # 1 appears on the screen.

   Type **1**
   Press <Return>

The LABEL LINE # prompt changes from 1 to 2.

   Type **2**
   Press <Return>

The LABEL LINE # prompt changes from 2 to 3.

   Type **3**
   Press <Return>

The LABEL LINE # prompt changes from 3 to 4.

Type **0** (zero)
Press <Return>

The prompt ENTER THE NUMBER OF SPACES BETWEEN LABELS appears at the bottom of the screen.

Type **4**
Press <Return>

The prompt DO YOU WISH TO HAVE A TEST RUN appears.

Type **N**
Press <Return>

The prompt INDEX FIELD NAME appears.

Type **Student Name**
Press <Return>

The prompt ENTER THE BEGINNING SEARCH VALUE appears at the bottom of the screen.

Type **A**
Press <Return>

The prompt ENTER THE ENDING SEARCH VALUE appears next.

Type **ZZ**
Press <Return>

The printer begins printing labels for the STUDENT file.

Summary of WestData 2.5 Functions

Function	Enables You To
Design a data file	create a file design.
Edit a data file definition	add, delete, or change the format of a field within a file.
Delete a data file	delete a data file from the directory.
Copy a data file	duplicate a data file under a new name.
Input data to a record	enter data into a record.
Edit data in a record	add, delete, or change the contents of a record.
Display a record	view the contents of records.
Delete a record	delete records in a file.
Design a report file	design headers and body style for reports.

Function	Enables You To
Display a report file	view the report design.
Copy a report file	duplicate a report file under a new name.
Print a report file	print hard copies of the report file.
Lock/Unlock files	lock files to protect them from accidental changes.
Mailing labels	design and print labels for mailing.
Change drive	change the default directory (disk drive) to be used.
Exit program	return to the Opening Menu.

Summary Points

■ The basic design of a file can be changed using the EDIT A DATA FILE function, which enables users to add or delete fields in a file or change field definitions.

■ Occasionally it may be useful to copy a data file. For example, a user may want to experiment with editing a file design but may still want to retain the original file design. The COPY A DATA FILE option enables the user to duplicate a data file under another name.

■ The DELETE A DATA FILE option enables users to delete a file that is no longer needed.

■ The locking feature enables users to protect existing files from accidental changes. A locked file can be displayed and printed, but no changes can be made to it. In the directory, one asterisk appears in front of the names of files that have been locked by students; two asterisks appear in front of files that have been locked by instructors.

■ The link function enables users to take data from two or more existing files and create an entirely new data file. Because data often is stored in many different files, the LINK function is particularly useful in creating files for specialized purposes from data stored in existing files.

■ One of WestData's useful features is the ability to make customized mailing labels. This feature is extremely useful for mass mailings, but customized labels also can be used for other applications.

WestData 2.5 Exercises

To complete the following exercises, you will need a DOS disk, the West Instructional Software diskette, and your data disk. Boot up the computer, load the West Instructional Software diskette, and insert the data disk into drive B.

In this exercise, you are going to prepare the rosters for classes at a state university. The files are organized as follows:

■ A file called ENROLL contains general student information such as personal data, program, and major.
■ Another file contains registration information for each semester.

1. Design a new file and name it ENROLL. You are going to create a file that contains information about the students. The file should have the following design:

Field Name	Type	Length	Index	Link	Formula
STUDENT #	N	2	Y	N	N
LAST NAME	A	20	Y	N	N
FIRST NAME	A	20	N	N	N
ADDRESS	A	25	N	N	N
CITY	A	20	N	N	N
STATE	A	2	N	N	N
MAJOR	A	20	N	N	N
PROGRAM	A	3	N	N	N

Save the file design.

2. Input the following records into the ENROLL file.

Student #	Last Name	First Name	Address	City	State	Major	Program
1	Mansfield	Carolyn	190 Main Street	Bowling Green	OH	Education	BA
2	Magpoc	William	1200 Victory Blvd.	Toledo	OH	Business	BS
3	Rath	Alexis	221 Maple Ave.	Perrysburg	OH	Business	BS
4	Byrtum	Laura	849 Napoleon Rd.	Bowling Green	OH	History	BA
5	Burkett	Lynn	12 Central	Toledo	OH	Music	BA
6	Catayee	Monique	110 Main Street	Maumee	OH	Theater	BA
7	Marin	Bernard	12 King Rd.	Huron	OH	Accounting	BS
8	Byler	Diane	Anderson Hall	Bowling Green	OH	Business	BS
9	Heil	Pascal	302 West Hall	Bowling Green	OH	Education	BA
10	Jaccoud	Lynn	120 S. Main St.	Sandusky	OH	Finance	BS
11	Wegman	Nelly	430 Clough	Dearborn	MI	Accounting	BS
12	Pinkston	Mark	65 High St.	Detroit	MI	Statistics	BS
13	Burroughs	Beverly	26 S. Summit	Huron	OH	Journalism	BA
14	King	Stephen	201 E. Wooster	Bloomdale	OH	History	BA
15	Paulin	Jack	102 High	Sylvania	OH	Math	BS
16	Proctor	Christopher	34 Eighth St.	Lancaster	OH	Chemistry	BS
17	Priess	Ronald	120 Prout Hall	Bowling Green	OH	Marketing	BS
18	Atkins	Lee	12560 Euclid Ave.	Cleveland	OH	Education	BA
19	Asik	Jennifer	22 Mercer	Cleveland	OH	History	BA
20	Dowell	Gail	112 Ridge	Toledo	OH	Business	BS
21	Wacker	Annick	320 East Merry	Sandusky	OH	Economics	BS
22	Garret	Lynda	39 Vine Street	Detroit	MI	Music	BA
23	McGovern	Alice	12000 Sand Ridge	Bowling Green	OH	Theater	BA
24	McLaughlin	Francoise	210 Main Street	Tiffin	OH	Education	BA
25	Augustin	Liliane	333 Jeffers Rd.	Dearborn	MI	Finance	BS

3. Once all the records have been entered, select the DISPLAY A RECORD option from the Main Menu and review the data in the records. Make sure that everything is correct. Use the EDIT DATA IN A RECORD option to make any necessary corrections.

4. Now you are going to create a second file called MOVE that will be used for registration for the fall semester. The file should have the following design:

Field Name	Type	Length	Index	Link	Formula
LAST NAME	A	20	Y	N	N
CLASS	A	8	Y	N	N
SEMESTER	N	2	N	N	N
YEAR	N	2	N	N	N

Save the file design.

5. Input the following data to records in the MOVE file.

Records for the MOVE file

Last Name	Class	Semester	Year
Mansfield	EDCI421	01	87
Magpoc	ECON221	01	87
Rath	ECON222	01	87
Byrtum	ENG441	01	87
Burkett	ENG441	01	87
Catayee	ENG441	01	87
Marin	ECON222	01	87
Byler	ECON222	01	87
Heil	EDCI421	01	87
Jaccoud	ECON222	01	87
Wegman	ECON221	01	87
Pinkston	ECON222	01	87
Burroughs	ENG441	01	87
King	ENG441	01	87
Paulin	MATH350	01	87
Proctor	MATH350	01	87
Priess	ECON221	01	87
Atkins	EDCI421	01	87
Asik	ENG441	01	87
Dowell	ECON221	01	87
Wacker	ECON222	01	87
Garret	ENG441	01	87
McGovern	ENG441	01	87
McLaughlin	EDCI421	01	87
Augustin	ECON221	01	87

6.   Once all the records have been entered, select the DISPLAY A RECORD option from the Main Menu and review the data in the records. Make sure that everything is correct. Use the EDIT DATA IN A RECORD option to make any necessary corrections.

7.   Now you want to produce a third file called ROSTER that includes the last name, first name, program, and major for each student in all the classes. The data for the ROSTER file will come from data stored in the ENROLL and MOVE files. You need the following information from the ENROLL and MOVE files:

Enroll	**Move**
Last Name	Last Name
First Name	Class
Major	
Program	

Using the link function, create a file design for ROSTER that will contain data stored in the above fields in the ENROLL and MOVE files.

8.   Use the EDIT A DATA FILE DEFINITION option to make sure that all the fields have been correctly defined in the ROSTER file.

9.   Use the INPUT DATA TO A RECORD option to enter records 1 through 25 to the ROSTER file. Select the DISPLAY A RECORD OPTION and view the records in the ROSTER file.

10.   Create a report that lists the last name, first name, major, and class for each student in the ROSTER file. Print a hard copy of the report.

WestData 2.5 Problems

To complete the following problems, you will need your DOS disk, the West Instructional Software diskette, and the WestSoft/File disk. Boot up the computer, load the West Instructional Software diskette, and insert the WestSoft/File disk into drive B.

The Museum of Science and Industry, located in Toledo, Ohio, has two types of associates who participate in different programs:

■ *Exhibition Program.* Under this program, the public can get a membership that provides the following rights:
Free parking
Free access to all permanent and temporary exhibitions
Free publications (newsletter and quarterly magazine)
Discount at the gift shop

■ *Science Clubs*. Under this program, a member has access to a series of activities and can use the museum facilities allocated to each club. Currently there are three science clubs:
Club A, for specific events and lectures by major scientists
Club B, for in-house workshops
Club C, for field trips

In addition, the members of each club have the right to free parking and a discount at the gift shop. They also receive a bi-monthly publication issued by the club.
An associate can be a member of one program or of both programs.

1. A permanent file called MASTER, with general information on all associates, already exists. It has the following structure:

Field #	Field Name	Type	Length	Index	Link	Formula
1	NUMBER	N	3	Y	N	N
2	LAST NAME	A	15	Y	N	N
3	FIRST NAME	A	15	N	N	N
4	DATE BIRTH	N	8	N	N	N
5	ADDRESS	A	20	N	N	N
6	CITY	A	15	N	N	N
7	STATE	A	2	N	N	N
8	TYPE	N	1	Y	N	N

(TYPE includes 1 for exhibition membership, 2 for club membership, and 3 for both.)
Copy the MASTER file and name the copy MASTER1. Use the MASTER1 file for the remaining problems.

2. Select the DISPLAY A RECORD option and open the MASTER1 file. Enter **LAST NAME** in response to the INDEX FIELD NAME prompt. Type BAKER when the cursor moves to the field LAST NAME. Scroll through the MASTER file. How many data records are in the MASTER1 file? What is the name, address, city, and type of the associate in the last record? How do you return to the Main Menu after viewing the records?

3. Select the EDIT A DATA FILE DEFINITION option from the Main Menu and edit the file design for the MASTER1 file. Change the field lengths for the LAST NAME and FIRST NAME fields from 15 to 20. What steps did you take to do this?

4. Assume the director of the museum asks you to provide her with a report that includes all the associates. Create and then print a report that includes the following information: LAST NAME, FIRST NAME, TYPE.

5. Once again, use the DISPLAY A RECORD option and the LAST NAME BAKER to view the records in the MASTER1 file. How many associates are in both programs (TYPE 3)? Print a report listing just the first and last name of all TYPE 3 members.

6.   Copy the MASTER1 file and name the copy MASTER2. Lock the MASTER2 file. How does the locked file appear on the directory?

7.   Select the DELETE A DATA FILE option from the Main Menu and try to delete the MASTER2 file. What happens?

8.   Unlock the MASTER2 file and try to delete it again. Describe the steps needed to complete this procedure.

9.   The director of the museum now wants you to design mailing labels that include each member's last name, first name, address, city, and state. Select the MAILING LABELS option from the Main Menu and design the labels. Print out labels for all the members.

PART THREE

BASIC
Supplement

SECTION I

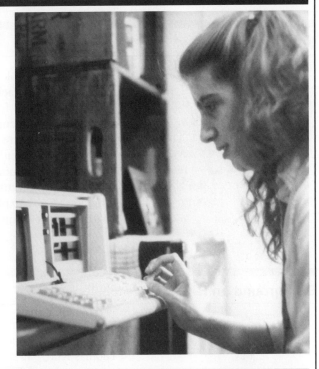

Introduction
to BASIC

Introduction

Part III of this book shows you how to write programs using Microsoft BASIC on the IBM PC. Each chapter introduces new topics in a readable, easily understood, step-by-step format. In time, you will become proficient in writing BASIC programs, but remember that learning to write computer programs is like building a house: unless there is a solid foundation, the entire house will collapse. For the time being, you should not skip around the book. Once you have a firm foundation, you can move to more advanced techniques.

This section discusses the process programmers follow to develop well-designed programs. It also explains several commands that enable you to manipulate BASIC programs—for example, to save them on a diskette or to execute them.

Background on BASIC

BASIC, an acronym for *Beginner's All-Purpose Symbolic Instruction Code*, was developed in the mid-1960s at Dartmouth College by Professors John Kemeny and Thomas Kurtz. It is a high-level language that uses English-like words and statements, such as LET, READ, and PRINT. It is easy to learn and is considered a general-purpose programming language, because it is useful for a wide variety of programming tasks.

BASIC, like English and other languages used for communication, includes rules for spelling, grammar, and punctuation. In BASIC, however, these rules are very precise and allow no exceptions. They enable the programmer to tell the computer what to do in such a way that the computer is able to carry out the instructions.

The Programming Process

A computer program is a step-by-step series of instructions which a computer can use to solve a problem. Because the computer can perform only the instructions submitted to it the program must be written precisely. In order to know what instructions are required to solve a problem efficiently, the programmer follows four steps, commonly referred to as the programming process:

1. Define the problem.
2. Design a solution.
3. Write the program.
4. Submit the program to the computer and debug and test the program.

To show how these steps are used in the programming process, we will describe a sample data processing problem: calculating a distance in miles, given the distance in kilometers.

Defining the Problem

INPUT
The data needed to solve a problem.

PROCESSING
The producing of output or information from the input or data.

OUTPUT
Information that is the result of processing.

The first step is to define the problem. To do so, we analyze it by using the basic steps involved in all data processing: **input, processing,** and **output.** Input is data used to solve the problem, output is the information that results when the problem is solved, and processing includes the steps needed to convert the input to output.

Often it is easier to determine what processing is needed by working backward: first determine what output is required, and then determine what input is needed to obtain the output. The gap between the available input and the required output is the processing needed in the program.

Determining the output for this sample is quite simple: we need to know the distance in miles. The input available is the distance in kilometers. The processing step requires a conversion factor that translates the distance in kilometers to the distance in miles. One kilometer equals 0.621 miles; hence, to calculate the distance in miles, we multiply the distance in kilometers by 0.621.

Designing a Solution

ALGORITHM
The sequence of instructions needed to solve a problem, arranged in a specific, logical order.

TOP-DOWN DESIGN
A method of solving a problem which proceeds from the general to the specific.

The second step, designing a solution, requires developing an **algorithm,** a sequence of instructions or statements arranged in a specific, logical order to solve the problem. Using **top-down design** to accomplish this step produces the most logical and efficient algorithm. When using top-down design, the programmer looks first at the most general task to be performed, then breaks this task into smaller, more specific subtasks. Top-down design makes the programmer's job easier by reducing a large task into smaller, more manageable portions that can be dealt with one at a time.

Applying this approach to the distance conversion problem, we see that the most general task is to calculate the distance in miles given the distance in kilometers. We can divide this task into at least three subtasks:

1. Input the number of kilometers to be converted.
2. Convert the distance from kilometers to miles.
3. Display the distance in miles.

Next, we examine each of these subtasks to see if any of them can be divided into smaller tasks. Because each of these three subtasks is very simple, we will not subdivide them further.

STRUCTURE CHART
A diagram that visually illustrates how a problem solution has been developed using stepwise refinement.

FLOWCHART
A graphic representation of the solution to a programming problem.

The design step of the programming process always should be accompanied by good documentation. Documentation can consist of either written or graphic descriptions of the solution. A **structure chart** graphically depicts the step-by-step breakdown, or refinement, of a problem. Figure I–1 shows a structure chart for the distance conversion problem. Because this problem is so simple, there are only two levels to this chart: Level 0 contains the general statement of the problem, and Level 1 contains the three basic steps. More complex programming problems usually contain many levels of refinement.

Once the various tasks making up the problem have been determined, we must decide what program steps are needed to perform those tasks. One way of visualizing these steps and their logical order is by using a **flowchart.** A flowchart

Figure I–1
Structure Chart for Distance
Conversion Problem

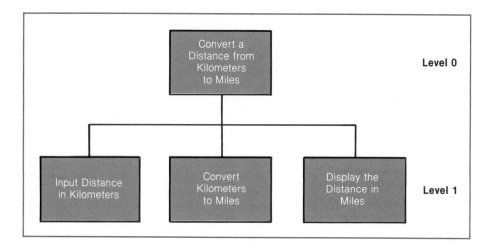

shows the actual flow of the logic of a program, whereas a structure chart simply contains statements of the levels of subproblems used to reach a solution. Flowcharts are composed of symbols that stand for various types of program operations. Figure I–2 shows some of the symbols and the steps they represent.

Figure I–3 shows a flowchart depicting the steps of the programming example. Notice how the symbols are shown in logical top-down order and connected by arrows. The first symbol shows the start of the program. The second symbol shows an input step: the distance in kilometers is entered. The third symbol shows the processing done by the program; that is, the conversion of the distance in kilometers to the distance in miles. Next, the result is displayed on the monitor. Finally, another terminal symbol signifies the end of the program. The flowchart makes it easy to see the input, processing, and output steps of the program.

Writing the Program

If the solution has been designed carefully, the next step—coding (writing) the program in a programming language—should be relatively easy. All that is required is to translate the flowchart into program statements. Figure I–4 shows the sample program written in BASIC. As you can see, many BASIC words, such as INPUT and PRINT, are easy to interpret.

Compare the coded BASIC statements in Figure I–4 to the flowchart in Figure I–3. The correspondence between the two is obvious. The remaining sections of this supplement will explain the exact meaning and use of the program statements shown in the sample program.

Submitting the Program to the Computer

The fourth step of the programming process involves sitting down at the keyboard and typing the program, line for line, into the computer. After this is done, the program can be executed. In order to execute a program, the programmer enters

Terminal symbol: Used to indicate the start or end of a program.

Process symbol: Used to represent calculations or other processing operations.

Input/Output symbol: Represents either input or output.

Decision symbol: Represents a comparison. The action taken next depends on the results of the comparison.

Connection symbol: Indicates exit from or entry to another part of the flowchart.

Preparation symbol: Indicates the dimensions of arrays, or represents initialization procedures.

Subroutine: Indicates the execution of a subroutine.

**Figure I–2
Flowcharting Symbols**

**Figure I–3
Flowchart for Distance Conversion Problem**

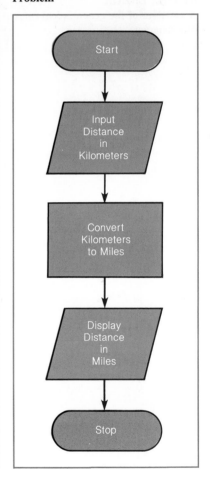

the RUN command and presses the Return key. This process will be discussed in more detail later in this chapter.

Few programs of significant length are error-free when first written. **Debugging** is the process of finding and correcting errors. Debugging should begin before the program is entered to the computer. Once the program code has been written, the

**DEBUG
To locate and correct program errors.**

Figure I–4
Distance Conversion Program

```
10  INPUT "ENTER KILOMETERS";KILOMETERS
20  LET DISTANCE = KILOMETERS * .6210001
30  PRINT "THE DISTANCE IN MILES IS ";DISTANCE
99  END
```

programmer should carefully check the typing and logic of each program statement. Errors detected in this way are far easier to correct than those found by the computer once the program has been submitted.

There are three basic types of program errors. **Syntax errors** are violations of the grammar rules of a language. Programming languages, like natural languages such as English, are governed by rules that determine how the language must be written. A frequent source of syntax errors is typing mistakes. For example, if the following BASIC statement were entered to the computer, a syntax error would occur because of the misspelling of PRINT:

SYNTAX ERROR
A violation of the grammatical rules of a language.

```
10  PRING "THE DISTANCE IN MILES IS ";D
```

RUN-TIME ERROR
An error that causes program execution to stop prematurely.

A **run-time error** occurs when the computer is unable to execute the program instructions as given. If the sample program instructed the computer to input two numbers but the user entered only one, a run-time error would occur, causing program execution to stop prematurely.

LOGIC ERROR
A flaw in an algorithm which results in the program's output being incorrect.

The worst type of error is a **logic error.** A program may be free from syntax errors and execute with no problems, yet produce incorrect output because the logic does not properly solve the problem. For instance, if an incorrect formula for converting kilometers to miles were used in the sample program, the output would be incorrect even though no error messages appeared. Logic errors can be detected only by carefully examining the program output and comparing it to the expected results. Figure I–5 shows the execution results of the distance conversion program. Check the answer by hand to see if it is correct.

Testing a program involves running it with a variety of data to determine if the results are always correct. A program may produce correct results when it is run with one set of data, but incorrect results when run with different data. The distance conversion program could be tested by using a variety of values for the number of kilometers to be converted.

This sample program is relatively simple, but it shows each of the steps required to complete a program. Although other problems may be more complex, the steps involved are the same. Successful programming can come about only through the diligent application of the four steps in the programming process.

Getting Started

The IBM Personal Computer runs an enhanced version of Microsoft BASIC. There are two versions of BASIC on the IBM Personal Computer: Disk and Advanced.

**Figure I–5
Output of Distance Conversion
Program**

```
RUN
ENTER KILOMETERS? 500
THE DISTANCE IN MILES IS    310.5001
```

Disk BASIC (referred to simply as BASIC) has the ability to input data from diskette and to output data to diskette, and an internal clock that keeps track of the date and time. Advanced BASIC, known as BASICA, has these same capabilities but also offers advanced graphic and sound support. The commands and statements for BASIC and BASICA are the same, except for some graphics and sound features that are offered only in BASICA. Because the last chapter of this

Learning Check

1. The steps in an algorithm can be listed in any order. True or false?

2. Top-down design always proceeds from the _____ to the _____.

3. A(n) _____ _____ is a diagram that depicts the levels of refinement of a problem solution.

4. A(n) _____ is used to represent the logic of a programming problem solution visually.

5. _____ is the process of writing a problem solution in a programming language.

Answers

1. false 2. general, specific 3. structure chart 4. flowchart 5. coding

section deals with graphics and sound, we will use BASICA in that chapter; until then, however, we will use BASIC.

To start BASIC on an IBM PC with standard configuration (two external drives, no hard disk), you need to start DOS (disk operating system). To do so, place the DOS diskette into Drive A, the left drive. Then turn on the computer. The power switch is located at the right rear of the machine. Remember to turn on the monitor and to turn up the brightness dial, too. Once the DOS has been booted, or loaded, the computer asks for the date and time. If you do not wish to enter the date and/ or time, merely press the [↵] (Return) key after each of the prompts, which appear as follows:

```
Current date is Tue  1-01-1980
Enter new date:
Current time is  0:00:08.95
Enter new time:
```

After you have responded to the time prompt and pressed [↵] , the computer responds with a display similar to the following:

```
The IBM Personal Computer DOS
Version 2.10 (C)Copyright IBM Corp 1981,1982,1983
A>
```

The A> is the DOS prompt. Type BASIC and press [↵] to load the disk BASIC interpreter. The screen will look similar to this:

```
The IBM Personal Computer Basic
Version D2.10 Copyright IBM Corp. 1981, 1982, 1983
61327 Bytes free
Ok
```

Notice the word "Ok" on the screen. It is the BASIC prompt, which tells you the computer is ready to accept BASIC commands and statements.

DOS Commands

Chapter 3 introduced DOS commands, which we will review in this section. These commands are executed at the DOS level (that is, at the A> symbol).

The FORMAT command enables you to prepare a disk so that files can be stored on it. The command

FORMAT *drive:*

allows you to specify the drive the disk to be formatted is in. For example,

FORMAT B:

would format the disk currently in Drive B.

The DISKCOPY command enables you to make backup copies of disks, as a precaution in case a disk is damaged. The command

DISKCOPY A: B

copies the contents of the disk currently in Drive A to the disk in Drive B. If your system only has one drive, use the following command:

DISKCOPY A:

You will then be instructed to remove the disk being copied and to place the target disk into the drive. Both commands, FORMAT and DISKCOPY, can be used without qualifiers. If you do use only the FORMAT or DISKCOPY command, a prompt will appear on the screen telling you what to do next.

The DIR (short for directory) command displays the names of all files stored on the disk.

To remove a file from a disk, use either the ERASE or the DEL command:

ERASE *filename*

or

DEL *filename*

A file can easily be copied by using the COPY command:

COPY *sourcedrive: filename targetdrive:*

To change the name of a file, use RENAME:

RENAME *drive: oldfilename newfilename*

BASIC Commands

Whereas DOS commands are entered at DOS level (A>), BASIC commands are entered while you are in BASIC mode, which is indicated by the Ok prompt. To get into the BASIC mode, simply type BASIC, as we showed you before:

A>BASIC

IMMEDIATE MODE
The BASIC mode in which commands are executed as soon as the RETURN key is pressed: it is used without line numbers.

and press ⏎ . You must be in the BASIC mode to enter BASIC commands and programs. BASIC commands are **immediate-mode** instructions; that is, they are executed as soon as the carriage control key (⏎) is pressed. They differ from BASIC language statements, which usually are not executed until the program is run. The most commonly used BASIC commands are discussed in this section.

NEW

The NEW command tells the computer that the programmer is ready to enter a new program. It does so by instructing the computer to erase any programs in main memory, thereby making room for the new program. The syntax is as follows:

NEW

If you want to store the program currently in main memory for future use, you must save it on a diskette (see SAVE) before entering the NEW command. Otherwise, the NEW command will erase the old program from main memory to make room for the new program, and you will not be able to recover it.

RUN

EXECUTE
To carry out the instructions in a program.

To see if a program works, use the RUN command. This command will cause the computer to **execute** the program currently in main memory. That is, the computer will carry out the instructions in the program.

There are three forms of the RUN command. The first form simply executes the program currently in memory from start to finish (unless an error is encountered). In the following example the last line is the output from the one line program that is executed when the computer receives the RUN command.

RUN ↵

For example:

```
10 PRINT "THIS IS A TEST"
RUN
```

```
THIS IS A TEST
```

The second form also executes the program currently in main memory, but it begins at the line number that you indicate. (A line number accompanies every program statement, as discussed in the next chapter.) The syntax is as follows:

RUN line number ↵

For example:

```
10 PRINT "THIS IS"
20 PRINT "A TEST"
30 PRINT "ON RUN"
40 PRINT "COMMANDS"
```

RUN 30

ON RUN
COMMANDS

The third form gets a program from the diskette, puts it into main memory, and runs it. This form erases any program currently in main memory. The syntax is as follows:

RUN ''filename'' ⏎

(The ''filename'' is the name given to the program when it is saved on diskette, as discussed later in this chapter.)
For example:

RUN "PAYROLL"

This command gets the program PAYROLL from the diskette, places it into main memory, and executes it.

Notice that quotation marks have been placed around the filename. The set of quotation marks on the right side of the filename is optional. Thus the file PAYROLL could also be executed by this statement:

RUN "PAYROLL

SAVE

Once a program has been entered into main memory, you can save it on a diskette by using the SAVE command. This command copies the program from main memory, which is temporary, to a diskette for long-term storage. Once the program is copied to a diskette, the programmer can perform other tasks that access the computer's main memory without worrying about erasing or changing the program. The syntax is

SAVE ''filename''

For example:

SAVE "PAYROLL"

This command saves the program in main memory under the filename PAYROLL. As with the RUN command, the set of quotation marks on the right side of the filename is optional. Thus the filename PAYROLL could also be saved by this statement:

SAVE "PAYROLL

The filename is the name given to the program to be saved on the diskette. It must contain eight or fewer characters. If a file already on the diskette has the same name as the filename just used, the old file will be written over and lost.

LOAD

A program that has been saved is stored on a diskette. When it is needed, it can be retrieved from the diskette and placed into the computer's main memory. This procedure is called loading a program, and it is carried out by the BASIC command LOAD. When the program you request is retrieved from the diskette and placed into main memory, any program currently in main memory is erased.

There are two basic forms of the LOAD command. The first form simply loads the specified program from the diskette into main memory. The syntax is as follows:

LOAD ''filename'' ⏎

For example:

LOAD "PAYROLL"

The second form of the command loads the specified program from the diskette to the computer's main memory and then runs it. The syntax is as shown here:

LOAD ''filename'',R ⏎

For example:

LOAD "PAYROLL",R

This command loads the program PAYROLL and executes it.

LIST

It is often necessary to view part or all of a program that is being worked on. The LIST command displays the program that is currently in main memory, either on the screen or on the printer. There are two basic forms of the LIST command, one to list the entire program and the other to list only part of the program.

To view the entire program in main memory, use the following syntax:

LIST ⏎

This command lists on the screen the program that is in main memory.

SCROLL
To move vertically off the top of the monitor screen.

When the LIST command is used to display a program on the monitor screen, the program **scrolls;** that is, the display image moves vertically in such a way that the next line of the program appears at the bottom of the text already on the screen. If your program contains more lines than the number of lines your screen is capable of displaying, part of it will disappear off the top of the screen. For example, if your program contains 40 lines but your screen only has a 24-line capacity, the first 16 lines will move vertically off the top of the screen. Scrolling occurs so quickly that the program disappears from the screen before you can read it. There is a way to control the display, however, thus enabling you to see a portion of the program and then continue displaying the remaining portion of the program.

Table I-1
LIST Command

Command	Explanation
LIST	List the entire program on the screen.
LIST,"LPT1:"	List the entire program on the printer.
LIST 10	List line 10 on the screen.
LIST 10-20	List lines 10 through 20 on the screen.
LIST 10-20,"LPT1:"	List lines 10 through 20 on the printer.
LIST 100 -	List the program from line 100 to the end of the program.
LIST -200	List the program from beginning through line 200.

This is known as controlling the scroll, and it is done by holding down the <Ctrl> key and pressing the <NumLock> key *at the same time*. To continue scrolling, simply press any key other than [↑] , <Break>, or <Ins>. To stop the LIST command once it has been started, press the <Ctrl> and <Break> keys at the same time.

To view a portion of the program, use the following syntax:

LIST line1 - line2

The lines from line1 through line2 are displayed. This form of the LIST command has several options. If only line1 is given, with the hyphen following it, that line and all higher-numbered lines are listed. If only line2 is given, with the hyphen preceding it, all lines from the beginning of the program through line2 are listed. If only line1 is given and no hyphen follows it, only that line is printed. (See Table I–1 for the forms of the LIST command.)

All of the LIST commands discussed here can be used to print all or part of the program to a printer, if the "LPT1:" extension is added to the end of the LIST command before the [↵] key is typed. For example:

LIST,"LPT1:" [↵]

"LPT1:" stands for line printer. This extension, preceded by a comma, tells the computer to print to the printer.

FILES and KILL

The FILES command lists all of the files stored on a disk. It works in the same way as the DOS DIR command, except that the DIR command is used at DOS level (the A> symbol), whereas FILES is used in BASIC mode.

The KILL command is used to delete a file that is saved on disk. Again, it is used in BASIC mode, whereas DEL is used to remove files at DOS level. The format of the KILL command is as shown here:

KILL "filename"

Learning Check

1. When is the NEW command used?

2. What is the syntax of the instruction to execute a program that has been saved on a diskette?

3. The LOAD command erases anything currently in the computer's main memory. True or false?

4. What is the command to list a program through Line 990 on the printer?

Answers

1. When the programmer is ready to enter a new program.   2. RUN "filename"   3. true   4. LIST -990,"LPT1:"

Summary Points

- BASIC (*B*eginner's *A*ll-Purpose *S*ymbolic *I*nstruction *C*ode) was developed in the mid-1960s by Professors John G. Kemeny and Thomas E. Kurtz at Dartmouth College.
- The four steps in the programming process are (1) Define the problem, (2) Design a solution, (3) Write the program, and (4) Submit the program to the computer, and debug and test it.
- Programs are best designed by the top-down approach, in which a large task is divided into smaller and smaller subtasks, moving from the general to the specific.
- Program design can be documented by structure charts to show the results of the top-down design process, and by flowcharts to display the order and type of program steps to be performed.
- BASIC has rules of grammar (syntax) to which programmers must adhere.
- The BASIC NEW command clears any programs in the computer's main memory, in preparation for a new program.
- The RUN command causes the computer to execute a program.
- The SAVE command transfers a program from main memory to diskette.
- The LOAD command places a saved program into main memory.
- The LIST command is used to display on the screen or printer all or part of a program that is in main memory.
- The FILES command lists files on disk.
- The KILL command deletes a stated file.

Review Questions

1. What are the steps in the programming process?
2. What is an algorithm, and what is its importance to programmers?
3. What information is needed to define a problem?
4. Design a solution to the problem of making a pizza, using the top-down approach. Draw a structure chart to document your design.
5. List the three types of program errors.
6. Why are logic errors in a program difficult to detect?
7. Name the seven BASIC commands presented in this chapter.
8. Give examples of the three different ways the LIST command can be used.
9. What does the SAVE command do?
10. When is the NEW command used? What does it do?

SECTION II

Getting Started
with BASIC

Introduction

In this section, you will learn how to write simple BASIC programs, including those that perform mathematical operations. Four BASIC statements are covered: REM, assignment, PRINT, and END. These statements will build a strong foundation for future programming, so it is important that you understand clearly how to use them.

Data Types

Two general types of data values are used within a program: numeric and string. BASIC enables the programmer to use these data types in two different ways, as constants or as variables. The following discussion clarifies the uses of these data types and the differences between them.

Constants

CONSTANT
A value that cannot change during program execution.

Constants are values that do not change during the execution of a program. There are two types of constants: numeric and character string.

Numeric Constants

A numeric constant is a number that is included in a BASIC statement (other than line numbers, which are discussed later). Numeric constants can be represented as real or as integer numbers.

A real constant is a number with a decimal part. The following are valid real constants:

6.0	6.782
.95	0.58
-7.302	-0.09

Very small or very large numbers can be represented in scientific notation (also called exponential notation), which has the following form: $\pm x.xxxxE \pm n$. The symbol $\pm$ represents the sign of the number, positive or negative. The E in the number represents the number 10, and the signed number following the E is the power to which 10 is raised. The symbol x.xxxx is called the mantissa, and it represents a number that may be carried to a maximum of eight decimal places. Table II-1 gives some examples of numbers in exponential notation.

An integer constant is a number with no decimal portion. The following numbers are examples of integer constants:

B-21

Table II-1
Examples of Exponential Notation

Decimal	Power Equivalent	Scientific Notation
53860	5.386×10^4	5.386E + 04
0.00531	5.31×10^{-3}	5.31E − 03
− 658310	$−6.5831 \times 10^5$	− 6.5831E + 05

```
29      123765
453     − 25
204     − 101
```

The following rules must be observed when using numbers in BASIC.

1. No commas can be embedded within numbers, because the computer interprets the digits before and after a comma as belonging to two separate numbers. For example, the computer would interpret 3,751 as the number 3 *and* the number 751. The valid form of the number is 3751.
2. If a number is negative, it must be preceded by a minus sign, as in the example − 21.
3. If no sign is included, the number is assumed to be positive: 56 is the same as + 56.
4. Fractions must be written in decimal form. For example, 2.75 is the correct representation for 2¾.

Character String Constants

A character string constant is a collection of symbols called alphanumeric characters. These can include any combination of letters, numbers, and special characters. The character string is enclosed in double quotation marks. The following are examples of character string constants:

"April 25, 1986"
"Friday night we went out for dinner."
"My name is Sam!"

Variables

VARIABLE
A storage location whose contents can change during program execution.

Values that can change during the execution of a program are **variables.** Variable names can be of any length, but the IBM PC recognizes only the first 40 characters of a name. The name must begin with a letter, followed by letters, numbers and a decimal point, with no embedded blanks. There are two types of variables, numeric and string, as explained in the following paragraphs.

**Table II-2
Valid Numeric and String Variable
Names**

Numeric	String
SUM (Real)	HEADING$
D6E7% (Integer)	DAY$
M1% (Integer)	M1$
AMT (Real)	NME$

Numeric Variables

A numeric variable is used to store a number that is either supplied to the computer by the programmer or internally calculated during program execution. As with numeric constants, there are both integer and real numeric variables. Integer variable names have a percent sign (%) as the last character. Some examples of integer variable names are EMP%, PAY%, and X%. Real variable names do not have to end with a special character GROSSPAY, RTE, and PRCNT are all real variables. It is possible to assign an integer value to a real variable, however, because the computer can convert the integer to a real number without changing its value. For example, the integer 17 can be assigned to the real variable name NMBR because it can be changed to the real number 17.0.

Character String Variables

A character string variable is used to store a character string, such as a name, an address, or a social security number. A string variable name must be terminated with a dollar sign($). Table II-2 shows valid numeric and character string variable names.

Reserved Words

**RESERVED WORD
A word that has a specific meaning to the BASIC system and therefore cannot be used as a variable name.**

Certain words have specific meanings in the BASIC language. These are called **reserved words,** and they cannot be used as variable names. Table II-3 lists all the reserved words in PC BASIC.

Line Numbers

**INDIRECT MODE
The mode in which BASIC statements are not executed until the RUN command is given. The statements must have line numbers.**

As mentioned earlier, BASIC commands usually are executed in immediate or direct mode. BASIC statements, or instructions, can be executed in either direct mode or **indirect mode.** In indirect mode, the statements are executed until the RUN command is given. **Line numbers** tell the computer that the statements

Table II-3
Reserved Words in BASIC

ABS	EOF	LPRINT	RIGHT$
AND	EQV	LSET	RND
ASC	ERASE	MERGE	RSET
ATN	ERL	MID$	RUN
AUTO	ERR	MKD$	SAVE
BEEP	ERROR	MKI$	SCREEN
BLOAD	EXP	MKS$	SGN
BSAVE	FIELD	MOD	SIN
CALL	FILES	MOTOR	SOUND
CDBL	FIX	NAME	SPACE$
CHAIN	FN*xxxxx*	NEW	SPC(
CHR$	FOR	NEXT	SQR
CINT	FRE	NOT	STEP
CIRCLE	GET	OCT$	STICK
CLEAR	GOSUB	OFF	STOP
CLOSE	GOTO	ON	STR$
CLS	HEX$	OPEN	STRIG
COLOR	IF	OPTION	STRING$
COM	IMP	OR	SWAP
COMMON	INKEY$	OUT	SYSTEM
CONT	INP	PAINT	TAB(
COS	INPUT	PEEK	TAN
CSNG	INPUT#	PEN	THEN
CSRLIN	INPUT$	PLAY	TIME$
CVD	INSTR	POINT	TO
CVI	INT	POKE	TROFF
CVS	KEY	POS	TRON
DATA	KILL	PRESET	USING
DATE$	LEFT$	PRINT	USR
DEF	LEN	PRINT#	VAL
DEFDBL	LET	PSET	VARPTR
DEFINT	LINE	PUT	VARPTR$
DEFSNG	LIST	RANDOMIZE	WAIT
DEFSTR	LLIST	READ	WEND
DELETE	LOAD	REM	WHILE
DIM	LOC	RENUM	WIDTH
DRAW	LOCATE	RESET	WRITE
EDIT	LOF	RESTORE	WRITE#
ELSE	LOG	RESUME	XOR
END	LPOS	RETURN	

LINE NUMBER
A number preceding a BASIC statement which is used to reference the statement and determine its order of execution.

following them are to be executed in indirect mode. Therefore, the computer does not execute numbered statements until it is instructed to do so.

Line numbers determine the sequence of execution of BASIC statements. They also are used as reference points for branching and editing (which are discussed later). Figure II-1 gives an example of a program using line numbers.

Line numbers must be integers between 0 and 65529. No commas or embedded spaces can be included in a line number. Line numbers do not have to be in increments of 1. In fact, it is best to use increments of 10 or 20, in order to allow for insertion of lines at a later time if necessary. Here is a simple example:

```
60 LET NUMBER = 10
70 PRINT NUMBER,NUMBER1
```

If you determine later that a line has been omitted, you can enter it out of sequence as shown here:

```
60 LET NUMBER = 10
70 PRINT NUMBER,NUMBER1
65 LET NUMBER1 = 11
```

When this program segment is listed, the lines are rearranged in their numeric order.

If you find that you have made an error on a line, simply retype the line number and the correct BASIC statement. This procedure corrects the error because, if two lines are entered with the same line number, the computer saves and executes only the most recently typed one. To demonstrate this fact, assume that line 160 should print SUM, but the following was typed instead:

```
160 PRINT SUN
```

Figure II-1
Program Showing Use of Line Numbers

```
10 REM * * * THIS PROGRAM ADDS TWO NUMBERS * * *
20 LET A = 9
30 LET D1 = 4
40 LET P3 = A + D1
50 PRINT "THE ANSWER IS ";P3
99 END

RUN
THE ANSWER IS  13
```

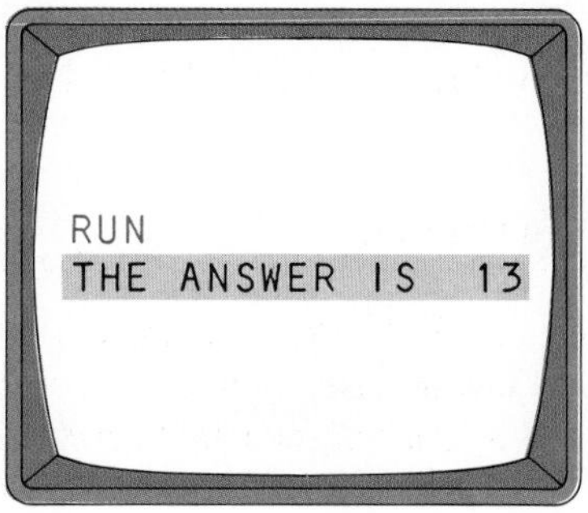

To correct this, simply retype line 160 as follows:

```
160 PRINT SUM
```

The computer discards the current line 160 and replaces it with the newest version of line 160.

Learning Check

1. Real numbers are numbers that do not include a decimal portion. True or false?

2. Which of the following are valid real variable names?
   a. CX   b. AA$ c. TOM%

3. How would you write the following in exponential notation?
   a. 73.92   b. 0.00010   c. 93240

4. Name the two ways numeric and character strings can be used in BASIC.

5. What are the two main purposes of line numbers?

Answers

1. false 2. a 3a. 7.392E-1 3b. 1.0E-4 3c. 9.3240E+4 4. Constants and variables
5. Line numbers tell the computer the order in which to execute program statements. They also tell the computer that the following statements are to be executed in indirect mode.

Elementary BASIC Statements

BASIC statements are composed of programming command words (special words recognized by the BASIC system) and elements of the language: constants, numeric and string variables, and operators. A BASIC program is a sequence of statements which tells the computer how to solve a problem. Figure II-2 is an example. This program calculates the gross pay of an employee whose wage rate is $4.50 an hour and who has worked 40 hours. We will now turn our attention to four elementary BASIC statements: REM, LET, PRINT, and END.

The REM Statement

DOCUMENTATION
Comments that explain a program to people; documentation is ignored by the computer.

REM, short for REMark, is a statement that provides information for the programmer or anyone else reading the program. It is ignored by the computer; in other words, it is a nonexecutable statement. This information is referred to as **documentation,** and its function is to explain the purpose of the program, what the variable names represent, or any special instructions for the benefit of human

Figure II-2
Gross Pay Program

```
10 REM * * * THIS PROGRAM COMPUTES AN * * *
20 REM * * * EMPLOYEE'S GROSS PAY.    * * *
30 REM
40 LET RTE = 4.5
50 LET HOURS = 40
60 LET PAY = RTE * HOURS
70 PRINT "GROSS PAY = $ ";PAY
99 END
```

```
RUN
GROSS PAY = $ 180
```

readers. Because REM statements do not affect program execution, they can be placed anywhere in the program. The only restriction is that the statement must begin with the reserved word REM.

The format for the REM statement is as follows:

line# REM comment

The comment can be any statement that the programmer regards as appropriate documentation. Figure II-3 is a sample program that uses the REM statement. Lines 10 and 20 describe the purpose of the program. Lines 30 through 70 explain the major variables that are used in the program. These lines are helpful to a reader who is not the original programmer. Notice that line 80 contains no comment after the REM statement. This statement makes the program listing easier to read by separating the opening remarks from the executable statements listed later in the program.

Notice the asterisks that surround the descriptive comments. Although this device is simply a matter of personal taste, many programmers use asterisks to separate comments from the rest of the program. This technique allows the REM statement to be identified easily when the programmer is looking through long program listings.

The Assignment Statement

ASSIGNMENT STATEMENT
A statement that causes a value to be stored in a variable.

The LET Statement is an **assignment statement**—that is, a statement that stores a value in the memory location allotted to the specified variable. In a flowchart, an assignment statement is illustrated by a processing symbol (☐). The general format of the LET statement is as follows:

line# LET variable = expression

```
10   REM * * * THE PURPOSE OF THIS PROGRAM IS    * * *
20   REM * * * TO COMPUTE AN AVERAGE TEST SCORE  * * *
30   REM * * * MAJOR VARIABLES:                  * * *
40   REM * * *    FTEST    FIRST TEST SCORE      * * *
50   REM * * *    STEST    SECOND TEST SCORE     * * *
60   REM * * *    TTEST    THIRD TEST SCORE      * * *
70   REM * * *    AV       AVERAGE               * * *
80   REM
90   LET FTEST = 89
100  LET STEST = 85
110  LET TTEST = 78
120  LET AV = (FTEST + STEST + TTEST) / 3
130  PRINT "AVERAGE ",AV
999  END
```

```
RUN
AVERAGE          84
```

**Figure II-3
Program Showing Use of the REM
Statement**

The variable can be a numeric or string variable. If it is a numeric variable, the expression can be a numeric constant, an arithmetic formula, or another numeric variable. If the variable is a string variable, the expression can be either a string constant or another string variable.

The LET statement can be used to assign values to numeric or string variables directly, or to assign the results of a calculation to a numeric variable. In either case, the expression on the right side of the equal sign is assigned to the variable on the left side. This operation causes the value of the expression to be placed in the memory location identified by the variable name on the left side of the LET statement.

In Figure II-3, lines 90 through 110 assign three numeric constants to three numeric variables. Line 120 assigns the result of an arithmetic calculation to the numeric variable AV, which represents the average of the three scores. Table II-4 shows some valid and invalid examples of the LET statements.

The use of the reserved word LET is optional. Therefore, the following two lines are equivalent:

```
10 LET X = A + B
10     X = A + B
```

For simplicity's sake, we will discontinue using the LET in programs after this chapter.

Table II-4
Valid and Invalid LET Statements

```
INVALID                                              VALID
LET 8 + B = X                                        LET X = 8 + B
LET T$ = A                                           LET T$ = A$
LET B$ = DON                                         LET B$ = "DON"
LET X = "PAUL"                                       LET X = 34
LET L + M = K                                        LET K = L + M
```

Arithmetic Expressions. In BASIC, arithmetic expressions are composed of constants, numeric variables, and arithmetic operators. Table II-5 shows the arithmetic operators that can be used.

Some examples of valid arithmetic expressions in assignment statements are shown here:

```
10 LET VOLUME = LNGTH * WDTH * HGHT
20 LET AREA = (BASE * HGHT) / 2
30 LET SUM = A + 7
```

Hierarchy of Operations. When more than one operation is to be performed within an arithmetic expression, the computer follows a **hierarchy,** or priority, **of operations.** If parentheses are present in an expression, as they are in line 20 of the preceding example, the operation within the parentheses is performed first. If parentheses are nested—that is, if one set of parentheses is inside another—the operation in the innermost set of parentheses is performed first. Thus, in the following expression, the first operation to be performed is to add 2 to the value in Y:

HIERARCHY OF OPERATIONS
The order in which arithmetic operations are performed. In BASIC the order is: (1) anything in parentheses, (2) exponentiation, (3) multiplication and division, and (4) addition and subtraction.

$$30 * (8 - 5 / (2 + Y) * 6)$$

In the absence of parentheses, operations are performed according to the rules of priority shown in Table II-6. Operations with high priority are performed before operations with lower priority (subject to parentheses). If more than one operation is to be performed at the same level, as in the following expression, the computer evaluates them from left to right:

Table II-5
BASIC Arithmetic Symbols

BASIC Arithmetic Operation Symbol	Operation	Arithmetic Example	BASIC Expression
+	Addition	A + B	A + B
−	Subtraction	A − B	A − B
*	Multiplication	A × B	A * B
/	Division	A ÷ B	A / B
^	Exponentiation	A^B	A ^ B

Table II-6
Rules of Priority

Priority	Operation	Symbol
First	Exponentiation	^
Second	Multiplication or division	*, /
Third	Addition or subtraction	+, −

$$5 * 4 / 2$$

In this example, the 5 would be multiplied by 4, and then the result, 20, would be divided by 2. The answer is 10.

The following are more examples of these hierarchical rules:

Statement	Computer Evaluation
1. Y = 2 * 5 + 1	First: 2 * 5 = 10 Second: 10 + 1 = 11 Result: Y = 11
2. Y = 2 * (5 + 1)	First: 5 + 1 = 6 Second: 2 * 6 = 12 Result: Y = 12
3. Y = (3 + (6 + 2) /4) + 10 ^ 2	First: 6 + 2 = 8 Second: 8 / 4 = 2 Third: 3 + 2 = 5 Fourth: 10 ^ 2 = 100 Fifth: 5 + 100 = 105 Result: Y = 105

Two operators cannot be placed next to each other. For example, the expression P/ − X is invalid, because parentheses should be used to separate the operators. Thus, P/(− X) is valid.

The PRINT Statement

The PRINT statement is used to print or display the results of computer processing. It also permits formatting, or arranging, of output. The PRINT statement can take several forms, depending on the output required. In a flowchart, a PRINT statement is illustrated by the input/output symbol (⬛). The general format of the PRINT statement is as shown here:

$$\text{line\# PRINT} \begin{cases} \text{variables} \\ \text{literals} \\ \text{arithmetic expressions} \\ \text{any combination of the above} \end{cases}$$

If more than one item is included in the PRINT statement, the items are separated by commas. These commas also are used to format or arrange the output; this topic is discussed in detail in the next chapter. For now, it is sufficient to know that the commas automatically space the items across the output line.

Printing the Values of Variables. We can tell the computer to print values assigned to storage locations by using the reserved word PRINT with the variables listed after it:

    100 PRINT AMOUNT,DAY,YEAR

Printing has no effect on the contents of the storage location. The PRINT statement only gets the value of a variable and prints it to the monitor screen.

LITERAL
An expression in a PRINT statement which contains any combination of letters, numbers, and/or special characters.

Printing Literals. A **literal** is an expression consisting of alphabetic, numeric, or special characters, or a combination of any of these. It is essentially the same as a constant, but the term *literal* is applied to constants used in PRINT statements. There are two types: character string literals and numeric literals.

A character string literal is a group of letters, numbers, or special characters enclosed in quotation marks. Whatever is inside the quotation marks is printed. For example,

    10 PRINT "EXAMPLES$%#"

would appear on the screen as

    EXAMPLES$%#

Note that the quotation marks are not printed.

Literals can be used to print headings in output. To print column headings, for example, put each heading in quotation marks and separate them with commas:

    50 PRINT "ITEM","PRICE","QUANTITY"

When line 50 is executed, the following output appears:

    ITEM   PRICE   QUANTITY

Numeric literals are numbers placed within the PRINT statement which are printed in the output. They do not have to be enclosed in quotation marks. For example, the statement

    40 PRINT 100

prints the following:

    100

Printing the Values of Expressions.   The computer can print not only the values of literals and variables, but also the values of arithmetic expressions. Consider the following program segment:

```
50 LET X = 15.0
60 LET Y = 26.0
70 PRINT (X + Y) / 2,X / Y
```

The computer evaluates each expression in line 70, according to the hierarchy of operations, and then prints the result:

```
20.5    .5769231
```

If the expression has an extremely large or small positive or negative value, the computer may print it in exponential notation.

Printing Blank Lines.   A blank line in output makes the output more readable, and can be achieved by using a PRINT statement alone:

```
100 PRINT
```

To skip more than one line, simply include more than one such statement:

```
110 PRINT
120 PRINT
```

The END Statement

The END statement instructs the computer to stop program execution. In a flow-chart, it is indicated by the termination symbol (⬭). The general format of the END statement is as follows:

line# END

To make the END statement readily identifiable, many programmers give it a line number of all 9's, such as 999. All programs in this supplement follow this practice.

Comprehensive Programming Problem

Problem Definition

Smith's Warehouse needs a program to calculate its monthly ending inventory and the value of that inventory. Smith's has provided you with the following inventory data:

Beginning inventory = 430 units
Receipts = 86 units
Orders issued = 112 units
Cost per unit = $11.50

The program should produce a report that displays the beginning inventory, receipts, orders issued, ending inventory, and the value of the ending inventory.

The input and output for the program are easily seen. The input is simply the data given, and the output consists of three of the input values, plus two calculated values: the ending inventory and its value. Because the output is in the form of a report, an appropriate heading also should be displayed. The processing requires a formula to calculate the ending inventory:

Ending inventory = Beginning inventory + Receipts − Orders issued

From the result, we can calculate the value of the ending inventory using the following formula:

Value of ending inventory = Ending inventory × Cost per unit

With the input, processing, and output defined, we must now design a solution.

Solution Design

We now consider the general problem of producing the specified report, and see if it can be divided into subproblems. Keeping in mind the flow of data processing, we can determine at least three smaller tasks to be performed:

1. Access the given data.
2. Perform the calculations.
3. Display the report.

The second step involves two formulas, so this step can be further divided as follows:

2.A. Calculate the ending inventory.
2.B. Calculate the ending inventory value.

The report should contain a heading plus the requested values, so the third step can be divided as follows:

3.A. Display a heading.
3.B. Display the requested values.

All of the tasks listed are pictured in the structure chart in Figure II-4.

Next we need to consider what program steps will accomplish these tasks. A flowchart of a possible solution is shown in Figure II-5. In order to use the given data, we assign the input values to variables. Next, the two calculations are performed. A heading is then printed, followed by the needed values.

Figure II-4
Structure Chart for Inventory
Program

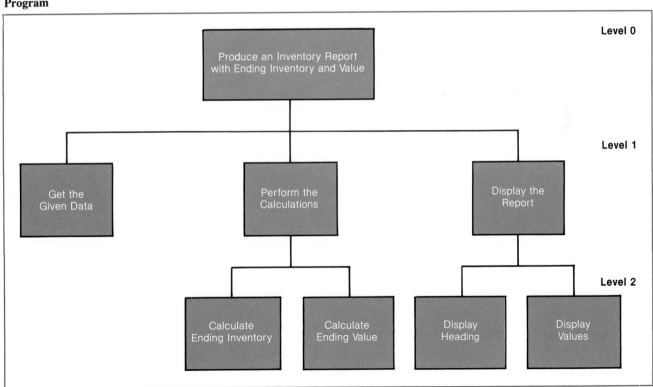

Figure II-5
Flowchart for Inventory Program

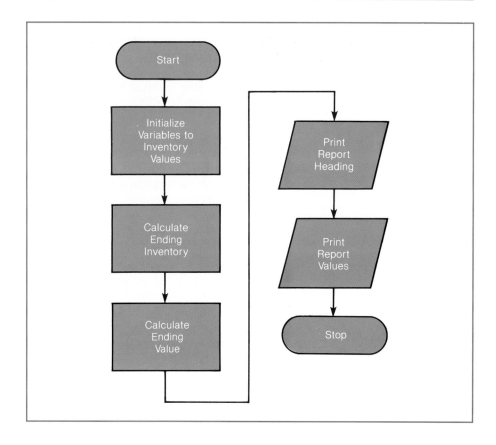

The Program

Figure II-6 shows the listing and output of this program. The REM statements in lines 10 through 110 document the purpose of the program and the contents of the variables. Lines 130, 190, and 230 give descriptions of the statements that follow them. Lines 140 through 170 assign the inventory values to variables. Line 200 calculates the ending inventory and assigns it to EINV. The result is then multiplied by the cost per unit in line 210. This operation yields the value of the ending inventory and assigns it to the variable VLUE.

Lines 240 and 250 improve the readability of the output by causing two blank lines to be printed before the next statement, line 260, prints the heading of the report. Each of the remaining PRINT statements prints a label for a field of output, followed by the field value. The program concludes with the END statement.

Summary Points

■ Constants are values that do not change during program execution. A valid numeric constant is any integer or real number. Character strings are alphanumeric data enclosed in quotation marks.

```
10   REM * * * THIS PROGRAM COMPUTES THE MONTHLY ENDING INVENTORY * * *
20   REM * * * AND VALUE FOR SMITH'S WAREHOUSE, AND PRINTS AN IN-  * * *
30   REM * * * VENTORY REPORT.                                     * * *
40   REM
50   REM * * * MAJOR VARIABLES:                                    * * *
60   REM * * *    BINV        BEGINNING INVENTORY                  * * *
70   REM * * *    EINV        ENDING INVENTORY                     * * *
80   REM * * *    ISSUED      NUMBER OF UNITS ISSUED               * * *
90   REM * * *    RECPT       NUMBER OF UNITS RECEIVED             * * *
100  REM * * *    CST         COST PER UNIT                        * * *
110  REM * * *    VLUE        ENDING INVENTORY VALUE               * * *
120  REM
130  REM * * * ASSIGN THE INPUT VALUES TO THE VARIABLES. * * *
140  LET BINV = 430
150  LET RECPT = 86
160  LET ISSUED = 112
170  LET CST = 11.5
180  REM
190  REM * * *  CALCULATE THE ENDING INVENTORY AND VALUE. * * *
200  LET EINV = BINV + RECPT - ISSUED
210  LET VLUE = EINV * CST
220  REM
230  REM * * * PRINT THE INVENTORY REPORT. * * *
240  PRINT
250  PRINT
260  PRINT "INVENTORY STATUS"
270  PRINT
280  PRINT "BEGIN INV.",BINV
290  PRINT "RECEIPTS",RECPT
300  PRINT "ISSUED",ISSUED
310  PRINT "ENDING INV.",EINV
320  PRINT "VALUE  $",VLUE
999  END
```

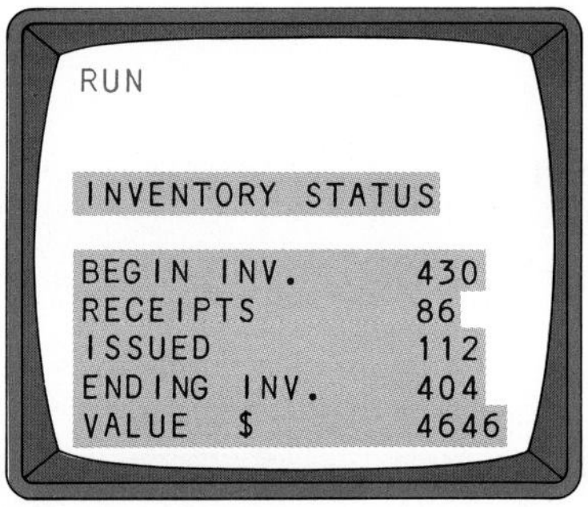

```
RUN

INVENTORY STATUS

BEGIN INV.      430
RECEIPTS         86
ISSUED          112
ENDING INV.     404
VALUE   $      4646
```

Figure II-6
Inventory Program

■ Variables are storage locations containing values that can change during program execution. Variable names are programmer-supplied names that identify specific variables. Numeric variables represent numbers. String variables contain character strings; their names are distinguished from those of numeric variables by the $ symbol used as the last character.

■ Line numbers serve to specify the order of execution of the program statements, and also to label statements so that they can be referenced.

■ Using line numbers in large increments, such as 10, permits easy insertion of new statements.

■ A BASIC statement is composed of reserved words, constants, variables, and operators.

■ REM statements document the program; they are not executed by the computer.

■ The purpose of the LET statement is to assign values to variables. The computer evaluates the expression on the right side of the equal sign and stores its value in the variable on the left side of the equal sign.

■ Arithmetic expressions are evaluated according to a hierarchy of operations: (1) operations in parentheses, (2) exponentiation, (3) multiplication or division, and (4) addition or subtraction. Multiple operations at the same level are evaluated from left to right.

■ The PRINT statement prints or displays the results of processing. It can be used to print the values of variables, literals, arithmetic expressions, or a combination of these.

■ The END statement causes program execution to stop and is the last statement executed.

Review Questions

1. What are the two main purposes of line numbers?
2. What is a constant? Name two types of constants.
3. What are numbers called which do not have a decimal portion?
4. What is alphanumeric data?
5. What is the name of a storage location that contains a value that can change during program execution?
6. What are the two types of variables?
7. What is the purpose of the REM statement?
8. What purpose does the LET statement perform?
9. What is the hierarchy of operations?
10. Define a literal, and give three examples.

Debugging Exercises

Examine the following programs and correct any programming errors.

```
1.  10 REM THIS PROGRAM PRINTS
    20 A NAME AND AGE OF A PERSON.
    30 REM
    40 LET A = 21
    50 LET N$ = STACY
    60 PRINT N$,A
    99 END
```

```
2.  10 REM *** THIS PROGRAM CALCULATES     ***
    20 REM *** THE AVERAGE OF TWO NUMBERS. ***
    30 LET A + 1 = 10
    40 LET B = 15
    50 LET X = A + B / 2
    60 PRINT X
    99 END
```

Additional Programming Problems

1. You want to know how much it would cost you to fly your plane to Hollywood for the Oscars. Hollywood is 2,040 nautical miles from your home. Your plane gets 14 miles per gallon, and you can get gas for $10.50 per gallon. Your output should have the following format:

DISTANCE   TOTAL COST
XXX $XXX.XX

2. A cassette tape with a list price of $8.98 is on sale for 15 percent off. Write a program that will calculate and output the sale price of the tape.

3. You own an apartment building with eight identical apartments, each having two rooms that need carpeting. One room has a length of twelve feet and a width of nine feet, and the other has a length of ten feet and a width of eight feet. The carpeting costs $9.50 a square yard. Write a program that will calculate the amount of carpeting needed to carpet the entire building, as well as the total cost of the carpeting. The output should include both figures. The area of a room is equal to the length multiplied by the width. Be sure to document your program.

4. Write a program that will print the date, time, and telephone number of the following telephone log entries:

8/9/90   8:09 am   (419) 353-7789
9/1/90   3:51 pm   (614) 366-6443
1/7/91   6:42 am   (313) 557-5864

The output should have the following format:

DATE   TIME   TELEPHONE #
X/X/X   X:XXxx   (XXX)XXX-XXXX

5. Write a program that converts 72 degrees Fahrenheit to its centigrade equivalent and prints the result, appropriately labeled. Use the formula $C = 5/9(F - 32)$, where C equals the degrees centigrade and F equals the degrees Fahrenheit.

SECTION III

Input and Output

Introduction

The first part of this section explains two methods of entering data to a program: the INPUT statement and the READ and DATA statements. The INPUT statement enables the user to enter data while the program is running. When the READ and DATA statements are used, the data is entered as part of the program itself.

The remainder of the section discusses ways of printing program output so that it is attractive and easy to read. It also explains how to print output in table form.

The INPUT Statement

In many programming situations, the data changes each time the program is executed. For example, think of a program that calculates the gas mileage for your car. Each time you run this program, you need to enter new values for the number of miles traveled and the amount of gas used. If such a program used assignment statements to assign these values to variables, the statements would have to be rewritten every time you wanted to calculate your gas mileage. A more practical approach to this programming problem is to use the INPUT statement.

The INPUT statement enables the user to enter data at the keyboard while the program is executing. The format of the INPUT statement is as follows:

line# INPUT variable1[,variable2,...]

Brackets ([]) indicate that the item enclosed is optional. In this statement, for example, it is not necessary to specify more than one variable.

The following are all valid INPUT statements:

```
110 INPUT STUDENT$,GPA,YR
120 INPUT ADDRESS$
130 INPUT PAY,TAX,NETPAY
```

The following are examples of invalid INPUT statements:

```
180 INPUT CITY$ ST$           (No comma separating variables)
INPUT BEANS,CARROTS,CELERY    (No line number)
240 TABLES,INPUT CHAIRS       (Reserved word INPUT in wrong place)
```

Note that one or more variables can be listed in a single INPUT statement. If there are two or more variables, their names must be separated by commas. The programmer places INPUT statements in a program at the point where user-entered data is needed, as determined by the logic of the program.

When a program is running and an INPUT statement is encountered, the program temporarily stops executing and a question mark appears on the monitor screen. The user then must enter the required data and press the Return key. After each value is stored in its corresponding variable, program execution continues at the next statement.

Figure III-1 shows a program that uses INPUT statements to enter the data needed to calculate the gas mileage. When this program is run, the computer encounters the INPUT statement in line 30, prints a question mark, and waits for the user to enter the distance traveled. Once the user has entered this value and pressed the Return key, the computer continues executing the program.

This process is repeated when the INPUT statement in line 40 is encountered. After the user has entered the amount of gas used and pressed the Return key, the program continues execution, calculates the mileage, and prints the results.

In Figure III-1 the INPUT statements request that a numeric value be entered by the user. If the user enters a character string instead, an error message is printed and program execution stops prematurely. If an INPUT statement requests a character string, the input need not be surrounded by quotation marks.

If an INPUT statement contains more than one variable, only one question mark appears on the screen when the program is run. In this case, the user needs to enter the correct number of data items and must separate them with commas. For example:

```
10 INPUT CITY$,ST$,ZIP
```

When this statement is executed, only one question mark appears on the monitor screen, but three data items must be entered by the user:

```
? CEDAR RAPIDS, IOWA, 12500
```

Figure III-1
Gas Mileage Program Using INPUT
Statements

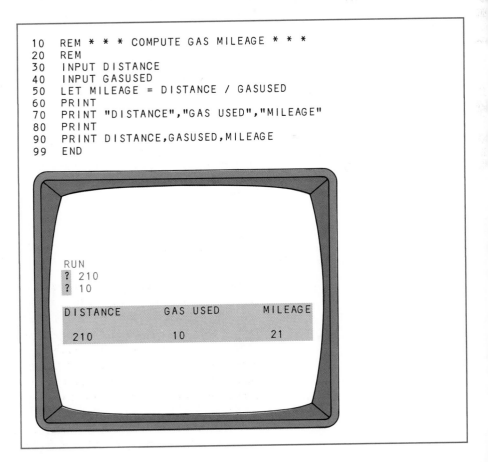

```
10  REM * * * COMPUTE GAS MILEAGE * * *
20  REM
30  INPUT DISTANCE
40  INPUT GASUSED
50  LET MILEAGE = DISTANCE / GASUSED
60  PRINT
70  PRINT "DISTANCE","GAS USED","MILEAGE"
80  PRINT
90  PRINT DISTANCE,GASUSED,MILEAGE
99  END
```

```
RUN
? 210
? 10

DISTANCE        GAS USED        MILEAGE

  210              10              21
```

The user must enter the exact number of data items needed by the INPUT statement and must include the commas. If fewer data items are entered, an error message is printed.

Printing Prompts for the User

PROMPT

A message telling the user to enter data. Usually a prompt also specifies the type of data to be entered.

In the previous example, when the INPUT statement was executed, only a question mark (?) appeared on the monitor screen when it was time for the user to enter data. The user was not told what type of data or how many data items to enter. Therefore, the programmer should also have included a **prompt** to tell the user what to enter.

A prompt can consist of a PRINT statement placed before the INPUT statement in the program, or it can be contained within the INPUT statement itself. Figure III-2 shows the program in Figure III-1 with prompts using PRINT statements preceding the INPUT statements.

Line 30 of the program prints the prompt:

```
30 PRINT "ENTER THE DISTANCE TRAVELED"
```

Figure III-2
Gas Mileage Program with Prompts

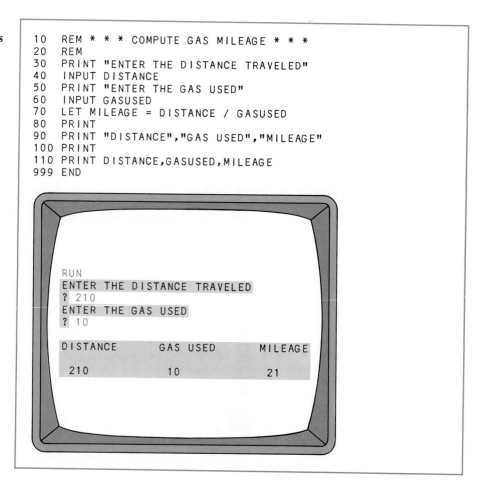

Line 40 is the INPUT statement:

```
40  INPUT DISTANCE
```

After line 40 is executed, the computer stops and waits for the user to enter the distance traveled. Then execution continues until the second INPUT statement is encountered. Again, the program waits for the user to enter the requested data and then continues execution.

The prompt can be included within the INPUT statement, using the following syntax:

line# INPUT prompt;variable1[,variable2,...]

Therefore, lines 30 and 40 of the program in Figure III-2 could be replaced with the following single statement:

```
30  INPUT "ENTER THE DISTANCE TRAVELED";DISTANCE
```

When the program is run with this modification, the question mark and the prompt appear on the same line as shown in Figure III-3. Using this format simplifies the writing of the program and makes the logic easy to follow.

Figure III-3
Gas Mileage Program with the
INPUT Statement and Prompts

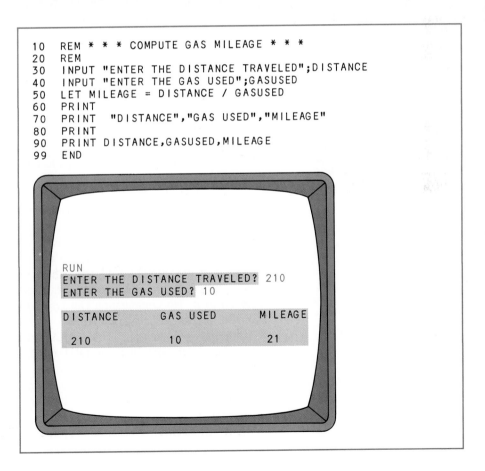

```
10   REM * * * COMPUTE GAS MILEAGE * * *
20   REM
30   INPUT "ENTER THE DISTANCE TRAVELED";DISTANCE
40   INPUT "ENTER THE GAS USED";GASUSED
50   LET MILEAGE = DISTANCE / GASUSED
60   PRINT
70   PRINT  "DISTANCE","GAS USED","MILEAGE"
80   PRINT
90   PRINT DISTANCE,GASUSED,MILEAGE
99   END
```

```
RUN
ENTER THE DISTANCE TRAVELED? 210
ENTER THE GAS USED? 10

DISTANCE          GAS USED          MILEAGE

   210               10               21
```

INQUIRY-AND-RESPONSE MODE (INTERACTIVE MODE)
A mode of operation in which the program asks a question and the user enters a response.

The method of data entry discussed in this section, in which the user enters a response to a prompt printed on the monitor screen, is called **inquiry-and-response, interactive mode,** or **conversational mode.**

The READ and DATA Statements

A second method of entering data to a BASIC program is to use the READ and DATA statements. The READ and DATA statements differ from the INPUT statement in that data values are not entered by the user during program execution, but instead are assigned by the programmer within the program itself.

The general formats for the READ and DATA statements are as follows:

line# READ variable1[,variable2,...]
line# DATA value1[,value2,...]

The values in the DATA statement are assigned to the corresponding variables in the READ statement. The following is a list of rules explaining the use of the READ and DATA statements.

■ A program can contain any number of READ and DATA statements.
■ The placement of READ statements is determined by the program logic. The programmer places these statements at the point where data needs to be read.
■ DATA statements are nonexecutable, and therefore can be placed anywhere in the program.
■ The computer collects the values from all the DATA statements in a program and places them in a single list, referred to as the **data list.** The values in this list are arranged in order, from the lowest to the highest line number and from left to right within a single DATA statement.
■ When two or more data values are placed in a single DATA statement, the values are separated by commas. Character strings require quotation marks only if they contain leading or trailing blanks, commas, or semicolons.
■ When the program encounters a READ statement, it goes to the data list and assigns the next value in that list to the corresponding variable in the READ statement. If the variable is numeric, the data value also must be numeric. If it is a character string variable, however, the computer allows a numeric value to be assigned to it. No computation can be performed with numbers that have been assigned to character string variables.
■ If there is inadequate data for a READ statement (that is, if there are no more data values in the data list), an OUT OF DATA error message appears and the program stops execution.
■ If there are more data values than variables, these extra data values remain unread. This condition does not result in an error message.

DATA LIST
A single list containing the values in all of the data statements in a program. The values appear in the list in the order in which they occur in the program.

Figure III-4 shows a program segment that contains READ and DATA statements. When the computer executes this segment, it first encounters the READ

**Figure III-4
READ/DATA Segment**

```
00100 READ NME$,S1,S2,S3
00110 READ NME$
00120 READ S1,S2
00130 READ S3
00140 DATA JACOBS,48
00150 DATA 60,53,GUINARD
00160 DATA 62,58
00170 DATA 54
```

statement in line 100. The statement instructs it to read four data values from the data list, and to assign these values to the variables NMNE$, S1, S2, and S3 respectively. After this task is completed, program execution continues at line 110, where the next value in the data list, GUINARD, is assigned to the variable NME$. This new value of NME$ replaces JACOBS, the previous value.

Note that the computer "remembers" where it is in the data list. Whenever it encounters another READ statement, it assigns the next value in the list to that variable. Study Figure III-4 to make certain you understand how the READ and DATA statements are used in reading data values.

Figure III-5 shows the sample gas mileage program rewritten using READ and DATA statements. Line 30 tells the computer to take the first value in the data list and put it in the storage location named DISTANCE. The statement also says to take the next value in the data list and assign it to the variable GASUSED. The program then goes on to calculate and print the gas mileage. To run this program again with different data, we would need to change line 100, the DATA line.

The RESTORE Statement

Usually, when READ and DATA statements are used, each data value is read only once. If it is necessary to use the same data value more than once, the RESTORE statement can be used. Consider the following program segment:

```
110 READ A,B
120 TT = A + A * B
130 RESTORE
140 READ C,D,E
150 SUM = C + D + E
160 DATA 44,790,1,,15,138
```

When line 110 of this program segment is executed, the value 44 is assigned to variable A and the value 790 is assigned to variable B. Normally, the next data value available to be read would be 1, but the RESTORE statement in line 130 returns the computer to the beginning of the data list. When line 140 is encountered, the value 44 will be read to variable C, 790 to variable D, and 1 to variable E.

Figure III-5
Gas Mileage Program Using READ and DATA Statements

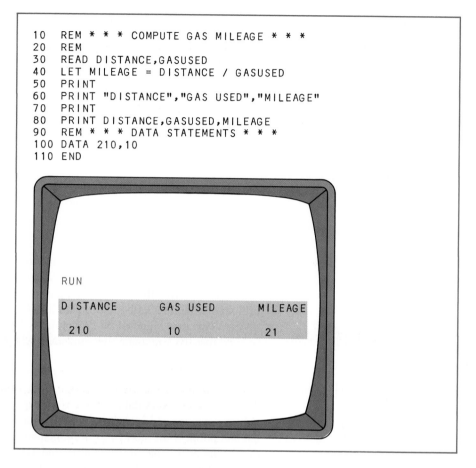

```
10   REM * * * COMPUTE GAS MILEAGE * * *
20   REM
30   READ DISTANCE,GASUSED
40   LET MILEAGE = DISTANCE / GASUSED
50   PRINT
60   PRINT "DISTANCE","GAS USED","MILEAGE"
70   PRINT
80   PRINT DISTANCE,GASUSED,MILEAGE
90   REM * * * DATA STATEMENTS * * *
100  DATA 210,10
110  END
```

```
RUN

DISTANCE          GAS USED          MILEAGE

   210               10                21
```

Comparison of the Two Data Entry Methods

The INPUT and the READ/DATA statements both can be used to enter data to BASIC programs. The relative advantages of the two methods depend on the application. Here are some general guidelines:

■ The INPUT statement is ideal when data values change frequently, because it allows the data to be entered at the keyboard during program execution.
■ The READ and DATA statements are well suited to programs that use large quantities of data, because the user does not have to enter a long list of data values during program execution, as would be necessary with the INPUT statement.
■ The READ and DATA statements are most useful when data values are the same for each program execution. When the data values change, however, the program itself must be altered.

Learning Check

1. When data must be entered to a program while it is executing, a(n) _____ statement is used.

2. A(n) _____ is used to tell the user what kind of data to enter a program.

3. _____ statements contain the data values that will be assigned to the variables listed in a READ statement.

4. There must be a DATA statement immediately after each READ statement. True or false?

5. The _____ statement causes the next READ statement encountered to start at the beginning of the data list.

Answers

1. INPUT 2. prompt 3. DATA 4. false. DATA statements can be anywhere within the program. 5. RESTORE

Clearing the Screen

User prompts and other program output should be as clear and attractive as possible. Before printing a user prompt, for example, you may want to clear the screen of any information previously displayed. On the IBM, the following statement clears the screen and places the cursor in the upper left corner of the screen:

line# CLS

In a flowchart, the clear screen instruction is contained in an input/output symbol (▱).

Printing Results

As discussed in the previous chapter, the PRINT statement enables us to print the results of processing. When more than one item is to be printed on a line, a variety of methods can be used to control the spacing and format of the output.

Print Zones and Commas

The IBM screen consists of 2,000 print positions: 80 columns across and 25 rows down. The 80 columns are divided into five print zones, each containing 14 print positions (columns). The zones are divided as follows:

Zone 1	Zone 2	Zone 3	Zone 4	Zone 5
(1–14)	(15–28)	(29–42)	(43–56)	(57–80)

Commas not only separate items within a PRINT statement, but also control the format of those items. A comma indicates that the next item to be printed will start at the beginning of the next empty print zone. The following example shows how this works:

```
10  READ NAM$,NUM,YEAR
20  PRINT NAM$,NUM,YEAR
30  DATA "JOHN",6,1968
```

The first item in the PRINT statement is printed at the beginning of the first print zone. The comma between NAM$ and NUM causes the computer to space over to the next unused print zone; then the value in NUM is printed. The second comma directs the computer to space over to the next zone (Zone 3) and print the value in YEAR. Thus the output is as follows:

```
JOHN            6              1968
```

If more items are listed in a PRINT statement than there are print zones in a line, the print zones of the next line also are used, starting with the first zone. Notice the output of the following example:

```
10  READ SEX$,AGE,CLASS$,MAJ$,HRS,GPA
20  PRINT SEX$,AGE,CLASS$,MAJ$,HRS,GPA
30  DATA M,19,JR,CS,18,2.5

RUN
```

```
M            19        JR          CS           18
2.5
```

If the value to be printed exceeds the width of the print zone, the entire value is printed, regardless of how many zones it occupies. The comma causes printing to continue in the next unused print zone, as shown in the following example:

```
10  LET SPOT$ = "BAGHDAD"
20  PRINT "YOUR NEXT DESTINATION WILL BE",SPOT$

ZONE 1          ZONE 2          ZONE 3
```

```
YOUR NEXT DESTINATION WILL BE          BAGHDAD
```

A print zone can be skipped by enclosing a space (the character blank) in quotation marks. This technique causes the entire zone to appear empty:

```
60  PRINT "NAME"," ","I.D.NUMBER"
```

It is also possible to skip a zone by typing consecutive commas:

```
60 PRINT "NAME",,"I.D.NUMBER"
```

Both techniques cause the literal NAME to be printed in the first zone, the second zone to be blank, and the literal I.D. NUMBER to be printed in the third zone:

```
ZONE 1              ZONE 2          ZONE 3
```

```
NAME                                I.D.NUMBER
```

If a comma appears after the last item in a PRINT statement, the output of the next PRINT statement encountered will begin at the next available print zone, as shown by the following statements and output:

```
10 READ NAM$,SEX$,VOICE$
20 PRINT NAM$,
30 PRINT SEX$,VOICE$
40 DATA "SHICOFF","M","TENOR"
99 END
```

```
RUN
```

```
SHICOFF          M              TENOR
```

Using Semicolons

Semicolons, like commas, can be used within a PRINT statement to control the format of printed output. The semicolon signals the computer to print the next item at the next available print *position,* rather than at the next print zone. In the following example, two strings in a PRINT statement are separated by a semicolon:

```
10 PRINT "JOHN";"DRAKE"
```

```
RUN
```

```
JOHNDRAKE
```

The first string is printed, and then the semicolon causes the next item to be printed in the next available print position, which is the next column.

To print these strings with a space between them, you can enclose a blank within the quotation marks of one of the strings:

```
10 PRINT "JOHN";" DRAKE"
```

```
RUN
```

```
JOHN DRAKE
```

A semicolon appearing after the *last* item in a PRINT statement prevents the output of the next PRINT statement from starting on a new line. Instead, the next item printed appears on the same line, at the next available print position:

```
10 PRINT "YVONNE DRAKE:";
20 PRINT 3567;" CHELSEA ST."

RUN
```

```
YVONNE DRAKE: 3567   CHELSEA ST.
```

The TAB Function

The comma and semicolon are easy to use, and many reports can be formatted in this fashion. There are times, however, when a report should be structured differently. The TAB function allows output to be printed in any column in an output line, thus providing the programmer greater flexibility in formatting printed output.

As with the comma and semicolon, one or more TAB functions are used within a PRINT statement. The general format of the TAB function is as follows:

TAB(expression)

The expression can be a numeric constant, a variable, or an arithmetic expression. When a TAB function is encountered in a PRINT statement, the computer spaces over to the column number indicated in the expression. The next variable value or literal found in the PRINT statement is printed starting in that column. The TAB prints blank spaces as it moves to the specified column, thereby erasing anything that was on the screen previously. The TAB function is separated from the items to be printed by semicolons. For example, the following statement causes the literal HELLO to be printed starting in column 10:

```
50 PRINT TAB(10);"HELLO";TAB(25);"GOODBYE"
```

Then, starting in column 25, the literal GOODBYE is printed.

The program in Figure III-6 illustrates the use of the TAB function. This program prints a simple table by using the TAB function to arrange the printed values in columns.

Note that the semicolon is used with the TAB function. If the comma is used instead, the computer uses the print zones by default, ignoring the columns specified in the parentheses. For example, if line 50 of the program in Figure III-6 had been

```
50 PRINT TAB(5),"ITEM";TAB(25),"GALLONS"
```

the output would have been as shown here:

```
            INVENTORY REPORT

            ITEM
                                GALLONS

ICE CREAM               50
TOPPING                 30
CHERRIES                10
```

Figure III-6
Program Using the TAB Function

```
10   REM * * * INVENTORY REPORT * * *
20   REM
30   PRINT TAB (10);"INVENTORY REPORT"
40   PRINT
50   PRINT TAB(5);"ITEM";TAB(25);"GALLONS"
60   PRINT
70   READ ITEM$,QUANT
80   PRINT TAB(5);ITEM$;TAB(25);QUANT
90   READ ITEM$,QUANT
100  PRINT TAB(5);ITEM$;TAB(25);QUANT
110  READ ITEM$,QUANT
120  PRINT TAB(5);ITEM$;TAB(25);QUANT
130  REM
140  REM * * * DATA STATEMENTS * * *
150  DATA ICE CREAM,50,TOPPING,30,CHERRIES,10
999  END
```

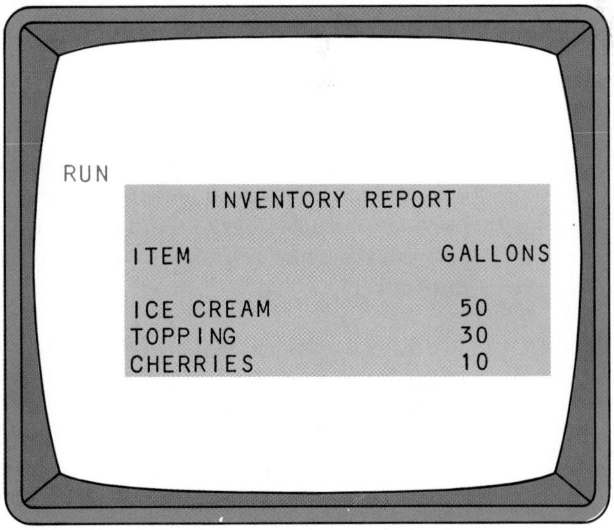

```
RUN
            INVENTORY REPORT

    ITEM                GALLONS

    ICE CREAM               50
    TOPPING                 30
    CHERRIES                10
```

In this example, the computer spaced over five columns as indicated by the first TAB function, but when it found the comma following the parenthesis, it skipped over to the next print zone to print ITEM. The comma following the quotation marks after ITEM causes the computer to skip to the next available print zone, which begins at column 30. The next TAB function instructs it to skip to column 25, but it has already passed that column, so it goes to the *next* line and skips to column 25. Then it finds the comma after the parenthesis, which causes it to continue to column 30, where the next available print zone starts. It prints GAL-LONS starting in column 30. This is why the second heading, GALLONS, is not on the same line with ITEM in this output.

The TAB function can be used only to advance the print position from left to right; backspacing is not possible. Therefore, if more than one TAB function appears in a single PRINT statement, the column numbers specified should increase from left to right. When a TAB function specifies a column to the left of the current print position, the computer spaces to that column on the next line, as shown in the previous example. Another example will illustrate this point:

Correct use of the TAB function

```
20 PRINT TAB(5);3;TAB(15);4;TAB(25);5

RUN
```

```
3            4            5
```

Incorrect use of the TAB function

```
20 PRINT TAB(25);3;TAB(15);4;TAB(5);5
RUN
```

```
                              3
                4
5
```

As already mentioned, the column number of the TAB function can be expressed as a numeric constant, a numeric variable, or an arithmetic expression. All of our previous examples have used numeric constants. The following examples, which perform the same operations, use numeric variables and arithmetic expressions respectively.

```
10 Y = 25
20 X = 10
30 PRINT TAB(X);7;TAB(Y);"MONDAY"

RUN
```

```
7                     MONDAY
```

```
10 Y = 20
20 X = 15
30 PRINT TAB(X - 5);7;TAB(Y + 5);"MONDAY"
```

RUN

```
7                        MONDAY
```

SPC

The SPC (space) function is similar to TAB in that it is used in controlling the printing of output. Instead of instructing the computer to print output in a specified column, however, it tells the computer how many spaces to advance beyond its current position before printing the output. Like the TAB function, the SPC function should be separated from other items in the PRINT statement by semicolons:

```
10 PRINT "WORD";SPC(10);"LETTER"
```
RUN

```
WORD          LETTER
```

When line 10 is executed, WORD is printed in columns 1 through 4. Then the computer leaves ten blank spaces between the end of WORD and the beginning of LETTER, so LETTER is printed starting in column 15.

Figure III-7 illustrates the difference between these two functions. When TAB is used, the output is printed in columns 5 and 10. With SPC, however, the output is printed in columns 5 and 15, because the SPC function spaces over ten columns from the last printed output (A) before printing B.

LOCATE

It is possible to specify where on the screen you want a message to be printed, or where you want to have an input value accepted. As we mentioned earlier, the display screen is divided into 2,000 positions, 80 columns across and 25 rows down. The LOCATE statement enables the user to specify the row and column in which to place the cursor.

The general format of the LOCATE statement is as follows:

line# LOCATE row,column

where the row is a number between 1 and 25, and the column is a number between 1 and 80. After a LOCATE statement has been executed, any subsequent input or output statement begins placing characters at the specified position.

Figure III-7
Program Segments Demonstrating
the Difference Between TAB and
SPC

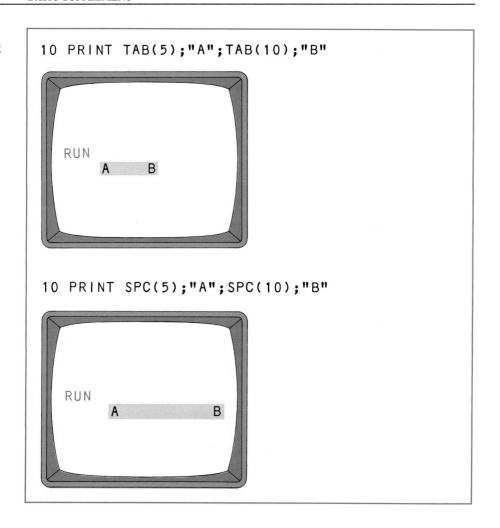

```
10 PRINT TAB(5);"A";TAB(10);"B"
```

```
RUN
    A     B
```

```
10 PRINT SPC(5);"A";SPC(10);"B"
```

```
RUN
     A          B
```

For example, suppose you want to print the message HAVE A NICE DAY in the center of the screen. The following statements would perform this task:

```
10 CLS
20 LOCATE 13,32
30 PRINT "HAVE A NICE DAY"
```

Line 10 clears the screen. Line 20 instructs the computer to move the cursor to row 13, column 32, thus causing the PRINT statement to begin printing in this specified position.

Normally, BASIC does not print text on line 25 because the KEY function display appears there. This display can be turned off by the command KEY OFF:

line# KEY OFF

This command enables you to print on line 25.

Table III-1
Format Control Characters

Character	Explanation
#	Numeric data; one symbol for each digit to be printed; zeroes are added to the left of the number to fill the field
$$	Two dollar signs cause the dollar sign to be floating, meaning that it will be in the first position before the number
\spaces\	This specifies the length of a string field to be 2 plus the number of spaces between the backslashes

The PRINT USING Statement

Another convenient feature for controlling output is the PRINT USING statement. This feature is especially useful when printing table headings or aligning columns of numbers. The general format of the PRINT USING statement is as follows:

line# PRINT USING ''format control characters''; expression list

The expression list consists of the string expressions or numeric expressions that are to be printed, separated by semicolons or commas. The format control characters are special formatting characters that determine the field and the format of the printed items. They must be enclosed by quotation marks. Table III-1 shows the most commonly used format control characters, which are explained in the remainder of this chapter.

String Expressions.   When PRINT USING is used to print strings, the most commonly used formatting characters are as shown here:

\n spaces\

where n blank spaces are enclosed by the backslashes. This format specifies that 2 + n characters from the string are to be printed. If the backslashes are types with no spaces, two characters are printed; if the backslashes are types with one space between them, three characters are printed, and so on. If the string is longer than the field, the extra characters are ignored. If the field is longer than the string, the string is left-justified in the field and padded with spaces on the right. For example:

```
10 A$ = "LOOK"
20 B$ = "OUT"
30 PRINT USING "\  \";A$;B$
40 PRINT USING "\   \";A$;B$
50 PRINT USING "\ \";A$;B$
RUN

LOOKOUT
LOOK OUT
LOOOUT
```

Line 30 creates a print field of four characters (the two backslashes plus the two spaces between). The string ''LOOK'' is four characters long, so it is printed in the field as is. The string ''OUT'' is only three characters long, however, so it is left-justified in the format field.

Line 40 creates a print field of five characters. Both strings are left-justified in the print field, but with this example you can see the padding at the end of the field. The string LOOK used only four characters, even though five characters were allotted in the format; thus it was left-justified and a blank was added at the right. This blank separates the string OUT from the string LOOK in the output.

The last example, line 50, allows only three characters to be printed. The string LOOK is longer, so when line 50 is executed, only the first three letters of LOOK are printed.

Numeric Expressions. When PRINT USING is used to print numbers, special characters can be used to format the numeric field. The most commonly used characters are the number sign and double dollar sign.

A number sign (#) is used to represent each digit position. Digit positions are always filled. If the number to be printed has fewer digits than the positions specified, the number is right-justified in the field and is preceded by spaces. A decimal point can be inserted at any position in the field. If the format string specifies that a digit is to precede the decimal point, a digit always is printed, even if it is 0. Numbers are rounded if necessary. The following examples illustrate these concepts:

Statement	Result	Reason
PRINT USING "####";78	78	More digit positions than digits.
PRINT USING "##.##";78	78.00	No decimal fraction specified.
PRINT USING "##.##";.78	0.78	No digits preceding the decimal.
PRINT USING "##.##";.788	0.79	Number rounded because there are more digits than specified positions following the decimal point.
PRINT USING "###";100.20	100	Number truncated because there are more digits than specified positions.

Another format character is the double dollar sign ($$), which causes a dollar sign to be printed to the immediate left of the formatted number. The $$ specifies two more digit positions, one of which is the dollar sign. Therefore, if you need to print a dollar value of four digits with a dollar sign, you would need only the double dollar sign and three number signs ($$###), as shown here:

Figure III-8
PRINT USING Example Program

```
10   REM * * * ILLUSTRATING PRINT USING * * *
20   REM
30   PRINT
40   PRINT USING "\          \          \     \";"ITEM","TOTAL"
50   PRINT USING "\          \          \      \";"PURCHASE","PRICE"
60   PRINT
70   READ A$,X
80   Y = X * .06
90   PRINT USING "\              \  $$##.##    $$#.##";A$,X
100  READ A$,X
110  Y = X * .06
120  PRINT USING "\              \  $$##.##    $$#.##";A$,X
130  READ A$,X
140  Y = X * .06
150  PRINT USING "\              \  $$##.##    $$#.##";A$,X
160  READ A$,X
170  Y = X * .06
180  PRINT USING "\              \  $$##.##    $$#.##";A$,X
190  READ A$,X
200  Y = X * .06
210  PRINT USING "\              \  $$##.##    $$#.##";A$,X
220  REM
230  REM * * * DATA STATEMENTS * * *
240  DATA TOASTER,27.50,BLENDER,18.45
250  DATA BLANKET,9.90,KNIVES,34.99,FAN,29.00
999  END
```

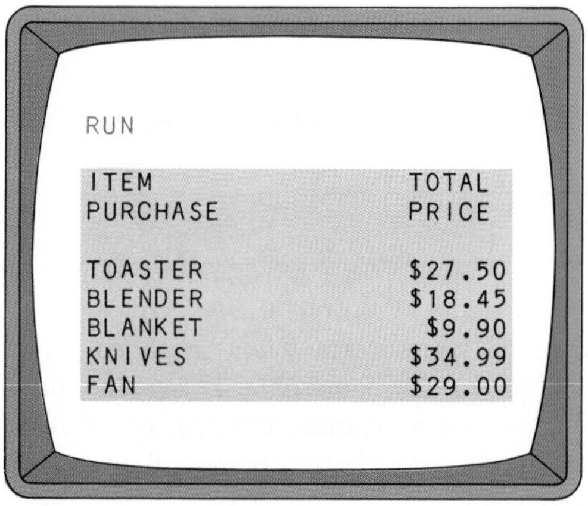

```
RUN

ITEM              TOTAL
PURCHASE          PRICE

TOASTER          $27.50
BLENDER          $18.45
BLANKET           $9.90
KNIVES           $34.99
FAN              $29.00
```

Statement	Result
`PRINT USING "$$###.##";4563.78`	$4563.78

Figure III-8 is a program that prints a table by implementing the PRINT USING statement.

Learning Check

1. The _____ function causes output to be printed in a column specified by the programmer.

2. A semicolon between items in a PRINT statement tells the computer to skip to the next available _____ to print the next item.

3. What output will the following statement produce? 110 PRINT "JOE IS";"NINETY".

4. When a PRINT statement ends with a comma or semicolon, the next value output begins _____.
   a. on the next line
   b. on the next page
   c. on the same line, if there is room

5. What would be the format used for printing a five-digit number, with a decimal point two positions to the left and with a dollar sign in front?

Answers

1. TAB 2. position 3. JOE ISNINETY 4. c 5. PRINT USING $$##.##

Comprehensive Programming Problem

Problem Definition

You are a loan officer for the local credit union. Your client, Ms. Rodgers, wants to borrow $70,000 to purchase a house. She wants to know how much her monthly payments will be. The annual interest rate for her loan will be 12 percent, and the term of the mortgage is 20 years. Because you must make this type of calculation often, you decide to write a program that reports the mortgage information and calculates payments for you.

The input for the problem consists of the given mortgage amount, interest rate, and term. The desired output is a report that lists this information along with the calculated monthly payment. To calculate the monthly payment from the given data, the program must determine the monthly interest rate, using the following formula:

Monthly interest rate = (Annual interest rate ÷ 100) ÷ 12.

The monthly interest rate then is used to calculate the mortgage multiplication factor:

Mortgage multiplication factor = Monthly interest rate ÷
[(1 + Monthly interest rate) ^
(Years of term × 12) − 1] +
Monthly interest rate.

The monthly payments then can be calculated based on the following formula:

Monthly payment = Mortgage multiplication factor × Mortgage amount.

Solution Design

The general problem is to produce a mortgage loan report. The flow of data processing determines three smaller problems to solve:

1. Enter the given data.
2. Calculate the monthly payment.
3. Display the report.

Three formulas are involved in calculating the monthly payment, so the second step can be divided as follows:

2.A. Calculate the monthly interest rate.
2.B. Calculate the mortgage multiplication factor.
2.C. Calculate the monthly payment.

The display of the report also can be divided into smaller tasks:

3.A. Display a heading.
3.B. Display the report values.

The structure chart in Figure III-9 shows this refinement of the problem.

Next we decide what program steps are needed to perform these tasks, and the order in which the steps should be performed. Figure III-10 shows the flowchart for a possible solution. We will make this an interactive program, because it will be used with frequently changing values.

The first step is to clear the screen so that the user prompts can be seen clearly. Next, the input values are entered. The calculations are performed, and the screen is cleared again to place the report at the top of the screen. Finally the report is printed.

The Program

The program in Figure III-11 documents its major variables in lines 30 through 100. Line 120 clears the screen. Lines 130 through 150 ask the user for the needed

Figure III-9
Mortgage Program Structure Chart

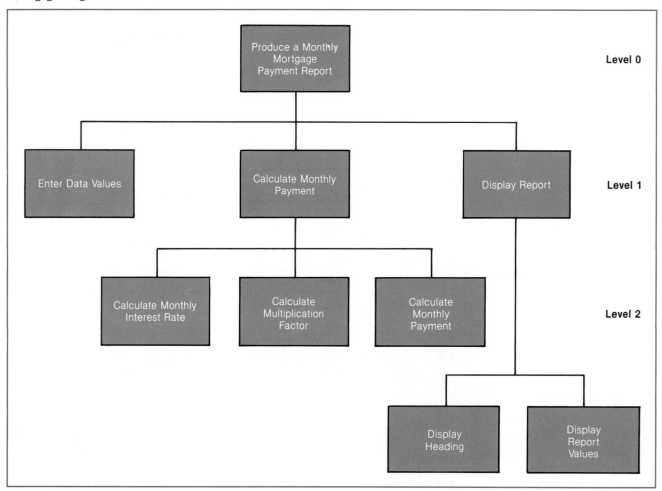

data values, accept these values, and store them in the appropriate variables. The computer is then instructed to perform the calculations by lines 180 through 200. Line 230 again clears the screen to make room for the report. The heàding and report information are indented to the second print zone by the commas in line 260 and lines 290 through 310.

Summary Points

■ The INPUT statement allows data to be entered at the keyboard during program execution. Each value entered is assigned to a corresponding variable in the INPUT statement. The variables must be separated by commas.

Figure III-10
Mortgage Program Flowchart

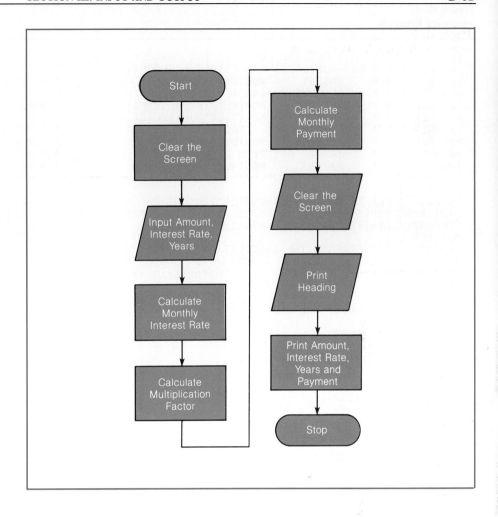

- Prompts should be used to tell the user what type of data to enter.
- Before prompts are printed on the monitor screen, it is good practice to clear the screen of any other printing. This can be done by using the CLS statement.
- The READ and DATA statements also can be used to read values to variables. In this case, the input is placed in DATA statements within the program. READ statements are used to read these values and assign them to variables.
- The INPUT statement is particularly well suited for situations in which data values change often. The READ and DATA statements are most useful when data values do not change often.
- The results of processing can be formatted by using commas in PRINT statement. A comma causes the next output to be printed in the next print zone. Using commas enables the programmer to print output in table form.
- A semicolon in a PRINT statement causes the next output to be printed in the next available print position.
- The PRINT USING statement allows string expressions and numeric values to be formatted for output. It is used primarily for printing tables.

Figure III-11
Mortgage Program

```
10   REM * * * THIS PROGRAM COMPUTES THE MONTHLY PAYMENTS * * *
20   REM * * * FOR MORTGAGES AND PRINTS A REPORT.         * * *
30   REM * * *    AMOUNT      MORTGAGE AMOUNT             * * *
40   REM * * *    ANNLRTE     ANNUAL INTEREST RATE        * * *
50   REM * * *    MNTHRTE     MONTHLY INTEREST RATE       * * *
60   REM * * *    MMFACTR     MORTGAGE MULTIPLICATION     * * *
70   REM * * *                      FACTOR                * * *
80   REM * * *    AMOUNT      MORTGAGE AMOUNT             * * *
90   REM * * *    YEARS       TERM OF MORTGAGE            * * *
100  REM * * *    PAYMNT      MONTHLY PAYMENT             * * *
110  REM
120  CLS
130  INPUT "ENTER MORTGAGE AMOUNT $";AMOUNT
140  INPUT "ENTER ANNUAL INTEREST RATE: ";ANNLRTE
150  INPUT "ENTER YEARS OF MORTGAGE: ";YEARS
160  REM
170  REM * * * PERFORM THE CALCULATIONS. * * *
180  LET MNTHRTE = (ANNLRTE / 100) / 12
190  LET MMFACTR = MNTHRTE / ((1 + MNTHRTE) ^ (YEARS * 12) - 1) + MNTHRTE
200  LET PAYMNT = MMFACTR * AMOUNT
210  REM
220  REM * * * PRINT THE REPORT. * * *
230  CLS
240  PRINT
250  PRINT
260  PRINT ,"MORTGAGE REPORT"
270  PRINT
280  PRINT
290  PRINT ,"MORTGAGE AMOUNT      $";AMOUNT
300  PRINT ,"ANNUAL INT. RATE      ";ANNLRTE;"%
310  PRINT ,"MONTHLY PAYMENT      $";PAYMNT
999  END
```

```
RUN
ENTER MORTGAGE AMOUNT $? 70000
ENTER ANNUAL INTEREST RATE: ? 12
ENTER YEARS OF MORTGAGE: ? 20


            MORTGAGE REPORT


            MORTGAGE AMOUNT     $ 70000
            ANNUAL INT. RATE      12 %
            MONTHLY PAYMENT     $ 770.7603
```

Review Questions

1. What is a data list, and how is it created?
2. Which statement should be used when there is an inquiry/response situation in a program?
3. What does the computer do when it comes to an INPUT statement?
4. What symbol separates the variables in an INPUT statement?
5. A _____ explains to the user what values are to be entered. It can be used either in an INPUT statement or in a PRINT statement that precedes an INPUT statement.
6. What happens if a program asks for a string value and the user enters a numeric value instead?
7. How does the RESTORE statement work?
8. The _____ statement is used with the READ statement, is nonexecutable, and can be located anywhere in a program.
9. What is the effect of a comma in a PRINT statement?
10. What is the difference between the TAB function and the SPC function?

Debugging Exercises

1.
```
10 INPUT "ENTER CITY AND STATE:",CITY$,ST
20 INPUT "AND ZIP CODE",ZIP$
30 PRINT TAB(5);CITY$;",";TAB(25);ST;TAB(35);ZIP$
```

2.
```
50 READ W1$,W2$,W3$
60 READ X,Y,Z
70 X = X - 10
80 Y = Y + 5
90 PRINT W1$;TAB(X);W2$;TAB(Y);W3$
100 DATA "WHAT","IS","LIFE?",8,5,15
```

Additional Programming Problems

1. Mrs. Mathey wants to know how much it would cost to fertilize her garden, which measures 15 by 20 feet. The economy fertilizer costs $1.75 per pound, and one pound covers 20 square feet. She also wants to know how much it would cost if she used the deluxe fertilizer, which is $2.00 per pound, and one pound covers 20 square feet. The program should output the cost of using each and the cost difference between the two.

2. Write a program that asks for a person's name and weight in pounds, and computes the weight in kilograms (1 pound = 0.453592 kilograms). The program

should print the name of the person, his/her weight in pounds, and weight in kilograms, each in a different print zone.

3. Write a program that will provide the user with an arithmetic quiz. The program should ask the user to enter two numbers. Then it should print a message telling the user to press any key when ready to see the sum, difference, product, and quotient of the two numbers. The program should then print the four results mentioned. Your output should be as follows:

```
ENTER ANY TWO NUMBERS
(SEPARATE THE NUMBERS WITH A COMMA) XXX, XXX
PRESS ANY KEY WHEN READY TO SEE THE ANSWERS: X
XXX + XXX = XXXX
XXX − XXX = XXX
XXX*XXX = XXXXXX
XXXX/XXX = XX
```

4. Tod Stiles has friends across the country, and would like to have a computerized address book. Write a program to read the following sample data and print it with the headings NAME, STREET, CITY, and STATE, using the TAB function:

Irene Bulas, 124 Columbia Hts, Brooklyn, NY
Monica Murdock, 778 Riverview Dr., New Orleans, LA
Link Case, 86 Eldorado Dr., Dallas, TX
Karen Milhoan, 799 Royal St. George, Naperville, IL

5. Write a program using READ/DATA statements to tally the cost of grocery list items. The program should calculate the total of the prices, a 6 percent tax on this amount, and the final total. Make use of the PRINT USING statement to print the prices and totals. Use the following data: 12.79, 9.99, 4.57, 3.99. The output should look like this:

```
                        12.79
                         9.99
                         4.57
                         3.99
        Subtotal        XX.XX
        Tax              X.XX
                        _____
Total                  $XX.XX
```

SECTION IV

Control Statements and Subroutines

Introduction

This section introduces the **control statement,** a powerful programming tool that will be used in all programs from this point on. Control statements enable the programmer to control the order in which program statements are executed. The GOTO, IF/THEN/ELSE, and ON/GOTO statements are control statements introduced in this section. The section also explains how programs are divided into subprograms or modules, which in BASIC are called **subroutines.** The GOSUB and ON/GOSUB statements are the two methods of executing a subroutine in BASIC.

The GOTO Statement: Unconditional Transfer

All of the programs we have written so far have been executed in a simple sequential manner. That is, they were executed from the lowest-numbered line to the highest-numbered line. To solve many programming problems, however, it is necessary to use control statements to alter the sequence in which statements are executed. One type of control statement is the GOTO statement. Its general format looks like this:

line# GOTO transfer line#

The transfer line number tells the computer the line number of the next statement to be executed, and control transfers to that program line regardless of its location in the program.

When a GOTO statement is executed, any of three possible actions may be taken:

1. If the statement indicated by the transfer line number is executable, it is executed, and program execution continues from that point.
2. If the statement indicated by the transfer line number is nonexecutable (such as a REM or DATA statement), control passes to the next executable statement after it.
3. If the transfer line number does not correspond to any statement in the program, an error message is displayed and execution is terminated.

The following is an example of a GOTO statement:

```
100 GOTO 60
```

This statement causes program execution to branch to line 60, execute if possible, and continue with the line following line 60.

Because control of the execution path *always* changes when the GOTO statement is encountered, such a statement is known as an **unconditional transfer.** The program segment in Figure IV–1 shows how execution paths are controlled with

Figure IV-1
GOTO Statement Execution Path

```
00030 X = 10
00040 Y = 20
00050 GOTO 70
00060 PRINT X
00070 PRINT Y
00080 -------
```

UNCONDITIONAL TRANSFER
Control is always passed to a specified line, regardless of any program conditions.

GOTO statements. The GOTO statement in line 50 causes control to pass to line 70. Therefore, only the value of Y is printed; line 60 is skipped.

At this point a word of caution is in order. Although the GOTO statement gives the programmer increased control over the logical flow of a program, unconditional transfers can produce an execution path so complex that the logic is virtually impossible to follow, and debugging becomes a nightmare. Later in this chapter and in the next chapter, you will be introduced to control statements that are preferable to the GOTO statement. The GOTO statement should be used only when it is not feasible to use another control statement.

The IF Statement: Conditional Transfer

CONDITIONAL TRANSFER
Program control is transferred to another point only if a stated condition is satisfied.

**SINGLE-ALTERNATIVE
DECISION STRUCTURE**
A decision step in which a specific action is taken if a stated condition is true; otherwise, execution proceeds to the next statement.

**DOUBLE-ALTERNATIVE
DECISION STRUCTURE**
A decision step in which a specific action is taken if a stated condition is true; otherwise, a different action is taken.

A second type of control statement is the **conditional transfer** or decision statement. A conditional transfer statement tells the computer that a decision must be made to determine which path of execution to take. This decision is based on the value of an expression. If the value meets a stated condition—that is, if the condition is true—then one path of execution is followed. If the condition is false, a different path is taken. Most program decisions fall into one of two categories:

1. Single alternative: A special set of one or more statements is executed if the condition is true. If the condition is false, these statements are ignored and the normal program flow continues. The flowchart for a single-alternative decision structure is shown in Figure IV–2.

2. Double alternative: There is a choice between two sets of statements or alternative paths. One path is executed if the condition is true, and the other is executed if the condition is false. Figure IV–3 shows the flowchart for a double-alternative decision structure.

**Figure IV-2
Single-Alternative Flowchart**

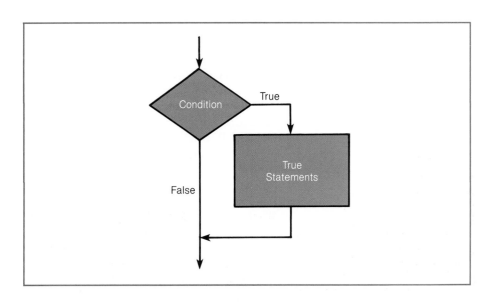

Figure IV-3
Double-Alternative Flowchart

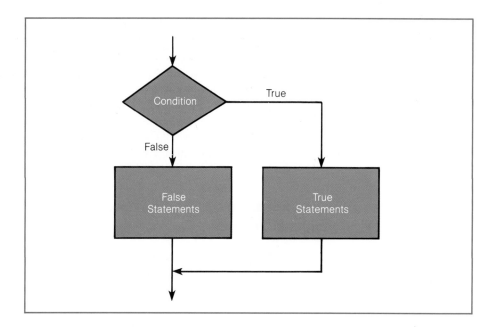

Single Alternative: IF/THEN

In BASIC, the IF/THEN statement is used for a single-alternative decision structure. The two general formats of the IF/THEN statement are as follows:

line# IF condition $\begin{Bmatrix} \text{THEN} \\ \text{GOTO} \end{Bmatrix}$ transfer line#

line# IF condition THEN statement(s) $\begin{Bmatrix} \text{transfer line}\# \\ \text{statement(s)} \end{Bmatrix}$

The brackets in the first statement indicate that one of the enclosed words is to be chosen when writing the statement. In other words, the first format of the IF/THEN can be worded in either of two ways:

line# IF condition THEN transfer line#
line# IF condition GOTO transfer line#

The execution of the IF/THEN statement follows these steps:

1. If the condition is true, the THEN or GOTO clause is executed. The program branches to the transfer line number and executes that statement (or the next executable statement).

Table IV-1
Relational Operators

Symbol	Meaning	Example
<	less than	small < BIG
<=	less than or equal to	1/2 <= .5
>	greater than	stock > 100
>=	greater than or equal to	X + 1 >= Y
=	equal to	NME$ = "BRUCE"
<>	not equal to	CODE$ <> "OK"

2. If the condition is false, the THEN or GOTO clause is ignored and execution continues with the next executable line following the IF/THEN statement.

The format of the condition looks like this:
expression1   relational symbol   expression2

RELATIONAL SYMBOL
(relational operator) A symbol used to specify a relationship between two values.

The values of the expressions can be either numeric or character strings (both must be the same type). The expressions can be constants, variables, and/or arithmetic expressions. The condition compares the two expressions by means of **relational symbols,** as defined in Table IV–1. In Table IV–1 the equals sign (=) is used to show both relational operations and assignment.

Figure IV–4 shows examples of valid IF/THEN statements. Notice the various conditions that are possible and the types of statements that can be used.

Double Alternative: IF/THEN/ELSE

Figure IV-4
Valid IF/THEN Statements

An extension of the IF/THEN statement is the IF/THEN/ELSE statement. Like the IF/THEN statement, it has two forms:

```
40   IF A = 6 THEN 60              10   IF X = Y THEN PRINT "X = Y"

70   IF A >= 10 THEN 90            30   IF C > 2 * D THEN LET A = A + 1

30   IF A <= 4 + B THEN 65         80   IF C$ <> "CONTINUE" THEN END

60   IF A = B + C THEN 10          20   IF X = 5 THEN Y = X + 1

90   IF G$ = "YES" THEN 80         50   IF N$ = "M" THEN PRINT "MONDAY"

50   IF X = Y / X THEN 85          55   IF A = 5 * A ^ B THEN PRINT X$
```

$$\text{line\# IF condition} \begin{Bmatrix} \text{THEN} \\ \text{GOTO} \end{Bmatrix} \text{transfer line\# ELSE} \begin{Bmatrix} \text{transfer line\#} \\ \text{statement(s)} \end{Bmatrix}$$

$$\text{line\# IF condition THEN statement(s) ELSE} \begin{Bmatrix} \text{transfer line\#} \\ \text{statement(s)} \end{Bmatrix}$$

The entire IF/THEN/ELSE statement must appear on one physical line (a physical line ends with a carriage return). If a statement exceeds the width of the screen, the computer causes the statement to "wrap around" to the next line without the use of the carriage return; thus it is still one physical line. A line can be up to 255 characters long. For example, the following program segment is invalid:

```
10 IF X > Y THEN Y = 0
20 ELSE X = 0
```

The statement should be written as follows:

```
10 IF X > Y THEN Y = 0 ELSE X = 0
```

The IF/THEN/ELSE statement is an example of the double-alternative decision structure mentioned earlier in this chapter. It is executed in this way:

1. If the condition is true, the THEN clause is executed and the ELSE clause is ignored.
2. If the condition is false, the THEN clause is ignored and the ELSE clause is executed.

The following are examples of the IF/THEN/ELSE statement:

```
70 IF X > 100 THEN PRINT "BIG" ELSE PRINT "SMALL"
80 IF X > Y THEN Z = X - Y ELSE Z = X + Y
40 IF X > Y THEN BIG = X ELSE BIG = Y
```

Nested IF Statements

It is possible to nest two or more IF/THEN or IF/THEN/ELSE statements. This means that an IF/THEN or IF/THEN/ELSE statement can be placed within the THEN or ELSE clause of another IF/THEN/ELSE statement. The following is an example of an IF/THEN/ELSE statement nested within the ELSE clause of another IF/THEN/ELSE statement:

```
10 IF N > 0 THEN PRINT "POSITIVE" ELSE IF N < 0 THEN
      PRINT "NEGATIVE" ELSE PRINT "ZERO"
```

Nesting statements in this manner can make a program difficult to follow. To avoid errors in logic, make sure that the nested IF/THEN/ELSE statements contain the same number of ELSE and THEN clauses; on execution, each ELSE is matched with the closest unmatched THEN. The following line illustrates this fact:

```
10 IF R = S THEN IF S = T THEN PRINT "R = T" ELSE "R <> T"
```

If R equals S and S equals T, this statement prints "R = T". This statement should print "R <> T" when either R is not equal to S or when S is not equal to T. As it is written, the statement does not print "R <> T" when R does not equal S because the ELSE clause is matched to the second THEN clause and thus is executed only when R equals S. The statement could be written correctly as follows:

```
10 IF R = S THEN IF S = T THEN PRINT "R = T" ELSE PRINT "R <> T"
   ELSE PRINT "R <> T"
```

AND/OR

The IF/THEN statement can be expanded by adding the AND and OR clauses to it. The program in Figure IV–5 contains examples of both these clauses. The IF/AND/THEN statement requires that *both conditions be true* before the THEN clause is executed. The IF/OR/THEN statement requires that *at least one of the conditions* be true before the THEN clause is executed. (If both conditions are true, the THEN clause also is executed.)

For example, the IF/AND/THEN statement in line 50 (Figure IV–5) requires that both conditions be true before control is transferred to line 90. By contrast, with the IF/OR/THEN statement in line 60, only one of the conditions must be true. If either A = 1 or B = 2 (or both), the computer skips to line 130 and continues from there. If neither statement is true, the computer continues onto line 70. If the appropriate conditions are not met for the corresponding IF/THEN statements, control of the program always passes to the next line in sequence.

The AND/OR clause also can be used with the double-alternative structure. The IF/AND/THEN requires that *all* the conditions be true for the THEN clause to be executed; if at least one condition is false, the ELSE clause is executed. The IF/OR/THEN requires that *at least one* condition be true for the THEN clause to be executed; otherwise, the ELSE clause is executed.

The ON/GOTO Statement

The ON/GOTO statement transfers control to other statements in the program. Any one of several transfers may occur, depending on the value computed for a mathematical expression. Because transfer depends upon the value of the expression, the ON/GOTO is another conditional transfer statement. Its general format is this:

line# ON expression GOTO line#1[,line#2,...]

The arithmetic expression is evaluated as an integer value; the expression is rounded if necessary. The execution of the ON/GOTO statement is as follows:

Figure IV-5
AND and OR Clauses

```
10   CLS
20   PRINT "ENTER THE NUMBERS 1,2,3"
30   PRINT "IN ANY ORDER"
40   INPUT N1,N2,N3
50   IF N1 = 1 AND N2 = 2 THEN 90
60   IF N1 = 1 OR N2 = 2 THEN 130
70   IF N1 <> N2 + N3 THEN 170
80   GOTO 200
90   PRINT
100  PRINT "BOTH CONDITIONS ARE MET"
110  PRINT "N1 = 1 AND N2 = 2"
120  GOTO 70
130  PRINT
140  PRINT "ONE OF THE CONDITIONS IS MET"
150  PRINT "EITHER N1 = 1 OR N2 = 2"
160  GOTO 70
170  PRINT
180  PRINT "N1 <> N2 + N3"
190  GOTO 999
200  PRINT
210  PRINT "N1 = N2 + N3"
999  END
```

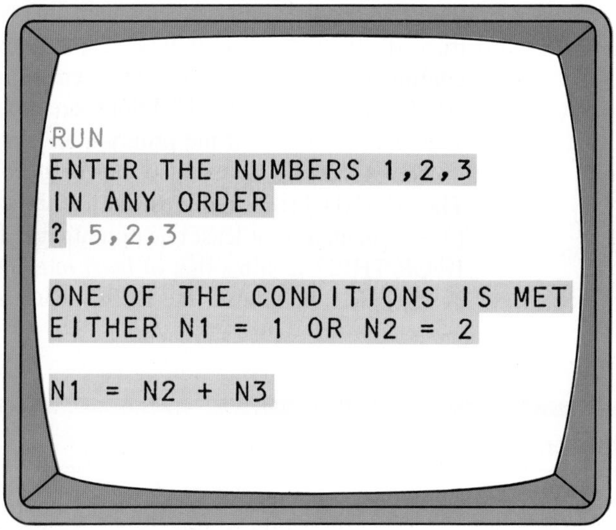

```
RUN
ENTER THE NUMBERS 1,2,3
IN ANY ORDER
? 5,2,3

ONE OF THE CONDITIONS IS MET
EITHER N1 = 1 OR N2 = 2

N1 = N2 + N3
```

1. The expression is rounded to an integer value.
2. Depending upon the value of the expression, control passes to the corresponding line number.

    a. If the value of the expression is 1, control passes to the first line number listed.

b. If the value of the expression is 2, control passes to the second line number listed.

c. If the value of the expression is *n*, control passes to the *n*th line number listed.

The following examples demonstrate the execution of the ON/GOTO statement.

Statement	Value of x	Execution
10 ON X GOTO 30,50,70	X = 1	Control passes to line 30
	X = 2	Control passes to line 50
	X = 3	Control passes to line 70
10 ON X − 2 GOTO 100,150	X = 3	3 − 2 = 1; control passes to line 100
	X = 4	4 − 2 = 2; control passes to line 150
20 ON X/3 GOTO 40,60,80	X = 7	7/3 = 2.33; result rounded to 2; control passes to line 60

Three additional rules apply to the ON/GOTO statement:

1. If the value of the expression is zero, the rest of the ON/GOTO statement is ignored and control passes to the next statement in sequence.

2. If the value of the expression is greater than the number of transfer lines listed, control passes to the next statement in sequence.

3. If the value of the expression is negative, an error message is displayed and execution stops.

Learning Check

1. A statement that always alters the execution path when it is encountered is a(n) _____ transfer statement.

2. A control statement that makes a decision based on the value of an expression is called a(n) _____ transfer statement.

3. Must the condition of an IF/THEN statement be evaluated only as true or false?

4. The expression in the ON/GOTO statement always is evaluated as a(n) _____.

5. The _____ clause indicates that *both* conditions must be true for the THEN/GOTO clause to be executed.

Answers

1. unconditional 2. conditional 3. yes 4. integer 5. AND

Figure IV–6 shows how to use the ON/GOTO statement in a program. If the expression N / 2 in line 30 equals 1 or is rounded to 1, control is transferred to line 100. If N / 2 equals 2 or is rounded to 2, control is transferred to line 200, and so on. Line 40 is inserted to prevent an error if N / 2 exceeds the values in the ON/GOTO statement. That is, if N / 2 is greater than S, the message requesting a number within bounds is repeated.

Menus

MENU
A screen display of a program's functions. The user enters a code at the keyboard to make a selection.

A **menu** is a displayed list of the functions that a program can perform. Just as a customer in a restaurant looks at the menu to choose a meal, so a program user looks at a menu displayed on the screen to choose a desired function. The user makes a selection by entering a code, usually a simple number or letter, at the keyboard. Figure IV–7 presents a simple example of a menu.

Figure IV-6
ON/GOTO Program

```
10 CLS
20   INPUT "ENTER A NUMBER FROM 1 TO 10";N
30   ON N / 2 GOTO 100,200,300,400,500
40   IF N / 2 > 5 THEN 20
100 PRINT "THE NUMBER WAS 1 OR 2"
110 GOTO 999
200 PRINT "THE NUMBER WAS 3 OR 4"
210 GOTO 999
300 PRINT "THE NUMBER WAS 5 OR 6"
310 GOTO 999
400 PRINT "THE NUMBER WAS 7 OR 8"
410 GOTO 999
500 PRINT "THE NUMBER WAS 9 OR 10"
999 END
```

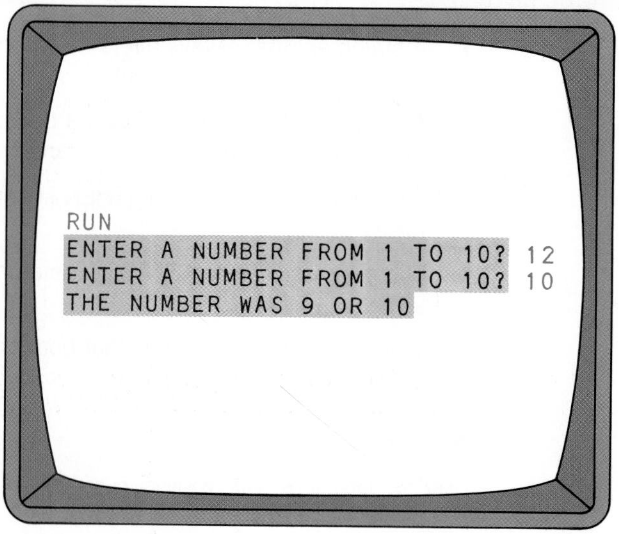

```
RUN
ENTER A NUMBER FROM 1 TO 10? 12
ENTER A NUMBER FROM 1 TO 10? 10
THE NUMBER WAS 9 OR 10
```

Figure IV-7
**Menu Program Using the ON/
GOTO Statement**

```
10   REM *** CONVERT DOLLARS TO FOREIGN CURRENCY ***
20   CLS
30   PRINT "           MONEY CONVERSION MENU"
40   PRINT
50   PRINT "ENTER NUMBER OF DOLLARS TO BE CONVERTED"
60   INPUT DOLLARS
70   PRINT
80   PRINT "PLEASE ENTER ONE OF THE FOLLOWING NUMBERS:"
90   PRINT "   1. TO CONVERT TO POUNDS"
100  PRINT "   2. TO CONVERT TO MARKS"
110  PRINT "   3. TO CONVERT TO FRANCS"
120  PRINT "   4. TO CONVERT TO LIRA"
130  PRINT
140  INPUT CODE
150  ON CODE GOTO 180,220,260,300
160  REM
170  REM *** POUNDS ***
180  RESULTS = DOLLARS * .94
190  GOTO 310
200  REM
210  REM *** MARKS ***
220  RESULTS = DOLLARS * 2.4
230  GOTO 310
240  REM
250  REM *** FRANCS ***
260  RESULTS = DOLLARS * 7.2
270  GOTO 310
280  REM
290  REM *** LIRA ***
300  RESULTS = DOLLARS * 1439!
310  PRINT "THE RESULT =";RESULTS
999  END
```

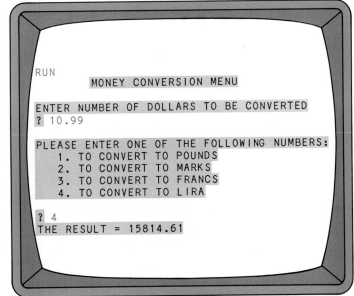

```
RUN
          MONEY CONVERSION MENU

ENTER NUMBER OF DOLLARS TO BE CONVERTED
? 10.99

PLEASE ENTER ONE OF THE FOLLOWING NUMBERS:
   1. TO CONVERT TO POUNDS
   2. TO CONVERT TO MARKS
   3. TO CONVERT TO FRANCS
   4. TO CONVERT TO LIRA

? 4
THE RESULT = 15814.61
```

The ON/GOTO statement often is used in menu programs such as the one in Figure IV–7. After entering the number of dollars to be converted, the user enters a 1, 2, 3, or 4 to indicate the currency desired. The ON/GOTO statement in line 150 then branches to the part of the program which performs the indicated conversion.

Subroutines: Structured Programming

STRUCTURED PROGRAMMING
A method of programming in which programs have easy-to-follow logic and are divided into subprograms, each designed to perform a specific task.

When computers were first developed, programming was extremely complex and programmers were happy just to get their programs to work. There was little concern about writing programs in a style that was easy for other people to understand. Gradually, however, programmers began to realize that working with such programs was very difficult, particularly when someone other than the original programmer had to alter an existing program.

Because of this problem, programmers began developing ways to make programs easier to understand and modify. These techniques, which have been developed over the past 20 years, are referred to as **structured programming.** Structured programming has two basic characteristics: (1) the program logic is easy to follow, and (2) the program is divided into smaller subprograms or modules, which in BASIC are referred to as subroutines.

Subroutines are modules in BASIC, each designed to perform a specific task. A subroutine is a sequence of statements which typically is located after the main body of the program. It can be executed any number of times in a given program.

The GOSUB Statement

The GOSUB statement transfers the flow of program control from the calling program to a subroutine. A subroutine can be called either from the main program or from another subroutine. The format of the GOSUB statement is as follows:

line# GOSUB transfer line#

The transfer line number must be the first number of the subroutine. This is very important, because the computer does not detect an error if it is instructed to branch to an incorrect line. It detects an error only if the transfer line number does not exist in the program.

The GOSUB statement causes an unconditional transfer to the specified line number. For example, the following statement causes a branch to the subroutine starting at line 1000:

```
100 GOSUB 1000
```

The RETURN Statement

After a subroutine is executed, the RETURN statement causes program control to return to the line following the one that contained the GOSUB statement. The format of the RETURN statement is as follows:

line# RETURN

Note that no transfer line number is needed in the RETURN statement. The computer automatically returns control to the statement immediately following the GOSUB statement that called the subroutine. If the line returned to is a nonexecutable statement, such as a REM statement, the computer simply skips it. Each subroutine must contain a RETURN statement as its last line; otherwise the program cannot branch back to the point from which the subroutine was called.

Example of Subroutine Usage

The program in Figure IV–8 prints a simple multiplication table. It contains a subroutine that prints a row of asterisks to divide the multiplication table into sections to make it more readable. The subroutine is called from three places in the main program: line 70, line 90, and line 210. Each time this subroutine is called, program control transfers to line 1000. Because lines 1000 through 1050 are nonexecutable statements, execution skips down to line 1060.

In this program, the subroutine is very short, so it would be easy to repeat the statements each time they are needed instead of using a subroutine. If the subroutine were longer, however, it would be tedious and wasteful to type it three times. Using subroutines simplifies program logic by organizing specific tasks into neat, orderly subsections.

The STOP Statement

When the STOP statement is executed, it causes the program to end. Sometimes a STOP statement is placed immediately before the subroutines of a program so that the subroutines are not executed after the last line of the main program is reached. The general format of the STOP statement is as follows:

line# STOP

In the program in Figure IV–8, the STOP statement in line 220 prevents the execution of the subroutines after the main program has been executed. Notice the message in the program output:

```
Break in 220
```

Figure IV-8
Multiplication Program Using a Subroutine

```
10    REM *** MULTIPLICATION PROGRAM ***
20    CLS
30    REM *** THE PURPOSE OF THIS PROGRAM IS TO SHOW ***
40    REM *** THE USE OF SUBROUTINES ***
50    REM
60    PRINT TAB(30);"MULTIPLICATION TABLE"
70    GOSUB 1000
80    PRINT TAB(5);"ONE";TAB(15);"TWO";TAB(25);"THREE"
90    GOSUB 1000
100   REM
110   REM *** PRINT TABLE ***
120   OUTER = 1
130   INNER = 1
140   PRINT OUTER;"*";INNER;"=";OUTER * INNER;
150   INNER = INNER + 1
160   IF INNER < 4 GOTO 140
170   PRINT
180   OUTER = OUTER + 1
190   IF OUTER < 11 THEN GOTO 130
200   PRINT
210   GOSUB 1000
220   STOP
1000  REM
1010  REM ************************
1020  REM ***SUBROUTINE ASTERISK***
1030  REM ************************
1040  REM *** PRINT ASTERISK ***
1050  REM
1060  COUNT = 1
1070  PRINT "*";
1080  COUNT = COUNT + 1
1090  IF COUNT <= 80 THEN 1070
1100  PRINT
1110  RETURN
9999  END
```

(Figure continued on the next page)

If an END statement were used in place of the STOP statement, this message would not be printed.

The ON/GOSUB Statement

Because the GOSUB statement is an unconditional transfer statement, it always transfers program control to the subroutine starting at the indicated line number. Sometimes, however, it is necessary to branch to one of several subroutines de-

Figure IV-8
Continued

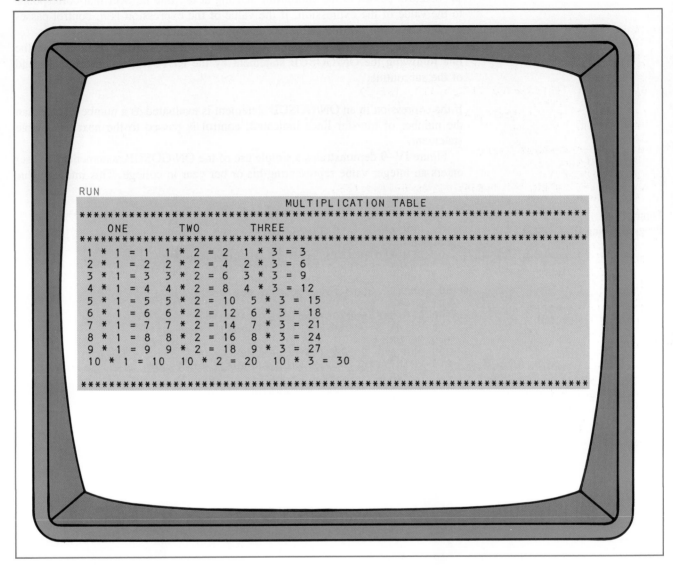

pending on existing conditions. The ON/GOSUB statement is useful for this purpose. The format of the ON/GOSUB statement is as follows:

line# ON expression GOSUB transfer line#1[transfer lines#2,...]

The ON/GOSUB is similar to the ON/GOTO statement in that it uses an arithmetic expression to determine the line number to which program control will transfer. The transfer line numbers in the ON/GOSUB statement, however, are not within the main program. Each transfer line number indicates the beginning of a subroutine.

The execution of the ON/GOSUB statement proceeds as follows:

1. The expression is evaluated as an integer, and is truncated if necessary.

2. Control passes to the subroutine starting at the line number that corresponds to the value of the expression. If the value of the expression is *n*, control passes to the subroutine starting at the *n*th line number listed.

3. After the specified subroutine is executed, control is transferred back to the line following the ON/GOSUB statement by the RETURN statement at the end of the subroutine.

If the expression in an ON/GOSUB statement is evaluated as a number larger than the number of transfer lines indicated, control is passed to the next executable statement.

Figure IV–9 demonstrates a simple use of the ON/GOSUB statement. The user enters an integer value representing his or her year in college. This integer value

Figure IV-9
Program Using ON/GOSUB

```
10   REM *** GRADUATION PROGRAM ***
20   CLS
30   REM *** PRINTS YEAR OF GRADUATION ***
40   INPUT "ENTER THE STUDENT'S NAME";STUDENT$
50   INPUT "ENTER CURRENT YEAR";YR
60   ON YR GOSUB 100,200,300,400
70   STOP
100  REM *** SUBROUTINE FRESHMAN ***
110  PRINT STUDENT$;" WILL GRADUATE IN 1991"
120  RETURN
200  REM *** SUBROUTINE SOPHOMORE ***
210  PRINT STUDENT$;" WILL GRADUATE IN 1990"
220  RETURN
300  REM *** SUBROUTINE JUNIOR ***
310  PRINT STUDENT$;" WILL GRADUATE IN 1989"
320  RETURN
400  REM *** SUBROUTINE SENIOR ***
410  PRINT STUDENT$;" WILL GRADUATE IN 1988"
420  RETURN
999  END
```

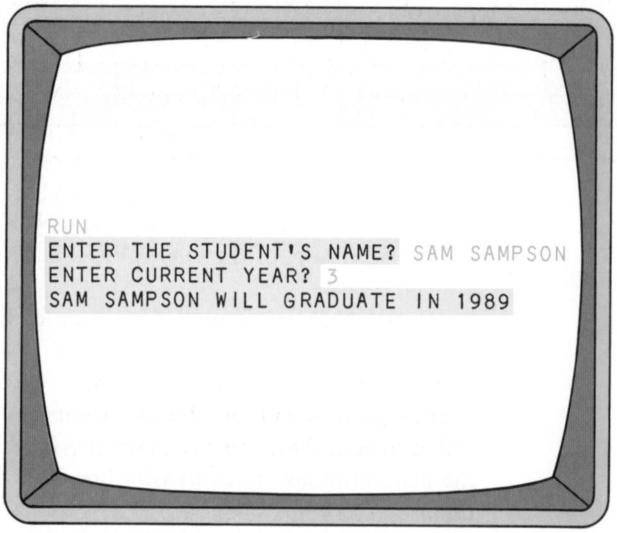

```
RUN
ENTER THE STUDENT'S NAME? SAM SAMPSON
ENTER CURRENT YEAR? 3
SAM SAMPSON WILL GRADUATE IN 1989
```

is assigned to the variable YR, which is used to determine which subroutine will be executed. After the appropriate subroutine is executed, control is returned to the main program, which then stops execution.

Learning Check

1. Subprograms in BASIC are called _____.

2. A(n) _____ statement causes an unconditional branch to a subroutine.

3. The _____ statement causes control to be transferred from a subroutine back to the calling program.

4. How many times can a given subroutine be called in a program?

5. The _____ statement is used to prevent unnecessary execution of subroutines or other statements.

Answers

1. subroutines 2. GOSUB 3. RETURN 4. There is no limit. 5. STOP

Comprehensive Programming Problem

The Problem

The math teachers at Stamm's Elementary school would like a program to help their students learn elementary arithmetic. The program should enable the user to enter a request to add, subtract, multiply, or divide two numbers (a menu can be used to display these options). After the operation is chosen, the program should ask for two numbers. Then it should use a subroutine to perform the computation and print the results.

Solution Design

The general problem we must solve is to calculate and print the results of a mathematical operation that is chosen by the user. The flow of data processing indicates that there are two smaller problems to solve:

1. Enter the necessary data.
2. Calculate the mathematical operation necessary.

Step 1 can be divided into two smaller units:

1.A.   Display the menu of mathematical operations.
1.B.   Enter the choice and the data values.

Because four mathematical operations are possible, the calculated results depend on a choice made by the user. Therefore, the second step can be divided into three steps:

2.A.   Determine which operation to perform.
2.B.   Calculate the results of the operation.
2.C.   Print the results.

The structure chart in Figure IV–10 shows this refinement of the problem.

Next we decide what program steps are needed to perform these tasks and the order in which they should be performed. Figure IV–11 shows the flowchart for a possible solution. The program needs to be interactive, so that the user can select the operation and the numbers.

Figure IV-10
Structure Chart for Mathematical
Operations Program

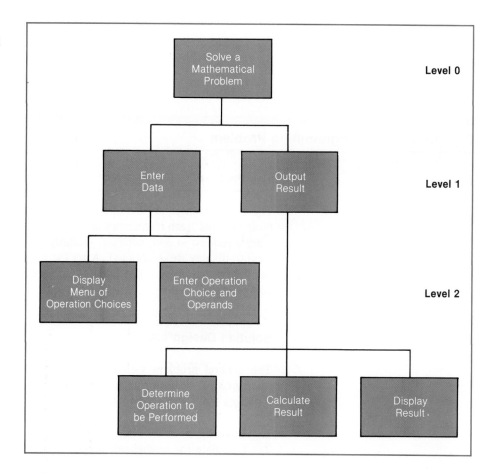

Figure IV-11
Flowchart for Mathematical Operations Program

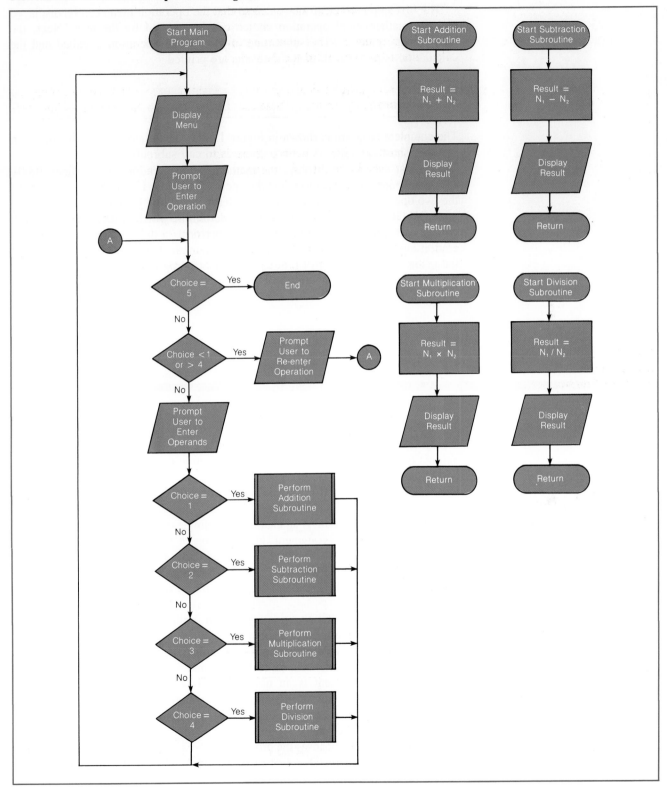

The first step is to clear the screen so that the operation menu can be displayed and the mathematical operation choice can be entered by the user. Next, the operands are entered. The subroutine of the chosen operation is called and the calculation is performed; then the results are printed.

The Program

The complete program is shown in Figure IV–12. The main body of this program is rather short, because its main purpose is to call subroutines.

The first subroutine displays the mathematical operations menu (lines 1000–1170) and enables the user to select the operation. In line 170 of the main program, the two operands are catered. The value that was entered for the operation is used in an ON/GOSUB statement in line 180 to determine which of the four subroutines will be executed. Each of the subroutines performs a different mathematical operation and prints the results. After the mathematical operation is executed and the result is printed, control returns to the main program (line 190), which calls the menu subroutine again and gives the user the option to perform another mathematical operation.

Summary Points

- The GOTO statement tells the computer to execute the statement whose line number follows the word GOTO. It is an unconditional transfer statement, because control is sent without regard to any condition.
- The IF/THEN evaluates a condition as true or false. If the condition is true, control passes to the THEN clause. If it is false, control passes to the next line.
- The IF/THEN statement is an example of a single-alternative decision structure.
- The IF/THEN/ELSE statement, an extension of the IF/THEN, passes control to the THEN clause if the condition is true and to the ELSE clause if the condition is false. IF/THEN and IF/THEN/ELSE statements can be nested.
- The IF/THEN/ELSE statement is an example of a double-alternative decision structure.
- When the IF/AND/THEN statement is used, both conditions specified must be true for the THEN clause to be executed.
- When the IF/OR/THEN statement is used, at least one (or both) of the conditions must be true for the THEN clause to be executed.
- The GOSUB statement is an unconditional branch that causes the flow of execution to be passed to the line number contained in the GOSUB statement.
- The RETURN statement causes control to be transferred back to the statement after the one that called the subroutine.
- The STOP statement causes the program to end at the point where it is executed. Usually it is placed immediately before the subroutines, to ensure that they are not executed when they are not needed.

Figure IV-12
Mathematical Operations Program

```
10    REM ***           MATHEMATICAL OPERATIONS               ***
20    CLS
30    REM *** THIS PROGRAM PERFORMS ADDITION, SUBTRACTION ***
40    REM *** MULTIPLICATION AND DIVISION OF TWO NUMBERS   ***
50    REM *** BASED ON THE USER'S CHOICE.                  ***
60    REM *** MAJOR VARIABLES:                             ***
70    REM *** CHOICE           MATHEMATICAL OPERATION      ***
80    REM *** N1,N2            TWO NUMBERS                 ***
90    REM *** ADD              RESULT OF ADDITION          ***
100   REM *** SUBTRACT         RESULT OF SUBTRACTION       ***
110   REM *** MULTIPLY         RESULT OF MULTIPLICATION    ***
120   REM *** DIVIDE           RESULT OF DIVISION          ***
130   REM
140   REM *** CALL SUBROUTINE TO PRINT MENU ***
150   GOSUB 1000
160   IF CHOICE = 5 THEN STOP
170   INPUT "ENTER TWO NUMBERS (SEPARATED BY A COMMA)";N1,N2
180   ON CHOICE GOSUB 2000,3000,4000,5000
190   GOTO 150
1000  REM
1010  REM ***********************
1020  REM *** SUBROUTINE MENU ***
1030  REM ***********************
1040  REM *** PRINT MATHEMATICAL OPERATION ***
1050  REM
1060  REM
1070  PRINT
1080  PRINT TAB(30);"MATHEMATICAL OPERATIONS"
1090  PRINT
1100  PRINT TAB(30);"1. ADDITION"
1110  PRINT TAB(30);"2. SUBTRACTION"
1120  PRINT TAB(30);"3. MULTIPLICATION"
1130  PRINT TAB(30);"4. DIVISION"
1140  PRINT TAB(30);"5. QUIT"
1150  PRINT
1160  INPUT "ENTER THE NUMBER OF DESIRED OPERATION";CHOICE
1170  RETURN
2000  REM
2010  REM ***************************
2020  REM *** SUBROUTINE ADDITION ***
2030  REM ***************************
2040  REM *** ADD TWO NUMBERS ***
2050  REM
2060  ADD = N1 + N2
2070  PRINT
2080  PRINT N1;" + ";N2;" = ";ADD
2090  PRINT
2100  RETURN
3000  REM
3010  REM ******************************
3020  REM *** SUBROUTINE SUBTRACTION ***
3030  REM ******************************
3040  REM *** SUBTRACT TWO NUMBERS ***
3050  REM
3060  SUBTRACT = N1 - N2
3070  PRINT
3080  PRINT N1;" - ";N2;" = ";SUBTRACT
3090  PRINT
3100  RETURN
4000  REM
4010  REM ******************************
```

(Figure continued on the next page)

Figure IV-12 Continued

```
4020 REM *** SUBROUTINE MULTIPLICATION ***
4030 REM ***********************************
4040 REM *** MULTIPLY TWO NUMBERS ***
4050 REM
4060 MULT = N1 * N2
4070 PRINT
4080 PRINT N1;" * ";N2;" = ";MULT
4090 PRINT
4100 RETURN
5000 REM
5010 REM ****************************
5020 REM *** SUBROUTINE DIVISION ***
5030 REM ****************************
5040 REM *** DIVIDE TWO NUMBERS ***
5050 REM
5060 DIVIDE = N1 / N2
5070 PRINT
5080 PRINT N1;" / ";N2;" = ";DIVIDE
5090 PRINT
5100 RETURN
9999 END
```

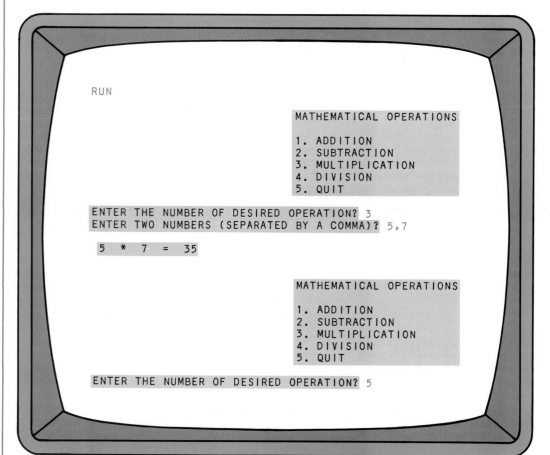

```
RUN

                          MATHEMATICAL OPERATIONS

                          1. ADDITION
                          2. SUBTRACTION
                          3. MULTIPLICATION
                          4. DIVISION
                          5. QUIT

ENTER THE NUMBER OF DESIRED OPERATION? 3
ENTER TWO NUMBERS (SEPARATED BY A COMMA)? 5,7

   5  *  7  =  35

                          MATHEMATICAL OPERATIONS

                          1. ADDITION
                          2. SUBTRACTION
                          3. MULTIPLICATION
                          4. DIVISION
                          5. QUIT

ENTER THE NUMBER OF DESIRED OPERATION? 5
```

Review Questions

1. What is a control statement?
2. Why is the GOTO statement an unconditional transfer statement?
3. Why is the IF statement a conditional transfer statement?
4. Which of the following are valid IF statements?

   a. 40 IF X$ = "FRANCO" THEN M = M + 1
   b. 50 IF Y$ <> "YES" THEN 40
   c. 20 IF Z = "NIENTE" THEN 100
   d. 70 IF Y THEN 20
   e. 60 IF "HOPELESS" >= "HOPEFUL" THEN 999

5. The expression of the ON/GOTO statement must be evaluated as an ____.
6. Control passes to what line when the following is executed, is SUM = 21?

   10 ON SUM/7 GOTO 50, 80, 110

7. What is a menu?
8. Where are RETURN statements placed in programs?
9. What happens if the transfer line number in a GOSUB statement is a non-executable statement?
10. Why is the GOSUB statement referred to as an unconditional branching statement?

Debugging Exercises

```
1.  10 READ A,B
    20 X = A + B
    30 IF X THEN 120
    40 PRINT X


2.  10 REM *** CALCULATES THE AVERAGE OF FIVE TEST SCORES **
    20 CNT = 1
    30 IF CNT > 5 THEN 80
    40    INPUT "ENTER SCORE";PTS
    50    TT = TT + PTS
    60 GOTO 30
    70 AVG = TT / 5
    80 PRINT "THE AVERAGE IS";PTS
    99 END
```

Additional Programming Problems

1. World Travel wants a program that displays a menu with a list of countries to which the agency can send a customer at special discount rates. After the user enters the name of a particular country, the program should print all cities in that country in which the special rates are available. Use the following data:

Country	Cities
France	Nice
	Cannes
	Nantes
	Chamonix
Italy	Milan
	Verona
	Venice
	Naples
U.S.A.	Chicago
	San Francisco
	New York
	Miami

2. Budget Balloons provides hot-air balloon rides for fairs, parties, and other special occasions. The basic fee is $65.00 for the first hour and $45.00 for every additional hour. The company needs a program to help calculate its clients' bills. The program should call a subroutine to do the actual calculating, and use a loop to allow as many bills to be calculated as desired. The output of the program should include the name of the client and his or her total bill.

3. R & R Railways wants a program to determine the cost for passengers to various cities. The cost per person for the following cities is as follows:

Columbus	$ 39.00
Denver	142.00
New York	108.00
New Orleans	158.00

A menu should display the names of the cities and ask how many people would like to purchase tickets. If a customer wants first-class tickets, there is an additional $30.00 flat fee. The cost of the needed tickets should be calculated in subroutines. Develop your own data to test the program.

4. As the manager of an apartment building, you need a program to help you keep track of the various apartments for rent. Write a program using subroutines which will give the user the choice of a studio, one-bedroom, or two-bedroom apartment. The monthly rent depends on the size of the apartment and whether it is to be furnished or unfurnished (this data should also be entered by the user). Use the following data:

| | | Rent | |
Type	Deposit	Furnished	Unfurnished
Studio	$ 75	$150	$135
One-bedroom	150	275	250
Two-bedroom	200	325	315

The program should print the apartment description, required deposit, and monthly rent according to the choices entered, using the following format:

Description:	One-bedroom furnished
Deposit:	$150
Rent:	$275

5. Write a program that will print current weather forecasts. A menu should be used to display the choices. Use the ON/GOTO statement and the following sample data:

Date	Forecast
9/01	Cloudy; 60% chance of afternoon showers; high 70–75°
9/02	Sunny and breezy; high 80–85°
9/03	Partly cloudy; 40% chance of rain; high 65–70°

SECTION V

Looping

Introduction

One of the most powerful features of the computer is its ability to perform repetitive tasks quickly and accurately. This process is referred to as looping. Two types of loops will be introduced in this section: the FOR/NEXT and the WHILE/WEND.

Looping Methods

Often a situation arises in which a single task must be performed several times. For example, a teacher may need a program to find the average test score of all the students in a given class. The job of processing a single student's data is simple enough:

    Read name, score
    Print name, score

Now consider the problem of repeating these steps for a class of thirty students:

    Read name, score
    Add score to total
    Print name, score
    Read name, score
    Add score to total
    Print name, score

            .
            .
            .

    Read name, score
    Add score to total
    Print name, score
    Divide total by 30
    Print class average

The same three statements to process a single student's data would have to be written thirty times, or they could be written once in a subroutine which the main program would call thirty times. The problem could be simplified greatly by writing the processing statements (or the subroutine call) just once, then executing those statements as many times as needed. This procedure, called looping, is flowcharted at the top of the next page.

One of the most important uses of control statements is the creation of loops. Control statements can determine which actions are to be repeated and the number of repetitions to be made. Some techniques for loop control include the use of trailer values, counters, and such looping statements as the FOR/NEXT statement.

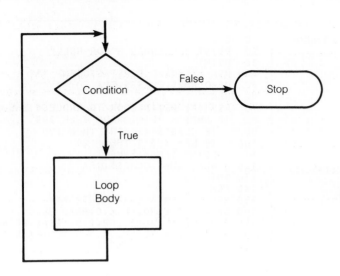

Trailer Values

TRAILER VALUE
A unique data value that signals the termination of a loop.

SENTINEL VALUE
See Trailer value.

A **trailer value** is a dummy value that follows or "trails" the data items to be processed. Sometimes it is referred to as a **sentinel value.** The trailer value signals the program that all the data has been read. The trailer can be either a numeric value or a character string, depending on the type of data being input, but it should always be a value outside the range of the actual data. For example, if a program reads people's ages, a good trailer value might be − 1. If names are being read, an example of a good trailer value would be the string FINISHED.

A trailer value can control a loop in the following way. Before the loop begins, a READ or INPUT statement reads the first data item or group of data items to a certain variable or variables. The loop begins with an IF/THEN statement, which checks one of the variables to see if its value equals the trailer value. If so, then all the data items have been read, and program control passes to the first executable statement following the loop. If the variable's value is not equal to the trailer value, however, then the statements in the loop are executed. At the end of the loop, the next data item or group of data items is read, and a GOTO statement passes control back to the beginning of the loop.

Trailer values also must be given for the other data items read by the READ statement, so that an out-of-data error does not occur; the computer expects a value to be present for each variable in the READ statement. This same principle is true when the INPUT statement is used to read data until the trailer value is entered.

Figure V-1 shows an honor roll program with a loop controlled by a trailer value. Because names are being read, the string FINISHED is appropriate for the trailer value. Notice the actions performed between the IF/THEN statement in line 80 and the GOTO statement in line 130; this is the loop. This loop continues processing data until the trailer value has been read and the condition in the IF/THEN statement evaluates as true. This event causes the branch statement in the THEN clause to be executed, and control passes out of the loop to the end of the program.

Figure V-1
Example of a Loop Using a Trailer
Value

```
10   CLS
20   PRINT "FRESHMAN HONOR ROLL"
30   PRINT
40   REM *** READ FIRST STUDENT ***
50   READ NME$,CLASS$,GPA
60   REM
70   REM *** BEGIN LOOP TO PROCESS ONE STUDENT PER PASS ***
80   IF NME$ = "FINISHED" THEN 999
90     IF CLASS$ <> "FR" THEN 120
100    IF GPA < 3.5 THEN 120
110    PRINT TAB(8);NME$
120    READ NME$,CLASS$,GPA
130  GOTO 80
140  REM
150  REM *** DATA STATEMENTS ***
160  DATA PAT LORD,FR,4.0,BRAD BUSCH,FR,3.7
170  DATA DERYL JONES,FR,2.9,IRENE DRAKE,SR,4.0
180  DATA CHLOE TULLY,JR,3.0,MONICA DYLAN,FR,3.8
190  DATA FINISHED,NONE,0
999  END
```

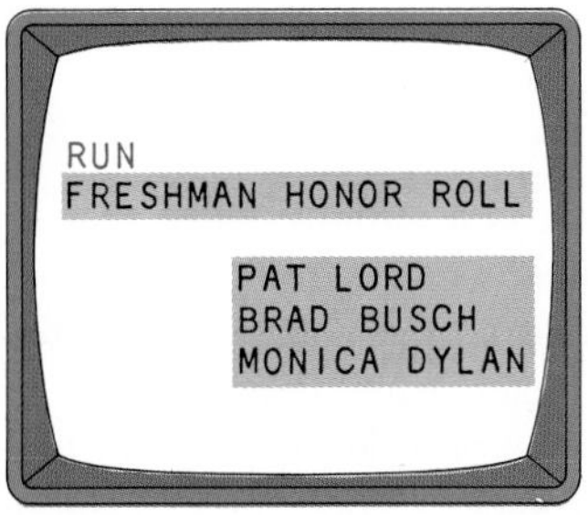

```
RUN
FRESHMAN HONOR ROLL

     PAT LORD
     BRAD BUSCH
     MONICA DYLAN
```

Care is needed when using GOTO statements in loops. An incorrect transfer line number can produce unexpected results. For example, study Figure V-1 and consider what would happen if the GOTO statement in line 130 were written like this:

```
220 GOTO 90
```

In this case, control would always be passed to the line after the IF/THEN statement. The students' names would not be tested for the trailer value, and there would be no way to end the loop. A loop such as this, without an exit, is called an **infinite** (or **endless**) **loop.** An infinite loop can cause an error or can prevent the program from continuing to a normal termination. Careful checking of all program branches helps the programmer to avoid infinite loops.

INFINITE LOOP
(endless loop) A loop with no exit point.

Counters

A second method of controlling a loop is to create a special variable to keep track of the number of times the loop has been executed. Such a variable is called a

COUNTER

A variable used to control loop repetition. Each time the loop is executed, the counter is tested to determine if the desired number of repetitions has been performed.

counter. The counter is increased, or incremented, by a fixed amount (usually 1) each time the loop is executed. When the programmer knows in advance how many times the loop should be repeated the counter can be tested by an IF/THEN statement after each loop execution to see if the proper number has been reached.

To set up a counter for loop control, you should perform the following steps:

1. Initialize the counter (before entering the loop) by setting it to a beginning value.
2. Increment the counter each time the loop is executed.
3. Test the counter each time the loop is executed to see if the loop has been performed the desired number of times.

The program in Figure V-1 has been rewritten in Figure V-2 to use a counter rather than a trailer value. There are six students, so the loop must be executed exactly six times. The counter is initialized to 1 in line 40, before the loop starts. Line 70 tests the counter to see if it is greater than 6, and exits the loop if the condition is true. Otherwise, the loop is executed and the counter is incremented in line 120 before branching to the top of the loop again.

Figure V-2
Example of a Counter Loop

```
10   CLS
20   PRINT "FRESHMAN HONOR ROLL"
30   PRINT
40   COUNT = 1
50   REM
60   REM *** BEGIN LOOP TO PROCESS ONE STUDENT PER PASS ***
70   IF COUNT > 6 THEN 999
80     READ NME$,CLASS$,GPA
90     IF CLASS$ <> "FR" THEN 120
100    IF GPA < 3.5 THEN 120
110    PRINT TAB(8);NME$
120    COUNT = COUNT + 1
130 GOTO 70
140 REM
150 REM *** DATA STATEMENTS ***
160 DATA PAT LORD,FR,4.0,BRAD BUSCH,FR,3.7
170 DATA DERYL JONES,FR,2.9,IRENE DRAKE,SR,4.0
180 DATA CHLOE TULLY,JR,3.0,MONICA DYLAN,FR,3.8
999 END
```

```
RUN
FRESHMAN HONOR ROLL

       PAT LORD
       BRAD BUSCH
       MONICA DYLAN
```

Elements of Looping

LOOP CONTROL VARIABLE
A variable whose value is used to determine the number of loop repetitions.

LOOP BODY
The statements that constitute the action to be performed by the loop.

The loop is an extremely powerful and vital programming tool. Many looping methods exist in various programming languages, but all these methods share some basic components. A **loop control variable,** for example, is a variable whose value is used to determine the number of times a loop is repeated. The counter variable is an example of a loop control variable. All loops contain some action that may be performed repeatedly; the statements that perform such an action make up the **loop body.**

Execution of the basic loop structure consists of the following five steps:

1. The loop control variable is initialized to a particular value before loop execution begins.

2. The program tests the loop control variable to determine whether it should execute the loop body or exit the loop.

3. The loop body, which can consist of any number of statements, is executed.

4. At some point during loop execution, the value of the loop control variable must be modified to allow exit from the loop.

5. The loop is exited when the test in Step 2 determines that the right number of loop repetitions has been made. Execution continues with the next statement following the loop.

Research has determined that the first statement of a loop always should contain Step 2, the condition controlling loop repetition. Therefore, the branch at the bottom of the loop transfers program control to this statement. This structure makes the boundaries of the loop readily identifiable. Also, the execution path of the loop is tightly controlled, and therefore easy to follow, because no actions of the loop can be performed unless the controlling condition is satisfied.

As an example of this concept, consider the following loop:

```
10 READ AGE
20 IF AGE > 18 THEN 99
30 PRINT AGE
40 GOTO 10
99 END
```

This loop begins with a READ statement, because the GOTO statement at the end of the loop always branches to line 10. The READ statement initializes and modifies the value of the variable AGE, but does not test it. The same loop is better designed as follows:

```
10 READ AGE
20 IF AGE > 18 THEN 99
30 PRINT AGE
40 READ AGE
50 GOTO 20
99 END
```

The extra READ statement within the loop makes line 20 the first statement of the loop, a good programming principle. Remember this when setting up a loop.

The FOR/NEXT Loop

FOR/NEXT statements are used together to form a loop that is repeated a stated number of times. Figure V-3 contains a single program that uses a FOR/NEXT loop to add ten numbers together. In this program, the value of SUM is initially set to zero. The FOR/NEXT loop is then entered.

The variable I is referred to as a loop control variable; it is the variable that determines if the loop will be executed. When the FOR statement is executed, the loop control variable is set to an initial value (in this case 1). This value is tested against the terminal value (10). As long as the value of I is less than or equal to the terminal value, the loop is executed. Each time the loop is executed, the value of I is incremented by 1. When I is greater than 10, the loop is not executed again.

The statements in lines 30 and 40 constitute the body of this loop contains the actions that the loop performs. For each execution of the loop, the next number is read from the DATA statement and added to SUM. Notice that the loop body is indented. Indenting control statements makes no difference to the computer, but makes the program more readable for humans.

When the NEXT statement in line 50 is reached, the value of I is incremented by one and program control is transferred to the top of the loop. If the current value of I is less than or equal to the terminal value, the body of the loop is executed again; if I is greater than the terminal value, program control is transferred to the first statement following the NEXT statement. In this example, after the loop has executed ten times, control is transferred to line 60 and the sum of the ten numbers is printed.

In the loop in Figure V-3, both the initial and terminal values are numeric constants. These values could be numeric expressions or variables instead. In the

Figure V-3
Program to Add Ten Numbers

```
10  SUM = 0
20  FOR I = 1 TO 10
30     READ NMBR
40     SUM = SUM + NMBR
50  NEXT I
60  PRINT SUM
70  DATA 4,15,72,80,6,29,34,42,96,9
99  END
```

```
RUN
387
```

next example, the initial value is numeric expression and the terminal value is a numeric variable:

```
30 A = 8
40 FOR I = 2 + 4 TO A
50    PRINT I
60 NEXT I
```

This loop executes three times, and the output appears as follows:

```
6
7
8
```

It is possible to alter the value by which the loop control variable is incremented. This is done by placing a step value at the end of the FOR statement. The FOR statement in the program at the top of Figure V-4 has a step value of 2.

If a FOR statement contains no step value, a step value of $+1$ is assumed. The following FOR statements are equivalent, because the default step value is $+1$:

```
FOR I = 10 TO 20            FOR I = 10 TO 20 STEP 1
```

The FOR/NEXT loop in Figure V-4 executes 10 times, and the even numbers from 2 through 20 are printed. It is also possible to have a negative step value, as shown in the program at the bottom of Figure V-4. When a negative step value is used, the loop control variable is decremented each time through the loop. This program prints the even numbers from 20 through 2.

Rules for Using the FOR/NEXT Loop

To avoid errors in using the FOR and NEXT statements, it is important to be aware of the following rules:

■ The body of the loop is not executed if the initial value is greater than the terminal value when using a positive step, or if the initial value is less than the terminal value when using a negative step. For example, a loop containing either of the following statements would not be executed at all:

```
10 FOR X = 10 TO 5 STEP 2
20 FOR COUNT = 4 TO 6 STEP -1
```

■ The initial, terminal, and step values cannot be modified in the loop body.
■ It is possible to modify the loop control variable in the loop body, but this should *never* be done. Note how unpredictable the execution of the following loop would be, because the value of I is dependent on the integer entered by the user:

```
30 FOR I = 1 TO 10
40    INPUT "ENTER AN INTEGER";X
50    I = X
60 NEXT I
```

Figure V-4
FOR/NEXT Loops Using Positive
and Negative Step Values

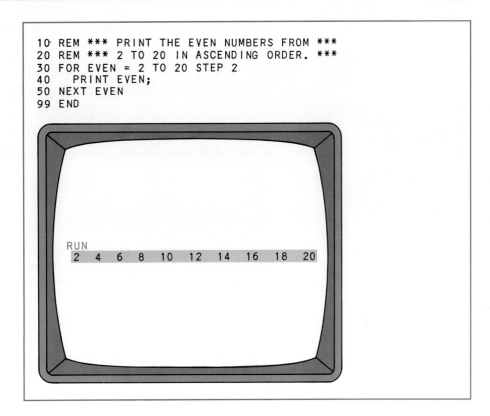

```
10 REM *** PRINT THE EVEN NUMBERS FROM ***
20 REM *** 2 TO 20 IN ASCENDING ORDER. ***
30 FOR EVEN = 2 TO 20 STEP 2
40   PRINT EVEN;
50 NEXT EVEN
99 END
```

```
RUN
 2   4   6   8   10   12   14   16   18   20
```

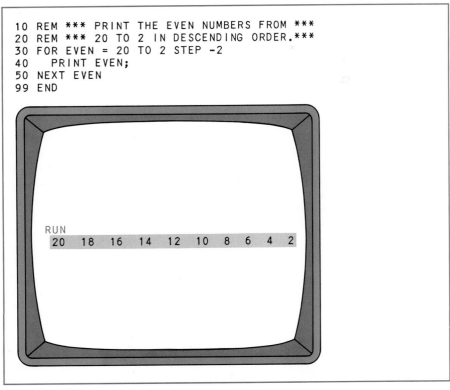

```
10 REM *** PRINT THE EVEN NUMBERS FROM ***
20 REM *** 20 TO 2 IN DESCENDING ORDER.***
30 FOR EVEN = 20 TO 2 STEP -2
40   PRINT EVEN;
50 NEXT EVEN
99 END
```

```
RUN
 20   18   16   14   12   10   8   6   4   2
```

■ If the step value is zero, an infinite loop is created:

```
10 FOR X = 10 TO 20 STEP 0
```

This loop could be rewritten so that it would execute ten times, as follows:

```
10 FOR X = 10 TO 20 STEP 1
```

■ Each FOR statement must have a corresponding NEXT statement.

Flowcharting the FOR/NEXT Loop

Figure V-5a shows the common method of flowcharting a FOR/NEXT loop. An alternate method, shown in Figure V-5b, shows a convenient shorthand symbol that we have developed. This symbol provides a concise way to indicate the initial, terminal, and step values. The symbol represents the actions of both the FOR and NEXT statements. As long as the terminal condition (indicated on the right portion of the symbol) is false, the execution path containing the loop body is followed. The arrow from the last loop body action to the step value portion of the symbol indicates the action of the NEXT statement. When the terminal condition is true, the path containing the actions following the loop is taken.

Advantages of Using the FOR/NEXT Loop

The FOR/NEXT loop often is used in programs because it performs many tasks automatically. The loop control variable is incremented or decremented automatically. Also, the condition that controls loop repetition is checked automatically each time the FOR statement is executed. Therefore, the programmer does not need to perform these tasks.

COUNTING LOOP
A type of loop in which repetition is controlled by a counter, which is a numeric variable that is tested each time the loop is executed to determine if the desired number of repetitions has been performed.

The FOR/NEXT loop is very useful when writing programs that use **counting loops,** in which the exact number of loop repetitions is known before the loop is executed for the first time. The program in Figure V-6 is an example of a situation in which it is appropriate to use a counting loop. In this program, the user is asked to enter the number of paychecks that need to be calculated for a village payroll. Then this number, which is assigned to the variable NMBR, is used to control the number of times the FOR/NEXT loop executes. In this way, the user can determine the number of paychecks calculated each time the program is executed.

Nested FOR/NEXT Loops

It is possible to nest two or more FOR/NEXT loops. This means that a FOR/NEXT loop can be placed within another FOR/NEXT loop, as shown in the following example:

```
FOR I = X TO Y STEP 2
  FOR J = 1 TO 2
      .
      .
      .
  NEXT J
NEXT I
```

Figure V-5
Flowcharting the FOR/NEXT Statements

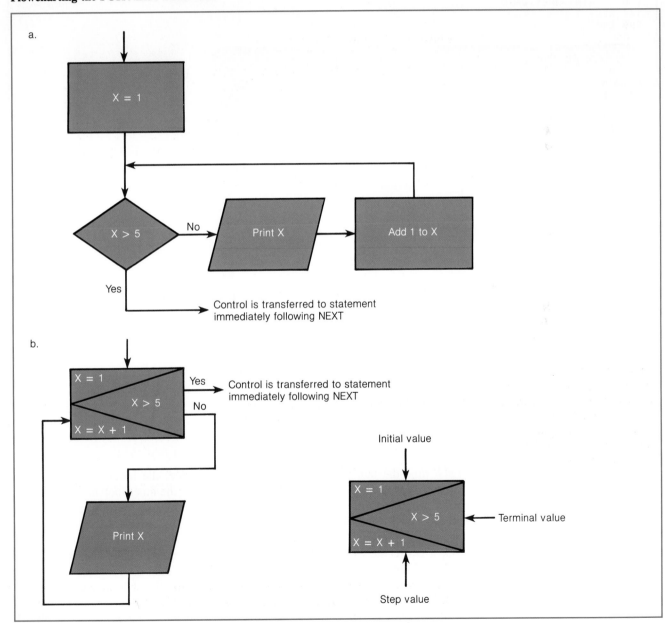

```
10   REM ***                    THE VILLAGE PAYROLL            ***
20   REM
30   LET RTE = 4
40   REM
50   CLS
60   REM *** DETERMINE HOW MANY PAYCHECKS ARE TO BE CALCULATED ***
70   INPUT "HOW MANY PAYCHECKS NEED TO BE CALCULATED";NMBR
80   REM *** LOOP TO PROCESS EACH EMPLOYEE'S PAYCHECK ***
90   FOR I = 1 TO NMBR
100    INPUT "ENTER NAME AND NUMBER OF HOURS WORKED";NME$,HOURS
110    WAGE = RTE * HOURS
120    PRINT "NAME","WAGE"
130    PRINT NME$,WAGE
140  NEXT I
999  END
```

```
RUN
HOW MANY PAYCHECKS NEED TO BE CALCULATED? 3
ENTER NAME AND NUMBER OF HOURS WORKED? JACOBSON,40
NAME            WAGE
JACOBSON         160
ENTER NAME AND NUMBER OF HOURS WORKED? SANCHEZ,43.5
NAME            WAGE
SANCHEZ          174
ENTER NAME AND NUMBER OF HOURS WORKED? ZOLLOS,38
NAME            WAGE
ZOLLOS           152
```

Figure V-6
Program to Calculate a Payroll

Each time the outer loop (loop I) is executed once, the inner loop (loop J) is executed twice, because J varies from 1 to 2. When the inner loop has terminated, control passes to the first statement after the NEXT J, which in this case is the statement NEXT I. This statement causes I to be incremented by 1 and tested against the terminal value of 4. If I still is less than or equal to 4, the body of loop I is executed again. The loop J is again encountered, the value of J is reset to 1, and the inner loop is executed until J is greater than 2. Altogether, the outer loop is executed I times (4 times in this case) and the inner loop is executed I × J times (4 × 2 = 8 times).

The following rules should be remembered when using nested FOR/NEXT loops:

■ Each loop must have a unique loop control variable. The following example is invalid, because execution of the inner loop modifies the value of the outer loop control variable:

```
FOR I = X TO Y STEP 2
  FOR I = Q TO R
      .
      .
      .
  NEXT I
NEXT I
```

These nested loops should be rewritten so that each uses a unique loop control variable:

```
FOR I = X TO Y STEP 2
  FOR J = Q TO R
      .
      .
      .
  NEXT J
NEXT I
```

■ The NEXT statements for an inner loop must appear within the body of the outer loop, so that one loop is entirely contained within another.

Invalid

```
FOR I = 1 TO 5
  FOR J = 1 TO 10
      .
      .
      .
  NEXT I
NEXT J
```

Valid

```
FOR I = 1 TO 5
  FOR J = 1 TO 10
      .
      .
      .
  NEXT J
NEXT I
```

In the invalid example, the J loop is not entirely inside the I loop, but extends beyond the NEXT I statement.

■ It is possible to nest many loops within one another. Figure V-7 illustrates multiple nested loops.

**Figure V-7
Multiple Nested FOR/NEXT Loops**

```
10   FOR I = 1 TO 3
20     PRINT I
30     FOR J = 1 TO 4
40       PRINT J
50       FOR K = 1 TO 2
60         PRINT K
70       NEXT K
80     NEXT J
90   NEXT I
```

Loop 3   Loop 2   Loop 1

Loop 1 is executed 3 times, loop 2 is executed $3 \times 4 = 12$ times, and loop 3 is executed $3 \times 4 \times 2 = 24$ times. Each loop is completely contained within its outer loop.

Figure V-8 shows an application of nested FOR/NEXT loops. The program prints the multiplication tables for the numbers 1, 2 and 3, with each table in a single column. The inner loop S controls the printing in each of the three columns, whereas the outer loop R controls the printing of rows. The first time the outer loop is executed, the first row is printed; the inner loop then prints three statements on that row. The first time the S loop is executed, $R = 1$ and $S = 1$, so the printed statement is $1 \times 1 = 1$. The comma at the end of line 90 causes a space to appear before the next output.

When the S loop has been completed (when three statements have been printed on the first 2 rows), the PRINT statement in line 110 causes the remainder of the line to remain blank; the next output starts at the left margin on the next line. As line 120 increments R and passes control back to the top of the R loop, this loop begins a second execution, during which a second row is printed. The program ends when the R loop has been executed ten times and ten rows have been printed.

Learning Check

1. When the terminal value is exceeded in a FOR/NEXT loop (using a positive step value), control passes to what statement?

2. When no step value is specified in a FOR statement, it is assumed to be _____.

3. A loop that is completely enclosed by another loop is called a(n) _____ loop.

4. Two or more nested loops can have the same loop control variable name. True or false?

5. The FOR statement serves to _____.
   a. initialize and test the loop control variable
   b. increment the loop control variable by the step value
   c. pass control to the NEXT statement

Answers

1. The first statement following the NEXT statement. 2. +1 3. nested 4. false 5. a

Figure V-8
Multiplication Table with Nested FOR/NEXT Loops

```
10    REM *** PRINT THREE MULTIPLICATION TABLES ***
20    CLS
30    REM *** MAJOR VARIABLES                    ***
40    REM ***    R         OUTER LOOP INDEX      ***
50    REM ***    S         INNER LOOP INDEX      ***
60    REM
70    FOR R = 1 TO 10
80      FOR S = 1 TO 3
90        PRINT S;" X ";R;" = ";S * R,
100     NEXT S
110     PRINT
120   NEXT R
999   END
```

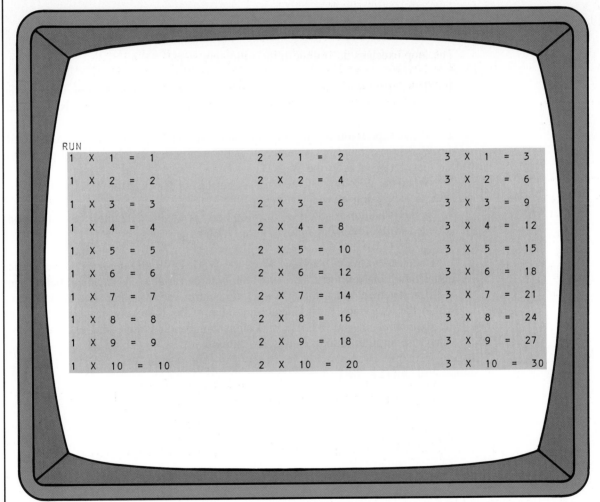

```
RUN
1  X  1  =  1          2  X  1  =  2          3  X  1  =  3

1  X  2  =  2          2  X  2  =  4          3  X  2  =  6

1  X  3  =  3          2  X  3  =  6          3  X  3  =  9

1  X  4  =  4          2  X  4  =  8          3  X  4  =  12

1  X  5  =  5          2  X  5  =  10         3  X  5  =  15

1  X  6  =  6          2  X  6  =  12         3  X  6  =  18

1  X  7  =  7          2  X  7  =  14         3  X  7  =  21

1  X  8  =  8          2  X  8  =  16         3  X  8  =  24

1  X  9  =  9          2  X  9  =  18         3  X  9  =  27

1  X  10  =  10        2  X  10  =  20        3  X  10  =  30
```

The WHILE/WEND Loop

Another type of loop available in BASIC is the WHILE/WEND. Unlike the FOR/NEXT, which executes a specified number of times, the WHILE/WEND continues to execute as long as a stated condition is true. The format of the WHILE/WEND loop is as follows:

    line# WHILE expression
        .
        .
        .
    line# WEND

The loop executes according to the following steps:

1. The expression, which can be a numeric expression or a numeric variable, is evaluated as true or false. If the expression is a variable, it is true if it is not equal to zero.

2. If the expression is true, the statements in the loop body are executed until the WEND statement is encountered. If the expression is false, control passes to the first statement after the WEND.

3. When the WEND is encountered, control passes back to the WHILE statement and the expression is evaluated again.

4. If the condition is still true, the loop body is executed again; if false, the loop is exited to the statement following the WEND.

In contrast to the FOR/NEXT loop, the WHILE/WEND involves no automatic initialization or incrementing of the loop control variable. A statement before the WHILE statement must initialize the loop control variable, and another statement within the loop body must change the value of the loop control variable so that the expression of the WHILE statement can become false and end the loop. Otherwise an infinite loop results, as shown here:

```
200 WHILE CNT < 50
210    PRINT CNT
220 WEND
```

This loop could be written correctly as follows:

```
190 CNT = 0
200 WHILE CNT < 50
210    PRINT CNT
220    CNT = CNT + 1
230 WEND
```

Figure V-9 implements the WHILE/WEND loop using an expression that consists of a single variable. The condition is true as long as the variable's value is not equal to XXX.

Figure V-9
Example of WHILE/WEND Loop

```
10   REM ***       LIBRARY LISTING OF NEW BOOKS     ***
20   CLS
30   REM *** THIS PROGRAM READS DATA FOR ALL NEW ***
40   REM *** BOOKS AND PRINTS A LISTING OF THEM. ***
50   REM
60   REM *** MAJOR VARIABLES                       ***
70   REM ***    TITLE$     BOOK'S TITLE            ***
80   REM ***    AUTHR$     BOOK'S AUTHOR           ***
90   REM ***    BNUM       NUMERIC RATING OF BOOK  ***
100  REM ***    INDEX      LIST NUMBER OF BOOK     ***
110  REM
120  REM *** PRINT HEADING ***
130  PRINT TAB(6);"TITLE";TAB(30);"AUTHOR";TAB(42);"RATING"
140  REM
150  REM *** INITIALIZE VARIABLES ***
160  INDEX = 0
170  READ TITLE$,AUTHR$,BNUM
180  REM
190  REM *** LOOP TO PROCESS ONE BOOK PER PASS ***
200  WHILE TITLE$ <> "XXX"
210    PRINT
220    INDEX = INDEX + 1
230    PRINT INDEX;". ";
240    PRINT TAB(6);TITLE$;TAB(30);AUTHR$;TAB(42);
250    FOR I = 1 TO BNUM
260      PRINT "*";
270    NEXT I
280    READ TITLE$,AUTHR$,BNUM
290  WEND
300  REM
310  REM *** DATA STATEMENTS ***
320  DATA "COMPETITIVE TANNING","HARRIS,Z.",1
330  DATA "BOMBAY","GOODTIME,C.",2
340  DATA "LEARNING TO LOVE C","LORD,P.",5
350  DATA "THE SURVIVOR","BULAS,I.",3
360  DATA "XXX","XXX",0
999  END
```

Comprehensive Programming Problem

Problem Definition

The film critic of the *Wopekeneta Daily News* would like a program to create a chart indicating the title and rating for each movie she has reviewed in the past week. This chart is to be printed in her weekly column. She assigns each movie a rating from 1 through 5, and she wants to be able to enter the movie title and its corresponding rating at the keyboard. The program should display a chart similar to the following:

Films Reviewed the Week of 4/24/87

Title	Rating
Dinner on Grounds	*****
Escape from The Amazon	****
Return of the Canal Beast	**
Love's Fury	***

Solution Design

This program must perform three major tasks:

1. Enter the date.
2. Read the data for each movie.
3. Display the chart.

The second and third tasks can be subdivided as follows:

2.B. Read the rating (1–5) for each movie.
3.A. Display the heading.
3.B. Display the title of each movie.
3.B. Display the title of each movie.
3.C. Display the number of stars for each movie.

The structure chart for this program is shown in Figure V-10.

The program can use READ statements to read each movie title and rating. Because it is not known in advance how many films will be read, this is a perfect situation in which to use an IF/THEN loop with a trailer value. This means that the last movie title value in the DATA statements must be DONE. Each movie rating is an integer value; therefore, this value can be used to determine how many times a FOR/NEXT loop should be executed to print the necessary number of stars. Figure V-11 depicts the flowchart for this program.

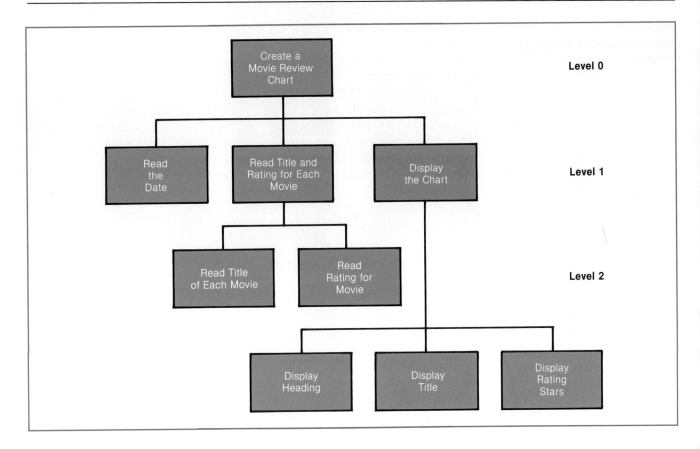

Figure V-10
Structure Chart for Movie Review
Program

The Program

The complete program is shown in Figure V-12. First the date is entered and a table heading is printed. Notice that the data for the first movie is read before the IF/THEN loop is entered for the first time. The title of the movie is printed; then a FOR/NEXT loop, contained in lines 240–260, is used to print a horizontal bar graph indicating the movie's rating. Data on each subsequent movie is read at the bottom of the IF/THEN loop, and execution then transfers to the top of the loop to determine if the sentinel value DONE has been read. The loop continues to execute until the sentinel value is encountered; then program execution terminates.

Summary Points

■ Control statements enable the programmer to alter the sequence in which program statements are executed. Loops are control statements that allow a given portion of a program to be executed as many times as needed.

Figure V-11
Flowchart of Movie Review
Program

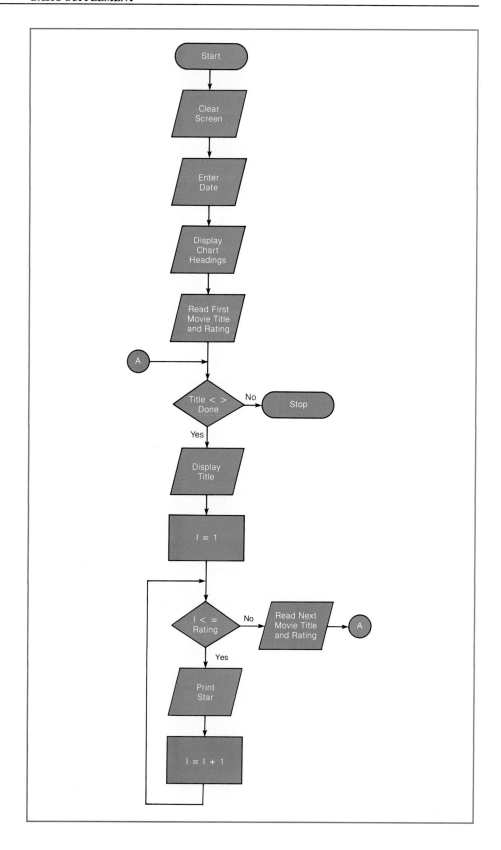

Figure V-12
Movie Review Program

```
10  REM ***                MOVIE REVIEW                    ***
20  REM ***  THIS PROGRAM READS THE TITLE AND RATING       ***
30  REM ***  (1-5) FOR EACH MOVIE REVIEWED IN A GIVEN      ***
40  REM ***  WEEK.  A CHART CONTAINING A BAR GRAPH FOR     ***
50  REM ***  EACH MOVIE REVIEWED IS THEN PRINTED.          ***
60  REM ***  MAJOR VARIABLES:                              ***
70  REM ***     DTE$              DATE                     ***
80  REM ***     TTLE$             TITLE OF THE MOVIE       ***
90  REM ***     RTE               RATING (1-5) OF MOVIE    ***
100 REM
110 CLS
120 PRINT
130 INPUT "ENTER THE DATE";DTE$
140 PRINT "Films Reviewed the Week of ";DTE$
150 PRINT
160 PRINT "Title","Rating"
170 PRINT
180 REM *** READ DATA FOR THE FIRST MOVIE. ***
190 READ TTLE$,RTE
200 REM *** LOOP TO READ AND PRINT EACH TITLE AND RATING. ***
210 WHILE TTLE$ <> "DONE"
220    PRINT TTLE$,
230    REM *** LOOP TO PRINT STARS FOR RATING BAR GRAPH. ***
240    FOR I = 1 TO RTE
250       PRINT "*";
260    NEXT I
270    PRINT
280    PRINT
290    READ TTLE$,RTE
300 WEND
310 REM *** DATA STATEMENTS ***
320 DATA "COLOR PURPLE",5,"OUT OF AFRICA",4,"SPIES LIKE US",2
330 DATA "GHOST BUSTERS",3,"DONE",0
999 END
```

```
RUN

ENTER THE DATE? 2/24/87
Films Reviewed the Week of 2/24/87

Title          Rating

COLOR PURPLE   *****

OUT OF AFRICA ****

SPIES LIKE US **

GHOST BUSTERS ***
```

■ The basic steps in loop execution are as follows:

1. The loop control variable is initialized to a particular value before loop execution begins.

2. The loop control variable is tested to determine whether the loop body should be executed or the loop should be exited.

3. The loop body, consisting of any number of statements, is executed.

4. At some point during loop execution, the value of the loop control variable must be modified to allow exit from the loop.

5. The loop is exited when the stated condition determines that the right number of loop repetitions has been performed.

■ The FOR/NEXT loop executes the number of times specified in the FOR statement. The NEXT statement increments the loop control variable, tests it against the terminal value, and returns control to the statement immediately following the FOR statement if another loop execution is required. Otherwise, execution continues with the statement following the NEXT statement.

■ A step value can be placed in a FOR statement to determine the value by which the loop control variable should be incremented (or decremented) with each loop repetition. The default step value is +1.

■ The FOR/NEXT loop is useful for counting loops, in which the number of repetitions needed can be determined before the loop is first executed.

■ The major advantage of the FOR/NEXT loop is that the loop control variable is initialized, incremented, and tested automatically. The FOR/NEXT loop cannot be used when the number of loop repetitions needed cannot be determined ahead of time.

■ The body of a loop, which contains the action that the loop performs, should be indented to make the program more readable.

■ The WHILE/WEND statement repeats execution of its loop body as long as the condition in the WHILE statement is true.

Review Questions

1. When should a loop structure be used in a program?
2. What are the five elements of a controlled loop?
3. What tasks are performed automatically by the FOR/NEXT loop?
4. Which of the following are valid FOR statements?

    a. 20 FOR I = 8 TO 12 STEP 3
    b. 100 FOR K = 15 TO 20 STEP 6
    c. 80 for $N\$$ = 3 TO 5 STEP .5
    d. 400 FOR X = -2 TO -1
    e. FOR I = 1 TO 100 STEP 20

5. When the step value in the FOR/NEXT loop is negative, does a loop stop executing when the loop control variable is greater than or less than the terminal value?

6. What happens when the step value of a FOR statement is zero?
7. What is a counting loop?
8. What happens if no step value is specified in a FOR statement?
9. When is the WHILE/WEND loop a more appropriate choice than a FOR/NEXT loop?
10. How many times is each of the following loops executed?

```
FOR I = 50 TO 10 STEP -5
    FOR J = 1 TO 6 STEP 2
        FOR K = 5 TO 5
        NEXT K
    NEXT J
NEXT I
```

Debugging Exercises

```
1.  10 REM *** READ AND PRINT TEN NAMES. ***
    20 FOR I = 1 TO 10
    30    READ NME$
    40 NEXT
    50 PRINT NME$
    60 DATA SAM,SARA,SUSAN,SALLY,SAMSON,SHAMERA,STEVEN
    70 DATA STEPHANIE,SMILEY,SONIA
    99 END
```

```
2.  10 FOR X = 1 TO 5
    20    FOR Y = 1 TO 10
    30       FOR Z = 1 TO 20
    40          PRINT X,Y,Z
    50          PRINT "*","*","*"
    60          SUM = X + Y + Z
    70          PRINT SUM
    80       NEXT Y
    90    PRINT "Z = ";Z
    100   NEXT Z
    110 PRINT "X = ";X
    120 NEXT X
```

Additional Programming Problems

1. Your landlord is considering a raise in rent of 5 percent, 7 percent, or 10 percent. To determine how much additional money you and your fellow tenants may have to pay, write a program to show sample rents of $200 to $600 (by

increments of $50) and the three proposed increased rents for each. Create a table like the following:

RENT	+5%	+7%	+10%
200	XXX	XXX	XXX
250	XXX	XXX	XXX
.	.	.	.
.	.	.	.

2. Write a program to display a multiplication table. Allow the user to enter the upper and lower limits of the table, then print the appropriate values. Use the following format for the table:

X	3	4	5	6
3	9	12	15	18
4	12	16	20	24
5	15	20	25	30
6	18	24	30	36

3. The high school tennis team is holding its annual tryouts. The coach selects the team members on the basis of the results of a series of matches. Each player is placed on a first, second, or third string team depending on his or her number of wins:

Number of wins	Team
10 or more	First string
4 to 9	Second string
3 or less	Third string

You are to write a program using a WHILE loop that indicates the team on which each player belongs. Use the following data:

Name	Wins
Sanders, S.	7
Crosby, D.	5
Casey, E.	9
Case, L.	12
Sandoval, V.	10
Coles, S.	3
Schnur, R.	2

4. Write a program to calculate X^N. This value should be found by multiplying X times itself N number of times (e.g., $X^4 = X \cdot X \cdot X \cdot X$). Use the following values for X and N to test your program:

X	N
1	2
6	3
5	4
2	6

The output should have the following format:

X raised to the $N = R$.

A trailer value should be used to determine the end of the data.

5. The Happy Hedonist Health Spa has asked you to write a payroll program that will calculate the weekly net pay for each of its employees. The employees have the option of participating in a medical insurance plan that deducts $10 per week. The income tax rate is 25 percent. Use a FOR/NEXT loop in your program. The following is the company pay code key:

Code	Wage Rate
1	$5.00
2	6.75
3	9.50

Use the following data:

Name	Medical Plan	Hours	Wage Code
Cochran, K.	Yes	40	2
Batdorf, D.	Yes	45	1
Jones, S.	No	38	3
Goolsby, L.	Yes	30	2
Halas, G.	No	35	1

The output should appear as follows:

NAME	NET PAY
XXXXXXXXX	$XXX.XX

SECTION VI

Arrays

Introduction

ARRAY
A collection of related data items. A single variable name is used to refer to the entire collection of items.

BASIC permits us to deal with many related data items as a group by means of a structure known as an **array**. The type of variable described in earlier chapters represented a single location in computer memory. For example, a variable B might represent the storage location of a numeric value, such as 500. An array, by contrast, is used to store a series of values in adjacent storage locations. When two or more related data items need to be entered, instead of giving each one a separate variable name, the programmer can give one variable name to the entire collection of data items. This capability is important when large quantities of data are needed in a program.

An array can be used to store integer, real, or string values, but the values in a given array must be of the same type. That is, if an array is given a numeric variable name, a string data item cannot be entered to it; only numeric values are allowed.

Subscripts

ELEMENT
An individual data item stored in an array.

Each individual data item within an array is called an **element**. An array consists of a group of consecutive storage locations, each containing a single value. The entire array is given one name; the programmer indicates an individual element in the array by referring to its position. For example, suppose that there are five test scores to be stored: 97, 85, 89, 95, and 100. The scores could be put in an array called TESTS, which we might visualize like this:

Array Tests

97	85	89	95	100

SUBSCRIPT
A value enclosed in parentheses which identifies an element's position in an array.

The array name TESTS now refers to all five storage locations containing the test scores. The gain acess to a single test score within the array, a **subscript** is used. A subscript is a value enclosed in parentheses which identifies the position of a given element in the array. For example, the first element of array TESTS (containing the value 97) is referred to as TESTS(1). The second test score is in TESTS(2), the third test score is in TESTS(3), and so on. Therefore, the following statements are true:

TESTS(1) = 97
TESTS(2) = 85
TESTS(3) = 89
TESTS(4) = 95
TESTS(5) = 100

The subscript enclosed in parentheses does not have to be an integer constant; it can be any legal numeric expression. When an array element subscript is an expression, the computer carries out the following steps:

- It evaluates the expression within the parentheses.
- It converts the result to an integer value, by truncation.
- It accesses the indicated element in the array.

SUBSCRIPTED VARIABLE
A variable that refers to a specific element of an array.

Variables that refer to specific elements of arrays, such as TEST(4), are called **subscripted variables**. A subscripted variable refers to one value in the array. It is possible to access a different value in the array by changing the subscript.

The same rules that apply to naming simple variables also apply to naming arrays. It is possible to use the same name for both a simple variable and an array in a program, but this is not good programming practice because it makes the logic of the program difficult to follow.

Assume that the array X and the variables A and B have the following values:

$$X(1) = 2 \quad X(2) = 15 \quad X(3) = 16 \quad X(4) = 17 \quad X(5) = 32$$

$$A = 3 \qquad B = 5$$

The following examples show how the various forms of subscripts are used:

Example	Reference
$X(3)$	Third element of X, or 16
$X(B)$	$B = 5$; thus the fifth element of X, or 32
$X(X(1))$	$X(1) = 2$; thus the second element of X, or 15
$X(B - A)$	$B = 5, A = 3$; $5 - 3 = 2$; thus the second element of X, or 15

The DIM Statement

When a program contains an array, the computer automatically sets aside eleven storage locations (0 through 10) for the elements in the array. The programmer does not have to fill all of the reserved array storage spaces with values; it is illegal, however, to refer to an array element for which space has not been reserved. For example, if only eleven storage spaces have been set aside, twelve data items cannot be entered to the array.

The DIM (dimension) statement enables the programmer to override this standard array space reservation and to reserve space for an array of any desired size. A DIM statement is not required for an array of eleven or fewer elements, but it is good programming practice to specify DIM statements for all arrays to help document the array usage.

The general format of the DIM Statement is as follows:

line# DIM variable1(limit1)[,variable2(limit2),...]

The variables are the names of the arrays. Each limit is an integer constant that supplies the maximum subscript value possible for that particular array. For example, if space is needed to store 25 elements in an array ITEM$, the following statement reserves the necessary storage locations:

```
10 DIM ITEM$(24)
```

Although it may seem that this statement sets aside only 24 positions, remember that array positions 0 through 24 are equal to 25 locations. For the sake of clarity and program logic, programmers often ignore the zero element. If we choose not to use the zero position, we dimension the array ITEM$ as follows:

```
10 DIM ITEM$(25)
```

As indicated in the statement format, more than one array can be declared in a single DIM statement. For example, the following statement declares the variables ACCNT, NME$, and OVERDRWN as arrays:

```
10 ACCNT(100),NME$(15),OVERDRWN(5)
```

ACCNT can contain up to 101 elements, NME$ up to 151 elements, and OVER-DRWN up to 51 elements.

DIM statements must appear in a program before the first reference to the arrays they describe. A good practice is to place them at the beginning of the program. The following standard preparation symbol generally is used to flowchart the DIM statement:

Learning Check

1. A subscript can consist of any legal numeric or character expression. True or false?

2. If an array is dimensioned as follows, it must contain 20 elements. True or false? 20 DIM X(20)

3. _____ are used with variables to identify a particular storage location within an array.

4. One array can be used to store more than one type of variable (string, real, and integer). True or false?

5. If a DIM statement is not used for an array, _____ storage locations are set aside automatically for the data elements.

Answers

1. false 2. false 3. Subscripts 4. false 5. eleven

One-Dimensional Arrays

ONE-DIMENSIONAL ARRAY
An array that has only one row.

All the arrays we have discussed so far in this chapter have been **one-dimensional arrays**, that is, arrays with a single row of elements. One-dimensional arrays can be thought of as lists of values. The following is a one-dimensional array named X:

15	20	27	8	16

In the next part of this chapter, we will learn how to manipulate the elements of one-dimensional arrays.

Reading Data to an Array

A major advantage of using arrays is the ability to use a variable rather than a constant as a subscript. Because a single name such as TESTS(I) can refer to any element in the array TESTS, depending on the value of I, this name can be used in a loop that varies the value of the subscript I. A FOR/NEXT loop can be an efficient method of reading data to an array if the exact number of items to be read is known in advance. The following program segment reads a list of five numbers into the array TESTS:

```
10 FOR I = 1 TO 5
20    READ TESTS(I)
30 NEXT I
40 DATA 85,71,63,51,99
```

The first time this loop is executed, the loop variable I equals 1. Therefore, when line 20 is executed, the computer reads the first number from the data list (which is 85) and stores it in TESTS(1). The second time through the loop, I equals 2. The second number is read to TESTS(2), the second location in the array. The loop processing continues until all five numbers have been read and stored. This process is outlined as follows:

For I =	ACTION	Array TESTS:
1	READ TESTS(1)	85
2	READ TESTS(2)	85 71
3	READ TESTS(3)	85 71 63
4	READ TESTS(4)	85 71 63 51
5	READ TESTS(5)	85 71 63 51 99

An array also can be filled using an INPUT statement or an assignment statement within a loop. To initialize an array of ten elements to zero, for example, the following statements could be used:

```
50 FOR I = 1 TO 10
60    SCORES(I) = 0
70 NEXT I
```

It is possible to read data to several arrays within a single loop. In the following segment, each data line contains data for one element of each of three arrays:

```
10 DIM NME$(5),AGE(5),SSN$(5)
20 FOR I = 1 TO 5
30    READ NME$(I),AGE(I),SSN$(I)
40 NEXT I
50 DATA TOM BAKER,41,268-66-1071
60 DATA LALLA WARD,28,353-65-2861
70 DATA MASADA WILMOT,33,269-59-9064
80 DATA PATRICK JONES,52,269-84-2834
90 DATA BERYL JONES,49,234-34-9382
```

When the exact number of items to be read to an array is unknown, a loop with a trailer value can be used. This method is demonstrated in the following segment, where the data contains a trailer value of −1. The programmer must ensure that the number of items read does not exceed the size of the array.

```
10 DIM X(5)
20 I = 1
30 INPUT X(I)
40 WHILE X(I) <> −1
50    I = I + 1
60    INPUT X(I)
70 WEND
99 END
```

Displaying the Contents of an Array

The FOR/NEXT loop can be used to print the contents of the array TEST, as shown in the following segment.

```
70 FOR T = 1 TO 5
80    PRINT TESTS(T)
90 NEXT T
```

RUN

```
85
71
63
51
99
```

Because there is no punctuation at the end of the PRINT statement in line 80, each value is printed on a separate line. As the loop control variable T varies from

1 to 5, so does the value of the array subscript, and the computer prints elements 1 through 5 of the array TESTS.

Computations on Array Elements

Figure VI-1 illustrates a program that might be used by a small business. The total sales for the day are calculated using three different arrays: arrays A and B are

Figure VI-1
Total Sales Program

```
10    REM ***        SALES PROGRAM       ***
20    DIM A(10),B(10),C(10)
30    PRINT "COST","SOLD","SALES"
40    PRINT
50    REM
60    REM *** ENTER DATA TO ARRAYS A AND B ***
70    FOR K = 1 TO 10
80      READ A(K),B(K)
90    NEXT K
100   REM
110   REM *** COMPUTE ARRAY C FOR ITEM SALES ***
120   FOR M = 1 TO 10
130     LET C(M) = A(M) * B(M)
140     PRINT A(M),B(M),C(M)
150   NEXT M
160   REM
170   REM *** CALCULATE TOTAL SALES ***
180   FOR N = 1 TO 10
190     LET S = S + C(N)
200   NEXT N
210   REM *** END OF CALCULATIONS ***
220   PRINT
230   PRINT "THE TOTAL SALES IS $ ";S
240   REM
250   REM *** DATA STATEMENTS ***
260   DATA .99,10,1.39,3,.59,17,.19,15
270   DATA 2.49,12,1,23,1.98,40
280   DATA .43,4,.39,63,9.49,37
999   END
```

```
RUN
COST              SOLD              SALES

.99               10                9.899999
1.39              3                 4.17
.59               17                10.03
.19               15                2.85
2.49              12                29.88
1                 23                23
1.98              40                79.2
.43               4                 1.72
.39               63                24.57
9.49              37                351.13

THE TOTAL SALES IS $   536.45
```

used to enter the unit cost and number sold respectively, and array C is used to hold the information obtained by multiplying the elements of arrays A and B together.

Line 20 dimensions the arrays to reserve storage space and to document the arrays used by the program. Lines 70 through 90 input the cost of the items and the number sold by using a FOR/NEXT loop. When the loop variable is set to 1, the first value entered is assigned to A(1) and the second value is assigned to B(1). As the loop continues to 2, the third and fourth pieces of data are input and assigned to A(2) and B(2) respectively. This process continues until the looping is completed. Control then passes to the next line.

The FOR/NEXT loop in lines 120–150 takes the information in arrays A and B, multiplies them together, and stores the results in array C. On the first pass through the loop, M = 1 and line 130 appears as follows:

LET C(1) = A(1)*B(1),

thus C(1) = .99*10 or 9.90.

This loop also contains a PRINT statement that displays what is contained in each array. The total sales for each item are stored in array C. Adding the contents of this array gives the total sales for all items (lines 180–200).

Learning Check

1. A(n) _____ array contains only one column.

2. What values are held in positions J(2) and J(3) in array J?

    ARRAY J

25	13	3	89	55

3. Write a loop that adds the corresponding elements of arrays A and B, each containing ten elements, and stores the results in array C.

4. Write a PRINT statement that displays the value 89 from array J in Question 2.

Answers

1. one-dimensional 2. 13 and 3, respectively 3. FOR I=1 TO 10 C(I) = A(I) + B(I) NEXT I 4. PRINT J(4)

Two-Dimensional Arrays

All the arrays shown so far in this chapter have been one-dimensional arrays; that is, arrays that store values in the form of a single list. A **two-dimensional array**,

TWO-DIMENSIONAL ARRAY
An array that can be compared to a table with both rows and columns.

by contrast, has both rows and columns. For example, suppose that a fast-food restaurant chain is running a four-day promotional T-shirt sale at each of its three store locations. It might keep the following table of data concerning shirts sold by each of the three restaurants:

	STORE		
DAY	1	2	3
1	12	14	15
2	10	16	12
3	11	18	13
4	9	9	10

Each row of the data refers to a specific day of the sale, and each column contains the sales for one store. Thus, the number of shirts sold by the second store on the third day of the sale (18) can be found in the third row, second column. A two-dimensional array named SHIRTS, containing the preceding data, can be pictured like this:

array SHIRTS

12	14	15
10	16	12
11	18	13
9	9	10

The array SHIRTS consists of twelve elements arranged as four rows and three columns. In order to reference a single element of a two-dimensional array such as this, two subscripts are needed: one to indicate the row and a second to indicate the column. For instance, the subscripted variable SHIRTS(4,1) contains the number of shirts (9) sold on the fourth day by the first store. In BASIC, the first subscript gives the row number and the second subscript gives the column number.

The rules regarding one-dimensional arrays also apply to two-dimensional arrays. A two-dimensional array is named in the same way as other variables and cannot use the same name as another array in the same program. A two-dimensional array can contain only one type of data; numeric and character string values cannot be mixed. As with one-dimensional arrays, two-dimensional array subscripts can be indicated by any legal numeric expression, as in the following examples:

```
SHIRTS(3,3)
SHIRTS(1,2)
SHIRTS(I,J)
SHIRTS(1,I + J)
```

Assume that I = 4 and J = 2, and that the array X contains the following 16 elements:

Array X

10	15	20	25
50	55	60	65
90	95	100	105
130	135	140	145

The following examples, based on this same array, show how the various forms of subscripts are used:

Example	Refers to
X(4,I)	X(4,4)—the element in the fourth row, fourth column of X, which is 145.
X(J,I)	X(2,4)—the element in the second row, fourth column of X, which is 65.
X(3,J + 1)	X(3,3)—the element in the third row, third column of X, which is 100.
X(I−1,J−1)	X(3,1)—the element in the third row, first column of X, which is 90.

As with one-dimensional arrays, the computer automatically reserves space for a two-dimensional array. By default, it reserves room for 11 rows and 11 columns, so the space for a two-dimensional array is $11 \times 11 = 121$ elements. As mentioned earlier, the 0 subscripted element often is ignored.

The DIM statement also can be used to set the dimensions of a two-dimensional array. The general format of such a DIM statement is as follows:

line# DIM variable1(limit1,limit2)[,variable2(limit3,limit4),...]

where the variable is the array name and the limits are the highest possible values of the subscripts for each dimension. For example, the following statement reserves space for the two-dimensional character array STDNT$, with up to 16 rows and 6 columns, for a total of $16 \times 6 = 96$ elements:

```
30 DIM STDNT$(15,5)
```

Reading and Displaying Two-Dimensional Arrays

As we explained in previous sections of this chapter, the FOR/NEXT loop is a convenient means of accessing all the elements of a one-dimensional array. The loop control variable of the FOR statement is used as the array subscript, as in the following example:

```
30 DIM X(5)
40 FOR I = 1 TO 5
50   READ X(I)
60 NEXT I
```

FOR/NEXT loops also can be used to read data to and print information from a two-dimensional array. It may be helpful to think of a two-dimensional array as a group of one-dimensional arrays, with each row making up a single one-dimensional array. A single FOR/NEXT loop can read values to one row. This process must be repeated for as many rows as the array contains; therefore, the FOR/NEXT loop that reads a single row is nested within a second FOR/NEXT loop that controls the number of rows being accessed.

The array SHIRTS of the previous example can be filled from the sales data table one row at a time, moving from left to right across the columns. The following segment shows the nested FOR/NEXT loops that do this:

```
30 FOR I = 1 TO 4
40    FOR J = 1 TO 3
50       READ SHIRTS(I,J)
60    NEXT J
70 NEXT I
80 DATA 12,14,15
90 DATA 10,16,12
100 DATA 11,18,13
110 DATA 9,9,10
```

Each time line 50 is executed, one value is read to a single element of the array; the element is determined by the current values of I and J. The outer loop (loop I) controls the rows, and loop J controls the columns. The READ statement is executed I $\times$ J = 4 $\times$ 3 = 12 times, which is the number of elements in the array.

Each time the outer loop is executed once, the inner loop is executed three times. While I = 1, J becomes 1, 2, and finally 3 as the inner loop is executed. Therefore, on the first pass through the outer loop, line 50 reads values to SHIRTS(1,1), SHIRTS(1,2), and SHIRTS(1,3), and the first row is filled:

	J = 1	2	3
I = 1	12	14	15

While I equals 2, J again varies from 1 to 3, and line 50 reads values to SHIRTS(2,1), SHIRTS(2,2), and SHIRTS(2,3) to fill the second row:

	J = 1	2	3
	12	14	15
I = 2	10	16	12

I is incremented to 3 and then to 4, and the third and fourth rows are filled in the same manner.

To print the contents of the entire array, the programmer can substitute a PRINT statement for the READ statement in the nested FOR/NEXT loop. The following segment prints the contents of the array SHIRTS, one row at a time:

```
40   BLANK = 10
50   FOR I = 1 TO 10
60     FOR J = 1 TO 3
70       PRINT TAB(BLANK * J);SHIRTS(I,J);
80     NEXT J
90     PRINT
100  NEXT I
```

The semicolon at the end of line 70 tells the computer to print the three values on the same line. After the inner loop is executed, the blank PRINT statement in line 90 causes a carriage return, so that the next row is printed on the next line. The program in Figure VI-2 shows how the data table for T-shirt sales results can be read to a two-dimensional array and printed in table form with appropriate headings.

Computations on Array Elements

Adding Rows   Once data has been stored in an array, often it is necessary to manipulate certain array elements. For instance, the sales manager in charge of the T-shirt promotional sale might want to know how many shirts were sold on the last day of the sale.

Because the data for each day is contained in a row of the array, it is necessary to total the elements in one row of the array (the fourth row) to find the number of shirts sold on the fourth day. The fourth row can be thought of as a one-dimensional array, so one loop is required to access all the elements in this row:

```
30 DAY4SALES = 0
40 FOR J = 1 TO 3
50   DAY4SALES = DAY4SALES + SHIRTS(4,J)
60 NEXT J
```

Notice that the first subscript of SHIRTS(4,J) restricts the computations to the elements in row 4, whereas the column J, varies from 1 to 3.

Adding Columns   To find the total number of T-shirts sold by the third store, for example, it is necessary to total the elements in the third column of the array. This time we can think of the column by itself as a one-dimensional array of four elements:

```
40 SALE3SHOP = 0
50 FOR I = 1 TO 4
60   SALE3SHOP = SALE3SHOP + SHIRTS(I,3)
70 NEXT I
```

Figure VI-2
Two-Dimensional Array Program

```
10   REM ***                    T-SHIRT SALES REPORT                    ***
20   REM
30   REM ***   THIS PROGRAM PRINTS A REPORT ON THE NUMBER OF   ***
40   REM ***   T-SHIRTS SOLD PER STORE FOR 4 DIFFERENT DAYS.   ***
50   REM ***   MAJOR VARIABLES:                                ***
60   REM ***      SHIRTS          ARRAY OF T-SHIRTS SOLD       ***
70   REM ***      I,J             LOOP CONTROLS                ***
80   REM
90   REM *** DIMENSION ARRAY ***
100 DIM SHIRTS(4,3)
110 REM
120 REM *** READ THE DATA ***
130 FOR I = 1 TO 4
140    FOR J = 1 TO 3
150       READ SHIRTS(I,J)
160    NEXT J
170 NEXT I
180 REM
190 REM *** PRINT TABLE OF QUANTITIES SOLD ***
200 PRINT "DAY #";TAB(10);"STORE 1";TAB(20);"STORE 2";TAB(30);"STORE 3"
210 BLANK = 10
220 FOR I = 1 TO 4
230    PRINT I;
240    FOR J= 1 TO 3
250       PRINT TAB(BLANK * J);SHIRTS(I,J);
260    NEXT J
270    PRINT
280 NEXT I
290 REM
300 REM *** DATA STATEMENTS ***
310 DATA 12,4,15,10,6,12,11,8,13,9,9,10
999 END
```

```
RUN
DAY #      STORE 1     STORE 2     STORE 3
 1           12           4          15
 2           10           6          12
 3           11           8          13
 4            9           9          10
```

In line 60, the second subscript (3) restricts the computations to the elements in the third column. The row, I, varies from 1 to 4.

Totaling a Two-Dimensional Array   Consider the problem of finding the grand total of all T-shirts sold during the entire four-day sale. The program must access all the elements of the array one at a time and add them to the grand total. Remember that nested FOR/NEXT loops were used to print or read values to a two-dimensional array. This same method can be used to total the elements of an array, by substituting an addition operation for the READ or PRINT statement:

```
50   TSHIRT = 0
60   FOR I = 1 TO 4
70      FOR J = 1 TO 3
80         TSHIRT = TSHIRT + SHIRTS(I,J)
90      NEXT J
100 NEXT I
```

This segment adds the elements in a row-by-row sequence. The same operation also can be performed in a column-by-column sequence:

```
50   TSHIRT = 0
60   FOR J = 1 TO 3
70      FOR I = 1 TO 4
80         TSHIRT = TSHIRT + SHIRTS(I,J)
90      NEXT I
100 NEXT J
```

Learning Check

1. What is the difference between a one-dimensional array and a two-dimensional array?

2. Given the statement
   10 DIM (20,10)
   how many elements could this array contain?

3. A(n) _____ stores values as a table consisting of rows and columns.

4. The first subscript of a two-dimensional array refers to the _____ of the elements, and the second subscript refers to the _____.

Answers

1. A one-dimensional array consists of only 1 row, whereas a two-dimensional array consists of rows and columns. 2. 231 3. two-dimensional array 4. row, column.

Manipulating Arrays

Sorting Arrays—The Bubble Sort

Many programming applications require data items stored in arrays to be sorted or ordered in some way. For example, names must be alphabetized, social security numbers must be arranged from lowest to highest, sports statistics must be arranged by numeric value, and so on. There are various methods the programmer can use to sort data items. We will examine only the **bubble sort**, as it is the easiest to understand.

The basic idea behind the bubble sort is to arrange the elements of an array in ascending or descending order by making a series of comparisons of the adjacent values in the array. If two adjacent values are out of sequence, they are exchanged.

When arranging an array in ascending order, the bubble sort "bubbles" the smallest value to the top of the array. The values of two adjacent array elements are compared, and the elements are switched if the value of the first is larger than that of the second. Then the next pair of adjacent elements is compared and switched if necessary.

This sequence of comparisons (called a pass) is then repeated, starting from the beginning of the array. After each complete pass through the array, the element moved to the end of the array need not be included in the comparisons of the next pass, because it is now in its proper position. Successive passes are performed until no elements are switched, indicating that the entire array is sorted.

As an illustration of this bubbling procedure, an array consisting of five integers is sorted into ascending order in Figure VI-3. Notice that, after each pass is completed, the largest of the numbers compared in that pass becomes the last of those numbers. After the first pass through the array, some of the numbers are close to their proper positions, but the array is not yet completely ordered. The largest value, 7, has been positioned successfully at the botton of the array and therefore is not included in the comparisons in the following passes.

After each pass through the array, the program checks a flag variable which indicates whether the array is in final order. After a fourth pass through this array, the array is completely arranged in ascending order, but another pass is required to set the flag value to indicate this fact. The actual code for a bubble sort is shown in Figure VI-4. This program sorts the names of ten astronauts into alphabetical order. The subroutine called at line 140 reads the astronauts' names into an array ASTRO$ and prints them. The subroutine starting at line 2000 performs the bubble sort. Let us examine this code carefully.

Line 2050 refers to the variable FLAG, which is initialized to 0. Its value is checked later by the computer to determine if the entire array has been sorted.

Notice the terminal value of the FOR/NEXT loop that sorts the array. The terminal value is one less than the number of items to be sorted, because two items at a time are compared. J varies from 1 to 9, which means that the computer eventually compares item 9 with item 9 + 1. If the terminal value were 10, the computer would try to compare item 10 with item 11, which does not exist in the array.

BUBBLE SORT

A sort that progressively arranges the elements of an array in ascending or descending order, by making a series of comparisons of the adjacent array values and exchanging those pairs of values which are out of order.

Figure VI-3
Bubble Sort Process

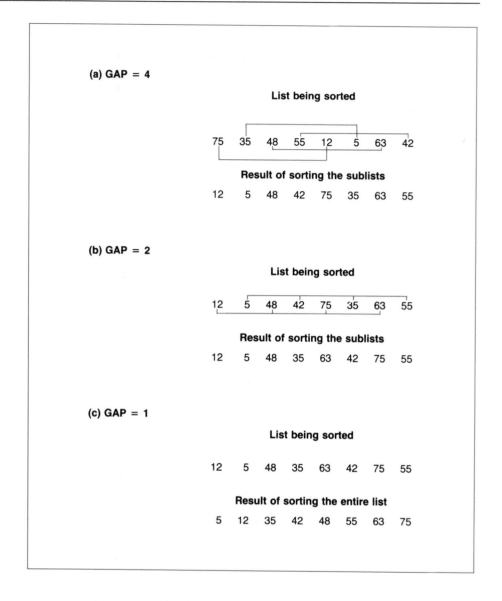

(a) GAP = 4

List being sorted

75   35   48   55   12   5   63   42

Result of sorting the sublists

12   5   48   42   75   35   63   55

(b) GAP = 2

List being sorted

12   5   48   42   75   35   63   55

Result of sorting the sublists

12   5   48   35   63   42   75   55

(c) GAP = 1

List being sorted

12   5   48   35   63   42   75   55

Result of sorting the entire list

5   12   35   42   48   55   63   75

The IF/THEN statement in line 2070 tells the computer whether to interchange two compared values. For example, when J = 1, the computer compares JET-SON, G. with SOLONG, H. Because J (the first letter of JETSON) is less than S, there is no need to switch these two items. The J is incremented to 2, and SOLONG, H. is compared with QUIRK, J. These two must be interchanged; the switch is performed by lines 2080 through 2100. Note that we have created a holding area, TEMP$, so that the switch can be made. SOLONG, H. is moved to TEMP$, and QUIRK, L. is moved to SOLONG, H.'s previous position. Now SOLONG, H. is placed in the position previously occupied by QUIRK, J.

Whenever the computer interchanges two values, FLAG is set to 1 in line 2110. This loop continues until every item in the array has been examined. After one pass through this entire loop, the array ASTRO$ looks like this:

Figure VI-4
Bubble Sort Program

```
10    REM ***                    ASTRONAUT'S MIX-UP              ***
20    REM
30    REM *** THIS PROGRAM SORTS THE ASTRONAUTS OF THE    ***
40    REM *** ASTRO AIR STATION INTO ALPHABETICAL ORDER.  ***
50    REM *** MAJOR VARIABLES:                            ***
60    REM ***     ASTRO          NAMES OF THE ASTRONAUTS   ***
70    REM ***     TEMP           TEMPORARY STORAGE OF NAME ***
80    REM
90    REM *** SET-UP NAME ARRAY SIZE ***
100   DIM ASTRO$(10)
110   REM
120   REM
130   REM *** READ NAMES INTO ARRAY AND PRINT THEM OUT ***
140   GOSUB 1000
150   REM
160   REM *** BUBBLE SORT ***
170   GOSUB 2000
180   REM
190   REM *** PRINT LIST ***
200   GOSUB 3000
210   GOTO 9999
1000  REM
1010  REM ***************************************************
1020  REM ****             SUBROUTINE ORIGINAL LIST       ****
1030  REM ***************************************************
1040  REM ***    READ NAMES INTO ARRAY AND PRINT THEM     ***
1050  REM
1060  PRINT "ASTRO AIR STATION -- UNSORTED"
1070  PRINT
1080  FOR I = 1 TO 10
1090    READ ASTRO$(I)
1100    PRINT ASTRO$(I)
1110  NEXT I
1120  PRINT
1130  PRINT
1140  RETURN
2000  REM
2010  REM ***************************************************
2020  REM ***             SUBROUTINE BUBBLE SORT          ***
2030  REM ***************************************************
2040  REM
2050  FLAG = 0
2060  FOR J = 1 TO 9
2070    IF ASTRO$(J) <= ASTRO$(J + 1) THEN 2120
2080    TEMP$ = ASTRO$(J)
2090    ASTRO$(J) = ASTRO$(J + 1)
2100    ASTRO$(J + 1) = TEMP$
2110    FLAG = 1
2120  NEXT J
2130  IF FLAG = 1 THEN 2050
2140  RETURN
3000  REM
3010  REM ***************************************************
3020  REM ****             SUBROUTINE SORTED LIST         ****
3030  REM ***************************************************
3040  REM ***         PRINT HEADING AND SORTED NAMES      ****
3050  REM
3060  PRINT "ASTRO AIR STATION -- SORTED"
3070  PRINT
3080  FOR I = 1 TO 10
3090    PRINT ASTRO$(I)
3100  NEXT I
3110  RETURN
3120  REM
```

(Figure continued on the next page)

```
3130 REM *** DATA STATEMENTS ***
3140 DATA "JETSON,G.","SOLONG,H.","QUIRK,J."
3150 DATA "SKYWALTZER,L.","MADER,D.","MCSOY,D."
3160 DATA "KANOBI,B.","SPECK,M.","OHORROR,L."
3170 DATA "CHECKUP,V."
9999 END
```

```
RUN
ASTRO AIR STATION -- UNSORTED

JETSON,G.
SOLONG,H.
QUIRK,J.
SKYWALTZER,L.
MADER,D.
MCSOY,D.
KANOBI,B.
SPECK,M.
OHORROR,L.
CHECKUP,V.


ASTRO AIR STATION -- SORTED

CHECKUP,V.
JETSON,G.
KANOBI,B.
MADER,D.
MCSOY,D.
OHORROR,L.
QUIRK,J.
SKYWALTZER,L.
SOLONG,H.
SPECK,M.
```

Figure VI-4
Continued

JETSON, G.
QUIRK, J.
SKYWALTZER, L.
MADER, D.
MCSOY, D.
KANOBI, B.
SOLONG, H.
OHORROR, L.
CHECKUP, V.
SPECK, M.

Although several switches have been made, the list is not sorted completely. That is why we need line 2050. As long as FLAG equals 1, the computer knows that switches were made in the previous pass and that the sorting process must continue. When the loop is completed without setting FLAG to 1—that is, when no switches are made—the computer finds FLAG equal to 0 and knows that the list is ordered. Numbers also can be sorted by this same method.

Merging

MERGE

A type of sort that combines two sorted arrays into a single sorted array.

It is possible to **merge**, or combine, two sorted arrays into one large sorted array. Suppose that two sorted integer arrays, A and B, need to be merged to form array C:

Array A

2	4

Array B

1	2	2

The first element in A is compared with the first element in array C, and the smaller of the two is placed in array C. Because 1 is less than 2, array C now looks like this:

Array C

1				

The integer placed in array C is not considered again. Next, the first element (2) in array A is compared with the second element (2) in array B. They are of equal value, so the array B is chosen arbitrarily to supply the next element of array C. The 2 in array B is no longer considered. Array C now appears this way:

Array C

1	2			

The first element of array A and the last element of array B are now compared. Because 2 is less than 3, 2 is moved into array C.

Array C

1	2	2		

The 2 in array A is no longer considered. Now the last elements of the two arrays are compared, and 3 is moved into array C:

Array C

1	2	2	3	

At this point, all of array B has been transfered into array C. The remaining element of array A is now moved into array C; if array A were larger, more than one integer would need to be moved. Array C now contains all the elements of both arrays A and B, in sorted order:

```
1000 REM ***********************************************
1010 REM ***          SUBROUTINE  MERGE  SORT       ****
1020 REM ***********************************************
1030 REM *** MERGE SORTED ARRAYS A AND B INTO C  ****
1040 REM
1050 REM ***          INITIALIZE ARRAY INDEXES          ***
1060 AINDX = 1
1070 BINDX = 1
1080 CINDX = 1
1090 REM
1100 REM *** MERGE UNTIL ALL OF ONE ARRAY IS READ ***
1110 WHILE (AINDX <= ASIZE) AND (BINDX <= BSIZE)
1120    IF A(AINDX) < B(BINDX) THEN C(CINDX) = A(AINDX):
       AINDX = AINDX + 1 ELSE C(CINDX) = B(BINDX):
       BINDX = BINDX + 1
1130    CINDX = CINDX + 1
1140 WEND
1150 REM
1160 REM *** ADD REMAINING ITEM TO END OF NEW ARRAY ***
1170 WHILE AINDX <= ASIZE
1180    C(CINDX) = A(AINDX)
1190    AINDX = AINDX + 1
1200    CINDX = CINDX + 1
1210 WEND
1220 REM
1230 WHILE BINDX <= BSIZE
1240    C(CINDX) = B(BINDX)
1250    BINDX = BINDX + 1
1260    CINDX = CINDX + 1
1270 WEND
1280 RETURN
```

Figure VI-5
Merge Subroutine

Array C

1	2	2	3	4

Figure VI-5 presents a subroutine that performs a merge sort. Is is assumed that the sizes of arrays A and B have been established in the main program, and that array C is large enough to hold the elements of both arrays. The loop of lines 1110 through 1140 places values into C until either A or B has no more elements left to be considered.

As indicated in the preceding example, if two compared integers are equal, this program places the integer from array B in array C. This comparison and the appropriate move into C are made in line 1120. The WHILE/WEND loop of lines 1170 through 1210 adds the remaining elements of array A (if any) to the end of C. If values of A run out before those of B, the loop of lines 1230 through 1270 adds the remaining values of B to C.

Searching

SEQUENTIAL SEARCH
A search that examines array elements from first to last, in the order in which they are stored. When the target element is located, the search terminates.

A given value in an array can be located by examining each array element until the desired value is found. This process is referred to as a **sequential search**. For example, you may want to know the number of scores greater than 89 in an array QUIZ, containing 40 test scores. The following segment performs this task:

```
50 CNT = 0
60 FOR I = 1 TO 40
70    IF QUIZ(I) > 89 THEN CNT = CNT + 1
80 NEXT I
```

The variable CNT holds a count of the scores greater than 89. The loop checks the value of each array element in numeric order, and the count is incremented only if the score being checked is greater than 89.

In another application, you might wish to locate a single value in an array. Suppose you wanted information regarding the August 19th concert at the local concert hall. The computer might prompt you to enter the date of the concert in which you are interested. It would then search an array of concert dates until it matched the given date. Finally, the computer would access the corresponding values from the arrays containing the rest of the concert information and display those values on the monitor screen.

If more than one array holds corresponding (related) data, the data must be contained in the same relative position in each array. In other words, if the desired date matches the third element of the date array, the third elements of the other arrays also are accessed. This process is shown in Figure VI-6.

Figure VI-6
Concert Information Example

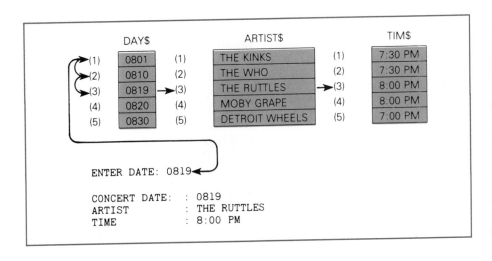

Learning Check

1. A(n) _____ consists of examining the elements of an array until the desired value or values are found.

2. In a sequential search of the following list, how many values will be examined before 236 is located?

   12   44   103   177   236   582   978   1235

3. What is indicated when a bubble sort makes an entire pass without making an exchange?

4. A(n) _____ combines two sorted lists into a single sorted list.

Answers

1. sequential search 2. 5 3. The array is sorted. 4. merge

Comprehensive Programming Problem

Problem Definition

The scorekeeper of the Centrovian Open Ice Skating Championships needs a program to determine the winner of the final round. Each competitor is given six scores, of which the highest and lowest are discarded. The remaining four scores then are averaged to obtain the final score. The maximum score for each event is 6.0. Write a program to read the names and scores of the ten finalists and produce a listing of the skaters' names and final scores in order of finish. Sample input and needed output are shown in the following table.

Input:

BALDUCCI, G.	5.7	5.3	5.1	5.0	4.7	4.8
CREED, A.	3.1	4.9	4.1	3.7	4.6	3.9
WILLIAMS, E.	4.1	5.3	4.9	4.4	3.9	5.4
HAMILTON, S.	5.1	5.7	5.6	5.5	4.4	5.3
LORD, P.	5.9	4.8	5.5	5.0	5.7	5.7
STRAVINSKY, I.	5.1	4.7	4.1	3.1	4.6	5.0
MONTALBAN, R.	5.1	5.1	4.9	3.4	5.5	5.3
SCHELL, M.	4.9	4.3	5.2	4.5	4.6	4.9
CRANSTON, T.	6.0	6.0	5.7	5.8	5.9	5.9
CROWLEY, S.	4.3	5.2	6.9	5.3	4.3	6.0

Needed Output

PLACE	NAME	SCORE
1	BALDUCCI, G.	5.7
•	•	•
•	•	•
•	•	•

Solution Design

The problem provides us with seven items of data for each skater—a name and six scores—and asks for a list of names, sorted by average. Once the data items have been read (the first step), two basic operations must be performed in order to produce the listing: the averages must be calculated, and these averages with their associated names must be sorted. Thus, the problem can be divided into four major tasks: (1) read the data, (2) calculate the averages, (3) sort the names and averages, and (4) print the sorted information. The structure chart is shown in Figure VI-7.

The input for this problem consists of two types of data, alphabetic and numeric, so two arrays must be used to store them. The output calls for the names already stored plus a new set of values, the averages; another array can be used to store these averages. In calculating the averages, variables also are needed to keep track of the high and low scores. These scores can be determined by means of a sequential search on the six scores of each skater.

A sort is required in the third step of our algorithm. A descending-order bubble sort could be used here. As the averages are rearranged, the corresponding skater's name must be carried with each average.

Figure VI-7
Structure Chart for Skating Scores Problem

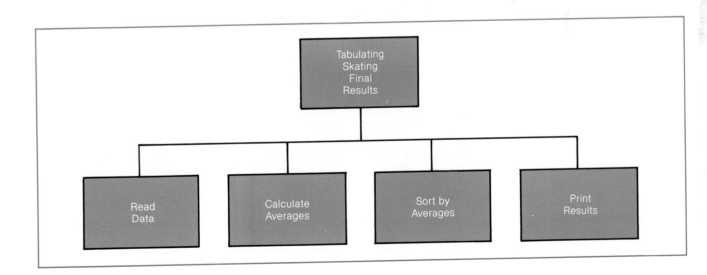

The Program

The program of Figure VI-8 shows the solution to the problem. Line 140 of the main program reserves space for a two-dimensional array of the scores, called PTS. Each row of array PTS contains the scores for one skater, so ten rows with six columns each are needed.

The first subroutine called by the main program reads the names and scores to their respective arrays. The second subroutine finds the average score for each skater, by performing a sequential search on each row of scores in PTS (lines 2050 through 2110). When the low and high scores for the row have been found, lines 2150 through 2170 add the scores for that row, except the low and high scores, to the total; then the average for that row is calculated.

The sorting of the final average is performed in the bubble sort in the third subroutine, lines 3000 through 3170. Notice that the flag, which indicates that a switch has been made, can be a string variable, as in line 3050. The actual value stored in the flag is unimportant; the critical factor is whether that value is changed during the sort.

The condition $AVG(I) > AVG(I+1)$ in line 3070 causes the averages to be sorted from highest to lowest. Every time an average is moved, its corresponding name from the array SKNM$ also is moved. The sorted results are printed by the fourth subroutine in lines 4000 through 4100.

Summary Points

■ An array is a collection of related values stored under a single variable name.
■ Individual array elements can be accessed by using subscripts.
■ A subscript of an array element can be any legal numeric expression.
■ The DIM statement sets up storage for arrays, and must appear before the first reference to the array it describes.
■ Array manipulation is carried out through the use of loops.
■ A two-dimensional array stores values as a table, grouped into rows and columns.
■ The first subscript of a two-dimensional array refers to the element's row, and the second subscript refers to the column.
■ The bubble sort places elements of an array in ascending or descending order by comparing adjacent elements.
■ The merge combines two sorted arrays into one sorted array.
■ A sequential search of an array consists of examining each element in the array sequentially until the desired value is located.

Review Questions

1. What is an array?
2. Give two advantages of using arrays.

**Figure VI-8
Skating Scores Program**

```
10    REM ***                    SKATING FINAL RESULTS          ***
20    REM
30    REM *** THIS PROGRAM COMPUTES THE AVERAGES OF SKATING   ***
40    REM *** SCORES, USING SIX SCORES AND DROPPING THE LOW   ***
50    REM *** AND HIGH SCORES.  IT THEN SORTS ALL THE AVERAGE***
60    REM *** SCORES IN ASCENDING ORDER.                      ***
70    REM *** MAJOR VARIABLES:                                ***
80    REM ***     SKNM$       ARRAY OF SKATERS' NAMES          ***
90    REM ***     PTS         ARRAY OF SCORES                 ***
100   REM ***     AVG         ARRAY OF AVERAGES               ***
110   REM ***     HI,LO       HIGHEST/LOWEST SCORES           ***
120   REM
130   REM *** DIMENSION THE ARRAYS ***
140   DIM SKNM$(10),PTS(10,6),AVG(10)
150   REM
160   REM *** READ NAMES AND SCORES ***
170   GOSUB 1000
180   REM
190   REM *** CALCULATE FINAL AVERAGE ***
200   GOSUB 2000
210   REM
220   REM *** SORT BY AVERAGE ***
230   GOSUB 3000
240   REM
250   REM *** PRINT RESULTS ***
260   GOSUB 4000
270   GOTO 9999
1000  REM ***********************************************
1010  REM ***                SUBROUTINE READ            ****
1020  REM ***********************************************
1030  REM ***         READS THE NAMES AND SIX SCORES     ***
1040  REM
1050  FOR I = 1 TO 10
1060    READ SKNM$(I)
1070    FOR J= 1 TO 6
1080      READ PTS(I,J)
1090    NEXT J
1100  NEXT I
1110  RETURN
2000  REM ***********************************************
2010  REM ***             SUBROUTINE AVERAGE            ***
2020  REM ***********************************************
2030  REM ***   DROP HIGH/LOW SCORES, THEN AVERAGE SCORE ***
2040  REM
2050  FOR I = 1 TO 10
2060    HI = PTS(I,1)
2070    LO = PTS(I,1)
2080    FOR J= 2 TO 6
2090      IF PTS(I,J) < LO THEN LO = PTS(I,J)
2100      IF PTS(I,J) > HI THEN HI = PTS(I,J)
2110    NEXT J
2120    REM
2130    REM *** AVERAGE REMAINING SCORES ***
2140    TPTS = 0
2150    FOR J = 1 TO 6
2160      IF PTS(I,J) <> LO OR PTS(I,J) <> HI THEN
            TPTS = TPTS + PTS(I,J)
2170    NEXT J
2180    AVG(I) = TPTS / 4
2190  NEXT I
2200  RETURN
3000  REM ***********************************************
3010  REM ***              SUBROUTINE BUBBLE SORT        ***
3020  REM ***********************************************
3030  REM ***           SORT AVERAGES IN ASCENDING ORDER  ***
3040  REM
3050  SWITCH$ = "N"
```

(Figure continued on the next page)

Figure VI-8
Continued

```
3060 FOR I = 1 TO 9
3070   IF AVG(I) > AVG(I + 1) THEN 3150
3080   TEMP = AVG(I)
3090   STEMP$ = SKNM$(I)
3100   AVG(I) = AVG(I + 1)
3110   SKNM$(I) = SKNM$(I + 1)
3120   AVG(I + 1) = TEMP
3130   SKNM$(I + 1) = STEMP$
3140   SWITCH$ = "Y"
3150 NEXT I
3160 IF SWITCH$ = "Y" THEN 3050
3170 RETURN
4000 REM *********************************************************
4010 REM ***                 SUBROUTINE PRINT                 ***
4020 REM *********************************************************
4030 REM ***        PRINT THE HEADINGS AND THE RESULTS        ***
4040 CLS
4050 PRINT "PLACE";TAB(10);"NAME";TAB(30);"SCORE"
4060 PRINT
4070 FOR I = 1 TO 10
4080   PRINT I;TAB(10);SKNM$(I);TAB(30);AVG(I)
4090 NEXT I
4100 RETURN
4200 REM
4210 REM *** DATA STATEMENTS ***
4220 DATA "BALDUCCI,G",5.7,5.3,5.1,5.0,4.7,4.8
4230 DATA "CREED,A",3.1,4.9,4.1,3.7,4.6,3.9
4240 DATA "WILLIAMS,E",4.1,5.3,4.9,4.4,3.9,5.4
4250 DATA "HAMILTON,S",5.1,5.7,5.6,5.5,4.4,5.3
4260 DATA "LORD,P",5.9,4.8,5.5,5.0,5.7,5.7
4270 DATA "STRAVINSKY,I",5.1,4.7,4.1,3.1,4.6,5.0
4280 DATA "MONTALBAN,R",5.1,5.1,4.9,3.4,5.5,5.3
4290 DATA "SCHELL,M",4.9,4.3,5.2,4.5,4.6,4.9
4300 DATA "CRANSTON,T",6.0,6.0,5.7,5.8,5.9,5.9
4310 DATA "CROWLEY,S",4.3,5.2,6.9,5.3,4.3,6.0
9999 END
```

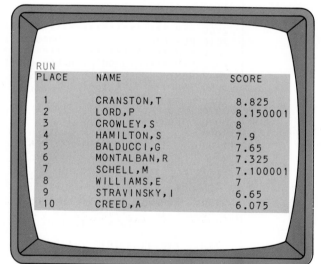

```
RUN
PLACE      NAME                    SCORE

  1        CRANSTON,T              8.825
  2        LORD,P                  8.150001
  3        CROWLEY,S               8
  4        HAMILTON,S              7.9
  5        BALDUCCI,G              7.65
  6        MONTALBAN,R             7.325
  7        SCHELL,M                7.100001
  8        WILLIAMS,E              7
  9        STRAVINSKY,I            6.65
 10        CREED,A                 6.075
```

3. What is a subscript?

4. Where must the DIM statement appear in a program?

5. Write a segment to sum the 10 values of a one-dimensional array of 10 elements.

6. How is the terminal value of the FOR/NEXT loop of the bubble sort determined?

7. How is a sequential search performed?

8. The _____ combines two sorted lists into a single sorted list.

9. How many elements can a one-dimensional array and a two-dimensional array hold if they have not been dimensioned?

10. The _____ statements provide an efficient method for manipulating arrays.

Debugging Exercises

```
1.  10 REM *** READ DATA TO ARRAY A ***
    20 FOR I = 1 TO 20
    30    INPUT A(I)
    40 NEXT I
    99 END

2.  10   DIM X(26)
    20   REM *** ASCENDING BUBBLE SORT ***
    30   F = 0
    40   FOR I = 1 TO 26
    50     IF X(I) <= X(I + 1) THEN 90
    60     T = X(I)
    70     X(I) = X(I + 1)
    80     X(I + 1) = T
    90     F = 1
    100  NEXT I
    110  IF F = 1 THEN 40
```

Additional Programming Problems

1. A stereo equipment store is holding a sale. The manager needs a program that will place the prices of all sale items in one array and the corresponding rate of discount in a second array. A third array should be used to hold the sale price of each item (sale price z price w (rate * price)). Use the following data:

Price	Rate of Discount
$178.89	0.25
59.95	0.20
402.25	0.30
295.00	0.25
589.98	0.30
42.99	0.20

Print the original prices and their corresponding sales prices.

2. Read 12 numbers to array A and 12 numbers to array B. Compute the product of the corresponding elements of the two arrays, and place the results in array C. Print a table similar to the following:

A	B	C
2	3	6
7	2	14

3. Your teacher has a table of data concerning the semester test scores for your class:

Name	Test 1	Test 2	Test 3
Mathey, S.	88	83	80
Sandoval, V.	98	89	100
Haggerty, B.	75	65	79
Drake, J.	60	85	99
Jenkins, J.	75	89	89

Your teacher would like to know the test average for each student, and the class average for each test. The output should include the preceding table.

4. The following list of employee names and identification numbers is in alphabetical order. Use a bubble sort to print the list in ascending order by I.D. number (Remember that when you change the position of a number in the array, the position of the name also must be changed so that they correspond.)

Name	I.D. #
Altt, D.	467217
Calas, M.	624719
Corelli, F.	784609
Kanawa, K.	290013
Lamas, F.	502977
Lehman, B.	207827
Shicoff, N.	389662
Talvela, M.	443279
Tousteau, J.	302621
Wymer, E.	196325

5. The manager of the Epitome Books store would like a program that will generate a report regarding the sales of the various types of books the store carries. The program should use the following data:

Year	Pop. Fiction	Classics	Biography	Instruction
1982	4,561	549	973	3,702
1983	5,140	632	1,375	4,300
1984	5,487	581	1,798	4,345
1985	5,952	605	2,204	5,156

The report should indicate what percentage of each year's total sales consisted of each book type. The format for the report is as follows:

SALES PERCENTAGES FOR EACH YEAR:

YEAR	POP. FICTION	CLASSICS	BIOGRAPHY	INSTRUCT.
1982	XX.XX%	XX.XX%	XX.XX%	XX.XX%
1983				
1984				
1985				

SECTION VII

Graphics and Sound

Introduction

Programming a computer for graphics and sound is enjoyable. Graphics can be used to enhance programs, making otherwise dull material interesting and readable. Sounds produced by the computer can be used to attract attention to specific prompts or displays, or to play music.

Display Modes

The IBM PC screen operates in three display modes: text, medium-resolution graphics, and high-resolution graphics. In previous chapters of this book, only the text mode has been used; however, graphics programming must be performed in the medium- and high-resolution graphics modes. In order to use these modes, you must equip your IBM PC with a special circuit board called a color/graphics interface and a color graphics monitor. The interface circuit board enables you to design detailed graphics that include a variety of colors. A monochrome graphics monitor allows you to design graphics, too, but the graphics will not appear in color.

The SCREEN command switches the format of the screen from one display mode to another. Its format is as follows:

line #SCREEN mode-number

The mode-number must be an integer between 0 and 2. The command SCREEN 0 activates the text mode, SCREEN 1 activates the medium-resolution graphics mode, and SCREEN 2 activates the high-resolution graphics mode. The screen is set automatically to the text mode when it is turned on.

In order to produce graphics displays that are clear and easy to read, you should first clear the screen of any existing characters through the use of the CLS command. Then you should remove the key functions displayed at the bottom of the screen by using the statement KEY OFF.

Medium-Resolution Graphics Mode

MEDIUM-RESOLUTION GRAPHICS
The graphics mode that divides the screen into 64,000 image points (320 across and 200 down).

PIXEL
An image point.

The **medium-resolution graphics** mode divides the screen into 320 image points across and 200 down, for a total of 64,000 image points. Each image point is referred to as a **picture element** or **pixel.** A pixel is specified by a pair of coordinates consisting of a column number (0 through 319) and a row number (0 through 199). In either the medium- or the high-resolution graphics mode, the column number must be specified *before* the row number. Notice also that the column and row numbers begin with 0, not 1 as in the case of the text mode.

Color Graphics

Of the three display modes for the IBM PC, the medium-resolution graphics mode is the only one that allows for color graphics. In order to use the available colors in your display, you must use the SCREEN statement to turn on the color switch for medium-resolution graphics mode:

```
line#   SCREEN 1,0
```

The number 1 puts you in the medium-resolution graphics mode, and the number 0 initiates the color capabilities. To turn the color off, you need to execute the following statement:

```
line#   SCREEN 1,1
```

Once the color capabilities have been turned on, you must select a background color and a foreground color. For the background color (the color of all 64,000 pixels *before* any pixels are lit up), there are 16 possible options, numbered 0 through 15. The foreground colors (the color that lights up as you specify particular pixels), however, are limited to only three options. These three colors are chosen from one of two groups of colors, or palettes. Palette 0 consists of the colors green, red, and brown, whereas palette 1 is made up of the colors cyan, magenta, and white. Table VII–1 lists the 16 background colors and defines the palettes of foreground colors.

**Table VII-1
Colors Used in Medium-Resolution
Graphics Mode**

Background Colors			
Color	Number	Color	Number
Black	0	Gray	8
Blue	1	Light blue	9
Green	2	Light green	10
Cyan	3	Light cyan	11
Red	4	Light red	12
Magenta	5	Light magenta	13
Brown	6	Yellow	14
White	7	Bright white	15
Foreground Colors			
Palette 0		**Palette 1**	
Color	Number	Color	Number
Green	1	Cyan	1
Red	2	Magenta	2
Brown	3	White	3

The COLOR statement is used to set both the background and foreground colors. Its format is as follows:

line # COLOR background color, foreground palette number

With the COLOR statement, you specify the number that corresponds to the color of the desired background. The foreground color, however, is not chosen directly using the COLOR statement. Instead, the palette of colors is designated. For example, the following statement sets the background color as blue (1) and selects palette 0 for the foreground:

```
10 COLOR 1,0
```

The PSET and PRESET statements are used to select the specific foreground color from the available options—in this case green, red, and brown (Table VII–1).

The PSET and PRESET Statements

The PSET statement is used to light up a specified pixel. Its format is as follows:

line # PSET (column, row),color-number

The column and row number are the coordinates of the specific pixel you wish to color, and the color-number is one of the available colors in the palette that was chosen in the COLOR statement.

To see how the PSET statement is used, look at the following program segment:

```
10 CLS
20 KEY OFF
30 SCREEN 1,0
40 COLOR 7,0
50 PSET(100,100),2
```

Line 30 switches the display mode to medium-resolution graphics. It also turns on the color capabilities. Line 40 selects white as the background color, and selects the foreground colors offered by palette 0. Line 50 causes the color of the pixel at column 100 and row 100 to be changed to red.

The PRESET statement is used to return a specific pixel to the background color. Its format is as follows:

line # PRESET (column,row)

The following statement returns the pixel at coordinate (100,100) to the background color. (It was colored red by the previous segment.)

```
60 PRESET(100,100)
```

The LINE Statement

Graphics displays often require the use of lines. It is possible to draw a line by using the PSET statement within a FOR/NEXT loop. Figure VII–1 is an example of a program that connects four lines to form a rectangle. The rows and columns are variables whose values depend on the value of the loop control variable of the FOR/NEXT loop. Notice that the GOTO statement in line 260 forms an infinite loop, which keeps the graphics display on the screen. (To terminate the program, hold down the <Ctrl> key and then press the <Break> key.)

Drawing in this manner is effective but not efficient. If you execute the program shown in Figure VII–1, you will notice that the lines are produced rather slowly. IBM BASIC offers the LINE statement as a more efficient alternative. Its format is as follows:

Figure VII–1
Rectangle Program Using the PSET Statement

line # LINE$(x_1,y_1) - (x_2,y_2)$,color number

```
10   REM *** PROGRAM RECTANGLE ***
20   REM *** X = COLUMN COORDINATE ***
30   REM *** Y = ROW COORDINATE ***
40   REM
50   REM *** PREPARE MEDIUM-RESOLUTION GRAPHICS SCREEN ***
60   CLS
70   KEY OFF
80   SCREEN 1,0
90   COLOR 7,0
100  REM *** DRAW TOP SIDE OF RECTANGLE ***
110  FOR X = 100 TO 200
120      PSET(X,75),2
130  NEXT X
140  REM *** DRAW RIGHT SIDE OF RECTANGLE ***
150  FOR Y = 75 TO 125
160      PSET(X,Y),2
170  NEXT Y
180  REM *** DRAW BOTTOM SIDE OF RECTANGLE ***
190  FOR X = X TO 100 STEP -1
200      PSET (X,Y),2
210  NEXT X
220  REM *** DRAW LEFT SIDE OF RECTANGLE ***
230  FOR Y = Y TO 75 STEP -1
240      PSET(X,Y),2
250  NEXT Y
260  REM *** INFINITE LOOP TO KEEP DISPLAY ON SCREEN ***
270  GOTO 270
999  END
```

```
10   REM *** PROGRAM RECTANGLE ***
20   REM *** X = COLUMN COORDINATE ***
30   REM *** Y = ROW COORDINATE ***
40   REM
50   REM *** PREPARE MEDIUM-RESOLUTION GRAPHICS SCREEN ***
60   CLS
70   KEY OFF
80   SCREEN 1,0
90   COLOR 7,0
100  REM *** DRAW TOP SIDE OF RECTANGLE ***
110  LINE (100,75)-(200,75),2
120  REM *** DRAW RIGHT SIDE OF RECTANGLE ***
130  LINE (200,75)-(200,125),2
140  REM *** DRAW BOTTOM SIDE OF RECTANGLE ***
150  LINE (200,125)-(100,125),2
160  REM *** DRAW LEFT SIDE OF RECTANGLE ***
170  LINE (100,125)-(100,75),2
180  REM *** INFINITE LOOP TO KEEP DISPLAY ON SCREEN ***
190  GOTO 190
999  END
```

Figure VII–2
Rectangle Program Using the LINE Statement

This statement is used to draw a line that connects the pixel at character position (x_1,y_1) to the pixel at (x_2,y_2). Specifying the color of the line is optional; if the color is not specified, the line is drawn in color 3 of the active palette. Using the LINE statement decreases the complexity of drawing lines and greatly increases the speed at which they are drawn. Figure VII–2 is a modified version of the rectangle program of Figure VII–1. It uses the LINE statement instead of the PSET statement inside a FOR/NEXT loop.

The LINE function has an extended format just for drawing rectangles. Before explaining its use, however, let's examine the rectangle diagrammed in Figure VII–3. This rectangle has corner A opposite corner C, and corner B opposite corner D. The sides meet at right angles (90°).

Figure VII–3
Drawing a Rectangle

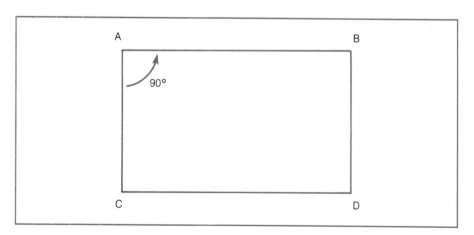

```
10    REM *** PROGRAM RECTANGLE ***
20    REM *** X = COLUMN COORDINATE ***
30    REM *** Y = ROW COORDINATE ***
40    REM
50    REM ** PREPARE MEDIUM-RESOLUTION GRAPHICS SCREEN ***
60    CLS
70    KEY OFF
80    SCREEN 1,0
90    COLOR 7,0
100   REM *** DRAW RECTANGLE ***
110   LINE (100,75)-(200,125),2,B
120   REM *** INFINITE LOOP TO KEEP DISPLAY ON SCREEN ***
130   GOTO 130
999   END
```

Figure VII–4
Rectangle Program Using the LINE
Statement and Box Parameter

One LINE statement can be used to draw this rectangle by specifying the coordinates of opposite corners, such as A and C.

The color number is followed by the letter B, which tells the computer to box in the two corners:

```
110 LINE (100,75) - (200,125),2,B
```

This statement draws the same rectangle that is produced by the four LINE statements in Figure VII–2. That is, it draws a 100×50 rectangle, with the top left corner at pixel (100,75) and the bottom right corner at pixel (200,125).

Using this form of the LINE statement greatly decreases the complexity of designing graphics displays. For example, the program shown in Figure VII–4 draws the same 100×50 rectangle produced by the program in Figures VII–1 and VII–2 with only a fraction of the statements.

Learning Check

1. The screen of the medium-resolution graphics mode is divided into _____ columns and _____ rows.

2. Each character position is called a(n) _____ and is specified by a pair of _____.

3. The _____ statement is used to illuminate a specified pixel.

4. A statement that draws a line connecting two pixels is a(n) _____ statement.

Answers

1. 320,200 2. pixel, coordinates 3. PSET 4. LINE

High-Resolution Graphics Mode

The **high-resolution graphics** mode divides the screen into 640 columns and 200 rows. Each of the 128,000 pixels can be controlled by any of the statements presented in the previous section. Although the high-resolution mode allows for sharper, more detailed graphics displays, each pixel can be only one of two colors: white(1) or black(0). The high-resolution graphics mode is activated by the statement SCREEN 2. There are no color capabilities to activate, because only two colors are available.

Although only two colors are available in this mode, it is possible to create different shades of white by turning on different combinations of pixels. For example, consider the rectangle position of the graphics screen shown in Figure VII–5. It is possible to color the rectangle pure white by lighting up all the pixels in the rectangle with the statement

```
10 LINE (X1,Y1) - (X2 - Y2),1,BF
```

where the letters BF (box fill) cause the entire box to be filled with the color specified (in this case white).

To fill the rectangle with a darker shade, the LINE statement could be used within a FOR/NEXT loop to color in every other column of pixels. The following program segment fills in the rectangle shown in Figure VII–5:

```
40 FOR X1 = X1 TO X2 STEP 2
50    LINE (X1,Y1) - (X1,Y2),1
60 NEXT X1
```

If the STEP value in line 40 is increased to 3, the program segment lights up every third column, thereby creating a still darker shade.

The program shown in Figure VII–6 divides the high-resolution screen into six 213 × 100 rectangles, each shaded differently. Study the algorithms used to shade each rectangle in order to understand how to create different shades of white.

Figure VII–5
Creating Different Shades of White

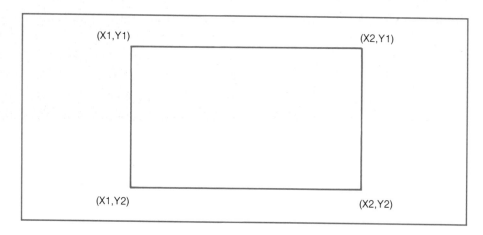

Figure VII–6
Program to Shade

```
10   REM *** PROGRAM SHADES ***
20   REM *** THIS PROGRAM DIVIDES THE SCREEN INTO SIX RECTANGLES ***
30   CLS
40   KEY OFF
50   SCREEN 2
60   REM *** BEGIN DRAWING IN TOP LEFT CORNER AT 0,0 ***
70   REM *** COLOR RECTANGLE I ***
80   LINE (0,0)-(212,99),1,BF
90   REM *** COLOR RECTANGLE II HORIZONTAL LIGHT GRAY ***
100  FOR Y = 0 TO 99 STEP 2
110      LINE (213,Y)-(425,Y),1
120  NEXT Y
130  REM *** COLOR RECTANGLE III VERTICAL LIGHT GRAY ***
140  FOR X = 426 TO 639 STEP 2
150      LINE (X,0)-(X,99),1
160  NEXT X
170  REM *** COLOR RECTANGLE IV VERTICAL DARK GRAY ***
180  FOR X = 0 TO 212 STEP 3
190      LINE (X,100)-(X,199),1
200  NEXT X
210  REM *** COLOR RECTANGLE V HORIZONTAL DARK GRAY ***
220  FOR Y = 100 TO 199 STEP 3
230      LINE (213,Y)-(425,Y),1
240  NEXT Y
250  REM *** INFINITE LOOP TO KEEP DISPLAY ON SCREEN ***
260  GOTO 260
999  END
```

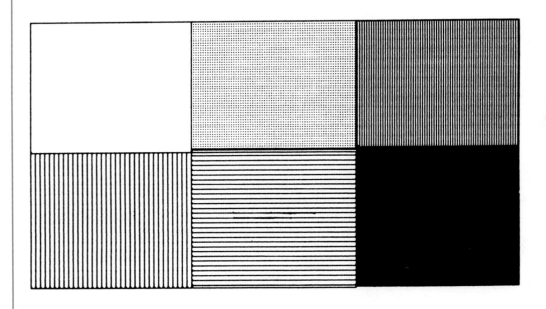

```
10   REM *** PROGRAM ROLLING BALL ***
20   CLS
30   KEY OFF
40   SCREEN 2
45   REM *** DRAW THE GROUND LINE ***
47   LINE (0,199)-(639,199),1
50   FOR X = 63 TO 574
60       CIRCLE (X+1,170),64,1
65       CIRCLE (X,170),64,0
70   NEXT X
80   REM *** INFINITE LOOP TO KEEP DISPLAY ON SCREEN ***
90   GOTO 90
99   END
```

Figure VII–7
Program for Rolling a Ball

The CIRCLE Statement

IBM BASICA also features a statement that enables you to create circles. This statement can be used in both medium- and high-resolution graphics mode, but because of the limited resolution of the medium-resolution mode, the circles produced in this mode are not smooth and often are unclear. For this reason, only a high-resolution example of the CIRCLE statement is provided here.

The format of this statement is as follows:

line # CIRCLE (column,row),radius,color

The column and row positions specify the coordinates of the center of the circle, and the radius specifies the distance from the center to any coordinate on the curve of the circle. For example, the statement

```
40 CIRCLE (100,75),40,1
```

draws a circle with a radius of 40 pixels, centered at column 100 and row 75.

The program shown in Figure VII–7 produces a circle that rolls slowly across the screen. The FOR/NEXT statement increases the X coordinate for the center of the circle, thus creating the horizontal rolling effect.

Graphics and Text

Many graphics displays require character string messages to clarify or explain their purpose. For this reason, BASIC enables you to include text with graphics displays. The PRINT and PRINT USING statements perform exactly as they would in the text mode, except that the cursor is hidden while in the graphics mode.

To print text within a graphics display, we suggest using the LOCATE statement (refer to Section III). A common mistake made by many beginning programmers is to specify the coordinates for the LOCATE statement in the sequence (column,row), as with the graphics statements. Remember that the LOCATE coordinates must be specified in the sequence (row, column) even while in the graphics modes. In the medium-resolution mode, text can be printed only within the first 40 columns and is displayed in color 3 of the active palette.

Learning Check

1. The high-resolution graphics mode divides the screen into _____ columns and _____ rows.

2. There are _____ possible colors for any high-resolution pixel.

3. The high-resolution graphics mode is activated by the statement _____.

4. The distance from the center of a circle to any point on the curve is called the _____ of a circle.

Answers

1. 640,200 2. two 3. SCREEN 4. radius

Sound on the PC

The BEEP Statement

Sounds can be produced on the IBM PC with any of three statements: BEEP, SOUND, and PLAY. The easiest and most often used is the BEEP statement. The BEEP does exactly what it says: when executed, it produces a single sound at 800 Hertz (cycles per second) which lasts for 1/4 of a second. (This frequency and duration cannot be changed when using the BEEP statement.) It is used most commonly in application programs when it is necessary to call attention to error messages or to request user input. Its format is as follows:

line# BEEP

Figure VII–8 shows how this command can be used to indicate user input.

The SOUND Statement

The SOUND statement enables the user to specify the frequency and length of tones. Its format is as follows:

Figure VII–8
Program Using the BEEP Statement

```
10   CLS
20   PRINT "PRESS Y FOR BEEP"
30   PRINT "PRESS N TO END PROGRAM"
40   INPUT "BEEP?",A$
50   IF A$ = "N" THEN 99
60      BEEP
70      GOTO 40
99   END
```

line# SOUND frequency, duration

Changing the frequency produces a beep at a higher or lower tone. The frequency can be set to any number between 37 and 32767 Hertz. The duration specifies how long the sound is to last. The duration actually is the number of clock ticks (remember that BASIC/BASICA features an internal clock), which can range between 0 and 65535; there are approximately 18.2 clock ticks per second.

The ability to change frequency and duration enables you to create a large variety of interesting sounds. The program in Figure VII–9 produces a series of increasingly high-pitched tones and a siren.

The PLAY Statement

The PLAY statement enables the user to program music. The sounds produced are sophisticated, yet the program is not difficult to use. Some background in

Figure VII–9
Program Using the SOUND Statement

```
10   REM *** TONES ***
20   FOR I = 300 TO 1200 STEP 100
30      SOUND I,8
40      FOR T = 1 TO 500
50      NEXT T
60   NEXT I
70   FOR T = 1 TO 600
80   NEXT T
90   REM *** SIREN ***
100  FOR I = 1 TO 3
110     FOR F = 450 TO 1200
120        SOUND F,.1
130     NEXT F
140     FOR F = 1200 TO 450 STEP -1
150        SOUND F,.1
160     NEXT F
170  NEXT I
999  END
```

Figure VII–10
Coded Music Strings

music is helpful; however, beginners also can create music easily. The format of the PLAY statement is as follows:

line# PLAY string

The string is a series of letters, numbers, and symbols which indicates a variety of musical information the computer needs in order to produce music. These combinations of letters and numbers are referred to as commands, and each command serves a specific purpose.

Figure VII–10 gives two examples of what coded music strings might be like. Although they may look difficult to code, actually they are quite simple. The following paragraphs contain an overview of how to code music on the IBM PC.

Octave   The octave is specified with the letter O followed by the octave number. There are seven possible octaves, from 0 to 6, with each octave ranging from C to B (octave 3 starts at middle C). For example: O3 means that all notes come from the third octave until another octave is specified. If no octave is specified, the notes are assumed to come from the fourth octave. Figure VII–11 shows octaves 1 through 4.

Notes   Just as with sheet music, notes are specified with the letters A through G, and each octave starts with C. A sharp is indicated by the symbol # or + following the note; a flat is indicated by the symbol − following the note. For a note to be sharp or flat, the note must correspond to a black key on the piano keyboard. For example, the notes B# and F− are invalid, whereas C# and B− are allowable.

Figure VII–11
Octaves 1 Through 4

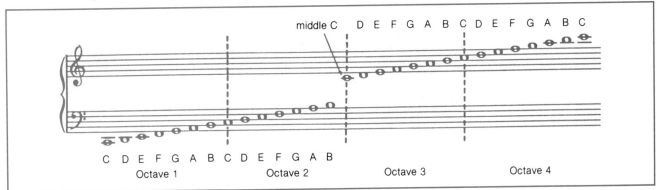

Length   The length is set in the same way as the octave. It is coded by the letter L, followed by a number that indicates the length of all subsequent notes until another length is specified. The length of the notes ranges from 1 to 64, where 1 indicates a whole note, 2 a half note, 4 a quarter note, and so on.

Pause   A pause, or rest, note is indicated with the letter P. It is set in the same manner as the length, that is, with the letter P followed by a number in the range 1 to 64. Therefore, P1 indicates a whole note rest, P2 a half note rest, and so on.

Tempo   The speed at which the music is played is called the tempo. Setting tempo is much like setting length. The user sets the number of quarter notes per minute, ranging from 32 to 255. For example, T60 sets the tempo at 60 quarter notes per minute. That tempo remains in effect until another tempo command is given.

Style   The IBM PC allows three styles of music to be played: staccato, legato, and normal. *Staccato* is indicated by the character MS; each note plays for three-quarters of the time specified by the L (length) command. *Legato* is indicated by the characters ML; each note plays for the full period set by the L command. *Normal* is indicated by the characters MN; each note plays for seven-eighths of the time specified by the L command. As with the other settings, the style remains in effect until the user changes it.

Repeating Strings   Almost all musical compositions contain sections that are repeated. Instead of recoding the same piece of music each time it is to be played, the IBM PC enables you to assign a string of coded music to a string variable:

```
100 M$ = "L4CEL2G"
```

To include this string with the string in the PLAY statement, the user types the letter X followed by the string variable name and semicolon. Thus, if M$ is defined as previously indicated, the following two statements are equivalent:

```
200 PLAY "O3L4CEL2GL4CEL2GL4GFED"
200 PLAY "O3XM$;XM$;L4GFED"
```

Comprehensive Programming Problem

The Problem

Your calculus professor wants you to produce a graph of the function $f(X) = 199 - \sqrt{X}$. X should range from 0 to 600.

Learning Check

1. The three commands on the IBM PC that produce sounds are _____, _____, and _____.

2. Music can be programmed by using the _____ statement.

3. If no octave is specified, all notes come from the _____ octave.

4. A sharp is indicated by following a note with a _____ or a _____.

Answers

1. BEEP, SOUND, PLAY 2. PLAY 3. fourth 4. number sign (#), plus sign (+)

Solution Design

The X axis must lie at the bottom of the screen, and the Y axis must lie on the left edge. Therefore, the dimensions of the graph will be 600 × 180. The input will be the value of X, between 0 and 600. The Y value will be the result of the calculation of the function. The output will be the plot of the coordinates (X,Y); therefore, a bottom and left edge of the graph should be displayed. The graph will appear the same whether in medium or high resolution, but with a high resolution, the graph will be crisper and clearer.

The Program

**Figure VII–12
Comprehensive Program—Function
Plotting**

Figure VII–12 shows the program that graphs the function f(X) = 199 − sqr(X), with X ranging from 0 to 600. The first thing necessary is to be in the graphics

```
10   REM *** PROGRAM PLOTTER ***
20   KEY OFF
30   CLS
40   SCREEN 2
50   REM *** DRAW X AXIS AT THE BOTTOM OF THE SCREEN ***
60   LINE (0,0)-(600,0),1
70   REM *** DRAW Y AXIS AT LEFT EDGE OF THE SCREEN ***
80   LINE (0,0)-(0,199),1
90   REM *** PLOT POINTS OF FUNCTION F(X) = X - 1 ***
100  FOR X = 0 TO 600
110      PSET(X,199-SQR(X)),1
120  NEXT X
999  END
```

mode, with a clear screen. Lines 20 through 40 perform this task. The LINE statements in lines 60 and 80 draw the border for the graph, across the bottom and down the left-hand side. Lines 100–120 use a FOR/NEXT loop to assign a value to X (from 0 to 600), calculate a value for Y, and light up the pixel indicated by the coordinate (X,Y).

Summary Points

■ The IBM PC has three display modes: text, medium-resolution graphics, and high-resolution graphics.

■ The medium-resolution graphics mode divides the screen into 320 pixels across and 200 down.

■ The medium-resolution graphics mode has 16 possible background colors (0–15) and two palettes (0–1), each with three foreground colors (0–2).

■ The PSET statement is used to illuminate a specific pixel.

■ The PRESET statement returns a specific pixel to the background color.

■ The LINE statement draws a straight line from one pixel to another.

■ The high-resolution graphics mode divides the screen into 640 pixels across and 200 down.

■ The high-resolution graphics mode has only two possible colors: white (1) and black (0).

■ The CIRCLE statement draws a circle of a specified radius, centered at a specified pixel.

■ Sounds can be produced by using the BEEP, SOUND, and PLAY statements.

Review Questions

1. Which display mode allows for the sharpest detail?

2. How many background colors are available in the medium-resolution graphics mode?

3. Which statement is used to program musical compositions?

4. Write the statement that lights up the pixel at column 80 and row 40 in the color green, assuming palette 0 is active.

5. What single statement draws a line from pixel (10,20) to pixel (40,80) in color 1 of the active palette?

6. What single statement draws a 50 × 40 rectangle whose top left corner is at (2,30) and whose color is option 2 of the active palette?

7. What statement draws a circle of radius 60 with its center at (100,100) in color 1?

8. When is the BEEP statement most commonly used?

9. How does the SOUND statement differ from the BEEP statement?

10. What does the *string* in the PLAY statement consist of?

Debugging Exercises

```
1.  10 CLS
    20 KEY OFF
    30 COLOR 7,0
    40 SCREEN ,1,0
    50 LINE (100,75) + (200,75),2
    60 LINE (200,125) - (100,125),2
    99 END
```

```
2.  100 PLAY "O3L4CE"
    110 M = "L4CEL2G"
    120 PLAY "O3XM$XM$L4GFED"
```

Additional Programming Problems

1. Write a program that produces the following graphics displays with the LINE statement:

    a. A straight line that connects pixels (10,40) and (100,90).

    b. A rectangle with corners at (30,50); (150,50); (150,100); (30,100).

    c. The rectangle described in b, colored in with color 2.

2. Write a program that creates a rectangle in the middle of the terminal screen and then enlarges it to twice its original size. Have the computer beep once after it has drawn the original rectangle, and twice after it has drawn the enlarged rectangle.

3. Write a program that produces the following graphics displays with the CIRCLE statement:

    a. A circle with radius 64 and center at pixel (100,71).

    b. A circle with radius 25 and center at pixel (100,100) in color 1.

4. Write a program that causes the computer to BEEP 25 times with a pause between each beep, and which enables the user to enter a certain frequency parameter and to hear the resulting sound for 1 second.

5. Use the PLAY statement to program the following four measures of Beethoven's Ninth Symphony:

BASIC Glossary

Algorithm The sequence of instructions arranged in a specific, logical order that are needed to solve a problem.

Array An ordered collection of related data items. A single variable name is used to refer to the entire collection of items.

Assignment statement A statement that causes a value to be stored in a variable.

Bubble sort A sort that progressively arranges the elements of an array in ascending or descending order by making a series of comparisons of the adjacent array values and exchanging those values that are out of order.

Conditional transfer Program control is transferred to another point only if a stated condition is satisfied.

Constant A value that cannot change during program execution.

Control statement A statement that allows the programmer to alter the order in which program statements are executed.

Conversational mode See **Inquiry-and-response mode.**

Counter A variable used to control loop repetition; each time the loop is executed, the counter is tested to determine if the desired number of repetitions has been performed.

Counting loop A type of loop in which repetition is controlled by a counter, which is a numeric variable that is tested each time the loop is executed to determine if the desired number of repetitions has been performed.

Data list A single list containing the values in all of the data statements in a program; the values appear in the list in the order in which they occur in the program.

Debug To locate and correct program errors.

Documentation Comments that explain a program to people; documentation is ignored by the computer.

Double-alternative decision structure A decision structure in which a specific action is taken if a stated condition is true; otherwise, a different action is taken.

Element An individual data item stored in an array.

Execute When the computer carries out the instructions submitted to it.

Flowchart A graphic representation of the solution to a programming problem.

Hierarchy of operations The order in which arithmetic operations are performed. In BASIC the order is (1) anything in parentheses; (2) exponentiation; (3) multiplication and division; (4) addition and subtraction.

High-resolution graphics The graphics mode that divides the screen into a total of 128,000 image points (640 across and 200 down).

Immediate mode The mode in which commands are executed as soon as the RETURN key is pressed; it is used without line numbers.

Indirect mode The mode in which statements are not executed until the RUN command is given. The statements must have line numbers.

Infinite loop A loop with no exit point.

Input The data needed to solve a problem.

Inquiry-and-response mode A mode of operation in which the program asks a question and the user enters a response.

Line number A number preceding a BASIC statement that is used to reference the statement and determine its order of execution.

Literal An expression in a PRINT statement that contains any combination of letters, numbers, and/or special characters.

Logic error A flaw in an algorithm developed to solve a programming problem; this results in the program's output being incorrect.

Loop body The statement(s) that constitutes the action to be performed by the loop.

Loop control variable A variable of which the value is used to determine the number of loop repetitions.

Medium-resolution graphics The graphics mode that divides the screen into a total of 64,000 image points (320 across and 200 down).

Menu A screen display of a program's functions. The user enters a code at the keyboard to make a selection.

Merge A type of sort that combines two sorted arrays into a single sorted array.

One-dimensional array An array that has only one column.

Output Information that is the result of processing.

Picture element See **Pixel.**

Pixel The smallest graphic point addressable by a computer, pixels are turned on or off to form characters and graphics images on a computer screen.

Processing The producing of output or information from the input or data.

Prompt A message telling the user that data should be entered at this point.

Relational symbol A symbol used to specify a relationship between two values.

Reserved word A word that has a specific meaning to the BASIC system and therefore cannot be used as a variable name.

Run-time error An error that causes program execution to stop prematurely.

Scroll To have lines move vertically off the top of the monitor screen.

Sentinel value See **Trailer value.**

Sequential search A search that examines array elements from the first to last in the order in which they are stored. When the target element is located, the search terminates.

Single-alternative decision structure A decision structure in which a specific action is taken if a stated condition is true; otherwise, execution proceeds to the next statement.

Structure chart A diagram that visually illustrates how a problem solution has been developed using stepwise refinement.

Structured programming A method of programming in which programs have easy-to-follow logic and are divided into subprograms, each designed to perform a specific task.

Subroutine A module in a BASIC program containing a sequence of statements designed to perform a specific task; it follows the main program.

Subscript A value enclosed in parentheses which identifies the position in an array of a particular element.

Subscripted variable A variable that refers to a specific element of an array.

Syntax error A violation of the grammatical rules of a language.

Top-down design A method of solving a problem that proceeds from the general to the specific.

Trailer value A method of controlling a loop in which a unique value signals the termination of the loop.

Two-dimensional array An array that can be compared to a table with both rows and columns.

Unconditional transfer Control is always passed elsewhere, regardless of any program condition.

Variable A storage location the contents of which can change during program execution.

BASIC INDEX

GLOSSARY

Access To get or retrieve data from a computer system.

Active cell The cell on a spreadsheet currently available for use; the active cell is indicated by the cell pointer.

Ada A high-level structured programming language developed for use by the Department of Defense and named for the "first programmer," Augusta Ada Byron, Countess of Lovelace and daughter of the poet Lord Byron.

Algorithm A set of well-defined instructions that outline the solution of a problem in a finite number of steps.

American Standard Code for Information Interchange (ASCII) A 7-bit standard code used for information interchange among data-processing systems, communications systems and associated equipment.

Analog computer A computer that measures the change in continuous electrical or physical conditions rather than counting data; contrast with digital computer.

Analytical Graphs Charts and graphics used for financial analysis and other types of numerical comparison.

Application program A sequence of instructions written for solving a specific user problem.

Arithmetic/logic unit The section of the processor, or CPU, that handles arithmetic computations and logical operations.

Artificial intelligence (AI) Intelligence exhibited by a machine or software; field of research currently developing techniques whereby computers can be used for solving problems that appear to require imagination, intuition, or intelligence.

Assembler program The translator program for an assembly language program; produces a machine language program (object program) that can then be executed.

Assembly language A low-level, symbolic programming language that uses convenient abbreviations called mnemonics rather than the groupings of 0s and 1s used in machine language. Because instructions in assembly language generally have a one-to-one correspondence with machine language instructions, assembly language is easier to translate into machine language than are high-level language statements.

Bandwidth Range, or width, of the frequencies available for transmission on a given channel; also known as grade.

Bar code A machine-readable code made up of bars and spaces of varying widths; often used on packaging of retail merchandise and read by wand readers or scanners.

BASIC (Beginners' All-purpose Symbolic Instruction Code) A high-level programming language commonly available with interpreter programs; widely implemented on microcomputers and often taught to beginning programmers.

Batch processing A method of processing data in which data items are collected and forwarded to the computer in a group; normally uses punched cards or magnetic tape for generating periodic output, e.g. payroll.

Baud Unit that describes transmission speeds.

G-1

Binary number system Base 2 number system that uses the digits 0 and 1; convenient for use in computer coding because it corresponds to the two possible states in machine circuitry, on and off.

Binary representation Use of a two-state, or binary, system for representing data, as in setting or resetting the electrical state of semiconductor memory to either 1 or 0.

Biomechanics Application of engineering methodologies to biological systems.

Bit Acronym for BInary digiT; the smallest unit of data that the computer can handle and that can be represented in the digits (0 and 1) of binary notation.

Boot To load an operating system into a computer's main memory.

Branch Program logic used to bypass or alter the normal flow of program execution.

Bubble memory A memory medium in which data is represented by magnetized spots (magnetic domains, or ''bubbles'') resting on a thin film of semiconductor material.

Byte A fixed number of adjacent bits, usually eight, operated on as a unit.

C A high-level structured programming language that includes low-level language instructions; C is popular because it is portable and is implemented on a wide variety of computer systems.

Cell A storage location within a spreadsheet.

Cell pointer The highlight that indicates the active cell in a spreadsheet.

Central processing unit (CPU) Acts as the ''brain'' of the computer; composed of three sections—arithmetic/logic unit (ALU), control unit, and primary storage unit.

Character A single letter, digit, or special sign (like $, #, or ★).

Chief programmer team (CPT) A method of organization used in developing software systems in industry in which a chief programmer supervises the development and testing of software; programmer productivity and software reliability are increased.

Clock speed The number of electronic pulses a microprocessor can produce each second.

COBOL (COmmon Business-Oriented Language) A high-level programming language generally used for business applications; well-suited for manipulating large data files.

Coding The process of writing a programming problem solution in a programming language.

Communication channel Pathway along which data is transmitted between sending and receiving devices.

Compatible Descriptive of hardware and/or software that can work together.

Compiler program The translator program for a high-level language such as FORTRAN or COBOL; translates the entire source program into machine language at once, creating an object program that is then executed.

Composite color monitor A color monitor that displays a composite of colors received in a single video signal.

Computer General-purpose electronic machine with applications limited only by the creativity of the humans who use it; its power is derived from its speed, accuracy, and memory.

Computer literacy General knowledge about computers; may include the ability to use computers for solving problems, technical knowledge about hardware and software, and awareness of how computers affect society.

Computer-aided design (CAD) Process of designing, drafting, and analyzing a prospective product using computer graphics on a video terminal.

Computer-aided manufacturing (CAM) Use of a computer to simulate or monitor the steps of a manufacturing process.

Computer-assisted instruction (CAI) Use of a computer to instruct or drill a student on an individual or small-group basis.

Computer-integrated manufacturing (CIM) Arrangement that links various departments within an organization to a central data base for the purpose of improving the efficiency of the manufacturing process.

Computerized axial tomography (CT or CAT) Form of noninvasive physical testing that combines x-ray techniques and computers to aid diagnosis.

Computer output microfilm (COM) A form of computer output in which information from a printer or magnetic tape is placed on microfilm or microfiche.

Control panel The portion of the spreadsheet which provides status and help information. The control panel is composed of a status line, an entry line, and a prompt line.

Control unit The section of the CPU that directs the sequence of operations by electrical signals and governs the actions of the various units that make up the computer.

Coordinate The location of a cell within a spreadsheet.

Coprocessor A microprocessor that can be plugged into a microcomputer to replace or work with the microcomputer's original microprocessor.

Cursor The marker on the display screen indicating where the next character can be displayed.

Daisy-wheel printer An output device resembling a daisy-wheel electronic typewriter; it has a removable flat wheel of petals or spokes, each having a character embossed at its tip; it is an impact printer and printing occurs one character at a time.

Data Facts; the raw material of information.

Data base A grouping of independent files that are commonly defined, consistently organized, and can be accessed through one central point; designed to fit the information needs of a wide variety of users in an organization.

Data manager A data management software package that consolidates data files into an integrated whole, allowing access to more than one data file at a time.

Data processing A systematic set of procedures for collecting, manipulating, and disseminating data to achieve specified objectives.

Data redundancy The repetition of the same data in several different files.

Debugging The process of locating, isolating, and resolving errors in a program.

Dedicated system A computer equipped to handle only one function, such as word processing.

Default setting The setting that a program automatically assumes when no other setting is designated by the user.

Deletion A word processing feature in which a character, word, sentence, or larger block of text can be removed from the existing text.

Demodulation Process of retrieving data from a modulated carrier wave.

Digital computer The type of computer that relies on counting for its operations and operates on distinct data (for example, binary digits) by performing arithmetic and logic processes on specific data units; commonly used in business and education.

Direct-access storage Secondary storage from which data can be retrieved at random; an example is a magnetic disk.

Directory A special kind of file that organizes the other files stored on a disk.

Disk drive The mechanical device used to rotate a disk, floppy disk, or disk pack past a read/write head during data transmission.

Documentation Written material that accompanies a program and includes definitions, explanations, charts, tests, and changes to the program.

Dot-matrix printer Impact printer that forms characters from a matrix of pins arranged in a rectangular shape. The matrix may consist of seven rows of five pins each and only the pins necessary for forming a particular character are selected from the matrix. (The dot-matrix formation may also be used in nonimpact printers.)

Editing window The area on a computer screen that contains the typed words in a document; also, the area in which changes can be made in a document.

Electronic bulletin board Smaller, user-run version of the commercial information services, offered at little or no cost to users.

Electronic data processing (EDP) Data processing performed largely by electronic equipment, such as computers, rather than by manual or mechanical means.

Electronic mail Transmission of messages at high speeds over communication channels.

Electronic spreadsheet A large computerized grid, or table, divided into rows and columns, which uses computer storage and capabilities for financial analysis.

Encryption The process of encoding data or programs to disguise them from unauthorized personnel.

Erasable programmable read-only memory (EPROM) A form of read-only memory that can be erased and reprogrammed, but only by being submitted to a special process such as exposure to ultraviolet light.

Expert system Software program that uses a base of knowledge in a particular field of study for decision-making and evaluation processes that result in suggestions for actions similar to those of human experts in that field.

Extended Binary Coded Decimal Interchange Code (EBCDIC) An 8-bit code for character representation.

Feedback A check within a system to see whether predetermined goals are being met.

Field A subdivision of a record that holds a meaningful item of data, such as an employee number.

File A group of related records stored together; a specific unit of data stored on a disk or tape such as a program or text file.

Filename A meaningful name given to a file.

Floppy disk A low-cost, direct-access form of secondary storage made of flexible plastic; a flexible magnetic disk currently made in 3 1/2-, 5 1/4-, and 8-inch diameters; also called flexible disk or diskette.

Flowchart A graphic representation in which symbols represent the flow of operations, logic, data, and equipment of a program or system.

Format See Initialize.

Formatting The function of a word processor which communicates with the printer to tell it how to print the text on paper.

Formula A mathematical expression used in a spreadsheet.

FORTH A high-level programming language that includes low-level language instructions; FORTH is the standard language used at astronomical observatories around the world.

FORTRAN (FORmula Translator) The oldest surviving high-level programming language; used primarily in performing mathematical or scientific operations.

Function A built-in formula or process included in a spreadsheet program. When a function is used in a formula, a calculation is automatically performed. For example, a sum function automatically adds a range of numbers.

Global search and replace A search and replace operation that is carried out throughout the entire document, without user intervention.

Hard copy Printed output.

Hardware Physical components that make up a computer system.

High-level language Languages that are oriented more toward the user than the computer system (contrast with low-level languages). High-level languages generally contain English words such as READ and PRINT and must be translated into machine language before execution. A single high-level language statement may translate into several machine language statements.

Impact printer A printer that forms characters by physically striking ribbon, paper, and embossed characters together.

Information Data that has been organized and processed so it is meaningful.

Information service Commercial service that offers information over communication lines to paying subscribers; also called information utility, information network, and commercial data base.

Initialize To prepare a disk so that data and programs can be stored on it.

Input Data submitted to the computer for processing.

Insertion A word processing feature in which a character, word, sentence, or larger block of text can be added to the existing text.

Instruction set The fundamental logical and arithmetic procedures that the computer can perform, such as addition and comparison, designed into the electronic circuitry of the CPU; the basic set of instructions built into a computer that tells it what to do.

Integrated circuit An electronic circuit etched on a small silicon chip less than 1/4-inch square, permitting much faster processing than with transistors and at a greatly reduced price.

Integrated software Two or more application programs that work together, allowing easy movement of data between the applications; they also use a common group of commands between the applications.

Interactive processing A data-processing method where the user enters input via a keyboard during processing.

Interactive video Multimedia learning concept that merges computer text, sound, and graphics by using a videodisk, videodisk player, microcomputer with monitor and disk drive, and computer software; allows the user to respond to questions from the system and input inquiries into the system.

Interpreter program A high-level language translator that evaluates and translates a program one statement at a time; used extensively on microcomputer systems because it takes less primary storage than a compiler.

Kilobyte (K) 1,024 (2^{10}) storage units (1024 bytes); often rounded to 1,000; K is the symbol used for representing kilobytes.

Label Information used for describing some aspect of a spreadsheet.

Language translator program System program that translates programming languages other than machine language (the source programs) into machine-executable code.

Large-scale integration (LSI) Method by which circuits containing thousands of electronic components are densely packed in a single chip.

Link A pointer that directs the program to search for a value in another file.

LISP (LISt Processing) A high-level programming language commonly used in artificial intelligence research and in the processing of lists of elements.

Load To put a program into a computer's primary memory from a disk or tape.

Local area network Specialized network of computers and peripherals that operates within a limited geographic area, such as a building or complex of buildings, with the stations being linked by communications cables; requires special software and allows the sharing of data and hardware.

Logo An education-oriented programming language designed to allow anyone quickly to begin programming and communicating with computers; it commonly uses an object such as a turtle for tracing the formation of images on the screen.

Loop Program logic that allows a specified sequence of instructions to be executed repeatedly as long as stated conditions are met.

Low-level language A machine-oriented language; machine language and assembly languages are low-level languages.

Machine language The only type of instructions that a computer can execute directly; a code that designates the proper electrical states in the computer as combinations of 0s and 1s.

Magnetic disk A direct-access storage medium consisting of a metal or plastic platter coated with a magnetic recording material upon which data can be stored as magnetized spots.

Magnetic-ink character recognition (MICR) The process that allows characters printed with ink containing magnetized particles to be read by a magnetic-ink character reader; used for sorting checks.

Magnetic tape A sequential storage medium consisting of a narrow strip of material treated with a magnetizable coating upon which spots are magnetized to represent data.

Mainframe A type of large, full-scale computer capable of supporting many peripheral devices.

Management information system (MIS) A formal network that uses computers to provide information that supports structured managerial decision making; its goal is to get the correct information to the appropriate manager at the right time.

Mass storage A type of storage developed for recording huge quantities of data; typically each unit of storage medium is retrieved mechanically and mounted on a drive for reading or writing.

Materials Requirement Planning (MRP) Computerized method of inventory control that involves entering data into a computer and receiving a report based on the data.

Megahertz (MHz) One million times per second; the unit of measurement for clock speed.

Menu A display of available choices or selections to help guide the user through the process of using a software package.

Microcomputer A small, low-priced computer used in homes, schools, and businesses; also called a personal, or home, computer.

Microprocessor A programmable processing unit, placed on a chip made of silicon or similar material, containing arithmetic, logic, and control circuitry; used in microcomputers, calculators, and microwave ovens and for many other applications.

Minicomputer A type of computer with the components of a full-sized system but with smaller primary memory.

Mnemonics Symbolic names or memory aids; used in assembly and high-level programming languages.

Model A numeric representation of a real-world situation.

Modeling Process of making a prototype of an idea or object in order to design and test it.

Modem An acronym for modulator/demodulator; a device that modulates and demodulates signals transmitted over communication lines; allows linkage with another computer.

Modula-2 A high-level structured programming language that is a descendant of Pascal and is based on the concept of modules that are nested within one another. Modula-2 incorporates low-level language commands.

Modular approach A method of simplifying a programming project by breaking it into segments or subunits referred to as modules.

Modulation Technology used in modems to make data processing signals compatible with communication facilities.

Module Part of a whole; a program segment or subsystem; a set of logically related program statements that perform one specified task in a program.

Monitor A video display device or screen used for showing output.

Monochrome monitor A monitor that displays a single color, such as white, green, or amber, against a black background; used primarily for displaying text.

Natural language A language designed primarily for novice computer users that allows use of statements very much like everyday speech, usually for the purpose of accessing data in a data base.

Nondestructive read/destructive write The feature of computer memory that permits data to be read and retained in its original state, allowing repeated reference during processing; new data written over the old, however, destroys (replaced) the old.

Nonimpact printer Printer in which the printing process involves heat, laser, or photographic methods of producing images; since no hammering or striking is involved, it is a quiet means of printing.

Nuclear magnetic resonance (NMR) scanning Computerized diagnostic tool that involves sending magnetic pulses through the body in order to identify medical problems.

Object program A sequence of machine-executable instructions generated by a language translator program from source-program statements.

Office automation Integration of computer and communication technology with traditional office procedures in order to increase productivity and efficiency in the office.

Offline Not in direct communication with the central computer.

Online In direct communication with the computer.

Operating system (OS) A collection of system programs used by the computer to manage its own operations; provides an interface between the user, application program, and computer hardware.

Optical character recognition (OCR) Method of electronic scanning that reads numbers, letters, bars, or other characters and then converts the optical images into appropriate electrical signals; some OCR scanners can read only certain fonts, while others can read fairly well-formed handwritten characters.

Output Information that comes from the computer as a result of processing into a form that can be used by people.

Parallel processing A type of processing in which instructions and data are handled simultaneously by two or more processing units.

Parity bit A bit added to detect incorrect transmission of data within a computer system; used in conducting internal checks to determine whether the correct number of bits are present.

Pascal A high-level structured programming language originally developed for instructional purposes and now commonly used in a wide variety of applications; named in honor of the French mathematician Blaise Pascal.

Peripheral device Device that attaches to the central processing unit, such as secondary storage device, input device, or output device.

Pixels Individual dots on the display screen which can be turned on or off.

Plotter An output device that converts data emitted from the CPU into graphic forms; typically uses pens in producing hard copy graphic output such as drawings, charts, maps, and other picture images.

Point-of-sale (POS) terminal Computer terminal that serves as a cash register but also records data for such tasks as inventory control and accounting at the location where goods are sold; connected to a central computer.

Portable Describing a program that can be run on many different computers with minimal changes.

Portable computer A small microcomputer that is light enough to be carried easily and does not need an external source of power; may be divided further by size into briefcase and notebook.

Precedence In a spreadsheet program, the order in which calculations are executed in a formula containing several operators.

Primary memory Also known as internal storage, main storage, or primary storage; the section of the computer that holds instructions, data, and intermediate and final results during processing.

Print Enhancements Variations such as underlining and boldfacing; some word processors also include superscripting and subscripting as print enhancements.

Print formatting The function of a word processor which communicates with the printer to tell it how to print the text on paper.

Printer A machine that prints characters or other images on paper; may be categorized as impact and nonimpact, depending on whether printing occurs by the striking action of print elements against paper and ribbon or by laser, chemical, thermal, or other means.

Privacy The right of an individual to be left alone; as related to data processing, the right of an individual to control the collection, processing, storage, dissemination, and use of data about personal attributes and activities.

Process To transform data into useful information by classifying, sorting, calculating, summarizing, or storing.

Program A series of step-by-step instructions that tells the computer exactly what to do; of two types, application and system.

Programmable read-only memory (PROM) Read-only memory that can be programmed by the manufacturer or user for special functions in order to meet the unique needs of the user; can be programmed once.

Programmer The person who writes the step-by-step instructions that tell a computer exactly what to do.

Programming The process of writing the step-by-step instructions that direct a computer in performing a task.

Prompt A message or cue that guides the user during computer processing—it indicates to the user what type of input is needed, what might be wrong in case of error, or how the user can ask for help; in BASIC programming, the PRINT statement written before an INPUT statement is used for printing an explanation of what data are to be entered next.

Proper program A structured program in which each individual segment or module has only one entrance and one exit.

Pseudocode An informal, narrative language used for representing the logic of a programming problem solution.

Punched cards Heavy paper storage medium in which data is represented by holes punched according to a coding scheme much like that used on Hollerith's cards.

Query language See Natural language.

RGB monitor A monitor that receives three separate color signals, one for each of three colors—red, green, and blue.

RPG (Report Program Generator) A high-level language designed for producing business reports. RPG requires the programmer to record data and operations on specification forms; the generator program then builds the needed program. RPG requires little skill on the part of the programmer for use.

RAM disk A portion of RAM memory that is temporarily acting as a disk drive, but approximating the speed of the microprocessor; often used for holding utility programs that may be needed while the user is working with an application program; it appears like a disk to the computer but is not actually a disk.

Random-access memory (RAM) Form of primary memory into which instructions and data can be read, written, and erased; the contents may be changed many times during processing; directly accessed by the computer; volatile, or temporary, memory that is erased when the computer is turned off.

Range A rectangular block of one or more cells in the worksheet, which is treated as one unit.

Read-only memory (ROM) The part of computer hardware containing items (circuitry patterns) that cannot be deleted or altered by stored-program instructions.

Read/write head The electromagnet of a tape or disk drive; in reading, it detects magnetized spots and translates them into electrical pulses; in writing, it magnetizes appropriate areas, thereby erasing any previously recorded data.

Real time Descriptive of a system's capability to receive and process data, providing output fast enough to control the outcome of an activity.

Record A collection of related data fields that comprise a single unit, such as an employee record.

Register An internal computer component used as a temporary holding area for an instruction or data item during processing; capable of accepting, holding, and transferring that instruction or datum very rapidly.

Remote terminal A terminal that is placed at a location distant from the central computer.

Resolution The number of pixels on a display screen. The greater the number of pixels, the higher the resolution.

Robotics Science dealing with the construction, capabilities, and applications of robots.

Scrolling Moving a line or lines of text onto or off the screen.

Search and find A routine that searches for a specific string of characters and places the cursor at that location.

Search and replace A routine that searches for a specified character string and replaces it with a specified replacement string.

Secondary storage Also known as external or auxiliary storage; supplements primary memory and is external to the computer; data is accessed at slower speeds.

Selection Program logic that requires the computer to make a comparison; the result of the comparison determines which execution path will be taken next.

Semiconductor A substance (for example, silicon) whose conductivity is less that that of metals, but greater than that of insulators; conductivity is improved by the addition of certain substances or by the application of heat, light, or voltage.

Sequential-access storage Secondary storage from which data must be read one after another in a fixed sequence from the beginning until the needed data is located; an example is magnetic tape.

Silicon chip Solid-logic circuitry on a small piece of silicon.

Simple sequence Program logic in which one statement is executed after another, in the order in which they occur in the program.

Simulation The process of creating a model of an object on the display screen, thus making it easy to change the design without building an actual model.

Soft copy A temporary, or nonpermanent, record of machine output; for example, a display that appears on a screen or monitor.

Software Program or programs used to direct the computer in solving problems and overseeing operations.

Software package A set of standardized computer programs, procedures, and related documentation needed for a particular application.

Software piracy The unauthorized copying of a copyrighted computer program.

Source program A sequence of instructions written in a language other than machine language that must be translated into machine language before the computer can execute the instructions.

Source-data automation Approach to data collection in which data is gathered in computer-readable form at its point of origin.

Spatial digitizer An input device that can graphically reconstruct a three-dimensional object on a computer's display screen.

Spreadsheet A ledger or table used in a business environment for financial calculations and for the recording of transactions.

Spreadsheet analysis A mental process of evaluating information contained in an electronic spreadsheet; also called what-if analysis.

Spreadsheet program A set of computer instructions which generates and operates an electronic spreadsheet.

Status line A message line above or below the text area on a display screen which gives format and system information.

Stored program A program held in primary memory in electronic form so that no human intervention is required during processing; can be executed repeatedly during processing.

Stored-program concept The idea that program instruc- can be stored in primary memory in electronic form o human intervention is required during pro-

cessing; allows the computer to process the instructions at its own speed.

Structure chart A graphic representation of the results of the top-down design process, displaying the modules of the solution and their relationships to one another.

Structured programming A collection of techniques that encourage the development of well-designed, less error-prone programs with easy-to-follow logic. Structured programming techniques include top-down design and extensive documentation and program testing.

Supercomputer The largest, fastest, most expensive type of computer in existence, capable of performing millions of calculations per second and processing enormous amounts of data; also called maxicomputer or monster computer.

Supermicrocomputer A microcomputer powerful enough to compete with low-end minicomputers; usually built around 32-bit microprocessors.

System analyst The person who is the communication link or interface between users and technical persons (such as programmers and operators); responsible for system analysis, design, and implementation of computer-based information systems.

System program Instructions written for coordinating the operation of computer circuitry and helping the computer run quickly and efficiently.

Tape drive A drive that moves tape past a read/write head.

Telecommunications The combined use of communication facilities, such as telephone systems and data-processing equipment.

Telecommute To work at home and communicate with the office or send data to the office via electronic machines and telecommunications facilities.

Teleconference Meeting that occurs via telephone, electronic and/or image-producing facilities, thereby eliminating the need for travel.

Text editing The function of a word processor which enables the user to enter and edit text.

Timesharing An arrangement in which two or more users can access the same central computer resources and receive what seems to be simultaneous results.

Top-down design A method of defining a solution in terms of major functions to be performed, and further breaking down the major functions into subfunctions; the further the breakdown, the greater the detail.

Touch screen A computer screen equipped for detecting

the point at which it is touched by the user; it allows the user to bypass the keyboard.

Track One of a series of concentric circles on the surface of a magnetic disk.

Transportable A class of microcomputer smaller than the desktop models for easier carrying, but larger than the portables and therefore bulkier to carry.

Users group An informal group of owners of a particular brand of microcomputer or software who meet to exchange information about hardware, software, service, and support.

Value A single piece of numeric data used in the calculations of a spreadsheet.

Very-large-scale integration (VLSI) Method by which circuits containing hundreds of thousands of electronic components are densely packed on a single chip, packed even more densely than with LSI.

Voice recognition The ability of electronic equipment to recognize speech and voice patterns.

Voice recognition system An input system that recognizes certain speech and voice patterns; the user must follow only the patterns the system is programmed to recognize.

Voice response unit A device through which the computer "speaks" by arranging half-second records of phonemes, or voice sounds.

Voice synthesizer The output portion of a voice communication system; used to provide verbal output from the computer system to the user.

Window The portion of an electronic spreadsheet which can be seen on the computer display screen.

Word size The number of bits that can be manipulated at one time, for instance, an 8-bit microprocessor can manipulate 8 bits (one byte) of data at a time.

Word processing The act of composing and manipulating text electronically.

Word processing system The hardware and software used for word processing.

Word processor A program or set of programs designed to enable you to enter, manipulate, format, print, store, and retrieve text.

Word wrap The feature by which a word is automatically moved to the beginning of the next line if it goes past the right margin.

Worksheet The grid of rows and columns created using a spreadsheet software package. The worksheet falls within the row and column borders.

INDEX

by permission of Innovative Software, Inc., **Fig. 6-2a** Jay Freis, Courtesy of Planning Research Corporation, **Fig. 6-2b** Photo courtesy of Anderson Jacobson, Inc., **Fig. 6-5** Courtesy of International Business Machines Corporation, **Fig. 6-6** Courtesy of International Business Machines Corporation, **Fig. 6-7** Courtesy of Oberon International, **Fig. 6-8** Compression Labs, Incorporated, **Fig. 6-9** Courtesy of Apple Computer, Inc., **Fig. 6-10** Courtesy of Cincinnati Milacron, **Fig. 6-11a** Courtesy of SAFER Emergency Systems, **Fig. 6-11b** Courtesy of SAFER Emergency Systems, **Fig. 6-12** Courtesy of AT&T Bell Laboratories, **Fig. 6-13** Reproduced with permission of Medtronic, Inc., **Fig. 6-14** Reproduced with permission of Medtronic, Inc., **Fig. 6-15** Courtesy of National Severe Storms Forecast Center, **Fig. 6-16** Optronics International, Inc., **Fig. 6-17** Courtesy of Parkland Memorial Hospital, **Fig. 6-18** Photos courtesy of Rockwell International, **Fig. 6-19a** Courtesy of Visual Communications Network, Inc., **Fig. 6-19b** 1985 Time Arts Inc. *Artist:* John Dorry, **Fig. 6-20** Photograph by John Morgan, **Fig. 6-21** Courtesy of Blyth Software, **Fig. 6-22** Courtesy of Apple Computer, Inc., **Fig. 7-2** Courtesy of the F.B.I., **Fig. 7-7** Honeywell Inc., Building Services Division, **Fig. 7-8** Photo courtesy INTERMEC.

IMPORTANT: PLEASE READ BEFORE OPENING DISKETTE PACKAGE
THIS TEXT IS NOT RETURNABLE IF SEAL IS BROKEN

West Services, Inc.
58 West Kellogg Boulevard
St. Paul, Minnesota 55164

WEST SOFT PACK 2.5 VERSION (IBM/MS-DOS)
LIMITED USE LICENSE

Read the following terms and conditions carefully before opening this diskette package. If you do not agree, promptly return this package unopened to West Services for a full refund.

By accepting this license, you have the right to use West Soft Pack and the accompanying documentation, but you do not become the owner of these materials.

This copy of West Soft Pack is licensed to you for use only under the following conditions:

1. PERMITTED USES
You are granted a non-exclusive limited license to use West Soft Pack under the terms and conditions stated in this License. You may:

- a. Use West Soft Pack on a single computer.
- b. Make a single copy of West Soft Pack in machine-readable form solely for backup purposes in support of your use of West Soft Pack on a single machine. You must reproduce and include the copyright notice on any copy you make.
- c. Transfer this copy of West Soft Pack and the License to another user if the other user agrees to accept the terms and conditions of this License. If you transfer this copy of West Soft Pack, you must also transfer or destroy the backup copy you made. Transfer of this copy of West Soft Pack, and the License automatically terminates this License as to you.

2. PROHIBITED USES
You may not use, copy, modify, distribute or transfer West Soft Pack or any copy, in whole or in part, except as expressly permitted in this License.

3. TERM
This License is effective when you open the diskette package and remains in effect until terminated. You may terminate this License at any time by ceasing all use of West Soft Pack and destroying this copy and any copy you have made. It will also terminate automatically if you fail to comply with the terms of this License. Upon termination, you agree to cease all use of West Soft Pack and destroy all copies.

4. DISCLAIMER OF WARRANTY
Except as stated herein, West Soft Pack is licensed "as is" without warranty of any kind, express or implied, including warranties of merchantability or fitness for a particular purpose. You assume the entire risk as to the quality and performance of West Soft Pack. You are responsible for the selection of West Soft Pack to achieve your intended results and for the installation, use and results obtained from it. West Publishing, and West Services do not warrant the performance of nor results that may be obtained with West Soft Pack. West Services does warrant that the diskette(s) upon which West Soft Pack is provided will be free from defects in materials and workmanship under normal use for a period of 30 days from the date of delivery to you as evidenced by a receipt.

Some states do not allow the exclusion of implied warranties so the above exclusion may not apply to you. This warranty gives you specific legal rights. You may also have other rights which vary from state to state.

5. LIMITATION OF LIABILITY
Your exclusive remedy for breach by West Services of its limited warranty shall be replacement of any defective diskette upon its return to West at the above address, together with a copy of the receipt, within the warranty period. If West Services is unable to provide you with a replacement diskette which is free of defects in material and workmanship, you may terminate this License by returning West Soft Pack, and the license fee paid hereunder will be refunded to you. In no event will West be liable for any lost profits or other damages including direct, indirect, incidental, special, consequential or any other type of damages arising out of the use or inability to use West Soft Pack even if West Services has been advised of the possibility of such damages.

6. GOVERNING LAW
This Agreement will be governed by the laws of the State of Minnesota.

You acknowledge that you have read this License and agree to its terms and conditions. You also agree that this License is the entire and exclusive agreement between you and West and supersedes any prior understanding or agreement, oral or written, relating to the subject matter of this agreement.